COVENANT OF CHRIST

A Modern English Version of The Book of Mormon

COVENANT OF CHRIST

A Modern English Version of The Book of Mormon

Originally translated through Joseph Smith Jr.

Adopted by a conference in 2017 as the Covenant offered by Christ, who asked us "to accept the obligations established by the Book of Mormon as a covenant." Published in modern language to let the Lord's covenant terms be understood by this generation.

COVENANT EDITION

First Edition

ISBN: 978-1-951168-86-5
Text: CE 01.0 - 2024.06.20

CONTENTS

DEDICATION

An account engraved by Mormon on plates, taken from the plates of Nephi.

It is a summary of the record of the Nephites, and of the Lamanites, written to the Lamanites — who are a remnant of the house of Israel — and to the Jews and Gentiles; written by means of divine commandment and by the spirit of prophecy and revelation. The records were engraved, sealed, and hidden under the Lord's care so they wouldn't be destroyed, to come forth by God's gift and power to be translated. They were sealed up by Moroni and hidden under the Lord's care, to appear at the right time through the Gentiles, and their translation by the gift of God.

Additionally, includes a summary made from the Book of Ether, which is a record of Jared's people, who were scattered when the Lord confused the people's language as they were building a tower to get to heaven. The purpose of this account is to show the remnant of the house of Israel how the Lord has done great things for their ancestors; and so they can know the Lord's covenants, that they are not rejected forever; and to convince both Jews and Gentiles that Jesus is the Christ, the Eternal God, revealing Himself to all nations. If there are any errors, they are human mistakes. That being the case, do not condemn the things of God, so you can be found spotless at Christ's judgment seat.

Moroni

PREFACE

Background

In a 2017 revelation regarding the scriptures, the Lord declared the following referring to the following books: Old Testament, New Testament, The Doctrine and Covenants, and The Book of Mormon:

> The records you have gathered as scriptures yet lack many of my words, have errors throughout, and contain things that are not of me, because the records you used in your labors have not been maintained nor guarded against the cunning plans of false brethren who have been deceived by Satan.
>
> ...the records you have received have not transmitted that which was first written in holiness,
>
> ...many parts were discarded and other parts were altered. False brethren who did not fear me intended to corrupt and to pervert the right way, to blind the eyes and harden the hearts of others, in order to obtain power and authority over them.
>
> Conspiracies have corrupted the records, beginning among the Jews, and again following the time of my apostles, and yet again following the time of Joseph and Hyrum. As you have labored with the records you have witnessed the alterations and insertions, and your effort to recover them pleases me and is of great worth. You may remove the brackets from your record, as I accept your clarifications, and you are permitted to proceed to the end with your plan to update language to select a current vocabulary, but take care not to change meaning — and if you cannot resolve the meaning, either petition me again or retain the former words. Nevertheless, you labor with an incomplete text.

The work of recovering the scriptures took a group of volunteers years of work before its completion in 2017. The Joseph Smith Translation of the Bible had not been correctly recovered and published. A version provided by the Reorganized Church of Jesus Christ of Latter Day Saints (subsequently renamed the Community of Christ) did not include all of Joseph Smith's corrections to the text, and contained multiple inaccuracies. Removing errors and correcting the text required extensive research before the Bible was finished in 2017.

The Book of Mormon was published before The Church of Jesus Christ of Latter-day Saints was organized. It belongs to the entire Christian world and not a single denomination. When the text was recovered for the scripture project in 2017, the earliest surviving portion of the translation and the printer's copy were used. The printer's copy was a hand-copied version of the translation given to E. B. Grandin's print shop in 1829 to use for typesetting. That copying resulted in numerous copy errors, which Joseph Smith was attempting to correct in 1842 for a later edition. Not all those errors were corrected, and the 2017 project attempted to finish recovering the most correct text.

Joseph Smith translated the Book of Mormon from an unknown language based on Egyptian characters to record Hebrew ideas. The Egyptian script was selected because it was more efficient and required fewer characters. However, the translation of the resulting text into English by Joseph Smith used an older version of English, often referred to as *Elizabethan* or *Shakespearian English*, named *Early Modern English* and was used between A.D. 1485 and 1714. Many of the words were in common usage before the creation of the King James Bible in 1611. Accordingly, when the book first appeared in 1830, its formal language was already outdated. Instead of the early 19th century American English, the initial translation was awkward, yet sometimes poetic English language that dated from the 15th, 16th, and 17th centuries. Relying on Noah Webster's 1828 first edition of *An American Dictionary of the English Language* as a reference to understand the text proves inadequate and leads to a misunderstanding of the meaning of many words.

Seven years ago, a new edition of the scriptures was approved by a conference that accepted the corrected, updated, recovered, and more complete texts at a conference in Boise, Idaho, and adopted as scriptures. The Old Covenants (Joseph Smith's corrected Old Testament), the New Covenants (Joseph Smith's corrected New Testament), The Book of Mormon, and the Teachings and Commandments (containing numerous missing or discarded revelations and historical writings) comprised the finalized canon. Since 2017, work has continued on the Book of Mormon following the approved process and confining the work to the Lord's direction: "you are permitted to proceed to the end with your plan to update language to select a current vocabulary, but take care not to change meaning[.]" That instruction motivated this modern English version of the Book of Mormon.

When the recovered scriptures were presented to and accepted by the Lord in 2017, He offered a covenant to believers and asked of us to: "receive the scriptures approved by the Lord as a standard to govern you in your daily walk in life, to accept the obligations established by the Book of Mormon as a covenant, and to use the scriptures to correct yourselves and to guide your words, thoughts, and deeds[.]" For this reason, as the project to restate the Book of Mormon in modern English neared completion, the Lord gave it a new title: *Covenant of Christ*. That new title is the direct result of the Lord's 2017 Covenant.

The updated language is essential for those who accept the 2017 Covenant. During the final stage of the project, the Lord declared: "The original Book of Mormon translation was to get that generation to be willing to accept it as scripture. They needed it to mimic the King James Version language. But this has a different purpose. This is to help a new generation understand the content to help with the Lord's return. There is as much Divine attention and assistance in getting this new version completed as before." Inspiration from the Lord has assisted throughout the process of finalizing this updated volume of scripture.

This volume is not intended solely for those who accepted the 2017 Covenant but will have value for anyone who wants to read and understand the Book of Mormon.

INTRODUCTION

The *Covenant of Christ* is the most important volume of scripture for the present day. The original text from 1830 was not a commentary, not an interpretation, neither a narration nor an explanation. It presented itself as original, authentic, ancient scripture. This new edition renders the text into a modern or present-day language setting.

The Process Involved in Creating this Edition

The first, initial undertaking took four years to complete and involved treating every word in the text with care and diligence. Without guidance from the Lord, this initial work would not have been possible to complete. There were some archaic elements, words, and syntax that weren't recognized as archaic until going deep into the project. As the project progressed, the unique flavor and personality of the text became more noticeable. It became a challenge to update the language and still preserve the uniqueness of the text. It was apparent that some words and phrases struggle to yield an acceptable, modern equivalent. Each word has undergone numerous independent and collaborative verifications, ensuring precise accuracy.

Unfortunately, there doesn't exist a lexicon of archaic *Early Modern English* terms and their modern equivalents that would have been useful in this project. This phase is the result of many years and thousands of hours of research, utilizing a consulting scholar's experience and expertise who specializes in the etymological source of English word origins by looking at all of the earliest existing literature. His expertise in the field of philology and word origins provided interpretation of archaic and obsolete words that would have been otherwise unavailable. Painstaking care and inspiration were taken in the selection of vocabulary to replace archaic or outdated words, phrases, and idioms.

It was clear from the outset that there was a clear, limited mandate, set out in scripture: We were only "permitted to update language to select a current vocabulary," and were warned "not to change the meaning." We were also instructed: "Take care not to change meaning—and if you cannot resolve the meaning, either petition Me again or retain the former words."[1] This, therefore, became a very narrow, tightly confined assignment. This project had constraints set by the Lord. The criteria prohibited simply rewriting or interpreting and did not even permit clarifying the text. What already existed could not be changed, and therefore, the task was solely to render existing content into a modern, more readable format. That does not allow for any change. Some of the difficult or complex language structures from the original text could not be smoothed into modern language while maintaining fidelity to each verse in the original.

To remain faithful to the original, this modern English version tracks the versification provided by Orson Pratt to the LDS Book of Mormon. This allows a reader to make a verse-by-verse comparison if they choose to do so.

What resources were employed in the creation of this edition?

This book owes its existence to many things. The first is the nature of the original text. To create this new edition, we utilized *The Book of Mormon, The Earliest Text*, 2nd ed. (New Haven and London: Yale University Press, 2022), edited by Royal Skousen, as the base or foundation text, along with *The Book of Mormon, Restoration Edition*. These sources were very important in terms of textual accuracy. They present the book in its purest state, guiding us back to the original manuscript, carefully reconstructed, and even capturing the exact words as initially dictated by Joseph Smith. Other sources included *The Oxford English Dictionary*, Oxford University Press, 2nd ed. [1989], 3rd ed. [2010], and the online version at https://www.oed.com., *The Joseph Smith Papers: Revelations and Translations*, Volume 3, Parts 1 and 2: *Printer's Manuscript of the Book of Mormon* (Salt Lake City: Church Historian's Press, 2015), and other works from Royal Skousen including *The Book of Mormon Critical Text Project*, 6 vols.: Vol. I: *The Original Manuscript of the Book of Mormon*; Vol. III: *The History of the Text of the Book of Mormon*, Parts 1 and 2: Grammatical Variation; Parts 3 and 4: Nature of the Original Language; Part 5: The King James Quotations in the Book of Mormon; Part 6: Spelling in the Manuscripts and Editions; Vol. IV: *Analysis of Textual Variants of the Book of Mormon*.

After the initial undertaking was completed and an acceptable draft manuscript prepared, it was then given to Denver Snuffer to edit and finalize. It was a commission demanding intense mental focus and he meticulously examined the initial draft multiple times, making thousands of restatements and corrections. After several months, Denver Snuffer returned the text with instructions about formatting and usage consistencies. It was reviewed, formatted, and returned to him for another final pass-through. In that second review, he made hundreds of additional restatements and edit clarifications. During the entire process the Lord has been petitioned and has responded, and His influence is reflected in this current published volume. This book has been designed to be easier for a modern reader to understand than the original, which was the primary goal of this project.

Translation and the Language of the Original Text

One of the most revolutionary acts in Christian history was translating the Bible into common language and allowing everyone to read and understand the content. Other Protestant clergy translating it into English, French, and many other spoken languages followed Martin Luther's translation into German. Everyone should be able to read and understand scripture. Having it available into a common language benefits every believer.

A considerable amount of the language of the original Book of Mormon text was written in the *Early Modern English* language (the stage of the English language that began from the beginning of the Tudor period (1485) to the end of the Stuart dynasty (1714). *Early Modern English* (with many similarities to King James English) was employed in the original translation of the Book of Mormon to make it consistent with the already familiar language of scripture; it was a way to break down the resistance of having something new claiming to be scripture. The King James Bible was a very public text — being the most accessible and read aloud in the churches — familiar to the ears of churchgoers for over two hundred years. If the Book of Mormon read as the King James Bible (and it contains over twenty-five passages that either quote extensively or paraphrase biblical passages, including from Isaiah, Exodus, Deuteronomy, Micah, and Matthew), people would be willing to read it and recognize that it was God's word. The abundance of archaic words and phrases was not updated to 19th-century vernacular in the work, as a testament to its originality and authenticity.

There is no question that the effect of the King James Bible on Western culture and thought, in all areas of life and society, has been vast. Its influence on language is undeniable. "The King James Bible had been, at least in the mainstream, unchallenged for 270 years, eight or nine generations. Its language, even archaic in 1611, derived from a form of English current in the mid-sixteenth century, had come to seem like the language spoken by God."[2] So, the assumption would naturally arise that the 1830 Book of Mormon would also employ that same divine language transmitted by Deity. And it does to a degree, but only to the extent that it uses the same Elizabethan language of that period.

This modern English version is intended to make it accessible, clear, and as succinct as possible. It is once again a modern revelation from God to the world.

---

[1] Teachings and Commandments 157:15.
[2] Adam Nicholson, *God's Secretaries: The Making of the King James Bible* (New York: Harper Perennial, 2003), 233.

PRAYER

Heavenly Father, it is I whom you named David, asking you in the name of Jesus Christ to answer this petition. We are grateful for the covenant you ordained in 2017 and hope to obey it. We remember what you said about our scriptures in your Answer:

> The records you have gathered as scriptures yet lack many of my words, have errors throughout, and contain things that are not of me, because the records you used in your labors have not been maintained nor guarded against the cunning plans of false brethren who have been deceived by Satan.

> … the records you have received have not transmitted that which was first written in holiness,

> … many parts were discarded and other parts were altered. False brethren who did not fear me intended to corrupt and to pervert the right way, to blind the eyes and harden the hearts of others, in order to obtain power and authority over them.

> Conspiracies have corrupted the records, beginning among the Jews, and again following the time of my apostles, and yet again following the time of Joseph and Hyrum. As you have labored with the records you have witnessed the alterations and insertions, and your effort to recover them pleases me and is of great worth. You may remove the brackets from your record, as I accept your clarifications, and you are permitted to proceed to the end with your plan to update language to select a current vocabulary, but take care not to change meaning — and if you cannot resolve the meaning, either petition me again or retain the former words. Nevertheless, you labor with an incomplete text.

These words about how the scriptures have been treated by those in the past warn us about how we treat your scriptures today. We are afraid of making errors again by failing to maintain or guard the scriptures. We have acted on your permission to proceed to the end with our plan to update language to select a current vocabulary, and we took care not to change meaning of anything in the Book of Mormon. You promised us that you:

> … will lead all who come to me to the truth of all things. The fullness is to receive the truth of all things, and this too from me, in power, by my word, and in very deed. For I will come unto you if you will come unto me.

Therefore we have asked for your guidance, direction and inspiration to be able to fulfill obligations assigned to us. In the 2017 Covenant you asked:

> Do you have faith in these things and receive the scriptures approved by the Lord as a standard to govern you in your daily walk in life, to accept the obligations established by the Book of Mormon as a covenant, and to use the scriptures to correct yourselves and to guide your words, thoughts, and deeds?

Therefore, you ordained the Book of Mormon as the Covenant for us. But you also permitted us to proceed with our plan to update language to select a current vocabulary, while taking care not to change meaning.

You directed us to:

> … Seek to recover the lost sheep remnant of this land and of Israel and no longer forsake them. Bring them unto me and teach them of my ways, to walk in them.

To recover the lost sheep of Israel also requires a Hebrew language version of the Book of Mormon, and therefore we are doing that work and expect it to be completed soon and ask for it to be accepted when finished. As for other lost sheep of Israel the text needs to be updated for English language readers to understand it. Many passages use words and grammar that confuse rather than inform today's readers. To obey the Covenant requires people to first understand it, and the language has become a barrier.

You instructed us to:

> … study my words and let them be the standard for your faith, and I will add thereto many treasures.

Our study will be improved by rewriting the book into modern English. Therefore we ask you to approve the modern language version as an acceptable Covenant version of the Book of Mormon. We do not want to make any change that fails to maintain or guard the language. We do not want to make the same errors as in the past for which ancient Israel was condemned. Isaiah wrote:

> The earth also is defiled under the inhabitants thereof, because they have transgressed the laws, changed the ordinance, broken the everlasting covenant.

We will not use the new English language version as part of the Covenant without your approval. We are asking for that approval, keeping in mind your previous revelation stating:

> You have asked to know if the scriptures are acceptable and approved, or if there is more to be done:
>
> The work that has been done is acceptable and sufficient for the labor now underway. You were permitted to update language, select a current vocabulary, and you were warned not to change any meaning. I reminded you that you do not understand the glory to be revealed unto my covenant people. You were instructed to complete the agreed upon labors, and you have done as was required.
>
> These scriptures are sent forth to be my warning to the world, my comfort to the faithful, my counsel to the meek, my reproof to the proud, my rebuke to the contentious, and my condemnation of the wicked. They are my invitation to all mankind to flee from corruption, repent and be baptized in my name, and prepare for the coming judgment.

For four years following the Covenant we have continued working to update the language of the Book of Mormon, trying to not change any meanings. On December 10, 2023, after years of labor by others, that project was turned over to me, and I have been working to complete the work of restating the text in modern English language. As I worked with the book, on December 22, 2023, you informed me:

> The original Book of Mormon translation was to get that generation to be willing to accept it as scripture. They needed it to mimic the King James Version language. But this has a different purpose. This is to help a new generation to understand the content to help with the Lord's return. There is as much Divine attention and assistance in getting this new version completed as before.

I acknowledge your continuing assistance while laboring with the book, and now ask whether it has accomplished your will. You provided a new name for this version of the Book of Mormon, calling it *Covenant of Christ*. Therefore, we ask: will you authorize this *Covenant of Christ* updated version to be accepted as your Covenant?

[Before the Lord answered I was instructed to review the entire text, during which several changes were required to be made.]

ANSWER

On June 20, 2024, the word of the Lord came to me, saying:

It is enough. I have given to you my direction both now and as the work was underway, and therefore I say to you: It is enough.

I labored alongside you in this work. My word is truth. My word is spirit. As you worked with the text I gave you my word and it is to be kept as it was given. My word carries with it the power of truth, and you are not called to alter it, but are to defend it. As you have considered comments from others you have feared man more than me. The corruption of scripture has been caused by men fearing others and failing to heed my word. You were told to update the language, and that included restating my doctrine, sacrament and baptismal prayers but you hesitated and needed to be commanded to do so. Let your work of updating the language now end with the words I have given you.

Publish it for the people to read. Then, have the voice of the people determine if they will accept it as my Covenant, as they will be judged by their voice on this matter. Once the voice of the people has been heard, if they accept it let it be your Covenant version to guide you. No one should be forbidden from using the earlier text, nor compelled to use only one of these two, but if approved by their vote it will be your Covenant text to guide you.

As for my doctrine, sacrament and baptismal prayers, use the new language but you are not to forbid using the earlier language, as I will accept either wording for these ordinances.

In the future when translating the Book of Mormon into other languages, use this *Covenant of Christ* version as the source for that work.

Hear me now: Let every person take care in how they use my name, as if I had part in their every dispute, for many things provoking arguments among the people are born from pride, stubbornness, aspiring for control, and reckless indifference toward me and one another. I bear with the people still, and patiently await the return of natural fruit in my vineyard. Do not be misled by my patience, for the time is quickly approaching for the harvest of my vineyard.

Amen.

xiii

Numeric Navigation Tools in This Volume

The chapter divisions in this text reflect the structure and divisions found in the original publications of the Book of Mormon beginning in 1830. These have been preserved to honor the original (e.g., Chapter 6). The paragraph divisions were divided based on content by a group in 2017 while working to restore a version of the scriptures more true to Joseph Smith and his restoration efforts. Paragraphs are identified using Roman Numerals (e.g., XXVII) in the left hand margin of each page.

LDS chapter and verse numbering have also been included in this volume with LDS chapters being shown inline with the text in a bold font nominally larger than the surrounding text (e.g., **2**). LDS verse numbers are also shown inline with the text and are shown as superscripts (e.g., 7). These references have been included to assist with overall document and chapter navigation and to aid readers in easily identifying chapter and verse citations they may already be familiar with.

LDS chapter and verse headers are on the left pages with RE chapter and paragraph headers on the right pages.

These notations are intended as helpful, but non-intrusive aids and are for reference purposes only.

The First Book of Nephi

HIS RULE AND MINISTRY

An account of Lehi, his wife Sariah, and his four sons, named beginning with the oldest Laman, Lemuel, Sam, and Nephi. The Lord warns Lehi to leave the land of Jerusalem because he prophesies to the people about their iniquity and they attempt to kill him. He journeys for three days into the wilderness with his family. Nephi takes his brothers and returns to Jerusalem to get the record of the Jews. The account of their hardships. They marry Ishmael's daughters. They take their families and depart into the wilderness. Their suffering and troubles in the wilderness. The path of their travels. They come to the ocean. Nephi's brothers rebel against him. He proves them wrong and builds a ship. They name the place Bountiful. They cross the ocean to the promised land, etc. This is according to Nephi's account — that is, I Nephi engraved this record.

Chapter 1

I Nephi was born to excellent parents. As a consequence, my father taught me from all his knowledge. I've experienced many hardships during my life, while at the same time I've been greatly blessed by the Lord. I gained great understanding of God's goodness and mysteries. Therefore I'm making a record of the important events in my life. 2 I'm writing in my father's language, which consists of Jewish knowledge written using Egyptian script. 3 I know the record I'm making is true, written in my own hand, and based on what I know and experienced.

II 4 My father Lehi lived his whole life at Jerusalem. During the first year that Zedekiah king of Judah ruled, many prophets were warning that the people must repent or the great city of Jerusalem would be destroyed.

III 5 So my father, when he was alone, prayed to the Lord with his whole heart for his people. 6 As he prayed to the Lord, a pillar of fire descended and rested on a rock in front of him, and he saw and heard many things. What he saw and heard made him shake and tremble. 7 Afterward, he returned to his house in Jerusalem and collapsed on his bed, overwhelmed by the Spirit and what he had seen. 8 While overwhelmed by the Spirit, he was carried away in a vision. He saw the heavens open, and he thought he saw God sitting on His throne, surrounded by numberless rings of angels engaged in singing and praising Him. 9 He also saw a person descending from heaven who was brighter than the midday sun. 10 He then saw twelve others following Him, and they were brighter than the stars in the sky. 11 They came down to the earth. The first one came and stood in front of my father and gave him a book and told him to read. ¹² As he read, he was filled with the Spirit of the Lord. ¹³ He read: Woe, woe to Jerusalem, because I've seen your abominations! My father continued to read about Jerusalem; that it would be destroyed along with its inhabitants, many would be killed by the sword and many would be captured and taken to Babylon. ¹⁴ After my father read and saw many great and surprising things, he cried out to the Lord: O Lord God Almighty, You've done such great and awe-inspiring things! Your throne is high in the heavens, and Your power, goodness, and mercy are over everyone living on earth. And because You are merciful, You won't let those who come to You be lost. ¹⁵ This is an example of how my father praised God. He rejoiced and his heart was full because of what the Lord showed him.

IV ¹⁶ Now I won't provide a full account of what my father wrote since he's written many things he saw in visions and dreams. He also wrote many prophecies that he told to his children. I'm not including a full account of those things. ¹⁷ Instead, I'll write an account of important events in my life. First, I'll summarize my father's record on these plates I made with my own hands. Then, following my father's summarized record, I'll write an account of my life.

V ¹⁸ After the Lord showed my father Lehi the approaching destruction of Jerusalem and other astonishing things, he started prophesying about what he had seen and heard. ¹⁹ However, telling them the truth about their wickedness and abominations resulted in the Jews mocking him. But when he also testified that he saw, heard, and read in a book that a Messiah was coming to redeem the world, ²⁰ that made the Jews furious with him, just like they were with former prophets, whom they had thrown out, stoned, and killed. So they tried to kill my father too. But the Lord's tender mercies are shown to everyone He has chosen because of their faith. He uses His power to save their lives.

VI **2** Following this, the Lord spoke to my father in a dream and told him: You are blessed, Lehi, because of the things you've done. And because you've been faithful and declared the things I commanded you, they're trying to kill you. ² In that dream, the Lord commanded my father to take his family and make his way into the wilderness. ³ He obeyed the Lord's word and did what the Lord commanded him.

VII ⁴ He departed into the wilderness. He left his house, the land he had inherited, and his gold, silver, and valuables, and didn't take anything with him except his family, provisions, and tents, and left into the wilderness. ⁵ He came down by the mountains near the Red Sea shore, journeying through the wilderness until reaching the Borders of the Red Sea. He traveled with his family, consisting of my mother Sariah, and older brothers, who were Laman, Lemuel, and Sam. 6 After he traveled for three days across the wilderness, he pitched his tent in a valley by a river.

VIII
        7 Then he built a stone altar and made an offering to the Lord and gave thanks to the Lord our God. 8 My father named the river Laman, and it flowed into the Red Sea. The valley was in the mountainous area near its mouth. 9 When my father saw the river emptied into the source of the Red Sea, he said to Laman: I wish you would be like this river — always flowing into the source of all righteousness. 10 He also said to Lemuel: I wish you would be like this valley — firm, resolute, and immovable in keeping the Lord's commandments. 11 He said this because Laman and Lemuel were stubborn. They complained about their father over many things: that he was a man carried away by his imagination, and had taken them away from Jerusalem, making them leave their land, gold, silver, and valuables, only to die in the wilderness. They said he did this because of his foolish, delusional thinking. 12 This is how Laman and Lemuel, the oldest children, complained about their father. They complained because they didn't understand how the God who created them deals with mankind. 13 They also didn't believe the great city of Jerusalem could be destroyed like the prophets were saying. They were like the Jerusalem Jews who tried to kill my father. 14 But my father was inspired by the Spirit, speaking to them with such power in the valley of Lemuel that they shook with fear before him. He silenced them and they didn't dare speak against him. Therefore they submitted to him. 15 And my father occupied a tent.

IX
        16 Since I was very young — but large in build — and had a strong desire to know about God's mysteries, I cried to the Lord in prayer. He influenced me and softened my heart letting me believe everything my father had said. As a result, I didn't rebel against him like my brothers. 17 And I talked to Sam, telling him what the Lord had revealed to me by His Holy Spirit. And he believed my words. 18 But Laman and Lemuel refused to listen to me. Because their hard-heartedness troubled me, I cried to the Lord in prayer for them. 19 And the Lord replied: You are blessed, Nephi, because of your faith, having honestly approached Me with a humble heart. 20 And to the degree you keep My commandments, you will prosper and be led to a promised land, one that I've prepared for you, a specially chosen land, better than all other places on earth. 21 And to the extent your brothers rebel against you, they'll be cut off from the presence of the Lord. 22 And to the degree you keep My commandments, you will be made a ruler and

teacher over them. 23 When they rebel against Me, I'll curse them with a severe curse, and they won't have any power over your descendants unless they also rebel against Me. 24 And if your descendants rebel against Me, your brothers' descendants will afflict your descendants to help them remember.

X   **3** Then I returned from speaking with the Lord to my father's tent. 2 And he said to me: I've had a dream where the Lord commanded you and your brothers to return to Jerusalem. 3 The assignment is to go to Laban who has the record of the Jews and my forefathers' genealogy engraved on brass plates. 4 The Lord has commanded for you and your brothers to go to Laban's house, retrieve the records, and bring them down here in the wilderness. 5 Your brothers are complaining, saying it's a difficult thing I've asked them to do. But I haven't asked them to do it. To the contrary, it's a commandment from the Lord. 6 So go, my son, and you'll be blessed by the Lord because you haven't complained. 7 Then I told my father: I'll go and do what the Lord has commanded because I know the Lord doesn't give people any commandments without preparing a way for them to accomplish what He commands to be done. 8 When my father heard this, he was very pleased since he could tell my understanding came from the Lord.

XI   9 So my brothers and I returned with our tents back to Jerusalem. 10 And when we arrived, we discussed among ourselves 11 and drew lots for who was to go to Laban's house. The lot fell on Laman. So he went to Laban's house and talked with him inside. 12 He asked Laban for the records engraved on the brass plates, which contained my father's genealogy. 13 But Laban got angry and threw him out, refusing to give him the records. He accused him: You're a robber! I'm going to kill you! 14 But Laman ran away and told us what Laban had done. As a result, we were very discouraged, and my brothers were about to return to my father in the wilderness.

XII   15 But I told them: As surely as the Lord lives and we live, we won't return to our father in the wilderness until we've accomplished what the Lord has commanded us to do. 16 Therefore let's be faithful in keeping the Lord's commandments. Let's go down to our father's land, because he left gold, silver, and valuables there. And he left everything because of the Lord's commandments. 17 For he knows Jerusalem will be destroyed because of the people's wickedness, 18 because they've rejected the words of the prophets. Therefore if our father were to live in the land after having been commanded to flee, he would lose his life too; that being so, he had to flee from the place. 19 And it's God's wise plan for us to get these records so we can continue to keep our forefathers' language for our children 20 and preserve the words spoken by all the holy prophets, which have been given to them by the Spirit and power of God, containing everything from when the world began to the present time. ²¹ With these words I persuaded my brothers to be faithful in keeping God's commandments.

XIII ²² So we went down to our land and gathered our gold, silver, and valuables. ²³ After gathering them, we went back up to Laban's house. ²⁴ We came to see Laban and asked him to give us the records written on the brass plates in exchange for our gold, silver, and valuables. ²⁵ When he saw our considerable possessions, he wanted to have them so much that he drove us out by force and sent his servants to kill us so he could steal our property. ²⁶ We fled from Laban's servants and were compelled to drop our possessions, and Laban took them.

XIV ²⁷ We escaped into the wilderness where we hid in a cave, and Laban's servants didn't catch us. ²⁸ Laman was angry with me, and with my father as well — and so was Lemuel, since he listened to Laman. As a result, Laman and Lemuel blamed us, their younger brothers, and they beat us with a club. ²⁹ As they were hitting us, an angel of the Lord appeared before them and asked: Why are you hitting your younger brother with a club? Don't you realize that because of your iniquities the Lord has chosen him to be your leader? You must return to Jerusalem, and the Lord will hand Laban over to you. ³⁰ After the angel said this to us, he left. ³¹ After the angel left, Laman and Lemuel again began to complain: How is it possible the Lord will hand Laban over to us? He's a powerful man and can command fifty. In fact, he can kill fifty, so why not us?

XV **4** I said to my brothers: Let's go back up to Jerusalem and be faithful in keeping the Lord's commandments. He's more powerful than the whole earth, so why not more powerful than Laban and his fifty? Or even than his tens of thousands? ² So, let's go back there. Let's be strong like Moses, because he actually spoke to the waters of the Red Sea and they divided to the right and left, and our fathers came through on dry ground out of slavery, and Pharaoh's armies followed and were drowned in the Red Sea. ³ Now you know this is true. And you also know an angel has spoken to you. So why do you doubt? Let's go back. The Lord can protect us, just like our ancestors, and destroy Laban, just like the Egyptians.

XVI ⁴ When I said this, they were still very angry and kept complaining. Nevertheless, they followed me until we reached the wall of Jerusalem. ⁵ It was dark and I had them hide outside the wall. After they concealed themselves, I crept into the city and went toward Laban's house. ⁶ I was led by the Spirit, not knowing in advance what I would do. ⁷ Nevertheless, I continued on. As I approached Laban's house, I saw a man on the ground ahead of me who was drunk with wine. 8 When I approached him, I saw it was Laban. 9 I noticed his sword and removed it from its sheath. Its hilt was made of pure gold and the design was of superior quality. The blade was made from the most expensive steel.

XVII   10 And the Spirit urged me to kill Laban. But I said in my heart: I've never killed anyone. So I hesitated and drew back, not wanting to kill him. 11 But the Spirit told me again: The Lord has handed him over to you. And I was also aware he had tried to kill me, and that he refused to listen to and follow the Lord's commandments, and he had also taken our property. 12 Then the Spirit told me again: Kill him — the Lord has handed him over to you. 13 The Lord kills the wicked to accomplish His righteous purposes. It's better for one man to lose his life than for a nation to lose their way and fall into unbelief. 14 When I had heard these words, I remembered the words the Lord had spoken to me in the wilderness: To the degree your descendants keep My commandments, they'll prosper in the promised land. 15 And I also considered that they couldn't keep the Lord's commandments of the Law of Moses unless they had the Law. 16 And I knew that the Law was engraved on the brass plates. 17 Furthermore, I knew the Lord had handed Laban over to me so I could get the records as He commanded. 18 So I obeyed the Spirit's voice, took Laban by the hair of his head, and struck his head with his own sword.

XVIII   19 After I had cracked his head with his sword, I took Laban's clothes and put them on. I also secured his armor around my waist. 20 After doing this, I went to Laban's treasury. As I was going there, I saw Laban's servant who had the treasury keys, and imitating Laban's voice I ordered him to go with me into the treasury. 21 He believed me to be his master Laban since he saw the clothes and the sword fastened around my waist. 22 He talked to me about the Jewish elders, knowing his master had been out with them at night. 23 And I spoke to him as if I were Laban 24 and told him I was going to carry the engravings on the brass plates to my older brothers who were outside the walls. 25 I also ordered him to follow me. 26 He thought I referred to church elders and I really was Laban whom I had killed, so he followed me. 27 He talked to me many times about the Jewish elders as I went to my brothers outside the city wall.

XIX   28 When Laman saw me, he was very scared, and so were Lemuel and Sam. They ran away because they thought I was Laban and he had killed me and was coming to kill them too. 29 I called after them and they heard me; so they stopped running away. 30 When Laban's servant saw my brothers, he began to shake with fear and was about to run and return to Jerusalem. 31 Because I have a large build and had received great strength from the Lord, I grabbed Laban's servant and held him so he couldn't run away.

XX

32 I told him that if he would agree with my words, as surely as the Lord lives and I live, if he would agree with what we said, we would spare his life. 33 And I took an oath that he didn't need to be afraid; he would be a free person like we were if he was willing to go down with us into the wilderness. 34 I also told him: The Lord has certainly commanded us to do this. So shouldn't we be diligent in keeping the Lord's commandment? Therefore if you're willing to go down into the wilderness to my father, you'll have a place with us. 35 Then Zoram — which was the servant's name — was satisfied with what I said and promised to go down into the wilderness to our father. He also made an oath he would stay with us from then on. 36 Now we wanted him to stay with us so the Jews wouldn't know about our sudden departure into the wilderness to follow and kill us. 37 But once Zoram took an oath, our worries about him ended. 38 So we took the brass plates and Laban's servant and went into the wilderness, traveling to our father's tent.

XXI

5 After we came to our father in the wilderness, he was overjoyed. And my mother Sariah was extremely glad because she had actually mourned for us, 2 since she thought we died in the wilderness. She had also complained against my father, telling him he was a dreamer, saying: You've led us out from our own land, and my sons are dead, and we're going to die in the wilderness. 3 My mother complained like this against my father. 4 And my father told her: I know I'm a man of visions. However, if I hadn't seen the things of God in a vision, I wouldn't have known God's goodness but would have stayed at Jerusalem and lost my life with my people. 5 But I've obtained a promised land, and I rejoice in that. I know the Lord will protect my sons from Laban and bring them back down to us in the wilderness. 6 This was how my father Lehi comforted my mother Sariah about us while we went through the wilderness up to Jerusalem to get the record of the Jews. 7 When we had returned to my father's tent, their joy was complete and my mother was comforted. 8 She said: Now I know for sure the Lord has commanded my husband to escape into the wilderness. I also know for certain the Lord has protected my sons and rescued them from Laban and given them power so they were able to accomplish what He had commanded them to do. These were her new remarks.

XXII

9 They were very glad and offered sacrifice and burnt offerings to the Lord and gave thanks to the God of Israel. 10 After thanking the

God of Israel, my father Lehi took the records engraved on the brass plates and carefully studied them from the beginning. 11 He saw they contained the five books of Moses, which gave an account of the world's creation and of Adam and Eve, who were our first parents; 12 and a record of the Jews from the beginning down to the start of the rule of Zedekiah, king of Judah; 13 and the prophecies of the holy prophets from the beginning, all the way up to the start of Zedekiah's rule; and many prophecies of Jeremiah. 14 My father Lehi also found his ancestors' genealogy on the brass plates; therefore he knew he was a descendant of Joseph, that same Joseph who was Jacob's son, who was sold into Egypt and kept safe by the hand of the Lord so that he could keep his father and his whole household from dying of starvation. 15 They had also been saved from slavery and escaped from Egypt by that same God who kept them alive. 16 This was how my father discovered his ancestors' genealogy. Laban was a descendant of Joseph too; therefore he and his forefathers had kept the records. 17 When my father saw all these things, he was filled with the Spirit and began to prophesy about his descendants: 18 that these brass plates would go to all nations, tribes, languages, and people who came from his descendants. 19 Therefore he said these brass plates would never be lost or obscured any more by time. And he prophesied many things about his descendants.

XXIII   20 Up to this point, my father and I had kept the commandments the Lord had given us. 21 We had obtained the records the Lord had commanded us to obtain and had studied them carefully, finding they were valuable and important for us so that we could retain the Lord's commandments for our children. 22 That being the case, it was God's wisdom for us to take them with us as we traveled in the wilderness to the promised land.

Chapter 2

6 Now I'm not providing my ancestors' genealogy in this part of my record, and I'm not going to do so on these plates that I'm engraving since it's provided in my father's record; so it's not included here. 2 I'm content to say that we're descended from Joseph. 3 Moreover, I don't care to provide a detailed account of all the events involving my father, since they won't fit on these plates, because I need the space so I can write the things of God. 4 My whole intent is to persuade people to come to the God of Abraham and the God of Isaac and the God of Jacob and be saved. 5 Therefore I don't write what's pleasing to the world, but what's pleasing to God and important for those who aren't worldly. 6 And so I'll command my descendants not to fill these plates with things that aren't valuable to mankind.

II   **7** Now I want you to know that after my father had finished prophesying about his descendants, the Lord spoke to him again, saying it wasn't right for him to take his family into the wilderness alone, but that his sons were to marry suitable women so that they could raise up children to the Lord in the promised land. 2 The Lord commanded him that my brothers and I were to return to the land of Jerusalem and bring Ishmael and his family back across the wilderness. 3 So I went again with my brothers through the wilderness to go back up to Jerusalem. 4 We went to Ishmael's house and gained his confidence, then we told him the Lord's words. 5 And the Lord softened Ishmael's heart and also his whole household's, so that they went with us through the wilderness back down to our father's tent.

III   6 As we traveled in the wilderness, Laman, Lemuel, two of Ishmael's daughters, and two of his sons and their families rebelled against me, Sam, their father Ishmael and his wife, and his three other daughters. 7 They rebelled because they wanted to return to Jerusalem. 8 Now I was troubled because of the hardness of their hearts, so I spoke to them, to Laman and Lemuel, saying: You are my older brothers. Why are you so hard in your hearts and blind in your minds that you need me, your younger brother, to speak to you and set an example for you? 9 Why haven't you listened to the Lord's word? 10 How can you forget you've seen an angel of the Lord? 11 How have you forgotten the great things the Lord has done for us, in rescuing us from Laban and letting us obtain the record? 12 And how have you forgotten the Lord can do everything for mankind according to His will, if they exercise faith in Him? So let's be faithful to Him. 13 And if we're faithful to Him, we'll reach the promised land. At some time in the future, you'll know the Lord's word concerning Jerusalem's destruction will be fulfilled, since everything the Lord has said about Jerusalem's destruction is certain to happen. 14 The Spirit of the Lord will soon stop struggling with them, because they've rejected the prophets, thrown Jeremiah in prison, and tried to kill our father, driving him away. 15 Because of this, I tell you that if you choose to return to Jerusalem, you'll die with them as well. Now, if you want to make that choice, go back up there. But remember the words I tell you, that if you go, you're sure to lose your lives too. This is what the Spirit of the Lord compels me to say to you.

IV   16 When I said this to my brothers, they got angry with me. And they took me by force because they were extremely angry. They tied me up with ropes in order to leave me in the wilderness to be eaten by wild animals as their plan to kill me. 17 But I prayed to the Lord, saying: O Lord, according to my faith in You, please free me from my brothers! Give me strength so I can break these ropes that have me tied. 18 When I said this, the ropes around my hands and feet came undone, and I stood in front of my brothers and spoke to them again. 19 And they got angry with me again and started to attack me. But one of Ishmael's daughters and her mother and one of Ishmael's sons pled with my brothers, and it softened their hearts and they gave up their determined efforts to kill me. 20 They regretted their wickedness, so they bowed down in front of me and begged me to forgive them for how they had treated me. 21 And I freely forgave them all they had done and urged them to pray to the Lord their God for forgiveness. And they did so. After they had finished praying to the Lord, we traveled back to our father's tent.

V   22 We went down to our father's tent, and after my brothers and I and Ishmael's family arrived at my father's tent, they gave thanks to the Lord God and offered sacrifice and burnt offerings to Him.

VI   **8** And we had gathered all kinds of seeds: many kinds of both grains and fruit.

VII   2 While my father was there in the wilderness, he told us: I've had a dream, or in other words, I've seen a vision. 3 Because of what I've seen, I have reason to praise the Lord about Nephi, and about Sam as well. I have reason to think they will be saved along with many of their descendants. 4 But, Laman and Lemuel, I'm very concerned for you. Indeed, it seemed like I saw a dark and gloomy wilderness. 5 And I saw a man dressed in a white robe who stood before me. 6 He talked to me and said I should follow him. 7 As I followed him, I saw I was in a dark and dreary wasteland. 8 After I had traveled for many hours in darkness, I began to pray to the Lord to help me, because of His many tender mercies.

VIII   9 After I had prayed to the Lord, I saw a large and spacious field. 10 Then I saw a tree with fruit that would make people happy. 11 I went and ate some of the fruit, discovering it was sweet beyond measure, better than all that I had ever tasted before. I noticed its fruit was white, brighter than I had ever seen.

IX   12 As I ate the fruit, it made my soul very joyful. So I began to wish my family would eat some of it too, since I knew it was better than all other fruit. 13 As I looked around, trying to catch sight of my family, I saw a river. It ran beside the tree whose fruit I was eating. 14 I looked to see where it came from and saw its source a little way off. At its source I saw your mother Sariah, Sam, and Nephi, standing there and looking lost. 15 I waved to them and yelled for them to come over to me and eat some of the fruit, which was better than any other fruit. ¹⁶ And they came over to me and also ate the fruit. ¹⁷ And I wanted Laman and Lemuel to come and eat some of the fruit too. Therefore I looked toward the source of the river to try to locate them. ¹⁸ I saw them, but they refused to come over to me and eat the fruit.

X ¹⁹ Then I saw an iron railing extending along the riverbank, leading to the tree next to me. ²⁰ I also saw a straight and narrow path that ran along the iron railing all the way to the tree beside me. It also led by the source of the river to a large and spacious field, as big as the earth itself. ²¹ And I saw innumerable throngs of people, many of them pressing forward so they could reach the path that led to the tree I was standing next to. ²² They moved forward and started on the path leading to the tree. ²³ Then a great dark cloud came up and those who had started on the path lost their way, wandering off and becoming lost. ²⁴ And I saw others pressing forward. They came and caught hold of the end of the iron railing and moved forward through the dark clouds, clinging to the iron railing until they arrived and ate some of the fruit from the tree. ²⁵ After they had eaten fruit from the tree, they looked around as if ashamed.

XI ²⁶ I also looked around and saw on the other side of the river an impressive and large building. It stood like it was in the air, high above the earth, ²⁷ and it was filled with people — old and young, male and female — and they wore expensive clothing. They appeared to mock and point their fingers at those who had come up and were eating the fruit. ²⁸ Those who had tasted the fruit were ashamed because of people scoffing at them, and they left, following forbidden paths and were lost.

XII ²⁹ Now I don't write all my father's words. ³⁰ But to summarize, he saw other crowds coming forward. People came, grasped the end of the iron railing, and moved forward, continually holding firmly to the iron railing until they arrived, sat down, and ate some of the fruit from the tree. ³¹ He also saw other crowds of people moving toward that impressive and large building. ³² And many drowned in the deep river, and many disappeared from his view, wandering on unfamiliar roads. ³³ A large number of people entered the large building. After they entered the building, they pointed at and made fun of me, and those who were also eating the fruit, but we didn't pay attention to them. ³⁴ My father said the following: All those who paid attention to the insults fell away. ³⁵ And my father said that Laman and Lemuel didn't eat any of the fruit.

XIII ³⁶ After my father had recounted everything about his dream or vision — and there was a lot covered — he told us that because of what he had seen in the vision, he was very afraid for Laman and Lemuel; afraid they would be shut out from the Lord's presence. ³⁷ He then urged them with all the feeling of a loving parent to listen to his words, because then the Lord might be merciful to them and not reject them. My father sincerely preached to them. ³⁸ After he had preached and prophesied to them about many things, he pleaded with them to keep the Lord's commandments. Then he finished speaking to them. **9** My father saw, heard, and said all these things as he occupied a tent in the valley of Lemuel, and much more that can't be written on these plates.

XIV ² Since I've mentioned these plates, these aren't the ones on which I'm making a complete account of my people's history. The plates set aside for that purpose I've given the name of Nephi; so they're called the plates of Nephi after my own name. Well, these plates are also called the plates of Nephi. ³ Understand, the Lord commanded me to make these plates for the specific purpose of making a written account of my people's ministry. ⁴ On the other plates there's a written account of the kings' rule and my people's wars and in-fighting. So these plates focus on telling you about our ministry, and the other plates focus on the kings' rule and my people's wars and arguments. ⁵ I trust the Lord commanded me to make these plates for His wise purposes, but I can't tell you His reasons. ⁶ You see, the Lord knows all things from the beginning. Therefore He prepares in advance any needed response to accomplish all His plans for mankind, to fulfill all His words. That's exactly how He works. Amen.

Chapter 3

10 On these plates I'll provide an account of my life, rule, and ministry. So, continuing on, I need to say something about my father's and my brothers' concerns.

II ² After my father had finished recounting his dream and urging them to diligence, he spoke to them about the Jews, ³ that once they're destroyed, along with that great city of Jerusalem, and after many have been carried away as prisoners into Babylon, then when the Lord decided the time was right, they were to return home, brought back out of slavery. After they're freed from slavery to occupy their land again, ⁴ 600 years after my father left Jerusalem, the Lord God would raise up a prophet among the Jews, even the Messiah, that is, a Savior of the world. ⁵ He also explained that many of the prophets testified about this Messiah, the Redeemer of the world, that he mentioned. 6 Therefore all mankind was and always would be in a lost and fallen state unless they relied on this Redeemer.

III   7 He also spoke about a prophet who was to come before the Messiah to prepare the way for the Lord, 8 who would cry out in the wilderness: Prepare the way for the Lord and follow in His straight path. There's one standing among you whom you don't acknowledge, who's far greater than I; whose sandal strap I'm not worthy to even touch. My father spoke at length about this. 9 My father said that prophet would baptize in Bethabara on the other side of the Jordan River. He also said that he would baptize with water, including baptizing the Messiah with water, 10 and after he baptized the Messiah with water, he would testify that he had baptized the Lamb of God, who would redeem all of creation from the Fall.

IV   11 After my father said these things, he talked to my brothers about the gospel that would be preached among the Jews, and about the Jews falling away in unbelief. And after they kill the coming Messiah, following His death, He would rise from the dead and make Himself known to the Gentiles by the Holy Ghost. 12 Understand, my father spoke extensively about the Gentiles and about the house of Israel, comparing them to an olive tree whose branches would be broken off and scattered throughout the earth. 13 Therefore he said it was part of God's plan for us to go to our promised land, to fulfill the Lord's word that we would be scattered across the earth; 14 and after the house of Israel has been scattered, they would be gathered back together; or in other words, in the end, after the Gentiles receive the fullness of the gospel, that the olive tree's natural branches (meaning the remnants of the house of Israel), would be grafted in or learn to worship the true Messiah, their Lord and their Redeemer. 15 My father prophesied and taught my brothers this. He said many more things that I'm not writing in this book since I've written about it in my other book. 16 All of this happened as my father lived in a tent in the valley of Lemuel.

V   17 After I heard all my father's words about what he saw in a vision, and what he understood by the power of the Holy Ghost which he received by faith in the Son of God about the coming Messiah, I also wanted to see, hear, and know about these things by the power of the Holy Ghost. That is God's gift to those who diligently seek Him, both long ago as well as when He'll show Himself to mankind. 18 He is the same yesterday, today, and forever. And the way has been prepared for all mankind from the foundation of creation if they repent and come to Him. 19 Because those who diligently seek will find, and God's mysteries will be unfolded to them by the power of the Holy Ghost.

This is true yesterday, today, and tomorrow because the Lord's pathway is one eternal round. 20 So remember, everyone: You will be judged for all your actions. 21 As a result, if you've pursued and done evil during the days of your probation, then you'll be found unclean before God's judgment seat. And no unclean thing can live with God; therefore you'll be rejected forever. 22 The Holy Ghost authorizes me to tell you these things and never deny them.

VI　　**11** After I had asked to personally experience the things my father had seen, and believing the Lord could reveal them to me, as I sat pondering in my heart, I was carried away in the Spirit of the Lord to a very high mountain, one I had never seen or set foot on before. 2 The Spirit asked me: What do you want? 3 I replied: I want to see what my father saw. 4 The Spirit asked me: Do you believe your father saw the tree he has talked about? 5 I replied: Yes, you know that I believe all my father's words. 6 When I had said these words, the Spirit shouted: Hallelujah to the Lord, the Most High God! He is God over the whole earth, even above all! And you are blessed, Nephi, because you believe in the son of the Most High God; therefore you'll see the things you've asked to see. 7 And this will be given to you for a sign, that after you've seen the tree that bore the fruit your father tasted, you'll also see a man descending from heaven and you'll testify of Him. And after you've testified of Him, you'll testify that He is the Son of God.

VII　　8 Then the Spirit said: Look! And I looked and saw a tree, like the tree that my father had seen. Its beauty surpassed all beauty and its brightness exceeded the whiteness of the newly fallen snow. 9 After I had seen the tree, I said to the Spirit: I see you've shown me the tree that's more precious than anything else. 10 Then He asked me: What do you want? 11 I replied: To know what it means. I spoke to Him as a man speaks, because I saw His form was as a man, yet I still knew it was the Spirit of the Lord, and He talked with me just like talking to another person.

VIII　　12 Then He told me: Look! And I looked in His direction but didn't see Him, since He departed. 13 Instead, I looked and I saw the great city of Jerusalem and other cities as well. And I saw the city of Nazareth. And in the city of Nazareth, I saw a virgin, and she was very beautiful and pure. 14 Then I saw the heavens open, and an Angel came down and stood in front of me. He asked me: Nephi, what do you see? 15 I replied: The most beautiful, pure virgin. 16 He asked me: Do you understand God's condescension? 17 I replied: I know that He loves His children, but I don't understand everything. 18 Then He said to me: The virgin you see is the Mother of the Son of God when He becomes a mortal. 19 I saw She was carried away in the spirit.

IX   After She had been carried away in the spirit for some time, the Angel told me: Look! 20 Then I looked and saw the virgin again, now carrying a child in Her arms. 21 The Angel told me: Behold the Lamb of God, even the Son of the Eternal Father. Do you know the meaning of the tree your father saw? 22 I replied: Yes, it's God's love, which inspires the souls of mankind; so it's the most valuable of all things. 23 Then He told me: Yes, and the greatest joy for mankind's soul.

X   24 After He had said these words, He said: Look! And I looked and saw the Son of God mingling as a mortal with mankind. I saw many fall down at His feet and worship Him. 25 Then I realized the iron railing my father saw was God's word. It led to the source of living waters or to the tree of life, whose waters represent God's love. I also concluded the tree of life represented God's love.

XI   26 Then the Angel told me again: Look and observe the condescension of God! 27 And I looked and saw the Redeemer of the world, whom my father mentioned, and the prophet who would prepare the way for Him. The Lamb of God went to him and was baptized by him. After baptism, I saw the heavens open and the Holy Ghost came down out of heaven and rested on Him in the form of a dove. 28 I saw that He went out ministering to the people in power and great glory, and large numbers of people gathered to hear Him. But I also saw Him thrown out of meetings. 29 I also saw twelve others following Him who were removed by the Spirit from my view.

XII   30 Then the Angel told me: Look! And I looked and saw the heavens open again and angels descending to mankind, and they ministered to them.

XIII   31 And He spoke to me again, saying: Look! And I looked and saw the Lamb of God going out among the people. I saw many people who were sick and afflicted with all kinds of diseases and with demons and unclean spirits — the Angel spoke and showed all these things to me — and the power of the Lamb of God healed them, and the demons and unclean spirits were thrown out.

XIV   32 Then the Angel said again: Look! And I looked and saw the Lamb of God, the Son of the Everlasting God, was taken and judged by the world. I was a witness and testify: 33 I saw He was put up on the cross and killed for the world's sins. 34 After He was killed, I saw that great numbers of people had gathered to fight against the Lamb's witnesses (which is what the Angel of the Lord called the Twelve). 35 Crowds had assembled, and I saw they were in a large and spacious building, like the one my father saw. The Angel of the Lord said: Look at the world and its wisdom; notice the house of Israel has gathered to fight against the Lamb's Twelve witnesses. 36 I saw and testify that the large and spacious building was the world's pride, and its fall was terrible. Then the Angel of the Lord said to me: This is how the destruction will be of all people who fight the Lamb's Twelve witnesses, from every nation, tribe, and language.

XV   **12** Then the Angel told me: Look and see your descendants and your brothers' descendants also. And I looked and saw the promised land and many people — seemingly as many as the sands of the sea. 2 Then I saw many people gathered to fight against each other. I saw wars, reports of wars, and death by the sword among my people. 3 I saw many generations killed in wars and conflicts on the land. And I saw many cities, too many to count. 4 Then I saw a dark cloud upon the promised land. I also saw lightning and heard thunder, earthquakes, and many violent noises, the earth's solid surface being broken up, mountains falling down in rubble, and the plains of the earth being broken up. I also saw many cities get sunk, many burned, and many collapse because of the earthquakes. 5 After I saw these things, I saw the dark cloud lifted from the surface of the earth. I also saw the survivors who hadn't died from the Lord's great and terrible judgments. 6 And I saw the heavens open and the Lamb of God descend from heaven. He came down and showed Himself to them.

XVI   7 I also saw and testify the Holy Ghost fell on twelve others, and they were ordained by God and chosen. 8 Then the Angel said to me: See the Lamb's twelve witnesses who were chosen to minister to your descendants. 9 And He told me: You remember the Lamb's Twelve witnesses. They're the ones who are to judge the twelve tribes of Israel; therefore the twelve ministers of your descendants will be judged by them because you belong to the house of Israel. 10 The Twelve ministers you now see will judge your descendants. They are righteous forever and because of their faith in the Lamb of God, His blood cleanses their clothes.

XVII   11 Then the Angel said: Look! And I looked and saw that three generations of people lived and died in righteousness; their clothes were clean, just like the Lamb of God. The Angel told me: These are made clean through the Lamb's blood because of their faith in Him. 12 I also saw many of the fourth generation who died in righteousness. 13 And I saw great numbers of people gathered together. 14 Then the Angel said to me: Now notice your descendants and your brothers' descendants. 15 I looked and saw great numbers of my descendants gathered against my brothers' descendants — they prepared for war. 16 Then the Angel said to me: See the filthy river your father saw and talked about; its depths are the depths of hell. 17 And the dark mists are the temptations of the accuser, who blinds people's eyes, hardens their hearts, and leads them away into wide roads, to perish and be lost. 18 The large and spacious building your father saw represents false and foolish thinking and the pride of mankind. A great and terrible gulf divides them — which is the sword of the justice of the Eternal God and Messiah, who is the Lamb of God, whom the Holy Ghost testifies of, from the beginning of the world until now, and from this time forth and forever.

XVIII   19 While the Angel said this, I saw my brothers' descendants fought against my descendants, just like the Angel said. And because of my descendant's pride and the accuser's temptations, I saw my brothers' descendants overpowered my descendants. 20 Then I watched and saw my brothers' descendants defeated my descendants. And large numbers of them spread out over the land. 21 I saw them gather in great numbers, and witnessed wars and reports of wars among them; and I saw many generations of people die fighting wars and hearing reports of wars. 22 Then the Angel told me: These will fall away in unbelief. 23 And I saw that after they fell away in unbelief, they became a corrupt, repulsive, and sinful people, following a meaningless religion and full of all kinds of abominations.

XIX   **13** Then the Angel told me: Look! And I looked and saw many nations and kingdoms. 2 Then the Angel asked me: What do you see? I replied: I see many nations and kingdoms. 3 Then He told me: These are Gentile nations and kingdoms. 4 I saw among the Gentile nations a large and powerful church was built up. 5 Then the Angel said to me: Notice the building up of a fully corrupt church, worse than all other churches, which kills God's holy ones, and tortures them, ties them down, subjugates them, and enslaves them with an iron yoke. 6 I saw this corrupt and utterly wicked church, and I saw that the accuser was the foundation of it. 7 I also saw gold, silver, woven and scarlet clothing, fine knit linen, and all kinds of costly apparel, and I saw all kinds of corruption. 8 Then the Angel said to me: The gold, silver, woven and scarlet clothing, fine knit linen, costly apparel, and corruption are the things this utterly wicked church considers valuable. 9 And it's to get praise of the world that they destroy the holy ones of God and enslave them.

XX   10 Then I looked and saw a great ocean, and it separated the Gentiles from my brothers' descendants. 11 The Angel said to me: God's anger is directed at your brothers' descendants. 12 And I looked and saw a man among the Gentiles, who was separated from my brothers' descendants by the great ocean. I also saw that the Spirit of God came down and influenced the man. He went out upon the vast water, going all the way to my brothers' descendants, who were in the promised land. 13 Then I saw the Spirit of God inspired other Gentiles, who then fled captivity and crossed the vast ocean. 14 Following that I saw large numbers of Gentiles on the promised land. I also saw that God's anger was upon my brothers' descendants, and they scattered before the Gentiles and were slaughtered. 15 And I saw that the Spirit of the Lord was upon the Gentiles, and they prospered and obtained the land as their inheritance. I saw they were devout, faithful, and beautiful, like my people before they were killed. 16 Then I saw the Gentiles who fled from captivity humbled themselves before the Lord, and His power was with them. 17 I saw that their foreign government that controlled them gathered on both sea and land to fight them. 18 But I saw God's power was with them, and His wrath was upon those who came to fight them. 19 I saw the Gentiles who had left captivity were protected by God's power from all other nations. 20 Then I saw they prospered in the land.

XXI   I also saw they had a book. 21 The Angel asked me: Do you know the book's purpose? 22 I replied: I don't know. 23 So He said: It comes from the Jews. And I saw it. And He told me: The book you see is a record of the Jews; it contains the covenants the Lord has made to the house of Israel. It also contains many of the prophecies of the holy prophets. It's a record like the engravings on the brass plates, except it's less complete. Still, it contains the covenants the Lord has made to the house of Israel; therefore they're very valuable to the Gentiles. 24 Then the Angel of the Lord said: You've seen that the book came from the Jews. When it came from the Jews, it contained the fullness of the gospel of the Lamb, whom the Twelve witnesses testified about. And they testified truthfully of the Lamb of God. 25 So these things were delivered in purity from the Jews to the Gentiles, relating the truth of God. 26 After they're delivered by the Lamb's Twelve witnesses, from the Jews to the Gentiles, you see the establishment of that corrupt and utterly wicked church, which is the most detestable of all other churches. For they removed from the Lamb's gospel many clear and extremely valuable parts and they've also removed many of the Lord's covenants. 27 They've done all this in order to corrupt and pervert the right ways of the Lord, to blind people's eyes and harden their hearts. 28 Therefore you see that after the book has passed through the hands of that corrupt and utterly wicked church, many clear and extremely valuable things are gone from the book, which is the book of the Lamb of God. 29 And after these clear and valuable things are gone, it was passed along to all the Gentile nations.

XXII   And after all Gentile nations receive the book, a great number of people make a great number of mistakes that gives Satan power over them. That altered book is what the Gentiles who crossed the sea to escape captivity bring with them. It lacks many clear, understandable things about the Lamb of God. 30 Nevertheless, you see the Gentiles have left captivity and have been liberated by God's power to independently control the land. The land is better than all other places on earth. The Lord God covenanted with your father to inherit it, and your descendants will mix with your brothers' descendants and survive. 31 God won't let the Gentiles destroy all your brothers' descendants, 32 or leave the Gentiles in the awful blind condition you see that resulted from that utterly wicked church removing the clear and extremely valuable parts of the Lamb's gospel. 33 Therefore, the Lamb of God says, I'll have mercy for the Gentiles and will judge and punish the remnant of the house of Israel.

XXIII   34 Then the Angel of the Lord told me: The Lamb of God says: After I've judged the remnant of the house of Israel (referring to your father's descendants), after punishing them using the Gentiles, I'll show mercy to the Gentiles. They'll make a great many mistakes because of the extremely clear and valuable parts of the Lamb's gospel that have been removed by that utterly wicked church, which is the mother of harlots. But by My power I'll bring to light for them more of My gospel, which will be clear and very valuable, says the Lamb. 35 Indeed, says the Lamb, I'll personally appear to your descendants so they are able to write many things that I'll provide to them, which will be plain and very valuable. After your descendants are destroyed and fall away in unbelief, along with your brothers' descendants, these writings will be hidden and protected, to later be delivered to the Gentiles by the gift and power of the Lamb. 36 My gospel will be written in them, says the Lamb — My rock and My salvation. 37 I'll bless those who then want to bring about My Zion; they'll have the gift and power of the Holy Ghost. And if they continue faithful to the end, they'll be raised up on the last day and saved in the everlasting kingdom of the Lamb. Therefore, any who proclaim peace, the joyful news, how beautiful shall be their presence upon the mountains!

XXIV   38 Then I saw my brothers' descendants and the book of the Lamb of God, which had come from the Jews, and that it came from the Gentiles to my brothers' descendants. 39 After it had come to them, I saw other books that came by the Lamb's power from the Gentiles to them — these convinced the Gentiles and my brothers' descendants, and also the Jews who were scattered throughout the earth, that the records of the prophets and the Lamb's Twelve witnesses are true. 40 Then the Angel told me: The last records that you've seen among the

Gentiles will confirm the truth of the first ones — which come from the Lamb's Twelve witnesses — and will reveal the clear and valuable things which have been removed from them and reveal to all people of every tribe and language that the Lamb of God is the Son of the Eternal Father and Savior of the world and that all people must come to Him or they cannot be saved. 41 And according to the words of the Lamb they must come to Him. And the Lamb's words will be revealed in the records of your descendants as well as in the records of the Lamb's Twelve witnesses. So they'll both be witnesses together, because there's one God and one Shepherd over the whole earth. 42 At a future time, He'll reveal Himself to all nations, both to the Jews and to the Gentiles. And after He has revealed Himself to the Jews and to the Gentiles, He'll then appear to the Gentiles and to the Jews. The last will be first and the first will be last.

XXV   **14** If the Gentiles then obey the Lamb of God, He'll reveal Himself to them in word and power and in person, in order to remove barriers to their belief, 2 and if they don't harden their hearts against the Lamb of God, they'll be included with your father's descendants — indeed, they'll be included as part of the house of Israel. And they'll become a blessed family in the promised land forever. They won't be enslaved anymore, and the house of Israel won't be embarrassed anymore. 3 And the great pit dug for them by that utterly wicked church, which the accuser and his followers founded so that he could take people's souls down to hell — that great pit dug for people's destruction will be filled with those who dug it, to their complete destruction, says the Lamb of God — not the destruction of the soul, but throwing it into that endless hell. 4 This is according to the accuser's imprisonment, and according to God's justice as well, upon all those who insist on doing wicked and corrupt things in God's sight.

XXVI   5 Then the Angel told me: You've seen that if the Gentiles repent, it will turn out well for them. You also know about the Lord's covenants with the house of Israel. And you've also heard that whoever doesn't repent must perish. 6 As a result, if the Gentiles harden their hearts against the Lamb of God, I will afflict them. 7 Because the time will come, says the Lamb of God, when I'll bring about a great and awe-inspiring work among mankind, one that will be everlasting — one way or the other — either to convince them, resulting in peace and life eternal; or to give them up to their hard hearts and blind minds, bringing about their slavery and temporal and spiritual destruction, under the accuser's enslavement which I've spoken about.

XXVII   8 When the Angel had said this, He asked me: Do you remember
the Father's covenants to the house of Israel? I replied: Yes. 9 Then He
told me: Look and observe that utterly wicked church, which is the
mother of abominations, whose foundation is the accuser. 10 Then He
told me: There are only two churches: one is the congregation of the
Lamb of God and the other is the church of the accuser. Therefore
anyone who doesn't belong to the congregation of the Lamb of God
belongs to the other wealthy and corrupt church that is the mother of
abominations, and she is the whore of the whole earth.

XXVIII   11 Then I looked and saw the whore of the whole earth. She was
spread everywhere across the seas, ruling over the whole earth, among
all people of every nation, tribe, and language. 12 And I saw the
congregation of the Lamb of God; its numbers were few because of
the wickedness and abominations of the whore who was spread
everywhere across the seas. Nevertheless, I saw that the congregation
of the Lamb, who were God's holy ones, were also there throughout
the earth; but their presence was small because of the wickedness of
the great whore whom I saw. 13 And I saw the great mother of
abominations assembled in large numbers all over the earth among all
Gentile nations to fight against the Lamb of God. 14 Then I saw the
power of the Lamb of God descend upon the holy ones of the Lamb's
congregation and upon the Lord's covenant people, who were
scattered across the earth. They were armed with righteousness and
God's power in great glory.

XXIX   15 And I saw that God's wrath was poured out upon that wealthy
and utterly wicked church, so that wars and reports of wars arose
among the nations and tribes of the earth. 16 As these wars and reports
of wars arose among the nations that followed the mother of
abominations, the angel told me: God's wrath is upon the mother of
harlots. You're a witness to all these things. 17 When the time comes
that God's anger is poured out upon the mother of harlots — the
wealthy and utterly wicked church of the whole earth, whose
foundation is the accuser — then as that happens it will be part of the
Father's work to vindicate the covenants He has made with His people
who belong to the house of Israel.

XXX   18 Then the Angel told me: Look! 19 And I looked and saw a man,
and he was dressed in a white robe. 20 The Angel said to me: This is
one of the Lamb's Twelve witnesses. 21 He's been appointed to see and
write about the remainder of these things, and also about many other
things that have happened. 22 He'll also write about the end of the
world. 23 Therefore the things he will write are proper and true, and
they're written in the book you saw coming from the Jews. When they

came from the Jews, or when the book came from the Jews, what was written was clear and pure and extremely valuable and easy for all to understand. 24 The things this witness of the Lamb is to write are many of the things that you've seen, and you'll see the rest. 25 However, you must not write the things you'll see after this, since the Lord God has ordered the witness of the Lamb of God to write them. 26 He has shown all things to others who have lived, and they've written them as well. They're sealed up to come forward in their correct form to the house of Israel, when the Lord deems it to be the proper time, according to the truth that's in the Lamb.

XXXI 27 I heard and testify that according to the Angel's word, the name of the Lamb's witness was John. 28 I'm forbidden to write the rest of the things I saw and heard. So, I'm satisfied with what I've written, and I've only written a small part of what I saw. 29 I testify that I saw the things my father saw, and the Angel of the Lord revealed them to me. 30 Now I finish writing about what I saw while I was in contact with the Spirit. And even though everything I saw isn't written, the things I have written are true. So be it, Amen.

Chapter 4

15 After I had been carried away in the Spirit and seen all these things, I returned to my father's tent. 2 I saw my brothers, and they were arguing with each other about what my father told them. 3 He had told them many great things that were hard to understand unless a person asked the Lord. Because they were hard-hearted, they didn't look to the Lord as they should have. 4 I was troubled because of their stubbornness and because of the things I had seen, and I knew that it was inevitable that the things would happen because of the great wickedness of mankind. 5 Since I had seen their fall, I was overwhelmed by my troubles, thinking my sorrow was more than anyone else because of the destruction of my people.

II 6 After my strength had returned, I talked to my brothers, asking to know why they argued. 7 They said: We can't understand what our father has said about the olive tree's natural branches and about the Gentiles. 8 I said to them: Have you asked the Lord? 9 They replied: We haven't — the Lord doesn't reveal any such thing to us. 10 Then I asked them: Why don't you keep the Lord's commandments? Why are you determined to damn yourselves because of the hardness of your hearts? 11 Don't you remember what the Lord has said? — if you choose not to harden your hearts and ask Me in faith, believing you will receive, consistently keeping My commandments, these things will certainly be revealed to you.

III   12 Now, I tell you that the Spirit of the Lord within our father compared the house of Israel to an olive tree. Are we not broken off from the house of Israel? Are we not a branch of the house of Israel? 13 The thing our father means about the natural branches being grafted in through the fullness of the Gentiles is that in the last days, when our descendants have fallen away in unbelief for many years over generations, and after the Messiah will have appeared in person to mankind, then the fullness of the gospel of the Messiah will come to the Gentiles, and from the Gentiles it will go to our descendants. 14 At that time, they'll learn that they're from the house of Israel and are the Lord's covenant people. Then our descendants will learn about their forefathers and learn about the gospel of their Redeemer, which He taught their ancestors. So they'll come to know about their Redeemer and the correct details of His doctrine, so they can know how to come to Him and be saved. 15 At that time, won't they be glad and give praise to their everlasting God, their rock and their salvation? Won't they receive strength and nourishment from the true vine at that day? Won't they come to God's true fold? 16 Yes. They'll be included with the house of Israel again; they'll be grafted into the true olive tree, being a natural branch of it. 17 This is what our father means. He also means that it won't happen until they've been scattered by the Gentiles. And he means that it will come through the Gentiles, so the Lord can show His power to the Gentiles, specifically because He'll be rejected by the Jews or by the house of Israel. 18 Therefore our father hasn't just spoken about our descendants, but also about all the house of Israel, pointing to the covenant to be fulfilled in the last days; the covenant the Lord made with our father Abraham, having said to him, All the families of the earth will be blessed through your descendants.

IV   19 I spoke to them extensively about these things and about the restoration of the Jews in the last days. 20 I recounted Isaiah's words to them, which told of the restoration of the Jews or the house of Israel — that after being restored they weren't to be lost anymore or scattered again. I told my brothers so many things that they were satisfied, persuaded, and humbled themselves before the Lord.

V   21 Then they spoke to me again, asking: What do these things mean, which our father saw in a dream? What's the meaning of the tree that he saw? 22 I replied: It represented the tree of life. 23 Then they asked me: What's the meaning of the iron railing that our father saw leading to the tree? 24 I told them it was the word of God and that those who were willing to obey and hold firmly to the word of God would never perish, nor would the adversary's temptations and fiery darts be able to overpower them so as to blind them and lead them away to destruction. 25 Therefore I urged them to pay careful attention to the Lord's word. Indeed, I urged them — with all the energy of my soul and all my ability — to pay careful attention to the word of God and to always remember to keep His commandments in all things. 26 Then they asked me: What did the river that our father saw mean? 27 I told them the water our father saw was filthiness, but that his mind was so occupied with other things he didn't notice the water was filthy. 28 I told them it was a terrible divide that separated the wicked from the tree of life and from the holy ones of God. 29 I said to them it represented the awful hell the angel told me was prepared for the wicked. 30 I then told them our father also saw that God's justice also divided the wicked from the righteous, and its glare was like a blinding fire ascending to God from eternity to eternity that never ends.

VI   31 They also asked me: Does this mean the body's torment in the days of mortality, or does it mean the spirit's final state following the death of the earthly body, or does it speak of physical things? 32 I told them it represented both physical and spiritual things; that the time would come when they would be judged for what they did, for the things they did while on earth during their days of mortal life. 33 Therefore if they were to die in their wickedness, they would have to be outcast from spiritual things involving righteousness. They would certainly be brought to stand before God to be judged for what they did, and if the things they did involved filthy thoughts and behavior, they'll certainly be filthy. And if they're filthy, it's impossible for them to live in God's kingdom; if they did, God's kingdom would have to be filthy as well. 34 But I tell you God's kingdom isn't filthy, and no unclean thing can enter God's kingdom. So there has to be a place of filthiness prepared for the filthy. 35 There is such a place prepared — that awful hell I've spoken about — and the accuser is at the foundation of it. So the final state of a person's soul is to live in God's kingdom or to be thrown out because of the justice I've explained to you. 36 So the wicked are separated from the righteous and from the tree of life, whose fruit is the most valuable and desirable of any fruit and the greatest of all God's gifts. This is how I spoke to my brothers. Amen.

Chapter 5

16 When I had finished speaking with my brothers they told me: You've declared harsh things to us, more than we can stand. 2 I replied that I knew I had spoken blunt things against the wicked because it's the truth. But I've justified the righteous, testifying they would be lifted up on the last day. Therefore the truth wounds the guilty since it cuts them to the core. ³ Now, my brothers, if you were righteous and willing to listen and pay careful attention to the truth in order to live righteously before God, you wouldn't complain because of the truth and say: You speak harsh things against us. ⁴ Then I humbly urged my brothers to keep the Lord's commandments. ⁵ And they humbled themselves before the Lord, and that gave me joy and great hopes for them, that they would walk in the paths of righteousness. ⁶ All this was said and done as my father lived in a tent in the valley he called Lemuel.

II
⁷ And I married one of Ishmael's daughters, and my brothers married his other daughters also, and Zoram married his oldest daughter. ⁸ My father had in this way fulfilled all the Lord's commandments given to him. And I also had been greatly blessed by the Lord.

III
⁹ Then the Lord's voice spoke to my father at night and commanded him to travel into the wilderness the next day. ¹⁰ When my father got up in the morning and went to the tent door, to his great astonishment he saw a round object of detailed workmanship on the ground, made of fine brass. Inside the ball were two pins, and one of them pointed where we were to go in the wilderness.

IV
¹¹ We gathered everything we needed to take into the wilderness and the rest of the provisions the Lord provided for us. And we took seeds of every kind that we were able to bring into the wilderness.

V
¹² So we took our tents and set out into the wilderness across the Laman River. ¹³ We traveled for four days in nearly a south-southeast direction. Then we pitched our tents again and named the place Shazer.

VI
¹⁴ Following that, we took our bows and arrows and went into the wilderness to hunt game for our families. After we had obtained food, we returned to them in the wilderness at Shazer. Then we traveled again in the wilderness, following the same direction, keeping to the most fertile parts of the wilderness in the mountainous area near the Red Sea. ¹⁵ We traveled for many days, killing food along the way with our bows, arrows, stones, and slings. ¹⁶ And we followed the directions the ball gave which guided us through the more fertile parts of the wilderness. ¹⁷ After we had traveled many days, we pitched our tents again so we could rest and get food for our families.

VII
¹⁸ But as I went out to hunt, I broke my bow, which was made of sturdy steel. After I broke my bow, my brothers were angry with me because its loss meant we couldn't get food. ¹⁹ So we returned without

food to our families. And since everyone was exhausted because of our travels, they suffered greatly because of the lack of food. 20 And Laman, Lemuel, and Ishmael's sons began to complain a great deal because of their suffering and difficulties in the wilderness. My father also began to complain against the Lord his God; indeed, they were all very unhappy, to the point they complained against the Lord. 21 I was mocked and shamed by my brothers because my bow had broken and their bows had lost their recoil. Therefore it became dangerous, so much so we faced starvation. 22 And I talked to my brothers a great deal, because they had hardened their hearts again, to the point of complaining against the Lord who is God. 23 I then made a wooden bow and an arrow from a straight stick, arming myself with a bow, arrow, sling, and stones. Then I asked my father: Where should I go to find game? 24 In turn, he asked the Lord, because they had humbled themselves because of my words, since I had said many things to them from my heart. 25 And the Lord's voice came to my father, and he was rebuked for complaining against the Lord, making him regret deeply his error.

VIII   26 The Lord's voice told him: Look on the ball and observe what is written. 27 When my father saw the things written on the ball, he became afraid and trembled a great deal, and so did my brothers and Ishmael's sons and our wives. 28 I realized the pointers in the ball worked according to the faith, diligence, and attention we gave them. 29 And a new writing, plain to be read, was written on them, letting me understand the Lord's ways. It was written and changed from time to time according to the faith and diligence we gave to it. We see from this that the Lord can accomplish great things by ordinary means. 30 I then climbed the mountain according to the directions given on the ball. 31 And I harvested game animals, and I obtained food for our families. 32 Then I returned to our tents, carrying the animals I harvested. When they saw that I brought food, they were overjoyed. And they humbled themselves before the Lord and gave thanks to Him.

IX   33 Then we traveled again, in nearly the same direction as in the beginning. After we had traveled for many days, we again pitched our tents to stay for a while.

X   34 And Ishmael died and was buried in the place called Nahom. 35 Ishmael's daughters mourned a great deal because of the loss of their father and because of their hardships in the wilderness. They complained about my father because he had brought them from Jerusalem, saying: Our father is dead, and we've wandered a long way into the wilderness and we've endured many difficulties: hunger, thirst, and fatigue. And after all this suffering we're going to die from hunger in the wilderness. ³⁶ These were their complaints about my father and me. They wanted to return home to Jerusalem. ³⁷ Then Laman said to Lemuel and Ishmael's sons: Let's kill our father and our brother Nephi, who's taken it upon himself to be our ruler and teacher, instead of us, his older brothers. ³⁸ He says the Lord has talked with him and angels have ministered to him. But we know he's lying to us. He tells us this and invents many things by his clever tricks to mislead us, perhaps planning to take us to some remote, uninhabited land. And after he's taken us there, he's come up with a plan to make himself a king and ruler over us, so he can force us to submit to his will and control. This was how my brother Laman got them angry. ³⁹ But the Lord was with us — His voice came and said many words to them and chastised them severely. After being rebuked by the Lord, they turned away their anger and repented of their sins, and the Lord blessed us again with food, letting us survive.

XI   **17** We resumed our journey in the wilderness, traveling nearly eastward from then on. We went through many hardships in the journey, and our women gave birth to children in the wilderness. ² But the Lord's blessings were so great that while we lived on raw meat in the wilderness, our women produced plenty of milk for their children and were strong, like the men. So they began to bear their journey without complaint.

XII   ³ Accordingly, we see God's commandments are certain to be fulfilled, and if people keep God's commandments, He nourishes and strengthens them and provides ways and means so they can accomplish what He's commanded them. That being the case, He provided ways and means for us as we traveled in the wilderness.

XIII   ⁴ We lived in the wilderness for many years, eight in total. ⁵ Then we came to the land we named Bountiful because it had plenty of fruit and wild honey. The Lord prepared all these things so we wouldn't perish. We saw the sea, which we called Irreantum (which means many waters).

XIV   ⁶ We pitched our tents by the seashore. And despite having suffered many hardships and difficulties, so many we can't write all of them down, we were overjoyed when we came to the seashore. And we named the place Bountiful because it was fruitful.

XV   ⁷ After I had been in the land of Bountiful for many days, the Lord's voice came to me, saying: Get up and climb the mountain. So I got up and climbed the mountain and prayed to the Lord. ⁸ Then the Lord told me: You must build a ship in the way I'll show you so I can carry your people across the sea. ⁹ And I asked: Lord, where should I go to find iron ore to melt so I can make tools to build the ship in the way you've shown me? 10 In response, the Lord told me where to go to find ore so I could make tools.

XVI   11 I then made a pair of bellows from animal skins with which to blow the fire. And after I had made a pair of bellows, I struck two stones together to make fire. 12 Up to that point, the Lord hadn't allowed us to make many fires as we traveled in the wilderness. He said: I'll keep your food from spoiling, and you will not need to cook it. 13 I will also be your light in the wilderness and prepare the way in front of you if you keep My commandments. So to the degree you keep My commandments, you'll be led toward the promised land. And you'll know that you're led by Me. 14 The Lord also said: After you've arrived at the promised land, you will know that I the Lord am God, that I saved you from destruction and brought you out of the land of Jerusalem. 15 So I made a great effort to keep the Lord's commandments and urged my brothers to be faithful and diligent. 16 I made tools from the ore that I melted from the rock. 17 When my brothers saw I was preparing to build a ship, they began to mock me, saying: Our brother's a fool! He thinks he can build a ship! He also thinks he can cross this great sea. 18 These were some of my brothers' complaints about what I was doing, and they didn't want to work, since they didn't believe I could build a ship, and they refused to believe I was led by the Lord.

XVII   19 Now I was deeply distressed because of how stubborn they were. When they saw I began to be discouraged, they were delighted, so much so that they gloated over me, saying: We knew you couldn't build a ship, since we knew you lacked good sense; you'll never finish such a huge task. 20 You're like our father, persuaded by his foolish, deluded thinking. He's taken us from the land of Jerusalem, and we've wandered in the wilderness these many years. And our women have struggled to travel while pregnant, and they've had children in the wilderness and suffered everything but death. It would have been better for them to have died before they left Jerusalem than to have endured these difficulties. 21 We've undergone hardships all these years in the wilderness when we could have enjoyed our possessions and property, and we would have been happy. 22 We know the people in the land of Jerusalem were righteous, since they keep the Lord's statutes and judgments and all His commandments according to the Law of Moses; so we know they're a righteous people. But our father has judged them and taken us from home because we were willing to listen to him; and our brother is like him. These were my brothers' complaints about us.

XVIII   23 I asked them: Do you believe our ancestors, the children of Israel, would have been freed from slavery to the Egyptians if they hadn't listened to the Lord's words? 24 Do you think they would have left their bondage if the Lord hadn't commanded Moses to free them? 25 Now you know the children of Israel were enslaved and you know they were forced to do hard work. So you know it was obviously a good thing for them to be freed from slavery. 26 Now you know Moses was directed by the Lord to do that great and miraculous thing. And you know the waters of the Red Sea were divided to the right and left by his word and they passed through on dry ground. 27 But you know the Egyptians — Pharaoh's armed forces — drowned in the Red Sea. 28 And you also know they were fed with manna in the wilderness, 29 and Moses, through his word according to God's power which was in him, struck the rock and water came out, so that the children of Israel could quench their thirst. 30 And despite being led — with the Lord their God, their Redeemer, going ahead of them, leading them by day, giving light to them by night, and doing everything for them that was necessary for people to receive — they hardened their hearts, refused to understand, and complained against Moses and against the true and living God. 31 And according to His word He destroyed them, and according to His word He led them, and according to His word He did everything for them. And nothing was done except by His word. 32 After they had crossed the Jordan River, He made them so powerful that they were able to drive out the inhabitants of the land and scatter them until they were gone.

XIX   33 Do you think the prior inhabitants of the promised land who were driven out by our ancestors were righteous? No, they were not. 34 Do you think that if those prior inhabitants had been righteous, our ancestors could have driven them out? No, our ancestors couldn't have. 35 The Lord values all mankind equally; however, those who are righteous are blessed by God. But that nation rejected all of God's words; they were ripe in iniquity and God's full wrath was imposed upon them. So the Lord cursed the land against them and blessed it for our ancestors. He cursed it, resulting in their destruction, and He blessed it for our ancestors, to give them possession of it.

XX   36 The Lord has created the earth to be inhabited, and He's created His children to inhabit it. 37 He raises up a righteous nation and destroys the wicked nations. 38 He leads the righteous to favorable lands and He destroys the wicked, cursing the land against them because of their sins. 39 He rules high in the heavens because it's His throne, and this earth is His footrest. 40 He loves those who want Him to be their God. He loved our fathers and covenanted with them —

Abraham, Isaac, and Jacob — and remembered the covenants He had made; so He freed their children out of Egypt. 41 And He disciplined them in the wilderness with His rod because they hardened their hearts, just like you have. The Lord imposed afflictions because of their iniquity. He sent flying fiery serpents among them. But after they were bitten, He prepared a way to heal them. It required them to look. But because the cure was so simple, many died. 42 They hardened their hearts from time to time and dishonored Moses and also God. Still, you know they were led by His unequaled power into the promised land.

XXI 43 After all these things, they've now become wicked, almost completely ripe in wickedness. For all I know, they're now about to be destroyed; and it's certain they'll be destroyed except for only a few who will be taken away as slaves. 44 Because of this, the Lord commanded our father to depart into the wilderness. The Jews also tried to kill him. And you have too. So you are murderers in your hearts, and you are like them. 45 You're quick to commit iniquity but slow to remember the Lord who is God. You've seen an angel and he spoke to you. You've heard His voice from time to time, and He's spoken to you in a quiet, gentle voice; but you were no longer capable of feeling and you couldn't feel His words. So He's spoken to you in a thundering voice that made the earth shake as if it would split in two. 46 You also know that by His all-powerful word He can make the earth pass away. You know that by His word He can level mountains and break apart the stable ground. Then how can you be so hard in your hearts? 47 My soul suffers because of you, and my heart aches. I'm afraid you'll be rejected forever. I'm full of the Spirit of God, so much so that I've become exhausted.

XXII 48 When I said this, they got angry with me and wanted to throw me into the deep sea. As they approached me, I said: In the name of the Almighty God, I command you not to touch me. God's power fills every part of my frame, and if either of you put your hands on me, you'll shrivel up like a dried weed. You're nothing before God's power, and God will strike you down. 49 Then I warned them not to complain against their father or refuse to work with me anymore, since God had commanded me to build a ship. 50 I told them: Anything God has commanded me to do, I can do. If He were to command me to say to this water: Become earth! — then it would become earth. Whatever I say, if God commands it, it will happen. 51 Now if the Lord has such great power and has performed so many miracles among mankind, then why can't He teach me how to build a ship? 52 I told my brothers many things that silenced them and they were unable to argue with

me. They also didn't resist or dare lay hands on me or even touch me
with their finger for many days. The Spirit of God affected them so
powerfully that they were afraid of withering away by touching me.

XXIII   53 Then the Lord said to me: Reach out your hand to touch your
brothers. They won't shrivel and dry up from your touch, but I the
Lord will shock them. And I'll do this to let them know I'm the Lord
who is God. 54 So I stretched out my hand to my brothers and they
didn't shrivel and dry up, but the Lord shocked them, just as He said
He would. 55 Then they said: We know for sure that the Lord is with
you because we know His power has shocked us. Then they fell down
in front of me and were about to worship me, but I wouldn't let them
do it, saying: I'm your brother, and your younger brother at that.
Therefore worship the Lord who is God and honor your father and
mother so your days will be long in the land the Lord your God will
give you.

XXIV   **18** So they worshiped the Lord and began to work with me, and
we produced well-crafted timbers. And the Lord showed me from time
to time how to shape the ship's timbers. 2 Now I didn't pattern the
timbers in a way followed by men, and I didn't build the ship in the
way that shipbuilders would do it either, but I built it following the way
the Lord showed me; as a result, it wasn't a typical man-made ship.

XXV   3 And I often went to the mountain, and I prayed to the Lord
frequently; therefore He showed me great things.

XXVI   4 After I completed the ship following the Lord's instructions, my
brothers saw it was good and its workmanship was excellent; so they
humbled themselves again before the Lord.

XXVII   5 The Lord's voice then spoke to my father saying we were to get
ready and embark. 6 So the following day, after we had prepared
everything — plenty of fruit and meat from the wilderness, large
quantities of honey and provisions, obeying what the Lord
commanded us to prepare — we entered the ship with all our cargo,
seeds, and everything we brought with us, every one in order of their
age. Then we embarked with our wives and children. 7 Now my father
had had two sons in the wilderness: the older one was named Jacob
and the younger Joseph.

XXVIII   8 After we all entered the ship — bringing with us supplies and
other things we had been commanded to bring — we set out to sea
and were driven before the wind toward the promised land.

XXIX   9 After we sailed for many days, my brothers and Ishmael's sons
and their wives began to indulge in feasting and drinking, to such an
extent they started to dance, sing, and become disrespectful, until they
forgot the power that brought them there; indeed, they became

extremely insolent. 10 I became very afraid the Lord would be angry with us and strike us down because of our iniquity, and we would all drown in the sea. So I tried to sober them up by talking to them. But they got angry with me, saying: We refuse to have our younger brother control us.

xxx 11 Then Laman and Lemuel took me, tied me up with ropes, and were otherwise brutal to me. Nevertheless, the Lord allowed it to happen so He could remind us of His ability to accomplish everything He said warning the wicked. 12 After they tied me up and I couldn't move, the compass the Lord had prepared stopped working. 13 As a result, they didn't know where to steer the ship. So a strong, violent storm arose, and we were driven backward on the water for three days. They became very afraid they would be drowned in the sea. Nevertheless, they didn't untie me. 14 The storm became very severe on the fourth day driving us back, 15 and we were about to sink into the depths of the sea. After we were driven backward for four days, my brothers realized God's judgments were upon them, and that they would die unless they repented of their iniquities. So they came to me and untied the ropes on my wrists. They had swollen a great deal and my ankles were also very swollen; it was extremely painful. 16 Still, I looked to God and praised Him all day long; I didn't complain against the Lord because of my difficulties.

xxxi 17 Now my father Lehi had been saying many things to them and to Ishmael's sons, but they just threatened anyone who spoke on my behalf. And since my parents were old and had suffered many hardships over their children, they were physically sick and bedridden. 18 Because of their suffering and heartbreak over my brothers' iniquity, they were almost taken from this life to meet God. Their gray hair was about to be brought down to return to dust; they were at the point of being laid with sorrow into a watery grave. 19 Likewise Jacob and Joseph, since they were young and still breastfeeding, were impacted by their mother's suffering. And my wife, with her tears and prayers, along with my children, failed to soften my brothers' hearts and get them to untie me. 20 Nothing except for God's power, threatening them with destruction, was able to soften their hearts. Therefore when they saw they were about to sink into the depths of the sea, they repented of what they had done, and they untied me.

xxxii 21 After they untied me, I took the compass and it directed us to whatever place I needed. I prayed to the Lord, and after I prayed, the winds and storm stopped and there was a great calm. 22 Then I guided the ship so we sailed again toward the promised land. 23 After we had sailed for many days, we arrived at the promised land. We disembarked, pitched our tents, and called it the promised land.

XXXIII
24 We began to till the earth and plant seeds. We put all the seeds we had brought from the land of Jerusalem in the ground and they grew extremely well; so we were blessed abundantly. 25 As we explored the wilderness, we found there were forest animals of every kind: cows, oxen, donkeys, horses, goats, wild goats, and all kinds of wild animals for human use. We also found a variety of precious metals: gold, silver, and copper.

XXXIV
19 I made metal plates to engrave a record of my people in order to obey the Lord's command. I engraved my father's record, our travels in the wilderness, and my father's prophecies on the plates I made. I've also engraved many of my own prophecies on them. 2 I didn't know when I made them that the Lord would later command me to make these plates. Therefore my father's record, his ancestors' genealogy, and most of our activities in the wilderness are engraved on the first plates I mentioned. So the details of what happened before I made these plates are actually written on the first plates.

XXXV
3 After I was commanded to make these plates, I received another commandment that the ministry and prophecies — the most important parts of them — were to be written on these plates, and what is written was to be kept to instruct my people, who would inhabit the land, and for other wise purposes known to the Lord. 4 Therefore I made a record on the other plates, which gives a more complete account of my people's wars, struggles, and periods of destruction. I've done this and commanded my people to do this after I was gone and to hand these plates down from one generation to another, or from one prophet to another, until the Lord gave them further commandments. 5 I'll later give an account of my making these plates. So that's how I'll proceed. I'm doing this to preserve for my people a record of the more sacred things. 6 However, I haven't written anything on plates unless I think it's sacred. If I make mistakes, so did others long ago. I don't wish to excuse myself because of other men, but I would excuse myself because of the weaknesses of human nature.

XXXVI
7 What some people consider very valuable, both to the body and spirit, others disregard and trample under their feet. People even trample underfoot the very God of Israel. I say trample underfoot, but I should use other words: they regard Him as unimportant and don't hearken to His counsels. 8 According to the angel's words, He will come 600 years after my father left Jerusalem. 9 And the world, because of their iniquity, will judge Him to be of no worth. Therefore they'll

whip Him, and He'll submit to it; they'll strike Him, and He'll submit to it; and they'll spit on Him, and He'll submit to it, because of His loving-kindness and long-suffering toward mankind. 10 The God who led our fathers out of Egypt and from slavery, who kept them alive in the wilderness, the God of Abraham and the God of Isaac and the God of Jacob will give Himself up as a man into the hands of wicked men, according to the words of the angel. He'll be lifted up, according to the words of Zenoch; to be crucified, according to the words of Neum; and to be buried in a sepulcher, according to the words of Zenos. He also spoke about the three days of darkness — which was to be a sign of His death given to those who would be living on the islands of the sea, more particularly given to those who are from the house of Israel.

XXXVII   11 This is what the prophet said: The Lord God will certainly visit all of the house of Israel at that day, some with His voice because of their righteousness, to their great joy and salvation, and others with the thunder and lightning of His power: by storm, fire, smoke, mist of darkness, the earth splitting apart, and mountains raised up. 12 All these things will certainly happen, said the prophet Zenos, and earth's bedrock, or solid ground, will break apart. Because of the groaning of the earth, many kings living on the islands of the sea will be so affected by the Spirit of God they'll cry out: The God of nature suffers. 13 The prophet said: As for those at Jerusalem, because they crucified the God of Israel and closed their hearts, rejecting the signs, miracles, and the power and glory of the God of Israel, they'll become hated and persecuted. 14 Because they've turned their hearts aside, said the prophet, and treated the Holy One of Israel with contempt, their aimless path will lead to destruction, scorning, ridicule, and hatred from all nations. 15 Nevertheless, the prophet said when the time comes that they don't turn their hearts aside anymore against the Holy One of Israel, He'll remember the covenants He made to their fathers. 16 And then He'll remember those who live on the islands of the sea. According to the words of the prophet Zenos, the Lord said: I'll gather in all the people who are from the house of Israel, from the four quarters of the earth. 17 The whole earth will see the Lord's salvation and people of every nation, tribe, and language will be blessed.

XXXVIII   18 I have written these things to my people hoping to persuade them to remember the Lord their Redeemer. 19 Therefore I speak to all the house of Israel, if they read these things. 20 For I have overwhelming impressions from the spirit about those who live at Jerusalem; it makes all my joints weak. Because if the Lord wasn't merciful to warn me about these judgments, just as He had former prophets, I would have died alongside them. 21 He certainly showed former prophets everything about them. He also showed prophets about us; so we read about us in what's written on the brass plates.

Chapter 6

22 So, I taught my brothers these things. I also read to them from the brass plates, so they could learn what the Lord had done in other lands among former people. 23 I read to them many things from the books of Moses. But in order to more completely persuade them to believe in the Lord their Redeemer, I read to them what the prophet Isaiah had written. I applied all scriptures to us, to educate and benefit us. 24 Therefore I said to them: Listen to the prophet's words, you who are a remnant of the house of Israel, a branch that's been broken off. Listen to the prophet's words written to all the house of Israel and apply them to yourselves, so you can have hope as well as your Israelite relatives from whom you've been broken off.

II   This is what the prophet wrote: **20** Hear and follow this, O house of Jacob, who are called by the name of Israel and have been through the waters of Judah (or through the waters of baptism), who testify using the name of the Lord and refer to the God of Israel; but who testify falsely and never righteously. 2 Despite this, they call themselves part of the holy city, without obeying the God of Israel, who is the Lord of Hosts; indeed, the Lord of Hosts is His name. 3 Know this, I've announced prior events from the beginning; and they were established by My words, and I made them happen. I caused them exactly as foretold. 4 And I did it because I knew you are stubborn, and you refuse to bow your neck or your hard head like brass. 5 I have warned you, even from the beginning; before it happened, I forewarned you. I revealed them because I expected you would say: My idol accomplished this, my religious icon and my gold statue have accomplished it. 6 You've heard and seen all this, and won't you admit it? And I've revealed to you new things now, even hidden things, and will you claim you already know them? 7 They're revealed now, and not from the beginning; and you're learning it now and never before. I'm telling you now to prevent you from saying: I already knew about it. 8 But you won't hear, you won't understand, because you refuse to listen. I've always known you were deceitful and have been lawless from your birth. 9 Nevertheless, for My reputation I'll delay punishing you, and to show I'm merciful I won't cut you off. 10 But remember, I'll reform you through hardships you will suffer. 11 For My reputation — yes, to prove I'm trustworthy — I do these things. Should I be willing to let My name be dishonored? I won't let people worship another.

III   ¹² Listen to Me, descendants of Jacob, and Israel as I called you, for I Am: I Am the First, and I Am also the Last. ¹³ My hand has also laid the foundation of the earth, and My power upholds the organized heavens. I've ordained it all and the creation continually obeys Me. ¹⁴ All of you, gather together and hear this: Who among you has revealed these things to you? The Lord has loved Jacob; yes, He'll fulfill His promises He has revealed in prophecy. And He'll do as He pleases with Babylon, and He'll also confront the Chaldeans. ¹⁵ Also, says the Lord, I the Lord, indeed, I've spoken; I've called My prophet to declare; I've brought him, and he'll succeed in his mission.

IV   ¹⁶ Come near unto Me and hear this. From the beginning I haven't spoken in secret; from the time anything existed, I was there. (Now the Lord God has sent me, endowed with His Spirit.) ¹⁷ The Lord your Redeemer, the Holy One of Israel says: I the Lord am your God, teaching you for your own benefit. Guiding you in the way you should go. ¹⁸ If only you would obey My commandments! Then your peace would have been like a river and your prosperity uninterrupted like the waves of the sea. ¹⁹ Your offspring would be as many as the sand, their descendants as many as the grains of sand. Their name would never be cut off or end before Me.

V   ²⁰ Go away from Babylon, flee from Chaldea; loudly shout this, announce this, send this message to the ends of the earth! Say: The Lord has redeemed His servant Jacob! ²¹ They have never thirsted; He led them through the deserts, He made water flow out of the rock for them; He split the rock and the waters gushed out. ²² And despite all this and even greater things, the Lord states: There's no peace for the wicked.

VI   **21** Listen, scattered Israel, who have been divided and scattered because of your corrupt priests. Listen, you people who are far away: The Lord appointed me before I was born; He named me while I was in my mother's womb. ² He made my mouth like a sharp sword; He hid me in the shadow of His hand and made me a polished arrow, hiding me in His quiver. ³ And He said to me: You are My servant Israel in whom I glory. ⁴ Then I said: I thought I had labored without success, I've used my strength to produce only empty breath. But the Lord is the judge of it.

VII   ⁵ And now the Lord has decided — He who formed me in the womb to be His servant to bring Jacob back to Him, so that Israel may be restored, and has honored me in His sight, my God has given me strength. ⁶ And He said: Is it not enough that you should be My servant I use to raise up the tribes of Jacob and to restore the survivors of

Israel? Then I will also make you a light for the Gentiles, that My salvation may reach to the ends of the earth. 7 This is what the Lord said, the Redeemer of Israel, His Holy One, to the despised ones, to the hated nations, to the slaves of rulers: Kings will see and stand up, princes and nobles will fall down before you to honor the Lord, who is faithful, the Holy One of Israel. 8 The Lord said: In an hour of favor I answered you even if on the islands of the sea, and on a day of salvation I helped you. And I'll preserve My people and will yet show My will through them, to restore My covenant with a remnant upon the earth, and they'll inherit My renewed birthright as the chosen people, 9 Saying to the prisoners: Go free; and to those in darkness: Move yourselves into the light. They'll feed along the roadways, and on every high place will I feed them. 10 They won't be hungry or thirsty, hot winds and the sun won't oppress them; because He who loves them will lead them. He'll guide them to springs of water. 11 I'll make My temple a path to the heavens and the roads from it will exalt. 12 Then, O house of Israel, Look! They're coming from far away, amazingly, from the north, and from the west, and these from the far east.

VIII   13 Let the heavens shout, and rejoice on earth, for those scattered are returning; and begin shouting upon the mountains, for the Lord has brought comfort to His people and lovingly embraced His afflicted people. 14 But Zion says: The Lord has abandoned me, my Lord has forgotten me — but He'll show that He has not. 15 Can a woman forget her baby, or abandon her newborn? Even if she were to forget, I can never forget you, house of Israel. 16 Look, I have cuts in the palms of My hands to remember you; your cities are continually watched by Me. 17 Your children will return quickly, those who attacked and assaulted you will run from you.

IX   18 Look up and all around you and see: the scattered are gathering, coming back to you! As certain as I live, declares the Lord, you'll embrace them like necklaces around your neck, as welcome to you as a marrying bride. 19 As for your ruins and desolated places, and lands that were laid waste, they're recovered and soon to be crowded with settlers. While those who fought you will be driven away from you. 20 The children you thought had been lost will yet say to you: The place is too crowded for me, give me another place to settle. 21 And you'll say to yourself: Who's born these children for me? When I thought I was left barren and grieving, exiled and hated, who raised these children for me? I was alone; where have these children been?

X   22 The Lord God declares: I'll raise My hand to the Gentiles and set My banner flying to invite people to gather. And they'll bring your sons in their arms, and your daughters carried on their shoulders.

23 And kings will tend your children, and their queens will serve as nurses. They'll bow down to you, face to the ground, and clean the dust from your feet; and you'll know that I Am the Lord, for those who trust Me won't be ashamed. 24 Can the chains imposed by the powerful be broken or the enslaved be freed? 25 Yet the Lord proclaims: Even those suffering in terrible bondage will be freed, and all the chains binding down mankind will be broken. For I'll fight for you, and I'll liberate your children. 26 I'll make the tyrants eat their own flesh; they'll be drunk with their own blood as if it was wine. And everyone will realize that I the Lord am your Savior and Redeemer, the Mighty One of Jacob.

Chapter 7

22 After I had read these things written on the brass plates, my brothers came to me and asked: What do the things you've read mean? Are they to be understood according to spiritual things, or what will happen to the spirit and not the body? 2 I told them: They were revealed to the prophet by the voice of the Spirit, because the Spirit has revealed everything that will happen to mortal people to the prophets. 3 Therefore the things I've read pertain to both physical and spiritual matters.

II It appears that sooner or later the house of Israel will be scattered throughout the earth and among all nations. 4 Indeed, there are many who are already lost and unknown to those at Jerusalem: yes, most of the tribes have been led away, and they're scattered here and there on islands of the sea. None of us know where they are, but we do know they've been led away. 5 And since the time they've been led away, these things have been prophesied about them and about those who will be scattered and brought to ruin in the future because of the Holy One of Israel, since they'll harden their hearts against Him. Therefore they'll be scattered among all nations and hated by all people.

III 6 Nevertheless, after the Gentiles are benefited by the record of the Jews, and the Lord has blessed the Gentiles and set them up as an example of belief, and Jacob's descendants have been carried in their arms and their daughters have been carried on their shoulders — these references are physical, since that is the nature of the Lord's covenants with our fathers. And it refers to our future and all the others from the house of Israel. 7 It also means that, after the entire house of Israel has been scattered and brought to ruin, the Lord God will raise up a powerful nation among the Gentiles, here on this land, and our descendants will be scattered by them. 8 After our descendants are scattered, the Lord God will proceed with an amazing work among the Gentiles that will be very valuable to our descendants. So it's compared to them being cared for by the Gentiles and carried in their arms and on their shoulders. 9 And it will also be valuable to the Gentiles — not only to them but to the entire house of Israel — to reveal and restore the covenants that the Father of heaven made with Abraham, having told him: All the families of the earth will be blessed through your descendants. 10 And I want you to know, my brothers, that the families of the earth can't be blessed unless He shows His power to all nations. 11 Therefore the Lord God will proceed to uncover His restored truths in the sight of people from every nation, to restore again His covenants and His gospel to those who are from the house of Israel. 12 As a result, He'll bring them back out of captivity — they'll be gathered to the lands they first inherited, and they'll be brought out of confusion and darkness, and they'll know the Lord is their Savior and their Redeemer, the Mighty One of Israel.

IV   13 And the murderous guilt of that utterly wicked church — the whore of the entire earth — will come back upon their own heads, because they'll fight among themselves. The swords they wield will fall upon their own heads, and they'll be drunk with their own blood. 14 And every nation that fights against you, O house of Israel, will be turned against each other. They'll fall into the pit they dug to ensnare the Lord's people. Those who fight against Zion will be destroyed. And the great whore that's corrupted and perverted the right ways of the Lord — that utterly wicked church — will tumble to the dust, and its fall will be complete. 15 The prophet has said: The time is quickly coming that Satan will no longer have power over mankind's hearts. The time is soon coming that the proud and those who do evil will be like straw; and the time is coming that they will certainly be burned. 16 Indeed, the time is soon coming when the full extent of God's wrath will be poured out on all mankind, since He won't allow the wicked to destroy the righteous. 17 Therefore He'll keep the righteous safe by His power, even if it means that the full extent of His wrath must come while the righteous are preserved by God destroying their enemies by fire. Therefore the righteous don't need to be afraid, because the prophet has said: They will be saved, even if it requires fire. 18 My brothers, these things are coming soon; there will be blood, fire, and smoke here, covering the face of this land. It will happen to mortal people in this life if they reject the Holy One of Israel. 19 However the righteous won't be destroyed, because those who fight against Zion are who will be cut off.

V   20 And the Lord will absolutely prepare the way for His people. He'll fulfill the words of Moses, when he said: A prophet will the Lord your God raise up for you, like unto me. You're to hear Him in all things whatsoever He'll teach you. And then everyone who won't follow that prophet will be cut off from among the people. 21 Now I declare to you that this prophet that Moses spoke about was the Holy One of Israel. Given that, He'll execute judgment in righteousness. 22 The righteous don't need to be afraid because they aren't the ones to be brought to ruin. Instead, it's the accuser's kingdom built up by people, and established among those living on earth, that will fall. 23 The time will soon come when the churches built up for profit, built up to gain power over mankind, built up to become popular in the world, and those that try to gratify the lusts of the people and desire worldly things and indulge in all kinds of iniquity — in short, all those that belong to the accuser's kingdom — they're the ones who need to be afraid, tremble, and shake. They're the ones who will be thrown low in the dust. They're the ones who will be burned up like straw. This is according to the prophet's words. 24 The time will soon come when the righteous will be cared for like well-fed calves, and the Holy One of Israel will rule in dominion, strength, power, and great glory. 25 He'll gather His children from the four quarters of the earth and will count His sheep, and they will know Him. And they'll constitute one fold with one Shepherd; He'll feed His sheep and they'll find security in Him. 26 Because of His people's righteousness, Satan won't have any power. He won't be let loose for many years since he won't have any influence in people's hearts, because they'll live in righteousness and the Holy One of Israel will rule. 27 Now I tell you all these things will happen here in this world. 28 But people of every nation, tribe, and language will abide safely with the Holy One of Israel if they only repent.

VI   29 Now I'll finish, because I don't dare say anything more about this. 30 Therefore, my brothers, I want you to trust that the things written on the brass plates are true which testifies that every person must obey God's commandments. 31 Therefore you shouldn't think my father and I are the only ones who have testified and taught this. That being the case, if you're obedient to the commandments and stay faithful to the end, you'll be saved on the last day. And so it is. Amen.

The Second Book of Nephi

An account of Lehi's death. Nephi's brothers rebel against him. The Lord warns
Nephi to go away into the wilderness. His travels in the wilderness, and so forth.

Chapter 1

After I Nephi finished teaching my brothers, our father Lehi also
said many things to them, recounting to them how the Lord had done
great things for them through leaving the land of Jerusalem. 2 He
talked to them about their rebellion during the sea voyage and God's
mercy in sparing their lives, so that they weren't lying at the bottom of
the sea. 3 He also spoke to them about the promised land they had
been given: how merciful the Lord had been in warning us to flee from
the land of Jerusalem. 4 He said: I've seen a vision showing me
Jerusalem has been destroyed. If we had remained there, we also
would have died. 5 But, he said, despite our hardships, we've been
given a promised land, a land specially chosen over all other lands, a
land the Lord God has covenanted with me that my descendants will
inherit. Indeed, the Lord has consecrated this land for my children and
me forever, and also for those who will likewise be led out of other
countries by the Lord's power. 6 Therefore I prophesy under the
influence of God's Spirit over me, that no one will come to this land
unless they're brought by the Lord's power. 7 So this land is consecrated
to those He'll bring here. And if they serve Him according to the
commandments He has given, it will always be a land of liberty for
them; therefore they'll never be brought down into captivity — but if
they are, it will be because of iniquity; because if iniquity abounds, the
land will become cursed because of their failure to serve Him. It will
always be blessed for the righteous. 8 It's a wise thing for this land to
still be kept from other nations knowing about it. Otherwise, many
nations would overrun this land, so there wouldn't be any place for an
inheritance.

II
9 As a result, I've obtained a promise that to the degree they keep
His commandments — including anyone the Lord God brings from
the land of Jerusalem — they'll prosper in this land. And they'll be
hidden from all other nations, so they can have this land to themselves.
And if they keep His commandments, they'll be blessed upon this
land. No one will interfere or take away the land they receive as an
inheritance; they'll live here safely forever. 10 But when they fall away
in unbelief, after having received such great blessings from the Lord,

having knowledge about the earth's creation and mankind's history, knowing the great and awe-inspiring things the Lord has done since the world was created, having power given to them to live by faith, having all the commandments from the beginning, and having been brought by His infinite goodness into this precious land of promise — I say if the time comes that they choose to reject the Holy One of Israel, the true Messiah, their Redeemer and their God, the judgments of Him who is righteous will fall upon them. 11 He'll bring other nations to them, He'll give to these others power and He'll take their lands away from them. He will scatter and strike them down. 12 Indeed, as one generation passes to another, there will be slaughter and God's punishment as a reminder for them.

III   Therefore, my sons, I want you to remember; I want you to listen to me carefully. 13 I wish you would wake up, wake up from your deep sleep — the sleep of hell — and shake off the awful chains that restrain you, the spiritual chains that overtake people to enslave them, leading down to the endless abyss of misery and anguish. 14 Wake up, get up from the dust, and hear a trembling parent's words, whose body you'll soon bury in the cold, silent grave, from where no traveler returns. A few days from now I will die, leaving my life here like everything does on this earth. 15 But the Lord has redeemed my soul from hell. I've seen His glory, and I'm continually welcomed in the arms of His love. 16 I want you to remember to keep the Lord's statutes and judgments. This has been a deep concern of mine from the beginning. 17 My heart has been weighed down with sorrow from time to time, as I've been afraid that — because of the hardness of your hearts — the Lord who is God will have no choice but to punish you in His justified wrath, and cut you off and destroy you forever. 18 Then a cursing would follow your descendants for many generations, killing them by sword and famines because of anger and hatred that enslaves through iniquity because they rebel against God and follow the accuser. 19 My sons, may these things not come upon you! Instead, may you be a chosen and blessed people of the Lord.

IV   May you do His will, because His ways are righteousness forever. 20 He has said: To the degree you keep My commandments, you'll prosper in the land. But to the degree you don't keep My commandments, you'll be shut out from My presence. 21 And now, so that I can have joy in you, so my heart can gladly leave this world thinking of you, and so I don't die filled with grief and sorrow — get up from the dust, my sons, and be men, determined in one mind and one heart, united in all things, so you don't fall into captivity 22 and aren't afflicted with a severe cursing and don't provoke a righteous

God's judgment upon you to the eternal destruction of both spirit and body. 23 Wake up, my sons, clothe yourselves with righteousness, shake off the chains that bind you, come out of the darkness, and get up from the dust. 24 Don't rebel anymore against your brother, whose understanding and teaching have been glorious, who's kept God's commandments since we left Jerusalem, and who's been an instrument in God's hands in bringing us to the promised land. Had it not been for him, we would certainly have died of hunger in the wilderness. Nevertheless, you tried to kill him, and you've constantly hurt and fought him. 25 I'm very afraid and worried about you, expecting you'll make him suffer again. You've accused him of trying to get power and authority over you. But I know he hasn't tried to get power and authority over you; on the contrary, he has sought God's glory and your own eternal happiness. 26 But you've complained because he's been forthright with you. You say he has reprimanded you harshly and been angry with you. But his powerful rebuke came from God's word within him. And what you call anger was the truth of God, which he didn't hold back, honestly declaring your iniquities. 27 God's power was clearly with him, to such an extent that when he commanded you then you obeyed. That wasn't just him, but it was the Spirit of the Lord in him that led him to speak, so he couldn't remain silent.

V   28 Now, my sons Laman, Lemuel, and Sam, as well as my sons who are Ishmael's sons, if you'll listen to Nephi teach, you won't be lost. If you're willing to listen to him, I leave you a blessing, namely my first blessing. 29 But if you refuse to listen to him, I'll take away my first blessing — even my entire blessing — and it will rest upon him. 30 Now Zoram, I speak to you: You are Laban's servant; nevertheless, you've been brought out of the land of Jerusalem. I know you are a true friend to my son Nephi forever. 31 Because you've been faithful, your descendants will be blessed with his descendants — they'll live long upon this land in prosperity. And nothing but their own iniquity will harm or disturb their prosperity on this land forever. 32 Therefore if you keep the Lord's commandments, the Lord has consecrated this land for the security of your descendants with my son's descendants.

VI   2 Now Jacob, I speak to you: You are my first born during the times of my trouble and difficulties in the wilderness. In your childhood you've experienced hardships and a great deal of distress because of your brothers' harsh and violent behavior. 2 Nevertheless, my first born in the wilderness, you are familiar with the greatness of God. He'll consecrate your difficulties ultimately to benefit you. 3 Therefore your soul will be blessed, and you'll live safely with your brother Nephi, and your life will be spent serving God. Therefore I know you are redeemed because of the righteousness of your Redeemer, for you've seen that He'll come at the appointed time to bring salvation to mankind. 4 You've seen His glory in your youth, so you are blessed just like those He'll minister to personally on earth. Because the Spirit is the same yesterday, today, and forever, and the way is prepared since the Fall of mankind, and salvation is free. 5 People are instructed well enough to understand good from evil — the law is given to mankind. However, no one on earth is justified by the law — that is, mankind are cut off by the law, indeed, they were cut off by the earthly, temporal law. Likewise, they're shut out from good things by the spiritual law and become miserable forever. 6 This is because redemption comes in and through the Holy Messiah, because He is full of grace and truth. 7 He offers Himself as a sacrifice for sin, to fulfill the requirements of the law for all those who have a broken heart and a contrite spirit. Therefore the requirements of the law cannot be met for anyone else. 8 That being the case, how extremely important it is to declare these things to the inhabitants of the earth, so they can know that no flesh can live in God's presence except through the merits, mercy, and grace of the Holy Messiah, who lays down His mortal life, and takes it back by the power of the Spirit, so He can accomplish the resurrection of the dead, being the first who will rise from the grave. 9 He is the essential required sacrificial offering to God, since He'll intercede on behalf of all mankind; and those who believe in Him will be saved. 10 Because of the intercession for everyone, all mankind will be brought to God. They'll stand in His presence to be judged by Him according to the truth and holiness in Him.

VII   The Holy One has established the requirements of the law that impose a fixed punishment opposite to the available happiness. Happiness is the purpose of the atonement. 11 But there must be a balance or opposition for all things. If there were no balance, my first born in the wilderness, righteousness and wickedness couldn't exist, or happiness and misery, or good and bad. The result would be no contrast but only an unvarying sameness. That being the case, if everything were fixed into the same condition, there would be no difference between life or death, decay or growth, happiness or misery, awareness or unconsciousness. 12 Therefore everything would have been created for nothing — there would have been no purpose resulting from its creation. This failure to have opposites would destroy the wisdom of God and His eternal purposes, and also make the power, mercy, and justice of God mean nothing. 13 If you eliminate law, you must also eliminate sin. And if you eliminate sin, you must also eliminate righteousness. Then if there's no righteousness, there's no happiness. And if there's no righteousness or happiness, there's no punishment or misery. And if all these plans of God are destroyed, you must also destroy God. If you destroy God, then we wouldn't exist, and neither would the earth, since there couldn't have been a creation of things, either to act or be acted upon; therefore all things would have necessarily ceased to exist.

VIII   14 Now, my sons, I tell you these things to help and instruct you. Because there is a God and He has created all things: the heavens, the earth, and everything that's in them, both things to act and things to be acted upon. 15 And to bring about His eternal plans in His purpose for mankind — after He had created our first parents and the animals of the field and the birds of the air and, in short, all created things — there had to be a contrast: the forbidden fruit in opposition to the tree of life, the one sweet and the other bitter. 16 Therefore the Lord God gave mankind the ability to choose; but people couldn't choose unless they were presented with a decision to make.

IX   17 And based on what I've read, I must conclude an angel of God, according to what's written, fell from heaven. And he became the accuser, having pursued what was evil before God. 18 And because he fell from heaven and became miserable forever, he wants mankind to be miserable too. Indeed, that old serpent — who is the accuser, who is the father of all lies — said to Eve: Eat some of the forbidden fruit, and you won't die, but you'll be like God, knowing good and evil. 19 After Adam and Eve ate the forbidden fruit, they were driven out of the Garden of Eden to cultivate the earth. 20 Then, they had children, which is the family of the whole earth. 21 And mankind's lifespan was lengthened, according to God's will, so they could repent while living on earth. Therefore their condition became a probation, and their lives were lengthened to provide them time to keep the commandments the Lord God gave mankind. He commanded that everyone must repent, letting everyone know they were lost because of their parents' transgression.

X   22 Now if Adam hadn't transgressed, he wouldn't have fallen, but he would have stayed in the Garden of Eden. And all things that were created must have remained in exactly the same state as when first created. They would have continued forever and had no end, 23 and they wouldn't have had children. Therefore they would have remained in a state of innocence, having no joy, because they knew no misery, doing no good, because they weren't exposed to sin. 24 But all things have been done in the wisdom of Him who knows all things. 25 Adam fell for people to exist, and we exist to experience joy. 26 And the

Messiah comes at the appointed time to rescue mankind from the Fall. Then because they're rescued from the Fall, they're free to act, knowing good from evil, to act for themselves and not to be acted on. However, mankind will be punished based on the law on the great and last day, according to the commandments God has given. 27 So people act freely in this life, and this creation lets people choose freely. They're free to choose liberty and eternal life by obeying mankind's Mediator, or instead choose captivity and death by letting the accuser lead them. The accuser wants all mankind to become miserable like he is.

XI   28 Now, my sons, I want you to look to the great Mediator and follow His great commandments and be faithful to His words and choose eternal life according to the will of His Holy Spirit, 29 and not choose eternal death according to the will of our fallen and vulnerable bodies, with their weaknesses and appetites, which allows the accuser to tempt and mislead you to fall into hell, so he can rule over you in his own kingdom. 30 I've spoken these few words to all of you, my sons, in the final days of my life. I've chosen to follow those good principles taught in the prophets' words. I have no other objective than your souls' everlasting happiness. Amen.

Chapter 2

3 Now I speak to you Joseph, my youngest: You were born in the wilderness of my trouble and difficulties; indeed, your mother gave birth to you during my time of greatest despair. 2 May the Lord also consecrate this extremely precious land for you, as your inheritance and your descendants' inheritance along with your brothers; to be a safe land forever, if you keep the commandments of the Holy One of Israel.

II   3 Now Joseph, my youngest whom I've brought out of the wilderness of my trouble and difficulties, may the Lord bless you forever that your descendants won't be completely destroyed. 4 You are my child, and I'm a descendant of Joseph, who was taken as a prisoner to Egypt. The Lord made great covenants with Joseph. 5 As a result, Joseph was shown about us, and the Lord promised him that He would raise up righteous descendants of the house of Israel from his offspring — not the Messiah, but a separated branch, who would be included in the Lord's covenants — and the Messiah would make Himself known to them in the last days in the spirit of power in order to enlighten them. He'll move them from darkness into light, from dark confusion and being lost into freedom.

III   6 Joseph testified truthfully, saying: The Lord who is God will raise up a worthy and chosen seer for my offspring. 7 Indeed, Joseph truthfully said: This is what the Lord told me: I'll raise up a worthy, carefully chosen seer from your offspring who will be highly regarded among your offspring. I'll give him a commandment to do a work for your offspring, his brothers and sisters, which will be very valuable to them, restoring them to knowledge of the covenants I made with your fathers. 8 And I'll give him a commandment to only do the work I'll commission him to do and nothing else. And I'll regard him as great in My eyes, since he'll do My work. 9 He'll be great like Moses, whom I've said I would raise up for you, O house of Israel, to set you free. 10 I'll raise up Moses to free your people from Egypt, 11 but I'll raise up a seer from your offspring. And I'll give him power to bring to light My word for your descendants — not only to bring to light My word, but to convince them of My word previously given to them.

IV
12 Therefore your offspring will write, and Judah's offspring will write. The Lord says: The things your offspring write, and the things Judah's offspring write, will grow together in order to expose false doctrines, settle disputes, and establish peace among your offspring and bring them, in the last days, to understanding their ancestors and comprehending My covenants. 13 The Lord said: His weakness will be made strong. My work will then begin among all My people. I'll restore you, O house of Israel.

V
14 Joseph prophesied in this way: The Lord will bless that seer. And those who attempt to destroy him will be defeated, because the Lord will fulfill this promise about my offspring given to me by the Lord. I'm sure of the fulfillment of this promise. 15 He'll be named after me, and it will be after the name of his father. And he'll be like me, because the things the Lord will bring to light by his hand and by the Lord's power will bring my people to salvation. 16 This is how Joseph prophesied: I'm sure of this thing, just as I'm sure of Moses' promise. Because the Lord has said to me: I'll preserve your descendants forever. 17 And the Lord has said: I'll raise up Moses and give him power in a staff and judgment in writing; however, I won't make him fluent and articulate as a speaker. But I'll write My law for him with My own finger and provide a spokesman for him.

VI
18 The Lord also told me: I'll give your descendants also a prophet and make a spokesman for him. I'll inspire the one to write the record of your descendants to bless your offspring. And that spokesman will declare that record. 19 The words he'll write will be the words that, in My wisdom, I consider important for your offspring to read. It will be as if your descendants called out to them from the dust, because I know their faith. 20 They'll call out the need for repentance from the dust for their brothers and sisters many generations after they've died.

Their words will go forth in a way that is a direct, clear message.
21 Because of their faith, their words will go from Me to their brothers
and sisters who are your offspring. I'll make the simplicity of their
words result in strong faith as they learn about the covenant I made
with your fathers.

VII   22 Now, my son Joseph, this is how my forefather prophesied.
23 Therefore you are blessed because of this covenant, since your
descendants won't be destroyed, because they'll listen to the words of
the book. 24 And one powerful among them will rise up and do much
good in what he says and does, acting as an instrument in God's hands
with great faith to accomplish wonderful results in God's sight, to
bring a significant restoration for the house of Israel including your
brothers' descendants. 25 You are blessed, Joseph. And because you are
young, listen to the words of your brother Nephi, and your life will
unfold according to what I've spoken. Never forget the words of your
dying father. Amen.

Chapter 3

4 Now I'll write about the prophecies my father has spoken of
concerning Joseph, who was taken into Egypt. 2 Joseph prophesied
truthfully about all his descendants, and there aren't many greater
prophecies than those he wrote. He prophesied about us, and future
generations descended from us, and they're written on the brass plates.

II   3 After my father finished speaking about Joseph's prophecies, he
called Laman's children, his sons and daughters, and said to them: My
sons and daughters, who are the children of my first born, I want you
to listen to me carefully. 4 The Lord God has said: To the degree you
keep My commandments, you'll prosper in the land. But to the degree
you don't keep My commandments, you'll be cut off from My
presence. 5 However, my sons and daughters, I can't go down to my
grave without leaving a blessing upon you. I know that if you're
brought up in the way you should live, you won't stray from it.
6 Therefore if you're cursed, I leave my blessing upon you so that the
cursing will be taken from you and your parents will be responsible for
it. 7 And because of my blessing, the Lord God won't allow you to
perish: He'll be merciful to you and your descendants forever.

III   8 After my father had finished speaking to Laman's children, he
had Lemuel's children brought to him, 9 telling them: My sons and
daughters, who are the children of my second son, I'm giving you the
same blessing I gave Laman's children; therefore your posterity won't

be completely destroyed, and in the end, your descendants will be blessed.

IV   10 When my father had finished talking to them, he spoke to Ishmael's sons and his whole household. 11 After he had finished speaking to them, he said to Sam: You and your descendants are blessed, because you'll inherit the land like your brother Nephi, and your posterity will be included with his. You'll be blessed like your brother, and your descendants like his descendants. You'll be blessed your whole life.

V   12 After my father had spoken to his whole household according to the feelings of his heart and the Spirit of the Lord in him, his health failed and he died and was buried.

VI   13 Not many days after his death, Laman, Lemuel, and Ishmael's sons were angry with me because of the Lord's warnings and correction 14 that I was inspired to tell them based on His word. I taught them many things, as my father did before he died. Much of what was said is written on my other plates, since more historical details are written on them. 15 But on these plates I only write the things within my soul and quotes of the scriptures from the brass plates. My soul delights in the scriptures, and I ponder upon them and write them for my children's instruction and benefit. 16 My soul rejoices in the things of the Lord, and I continually ponder in my heart what God has shown and told me.

VII   17 Nevertheless — despite the Lord's great goodness in showing me His great and awe-inspiring works — my heart cries out: How wretched a man am I! Indeed, my heart mourns because of my human weakness. My soul is pained because of my shortcomings. 18 I'm surrounded on all sides because of the temptations and sins that so easily trap me. 19 When I want to be glad, I mourn over my sins. Nevertheless, I know whom I've trusted. 20 God has supported me. He's led me through my troubles in the wilderness and preserved me while crossing the deep waters. 21 He's filled me with so much of His love that it has completely overwhelmed me. 22 He's defeated my enemies, making them shake in front of me. 23 He's heard my prayer by day and given me knowledge by visions at night. 24 I've grown bold through powerful prayers offered to Him by day. I've sent up my voice to heaven, and angels have come down and taught me. 25 My body has been carried away on the wings of His Spirit upon very high mountains; and my eyes have seen great things — too great for man — and I was ordered not to write them.

VIII   26 Then, if I've seen such great things, if the Lord — who descends from His high position to help mankind — if He has visited me with so much mercy, then why does my heart weep and my soul linger in the valley of sorrow, why does my body cower and my strength fail me because of my difficulties? 27 Why should I ever submit to temptations because of weaknesses? Why should I let any temptation by the Evil One have a place in my heart to cause me regret and trouble my soul? Why am I angry with myself because of my enemy? 28 Wake up, my soul! Don't focus on sin any longer! Rejoice, my heart; don't give any attention to the enemy of my soul anymore. 29 Don't get angry because of my enemies. Don't lose resolve to obey God because I face troubles. 30 Rejoice, my heart; pray to the Lord, saying: O Lord, I'll praise you forever. My soul will rejoice in you, my God and the rock of my salvation. 31 O Lord, redeem my soul! Rescue me from my enemies! Make me shudder when sin appears! 32 May the gates of hell always be shut in front of me because my heart is broken and my spirit contrite. O Lord, don't shut the gates of your righteousness in front of me, let me walk in Your pathway and stay on Your safe road. 33 O Lord, cover me in the robe of Your righteousness, help me to escape from my enemies, clear the path in front of me! Don't let any obstacle hinder me, but clear the way in front of me so I can go on safely, and hinder my enemy. 34 O Lord, I've trusted in You and will trust in You forever. I won't put my trust in the scholarly arrogance of man, because I know those who trust in arrogant fools are cursed. Indeed, those who put their trust in the vain teachings of a man and trust them as if they were truth are cursed. 35 Yes, I know God will give freely and abundantly to those who ask; yes, God will give to me if I don't ask improperly. Therefore I'll lift up my voice to You; yes, I'll cry to You, my God, the rock of my righteousness. I'll never stop calling out to You, my rock and my everlasting God. Amen.

Chapter 4

5 I cried often to the Lord my God in prayer because of my brothers' anger, 2 but their anger against me grew to such an extent that they tried to kill me. 3 Indeed, they complained about me, saying: Our younger brother is planning to rule over us — we've put up with so much from him. Therefore let's kill him now, so we won't be bothered anymore by what he says. We refuse to have him be in charge of us, because it belongs to us, the older brothers, to rule over the people. 4 Now I don't write on these plates all of their accusations against me, I'll just leave it with they tried to kill me.

II   5 Then the Lord warned me and any who wanted to go with me, to leave them and escape into the wilderness. 6 Therefore I took my family, Zoram and his family, my older brother Sam and his family, my younger brothers Jacob and Joseph, my sisters, and anyone willing to go with me. Those willing to go with me were the people who believed in God's warnings and revelations; as a result, they listened to what I said. 7 We took our tents and everything we could and traveled in the wilderness for many days. After we had traveled for many days we set up our tents. 8 Those who accompanied me wanted to name the place Nephi, so we called it Nephi, 9 and they took the liberty of calling themselves Nephi's people. 10 We paid careful attention to follow the Lord's judgments, statutes, and commandments in all things, according to the Law of Moses. 11 The Lord was with us and we thrived, sowing seeds and harvesting abundantly. We began to raise flocks, herds, and animals of every kind. 12 I also brought the records engraved on the brass plates, and the ball or compass prepared for my father on which the Lord had written messages.

III   13 Then we began to have very good results on the land and our families multiplied. 14 I took Laban's sword and made many copies, to defend ourselves from the people who were now called Lamanites, fearing they would attack and kill us, because I knew they hated me, my children, and those called my people. 15 I taught my people to construct buildings and work in all kinds of wood, iron, copper, brass, steel, gold, silver, and useful metals, which were abundant. 16 And I built a temple, constructing it like Solomon's temple, except that it wasn't built of similar carved stonework — since we didn't have access to that in our new place — so it wasn't an exact copy of Solomon's temple. But the layout followed Solomon's temple, and it had our best workmanship.

IV   17 I encouraged my people to be industrious and work with their hands. 18 They wanted me to be their king, but I didn't want them to have a king. Nevertheless, I did for them everything in my power. 19 What the Lord predicted about my brothers happened when God said I would be a ruler and teacher. I actually had been their ruler and teacher, following the Lord's commandments, until they tried to kill me. 20 As a result, what the Lord told me was fulfilled, saying: If they refuse to listen to your words, they'll be cut off from God's presence. And they actually were cut off from His presence. 21 He imposed a cursing on them. It was a severe cursing because of their iniquity, because they had hardened their hearts against Him. They were unyielding, like flint. Therefore, although they had been pure and radiant and highly pleasing, the Lord God made their dark countenance show through so they wouldn't be attractive to my people. 22 The Lord God decreed: I'll cause them — unless they repent of their iniquities — to repulse your people. 23 And the descendants of anyone who joins their descendants will be cursed, since they'll receive the same cursing. The Lord spoke it, and it was done. 24 Because of the curse upon them, they became people without purpose and meaning, engaged in trifling and foolish behavior, full of mischief and subtlety, hunting predator animals in the wilderness. 25 The Lord God told me: They will afflict your descendants in order to remind your posterity to remember Me. And to the degree your posterity fails to remember Me and hearken to My words, they'll attack your people, threatening their complete destruction.

V   26 And I ordained Jacob and Joseph to be priests and teachers in the land of my people. 27 And we lived in a way that brought happiness, 28 thirty years having elapsed since we left Jerusalem. 29 And I had kept the record of my people up to this time upon the plates I had made.

VI   30 Then the Lord God told me: Make other plates. You are to engrave important things on them that I consider valuable for your people's benefit. 31 Therefore in order to obey the Lord's commandment, I went and made these plates on which I've written these things. 32 And I engraved what pleases God. So, if my people are pleased with the things of God, they'll be pleased with what I've written on these plates. 33 But if my people want to know details about our history, they'll need to study my other plates. 34 It's enough for me to say that forty years had come to an end, and we had already had wars and conflicts with our brothers.

Chapter 5

6 These words were taught by Nephi's brother, Jacob, to the Nephite people: 2 Be assured, my dear people, that I Jacob have been called by God and ordained into His Holy Order after I was consecrated by my brother Nephi. You trust Nephi as a king or protector and depend on him for safety. You also know I've taught you a great many things. 3 But I need to teach you again, because I'm worried about and want to save your souls. I'm very concerned about you. You already know and have heard my continual diligent teaching showing my concerns. I've taught you my father's words, and spoken to you about the teachings that go back to the creation of the world.

II   4 Now I'll speak to you about present and future matters. Therefore I'll read you Isaiah's words — the words my brother has asked me to discuss with you. I explain them for your benefit, so you can learn and glorify the name of God. 5 Now the words I'll read are those Isaiah wrote about the entire house of Israel. So they pertain to you, since you're from the house of Israel. Indeed, there are many things that have been spoken by Isaiah which are relevant to you because you're from the house of Israel.

III   6 And now these are the words: The Lord God declares: I'll raise My hand to the Gentiles and set My banner flying to invite people to gather. And they'll bring your sons in their arms, and your daughters carried on their shoulders. 7 And kings will tend your children, and their queens will serve as nurses. They'll bow down to you, face to the ground, and clean the dust from your feet; and you'll know that I Am the Lord, for those who trust Me won't be ashamed.

IV   8 Now I wish to say something about these words. The Lord has shown me that those who were at Jerusalem, where we came from, have been killed or taken away as prisoners. 9 Nevertheless, the Lord has shown me they will return home. He has also shown me that the Lord God, the Holy One of Israel, is Himself to come to them in the flesh. And after He comes Himself to live among them, they'll whip and crucify Him, according to the words of the angel who told it to me. 10 And after they've hardened their hearts and stiffened their necks against the Holy One of Israel, the judgments of the Holy One of Israel will fall upon them and they will be punished and afflicted. 11 So after they're driven here and there — this is what the angel said: Many will be afflicted in this life but they won't be entirely killed because of the prayers of the faithful. They'll be scattered, punished, and hated. But the Lord in His mercy will remember them, and when they begin to know their Redeemer, they'll be gathered back to the lands of their inheritance.

V   12 And the prophet wrote about the Gentiles who will be blessed. If they repent and don't fight against Zion nor join that powerful and utterly wicked church, they'll be saved, because the Lord God will fulfill the covenants He has made to His children. This is why the prophet has written these things. 13 As a result, those who fight against Zion and the Lord's covenant people will clean the dust from their feet. And the Lord's people won't be put to shame, because they're the ones who put their trust in Him and await the Messiah's coming. 14 According to the prophet's words, the Messiah will set about a second time to recover them. So when the time comes that they believe in Him, He'll reveal Himself to them in power and great glory, bringing about the destruction of their enemies. He won't destroy anyone who believes in Him. 15 But those who don't believe in Him will be destroyed by fire, storm, earthquake, slaughter, disease, and famine. They'll know the Lord is God, the Holy One of Israel. 16 Can the chains imposed by the powerful be broken or the enslaved be freed?

17 Yet the Lord proclaims: Even those suffering in terrible bondage will be freed, and all the chains binding down mankind will be broken. For I'll fight for you, and I'll liberate your children. The Lord declares: I'll fight those who fight you; 18 I'll make the tyrants eat their own flesh; they'll be drunk with their own blood as if it was wine. And everyone will realize that I the Lord am your Savior and Redeemer, the Mighty One of Jacob.

VI   7 Hear, for the Lord says: Have I left you? Or have I abandoned you forever? Where is the divorce decree from your mother? To whom have I sold you? You sold yourselves into slavery through your sins. Your mother was sent away because of your crimes. 2 Why, when I came, was there no one there. Why, when I called, would no one answer? Is My arm too weak to rescue you? Don't I have the power to save? With merely a rebuke I dry up the sea, and turn rivers into desert, their fish die and rot for lack of water, and they lie dead of thirst. 3 I cover the heavens in blackness as if mourning in sackcloth.

VII   4 The Lord God has inspired My words, letting Me speak undeniable truths to you, O house of Israel, when you're doubting Me. He awakens Me each morning, filling My ears with wisdom. 5 The Lord God has spoken into My ear, and I listened as His disciple, and didn't turn away. 6 I let My back be flogged and let the hair on My cheeks be ripped out. I didn't stay away from insults and spitting. 7 I know the Lord God will help Me, therefore I feel no disgrace. Accordingly, My face is fixed like flint, and I know I won't be ashamed. 8 My defender is nearby, supporting Me. Who dares fight with Me? Let's stand together. Who will be My opponent? Let him approach Me and My rebuke will humble him! 9 Watch, the Lord God will help Me. Any who dares to condemn Me will wear out like an old garment, and moths will eat them up. 10 Who among you reveres the Lord, and listens to the voice of His servant? Although you find yourself in darkness and with no light, you should trust in the Lord. 11 But all of you that light your own fire, that try to see using your sparks, go ahead and walk using the sparks which you've lit. But know this from Me: You will painfully fall down.

VIII   8 You who pursue justice, listen to Me. You who seek the Lord: Look to the quarry from where you came, and to the bedrock from which you are part. 2 Look back to Abraham your father, and to Sarah, who gave birth to you; for he was alone when I called him but I blessed him and have made him a multitude. 3 Truly the Lord has comforted Zion; repaired all her ruins, and He has made her wilderness like Eden and her desert like the Garden of the Lord. Joy and gladness will be found there, with praise and singing. 4 Listen to Me, My people, and understand Me, My nation, for I'll provide you teachings like a light to guide My people. 5 I'll provide it timely, when needed. Your eventual success will be provided although scattered on the islands of the seas, if you trust in My arms. 6 Raise your eyes to the heavens and look at the earth below, for if the heavens blew away like smoke, and the earth wore out like a garment, and the people living there were all to die, the victory I promise will still endure forever, and My triumph cannot be thwarted. 7 Listen to Me, you who care about what's right, you who remember My instructions in your heart! Don't be afraid of people's insults or their jeering at you. 8 For the moths will eat them up like a garment and the worm will eat them like wool. But My triumph will stand forever, and My salvation through all the ages.

IX

9 Wake up, wake up, dress yourself in glory, O arm of the Lord. Awaken as in former ages. It was You who cut Rahab to pieces and cast down the dragon. 10 It was You that dried the sea, the waters of the great deep, that made the abysses of the sea into a way for the redeemed to walk. 11 So let the redeemed of the Lord return and come with singing to Zion, crowned with everlasting joy and holiness. Let them be joyful and glad, while sorrow and mourning flee from them. 12 I am He who comforts you!

X

What's wrong that you're afraid of people who will die, mere mortals that perish like the grass? 13 You've forgotten the Lord your God who stretched out the heavens and established the earth. You live in constant dread because of your angry oppressor who wants to destroy you. What does your oppressor's anger matter? 14 Remember the captive has been freed, not cut down and slain, and he hasn't been left hungry. 15 I Am the Lord your God, I make the sea's roaring waves; the Lord of Hosts is My name. 16 I've put My words in your mouth and sheltered you with My hand. I, who organized the heavens and made the foundations of the earth, have said to Zion: You are My people.

XI

17 Wake up, rouse yourself, stand up, O Jerusalem, you who've drunk from the Lord's hand the bitter cup of His fury; you who've drained the dregs of the bitter cup of suffering — 18 she had no guide for her from among all the sons she bore, none of them took her by the hand from all her sons. 19 These two misfortunes come upon you — havoc and ruin — who can console you? Famine and destruction — how shall I comfort you? 20 Your sons have fainted on every street; like a deer caught in a net. They're drunk with the Lord's wrath, with your God's rebuke.

XII

21 Therefore listen to this, unhappy ones, who are drunk but not with wine. 22 This is what your Lord says — the Lord and your God who watches over His people: I'll take your bitter cup and you'll never

need to drink from it again. ²³ I'll then put it into the hands of your tormentors, who've commanded you to get down on the ground so they can walk over you — and you laid on the ground like a pathway for the passersby.

XIII   ²⁴ Wake up, wake up and clothe yourselves in virtue O Zion. The uncircumcised and the unclean will never enter again. ²⁵ Get up and shake off the dust. Return to your throne, O Jerusalem. Get the chains off your neck, O enslaved Zion.

Chapter 6

9 Now, my dear people, I've read these things so you would know about the covenants the Lord made with all the house of Israel. ² He has told His people, and the Jews preserved His holy prophets' words, from the beginning down from generation to generation. They tell of the time when they'll be restored to God's household and fold when they return home to the lands of their inheritance and settle in their promised lands.

II   ³ My dear people, I tell you these things so you can rejoice and look forward forever because of the blessings the Lord God will bestow on your children. ⁴ I know many of you have searched extensively to find out about things to come. Therefore I know you realize our physical bodies are certain to grow old and die; however, as I'll explain, in our bodies we'll see God. ⁵ Indeed, I know you realize He'll show Himself in a physical body to those at Jerusalem, where we came from, because it's necessary for that to happen among them. For it's required and absolutely necessary for the great Creator to allow Himself to become part of mankind and live on earth in order to die so He can benefit every person. Therefore all mankind can benefit from Him. ⁶ Because death has befallen us all, to accomplish the great Creator's merciful plan there needs to be a power of resurrection. The resurrection is required for all because of the Fall, and the Fall came about because of transgression. Because mankind fell, they were cut off from the Lord's presence. ⁷ Therefore it requires an infinite atonement to restore mankind. Without an infinite atonement our decaying bodies couldn't stop decay and death. Therefore the first judgment imposed upon man would have necessarily remained forever. If that were the case, our body would die, to rot and disintegrate to its mother earth, never to rise again.

III   ⁸ How great are God's wisdom, mercy, and grace! Because if our bodies never rose again, our spirits would necessarily become subject to that angel who fell from the presence of the Eternal God. He became the accuser to never rise again. ⁹ And our spirits would be doomed like him to remain fallen from heaven; we would have become devils, angels to the accuser — to be shut out from God's presence and remain with the father of lies, in misery like he is — angels to the one who deceived our first parents, who tries to imitate an angel of light and persuade mankind to enter into conspiracies to commit murder and to do all kinds of dark, secret works.

IV

10 How great is God's goodness, which prepared a way for our escape from the reach of this awful monster! — the monster of death and hell, by which I mean the death of the body and the death of the spirit. 11 But because of the deliverance of God — the Holy One of Israel — this physical death I've mentioned, which is the grave, will give up its dead. 12 And this spiritual death I've mentioned, which is hell, will give up its dead. Therefore death and hell will give up their dead: hell will give up its captive spirits and the grave will give up its captive bodies. And the bodies and spirits of mankind will be restored to each other by the power of the resurrection of the Holy One of Israel.

V

13 How great is God's plan! On the other hand, God's paradise will give up the spirits of the righteous, and the grave will give up the bodies of the righteous. The spirit and body will be restored to each other, and all mankind will be free from decay and immortal. They'll be living souls — having complete knowledge — alive like we are now on earth, except that then our knowledge will be complete. 14 Therefore we'll have a complete awareness of all our guilt, uncleanliness, and nakedness. And the righteous will have a complete awareness of their joy and righteousness, being clothed with purity — even wearing the robe of righteousness.

VI

15 When all mankind has passed from this first death to life, so that they've become immortal, they'll be brought before the judgment seat of the Holy One of Israel. Then judgment comes, when they'll be judged according to God's holy judgment. 16 And as sure as the Lord lives — because the Lord God has spoken it and it's His eternal word that cannot fail — those who are righteous will remain righteous and those who are filthy will remain filthy. Therefore those who are filthy are the accuser and his angels. They'll go away into everlasting fire prepared for them. Their torment will be like a fiery lake of lava, whose flames ascend from eternity to eternity without end.

VII

17 Oh the greatness and justice of our God! He carries out all His words; they've gone out from His mouth, and His law must be fulfilled. 18 But the righteous, the saints of the Holy One of Israel, those who have believed in the Holy One of Israel, those who have endured adversity and persecution and ignored the disgrace or dishonor, they

will inherit God's kingdom, which was prepared for them from the foundation of creation. Their joy will be complete forever. 19 How great is the mercy of our God, the Holy One of Israel! He sets His holy ones free from that awful monster: the accuser and death and hell, and that fiery lake that burns like lava that is endless torment. 20 How great is the holiness of our God! He knows all things — there's nothing that He doesn't know. 21 And He comes into the world in order to save all mankind, if they choose to listen to His voice. He suffers the pains of all mankind, yes, the pains of every living being — men, women, and children — all who belong to the family of Adam. 22 And He suffers this to provide the resurrection for everyone, so all can stand before Him at the great judgment day. 23 He commands all people to repent and be baptized in His name, and to have complete faith in the Holy One of Israel, or they can't be saved in God's kingdom. 24 But if they won't repent and believe in His name and be baptized in His name and persevere to the end, they will certainly be damned, because the Lord God, the Holy One of Israel, has spoken it. 25 Therefore He has given a law. And where there's no law established there's no punishment, and where there's no punishment there's no condemnation. And where there's no condemnation, the mercy of the Holy One of Israel has claim upon them because of the atonement, since they're set free by His power. 26 The atonement satisfies the demands of His justice for those to whom the law hasn't been given, so that they're freed from that awful monster: death and hell and the accuser, and the fiery lake that burns like lava which is endless torment. Instead they're restored to that God who gave them breath, who is the Holy One of Israel.

VIII   27 But woe to those who have been given the law, who have all of God's commandments, like we do, and who transgress them and waste the days of their probation — because their state is awful.

IX   28 How crafty is the Evil One's plan! How vain, weak, and foolish are mankind! If they're educated, they think they're wise, and they don't follow God's counsel. They set it aside, thinking they know better themselves. As a result, their wisdom is foolishness, and doesn't benefit them, and they will perish. 29 But it's good to be educated if they also follow God's counsels.

X   30 But woe to those who are rich in worldly things and who, because they're rich, show contempt for the poor and persecute the meek. They've set their hearts upon their wealth; therefore their money is their god. But their money will perish along with them. 31 Woe to the deaf who refuse to hear, because they will perish. 32 Woe to the blind who refuse to see, because they will perish. 33 Woe to the unconverted in heart, because a knowledge of their iniquity will torment them on the last day. ³⁴ Woe to the liars, because they will be thrown into hell. ³⁵ Woe to the murderers who kill deliberately, because they will die. ³⁶ Woe to those who commit whoredoms, because they will be thrown down to hell. ³⁷ Indeed, woe to those who worship idols, because the accuser of us all delights in them. ³⁸ And in short, woe to those who die in their sins, because they will return to God, see His face, and remain without forgiveness of their sins.

XI ³⁹ My dear people, remember how awful it is to transgress against that holy God and how awful it is to yield to the temptations of that crafty one. Remember, to be carnally minded is death but to be spiritually minded is life eternal. ⁴⁰ My dear people, listen carefully to my words and remember the greatness of the Holy One of Israel. Don't claim I've spoken harshly against you. Because if you do, you'll reject the truth, since I've spoken your Maker's words. I know the truth is blunt about all uncleanliness, but the righteous aren't afraid of it, because they love the truth and aren't shaken. ⁴¹ Then, my dear people, come to the Lord, the Holy One. Remember that His paths are righteousness. The way for man is narrow, but it lies in a straight course before him. And the gatekeeper is the Holy One of Israel, and He doesn't use any servant there. There's no other way except through the gate, and He can't be deceived since His name is the Lord God. ⁴² He'll open to whoever knocks. And the worldly, the educated, and those who are rich, who are inflated with pride because of their knowledge, education, and wealth — they're the ones He looks down upon. And unless they abandon these things and consider themselves fools before God, and come down in the depths of humility, He won't allow them through the gate. ⁴³ Real wisdom and real understanding will be hidden from them forever, and shared only with the holy ones to give them joy.

XII ⁴⁴ My dear people, remember my words. I take my coat off and shake off the dust before you. I humbly ask the God of my salvation to evaluate me with His all-searching eye. I tell you that you'll realize on the last day, when all people are judged for what they did in this life, that the God of Israel saw me shake your iniquities from my soul and I stand clean before Him and am free of your blood. ⁴⁵ My dear people, turn away from your sins. Shake off the chains of him who wants to enslave you so you can't escape. Come to that God who is the rock of your salvation. ⁴⁶ Prepare your souls for that glorious day when justice will be administered to the righteous — the day of judgment — so you won't cower with awful fear as you fully remember your awful guilt or be compelled to cry out: Holy, holy are Your judgments, O

Lord God Almighty, but I know my guilt. I transgressed Your law and my transgressions are mine, and the accuser has taken hold of me so that I've become a victim of his awful misery. ⁴⁷ My brothers and sisters, is it still necessary for me to wake you up to the awful reality of all this? Would I trouble your souls if you were pure-minded? Would I need to tell you bluntly the truth if you were free from sin? ⁴⁸ If you were holy, I would speak to you about holiness. But since you aren't holy and you look to me as a teacher, it's absolutely necessary that I teach you the consequences of sin.

XIII   ⁴⁹ My soul hates sin, and my heart delights in righteousness. And I'll praise the holy name of God. ⁵⁰ Come, my people; everyone who's thirsty, come to the waters. And those who don't have any money, come, buy and eat; yes, come, buy wine and milk without money and without cost. ⁵¹ Don't spend money on worthless things, or work for things that can't satisfy. Listen carefully and remember the words I've spoken and come to the Holy One of Israel, and feast on things that don't perish and can't be spoiled; let your soul rejoice in the best part. ⁵² My dear people, remember the words of God. Pray to Him continually by day and give thanks to His holy name by night. Let your hearts be glad! ⁵³ How great are the Lord's covenants! How great are His sufferings for mankind! Because of His greatness, grace, and mercy, He has promised us that our descendants won't be altogether removed from the earth, but He'll preserve them. They'll become a righteous branch to the house of Israel in future generations.

XIV   ⁵⁴ Now I want to tell you more, my people, but I'll declare the rest of my words to you tomorrow. Amen.

Chapter 7

10 Now I Jacob speak to you again, my dear people, about the righteous branch I've mentioned. ² The promises we've obtained are promises to us here on earth. Therefore I've been shown that many of our descendants will be lost here on earth because of unbelief. Nevertheless, God will be merciful to them, and our descendants will be recovered, so they can have revealed to them the truth about their Redeemer. ³ Therefore, as I told you, it must necessarily be that Christ — and last night the angel told me this was to be His name — should come among the Jews, among those who are the more wicked part of the world. And they will crucify Him — because it's essential for God — and no other nation on earth would crucify their God. ⁴ Because if the mighty miracles were performed among other nations, they would repent and know He was God. ⁵ But because of priestcrafts and iniquities, those at Jerusalem will be stubborn and hardened against Him, resulting in His crucifixion. 6 As a result, destruction, famine, disease, and slaughter will befall them because of their iniquities. And those who aren't destroyed will be scattered among all nations.

II   7 But this is what the Lord God said: When the day comes that they believe in Me, that I Am the Messiah — for I've covenanted with their fathers — then they will be restored here on earth to the lands of their inheritance. 8 And they will be gathered in from their long scattered state from islands and from the four corners of the earth. God has said: The Gentile nations will be great in My eyes in returning them to the lands of their inheritance. 9 Indeed, the Gentile kings will be like foster fathers to them, and their queens will be like nursing mothers. Therefore the Lord has made great promises to the Gentiles, because He has decreed it, and who can argue against it? 10 But God has said: This land will be a land for your inheritance and the Gentiles will also be blessed upon the land. 11 This land will be a land of liberty for the Gentiles, and there won't be any kings on the land who will oppress the Gentiles. 12 I'll fortify this land against all other nations. 13 God has said: Those who fight against Zion will be destroyed. 14 Those who try to establish a king in place of Me will perish, because I the Lord, the King of Heaven, will be their king; and I'll be a light to those who hear My words forever.

III   15 Therefore I must destroy secret works of darkness, murder, and abominations so that the covenants I've made with mankind can be fulfilled, which I'll do for them while they're living on earth. 16 So those who fight against Zion — Jews or Gentiles, enslaved or free, male or female — will be destroyed. God has said: They are the whore of all the earth — those who aren't for Me are against Me. 17 I'll fulfill the promises I've made to mankind, which I'll do for them while they're here on earth.

IV   18 So, my dear people, this is what God has said: I'll use the Gentiles to afflict your descendants. Nevertheless, I'll soften the Gentiles' hearts, so they'll be like a father and a mother to them. As a result, the Gentiles will be blessed and included with the house of Israel. 19 I'll dedicate this land to your descendants forever — and to those who are included with them — as their inherited land; because it's a choice land to Me, more than all other lands. Therefore I'll require all who live there to worship Me.

V   20 Now, my dear people, since our merciful God has given us such great information about these things, let us remember Him and abandon our sins and not hang our heads down, because we aren't rejected. Although we've been removed from our inherited land, we've been led to a better land; the Lord has made the sea our path and we're on an island of the sea. 21 But the Lord's great promises include those who live on the islands of the sea. Therefore since it says islands, there have to be more than this one, and our fellow Israelites also inhabit them. 22 The Lord God has led some of the house of Israel away from time to time according to His plan and faithfulness. And the Lord remembers all those who have been broken off; consequently, He remembers us also. 23 So be of good cheer and remember you're free to act for yourselves, to choose the way of everlasting death or the way of eternal life. 24 So, my dear people reconcile yourselves to God's will, not to the will of the accuser and the flesh. And remember that after you're reconciled to God, it's only in and through God's grace that you're saved. 25 Therefore may God raise you from death by the power of the resurrection, and from everlasting death by the power of the atonement, so you can be received into God's eternal kingdom, so you can thank Him for divine grace. Amen.

Chapter 8

11 Now Jacob spoke many more things to my people at that time. However, I've only caused these things to be written, and I'm satisfied with what I've written.

II
2 Now I'll write more of Isaiah's words since my soul takes comfort from his words. I'll apply his words to my people and record them for all my descendants, because he truly saw my Redeemer, just as I've seen Him. 3 And my brother Jacob has also seen Him, as I've seen Him. Therefore I'll proclaim their words for my descendants in order to show them that my words are true. God has said: I'll confirm My word by testimony from three witnesses. However, God sends more witnesses, establishing the truth of all His words. 4 I take great joy in demonstrating to my people the truth of Christ's coming, and the Law of Moses has been given for this purpose. And all things given to man by God from the beginning of the world foretell of Him. 5 I also take great joy in the Lord's covenants made to our fathers; yes, my soul delights in His grace, justice, power, and mercy; and in the great and eternal plan of redemption from death. 6 I take great joy in demonstrating to my people that unless Christ comes, all mankind will certainly be lost. 7 Because if there's no Christ there's no God. And if there's no God we don't exist since there couldn't have been any creation. But there is a God and He is Christ, and He comes at His own appointed time.

III
8 Now I write some of Isaiah's words, so that any of my people who see these words can lift up their hearts and rejoice for all

mankind. Here are the words; you can relate them to yourselves and to all mankind.

12 *The prophecy of Isaiah the son of Amoz, about Judah and Jerusalem:*

IV ² In days to come the mountain of the Lord's House will stand unchanging above the mountains, and tower above the hills, and all the nations will look joyfully at it. ³ And many people will go and say: Come, let's go up to the mountain of the Lord, to the house of the God of Jacob, that He may instruct in His ways and we'll walk in His paths. For instruction will come out of Zion, and the word of the Lord from Jerusalem. ⁴ In this way He'll govern the nations and settle matters between people. And they'll exchange their swords for plowshares and their spears for pruning tools; nation won't take up sword against nation, they'll never again experience war.

V ⁵ O house of Jacob! Come all of you and let's walk by the light of the Lord, because you've abandoned the right way. ⁶ O house of Jacob! They've adopted the practices from the east, and fortunetelling like the Philistines, and they overflow with foreign customs. ⁷ Their land is full of silver and gold, there's no end to their treasures. Their land is also full of horses, there's no end to their chariots. ⁸ And their land is full of idols; they bow down to the work of their own hands, that which their own fingers have made. ⁹ But mankind will be humbled, and mortals humiliated — O do not forgive them!

VI ¹⁰ You wicked ones, hide yourselves deep in the rock and bury yourselves in the ground before the terror of the Lord and His glorious majesty! ¹¹ The Lord alone will be exalted in that day. ¹² For the Lord of Hosts has planned a day against all the proud and arrogant, against everyone who thinks themselves elect; and they'll be brought down. ¹³ The day of the Lord will come against those acting like the cedars of Lebanon, lofty and proud, and like the oaks of Bashan, ¹⁴ against the high mountains, and the lofty hills, and against all the arrogant nations, ¹⁵ and every defense barrier, and every fenced wall, ¹⁶ and all the ships of Tarshish and other ships of the sea. ¹⁷ For mankind's conceit will be humbled and their pride brought down, and the Lord alone will be exalted on that day. ¹⁸ And all the idols will vanish. ¹⁹ They'll cower in caves of the earth, for the fear of the Lord will fill them with dread, and His majesty will overwhelm the earth. ²⁰ At that time, mankind will throw away their idols of silver and idols of gold, which they worshiped, to the places where moles and bats are found, ²¹ to then hide in the gaps of the rocks and the lonely canyons; for fear of the Lord will fill them with dread, and His majesty will overwhelm the earth. ²² Stop glorifying mankind, who only have breath in their nostrils, for what basis is there to admire them?

VII   **13** Watch this happen: the Lord, the Lord of Hosts, takes away from Jerusalem and from Judah His word, the inspired voices and ordinances of salvation, ²,³ the prophet and prophetess, the priest and priestess, wisdom from the counselors, knowledge from the teacher, and they'll be left without prudence, insight, and understanding. ⁴ He'll let their boys lead them, babies will govern them. ⁵ The people will oppress one another, everyone abusing their neighbor. Young people will bully the elderly, and those without status will bully the honorable. ⁶ When a man will grab ahold of his brother in his father's house, and say: You at least have a cloak, you lead us and get us out of these ruins — ⁷ but he'll protest, saying: I have no remedy, for in my house I have no food or clothing; don't think I can be your ruler. ⁸ Jerusalem staggers and Judah has fallen because what they say and what they do fights against the Lord, defying Him in front of His glorious presence. ⁹ The look of their faces shows their defiance, they parade and celebrate sins like Sodom, and they don't hide it. Woe to them, for they've provoked disaster for themselves. ¹⁰ Tell the righteous that it will be well with them, for they will be spared for their righteousness. ¹¹ Woe to the wicked, for their defiance will be repaid.

VIII   ¹² And as for My people, the youth oppress you, foolish women control you. O My people, those who lead you bring you confusion and away from My path. ¹³ The Lord stands up to announce His judgment against the people. ¹⁴ The Lord will accuse the elders and leaders of His people, announcing: It's you who've wrecked My vineyard and taken the property belonging to the poor into your houses. ¹⁵ How dare you do this? Why do you crush My people and hit the poor in their faces, demands the Lord God of Hosts. ¹⁶ The Lord adds: The women of Zion are uppity, parading with their noses in the air, flirting with roving eyes, strutting with swaying hips, clattering bracelets on their ankles, ¹⁷ therefore the Lord will cover their heads with sores and scabs, and the Lord will make these women of Zion bald. ¹⁸ In that day, the Lord will strip away their fine outfits, tearing off their earrings, bracelets, astrological jewelry, ¹⁹ necklaces, scarves, and the charm bracelets, ²⁰ the wigs and hair extensions, anklets, girdles, perfumes, and scents, ²¹ the sorority rings, and nose rings, ²² the evening gowns, furs, and purses, ²³ their mirrors, linen undergarments, lace, and scarves. ²⁴ And then, instead of perfume there will be rot; and instead of a belt, a rope; and instead of groomed hair, baldness; and instead of expensive clothing, a worn bag; scarring instead of beauty. ²⁵ Their men will fall in battle, and those in the prime of life will die in the war. 26 And her streets will be filled with crying and mourning, and destitute she will sit on the ground.

IX   **14** In that coming day, seven women will sustain the priesthood authority of a man and say: We are self-sufficient; but let us be called by the name of our Messiah through baptism because the Messiah removes our sins.

X   2 In that day the people of the Lord will become pure and reflect His glory, the beauty of the land will make the survivors of Israel grateful and humble. 3 And those left in Zion and the survivors in Jerusalem will be called holy, everyone whose name is listed among the living in Jerusalem 4 after the Lord will have washed away the filth of the daughters of Zion, and will have removed the blood staining Jerusalem by His judgment, using fire to remove the wicked. 5 And the Lord will establish a glowing cloud by day, and a pillar of fire by night over the Temple and meeting place on Mount Zion; and the glory of Zion will be a defense, for none will go up to battle against Zion because it's glorious and terrible and we can't stand against her. 6 And there will be a canopy to protect Zion from drought and storms, to make a shelter for God's people.

XI   **15** Let me sing a song for the one I loved, about his vineyard: My loved one had a vineyard on a fertile hillside. 2 And he fenced it, and cleared away the rocks, and planted it with the very best vines, and built a watchtower in it, and also installed a winepress. And he expected it to produce good grapes, but it grew bad grapes. 3 And now O people living in Jerusalem and those of Judah, judge between Me and My vineyard. 4 What more could have been done for My vineyard than I've done for it? When I expected it to produce good grapes, why did it produce only bad grapes? 5 Now I'll tell you what I'll do to My vineyard: I'll take away the protecting hedge and let it be destroyed, and I'll break down the wall and let it be trampled; 6 and I'll make it a wasteland; neither pruned nor cultivated, but weeds and thorns will grow there. I'll also command the clouds not to rain upon it. 7 The Lord of Host's vineyard is the house of Israel, and the people of Judah His vine. And He looked for judgment, but saw violence; for righteousness, but saw only iniquity.

XII   8 Woe to you that build house to house until everything is crowded and yet you live isolated in the place. 9 The Lord of Hosts said directly in my ear: Truly many families will become desolate, and fine mansions abandoned. 10 A ten-acre vineyard will hardly produce six gallons of wine, and 360 pounds of seed will only produce 36 pounds of grain.

XIII   11 Woe to those who get up early in the morning to begin drinking
and continue until nighttime as pitiful drunkards. 12 They listen to loud
music and get drunk at their parties, but have no respect for the Lord's
work, nor do they give any thought to His creation. 13 Therefore I'll
exile My people because they have no understanding, and the leaders
they now respect will die of starvation, and their followers will die of
thirst. 14 Therefore death will gobble them up, eating their leaders,
commoners, partiers, and celebrities. 15 And the arrogant will be
humbled, and the wealthy put into poverty, and they'll be made to bow
down; 16 but the Lord of Hosts will be respected because of His
judgment, and His actions will be understood to be right. 17 Then
sheep will graze on their abandoned homeland, and livestock will
occupy their ruins.

XIV   18 Woe to those who pull sin along with ropes of deceit, and
iniquity with strong cables, 19 that say: Let God hurry up; make Him
do His work now so that we can see it; and let the plans of the Holy
One of Israel come into our view, so we can see it happen.

XV   20 Woe to them that call evil good and good evil, that call darkness
the light and call light the darkness, that call bitter the sweet and call
sweet the bitter.

XVI   21 Woe to those who believe themselves wise and see themselves as
clever.

XVII   22 Woe to the drinking champions, and skilled bartenders, 23 who
take bribes from the guilty, and deny justice to the innocent.
24 Therefore, like the fire consumes straw, and dry grass ignites, their
roots will rot and their descendants will decay into dust, because they
have rejected the law of the Lord Almighty, and ignored the word of
the Holy One of Israel. 25 Therefore the Lord's anger has been stirred
against His people, and this is why He has hit and punished them. And
the earth quaked, and dead bodies piled up in the streets. Despite this
His anger remains, and His control over everything remains intact.

XVIII   26 And He'll raise a banner to the distant nations, and will whistle
for them to come from the end of the earth. Here they return, swiftly
and speedily; not one of them will be tired or stumble; 27 none of them
slumber or sleep; no belt is loosened, nor sandal strap broken; 28 their
arrows are sharpened, and all their bows ready, and their horses'
hooves seem like flint, and their wheels spin like a whirlwind, they roar
like a lion. 29 They're as loud as young lions; they'll roar like wild
beasts, and capture their prey, and carry it away and no one can rescue
them. 30 And on that day, they'll roar over them like the crashing of the
sea; and if one looks at the land, there's great darkness and mourning,
and the sun will be hidden behind the clouds.

Chapter 9

16 In the year that king Uzziah died, I saw the Lord sitting upon a throne, high and lifted up, and His robe filled the temple. 2 Seraphs gathered around Him. Each one had six wings: with two he veiled his face, and with two he covered his legs, and with two he would fly. 3 And one would call to the other, saying: Holy, holy, holy! The Lord of Hosts! The whole earth is within His view! 4 And the doorframe would shake at the sound of that voice, and clouds billowed around God's throne.

II 5 Then I said: Woe is me, I'm lost, for my lips are unclean, and I live among people whose lips are also unclean, and my eyes have seen the King, the Lord of Hosts. 6 Then one of the seraphs flew to me with a live coal in his hand, which he used tongs to take from the altar. 7 And he touched my lips and declared: Hear now, this has touched your lips, your guilt is taken away, and your iniquity cleaned away. 8 Then I heard the voice of the Lord asking: Whom do I send? Who will go for us? And I said: Here am I; send me. 9 And He said: Go tell the people: Listen to this message — but they won't understand what you tell them; and tell them to see your message — but they'll fail to perceive its meaning. 10 Their minds have become dull, their ears plugged, and their eyes closed, otherwise they would see with their eyes, hear with their ears, and understand with their heart, and be converted, and be healed. 11 Then I asked: Lord, how long will they remain like this? And He said: Until their cities have been destroyed and left desolate, and their houses abandoned, and the land deserted, 12 until the Lord has driven everyone far away, and there are many abandoned places throughout the land. 13 But a tithe of the people will remain and will be burned. Like a linden tree or oak tree, leaving a stump with living roots although cut down, likewise a holy remnant to be restored still survives in the residue.

III **17** When Ahaz son of Jotham, the son of Uzziah, was king of Judah, king Rezin of Syria, and Pekah the son of Remaliah king of Israel marched up to fight against Jerusalem, but they couldn't defeat it. 2 When the report reached the house of David that Syria is allied with Ephraim, they all panicked and trembled like the trees of the forest wave in the wind.

IV 3 Then the Lord directed Isaiah: Go out with your son Shear-jashub to meet Ahaz at the end of the channel of the upper pool on the road to the Laundry Field. 4 Tell him: Relax and be quiet; don't be afraid of these two smoldering embers of firewood because of the anger of Rezin of Syria and Remaliah's son. 5 Syria, Ephraim, and

Remaliah's son have plotted your defeat, saying: 6 Let's invade Judah, tear it apart, and divide it up between us, and put the son of Tabeal over it as the king. 7 The Lord God says: It won't happen, I won't let it take place. 8 For the center of Syria is Damascus, and the king of Damascus is Rezin. And within 65 years Ephraim will be shattered, no longer identifiable. 9 The center of Ephraim is Samaria, and the king of Samaria is Remaliah's son. If you won't stand faithful, you won't stand at all.

V   10 The Lord invited Ahaz to: 11 Ask the Lord your God for a sign; anything from the deepest to the highest place. 12 But Ahaz said: I won't ask, nor will I test the Lord. 13 Then Isaiah said: Listen now, you house of David: Is it not enough you try the patience of men? Now you want to try God's patience also? 14 Therefore the Lord Himself will give you a sign: The virgin will conceive and give birth to a son and will call Him Immanuel. 15 By the time He learns to reject the bad and choose the good, people will be eating butter and honey. 16 Before the lad learns to reject evil and choose good, the land of these two kings will be wasted. 17 The Lord will bring upon you and your people and your father's house the worst days since Ephraim broke away from Judah — that king of Assyria. 18 In that day the Lord will whistle for flies from the Nile delta in Egypt, and for bees from the land of Assyria. 19 They'll come and land in the rugged valleys, and in the cracks of the rocks, and on thorn bushes, and beside your ponds. 20 On the same day the Lord will hire the king of Assyria like a razor to shave your head, legs, and beard.

VI   21 And in that day, a man will raise a young cow and two sheep. 22 And because of the abundance of milk they produce, he'll have butter. Everyone remaining in the land will have butter and honey. 23 And at that time, every place where there were 1,000 grapevines worth 1,000 silver coins, there will only be weeds and thorns left. 24 Hunters will go there with bows and arrows because the land is covered with weeds and thorns. 25 As for the once plowed and cultivated hills, you'll no longer go there to see weeds and thorns, since only cattle will graze and only sheep will roam on these places.

VII   **18** The Lord said to me: Take a large scroll and write on it with a pen: For Maher-shalal-hash-baz. 2 Call two reliable witnesses, Uriah the priest and Zechariah the son of Jeberechiah, to witness it. 3 I then impregnated the prophetess, and she gave birth to a son. The Lord told me: Name him Maher-shalal-hash-baz. 4 Before the child learns to call, Father and Mother, the wealth of Damascus and the plunder of Samaria will be carried off by the king of Assyria.

VIII

⁵ The Lord spoke to me again, saying: ⁶ Because this people are ungrateful for the gentle waters of Shiloah, and admire Rezin and Remaliah's son, ⁷ know this, the Lord will bring to them a flood of violent water from the Euphrates, indeed, the king of Assyria and his army. He'll flood over the riverbanks, ⁸ like a flash flood upon Judah, reaching up to the neck. Surely the wings of Immanuel will stretch out as wide as the land. ⁹ Even if you people gather together people, you'll too be broken into pieces. Listen, those who are in distant lands: Even if you prepare for battle, you'll be broken into pieces; you may prepare for battle, but you'll be broken in pieces! ¹⁰ Though you prepare your battle strategy, it will be defeated; though you make your plans, they won't stand, because God is with us.

IX

¹¹ The Lord said to me, taking me by the hand, and telling me to not walk in the path this people follow, saying: ¹² Don't say: A conspiracy! to everything this people says is a conspiracy; don't be afraid of what they fear. ¹³ Only the Lord of Hosts is to be regarded as holy, and He alone inspires awe. ¹⁴ He can make things holy, but for the people of Jerusalem, He'll be a stumbling stone and a rock that trips both houses of Israel, and a trap and a snare for the inhabitants of Jerusalem. ¹⁵ Many of them will stumble, fall down, and be injured, and be caught and taken captive.

X

¹⁶ Deliver the testimony, seal up the law among My disciples. ¹⁷ I'll wait for the Lord who hides His face from the house of Jacob, and I'll put my trust in Him. ¹⁸ Here am I and the children the Lord has given me. We are signs and symbols in Israel from the Lord of Hosts, who lives on Mount Zion. ¹⁹ When people advise you to ask gurus and false spirits that whisper and moan — shouldn't people instead ask God? Why ask the dead for advice for the living? ²⁰ Shouldn't people look for direction from God's law and His warning testimony? And if anyone speaks contrary to this word, it's because there's no light in them. ²¹ And they'll wander lost, wretched, and hungry; and when they're hungry, they'll become angry, look up to heaven and curse their King and their God. ²² And they'll look at the earth and see trouble and darkness, gloom and fear, and won't see the dawn.

XI

19 Nevertheless, the gloom will depart from those who were in distress. In the past, He humbled the land of Zebulun, and the land of Naphtali, but in the future, He'll honor Galilee by the Way of the Sea, on the other side of the Jordan. ² The people walking in darkness have seen a great light; those living in the land of deep darkness have had the light dawn on them. ³ You've enlarged that nation and given it great joy; they rejoice before You like the harvest celebration, and like warriors are happy when dividing their loot. 4 Because you've broken their chains, and the bar across their shoulders, the club used by their oppressor, 5 every warrior's boot worn in battle and all the bloodstained clothes will become fuel for the fire. 6 For unto us a child is born, unto us a son is given, and the government will be upon His shoulder. And His name will be called Wonderful Counselor, the Mighty God, the Everlasting Father, the Prince of Peace. 7 His government and peace will endlessly increase, He'll sit on the throne of David and reign over His kingdom, establishing and upholding it with righteousness and with justice from that time continuing forever. The zeal of the Lord of Hosts will cause this to happen.

XII   8 The Lord sent a message condemning Jacob, and it will fall upon Israel. 9 Everyone will know it — Ephraim and the inhabitants of Samaria — who say in their pride and arrogance: 10 The bricks are fallen down, but we'll rebuild with cut stones; the sycamores are cut down, but we'll replace them with cedars. 11 So the Lord allowed the enemies of Rezin to come against him, and his enemies joined together — 12 the Syrians from the east and the Philistines from the west — and they'll swallow up Israel. Despite this His anger remains, and His control over everything remains intact.

XIII   13 But His people haven't returned to Him who punished them; they reject the Lord of Hosts. 14 Therefore the Lord cut off the head and tail from Israel, palm branch and reed, in a single day. 15 The leaders and teachers are the head, and the lying prophets are the tail. 16 The guides of this people mislead them, and those who follow stumble in the dark. 17 Therefore the Lord will have no sympathy for their young men, nor pity the orphans and widows; for every one of them is a hypocrite and ungodly, and every mouth speaks foolishness. Despite this His anger remains, and His control over everything remains intact.

XIV   18 Wickedness burns like a fire destroying weeds and thorns, and sets ablaze the forests, rolling forward like a pillar of smoke. 19 It's the wrath of the Lord of Hosts that scorches the land and the people become fuel for the fire; they won't spare one another. 20 On the right hand they gobble up but remain hungry, on the left they eat but are never satisfied. They'll eat their own families — 21 Ephraim eating Manasseh's, and Manasseh eating Ephraim's — and together they eat Judah's. Nevertheless, His anger remains, and His control over everything remains intact.

XV   20 Woe to those who make unjust laws, and to those who issue oppressive orders, 2 subverting the rights of the poor, denying justice and imposing tyranny, victimizing widows and orphans. 3 What will you do on the day of judgment, when disaster comes from far away? Where will you run for help? Where will you hide your riches? 4 You'll have no choice but to cower among the prisoners or be killed with the others. Despite this His anger remains, and His control over everything remains intact.

XVI   5 But the Assyrians are only the club I use to impose My discipline. 6 I send them against a godless nation, and against the people who have angered Me, to loot and plunder, and trample over them like mud in the streets. 7 But this isn't what the Assyrians intend, not at all what they have in mind. They intend to destroy and defeat many nations. 8 Their king tells himself: Aren't my commanders all kings? 9 Hasn't Calno fallen just like Carchemish? Isn't Hamath just like Arpad? Isn't Samaria just like Damascus? 10 My hand has conquered the kingdoms of the idols, kingdoms whose idols are better than those of Jerusalem and Samaria. 11 Should I not deal with Jerusalem and her idols as I dealt with Samaria and her idols?

XVII   12 But when the Lord has finished all His discipline of Mount Zion and Jerusalem, He'll then punish the prideful king of Assyria for his arrogance. 13 For he says it's his strong hand and his wisdom that accomplished this, because he claims understanding. He says he's the one that changed national boundaries and pilfered their wealth, like a great hero, saying: 14 I've taken the wealth of other countries like reaching your hand into a nest to gather eggs, and they didn't flap a wing or cluck when I took it all. 15 Is the ax greater than the one who swings it? Does the saw brag it cuts wood without the one using it? As if a club could control the one holding it, or a staff steer the person as if it weren't mere wood. 16 Therefore, the Lord, the Lord of Hosts will inflict disease on his army; and under his pomposity a fire will be kindled. 17 The Light of Israel will be that fire, and Israel's Holy One the flame, and in a single day it will turn his weeds and thorns to ash 18 and burn up his splendid forest and fertile fields, everything. It will be like a gravely ill person wastes away. 19 What's left of his forest will be so small that a little boy can count them all.

XVIII   20 When that happens the remnant of Israel and survivors of the house of Jacob will no longer fear those who struck them down, but will truly trust in the Lord, the Holy One of Israel. 21 A remnant will return, a remnant of Jacob will return to the Mighty God. 22 Even though Israel's people are like the sand of the sea, only a remnant will return. The destruction decreed is overwhelming and righteous. 23 The Lord God of Hosts will carry out the destruction decreed upon the whole land.

XIX   ²⁴ Therefore the Lord God of Hosts tells you: My people who live
in Zion, don't fear the Assyrians who beat you with a club and capture
you like Egypt once did. ²⁵ Very soon My anger with you will end and
I'll impose destruction upon them. ²⁶ The Lord of Hosts will
horsewhip them like He struck down Midian at the rock of Oreb; and
He'll raise His staff to part the waters, as He did in Egypt. ²⁷ And at
that time the burden will be removed from your shoulders, and their
chains taken off your neck, because of the anointing.

XX   ²⁸ They enter Aiath, they pass through Migron; they store supplies
at Michmash. ²⁹ They go through the pass, and they plan to camp
overnight at Geba. Ramath is afraid, and Gibeah of Saul runs in fear.
³⁰ Shout out daughter of Gallim; listen Laish! Poor Anathot!
³¹ Madmenah is running in fear; take cover people of Gebim! ³² They
will be stopped at Nob that day; they'll shake their fist at the mount of
Daughter Zion, at the hill of Jerusalem. ³³ Just watch as the Lord, the
Lord Almighty chops down the mighty branches with power, and the
tall trees will be cut down, and the arrogant will be humbled. ³⁴ He'll
cut down the thick forests with an ax, and Lebanon will fall before the
Mighty One.

XXI   **21** A shoot will come up from the stump of Jesse, and from his
roots a Branch will produce fruit. ² The Spirit of the Lord will rest
upon Him — the Spirit of wisdom and understanding, the spirit of
counsel and might, the spirit of knowledge and of respect for the Lord
— ³ and He'll have insight and love for the Lord. He won't judge by
what He sees with His eyes, nor decide by what He hears with His ears,
⁴ but with righteousness He'll judge the needy, and with justice decide
matters for the poor. He'll control the earth with words from His
mouth, and with His breath He'll slay the wicked. ⁵ And righteousness
will be His belt, and faithfulness the sash around His waist. ⁶ Wolves
will live beside lambs, leopards will lay beside goats; and the calf,
young lion, and yearling together, and a little child will lead them.
⁷ And the cow will eat beside the bear, their young will lie down to rest
together, and the lion will eat straw like the ox. ⁸ The infant will play at
the cobra's den, and a young child will put his hand in the viper's nest.
⁹ They'll neither harm nor destroy on all My holy mountain, because
the earth will be filled with the knowledge of the Lord like the waters
cover the sea.

XXII   ¹⁰ In that day the Root of Jesse will stand as a banner for the
people; the Gentiles will rally to Him, and His peace will be glorious.
¹¹ On that day the Lord will reach out His hand a second time to
reclaim the remaining remnant of His people from Assyria — also
from Lower and Upper Egypt, Cush, Elam, Shinar, Hamath, and

from the islands of the sea. 12 He'll set up a banner for the Gentiles, and will gather the lost people of Israel, and assemble the scattered people of Judah from the four corners of the earth. 13 All the outcasts of Israel will be gathered to His house, and the jealousy of Ephraim and Judah will end; Ephraim won't envy Judah and Judah won't provoke Ephraim. 14 They'll pounce upon the shoulders of the Philistines to the west, together they'll take the wealth of the east, they'll subdue Edom and Moab, and the Ammonites will obey them. 15 The Lord will dry up the gulf of the Egyptian Sea, and dry up the Euphrates River to let His returning people step over the remaining seven brooks. 16 There will be a highway for the returning remnant of His people from Assyria, as there had been earlier when Israel departed from Egypt.

XXIII   **22** And on that day, people will proclaim: Give praise to the Lord; although You were angry with me, Your anger has turned away and You've comforted me. 2 God is my Savior. I'll trust and not fear, for the Lord Jehovah is my strength and my defense; He provided my salvation. 3 You'll joyfully draw water from the wells of salvation. 4 And on that day you'll say: Give praise to the Lord, Proclaim His name, testify about the great things He's done for His people. 5 Sing hymns to the Lord, for He's done glorious things; let it be known throughout the world. 6 Shout joyfully and sing, people of Zion, for the Holy One of Israel dwells among you.

Chapter 10

23 The decree about Babylon, that Isaiah the son of Amoz was shown.
2 Lift up a banner on the high mountain, shout to them, beckon them to enter the royal gates. 3 I've commanded the ones I've prepared for battle, and assembled warriors to execute My judgment, those who rejoice in My triumph. 4 Listen to the noise on the mountains, like a great multitude preparing and massing together, for the Lord Almighty is marshaling an army for war. 5 They come from distant lands, from the end of heaven — the Lord and the weapons of His wrath — to destroy the whole country.

II   6 Start wailing, for the day of the Lord is coming; it will come like destruction from the Almighty. 7 Everyone will faint, everyone's heart will sink, 8 and they'll be overcome by terror. Pain and fear will seize them, they'll thrash about like a woman in childbirth, looking in horror at each other's shocked faces. 9 See, the day of the Lord is coming, cruel, wrathful, and full of fierce anger, to make the land desolate and destroy the sinners occupying it. 10 For the stars above and the constellations won't be seen; the rising sun will be darkened, and the moon won't permit her light to shine. 11 I'll punish the world for its evil and the wicked for their iniquity. I'll put an end to the arrogance of the proud and knock down the cruelty of the ruthless. 12 Survivors will be more refined than pure gold, and it will be harder to find people than the gold of Ophir. 13 Therefore I'll shake the heavens, and the earth will violently quake in response to the anger of the Lord of Hosts on that day. 14 Then like chased deer or wild sheep, everyone will try to gather with friends and flee to a safe place. 15 Whoever is captured will be torn apart, men will be slaughtered. 16 Their infants will be dashed to pieces while they watch, their houses will be robbed, and their wives abused. 17 I'll bring the Medes against them, who don't value silver and gold. 18 Their weapons will massacre the young men, and they'll have no pity for infants; they won't spare the children.

III
19 Then Babylon, jewel of kingdoms, the pride and joy of the Babylonians, will be destroyed by God like Sodom and Gomorrah. 20 She'll never be inhabited or lived in from generation to generation, nomads won't pitch a tent there, and shepherds won't rest their flocks there. 21 Instead, wild desert animals will occupy it, jackals will enter their abandoned houses, and owls will live there, and wild goats will leap about. 22 Hyenas and jackals will roam within her abandoned walls. Her time is close at hand, and her days won't continue. I'll destroy her speedily. Indeed, I'll be merciful to My people, but the wicked will perish.

IV
24 The Lord will have compassion for Jacob, and will again choose Israel, and bring them back to their own land. Foreigners will join and be included with the house of Jacob. 2 Nations will bring them back to their homeland from the ends of the earth, and they'll return to their lands of promise. The house of Israel will allow them to become the Lord's servants and handmaids; and Israel will be captors instead of captives, masters without taskmasters. 3 On that day the Lord will give you rest from your sorrow and trouble, from the hard times you had to endure,

V
4 You'll tell this proverb to the king of Babylon, saying: How has the taskmaster vanished, and how has the oppression ended? 5 The Lord has broken the staff of the wicked, the scepter of the king, 6 used to abuse people in wrath with continual beatings, and in fury conquered nations with his aggression; he's now persecuted, and no one is stopping it. 7 The whole earth is at rest and peaceful; they begin singing. 8 Even the junipers and the cedars of Lebanon gloat over your fall, saying: Now that you've been dropped to the ground no one will come to cut us down! 9 The dead in hell are looking forward to your

arrival. The departed anticipate greeting you. Former leaders and kings are rising from their thrones in anticipation of you joining them in hell. 10 They'll all say to you: You're as weak now as we are; you're now one of us. 11 All your magnificence fell into the grave, along with the noise of your harps; maggots and worms are now covering you.

VI   12 How have you fallen from heaven, O Lucifer, son of the morning! You've been cast down to the earth, you who once destroyed whole nations! 13 You said in your heart: I'll ascend into heaven; I'll sit on a throne above the stars of God; I'll be enthroned on the mount of the congregation, in the northern sky; 14 I'll ascend above the highest clouds; I'll make myself like the Most High! 15 But you've been brought down to hell, to the deepest pit. 16 Those who notice you stare at you, pondering your fate. They ask: Is this the man who shook the earth, who controlled kingdoms, 17 and turned the world into a wilderness, and overthrew its cities and didn't let his prisoners return home?

VII   18 All the kings of the nations lie in state, each buried in their own tomb. 19 But you've been left on the ground like a rejected branch; your unburied carcass now rotting on the ground, stabbed through by a sword. 20 You weren't mourned or buried because you destroyed your land and killed your people. Let the children of your wicked people never remember your name. 21 Prepare a place to slaughter your children for the sins you committed, they are never to rise to inherit any land or ever again control a city. 22 I'll prevent it, says the Lord of Hosts, I'll wipe out Babylon's name and any of her survivors or descendants, declares the Lord. 23 I'll turn it into an abandoned swampland, and I'll make its destruction complete, says the Lord of Hosts.

VIII   24 The Lord of Hosts has promised, saying: Just as I've planned, it will happen; and My purposes will control events. 25 I'll defeat the Assyrian in My land, and on My mountains trample him down. Then his chains will be removed from My people, and his burdens taken off their shoulders. 26 This is My plan set for the whole earth, and this is My hand stretched out over all nations. 27 For the Lord of Hosts has a plan, and who can thwart it? Who's able to fight against His hand?

     28 *The year king Ahaz died I received this prophecy from the Lord:*

IX   29 You Philistines shouldn't rejoice over the club that struck you being broken, because from that snake's root will come a viper, a darting, poisonous serpent. 30 And the poorest of the poor will be fed, and the needy will rest safely. And I'll kill your root with famine, killing all your survivors. 31 Wail at your gate; howl in your city; melt away all you Philistines, for a cloud of smoke is coming from the north against you at the appointed time. ³² What's the message to all the nations? That Zion has been established and there His people will find safety.

Chapter 11

25 Now I'll explain Isaiah's words that I've included in my record. He said many things that are hard for many of my people to understand, since they don't understand the method of Jewish prophesying. ² And I haven't bothered to teach them much about Jewish ways since they fell into dark paths and their practices became an abomination. ³ I'll explain the prophecy to my people who will receive my record in the future, so they can come to understand that God's judgments involve all nations according to the words that He's spoken. ⁴ Therefore pay careful attention, my people who are from the house of Israel, think about my words, because Isaiah's words are difficult for you — nevertheless, they deliver a message to those who are inspired with the spirit of prophecy. Let me give you a prophecy according to the Spirit that's in me — I'll prophesy using the clarity that's been with me since my father and I left Jerusalem. For I take great joy in being straightforward and clear to my people, so they can learn.

II   ⁵ I tell you I take great joy in Isaiah's words, since I came from Jerusalem and understand Jewish ways from my direct experience. I know the Jews understand the approach of the prophets. No other nation understands what was said to the Jews like they do, unless they get taught in the Jewish system. ⁶ But I haven't provided my children an education in Jewish customs; however, I lived at Jerusalem, so I know about the place. I've explained to my children about God's judgments that have happened to the Jews that have fulfilled everything that Isaiah prophesied; yet I haven't written that down.

III   ⁷ But I continue with my prophecy, being direct and clear, and I know that no one can go wrong by it. Nevertheless, when Isaiah's prophecies are fulfilled, people will understand them, once they've actually happened. ⁸ Therefore they're valuable for mankind. And I'll mainly speak to those who don't value them, and limit the discussion to my own people, because I know they'll be very valuable to them in the last days, since they'll understand them at that time. Therefore I've written it down to benefit them.

IV   ⁹ And as one generation of the Jews has been destroyed because of iniquity, so too have they been destroyed from generation to generation because of their iniquities. But no generation has ever been destroyed without warning them beforehand by the Lord's prophets.

¹⁰ Therefore they were told about the destruction that would happen to them right after my father left Jerusalem. Despite that, they hardened their hearts; and according to my prophecy, they've been destroyed, except for those who've been taken as prisoners into Babylon. ¹¹ I say this because of the Spirit that's in me. And although they've been taken away, they'll return and live in the land of Jerusalem. Therefore they'll be restored to the lands of their inheritance. ¹² But they'll have wars and reports of wars.

V   And when the time comes that the Only Begotten of the Father — the Father of heaven and of earth — lives with them in the flesh, they'll reject Him because of their iniquities, hard hearts, and their stubbornness. ¹³ It's certain that they will crucify Him. After He's been buried in a sepulcher for three days, He'll rise from the dead with healing in His wings, and those who believe in His name will be saved in God's kingdom. Therefore my soul takes great joy in prophesying about Him, since I've seen His day, and my heart praises His holy name. ¹⁴ After Christ has risen from the dead and shown Himself to His people (meaning to all those who are willing to believe in His name), Jerusalem will again be destroyed because cursing befalls those who fight against God and His people who obey Him. ¹⁵ As a result, the Jews will be scattered among all nations and Babylon will be destroyed. Then other nations will likewise scatter the Jews.

VI   ¹⁶ After they've been scattered and the Lord God has afflicted them through other nations for many generations — from one generation to another until they're persuaded to believe in Christ the Son of God, and the infinite atonement provided for all mankind — when the time comes that they believe in Christ and worship the Father in His name with pure hearts and clean hands and don't expect there to be any other Messiah — then it will clearly benefit them to believe these things — ¹⁷ the Lord will reach out His hand a second time to restore His people from their lost and fallen state. He'll proceed to do an awe-inspiring and amazing work among mankind. ¹⁸ He'll bring to light and publish His words for them, words that will be used to judge them on the last day. The words will be provided to them in order to convince them of the true Messiah, who was rejected by them. Also, to convince them they don't need to expect a different Messiah to come because any other is a false Messiah to deceive the people. Indeed, there's only one Messiah the prophets have spoken about, and that Messiah is the one who will be rejected by the Jews. ¹⁹ According to the words of the prophets, the Messiah comes 600 years after my father left Jerusalem. And according to the words of the prophets and the words of the angel of God, His name will be Jesus Christ, the Son of God.

VII   20 My people, I've spoken clearly so you can't make a mistake. As the Lord God lives who brought the Israelites out of Egypt and gave Moses power to heal the tribes of Israel after they were bitten by poisonous snakes, if they were willing to look at the snake he lifted up in front of them. The Lord who gave Moses power to strike the rock and have water come out — I tell you that as these things are true and as the Lord God lives, there isn't any other name given under heaven that mankind can be saved by, except for Jesus Christ, whom I've spoken about. 21 This is why the Lord God has promised me the things I'm writing will be kept safe and handed down to my descendants from generation to generation. This will fulfill the promise to Joseph that his descendants would never die out as long as the earth lasted. 22 Therefore these records will endure from generation to generation for as long as the earth exists, and they'll be available according to God's will and design. And the nations that have them will be judged based upon them according to the scriptures.

VIII   23 So we work diligently to write, to persuade our children and our people to believe in Christ and be reconciled to God, because we know that it's by grace we are saved, despite all that we can do. 24 Although we believe in Christ, we keep the Law of Moses and look forward with firm resolve to follow Christ, until the Law is fulfilled, 25 because the Law was given for this purpose. Therefore the Law has become dead to us, and we're made alive through Christ because of our faith; still, we keep the Law because of the commandments. 26 And we talk of Christ, we rejoice in Christ, we preach of Christ, we prophesy of Christ, and we write according to our prophecies so that our children can know to what source they can look for a remission of their sins. 27 Therefore we speak about the Law, so our children understand the Law is dead. And by knowing the deadness of the Law, they can look forward to the life that is in Christ and know for what purpose the Law was given, and after the Law is fulfilled in Christ, they don't need to harden their hearts against Him when the Law must be abandoned.

IX   28 Now, my people, you are stubborn. Therefore I've spoken to you plainly so you can't misunderstand. And the words I've spoken will stand as a testimony against you, because they're enough to teach anyone the true way. And the true way is to believe in Christ and not deny Him, because by denying Him you also deny the prophets and the Law. 29 Now I tell you that the true way is to believe in Christ and not deny Him. And Christ is the Holy One of Israel. Therefore you must bow down before Him and worship Him with all your power, mind, and strength, and your whole soul. If you do this, you'll in no way be thrown out. 30 And to the degree it's suitable and proper, you must keep God's performances and ordinances until the Law that was given to Moses is fulfilled.

X   **26** After Christ has risen from the dead, He'll visit with you, my children and my dear people, and the words that He'll speak to you will be the law you follow. 2 I tell you that I've seen many generations will come and go and there will be great wars and conflicts among my people. 3 And after Christ comes, there will be signs given to my people of His birth, His death, and His resurrection. That time will be great and terrible for the wicked since they will die: they will be killed because they drive out the prophets and holy ones and stone them and kill them. The cry that comes up from the ground from the blood of the holy ones will ascend to God against them. 4 Therefore all those who are proud and do evil — the Lord of Hosts says that the day that is coming will burn them up; they'll be like straw. 5 And those who kill the prophets and holy ones — the Lord of Hosts says that the depths of the earth will swallow them, mountains will cover them, tornadoes will carry them away, and buildings will fall upon them and crush them into pieces and grind them into powder. 6 They'll be visited with thunder, lightning, earthquakes, and all kinds of destruction, because the fire of the Lord's anger will be kindled against them and they'll be like straw. The time that is coming will burn them up, says the Lord of Hosts.

XI   7 How great the pain and anguish of my soul for the loss of my slain people! I've seen it, and it very nearly overwhelms me before the Lord's presence. But I have to admit to God: Your ways are righteous! 8 But the righteous who hearken to the words of the prophets and don't destroy them but anticipate Christ and wait for the signs to be given, despite every persecution, are the ones who won't be killed. 9 On the contrary, the Son of Righteousness will appear to them and He'll heal them. They'll have peace with Him for three generations, and many of the fourth generation will have lived and died in righteousness. 10 Once these things have come to an end, a rapid destruction will come upon my people. And despite the pains of my soul, I've seen it, so I know that it will happen. They will sell themselves for nothing, and in return for their pride and foolishness they will receive destruction. Because they yield to the accuser and choose works of darkness rather than light, they will certainly go down to hell. 11 The Spirit of the Lord won't always help mankind fight temptation. And when the Spirit stops helping mankind fight temptation, a rapid destruction will come, and this distresses my soul.

XII   12 Just as I spoke about convincing the Jews that Jesus really is the Messiah, it's also necessary for the Gentiles to be convinced that Jesus is the Christ, the Eternal God, 13 and that He'll reveal Himself by the power of the Holy Ghost to those who believe in Him — to people of every nation, tribe, and language — performing powerful miracles, signs, and amazing things among mankind according to their faith.

XIII   14 But I prophesy to you about the last days, concerning the time when the Lord God brings these records to light for mankind. 15 After my descendants and my brothers' descendants have fallen away in unbelief and been defeated by the Gentiles — after the Lord God has surrounded them on every side, besieged them with fortifications, and raised towers against them, and after they've been humbled to the dust, to the point that they're considered as nothing — in spite of that, the words of the righteous will be written and the prayers of the faithful will be heard and those who have fallen away in unbelief won't be forgotten. 16 Those who have been slain will leave for them a message to be read after their bodies have turned to dust in the grave, and their message will bring a familiar testimony because the Lord God will have inspired the writings, so that the message will come with conviction, as if they were speaking from the dust.

XIV   17 This is what the Lord God has said: They will write the things that take place among them; they'll be written and sealed away in a book. And those who have fallen away in unbelief won't have them, since they try to destroy the things of God. 18 Therefore, just as those who have been destroyed have been destroyed quickly, the ruthless enemies will also be tossed away like dust in the wind. Indeed, the Lord God says: It will happen suddenly, in an instant.

XV   19 Then those who have fallen away in unbelief will be struck down by the Gentiles. 20 But the Gentiles will proudly view themselves as superior and will have stumbled because they have a great stumbling block: They build up to themselves many churches, but they have no faith in God's power and miracles. They praise themselves — their own wisdom and knowledge — in their preaching, so they can make money and oppress the poor. 21 Many churches will be established, causing envy, antagonism, and malice. 22 And there will also be secret conspiracies, as in former times, using the accuser's plan for conspiracies, because he's involved in the foundation of all these things — the foundation of murder and works of darkness — and he leads them by the neck with a strong rope at the start made of flax, until he enslaves them with his strong ropes forever.

XVI   23 My dear people, I tell you the Lord God doesn't act in darkness or do evil. 24 He doesn't do anything unless it's for the world's benefit, since He loves the world, even laying down His own life so He can draw all mankind to Him. As a result, He doesn't command anyone to reject His salvation. 25 Does He cry out to anyone: Go away! I tell you: No. On the contrary, He says: Come to Me, everyone on earth; buy milk and honey for free. 26 Has He commanded anyone to get out of synagogues or houses of worship? I tell you: No. 27 Has He commanded anyone not to share in His salvation? I tell you: No. On the contrary, He's given it freely to all mankind. And He's commanded His people to lead everyone to repentance. 28 Has the Lord commanded anyone not to share in His goodness? I tell you: No. On the contrary, all people are equally invited, one like the other, and no one is forbidden.

XVII
29 He commands there to be no priestcrafts. Priestcrafts are when preachers set themselves up as a light to the world, so they can make money and receive praise from the world, but they have no desire for Zion to advance. 30 The Lord has forbidden priestcrafts. So the Lord God has commanded everyone to have charity — that is, love — and unless they have charity, they're nothing. As a result, if they had charity, they wouldn't allow those who labor in Zion to waste away. 31 But laborers in Zion must work for the good of Zion since they'll perish if they work only for money. 32 Again, the Lord God has commanded people not to murder, not to lie, not to steal, not to misuse His name, not to envy, not to hate, not to fight with each other, not to commit whoredoms — not to do any of these things. Because whoever does them will perish, 33 since none of these iniquities come from the Lord. Indeed, He does what's good among mankind. And He doesn't do anything without it being clear to mankind. He invites everyone to come to Him and share in His goodness and doesn't deny anyone who comes to Him, black or white, enslaved or free, male or female; and He remembers those who don't worship Him or know anything about Him. All are the same to God — Jews and Gentiles.

XVIII
27 But in the last days or in the time of the Gentiles, every nation of Gentiles and Jews — both those who come upon this land and those who live on other lands, indeed, on every land throughout the earth — will be drunk with iniquity and all kinds of abominations. 2 And when that day arrives, the Lord of Hosts will send thunder, and earthquakes, and loud noises, and storms, and tempests, and uncontrolled fires. 3 And all the nations that fight against Zion and interfere with her will be like a mere dream of the nighttime. It will be to them like a hungry man who dreams that he ate his fill, but when he wakes up he remains hungry. Or like a thirsty man who dreams he gets a drink, but when he wakes up he's still thirsty and starving and he craves relief. Yes, this

is how it will be for all the people who fight against Mount Zion. 4 Those of you who commit iniquity, stop and marvel; you'll cry out and wail. You'll be drunk, but not with wine; you'll stagger, but not with hard liquor. 5 The Lord has poured out a spirit of deep sleep upon you. You've closed your eyes and rejected the prophets, and He's taken away your teachers and seers because of your iniquity.

XIX   6 Then the Lord God will bring forward for you the words of a book, and the words will be from those who have died. 7 The book will be sealed, and a revelation from God from the beginning to the end of the world will be in the book. 8 And because of what's sealed up, the sealed things won't be made known while people remain wicked and practice abominations. So the book will be kept from them. 9 But the book will be given to a man, and he'll write down the words of the book, the words of those who have died, and he'll dictate these words to another. 10 But he must not dictate the sealed words or give the book to anyone else since the book will be sealed by God's power. And the sealed revelation — which discloses all things, from the foundation of the world to its end — are to be left in the book until the Lord determines it's the proper time for them to be revealed. 11 Eventually the words of the book that were sealed will be read upon the housetops, and they'll be read by the power of Christ. Everything will be revealed to mankind, everything that's ever happened among mankind and everything that will happen, all the way to the end of the earth. 12 When the book is given to the man I've just mentioned, the book will be hidden from the eyes of the world, so that no one will see it — besides the one to whom the book will be entrusted — except for three witnesses who will see it by God's power. They'll testify to the truth of the book and the things in it. 13 No one else will view it, except for a few according to God's will, to testify of His word to mankind. The Lord God has said the words of the faithful would speak as if from the dead. 14 Therefore the Lord God will proceed to bring the words of the book to public view. And He'll confirm His word with as many witnesses as seems right to Him. And woe to those who reject God's word!

XX   15 However, the Lord God will tell the one to whom He'll entrust the book: Take these words that are unsealed and give them to another, so he can show them to the well educated, saying: Please read this. And the well educated will say: Bring the book here and I'll read the words. 16 Now he'll say this because he wants attention from the world and to make money, not for God's glory. 17 And the man will reply: I can't bring the book because it's sealed. 18 Then the well educated will say: I can't read it. 19 Therefore the Lord God will give back the book and its words to the one who isn't well educated. Then the man who isn't well educated will say: I'm not well educated. 20 And the Lord God will tell him: The well educated won't read the words — they've rejected them. But I'm able to do My own work; so you must read the words that I'll give you. 21 Don't do anything with the sealed things; I'll reveal them at the right time. I'll show mankind that I'm able to do My own work. 22 When you've read the words I've assigned you, and obtained the witnesses I've promised you, then you must seal up the book again and hide it away to Me, so I can keep the words you haven't read safe until I see fit in My own wisdom to reveal all things to mankind. 23 For I Am God, and I Am a God of miracles. I'll show the world I Am the same yesterday, today, and forever; that I don't do anything among mankind unless it's according to their faith.

XXI   24 And the Lord will also tell the one who will read the words assigned to him: 25 Because these people draw near to Me with their mouths and honor me with their lips, but have removed their hearts far from Me, and their respect for Me is taught by the doctrines of men, 26 therefore I'll proceed to do a marvelous work among these people, yes, a marvelous work and a wonder; for the wisdom of their wise and learned will pass away, and the understanding of their prudent will become confused. 27 And woe to them who work carefully to hide what they're up to from the Lord, and they scheme in the dark, and they say: Who can see what we're doing? And who can identify us? They're perverse, regarding the potter as if he were the clay. But I'll show unto them, says the Lord of Hosts, that I know all their works. For should what's made say of his maker: You didn't make me? Or should what's formed say of him who formed him: He doesn't understand? 28 But listen, says the Lord of Hosts, I'll show you that in a very short time Lebanon will be turned into farmland, and the farmland will be regarded as merely a thicket. 29 And in that day the deaf will hear even written words, and the eyes of the blind will see even in the darkness. 30 Then the humble will have increasing happiness because of the Lord, and the poor will rejoice in the Holy One of Israel. 31 For as certain as the Lord lives, they'll see that the tyrant is brought to nothing, and the scoffer is removed; and all that are eager to do iniquity are wiped out, 32 along with those that testify falsely in court to make the innocent guilty in order to pervert justice. 33 Therefore the Lord who redeemed Abraham declares, concerning the house of Jacob: Jacob will no longer be ashamed, neither will his face grow pale. 34 But when he sees his children, the work of My hands, they'll keep My name holy, and acknowledge the Holy One of Jacob, and will be in awe of the God of Israel. 35 Those who strayed from the truth will return and be willing to accept instruction without complaining.

Chapter 12

28 Now, my people, I've spoken to you as the Spirit has inspired me; so I know these things will certainly happen. 2 The things that will be written from the book will be very valuable for mankind and especially for our descendants, who are a remnant of the house of Israel. 3 Then at that time, among churches that aren't established by the Lord, one church will say to the other: I, I'm the Lord's! And the other will reply: I, I'm the Lord's! — this is how everyone will talk who's built up churches that aren't established by the Lord. 4 They'll argue with each other, and their priests will contradict each other. They'll teach according to what they've learned and deny the Holy Ghost, which inspires people to speak truth. 5 And they'll deny the power of God, the Holy One of Israel. They'll tell the people: Listen to us and follow our directions. God isn't around today; the Lord and the Redeemer has done His work, and He's given men His power. 6 Believe what we teach: If they say that there's a miracle performed by the hand of the Lord, don't believe it! He's not a God of miracles today; He's finished His work. 7 There will be many who will say: Eat, drink, and enjoy yourselves; because we'll soon die and it will turn out fine for us. 8 And there will also be many who will say: Eat, drink, and enjoy yourselves, but praise God. He'll justify committing a little sin. Lie a little, take advantage of someone because of their mistakes, set a trap for your neighbor; there's no harm in any of this. And do all these things, because we'll soon die. But if it turns out we're guilty, God will spank us with a few strokes, and in the end, we'll be saved in God's kingdom. 9 Many will teach in this way false, powerless, and foolish doctrines, and will be filled with pride to their very center and go to great lengths to hide their secret plans from the Lord. They'll try to hide the things they do from public view. 10 And the blood of the holy ones will cry out from the ground against them.

II   11 Indeed, they've all departed from the pathway and become corrupted because of pride. 12 And because of false teachers and false doctrines, their churches will have become corrupted and prideful; because of pride they're full of conceit. 13 They rob the poor because of their fine places of worship and they rob the poor because of their expensive clothing. They persecute the humble and poor in heart because they're inflated with pride. 14 They're unyielding and arrogant; and because of pride, wickedness, abominations, and whoredoms, they've all gone astray except for a few who are Christ's humble followers. However, they're led by false teachings, so that in many cases they go astray because they're taught to obey man-made rules and principles.

III   15 The Lord God Almighty has said: Woe, woe, woe to the wise, the well-educated, and the rich who are prideful to their very center, and to all those who preach false doctrines, practice whoredoms, worship idols, and corrupt and pervert the Lord's right way! They will be thrown down to hell.

IV   16 Woe to those who disregard the just for something of no value and loudly condemn what's good and say it's worthless, because the time is soon coming when the Lord God will visit the inhabitants of the earth in judgment. And when they're fully ripe in iniquity, they will be destroyed. 17 However, the Lord of Hosts has said, if the inhabitants of the earth repent of their wickedness and abominations, they won't be destroyed. 18 But that powerful and utterly wicked church — the whore of all the earth — will fall to the ground in ruins; and its fall will be impressive. 19 Indeed, the accuser's kingdom must shake. And those who belong to it must be motivated to repent, or the accuser will grab them with his everlasting chains and they'll become angry and be lost, 20 since at that time he'll rage in mankind's hearts and cause them to be angry against all that is good. 21 And he'll pacify others, lulling them into worldly security, so that they'll say: Everything is fine in Zion; in fact, Zion is prospering. Everything is fine! And so the accuser swindles them and leads them away carefully down to hell. 22 And he beguiles others, telling them: There's no hell. He says to them: I'm not the accuser — because there isn't one. This is how he whispers in their ears until he imprisons them with his awful chains, from which there's no rescue. 23 They're imprisoned by death and hell and the accuser; and all those who have been captured by these will stand before God's throne and be judged according to their works. From there they'll go to the place prepared for them — a fiery lake that burns like lava, which is endless torment. 24 Therefore, woe to those who are at ease in Zion!

V   25 Woe to those who cry out: Everything is fine! 26 Woe to those who follow the worthless teachings of men and deny God's power and the gift of the Holy Ghost. 27 Woe to those who say: We've received enough of the truth and we don't need any more. 28 In short, woe to all those who shake with anger because of God's truth. Because those built on God's rock are glad to receive truth. But those built on a sandy foundation are afraid of falling.

VI   29 Woe to those who say: We've received God's word; we don't need more of God's word because we have enough. 30 This is what the

Lord God has said: I'll give mankind line upon line, a teaching here and a teaching there, a little here and a little there. Those who follow My teachings and listen to My counsel are blessed since they'll learn wisdom. And I'll give more to those who receive; but from those who say we have enough, even what they have will be taken away. 31 Those who put their trust in the scholarly arrogance of men or follow the false teachings of a man are cursed, because only those teachings given by the power of the Holy Ghost are true.

VII   32 The Lord God of Hosts has said: Woe to the Gentiles; because despite extending My welcoming arm to them from day to day, they will deny Me. Nevertheless, I'll be merciful to them, says the Lord God, if they repent and come to Me. My arm beckons to them all day long, says the Lord God of Hosts.

VIII   **29** But there will be many who are uninterested when I proceed to do an awe-inspiring work among them, in order to fulfill the covenants I've made with mankind. When I beckon them a second time to recover My people who belong to the house of Israel; 2 when I fulfill the promises I've made to you, Nephi, and to your father as well. I said I would remember your descendants, and the words of your record would be made available by My power to your descendants. My words will whistle to the ends of the earth as a standard to My people who belong to the house of Israel. 3 And because My words will ring out, many of the Gentiles will say: A Bible? A Bible? We have a Bible! There can't be another Bible! 4 But this is what the Lord God has said: These fools will have a Bible, and it will come from the Jews, My ancient covenant people. But what thanks do they give the Jews for the Bible they received from them? What do the Gentiles mean? Do they remember the Jews' struggles, efforts, and pains, and their diligence toward Me in making news of salvation known to the Gentiles?

IX   5 You Gentiles, have you remembered the Jews, My ancient covenant people? No, on the contrary, you've cursed and hated them and haven't tried to recover them. But I'll turn all these things back on your own heads, because I, the Lord, have never forgotten My people. 6 You fool who says: A Bible? We've got a Bible! We don't need another Bible! Have you obtained a Bible from anyone but the Jews? 7 Don't you know there are more nations than one? Don't you know that I the Lord your God have created all people and remember those on islands of the sea, and that I rule in the heavens above and on earth beneath, and I bring forth My word for mankind, for every nation of the world? 8 So why do you complain that you receive more of My word? Don't you know that the testimony of two nations is a witness to you that I Am God, and I remember one nation like another? That being the case, I speak the same words to one nation as I do to another; and when the two nations unite, their testimonies will also unite. 9 I do this to prove to everyone that I Am the same yesterday, today, and forever, and I deliver My words according to My own pleasure.

x   And because I've spoken one word, there's no need for you to conclude that I can't speak another. Because My work isn't finished yet, and it won't be until the end of mankind, or even from then on and forever. 10 So, because you have a Bible, there's no need to conclude it contains all My words or that I haven't caused more to be written. 11 I command all people — in the east, the west, the north, the south, and on the islands of the sea — to write the words I speak to them, because I'll judge the world from the books that will be written, each person according to what they do measured against what's written. 12 I'll speak to the Jews, and they'll write it; I'll also speak to the Nephites, and they'll write it; I'll also speak to the other tribes of the house of Israel I've led away, and they'll write it; I'll also speak to every nation on earth, and they'll write it. 13 The Jews will have the Nephites' records and the Nephites will have the Jews' records; and the Nephites and Jews will have the records of the lost tribes of Israel, and the lost tribes of Israel will have the records of the Nephites and the Jews. 14 And My people who belong to the house of Israel will be gathered home to their own lands. And the testimonies of Me will also be united as one, and I'll show those who fight against My word and against My people who belong to the house of Israel that I Am God, and I covenanted with Abraham to remember his descendants forever.

xi   **30** Now, my dear people, I wish to talk to you. I don't want to let you think you are more righteous than the Gentiles will be. Unless you keep God's commandments, you'll all likewise be lost. And because of the words provided to you, don't conclude the Gentiles will be completely destroyed. 2 I tell you: All the Gentiles who repent are the Lord's covenant people, and all the Jews who refuse to repent will be rejected. The Lord only covenants with those who repent and believe in His Son, who is the Holy One of Israel.

xii   3 Now I wish to prophesy a little more about the Jews and Gentiles. After the book I've mentioned appears, and is set down in writing for the Gentiles, and is sealed up again to the Lord, there will be many who will believe the words that are written. And they'll take the words to the remnant of our descendants, 4 who will then know about us, that we came from Jerusalem, and they descend from the Jews. 5 And the gospel of Jesus Christ will be taught to them; so they will be restored to the knowledge of their forefathers and also to knowledge of Jesus Christ, knowledge that their ancestors had among them. 6 Then they'll rejoice since they'll know it's a blessing to them from the hand of God. Their blindness will begin to be removed from their eyes. And after only a few generations they'll become a pure and delightful people. 7 The scattered Jews will also begin to believe in the Messiah, and they'll begin to gather together on the land. And all who believe in Christ will become a delightful people.

XIII

8 The Lord God will begin His work among people of all nations, tribes, and languages, to bring about His people's restoration upon the earth. 9 And with righteousness He'll judge the needy, and with justice decide matters for the poor. He'll control the earth with words from His mouth, and with His breath He'll slay the wicked. 10 For it will soon be time when the Lord God will cause a great division among the people, and He'll destroy the wicked. And He'll spare His people, even if He needs to use fire to destroy the wicked. 11 And righteousness will be His belt, and faithfulness the sash around His waist. 12 Wolves will live beside lambs, leopards will lay beside goats; and the calf, young lion, and yearling together, and a little child will lead them. 13 And the cow will eat beside the bear, their young will lie down together, and the lion will eat straw like the ox. 14 The infant will play at the cobra's lair, and a young child will put his hand in the viper's nest. 15 They'll neither harm nor destroy on all My holy mountain, because the earth will be filled with the knowledge of the Lord like the waters cover the sea. 16 So the true history of all nations will be made known; indeed, everything will be made known to mankind. 17 There isn't anything secret that won't be revealed, and there isn't any hidden event that won't be shown in the light. And there isn't anything sealed on earth that won't be unsealed. 18 Therefore all things that have happened to mankind will, at that time, be revealed. And Satan won't have power over people's hearts anymore, for a long time. Now, my dear people, I finish my words.

Chapter 13

31 Now I finish my prophesying to you, my dear people. I can only write a few things about what I know will certainly happen, and also a few of my brother Jacob's words. 2 I'm satisfied with what I've written, except for a few words I must say about Christ's doctrine. Therefore I'll speak to you clearly and directly so you'll understand my prophesying. 3 My soul delights in clarity and candor since this is how the Lord God works among mankind. The Lord God gives light to the intellect, speaking to people in their language so they can understand. 4 I want you to remember that I've told you about the prophet the Lord showed to me who would baptize the Lamb of God, the Redeemer of this fallen creation.

II

5 Now if the Lamb of God, being holy, needed to be baptized by water to fulfill all righteousness, then how much more do we, being unholy, need to be baptized by water! 6 I want to ask you, my dear people, how did the Lamb of God fulfill all righteousness by being baptized by water? 7 Don't you know that He was holy? However, despite being holy, He showed mankind that in the flesh He humbled Himself before the Father and witnessed to the Father that He was willing to obey Him by keeping His commandments. 8 After He was baptized with water, the Holy Ghost descended upon Him in the form of a dove. 9 This shows mankind the precise path and the exact gate through which they were to enter, since He provides the example for them. 10 He has told mankind: Follow Me. Therefore, my dear people, can we follow Jesus without being willing to keep the Father's commandments? 11 The Father says: Repent, repent, and be baptized in the name of My Beloved Son. 12 And the voice of the Son also spoke to me, saying: The Father will give the Holy Ghost to those who are baptized in My name, just like He did to Me. Therefore follow Me and do the things you've seen Me do. 13 So, my dear people, I know if you follow the Son with all your heart — without being hypocritical or deceptive before God but acting with pure intent, repenting of your sins, showing to the Father you are willing to take upon yourselves the name of Christ by baptism, by following your Lord and Savior down into the water according to His word — then you will receive the Holy Ghost. Then the baptism of fire and of the Holy Ghost comes, and then you can speak the words of angels and shout praises to the Holy One of Israel.

III

14 But, my dear people, the Son's voice came to me, saying: After you've repented of your sins and shown to the Father by the baptism of water that you're willing to keep My commandments and have received the baptism of fire and of the Holy Ghost and can speak in a new language — indeed, even in the language of angels — and then you deny Me, it would have been better for you not to have known Me. 15 And I heard the Father's voice, saying: Yes, the words of My Beloved are true and faithful: Anyone who endures to the end will be saved. 16 Now, my dear people, I know by this that unless a person endures to the end in following the example of the Son of the living God, they can't be saved. 17 Therefore do the things I've told you that I saw your Lord and Redeemer will do. They've been shown to me for this purpose, so you'll know the gate through which you're to enter. And the gate you're to enter is repentance and baptism by water, and then

a remission of your sins comes by fire and by the Holy Ghost. 18 Then you're on the straightforward and narrow path that leads to eternal life — indeed, you've entered through the gate. You've acted in accordance with the commandments of the Father and the Son, and you've received the Holy Ghost promised to you once you entered through the way, which testifies of the Father and Son.

IV   19 Now, my dear people, after you've made your way onto this straightforward and narrow path, I want to ask if everything is done? I tell you: No. Because you've only come to this point by Christ's word, with unshaken faith in Him, relying exclusively on the merits of Him who's powerful to save. 20 Therefore you must press on resolutely with constancy, purpose, and a firm belief in Christ, having a complete brightness of hope and a love for God and for all mankind. This is what the Father has said: If you press forward, feasting on Christ's word, and persevere to the end, you will have eternal life.

V   21 Now, my dear people, this is the way. And there's no other way or name given under heaven by which mankind can be saved in God's kingdom. This is Christ's doctrine, and the only true doctrine of the Father, and of the Son, and of the Holy Ghost, which are united as one God without end. Amen

Chapter 14

32 Now, my dear people, I believe you're wondering a little in your hearts about what you should do after you've entered through the way. But why do you wonder over these things in your hearts? 2 Don't you remember I told you that after you had received the Holy Ghost, you could speak the words of angels? Now, how could you speak the message of the angels unless you did it by the Holy Ghost? 3 Angels speak by the power of the Holy Ghost; as a result, they speak Christ's words. Therefore I told you: Feast on Christ's words — because the words of Christ will tell you everything that you should do. 4 After I've said these words, if you can't understand them, it will be because you don't ask or knock. Consequently, you aren't brought into the light but are certain to perish in the dark. 5 I tell you again, if you will enter through the way and receive the Holy Ghost, it will show you everything you should do. 6 This is Christ's doctrine. No more doctrine will be given until after He visits you here on earth. Once He shows Himself to you here on earth, you must obey what He tells you.

II   7 Now I can't say anything else. The Spirit keeps me from going on, and I'm left to mourn because of mankind's unbelief, wickedness, ignorance, and stubbornness. They refuse to search for knowledge, or comprehend great knowledge when it's given plainly to them, just as plain as words can be.

III   8 Now, my dear people, I sense you're still wondering in your hearts. And it distresses me that I have to speak about this. Because if you were willing to listen to the Spirit that teaches a person to pray, you would know you must pray. Because the evil spirit doesn't teach a person to pray; on the contrary, it teaches a person they must not pray. 9 But I tell you that you must always pray and not be discouraged, and you must not begin to work on anything for the Lord unless you first pray to the Father in the name of Christ that He'll consecrate your performance to you, so your performance can be for your soul's well-being.

Chapter 15

33 Now I can't write everything that was taught to my people, and I'm also not as effective a writer as I am a speaker. Because when anyone speaks by the power of the Holy Ghost, the power of the Holy Ghost impresses people's hearts. 2 But there are many who harden their hearts against the Holy Spirit, so there is no room for it within them. So they reject many written things, regarding them as worthless. 3 But I've written what I've written, and I think it's very valuable, especially for my people. I pray continually for them by day, and my tears wet my pillow at night over them. I cry to God in faith, knowing He'll hear my cry. 4 I know the Lord God will consecrate my prayers for the benefit of my people. He'll make what I've written in weakness powerful for them, since it persuades them to do good, tells them about their ancestors, speaks about Jesus, and persuades people to believe in Him and to persist to the end, which is life eternal. 5 And it speaks harshly against sin in plain truth. So no one will be angry at the words I've written unless they embrace the spirit of the accuser. 6 I glory in plainness, I glory in truth, and I glory in Jesus, because He has redeemed my soul from hell. 7 I have charity for my people and great faith in Christ that I'll meet many souls spotless at His judgment seat. 8 I have charity for the Jews — I say Jews referring to those who I came from. 9 I also have charity for the Gentiles. But I can't hope for any of these unless they're reconciled to Christ, enter through the narrow gate, walk in the precise pathway that leads to life, and stay on that path until their probation ends.

II   10 Now, my dear people, and the Jews as well, and all of you in the farthest reaches of the earth, trust these words and believe in Christ. And if you don't believe in these words, believe in Christ; and if you believe in Christ, you'll believe in these words since they're Christ's words. He's given them to me, and they teach all mankind to do good. [11] If they aren't Christ's words, you be the judge. Because on the last day, Christ will show you with power and great glory that they are His words. You and I will stand face to face before His judgment bar, and you'll know then that I've been commanded by Him to write these things, despite my weakness. [12] And I ask the Father in the name of Christ that many of us, if not all, may be saved in His kingdom on that great and last day.

III   [13] Now, my dear people, and those who belong to the house of Israel as well as all of you in the farthest reaches of the earth, I speak to you like the voice of one crying out from the dust. Farewell until that great day comes. [14] To you that refuse to share in God's goodness or show respect for the Jews' words, my words, and every word that will come from the Lamb of God, I say goodbye forever, since these words will condemn you on the last day. [15] What I seal on earth will be brought against you at the judgment bar. This is what the Lord has commanded me to say, and so I obey. Amen.

THE BOOK OF JACOB

THE BROTHER OF NEPHI

The words of his preaching to his people. He silences a man who attempts to overthrow Christ's doctrine. A few words about Nephite history:

Chapter 1

After fifty-five years had ended since Lehi left Jerusalem, Nephi gave me, Jacob, a commandment regarding the small plates on which these writings are engraved. [2] He commanded me to only write a few things on these plates that I considered to be extremely valuable, and to only touch lightly on the history of this people, who are called Nephites. [3] He said his people's history was to be engraved on his other plates and I was to keep these plates safe and hand them down to my descendants from generation to generation. [4] If there was sacred preaching or any great revelation or prophecy, I was to engrave their main points on these plates and write about them as much as possible, on behalf of Christ to benefit our people. [5] The things to happen to our people were accurately shown to us as a result of faith and our great concern. [6] We also had many revelations and the spirit of great prophecy; so we knew about Christ, who was appointed to come, and His kingdom. [7] Therefore we worked diligently among our people to persuade them to come to Christ and share in God's goodness, so they could enter His rest. Then there wouldn't be any reason for Him to declare in His wrath that they would not enter His rest, as He had been provoked during the days testing the children of Israel in the wilderness. 8 Therefore we pray to God we could persuade all mankind not to rebel against God, not to provoke Him to be angry; rather, we pray that all people would believe in Christ, contemplate His death, endure your cross along with Him, and patiently go through the persecution and dishonor that come from the world. And so I Jacob intend to fulfill my brother Nephi's commandment.

II   9 Then Nephi grew old, and he sensed he would soon die. So he anointed a man to be a king and ruler over his people. Now according to the rule of the kings — 10 the people loved Nephi tremendously since he had been a great protector for them and had wielded Laban's sword in their defense and had worked his whole life for their well-being — 11 as a result, the people wanted to memorialize his name, calling those who ruled as his successors Second Nephi, Third Nephi, etc., according to the rule of the kings. So this is the title the people called them, whatever their name happened to be.

III   12 Then Nephi died. 13 Now the people who weren't Lamanites were Nephites; however, there were also those called Nephites, Jacobites, Josephites, Zoramites, Lamanites, Lemuelites, and Ishmaelites. 14 But I won't distinguish them by these names after this; instead, I'll call those who attempt to kill the Nephites Lamanites, and those who are friendly to Nephi I'll call Nephites, or the people of Nephi, according to the rule of the kings.

IV   15 Now the Nephites under the second king's rule began to grow hard in their hearts and indulge in wicked practices to a certain degree, like David of old and his son Solomon did, wanting to have many wives and concubines. 16 They also began to spend their time searching for gold and silver and began to be filled with pride. 17 Therefore I Jacob addressed the following words to them as I taught them in the temple, having first obtained from the Lord the message I was to give them, 18 since my brother Joseph and I had been ordained as priests and teachers of this people by Nephi. 19 We honored our callings for the glory of the Lord, taking upon ourselves the responsibility, viewing the people's sins as our responsibility if we didn't diligently teach them God's word. That being the case, by laboring with our strength their blood wouldn't stain our clothes, otherwise their blood would stain our clothes and we wouldn't be found spotless on the last day.

Chapter 2

2 The words Jacob, Nephi's brother, spoke to the Nephites following Nephi's death. 2 Now, my dear people, I come to the temple today to declare God's word to you according to the responsibility I owe to God to honor my calling in all seriousness, and to avoid being accountable for your sins. 3 You know I've been diligent up to now in performing my calling, but today I'm far more concerned and uneasy about your souls' welfare than I've been before. 4 You've obeyed the Lord's word I've given you until now. 5 But listen and with the help of the all-powerful Creator of heaven and earth, I will tell you about your thoughts, how you're beginning to commit sin — one I find very abhorrent, and is also offensive to God. 6 It weighs heavily on my soul and I am ashamed before God to need to confront you about the wickedness of your hearts. 7 It also pains me to use such blunt language about you in front of your wives and children. Many of their feelings are very tender, chaste, and delicate before God, which pleases Him. 8 I suppose they came here to listen to an encouraging and healing message from God.

II
9 Therefore it weighs down my soul to be compelled by the strict commandment I've received from God to admonish you for your sins. This will reinjure those who are already wounded, instead of comforting and healing their injuries. The rest who are innocent, instead of being fed on good tidings from God, will hear condemnation that will break their hearts and trouble their minds. 10 But despite the challenge of this, I must obey God's strict commands and tell you about your wickedness and abominations in front of those pure in heart and broken-hearted, and under the piercing glance of Almighty God's eye.

III
11 I must tell you the truth and deliver God's blunt message. I asked the Lord, and He answered me, saying: Jacob, go up to the temple tomorrow and deliver the message I'll give you.

IV
12 Now, my people, this is the message to you: Many of you have begun to search for gold, silver, and all kinds of precious metals this promised land, which is for you and your descendants, has in generous amounts. 13 God, in His foreknowledge and generosity, has blessed you and allowed you to become wealthy. Because some of you have acquired more than your brothers and sisters, you're filled with pride to your core, are stubborn and arrogant, because of your expensive clothing, and you look down on those around you because you think you're better than them.

V   14 My friends, do you think God justifies you thinking and acting this way? I tell you: No; He condemns you. If you continue doing this, His judgments will crash down on you. 15 I wish He would show you He can pierce you and with one glance of His eye strike you down to the dust! 16 If only He would rescue you from this foolish sin and abomination! If only you would pay attention to His commandments and not let pride destroy your souls! 17 Care for those around you like you care for yourselves and treat everyone like family and be generous with your money and possessions, so they can prosper like you. 18 Before you ever try to be wealthy, seek God's kingdom. 19 And after you've obtained a hope in Christ, you'll have wealth, if that's your goal; and you will want it as the means to do good to others: to clothe the naked, feed the hungry, free the enslaved, and to help cure the sick and injured.

VI   20 My people, I've spoken to you about pride. Those of you who have reviled your neighbors, looking down on them because you were proud in your hearts for what God has given you, how can you explain this? 21 Don't you think such things are offensive to the One who created all mankind? Each person is as precious to Him as another. Mankind was made from the dust; and He has created everyone for the very same purpose: to keep His commandments to glorify Him forever. 22 Now I'm done speaking to you about this pride. And if I didn't have to speak to you about a worse sin, my heart would be very glad because of you. 23 But God's word weighs me down because of your more obscene sins. The Lord says: This people are beginning to increase in iniquity; they don't understand the scriptures, trying instead to excuse themselves in committing whoredoms because of what's written about David and his son Solomon. 24 Indeed, David and Solomon had many wives and concubines — something offensive to Me, says the Lord.

VII   25 Therefore the Lord says: I led this people from the land of Jerusalem by My power so I could make from Joseph's offspring a righteous branch that will follow Me. 26 Therefore I won't let this people do like others did in the past. 27 So, my people, listen to me and hearken to the Lord's word: No man among you is to have more than one wife — and he is not to have any concubines. 28 I the Lord God delight in women's chastity and prostitution is an abomination to Me — says the Lord of Hosts. 29 Therefore this people must keep My commandments, says the Lord of Hosts, or the land will be cursed on their account.

VIII   30 For in My Wisdom I will have covenant people, says the Lord of Hosts, whom I'll command and lead, and they will hearken to this commandment to have only one wife. ³¹ I the Lord have seen the sorrow and heard the sobbing of the daughters of My people in the land of Jerusalem, and elsewhere in My people's lands, because of the wickedness and abominations of their husbands. ³² The Lord of Hosts says: I won't let the cries of the beautiful daughters of this people, whom I've led out of the land of Jerusalem, come up to Me against the men of My people, says the Lord of Hosts. ³³ They're not to mislead the daughters of My people — because of their kind, gentle nature — and use their vulnerabilities to subjugate them. If they do this, I will chastise them, even destroy them if needed, because I've commanded them not to commit whoredoms like others did in the past, says the Lord of Hosts.

IX   ³⁴ Now, my brothers and sisters, you know these commandments were given to our father Lehi; so you are familiar with them. And you've come under great condemnation, since you've violated what you were taught. ³⁵ You've committed greater iniquity than the Lamanites, our brothers and sisters. You've broken the hearts of your tender wives and lost your children's confidence because of your bad examples to them. The sobbing of their hearts goes up to God against you and many hearts are broken, cut with deep wounds. Because God's word is clear, it condemns you, because of your disobedience.

X   **3** But I also want to speak to those who are pure in heart. Look to God with a firm mind and pray to Him with great faith. He'll comfort you in your distress and plead your cause and send down justice upon those who seek to destroy you.

XI   ² All of you pure in heart: Look up, receive the pleasing word of God, and feast on His love, because if your minds are firm, it's always available. ³ But woe, woe to those of you that aren't pure in heart, who are filthy before God today. Unless you repent, the land has been cursed because of you. And the Lamanites, who aren't filthy like you are — even though afflicted with a bitter curse — will punish you and be allowed to destroy you. ⁴ Unless you repent, the time will quickly come when they'll take possession of your inherited land, and the Lord God will guide the righteous to leave you. ⁵ You hate your brothers and sisters, the Lamanites, because of their filthiness and darkened countenances, but they're more righteous than you. They haven't forgotten the Lord's commandment, given to our father, to have only one wife and no concubines, and forbidding whoredoms. ⁶ They make a point of keeping this commandment. And so, because they stay obedient to this commandment, the Lord God won't destroy them but will be merciful to them, and one day they'll become a blessed people. ⁷ Their husbands love their wives, their wives love their husbands, and their husbands and wives love their children. And their unbelief and hatred for you is due to the iniquity of their forefathers; so why do you think you're better than them in the sight of your great Creator?

XII   8 My brothers, I'm afraid that unless you repent of your sins, their countenance will be more pure than yours when you and they are brought before God's throne. 9 Therefore I give you a commandment, which is God's word, not to insult them anymore because their countenance is darkened. You must not speak disparagingly of them because of their filthiness, but remember your own filthiness and that theirs is due to their forefathers. 10 Therefore you must remember your children, how you've injured their hearts because of your example. Remember that because of your filthiness you would be responsible for their sins and may cause your children's destruction. When God judges you, you'll be condemned for both your sins and theirs.

XIII   11,14 My people, listen carefully to me. Awaken the power of your souls, shake yourselves so you can wake up from the slumber of death, and free yourselves from the pains of hell, so you don't become angels to the accuser, to be thrown into that fiery lake that burns like lava, which is the second death. This concludes what I said following Nephi's death. 12 Now I Jacob spoke many more things to the Nephites, warning them against fornication and adultery, the inciting of lust, and every kind of sin, explaining to them their awful consequences. 13 And not even one percent of the doings of this people, who are now becoming numerous, can be written on these plates; but many of their doings are written on the larger plates, including their wars, conflicts, and the rule of their kings. 14 These plates are called the plates of Jacob, and they were made by Nephi himself.

Chapter 3

4 Now I Jacob had spoken a great deal to my people — but I can only write a few of my words because of the difficulty of engraving metal plates. We know what we put on plates will last, 2 and whatever we write on anything other than plates will be lost and fade away. So we write a few words on plates, and they'll give our descendants and dear brothers and sisters a little knowledge about us or their forefathers. 3 We're pleased to do this, and we work carefully to engrave these words, hoping our dear people and our descendants will be thankful for them. We hope they'll study them carefully so they can understand their ancestors, be grateful, and not disregard them. 4 We've written these things for this purpose: so they learn we knew about Christ and had a hope of glory in Him hundreds of years before

His coming. And it wasn't just us who had a hope of His glory, but so did the holy prophets before us.

II   5 They believed in Christ and worshiped the Father in His name, and we also worship the Father in His name. This is the reason we keep the Law of Moses, since it points our souls to Him. This lets us honor Him and His righteousness, just as it was credited to Abraham, in the wilderness, for being obedient to God's commands in offering his son Isaac. That event symbolized God and His Only Begotten Son. 6 Therefore we carefully study the prophets and have many revelations and the spirit of prophecy. Because we have all these witnesses, we obtain hope and our faith becomes unshaken, so we can actually command in Jesus' name and even the trees, mountains, or waves of the sea obey us. 7 Nevertheless, the Lord God shows us our weaknesses so we know it's by His grace and great acts of condescension for mankind that we receive power to do these things.

III   8 The Lord has done such great and awe-inspiring things! How unsearchable are His deep mysteries! It's impossible for mankind to discover all His ways. And no one knows His ways unless they're revealed to them. Therefore, brothers and sisters, don't disregard God's revelations. 9 By the power of His word, mankind inherited the earth, and the earth was created by the power of His word. So if God was able to speak and the world came into existence and able to speak and mankind was created, then why can't He command the earth or His handiwork upon it, according to His will and purposes? 10 Therefore, brothers and sisters, don't attempt to give advice to the Lord, but decide to take advice from Him. Indeed, you know He counsels wisely, justly, and very mercifully over His creation. 11 Therefore, dear people, be reconciled to God through the atonement of Christ, His Only Begotten Son, so you can receive a resurrection according to the power of the resurrection which is in Christ and so you can be presented to God as Christ's first harvest, having faith and receiving the promise of glory in Him before He reveals Himself in the flesh.

IV   12 Now, dear people, don't let this surprise you. Why shouldn't we speak of Christ's atonement and have perfect knowledge about Him? Why not have understanding of the resurrection and the world to come? 13 My people, those who prophesy, let them prophesy so people can understand, because the Spirit speaks the truth, not lies. Therefore it speaks of things as they really are and really will be. These things are shown to us plainly to save our souls. But we aren't the only witnesses of these things, since God told them to former prophets.

V　　　14 However the Jews were a stubborn group, and they treated plain words with disdain and killed the prophets, and only wanted things they couldn't understand. Therefore because of their blindness, which came from looking beyond the mark, they couldn't help but fall. So God removed His plain word from them and left them with things they can't understand, like they wanted. Therefore God lets them puzzle and argue.

VI　　　15 Now I prophesy by the Spirit, from the inspiration given to me, that because of the Jews' confusion, they'll reject the stone on which they could build a safe foundation. 16 According to the scriptures, this stone will prove to be the great, last, and only sure foundation offered to the Jews. 17 Now, dear people, how is it possible these people, after having rejected the sure foundation, can ever build on it as their safe cornerstone? 18 My dear people, I'll explain this mystery to you if I don't lose the Spirit of revelation and get distracted by my worry over you.

VII　　　**5** My people, let me remind you of the words the prophet Zenos spoke about the house of Israel, saying: 2 Hearken, O house of Israel, and hear my words, the words of a prophet of the Lord. 3 This is the Lord's message: I'll compare you, O house of Israel, to a tame olive tree a man took and nourished in his vineyard. And it grew, became old, and began to decay. 4 And the lord of the vineyard went out and saw his olive tree started to decay, so he said: I'll prune it and loosen the soil around it and tend it, so perhaps some young, tender branches will sprout and it won't die. 5 So he pruned it, loosened the soil around it, and tended it according to his word. 6 After many days it began to sprout a few young and tender branches, but the main top was dying. 7 And the lord of the vineyard saw it and said to his servant: It makes me sad to lose this tree. So go and retrieve branches from a wild olive tree and bring them here to me. Then we'll cut off the main branches that are starting to wither away and throw them into the fire to be burned. 8 And the lord of the vineyard said: I'll remove many of these new, tender branches and graft them in places I choose; then it won't matter if the original tree root dies, because I can still save its fruit for myself. Therefore I'll take these young, tender branches and graft them in places I choose. 9 Now take the branches of the wild olive tree and graft them in to replace them. Then I'll throw the ones I've cut off into the fire and burn them, so they won't take up space in my vineyard.

VIII　　　10 And the servant of lord of the vineyard followed the lord of the vineyard's plan and grafted in the branches of the wild olive tree. 11 And the lord of the vineyard had it tilled, pruned, and tended, saying to his servant: It makes me sad to lose this tree; so I've done this to perhaps be able to keep its roots alive, so they don't die, because I would like to save them for myself. 12 Therefore follow the plan; watch the tree and tend it following my instructions. 13 And I'll place these branches in the lowest parts of my vineyard, where I choose, and that isn't your concern. I'll do this in order to save the tree's natural branches for myself and to store its fruit for myself in preparation for the harvest time. Because it would make me sad to lose this tree and its fruit.

IX   14 And the lord of the vineyard went his way and hid the natural branches of the tame olive tree in the lowest parts of the vineyard, some in one part and some in another, according to his deliberate plan. 15 After a long time had elapsed, the lord of the vineyard said to his servant: Come, let's return to the vineyard to work there.

X   16 Then the lord of the vineyard with his servant returned to work in the vineyard. The servant said to his master: Oh good! Look here! Inspect this tree. 17 And the lord of the vineyard looked and saw the tree where the wild olive branches had been grafted in. It had sprouted and begun to produce fruit. He saw it was good and its fruit was like the natural fruit. 18 He said to his servant: See, the wild tree's branches have taken hold of the root's vitality, so that the root has provided them with vigor. And because of the root's vitality, the wild branches have produced tame fruit. If we hadn't grafted in these branches, the tree would have died. Therefore I'll store plenty of fruit that this tree has now produced. I'll store the fruit for myself as part of the harvest.

XI   19 The lord of the vineyard then told the servant: Come, let's go to the lowest parts of the vineyard and see if the tree's natural branches have also produced a lot of fruit, so I can store the fruit for myself as part of the harvest. 20 And they went out to where the lord of the vineyard had hidden the tree's natural branches, and he said to the servant: Look at these! He saw the first tree had produced plenty of fruit, and he saw it also was good. Then he told the servant: I've tended it a long time, and it has produced plenty of fruit. So take the fruit of the tree and store it as part of the harvest, so I can save it for myself.

XII   21 The servant asked his master: How was it that you came to plant this tree or this tree branch here? It was the poorest spot in the whole vineyard. 22 But the lord of the vineyard replied: Don't complain about it, I knew it was a poor spot of ground. That's why I told you that I gave it attention and cared for it a long time, and you see it has produced plenty of fruit.

XIII   23 Then the lord of the vineyard said to his servant: Look here! I've also planted another branch of the tree, and you know this spot of ground was poorer than the first. But look at the tree! I've tended it a long time and it has produced plenty of fruit. Therefore gather it and store it as part of the harvest, so I can save it for myself.

XIV   24 Then the lord of the vineyard said again to his servant: Look here and see another branch I've planted. I've tended it too, and it has produced fruit. 25 And he told the servant: Look here and see the last one! I've planted this one in a very favorable spot and tended it a long time. And only part of the tree has produced tame fruit, but the other part of the tree has produced wild fruit. I've tended this tree like the others.

XV   26 Later the lord of the vineyard told his servant: Cut off the branches that haven't produced good fruit and throw them into the fire. 27 But the servant said to him: Let's prune it, loosen the soil around it, and tend it a little longer, so it will perhaps produce good fruit for you, so you can store it as part of the harvest. 28 So the lord of the vineyard and his servant cared for all the vineyard's fruit.

XVI   29 After a long time had passed, the lord of the vineyard told his servant: Come, let's return to the vineyard to work there again. Because the time approaches and the end is coming soon, therefore I must store fruit before the final harvest arrives. 30 Then the lord of the vineyard and the servant returned to the vineyard and came to the tree whose natural branches had been taken off and which had wild branches grafted in, and all kinds of fruit weighed down the tree.

XVII   31 And the lord of the vineyard tasted the fruit, every kind that had grown there. And the lord of the vineyard said: We've tended this tree a long time, and I've stored plenty of fruit for myself in preparation for the harvest. 32 Now it has produced plenty of fruit, although none of it's good; there are all kinds of bad fruit, and it's of no use to me, despite all our work. Now it makes me sad to lose this tree. 33 And the lord of the vineyard said to the servant: What else can we do for the tree so that I can again obtain good fruit for myself? 34 And the servant said to his master: Because you grafted in the wild olive tree's branches, they've saved the roots, so they're still alive and haven't died; and you can see they're still good.

XVIII   35 Then the lord of the vineyard told his servant: The tree is of no use to me and its roots are of no use to me so long as it produces bad fruit. 36 However, I know the roots are good, and I've kept them alive as part of my plans. And because of their great vitality, they've produced good fruit from the wild branches until now. 37 But the wild branches have grown and overrun the roots. And because the wild branches have overcome the roots, the tree has produced a lot of bad fruit. And because it has produced so much bad fruit, you see it's beginning to die. It will soon be lost, reaching the point that we'll need to throw it into the fire unless we do something to keep it from dying.

XIX   38 Then the lord of the vineyard told his servant: Let's go down into the lowest parts of the vineyard and see if the natural branches have also produced bad fruit. 39 So they went down into the lowest parts of the vineyard and saw the fruit of the natural branches had also become corrupt — the first, second, and last — they had all become corrupt. 40 And the wild fruit of the last one had overcome that part of the tree that once produced good fruit, to the point that the good branch had withered away and died.

XX   41 Then the lord of the vineyard mourned and asked the servant: What more could I have done for my vineyard? 42 I knew that all the vineyard's fruit, except for these, had become corrupt. Now these that once produced good fruit have also become corrupt. All my vineyard's trees are now good for nothing and will need to be cut down and thrown into the fire. 43 I planted this last one, whose branch has withered away, in a good spot of ground — indeed, a place I valued above all other parts of my vineyard.

XXI   44 And you see I also cut down what was growing in this spot of ground so I could plant this tree in its place. 45 You can see that part of it produced good fruit and the other part produced wild fruit. Because I didn't cut off its bad branches and throw them into the fire, they've overcome the good branch, so it has withered away. 46 Now, despite all the care we've given to my vineyard, all its trees have become corrupt, so they don't produce any good fruit. I was hoping to save these, to have stored up fruit for myself as part of the harvest. But they've become like the wild olive tree, and they're of no value except to be cut down and thrown into the fire. And it makes me sad to lose them. 47 But what more could I have done in my vineyard? Have I neglected my work and failed to tend it? No, I've tended it and I've loosened the soil around it, I've pruned it, I've fertilized it, and I've worked my hand almost the whole day, and now the end is approaching. It makes me sad that I must cut down all my vineyard's trees and throw them into the fire to be burned. What's ruined my vineyard?

XXII   48 Then the servant asked his master: Isn't it your vineyard's ambitious overgrowth? Haven't the branches overgrown the good roots? And because the branches have overgrown their roots — growing faster than the strength of their roots, taking strength to themselves — I ask, Isn't this the reason your vineyard's trees have become corrupted?

XXIII   49 The lord of the vineyard told his servant: Let's go ahead and cut down the vineyard's trees and throw them in the fire, so they don't take up space in my vineyard — I've done everything I could. What more could I have done? 50 But the servant said to the lord of the vineyard: Wait a little longer. 51 And the lord of the vineyard replied: Yes, I want to give it more time, because it makes me sad to lose my vineyard's trees. 52 Therefore let's take some of the original branches I've transplanted to the lowest parts of my vineyard and graft them into the tree they came from. And let's cut from the tree the branches with the most bitter fruit and graft in the tree's original branches in their place. 53 I'll do this so the tree won't die, so that perhaps I might save the roots for myself and for my own purpose. 54 And the roots of the tree from which I took the original branches are still alive; therefore, to also save them as part of my plan, I'll take some of the tree's original branches and graft them back. I'll graft the original branches back to the roots of the original tree, so I can also save the roots for myself, so that when they're strong enough, they might produce good fruit for me, and I can still celebrate my vineyard's fruit.

XXIV   55 So they took branches from the original tree that had become wild and grafted them into the original tree that also had become wild. 56 They also took branches from the original tree that had become wild and grafted them into their original tree's root. 57 And the lord of the vineyard said to the servant: Only cut away the most bitter, wild branches from the trees. And graft in their place according to my instructions. 58 We'll tend the vineyard's trees again and trim their branches and cut from the trees the ripe branches, which have to be destroyed, and throw them into the fire. 59 I'm doing this to let their roots perhaps regain strength because they're still promising and because changing the branches will let the good overcome the evil. 60 Now I've saved the natural branches and their roots and grafted the natural branches into their mother tree again and kept the mother tree's roots from dying. That way my vineyard's trees can perhaps produce good fruit again, and so I can celebrate with my vineyard's fruit. Maybe I'll be able to have great results because I've kept the roots and branches of the original plant alive. 61 Now go ahead and call servants, so we can work diligently with our strength in the vineyard, so we can prepare the vineyard to again yield the best good fruit as I originally had in my vineyard.

XXV   62 Therefore let's go work hard this last time — the end is approaching, and this is the last time I'll prune my vineyard. 63 Graft in the branches — begin with the last so they can be first and so the first can be last — and loosen the soil around the trees, both old and young — the first and the last, and the last and the first — so everything can be tended again for the last time. 64 Loosen the soil around them and prune them and fertilize them once more for the last time — the end is approaching. And if it turns out these last grafts grow and produce natural fruit, then you will trim away so they can grow. 65 As they begin to grow, you must clear away the branches that produce bitter fruit, as the good gains size and strength. But you must not clear away the bad all at once as that would let the roots be too strong for the graft, because we don't want the graft to die, and I don't want to lose my vineyard's trees. 66 It would make me sad to lose the trees of my vineyard. Therefore you must clear away the bad in proportion to the growth of the good, so the root and top will be equal in strength until the good overgrows the bad and the bad is cut down and thrown in the fire, so they don't take up space in my vineyard. This will be how I'll rid my vineyard of the bad. 67 I'll graft the branches of the original tree back into the original tree, 68 and I'll graft the branches of the original tree into the tree's original branches. This is how I'll bring them back together, so they will produce the original fruit again and be united. 69 The bad will be thrown out — including from my entire vineyard. I'll prune my vineyard just this last time.

XXVI   70 Then the lord of the vineyard sent his servant, and the servant went and did as the lord had commanded him and brought a few other servants. 71 And the lord of the vineyard told them: Get started and work hard in the vineyard. This is the last time I'll tend my vineyard — the end is near and the harvest is coming quickly. If you work hard with me, you'll have joy in the fruit that I'll harvest for myself at the end of the growing season.

XXVII   72 Then the servants went ahead and worked hard, and the lord of the vineyard also worked with them. And they obeyed the lord of the vineyard's direction in all things. 73 And original fruit again grew in the vineyard, and the original branches began to grow and produce abundantly, and the wild branches began to be cut off and thrown away. And they kept the root and the top equal based on their strength. 74 This is how they worked with all diligence according to the lord of the vineyard's commandments, until the bad had been thrown out of the vineyard and the lord had saved the good for himself, so the trees had again produced the original fruit. And they became like one body and the fruit was equally good; and the lord of the vineyard had saved the original fruit for himself, which was most valuable to him from the beginning.

75 When the lord of the vineyard saw his fruit was good and his vineyard was no longer corrupt, he called up his servants and told them: We've tended my vineyard for the last time. You see I've followed my plans and have saved the original fruit, so it's good just like it was in the beginning. And you are blessed since you've been diligent in working with me in my vineyard and have followed my instructions — and it has produced the original fruit for me again, so that my vineyard is no longer corrupt and the bad is thrown away — and you'll celebrate with me over my vineyard's fruit. 76 I'll store my vineyard's fruit for myself for a long time as we prepare for the end of the growing season, which is coming quickly. I've tended my vineyard for the last time and pruned, tilled, and fertilized it. Therefore I'll store the fruit for myself for a long time, as I had planned. 77 And when the time comes that evil fruit again grows in my vineyard, then I'll have the good and bad gathered, and I'll store the good for myself and throw the bad away into its own place. And then the final season ends, and it will be time for my vineyard to be burned with fire.

Chapter 4

6 Now, my people, since I said that I would prophesy, this is my prophecy: That the things this prophet Zenos said about the house of Israel, comparing them to a tame olive tree, will certainly happen. 2 When He sets about a second time to recover His people, that will be the very last time the Lord's servants will go out in His power to tend and prune His vineyard — following that, the end will happen quickly. 3 And how blessed are those who have worked diligently in His vineyard! But how cursed are those who will be thrown out to where they belong! And the world will be burned with fire. 4 How merciful God is to us! He remembers the house of Israel, both roots and branches, and reaches out His hands to them all day long. But they're a stubborn, quarrelsome people. Nevertheless, all those who don't harden their hearts will be saved in God's kingdom.

5 So, my dear people, I solemnly urge you to repent and come with all your heart and remain as devoted to God as He is devoted to you. And while His arm of mercy reaches out to you in the light of the day, don't harden your hearts. 6 Do it right now if you're willing to respond to His voice. Don't harden your hearts. Why would you choose to die? 7 After you've been nourished by God's good word all day long, why are you willing to choose to produce evil fruit, which will result in you being cut down and thrown in the fire? 8 Will you reject my words? Will you reject the prophet's words? Will you reject all the words spoken about Christ after so many have spoken about Him, and deny the

good word of Christ and God's power and the gift of the Holy Ghost? Will you suppress the Holy Spirit, and mock the great plan of redemption provided for you? 9 If you choose to do this, then you should realize that when, through Christ's power, you've been redeemed and resurrected and brought before God's judgment bar, you'll be filled with shame and guilt. Is that what you want? 10 Based upon what's just, and justice won't be denied, you'll be destined for the fiery lake that burns like lava. Its flames are unquenchable, and its smoke ascends from eternity to eternity; and this fiery, burning lake is endless torment. 11 Therefore, my dear people, repent and enter through the strict, narrow gate and stay on the narrow path until you gain eternal life. 12 Be wise! What more can I say? 13 Finally, I say goodbye until I come face to face with you during God's judgment, an event that strikes the wicked with awful dread and fear. Amen.

Chapter 5

7 Some years later, a man came among the Nephites named Sherem. 2 He began to preach among the people and tell them there would be no Christ. He preached many things to deceive the people, and he did this to overthrow Christ's doctrine. 3 He worked hard to mislead the hearts of the people, and he deceived many of them. Because he knew that I, Jacob, had faith in Christ who was to come, he sought every opportunity to confront me. 4 He was well educated with a comprehensive vocabulary and spoke eloquently; as a result, he could be very persuasive and convincing when speaking, inspired by the accuser's power. 5 He was hoping to shake me from the faith, despite the many revelations and numerous things God had given to me. I had in fact seen angels who ministered to me. I had also heard the Lord's voice actually speaking to me from time to time; therefore I couldn't be shaken.

II   6 He came to see me and said this: Brother Jacob, I've sought repeatedly to come and see you, because I've heard and understand you travel a great deal, preaching what you call the gospel or Christ's doctrine. 7 You've misled many of the people, so they corrupt and pervert God's right way and don't keep the Law of Moses, which is the right way. You misinterpret the Law of Moses into the worship of a being who you say will come hundreds of years from now. Now I Sherem declare to you this is blasphemy; no one knows about such things because it's impossible to predict future events. Sherem argued this way with me. 8 But the Lord God poured His Spirit into my soul to such a degree that I proved him wrong in everything he said. 9 I asked him: Do you deny Christ, who is to come? He replied: If there were a Christ, I wouldn't deny Him; but I know that there's no Christ — there hasn't been a Christ, and there will never be a Christ. 10 I asked him: Do you believe the scriptures? He replied: Yes. 11 I said to him: Then you don't understand them since they testify truthfully of Christ. I tell you that no prophet has written or prophesied without speaking about Christ. 12 And this isn't everything. I've been shown, have heard, and seen by the power of the Holy Ghost and therefore I know that if there were no atonement made, all mankind would certainly be lost.

III   13 Then he said to me: Show me a sign by this power of the Holy Ghost that lets you know so much.

IV   14 I said to him: Who am I to put God to the test to show you a sign about things you already know to be true? You would still deny it because you belong to the accuser. Nevertheless, I don't want it, but if God strikes you, let that be a sign to you that He has power in both heaven and earth and that Christ will come. And may it happen, O Lord, according to Your will, not mine.

V   15 When I had said these words, the Lord's power descended on him and he collapsed helplessly onto the ground. He received care for many days. 16 Then he asked the people: Come together tomorrow because I'm going to die — I would like to speak to the people before I die.

VI   17 On the following day, when a crowd had assembled, he spoke openly to them, denying what he had taught them and acknowledging Christ, the power of the Holy Ghost, and the ministering of angels. 18 He admitted openly that he had been deceived by the accuser's power. He also spoke about hell, eternity, and eternal punishment. 19 Then he said: I'm afraid I've committed the unpardonable sin, because I've lied to God, denied Christ, and claimed I believed the scriptures — and they testify truthfully of Him. Because I've lied to God in this way, I'm very afraid of my position before Him, so I'm making this confession before God.

VII   20 After he said this, he was unable to speak anymore and he died. 21 When the crowd heard him say this as he was about to die, they were very astonished, so much so that God's power descended on them and they were overcome, bowing down to the ground. 22 Now this pleased me, because I asked my Father in heaven for it to happen. He heard my cry and answered my prayer.

VIII   23 And so peace and God's love were restored among the people. They carefully studied the scriptures and stopped listening to this evil man's words. 24 There were many plans made to reclaim and restore the Lamanites to the knowledge of the truth; but our plans were all fruitless because they had permanent hatred for us, their relatives, and took pleasure in wars and slaughter, frequently trying to kill us with their weapons. 25 So the Nephites prepared to defend themselves with their weapons and all their strength, trusting in God, the Rock of their Salvation. As a result, up to this time, we were able to defeat our enemies.

IX   26 Then I began to grow old. And because this people's history is kept on Nephi's other plates, I'll conclude this record. I declare I've written to the best of my knowledge. Our time and lives came and went like a dream to us, since we're a lonesome, careful people, wanderers thrown out of Jerusalem, born in difficulty in wild, unsettled lands, and hated by our relatives, which has led to wars and conflicts. Therefore our lives were filled with sorrow.

X   27 When I sensed I was going to die soon, I told my son Enos: Take control of these plates. I related to him the things my brother Nephi had commanded me to do, and he promised to obey the same commands. So I conclude my brief writing on these plates and say goodbye to the reader, hoping many of my people will respect my words. Brothers and sisters, farewell.

THE BOOK OF ENOS

I Enos respected my father because he taught me to read and understand his language, and that allowed me to be guided and corrected by the Lord. May the name of God be blessed for it. 2 I'll tell you about the struggle I had with God before receiving forgiveness of my sins. 3 I went to hunt animals in the forest, and the lessons I had often heard from my father about eternal life and the joy of the holy ones sank deep into my heart, 4 and I wanted that to my very soul. Therefore I knelt down before my Maker and cried out to Him in powerful prayer in an appeal for my own soul. I prayed to Him all day long. When the night came, I continued to pray out loud to get the attention of heaven. 5 Then a voice came to me, saying: Enos, your sins are forgiven, and you will be Blessed. 6 And because I knew God couldn't lie, I felt no more guilt. 7 Then I asked: Lord, how did it happen? 8 And He replied: Because of your faith in Christ, whom you haven't heard or seen before this. Many years from now He'll reveal Himself as a man. Press on, your faith has made you whole.

II   9 When I heard this, I began to be concerned about the well-being of my Nephite brothers and sisters; so I prayed from my whole heart to God for them. 10 While I was laboring like this in the spirit, the

Lord's voice came into my mind again, saying: I'll bless or punish them according to their diligence in keeping My commandments. I've given them this land, and it's a holy land; and I'll only curse it because of iniquity. Therefore I'll bless or punish your people just as I've said, and bring their transgressions down with sorrow on their own heads. 11 And after I had heard these words, my faith became unshaken in the Lord. And I prayed to Him with greater intensity for my Lamanite brothers and sisters.

III   12 After I prayed and diligently stated my concerns, the Lord told me: I'll grant your request because of your faith. 13 Now this was what I requested of Him: that if it turned out my people the Nephites fell into transgression and were destroyed, but the Lamanites weren't destroyed, that the Lord God would keep a record of my people the Nephites safe, even if it's done by His own power, so it could be brought to light at some time in the future for the Lamanites. Then they might be able to learn and be saved. 14 Because at present our struggles to restore them to the true faith were hopeless. They swore an oath in anger that if possible, they would destroy our records and us and all the traditions passed down to us by our forefathers.

IV   15 Since I knew the Lord God was able to preserve our records, I prayed to Him continually, because He had told me: Anything you ask in faith, in the name of Christ, believing you will receive, you will receive it. 16 And I had faith and prayed to God that He would keep the records safe. He covenanted with me that He would provide them for the Lamanites when He decided it was the right time. 17 I knew it would happen according to the covenant He had made; so my soul was at peace. 18 Then the Lord told me: Your fathers have also asked Me to do this. And it will be done for them according to their faith, because their faith was like yours.

V   19 Now I returned to the Nephites, prophesying of things to come and testifying of what I had heard and seen. 20 I tell you the Nephites sincerely tried to restore the Lamanites to the true faith in God, but our efforts were pointless. Their hatred was fixed, and they couldn't change their corrupt outlook, therefore they became an uncivilized and savage people, who were eager to kill and preoccupied by idolatry and moral filth, who ate predator animals, lived in tents, and camped in the wilderness with a short skin strapped around their waists and their heads shaven. Their skill was in the bow, blade, and ax, and many of them ate nothing but raw meat. They were always trying to kill us.

VI   21 The Nephites tilled the ground and raised all kinds of grain and fruit, and large herds — cattle of every kind, goats, wild goats, and many horses. 22 And we had a great many prophets, but the people were stubborn and hard to persuade. 23 Nothing kept them from destruction except for blunt and unequivocal language preaching and prophesying about wars, conflicts, and destruction, and constantly reminding them of death and the length of eternity and God's judgments and power — all this continually threatening them to keep them in the fear of the Lord — I say there was nothing except for unmistakable blunt language that could keep them from quickly being destroyed. This is how I would describe them. 24 I personally experienced wars between the Nephites and Lamanites during my life.

VII   25 Then I got old. And 179 years had passed since our father Lehi left Jerusalem. 26 I realized I would soon die. God's power influenced me to preach and prophesy to this people and declare the word according to the truth that is in Christ — and I've testified my whole life. This mattered more to me than worldly things. 27 I soon go to the place of my rest, to join my Redeemer — and I know I'll rest in Him. I rejoice in the day when my mortal body will become immortal and stand before Him. Then I'll see His face with pleasure, and He'll say: Come to Me, Blessed one; there are places prepared for you in My Father's realms. Amen.

THE BOOK OF JAROM

Now I Jarom write a few words to obey my father Enos' commandment, so that our genealogy can be maintained. 2 Because these plates are small, and because these things are written to benefit our relatives the Lamanites, it requires me to write a little. But I won't write about my prophesying or revelations. Indeed, what more could I write than my forefathers have written; haven't they revealed the plan of salvation? I say: Yes, and I'm satisfied with this.

II   3 It requires a lot of effort to help this people — because of their hard hearts, deaf ears, blind minds, and stiff necks. Nevertheless, God is very merciful to them and hasn't swept them off the land yet. 4 Many of us have many revelations, because not everyone is stubborn. All who are not stubborn, and have faith, have fellowship with the Holy Spirit, which reveals things according to mankind's faith.

III   5 Now 200 years had elapsed, and the Nephites had become strong in the land. They paid careful attention to keeping the Law of Moses and the Sabbath day holy to the Lord, and they didn't treat or speak about the things of God profanely or with contempt. The laws of the land were very strict. 6 And they had spread out over most of the land,

and the Lamanites as well, who were much more numerous than the Nephites. They loved murder and would drink animal blood.

IV ⁷ They attacked us, the Nephites, many times in battle. But our kings and leaders were faithful to the Lord and they taught the people the Lord's ways. So we successfully resisted the Lamanites and removed them from our lands, began fortifying our cities, and defending all the land we inherited. ⁸ We greatly increased in numbers and spread across the land and became very rich in gold, silver, and valuables; in fine woodworking, buildings, and clever devices; in iron, copper, brass, and steel; making all kinds of tools to till the ground and weapons as well — sharp, pointed arrows, quivers, light spears, and heavy spears — and prepared for war. ⁹ Because we were prepared to fight the Lamanites, they didn't succeed against us. But the Lord's warning to our fathers was verified, which said: To the degree you keep My commandments, you'll prosper in the land.

V ¹⁰ The Lord's prophets sternly warned the Nephites according to God's word, that if they didn't keep the commandments but fell into transgression, they would be removed from the earth. ¹¹ Therefore, the prophets, priests, and teachers taught continually, patiently urging the people to be diligent. They taught the Law of Moses and the purpose behind it, persuading them to anticipate Christ and believe in Him who was to come as if He had already come. This is how they taught them. ¹² By teaching this to penetrate their hearts with the word and continually urging them to repent, they prevented them from being destroyed.

VI ¹³ Now 238 years had come and gone — and wars, conflicts, and violent fighting happened frequently. ¹⁴ And I Jarom don't write anything more since the plates are quite limited. But, my people, you can go to Nephi's other plates. The records of our wars are engraved there, according to what the kings wrote or caused to be written. ¹⁵ Now I'll deliver these plates to the care of my son Omni so they can be kept according to my forefathers' commandments.

THE BOOK OF OMNI

I Omni was commanded by my father Jarom to write a little on these plates in order to maintain our genealogy. ² Therefore I want you to know I fought a lot with the sword during my life to keep my people the Nephites from being defeated by their enemies the Lamanites. But I myself am a wicked man — I haven't kept the Lord's statutes and commandments as I should have.

II   3 Now 276 years had elapsed; and we had many periods of peace and many periods of serious war and slaughter. Briefly, 282 years had come to an end; and I kept these plates, obeying my forefathers' commandments. Then I conferred them on my son Amaron, and I end it there.

III   4 Now I Amaron write the few things I add to my father's book. 5 320 years had come and gone, and most Nephites were killed. 6 For the Lord — after He had led them out of the land of Jerusalem and protected and kept them from falling into their enemies' hands — wouldn't allow the words He told our forefathers fail to be proven true, having said that to the degree you don't keep My commandments, you won't prosper in the land. 7 Therefore the Lord punished them according to His justice. Nevertheless, He spared the righteous, so they didn't die, saving them from their enemies. 8 And I handed the plates over to my brother Chemish.

IV   9 Now I Chemish will write the few things I add in the same book as my brother. Indeed, I watched the last things he wrote when he wrote them with his own hand; and he wrote them on the day he handed them over to me. This is how we keep the record — according to our forefathers' commandments. And so I end.

V   10 I Abinadom am Chemish's son. I experienced many wars and conflicts between my people the Nephites, and the Lamanites. And I've taken many Lamanite lives with my own sword while defending my people. 11 This people's record is engraved on plates, which the kings hold from one generation to another. And I don't know about any other revelation or prophecy besides what has been written. Therefore what's written is adequate. And so I finish.

VI   12 I'm Amaleki, Abinadom's son. I'll tell you something about Mosiah, who was made king over Zarahemla. He was warned by the Lord to flee from the land of Nephi — and all those who were willing to respond to the Lord's voice were also warned to go with him into the wilderness. 13 And he did what the Lord commanded him, and all those who were willing to respond to the Lord's voice went into the wilderness. They were led by continual preaching and prophesying and were constantly admonished by God's word. They were led through the wilderness by His power, until they came down to the land called Zarahemla. 14 There they discovered a people who were called Zarahemla's people. Now Zarahemla's people rejoiced greatly and so did Zarahemla, because the Lord had sent Mosiah's people with the brass plates containing the record of the Jews.

VII   15 Mosiah discovered Zarahemla's people left Jerusalem at the time Zedekiah, king of Judah, was taken away as a prisoner to Babylon.

16 They traveled across the wilderness and were brought by the Lord's hand across the sea to the land where Mosiah discovered them; and they had lived there since their arrival. 17 When Mosiah discovered them, they had become very numerous. Nevertheless, they had many wars and serious conflicts and had been killed by the sword from time to time. Their language had become corrupted, and they hadn't brought any records with them. In addition, they denied their Creator's existence, and Mosiah and his people couldn't understand them. 18 But Mosiah had them taught to understand his language. After they were taught Mosiah's language, Zarahemla gave his ancestors' genealogy from memory; and it's written down, but not in these plates.

VIII   19 Zarahemla's people and Mosiah's people united, and Mosiah was accepted as their king. 20 During Mosiah's rule, a large stone containing engravings was brought to him and he translated the engravings by God's gift and power. 21 They gave an account of a man named Coriantumr and his slaughtered people. This Coriantumr was discovered by Zarahemla's people and he lived with them for nine months. 22 The stone also mentioned Coriantumr's ancestors — that the earliest ones had come from the tower when the Lord confused the people's language. But the Lord's justice resulted in severe judgments on them, and their bones lay scattered in the land northward.

IX   23 Now I was born in Mosiah's days, and I've lived to see his death; and Benjamin his son now rules in his place. 24 During king Benjamin's time I've seen a serious war and tremendous slaughter between the Nephites and Lamanites. But the Nephites won a great victory over them, and king Benjamin drove them out of the land of Zarahemla.

X   25 I got old. And since I don't have any posterity and because I know king Benjamin is a righteous man before the Lord, therefore I'll hand these plates over to him, urging all people to come to God, the Holy One of Israel, and to believe in prophesying, revelations, the ministering of angels, the gift of speaking with tongues and translating languages, and everything that's good. Because everything that's good comes from the Lord, and everything that's evil comes from the accuser. 26 Now, my dear people, I want you to come to Christ, who is the Holy One of Israel, and share in His salvation and the power of His redemption. Come to Him, offer your whole souls as an offering to Him, continue fasting and praying, and persevere to the end. And as the Lord lives, you will be saved.

XI   27 Now I would like to say a little about a large group of people who went into the wilderness to return to the land of Nephi, since there were many who wanted to settle in their ancestral land.

28 Therefore they traveled into the wilderness. And because their leader was a strong, powerful, stubborn man, he started a conflict among them. All but 50 of them were killed in the wilderness — the survivors returned to Zarahemla. 29 Then they took a considerable number of others and once more departed into the wilderness. 30 I had a brother who went with them as well, and I haven't heard about them since they left. Now I'm about to die, and these plates are full, so I'm finished with this.

THE WORDS OF MORMON

I Mormon, in preparing to hand over the record I've been making to my son Moroni, wish to make clear that I've witnessed almost the complete destruction of my people the Nephites. 2 It's hundreds of years after Christ's coming when I'm entrusting these records to my son. I expect he'll see my people's complete destruction. But may God allow him to survive so he can write a little about them and about Christ, to perhaps benefit them some day.

II   3 Now I'll speak a little about this record. After I had made a summary from the plates of Nephi down to the rule of this king Benjamin whom Amaleki mentioned, I searched among the records entrusted to me and found these plates containing this short account of the prophets from Jacob down to king Benjamin's rule, and also Nephi's message. 4 Since the things on these plates are impressive to me, because of the prophecies about Christ's coming, and since my forefathers know many of them have happened — indeed, I too know that all the prophecies about us until now have happened, and that all of them about the future will certainly happen — 5 therefore I choose to finish my record by adding this record from the plates of Nephi. I can't write one percent of my people's activities.

III   6 I'll take these plates containing these prophecies and revelations and put them with the rest of my record because they're especially valuable to me, and I know they'll be very valuable to my people. 7 I do this for a wise purpose since the influence of the Spirit of the Lord persuades me they need to be added. Now I don't know all things, but the Lord knows everything that will happen, and so He impresses me to act according to His will. 8 My prayer to God is about my relatives the Lamanites, so they can once again come to the knowledge of God and Christ's redemption and be a delightful people again.

IV   9 Now I'll go on to finish the record I'm taking from the plates of Nephi, making it according to the knowledge and understanding God has given me. 10 After Amaleki handed these plates over to king Benjamin, the king took them and put them with the other plates, containing records handed down by the kings from generation to generation until the time of king Benjamin. 11 They were then handed down from king Benjamin from one generation to the next until they came into my possession. I pray to God they can be preserved from now on. I know they'll be kept safe, because there are great things written on them from which my people and their Lamanite relatives will be judged on the great and last day, according to God's written word.

v   12 As for king Benjamin, he had some conflicts among his own people. 13 In addition, Lamanite armies came down from the land of Nephi and attacked his people. But king Benjamin assembled an army and opposed them, personally joining the fight and using Laban's sword. 14 They fought their enemies with the Lord's strength until they had killed many thousands of Lamanites. They fought them until they had driven them from their lands.

VI   15 And after there had been false christs — who had been silenced and who had been punished according to their crimes. 16 After false prophets, preachers, and teachers among the people — who had also been punished consistent with their crimes — and after many conflicts and disputes, resulting in some joining the Lamanites, king Benjamin, joined by holy prophets, taught his people repentance. 17 Now because king Benjamin was a holy man and ruled over his people in righteousness, and was joined by many holy men in the land who spoke God's word with power and authority, rebuking the people because of their stubbornness, 18 with their help, king Benjamin again established peace. It required him to exert all his physical strength, and all his soul. He was helped by the prophets as well.

THE BOOK OF MOSIAH

Chapter 1

Because there were no more conflicts among king Benjamin's people in Zarahemla, he had continual peace during the rest of his rule. 2 He had three sons, whom he named Mosiah, Helorum, and Helaman. He had taught them the written language of his forefathers so they could become men of understanding and comprehend the Lord's prophecies spoken by their forefathers. 3 He also taught them about the records engraved on the brass plates, saying: My sons, I want you to remember if it weren't for these plates containing these records and commandments, we would have remained ignorant, even now, not knowing God's mysteries. 4 Without the help of these plates, it would have been impossible for our father Lehi to have remembered all these things and taught them to his children. Since he could read the written language of the Egyptians, he was able to read these engravings and teach them to his children so they could teach them to their children, and by this fulfill God's commandments from then until now. 5 I tell you, my sons, if it weren't for these records that have been kept and preserved by God, so we could read and understand His mysteries and have His commandments always with us, even our forefathers would have fallen away in unbelief. Then we would have been like our Lamanite relatives, who, because of the incorrect traditions of their ancestors, know nothing about these things, and don't believe them when they're taught. 6 My sons, I want you to remember these words are true and these records are true. The plates of Nephi, containing the records and teachings of our ancestors from the time they left Jerusalem until now, are also true. We have them and can study them to know their value. 7 Now my sons, remember to study them carefully, and you'll benefit from them. I want you to keep God's commandments so that, according to the promises of the Lord to our fathers, you can prosper in the land. 8 King Benjamin taught his sons many other things not written in this book.

II   9 After he had finished teaching his sons, he grew old and knew that, like all men, he would soon die. Therefore he thought it advisable to confer the kingdom on one of his sons. 10 He had Mosiah brought before him and told him: My son, I want you to make an announcement to all the people throughout this land — the people of Zarahemla and the people of Mosiah — all who live in this land, to gather as a group. Tomorrow I'll announce to my people, by my own mouth, that you are a king and ruler over this people, which the Lord our God has given us. 11 Furthermore, I'll give the people a name to distinguish them from the other people the Lord God brought from the land of Jerusalem. I'm doing this because they've been diligent in keeping the Lord's commandments. 12 I'll give them a name that can only be erased by transgression. 13 In addition, I tell you that if this people, who are greatly blessed by the Lord, fall into transgression and become evil and adulterous, the Lord will hand them over, and they'll become weak like their Lamanite relatives. He'll no longer protect them like He preserved our ancestors until now, using His unmatched and almighty power. 14 If He hadn't intervened with His power to preserve our ancestors, they would have been conquered by the Lamanites and become victims of their hatred.

III   15 After king Benjamin had finished saying this to his son, he gave him responsibility over the affairs of the kingdom. 16 He also gave him responsibility over the records engraved on the brass plates, the plates of Nephi, Laban's sword, and the ball or director that led our ancestors through the wilderness. To the extent they each gave careful attention and diligence to Him, that instrument was provided by the Lord to lead them. 17 Therefore when they were unfaithful, they didn't prosper or progress in their journey, but were driven back and provoked God's disapproval upon themselves. In this, they encountered hunger and suffering as a reminder of their responsibility.

IV   18 Now Mosiah went and did what his father commanded and announced to the people in the land of Zarahemla to gather at the temple to hear his father.

V   **2** After Mosiah did as his father had commanded and made an announcement throughout the land, people gathered at the temple from all over to hear king Benjamin. 2 The population in the land had grown, increasing so much that there was no way to count those who gathered. 3 They brought the firstborn of their flocks to offer sacrifice and burnt offerings according to the Law of Moses 4 and to give thanks to the Lord who is God. They thanked God for bringing them out of the land of Jerusalem, for keeping them free from their enemies, and for appointing just men to be their teachers and a righteous man to be their king. They were also thankful for the peace in the land of Zarahemla, and that their king taught them to keep the commandments of God so they could rejoice and be filled with love toward God and all mankind.

VI   5 When they arrived at the temple, they set up their tents around it. Each man had his own family with him, including his wife, sons, daughters, and grandchildren of all ages. Each family gathered in their own separate area. 6 Everyone pitched their tents facing the temple, allowing them to hear king Benjamin while remaining inside their tents. 7 Due to the large number of people, not all could fit inside the temple walls, so king Benjamin had a tower built so they could hear what he intended to say.

VII   8 He began speaking from the tower, but because so many had gathered, they couldn't all hear him. Therefore he had his words written down and sent out to those beyond his voice so all could receive his words. 9 This is what he said and had written: My people, all who have gathered and can hear the words I speak to you today, I haven't called you here to trifle with what I will say. Rather, I want you to listen carefully and not just with your ears, but also with your hearts. By doing so, you'll be able to comprehend God's mysteries, and I can help you see His grace. 10 I haven't commanded you to come up here to threaten you, or to have you think that I'm more than a mortal man. 11 I'm like you, dealing with all kinds of infirmities in body and mind. Nevertheless, I've been chosen by this people, consecrated by my father, and allowed by the Lord to be a ruler and king over this people. I've been watched over and helped by His unmatched power to serve you with all the power, mind, and strength the Lord has granted to me. 12 I tell you that I've been permitted, up to now, to spend my days in your service. I haven't wanted gold, silver, or anything of value from you. 13 I haven't allowed you to be imprisoned in dungeons or to enslave each other or to murder, plunder, steal, or commit adultery. I haven't allowed you to commit any kind of wickedness. I've taught you to keep the Lord's commandments in everything He's commanded you. 14 I've even worked with my own hands to serve you so you wouldn't be burdened with taxes, and so nothing difficult or distressing to bear would be imposed upon you — and today you know everything I've said to be true. 15 But, my people, I haven't done these things to boast, nor do I tell you this to complain about you. I tell you this so you know I can answer before God today with a clear conscience. 16 Now I told you I had spent my days in your service, but I don't say that to brag, for I've only been in the service of God.

VIII 17 I tell you this so you can learn wisdom, and so you can learn that when you're in the service of your fellow man, you're only in the service of God. 18 You've called me your king, and if I, whom you call your king, work to serve you, then shouldn't you also work to serve each other? 19 As your king, I've served both you and God. If you feel grateful towards me, direct your gratitude towards our heavenly King instead. 20 My dear people, I want to remind you that if you used all your energy to thank God and praise Him to the fullest, acknowledging He has created you, watched over and preserved you, filled you with joy, and given you the ability to live in peace with one another, 21 you would still not be able to repay Him for all He's done for you. God is the one who created you from the very beginning, and He's the one who continues to preserve you day by day by giving you breath so that you can live, move, and act according to your own will. He's even supporting you from one moment to the next. Therefore I urge you to serve Him with your entire soul. Even if you do this, you'll still be unprofitable servants. 22 All that He requires of you is to keep His commandments. He's promised you that if you would keep His commandments, you would prosper in the land. He never deviates from what He has said, therefore if you keep His commandments, He blesses you and causes you to prosper.

IX   23 First, remember God has created you and given you your life,
and for that, you're indebted to Him. 24 Second, He has given you
commandments to follow, and when you do so, He blesses you
immediately, which is His reward for your obedience. However,
despite receiving His blessings, you remain in debt to Him from the
beginning of time till the end. Therefore there's nothing to brag about.
25 So I ask: Can you say anything of yourselves? I answer you: No. You
can't say you're even as much as the dust of the earth, because you
were created from the dust of the earth, and it belongs to Him who
created you. 26 Even I whom you call your king am no better than you
are, because I'm also made from dust. You can see that I'm old, and
my life is about to end and my body about to return to dust of the
earth. 27,28 I told you that I've served you with a clear conscience before
God. I've asked you to gather here today so I can be found innocent,
and your blood won't be upon me when I stand to be judged by God.
He's commanded me to tell you some things, and I want to rid my
clothes of your blood before I enter my grave. I wish to die in peace so
my immortal spirit can join the choirs above in singing the praises of
a righteous God. 29 Furthermore, I've asked you to come today so I can
announce that I can no longer be your teacher or your king. 30 Even at
this moment my whole body trembles as I address you, but the Lord
God supports me. He's let me talk to you and has commanded me to
now announce that my son Mosiah is a king and ruler over you.

X   31 My people, continue living your lives as you've been doing until
now. You've been successful thus far because you've followed my
commandments and those of my father. If you continue to obey the
commandments of my son or the commandments of God that will be
communicated to you through him, you'll continue to prosper in the
land and your enemies won't have any power over you. 32 My people,
please make sure you don't let any conflicts arise among yourselves,
and that you don't follow the evil spirit mentioned by my father
Mosiah. 33 A woe is pronounced on anyone who chooses to obey that
spirit, and if they remain and die in their sins, that person drinks
damnation to their own soul. By disobeying God's law, they'll receive
an everlasting punishment as their wages, and nothing else. Therefore
it's crucial to stay on the right path and avoid the ways of evil spirits.
34 I want to remind you that every one of you, except for your little
children, has been taught about our indebtedness to our Heavenly
Father. We know we must give Him everything we have and are. We've
also learned about the records that contain the prophecies spoken by
the holy prophets. These records go all the way back to the time when
our father Lehi left Jerusalem. 35 The records include everything our

ancestors have spoken, and they also teach what the Lord has commanded them. Because of this, we can trust that their records are reliable and true.

XI   36 Now, my people, I tell you that after you've been taught and therefore know all this, if you're disobedient to what I've taught you, you'll withdraw yourselves from the Spirit of the Lord. By not allowing the Spirit of the Lord to guide you towards Wisdom, you're hindering your own chances of being blessed, prospered, and preserved. 37 This behavior is in open rebellion against God, as it shows that you choose to obey the evil spirit and become an enemy of all righteousness. Consequently, the Lord has no place in you, as He doesn't dwell in unholy temples. 38 Then if that person chooses not to repent and instead dies as God's enemy, divine justice demands that their immortal soul feel the weight of their own guilt. This causes them to recoil from the Lord's presence, leading to intense regret, pain, and anguish. This state is like an unquenchable fire whose flames rise from eternity to eternity. 39 Sadly, mercy doesn't provide any relief for such a person, and their final fate is to endure never-ending torment.

XII   40 Now, whether you're old, young, or a little child, I've spoken plainly so you can understand my words. I pray that you'll wake up and remember the awful position of those who've fallen into transgression. 41 In contrast, consider the blessed and happy state of those who keep God's commandments — they're blessed in all things, both physical and spiritual. If they're faithful to the end, they're received into heaven, and they can live with God in a state of never-ending happiness. Remember, remember these things are true, because the Lord God has spoken it.

XIII   3 My dear people, I have more news to share with you about coming events. 2 These revelations were given to me by an angel sent from God. He commanded me to wake up, and as I did, he appeared before me. 3 The angel said: Wake up. And then he proceeded to declare to me the good news of great joy, 4 saying that the Lord has heard your prayers, judged you to be righteous, and sent me to make this announcement. You can rejoice and share this news with your loved ones.

XIV   5 In the near future, the Lord Omnipotent, who reigns from eternity to eternity, will come down from heaven and dwell among mankind in a tabernacle of clay. He'll perform impressive miracles such as healing the sick, raising the dead, causing the lame to walk, restoring sight to the blind, hearing to the deaf, and curing all kinds of diseases. 6 He'll also rebuke the evil spirits that influence the hearts of the people. 7 Amazingly, He'll suffer temptations, bodily pain, hunger, thirst, and fatigue, to a greater extent than any person could bear without dying. His anguish for His people's wickedness and abominations will be so great that blood will come from every pore. 8 Know that He'll be called Jesus Christ, the Son of God the Father of heaven and earth, and the Creator of all things from the beginning. His Mother will be called Mary. 9 It's amazing that He'll come into His own creation so that salvation can come to mankind through faith in His name. However, even after all this, people will consider Him a man, say He's possessed by a devil, and ultimately whip and crucify Him. 10 But He'll rise from the dead on the third day.

xv   And then He'll judge the world. All these things will happen so that a righteous judgment can come upon mankind. 11 His blood atones for the sins of those who have fallen due to Adam's transgression, and for those who have died without knowing God's will or have sinned ignorantly. 12 However, woe, woe to anyone who knowingly rebels against God, as salvation can only be attained through repentance and faith in Jesus Christ. 13 God has sent His holy prophets to all people, every tribe, nation, and language. The prophets announce that everyone who believes in the coming of Christ can receive a remission of their sins, and rejoice with immense joy, as if Christ had already come among them.

xvi   14 Because the Lord God saw that His people were stubborn, He gave them the Law of Moses. 15 Many signs, wonders, types, and symbols foreshadowed His coming. Additionally, holy prophets also spoke to them about His coming. However, the people hardened their hearts and failed to understand that the Law of Moses alone couldn't provide forgiveness. Forgiveness comes exclusively through the atonement of Jesus Christ's blood. 16 Even if it were possible for children to sin, they couldn't be saved. However, I tell you that they're blessed. Even though by Adam or by nature they fall, Christ's blood is sufficient to atone for their sins. 17 I want to share with you that there's no other way for mankind to attain salvation except through the name of Christ, the Lord Omnipotent. 18 He'll be the righteous judge. While infants who pass away won't be lost, mankind must humble themselves and believe in the atoning blood of Christ to avoid damnation. This belief is necessary for salvation and must be held steadfastly. 19 Men and women, in their natural state, are out of harmony with God and have been since the Fall of Adam. This disharmony will continue from eternity to eternity, unless they yield to the guidance of the Holy Spirit, abandon their fallen nature, and become holy through the atonement of the Lord Jesus Christ. They should strive to become like a child, humble, meek, patient, and full of love, willing to accept everything that the Lord deems appropriate for them, as a child obeys their parents.

XVII   20 Furthermore, I tell you there will come a time when the knowledge of a Savior will be spread among people of every nation, tribe, and language. 21 At that time, men and women can only be declared innocent before God — with the exception of little children — through repentance and faith in the name of the Lord God Omnipotent. 22 Even now, when you've taught your people what the Lord God has commanded you, they can only be deemed innocent in God's sight according to the words I've taught you.

XVIII   23 I've now taught the words the Lord God has commanded me to say. 24 The Lord God says my words will be a bright testimony against the people at judgment day. Each person will be judged based on their works, whether they're good or evil. 25 Those who have done evil will be condemned to suffer terrible regret and guilt because of their abominations, making them recoil from the Lord's presence into a state of misery and endless torment. They've chosen to drink from the cup of God's wrath, damning their souls, 26 something that justice can't deny any more than it could deny that Adam had to fall because he ate the forbidden fruit. Therefore mercy won't be available to them any longer, forever. 27 Their punishment will be like a fiery lake of lava, whose flames are unquenchable and whose smoke ascends from eternity to eternity. This is what the Lord has commanded me to say. Amen.

Chapter 2

4 Now when king Benjamin had finished speaking the words that had been delivered to him by the angel of the Lord, he looked around at the crowd. Because the fear of the Lord overcame them, they had fallen to the ground. 2 They looked at themselves in their carnal state, feeling no better than dust on the ground. In unison, they cried out: Have mercy on us and purify our hearts with Christ's atoning blood, that we might receive a remission of our sins. They believed in Jesus, the Son of God who created all things, heaven, and earth, and who would come down to mankind.

II   3 After they had said these words, the Spirit of the Lord embraced them and they were filled with joy, having received a remission of their sins. And according to what king Benjamin had taught them, and because of the great faith they had in Jesus Christ, they gained peace of conscience. 4 And king Benjamin resumed teaching them, saying: My friends, my brothers and sisters, my relatives, and my people, please listen for I have more to say. 5 If you've come to realize, upon hearing about God's goodness, that you're nothing, worthless, and fallen, 6 then I say, if you also understand God's unmatched power, wisdom, patience, and long-suffering for mankind and comprehend that the atonement was planned at the outset of creation to provide salvation for anyone who puts their trust in the Lord, keeps His commandments diligently, and continues in faith until the end of their life, the life of the mortal body, 7 then you're the one who receives salvation through the atonement. Salvation was prepared for mankind when creation was first planned. It's available to all individuals who have lived since the Fall of Adam, those who are currently living, and those who will live in the future until the end of the world. 8 There's no other means of obtaining salvation besides what I've taught you.

III

9 Believe in God! Believe that He exists and that He created all things, both in heaven and on earth. Believe He has all wisdom and power, both in heaven and on earth. Mankind can't comprehend everything the Lord can comprehend. 10 In addition, believe that repentance, humility, and sincerity of heart before God are required for Him to forgive you. Now if you believe all these things, make sure you do them. 11 Additionally, as I've mentioned earlier, now that you've learned about God's glory, known about His goodness, felt His love, and received a remission of your sins, which brings great joy to your souls, I want you to always remember God's greatness. Remember you're nothing without Him and acknowledge His grace and patience even though we are unworthy creatures. Let this humble you deeply. Every day, pray using the Lord's name and remain steadfast in your confidence in what's to come, which was foretold to us by the angel. 12 If you do this, you'll always rejoice and be filled with God's love, and you'll continue to receive forgiveness for your sins. Moreover, you'll grow in your understanding of the glory of the One who created you and gain knowledge of what's righteous and true. 13 You won't wish to hurt each other. You'll be honest, pay your debts, and live in peace. 14 You won't let your children go hungry or naked or let them violate God's laws and fight and quarrel with each other. Nothing will be tolerated that serves the accuser, the evil spirit referred to by our forefathers, who's the master of sin and an enemy of all righteousness. 15 However, you should teach your children to always walk in the path of truth, to be considerate and kind, and to love and serve one another.

IV

16 Remember to always help those who need it and give what you can to those in need. Don't ignore beggars and turn them away to perish. 17 You may think they brought their suffering upon themselves and therefore you don't want to help them, or give them food, or share any of your belongings. You may not want to end their suffering,

thinking they deserve to suffer. 18 But I say to each of you: Whoever does this has a great need to repent. Unless they repent of what they've done, they'll perish forever and won't have any part in God's kingdom. 19 Indeed, aren't we all beggars? Don't we all depend on the same Being, who is God, for everything we have — food, clothing, gold and silver, and everything we own? 20 You've been calling on His name, asking for forgiveness for your sins. Has He refused your request? No, He's poured out His Spirit upon you, filling your heart with joy and leaving you speechless due to the overwhelming happiness you feel.

V   21 If God has created you and you rely on Him for your lives and everything you have, and if He grants you whatever you ask for in faith, believing that you will receive it, then you should share the things you have with each other even more. 22 If you judge someone who asks you for something that you possess, and you refuse to help them in order to prevent their suffering, then you deserve even greater condemnation for withholding what you have. Everything you possess ultimately belongs to God, including your own life, and yet you didn't need to ask Him for it, nor are you willing to repent of your greed. 23 Therefore I warn you: Woe to those who have abundance and the ability to share and help others but choose not to. They'll face dire consequences. Woe to that person, for they will lose all their possessions when they die. 24 On the other hand, I want to address those who are poor and have very little, barely surviving day-to-day. I mean all you who don't help the beggar because you don't have anything to give — I want you to know that in your hearts, you refrain from giving because you lack the means to do so. If you had the resources, you would give. 25 If you acknowledge this truth, you aren't guilty. However, if you deny it, you're condemned, and rightfully so, because you covet other people's belongings.

VI   26 In light of the things I've told you — to maintain a remission of your sins daily and to walk guiltless before God, it's important to share your belongings with the poor. Each person should give based on what they have, by feeding the hungry, clothing the naked, visiting the sick, and providing spiritual and temporal relief according to their circumstances. 27 See that all these things are done with patience and wisdom. No one is required to work beyond their capacity. Diligent efforts can lead to success. Therefore live your life thoughtfully, being mindful of order and diligence. 28 Remember that when you borrow something from your neighbor, it's important to return it as promised. Not doing so would be considered a sin, and it may even cause your neighbor to commit a sin as well. 29 Finally, there are countless ways to commit sin and I can't possibly list them all. 30 However, I can warn you that if you don't remain vigilant and pay close attention to your thoughts, words, and actions, and if you don't follow God's commandments and maintain your faith in the Lord until the end of your life, you will perish. So please, remember this and avoid perishing!

Chapter 3

5 After king Benjamin had said all these things to his people, he sent out a message, asking his people if they believed what he taught them. 2 And they all cried out with one voice, saying: Yes, we believe everything you've taught us. And we know these things are true because of the Spirit of the Lord Omnipotent, which has caused a big change in our hearts. We're not inclined to do evil anymore, but rather want to continually do good. 3 We, through God's infinite goodness and the manifestations of His Spirit, can clearly envision what's to come. And if necessary, we could even prophesy about all of it. 4 And it's our faith in the things our king has taught us that's given us this valuable knowledge, which makes us rejoice! 5 We're willing to enter into a covenant with God, promising to obey His commandments and do His will for the rest of our lives. We don't want to cause ourselves the never-ending torment described by the angel, nor do we want to incur God's anger.

II   6 Now these are the words king Benjamin hoped to hear from them. Therefore he told them: You've said the words I wanted to hear, and the covenant you've made is a righteous covenant. 7 Now because of the covenant you've made, you'll be called the sons and daughters of Jesus Christ. Today, He has spiritually begotten you. You've said your hearts have changed through faith in His name. As a result, you're born of Him and have become His sons and daughters. 8 You're now free under His wings, and there's no other Savior under whose wings you can be sheltered. There's no other name given through which salvation comes. Therefore all of you who have made the covenant with God to be obedient for the remainder of your lives, take upon yourselves the name of Christ. 9 Those who do this will be found at the right hand of God and will answer to the name of Christ.

III   10 However, anyone who doesn't answer to the name of Christ will have to answer to some other name and will be found on God's left hand. 11 I want to remind you that I provided you with a name that should never be erased except through transgression. Therefore please be careful not to transgress, so that the name remains in your hearts. 12 Remember to always keep the name of God in your hearts. This way, you won't be found on His left hand, but rather you'll hear and recognize the voice He uses to call you forth and the name He'll use to call you. 13 Indeed, how can a person recognize a master they haven't served, a stranger who's far from the thoughts and intents of their heart? 14 Also, would someone take their neighbor's donkey and keep it? No, they wouldn't even let it feed among their flocks; they would drive it away and remove it. Therefore I tell you that it will be the same for you if you don't know the name used to call you. 15 Thus, I want you to be firm and immovable, always filled with good works, so Christ, the Lord God Omnipotent, can seal you as His own. This way, you can be brought to heaven and have everlasting salvation and eternal life through the wisdom, power, justice, and mercy of Him who created all things in heaven and on earth, who's God above all. Amen.

Chapter 4

6 After finishing his speech to the people, king Benjamin decided to make a record of the names of everyone who had made a covenant with God to keep His commandments. 2 It turned out that everyone except the little children had made this covenant and had taken upon himself or herself the name of Christ. 3 After king Benjamin had completed all his duties and consecrated his son Mosiah as the new ruler and king over his people, he transferred all the kingdom's responsibilities to him. Additionally, he appointed priests to teach the people, so that they could hear, learn, and understand God's commandments, and to remind them of the covenant they made. Finally, he dismissed the crowd, and everyone returned home with their families.

II   4 Mosiah took his father's place as king at the age of 30, which was approximately 476 years since Lehi and his family left Jerusalem. 5 King Benjamin lived for three more years after his son took the throne, and then passed away. 6 King Mosiah was a righteous ruler who followed the Lord's ways, obeyed His commandments, and kept His judgments and statutes.

III   7 He encouraged his people to cultivate the land, and he himself worked hard on the crops to set a good example and not be a burden on his people. He followed his father's example. As a result, there were no conflicts among his people for three years.

Chapter 5

7 King Mosiah enjoyed three years of peace, but he became curious about the people who had left Zarahemla to live in the land of

Lehi-Nephi. He and his people hadn't heard from them since their departure, and his people constantly asked him to find out what happened to them.

II   2 Eventually, king Mosiah gave his permission for 16 strong men to search for them in the land of Lehi-Nephi and find out what happened to them. 3,4 The next day, a man named Ammon, who was a descendant of Zarahemla and a strong leader, led them on their journey to the land of Lehi-Nephi. 4 However, they didn't know which way to go, and wandered aimlessly in the wilderness, traveling in various directions for forty days. 5 Finally, after forty days of wandering, they arrived at a hill north of Shilom, where they set up camp. 6 Ammon, along with three of his men named Amaleki, Helem, and Hem, went down to the land of Nephi. 7 While they were there, they met the king of the people living in the lands of Nephi and Shilom. While there, they were surrounded by the king's guard, captured, tied up, and imprisoned.

III   8 After they had been in prison for two days, their hands were untied, and they were again brought before the king. They stood before the king and were permitted — or rather ordered — to answer the questions he asked them. 9 He said to them: I'm Limhi, the son of Noah, son of Zeniff, who came as a rightful heir from Zarahemla to take these ancestral lands. By the voice of the people, I've been made king over this land. 10 I would like to know why you boldly approached the city walls while I was outside the gate with my guards. 11 I've only spared your life so that I can inquire about this; otherwise, my guards would have killed you. You may now explain yourselves.

IV   12 When Ammon saw that he was allowed to speak, he stepped forward and bowed before the king. Rising, he said: O king, I'm very grateful to God today that I'm still alive and able to speak. I'll speak honestly. 13 I'm certain if you had known who I was, you wouldn't have wanted me tied up. My name is Ammon, I'm a descendant of Zarahemla, and I've come from the land of Zarahemla to inquire about our relatives whom Zeniff led from that land.

V   14 After hearing Ammon's words, Limhi was thrilled and said: Now I know for certain my relatives who were in the land of Zarahemla are still alive. Tomorrow, I'll have my people celebrate this news. 15 We are currently in servitude to the Lamanites and are forced to pay a heavy tax that is difficult to bear. But when our relatives free us from this slavery, we'll willingly become their slaves. We would rather be Nephite slaves than continue paying tribute to the king of the Lamanites.

VI   16 King Limhi gave orders to his guards to release Ammon and his men from detention. He then commanded his guards to go to the hill north of Shilom and bring Ammon's men into the city so they could eat, drink, and rest from their difficult journey. They had been through numerous hardships, including hunger, thirst, and fatigue.

VII   17 King Limhi sent out an announcement to his people on the following day, asking them to gather at the temple to hear what he had to say. 18 When they had all gathered, he spoke to them, saying: My people, look up and take courage. The time has come when we'll escape from our enemies, even though we've failed in our previous attempts. Nevertheless, I'm confident we'll succeed this time. 19 So look up, rejoice, and trust in God — in the God of Abraham, the God of Isaac, and the God of Jacob. He's the one who brought the Israelites out of Egypt and led them through the Red Sea on dry ground. He fed them with manna to keep them alive in the wilderness and did many more things for them. 20 That same God led our ancestors out of the land of Jerusalem, and has continuously watched over and preserved His people, up until now. It was our sins and abominations that brought us into slavery.

VIII   21 You're all witnesses today that Zeniff, who was made king over this people, was ambitious to reclaim his ancestral land as an inheritance. He was misled by the careful fraud of king Laman, who made a treaty with king Zeniff, giving him part of the land — including the city of Lehi-Nephi, the city of Shilom, and the surrounding area. 22 He did all this for the sole purpose of bringing us under their total control. Now, we pay taxes to the king of the Lamanites, giving them one-half of our corn, barley, and grain of every kind, as well as one-half of the increase of our flocks and herds. The king of the Lamanites even demands one-half of all that we own and threatens to take our lives if we fail to pay. 23,24 Aren't we suffering? Isn't this intolerable? Think what a miserable situation we're in. I don't need to remind you that we have many reasons to mourn! To begin with, many of our people have been killed and have died needlessly — all because of our iniquity! 25 If this people hadn't fallen into transgression, the Lord wouldn't have let this misery happen to us. But the people wouldn't listen to His words. As a result, we turned against one another to such an extent that we've resorted to killing each other.

IX   26 We've killed a prophet of the Lord. He was a chosen man of God who exposed our wickedness and abominations. He prophesied about many future events, including the coming of the Messiah. 27 He taught that the Messiah was God, the Father of all things, who would come down in a mortal body, resembling the image after which mankind was created in the beginning. In other words, he taught that mankind was created in the image of God, and that God would come down to earth in a mortal body. 28 Because of his teachings, they killed him. And they committed many other sins that angered God.

X   Therefore how can we be surprised to find ourselves in slavery and afflicted with terrible troubles? 29 The Lord has warned: I won't help my people while they continue in transgression, but instead will block their ways, preventing them from prospering, and their own behavior will be a hindrance to them. 30 He has also said: If my people plant wickedness, they'll harvest a tornado of rubbish; and the results are poisonous. 31 If my people plant filthiness, they'll reap a scorching wind, which brings immediate destruction. 32 Now the promise of the Lord has been fulfilled, and you are driven and afflicted. 33 However, if you return to the Lord with all your heart, trust in Him, and serve Him with determination, He'll free you from slavery in His own due time.

XI   **8** After king Limhi finished addressing his people, saying more than what's recorded here, he informed them about their relatives in the land of Zarahemla. 2 And he had Ammon stand before the crowd and tell them all that had happened to their relatives since Zeniff departed, up to the time Ammon arrived in this land. 3 Additionally, Ammon explained to king Limhi's people the final teachings of king Benjamin, to familiarize them with what he taught. 4 After finishing, king Limhi dismissed the crowd and allowed them to return to their homes.

XII   5 Then he had the plates containing the record of his people from when they left the land of Zarahemla brought to Ammon for him to read. 6 As soon as Ammon finished reading the record, the king asked him if he could interpret languages. Ammon told him that he could not. 7 Then the king said to him: Because I was troubled by the suffering of my people, I sent 43 of them to explore the wilderness in search of the land of Zarahemla, hoping our relatives there could help free us from slavery. 8 However, despite their best efforts, they were lost in the wilderness for many days and couldn't locate Zarahemla. They returned after wandering through a land dotted with many lakes, where they also found a place scattered with the bones of men and animals, as well as other objects. They stumbled upon the ruins of various types of buildings that were once inhabited by many people, as numerous as the Israelites. 9 To prove their claims, they brought back 24 plates made of pure gold, filled with engravings. 10 They also brought back intact breastplates made of brass and copper, 11 as well as swords with rusted hilts and corroded blades. No one here can translate the language or engravings found on these plates. Therefore

I'm asking you: Can you translate them? 12 Additionally, do you know anyone who can translate them? I want these records to be translated into our language so we can learn more about the people who were destroyed, potentially the same people whose bones were found with these records. It would be valuable to understand what caused their destruction.

XIII   13 Ammon then replied: I can confidently inform you, king, about a man who's able to translate the records. He possesses the means that allow him to see and translate ancient records, and this ability is a gift from God. These things are known as Interpreters, and no man can look into them unless God commands him to do so, in order to prevent him from seeing something he shouldn't see and perishing. Whoever is commanded to look in them is called a seer. 14 The king in Zarahemla is the one who's been commanded to perform these tasks; he's been given this special gift from God. 15 The king declared that a seer is greater than a prophet. 16 Ammon explained that a seer is both a revelator and a prophet. No one can have a greater gift unless they possess God's power, which is impossible, but a man can receive great power from God. 17 A seer can know about the past and the future; the Interpreters can reveal everything — hidden secrets can be revealed, and unknown things can be uncovered. A seer can discover the unknown and reveal things that would otherwise remain unknown to us. 18 This is how God has established a way for mankind to perform great miracles through faith; therefore seers are a benefit to their fellow men.

XIV   19 When Ammon had finished speaking, the king was overjoyed and thanked God, saying: These plates surely hold a great mystery, and these Interpreters must have been prepared for the purpose of uncovering such mysteries for mankind. 20 How awe-inspiring are the Lord's works! How patient He is with His people! In contrast, how blind and stubborn are people in their understanding. They won't seek Wisdom and don't want Her to rule over them. 21 Yes, they're like a wild flock fleeing from the shepherd, scattered, hunted, and eaten by forest predators.

Chapter 6

THE RECORD OF ZENIFF

The earlier account of his people from the time they left the land of Zarahemla until they were freed from Lamanite control. [Comprising chapters 6-9 RE.]

9 I Zeniff was educated using the Nephite language and was familiar with the land of Nephi — the land our ancestors first inherited. I was sent as a spy among the Lamanites to investigate their forces, so our army could attack and destroy them. But when I saw what was good among them, I didn't want them to be destroyed. 2 I argued with the other soldiers in the wilderness because I wanted our leader to make a peace treaty with them. But because he was inflexible and violent, he ordered my death. But I was rescued in a bloody fight, with father fighting against father and brother against brother, until most of our army was killed in the wilderness. Those of us who survived returned to the land of Zarahemla to relate the account to the widows and children. 3 I was still very eager to return to our ancestral land, so I gathered all who wanted to return to that land and traveled back again. We were struck with hunger and serious difficulties, since we failed to remember the Lord, who is God. 4 However, after wandering many days in the wilderness, we camped where our fellow soldiers were killed, near our ancestral lands.

II   5 I went out with four of my men and entered the city to see the king, to find out what the king thought, to learn if I could enter the land with my people and settle there peacefully. 6 I went to the king and he made a pact with me that I could have the land of Lehi-Nephi and the land of Shilom. 7 He also ordered his people to leave those lands, letting my people and I settle there. 8 We started constructing buildings and repairing the city walls of both the city of Lehi-Nephi and the city of Shilom. 9 And we began to farm the ground with all kinds of seeds: corn, wheat, barley, neas, sheum, and seeds of various fruits. And we began to increase in numbers and prosper in the land. 10 Now king Laman, in his clever fraud, provided the land for us to live on while planning to make my people his slaves.

III   11 After we had lived there for 12 years, king Laman began to grow uneasy fearing my people were getting too strong for his plan to overpower them and enslave them. 12 Now his people were lazy and worshiped idols. Therefore they wanted to enslave us so they could take the things we produced and feed themselves from the flocks we raised.

IV   13 So king Laman began to provoke his people to get them to attack us; as a result, there were wars and conflicts. 14 Then in the 13th year of my rule in the land of Nephi, south of Shilom, while my people were watering and feeding their flocks and farming their lands, a large Lamanite army attacked and started killing them. They stole from their flocks and grain. 15 All who survived fled directly to the city of Nephi, entering the city and asking me for protection.

V   16 So I armed them with bows, arrows, swords, cimeters, clubs, slings, and any kind of weapon we could think of. Then my people and

I went to fight against the Lamanites, 17 asking God to be with and strengthen us. My people and I humbly appealed to the Lord, asking that He would deliver us from our enemies, since we were reminded of our ancestors' deliverance. 18 God heard our appeal and answered our prayers, and we went to battle in His strength against the Lamanites. We killed 3,043 of them in one day and night, until we had driven them out of our land. 19 And I helped bury their dead with my own hands. But 279 of our brothers were killed, to our great sorrow and mourning.

VI   **10** Then we fortified the kingdom and lived peacefully in the land. And I had every kind of weapon made, so that I could arm my people whenever the Lamanites came back up to attack us. 2 I also set guards all around the land so the Lamanites couldn't mount a surprise attack and kill us. This is how I guarded my people and my flocks and kept them from falling into our enemies' hands.

VII   3 We occupied our forefathers' land for many years — 22 years to be exact. 4 I assigned the men to farm and raise all kinds of grain and fruit. 5 And I assigned the women to weave, and work patterns of fine linen and cloth, to produce quality clothing for the people to wear. And so we were comfortable and had stable peace in the land for 22 years.

VIII   6 Then king Laman died, and his son replaced him. He started provoking his people to be hostile to my people. As a result, they got ready for war and prepared to attack us. 7 But I had spies inside of Shemlon to learn about their preparations and put together a defense, so they couldn't attack unexpectedly and destroy us.

IX   8 They approached from north of the land of Shilom with their large armies — men armed with bows, arrows, swords, cimeters, stones, and slings — with their heads shaved clean and wearing a leather cloth around their waists.

X   9 I had the women and children hide in the wilderness for their safety. Any of the men, young or old, who could fight were gathered for battle against the Lamanites. I put them in ranks, based on age.

XI   10 Then we engaged in battle against the Lamanites — even though I was old, I fought too. We were fighting with the Lord's strength on our side.

XII   11 Now the Lamanites didn't know anything about the Lord or the Lord's strength; therefore they depended on their own strength, but still they were strong men. 12 They were wild, ferocious people, eager to kill. They believed their ancestors' tradition, which is this: They were driven from the land of Jerusalem because of their forefathers' sins and offenses there. Then, their brothers mistreated them in the wilderness, and again while crossing the sea, 13 and they were oppressed while in their original inheritance after crossing the sea. But the truth is that Nephi was more faithful in keeping the Lord's commandments. Therefore the Lord blessed him, since the Lord heard his prayers and answered them. That resulted in him taking the lead in their journey in the wilderness. 14 And Nephi's brothers were furious with him because they didn't understand how the Lord works. They were also furious with him on the sea because they hardened their hearts against the Lord. 15 They were also angry with him once they arrived in the promised land because they claimed he had wrongly asserted authority over the people taking it away from them; therefore they tried to kill him. 16 They were also furious with him because he departed into the wilderness as the Lord had commanded him, taking the records engraved on the brass plates — so they said he robbed them. 17 Therefore they taught their children to hate, murder, rob, and plunder them, and to do all they could to destroy them. They have an eternal hatred for the children of Nephi. 18 And because of this, king Laman has — by his sly, devious lies and tempting promises — deceived me, so that I led my people up into this land, and now they want to destroy them. We've suffered here for many years.

XIII   19 After explaining this to my people about the Lamanites, I Zeniff urged them to go to battle with all their strength, putting their trust in the Lord. So we fought with them face to face. 20 And we drove them again out of our land. We killed a great number of them, but this time we didn't count them.

XIV   21 And we returned to our own land, and my people returned to tend their flocks and farm their land. 22 Then, since I was old, I conferred the kingdom upon one of my sons; so I end my record. And may the Lord bless my people! Amen.

Chapter 7

11 Now Zeniff conferred the kingdom on Noah, one of his sons; and Noah began to rule in his place. But he didn't follow his father's ways. 2 He didn't keep God's commandments; instead, he followed his own ambitions. He had many wives and concubines. And he led his people to commit sin, to do things the Lord hated; they committed whoredoms and all kinds of evil. 3 In addition, he put a 20 percent tax on everything they owned: one-fifth of their gold, silver, ziff, copper, brass, and iron; and one-fifth of their fattened calves and grain. 4 He took all this to support himself and his wives and concubines, and to support his priests and their wives and concubines. And so he changed the management of the kingdom, 5 removing all the priests ordained by his father and ordaining new ones in their place, priests who were filled with pride to their core. 6 In this way they were supported in their laziness, idolatry, and whoredoms by the taxes king Noah imposed on his people. So the people's hard work was used to support iniquity. 7 They were deceived by the king's and priests' lying praise and reassurances, appealing to their pride, so much that they reverted to idolatry.

II   8 And king Noah built many impressive and large buildings, covering them with fine woodwork and a variety of valuable things: gold, silver, iron, brass, ziff, and copper. 9 He also built for himself a great palace with a prominent throne in it, the whole thing made of fine wood and adorned with gold, silver, and valuable things. 10 He also had his workmen make all kinds of fine work within the temple walls: fine woodwork, copper, and brass. 11 And he decorated the seats set apart for the high priests — placed above the other seats — with pure gold. He had a pulpit built in front of them so they could rest their bodies and arms on it while telling lies and praising his people.

III   12 And he built a tall tower near the temple, a very high tower, so high that he could stand on the top of it and overlook the land of Shilom and also the land of Shemlon occupied by the Lamanites. From there he could survey all the surrounding land.

IV   13 He had many buildings built in the land of Shilom and a great tower built on the hill north of Shilom, which had been a refuge for the children of Nephi when they fled the area. This is how he used the money he obtained by taxing his people.

V   14 And he loved his money and spent his time in extravagant living with his wives and concubines; and his priests also spent their time with whores. 15 He planted vineyards all around the land, and he built winepresses and produced a great volume of wine. As a result, he and his people became drunkards.

VI   16 Then the Lamanites started attacking small numbers of his people, killing them in their fields while they were tending their flocks. 17 So king Noah sent guards on all sides of the land to protect against them, but he didn't send enough. The Lamanites attacked them and killed them, stealing many herds away. In this way the Lamanites began to kill them and act on their hatred of them.

VII   18 Then king Noah sent his armies against them, and they forced them back at first. And so they returned happy about what they had gained in battle. 19 Now because of this great victory they arrogantly bragged about their strength, claiming that 50 of them could stand against thousands of the Lamanites. Then they bragged and enjoyed war, and wanted to attack and kill their Lamanite relatives — because of the wicked leadership of their king and priests.

VIII   20 But a man who lived among them, named Abinadi, went out and began to prophesy, saying: This is the Lord's message for me to give to you: Go and tell this people, this is what the Lord says: Woe to this people. I've seen their abominations, wickedness, and whoredoms! Unless they repent, I'll punish them in My anger. 21 Unless they repent and turn to the Lord who is God, I'll let their enemies overpower them; indeed, they'll be brought into slavery, and be punished by their enemies. 22 They will know that I Am the Lord their God — a God who requires faithfulness, punishing My people for their iniquities. 23 Unless these people repent and turn to the Lord who is God, they'll be brought into slavery; no one will set them free except for the Lord the Almighty God. 24 When they cry to Me, I'll be slow to hear their cries. I'll let them be killed by their enemies. 25 Unless they repent in sincere humility and regret, and honestly ask the Lord their God in faith to forgive, I won't hear their prayers or save them from their punishment. This is what the Lord says and this is what He's commanded me to say.

IX   26 Now when Abinadi had spoken these words to them, they were furious with him and tried to kill him; but the Lord rescued him. 27 When king Noah had heard about the things Abinadi said to the people, he was also very angry and said: Who does Abinadi think he is, judging me and my people like this? Or who is the Lord that He should bring such great trouble on my people? 28 I order you to bring Abinadi here so I can kill him. He's said these things to stir up my people to be angry with each other and to cause conflict among my people; therefore I'll kill him. 29 Now the people were deceived; so they ignored Abinadi's words and tried to arrest him from that time forward. And king Noah completely ignored the Lord's word and didn't change his evildoing.

X   **12** Two years later, Abinadi returned in disguise, and they didn't recognize him. He once more began to prophesy to them, saying: This is what the Lord has commanded me: Abinadi, go and prophesy to My people: Because you've ignored My words and haven't repented of doing evil, therefore I'll punish you in My anger, yes, I'll punish you in My fierce anger for your iniquities and abominations. 2 Woe to this generation! And the Lord told me: Stretch out your hand and prophesy: This is what the Lord says: Because of their iniquities, this generation will be enslaved, struck on the cheek, hunted by men, and killed. Vultures, dogs, and wild animals will devour their flesh.

XI

³ And king Noah's life will have the same future as a piece of cloth thrown in a furnace fire; he'll know that I Am the Lord. ⁴ I'll strike My people with terrible afflictions: famine and disease. I'll make them cry out in pain and sorrow all day long. ⁵ I'll cause them to carry heavy loads tied on their backs, and they'll be made to work like pack mules.

XII

⁶ I'll send hail to beat upon them. They'll also encounter burning, dry winds, and insects will plague their land and eat all their grain. ⁷ They'll be plagued with sicknesses. I'll do all this because of their iniquities and abominations.

XIII

⁸ Unless they repent, I'll wipe them off of the earth. However, they'll leave a record behind, and I'll protect it so other nations that follow in the land can learn. I'll do all this to expose this people's failures to other nations. And Abinadi prophesied many things against the people.

XIV

⁹ So they were angry with him. And they took him, tied him up, and brought him before the king, and said to the king: We've brought a man before you who's prophesied evil about your people saying God will destroy them. ¹⁰ He also prophesies evil about your life and says that your life will end up like a piece of cloth in a fiery furnace. ¹¹ He also says you'll be like a stalk, a dry stalk in a field, which gets run over by animals and trampled underfoot. ¹² Furthermore, he also says you'll be like a thistle's blossoms, which, when it has matured and the wind blows, are scattered over the land. And he claims the Lord has spoken it. He also says all this will happen to you unless you repent — because of your iniquities.

XV

¹³ Now, your majesty, what great evil have you done? Or what great sins have your people committed that we should be condemned by God or judged by this man? ¹⁴ We know, your majesty, we are innocent. And you, your majesty, haven't sinned. Therefore this man has lied about you and prophesied falsehoods. ¹⁵ We are strong and can't be enslaved or be taken captive by our enemies. And you've prospered in the land and will continue to prosper. ¹⁶ Here is the man. We're handing him over to you. You may do with him as you wish.

XVI

¹⁷ Then king Noah had Abinadi thrown in prison and he ordered his priests to assemble so that he could hold a council with them about what to do with him. ¹⁸ They said to the king: Bring him here so we can question him. And the king ordered him to be brought to them. ¹⁹ They started questioning him, to get him to contradict himself and have something to accuse him with. But he answered them boldly and to their astonishment defended against all their claims, proving them wrong in everything they said.

XVII

20 One of them asked him: What do the following words from scripture mean, that were taught to us by our fathers? 21 How welcome on the mountain are the footsteps of those announcing good news, that proclaim peace, that report coming good fortune, announcing victory, telling Zion: Your God reigns! 22 Listen, your border guards shout out together their joyful praise, for everyone will witness the Lord's return to Zion. 23 Everyone will proclaim together, O ruins of Jerusalem! The Lord now comforts you His people, coming to redeem Jerusalem. 24 The Lord will bare His holy arm in the sight of every nation, and all will see God's victory to the very end of the earth. 25 Then Abinadi asked them: Aren't you priests who claim to teach this people and to understand the spirit of prophesying, and yet you need me to explain to you what these things mean? 26 I tell you: Woe to you for perverting the Lord's ways! Because, if you understand these things, you haven't taught them. Therefore you've perverted the Lord's ways. 27 You haven't devoted yourselves in order to understand; therefore you are unwise. What then do you teach this people? 28 And they replied: We teach the Law of Moses. 29 Then he asked them: If you teach the Law of Moses, why don't you keep it? Why do you set your hearts on being rich? Why do you commit whoredoms and dissipate yourselves with prostitutes and lead this people to commit sin, making it necessary for the Lord to send me to prophesy against this people — indeed, a terrible judgment coming for this people? 30 Don't you know I speak the truth? Yes, you know that I speak the truth; and you ought to tremble before God.

XVIII

31 You'll be afflicted because of your iniquities, since you've said that you teach the Law of Moses. But what do you know about the Law of Moses? Does salvation come by the Law of Moses? What do you think? 32 And they responded, saying salvation did come by the Law of Moses. 33 But Abinadi said to them: I know if you keep God's commandments, you will be saved — if you keep the commandments the Lord gave Moses on Mount Sinai, saying: 34 I Am the Lord your God, who have saved you from the land of Egypt, out of slavery. 35 You shall have no other God besides Me. 36 You shall not make for yourself any sculptured image, or any imitation of what is in heaven above, or upon the land or under water. 37 Now Abinadi asked them: Have you done all this? I tell you: No, you haven't. Have you taught this people to do all this? I tell you: No, you haven't.

XIX

13 When the king had heard these words, he told his priests: Take this man away and kill him! Why are we wasting our time with him? — he's crazy! 2 And they stepped forward and tried to grab him, but he resisted, telling them: 3 Don't touch me! God will strike you if you

lay your hands on me; I haven't yet given the message the Lord sent me to give, and I haven't answered your question yet. Therefore God won't allow you to kill me at this time. 4 But I must complete the commandments God has given me. And because I've told you the truth, you're angry with me. Because I've spoken God's word, you've concluded that I'm crazy.

XX   5 After Abinadi had said this, king Noah's people didn't dare seize him, since the Spirit of the Lord was upon him. His face was shining brightly like Moses' face did while he was on Mount Sinai speaking with the Lord. 6 And he spoke with power and authority from God. Then he continued with his message, saying: 7 You see that you don't have power to kill me. So I'll finish my message. I sense that it cuts you to your core because I'm telling you the truth about your iniquities. 8 My words fill you with wonder, amazement, and anger. 9 But I'll finish my message, and then it doesn't matter what happens next, or if I survive at all. 10 But I tell you this much: What you do with me after this will be the same fate you will suffer. 11 Now I'll read to you the rest of God's commandments, because I can tell they aren't written in your hearts. It's clear to me that you've devoted yourselves to and taught iniquity the majority of your lives.

XXI   12 And now you remember I said: You shall not make for yourself any sculptured image, or any imitation of what is in heaven above, or upon the land or under water. 13 Furthermore: You shall not worship them or serve them, because I, the Lord your God, am a jealous God, visiting the guilt of the fathers on the children through the third and fourth generation of those that abandon Me, 14 but giving forgiveness to the thousandth generation of those that obey Me and keep My commandments. 15 You shall not use the name of the Lord your God to accomplish your ambitions, for the Lord will not forgive him who advances himself using God's name. 16 Remember to keep the Sabbath holy. 17 Six days you shall work and do all your laboring; 18 but the seventh day, the Sabbath of the Lord your God, you shall not do any work, not you or your son, or your daughter, any male or female servant, nor your cattle, nor any visitor within your settlement. 19 For in six days the Lord made heaven, and earth, and the sea, and everything in them; the Lord rested and blessed the seventh day. 20 Respect your father and your mother, so that your life is prolonged on the land the Lord your God assigns to you. 21 You shall not murder. 22 You shall not commit adultery. You shall not steal. 23 You shall not testify falsely as a witness against your neighbor. 24 You shall not covet your neighbor's house; you shall not covet your neighbor's wife, nor his

male or female servant, nor his ox, nor his donkey, nor anything that
is your neighbor's.

Chapter 8

25 After Abinadi had finished saying this, he asked them: Have you
taught these people to take care to do all these things, to keep these
commandments? 26 I tell you: No. Because if you had, the Lord
wouldn't have had me come and prophesy evil about this people.
27 Now you've said that salvation comes by the Law of Moses. I tell
you, while it's still necessary for you to keep the Law of Moses, the
time will come when it won't be necessary to keep it anymore.
28 Furthermore, I declare that salvation doesn't come by the Law alone.
If it weren't for the atonement God Himself will make for His people's
sins and iniquities, they would unavoidably perish, despite the Law of
Moses. 29 You should understand that it was necessary for there to be a
very strict law given to the Israelites. They were a stubborn people,
quick to commit iniquity and slow to remember the Lord who is God.
30 So a law of performances and ordinances was given to them, one
they were to strictly follow on a daily basis to remind them of God and
their duty toward Him. 31 But I tell you all these things symbolized
what was to come.

II   32 Now, did they understand the Law? I tell you: No, not all of
them understood the Law — because of the hardness of their hearts.
They didn't understand that no one could be saved except through
God's redemption. 33 Didn't Moses prophesy to them about the
coming Messiah and that God would redeem His people? Yes, and
even all the prophets that have prophesied ever since the world began,
haven't they spoken more or less about these things? 34 Haven't they
said that God Himself would come down among mankind and take
upon Himself the form of a man and go about in great power on the
earth? 35 And haven't they also said He would enable the resurrection
of the dead and that He Himself would be oppressed and afflicted?

III   14 Of course, doesn't Isaiah say: Who believes what we've heard?
Who's heard the Lord's revelation? 2 For He'll grow up with His favor
like a lively vine springing from the desert ground. He has no rank or
position deserving respect, and when we notice Him, there's nothing
about Him to please us. 3 He is despised and rejected by men — a man
of sorrow and familiar with disease. And we turned our faces away,
ignoring Him. He was despised and thought to be of no value. 4 Yet it
was our sickness He took upon Himself, our suffering He endured.

IV   5 He suffered for our sins, healed our sickness; was punished for
our iniquities, bearing our guilt to completely restore us. 6 We all
strayed like sheep, wandering off — each one going their own way;
and the Lord has imposed on Him the guilt belonging to us all. 7 He
was oppressed and submitted, without complaining; like a lamb
brought to be slaughtered, and as a ewe is silent while they shear her,
so He endured without opening His mouth. 8 He was condemned by
an unjust judgment. There were none who defended Him. For He was
slain as a sacrifice for the transgressions of My people, who deserved
the punishment. 9 He died with the wicked, and was buried with the
rich. Though He had done no evil, nor had He declared anything
untrue; 10 but the Lord was content with His offering; satisfied with His
healing.

V   After He made himself a sin offering, He'll inherit offspring,
obtain eternal life, and vindicate God's promises. 11 He'll see His
sacrifice and will be satisfied; by the understanding He gains, the
righteous Servant will make many others righteous, for He'll remove
their iniquities. 12 Therefore I intend for Him to inherit multitudes, and
His triumph will endow Him eternally — because He submitted
willingly to death, and He was regarded as a sinner; but instead, He
took on other's guilt while making intercession for sinners.

VI   **15** Then Abinadi said to them: I want you to understand that God
Himself will come down among mankind and redeem His people.
2 And because He'll dwell in the flesh, He'll be called the Son of God.
He'll subject the flesh to the Father's will, gaining the role of the Father
and the Son: 3 the Father because He was conceived by God's power
and the Son because of the flesh, becoming the Father and Son in this
way. 4 And they're united as one God — indeed, the very Eternal
Father of heaven and earth. 5 So the flesh becomes subject to the
Spirit, or the Son to the Father, being one God, suffering temptation
and not yielding to it, but allowing Himself to be mocked, whipped,
thrown out, and disowned by His people.

VII   6 After all this, and after performing many mighty miracles among
mankind, He'll be led, just as Isaiah said, as a ewe is silent while they
shear her, so He endured without opening His mouth. 7 Yes, He'll be
led, crucified, and killed, the mortal flesh fully surrendering to death,
the Son's will submitting entirely to the Father's will. 8 And so God
breaks the chains of death, gaining victory over death, giving the Son
power to make intercession for mankind, 9 having ascended into
heaven, showing tender mercy, being filled with compassion toward
mankind, standing between them and justice, having conquered

death, Himself assuming responsibility for their transgressions and
iniquity, having redeemed them, and satisfied the demands of justice.

VIII   10 Now I ask you: Who will identify His sons and daughters? I tell
you that after His life has been made a sin offering, He'll reclaim His
children. Now, what do you say? Who will be His children? 11 I tell you
that whoever has believed the prophet's words — moreover, all the
holy prophets who have prophesied about the Lord's coming, I tell you
that all those who have followed their words and believed that the Lord
would redeem His people and have looked forward to that day for a
remission of their sins, I tell you that these are His children, or they are
heirs of God's kingdom. 12 These are the ones whose sins He has
borne; these are the ones He has died for, to redeem them from their
transgressions. And now, are they not His children? 13 And the
prophets, every one who's proclaimed His messages, who hasn't fallen
into transgression — I mean all the holy prophets since the world
began — I tell you that they are His children. 14 These are the ones
announcing good news, that proclaim peace, that report coming good
fortune, announcing victory, telling Zion: Your God reigns! 15 How
welcome on the mountain are their footsteps! 16 And how welcome on
the mountain are the footsteps of those who are still announcing
victory! 17 Again, how welcome on the mountain are the footsteps of
those who will continue announcing victory from now on and forever!

IX   18 I tell you: This isn't all. Again, how welcome on the mountain
are the footsteps of Him who brings good news and is the Founder of
peace — meaning, the Lord who's redeemed and granted His people
salvation. 19 If it weren't for the redemption He has made for His
people, which was planned from the start of creation, I say that if it
weren't for this — all mankind would be doomed. 20 But the chains of
death will be broken. And the Son's authority includes power over the
dead; therefore He owns the resurrection of the dead. 21 And a
resurrection is coming, that is a first resurrection, of those who have
lived, now live, and will live, up until the resurrection of Christ (and
that is His name). 22 Now the resurrection of all the prophets and those
who have believed their messages — or those who have kept God's
commandments — are the ones who will come forth in the first
resurrection; therefore that is the initial resurrection. 23 They're raised
to live with God, who's redeemed them. So they have eternal life
through the Messiah, who's broken the chains of death.

X   24 And those who have died in ignorance before the Messiah came,
not having salvation taught to them, are also included in the first
resurrection. So the Lord brings about their restoration, and they're

included as part of the first resurrection, or have eternal life, being redeemed by the Lord. 25 And little children also have eternal life.

XI   26 However, beware and fearful of God's judgment of you — as you should — because the Lord doesn't redeem anyone who rebels against Him and dies in their sins. Understand that everyone, from the beginning, who deliberately refuses to follow God while knowing His commandments, won't be redeemed by Him. These people don't have any part in the first resurrection. 27 Therefore shouldn't you be afraid? Because the Lord hasn't redeemed anyone like that, and salvation doesn't come to anyone like that. And He can't redeem them either, for He can't go back on His word or deny justice when it applies.

XII   28 Now I tell you that the time will come when the Lord's salvation will be declared to all people of every nation, tribe, and language. 29 Listen, your border guards shout out together their joyful praise, for everyone will witness the Lord's return to Zion. 30 Everyone will proclaim together, O ruins of Jerusalem! The Lord now comforts you His people, coming to redeem Jerusalem. 31 The Lord will bare His holy arm in the sight of every nation, and all will see God's victory to the very end of the earth.

XIII   **16** After Abinadi had spoken these words, he reached out his arms and said: The time will come when everyone will see the Lord's salvation, when all people of every nation, tribe, and language will see with their own eyes and acknowledge before God that His judgments are correct. 2 Then the wicked will be thrown out, and they'll have a reason to howl, weep, wail, and grind their teeth — because they wouldn't hearken to the Lord's voice. Therefore the Lord won't redeem them. 3 Because they're carnal and devilish; and the accuser has power over them. Indeed, that old snake who deceived our first parents, which was the cause of their fall, resulting in mankind becoming carnal, sensual, devilish, knowing evil from good, and subjecting themselves to the accuser. 4 All mankind was then lost and they would have been permanently lost if God hadn't redeemed His people from their lost and fallen state. 5 But remember that those who persist in their own carnal nature and follow sin and rebellion against God will remain in their fallen state, and the accuser has influence over them. So they're as if no redemption had been made — effectively enemies of God; and the accuser is clearly an enemy of God.

XIV   6 Now if the Messiah had not come into the world — speaking of future events as if they had already happened — there would have been no redemption. 7 And if the Messiah hadn't risen from the dead or broken the chains of death — so that the grave had no victory and death no bite — there would have been no resurrection. 8 But there is a resurrection. Therefore the grave doesn't have any victory, and death's bite is swallowed up through the Messiah. 9 He is the light and life of the world, an endless light that can never be darkened and an endless life so there is no more death. 10 This mortal body will become immortal, and our decaying flesh will become free from decay, and in our bodies we'll stand before the judgment seat of God to be judged by Him. Judged based on our works, whether they're good or evil: 11 if good, to the resurrection of endless life and happiness; and if evil, to the resurrection of endless damnation, handed over to the accuser, who has authority over the condemned, which is damnation. 12 They lived unworthy, selfish lives, never repenting and asking forgiveness from the Lord, although He was always ready to forgive; they refused His mercy. They ignored warnings about their iniquities, and they wouldn't abandon them. And though they were commanded to repent, they refused to repent.

xv   13 Now shouldn't you fear God's judgment and repent of your sins? Remember, you can be saved only in and through the Messiah. 14 Therefore if you teach the Law of Moses, also teach that it foreshadows what's coming. 15 Teach them that redemption comes through Christ the Lord, who is the very Eternal Father. Amen.

Chapter 9

17 When Abinadi had finished speaking, the king ordered the priests to take him and have him put to death. 2 But there was one among them named Alma, a young man and a descendant of Nephi, who believed Abinadi's words, since he could see the iniquity Abinadi had testified against them. Therefore he started to plead with the king not to be angry with Abinadi, but to let him leave in peace. 3 But the king became even angrier and had Alma thrown out and sent servants to kill him. 4 But he escaped and hid and they didn't find him. While in hiding for many days, Alma wrote down everything Abinadi had said.

II   5 The king had his guards surround Abinadi and take him, tie him up, and throw him in prison. 6 The king consulted with his priests and after three days, he had Abinadi brought back. 7 Then he announced: Abinadi, we've found you guilty, and you deserve to be executed. 8 You claim that God Himself would come down among mankind. And now for saying this, you'll be put to death unless you retract everything you've falsely testified about me and my people.

III   9 And Abinadi said to him: I won't retract anything I've said to you, because it's all true. To prove I'm testifying of the truth, I've let you capture me. 10 And I will let you execute me, but I won't retract my words, and they'll stand as a testimony condemning you. If you kill me, you will shed innocent blood, which will also condemn you on the last day.

IV   11 Now king Noah was about to release him, because he was afraid of what he had been told, and worried God's judgments would fall on him. 12 But the priests cried out loudly in opposition, accusing and claiming: He's insulted the king! So the king was provoked to anger against him, and he instead decided to have him executed.

V   13 They then took him, tied him up, set him atop firewood, and burned him to death. 14 And when the flames began to burn him, he yelled to them, saying: 15 Just as you've done to me, your descendants will also do to many others who will suffer the same pain that I suffer — painful death by fire — because they believe in the salvation of the Lord who is God. 16 You'll be infected by many diseases because of your iniquities. 17 You'll be attacked on all sides and driven and scattered, just like a wild flock driven by hungry predators. 18 At that time you'll be hunted and taken by your enemies. Then you will, like me, feel the pain of being executed by burning. 19 This is how God repays those who destroy His people. O God, receive my spirit! 20 Now when Abinadi had said this, he collapsed, dying in the fire, having been executed because he wouldn't deny God's commandments, having sealed the truth of his words through his death.

VI   **18** Now Alma, who escaped from king Noah's servants, repented of his sins and iniquities and began secretly teaching Abinadi's words to others: 2 about what was coming, the resurrection of the dead, and the redemption of mankind, which was accomplished through Christ's power, suffering, death, resurrection, and ascension into heaven. 3 He taught all those who would listen to him, teaching them privately so it wouldn't become known to the king. And many believed what he taught. 4 Those who believed him went to a place called Mormon, which was in the frontier of the land. It had received its name from the king and was sometimes overrun by wild animals. 5 There was a spring of pure water in Mormon, and Alma hid there during the day in a thicket of small trees near the water, to avoid the king's pursuit. 6 And all those who believed him went there to hear him teach. 7 After many days, a large group who believed gathered at Mormon to hear Alma's teaching. He instructed them about repentance, redemption, and faith in the Lord.

VII   8 He told them: Here are the waters of Mormon (referring to what they were called). Do you have a desire to enter God's fold and be called His people? Are you willing to help carry each other's burdens, to lighten them for one another? 9 Are you willing to mourn with those who mourn, and comfort those who need comforting? Will you stand and testify as witnesses of God at all times, in all things, wherever you go, for the rest of your lives? Do you want to qualify for redemption by God and be included with those of the first resurrection, receiving eternal life? 10 If this is the desire of your hearts, are you now willing to be baptized in the Lord's name, as a witness before Him that you've made a covenant with Him? Are you willing to commit to serve Him and keep His commandments, so He can pour out His Spirit more abundantly upon you? 11 Now when the people heard this, they applauded and shouted: This is our heart's desire!

VIII   12 Then Alma took Helam — one of the first — and went and stood in the water and prayed: O Lord, pour out Your Spirit upon Your servant, so he can do this work with holiness of heart. 13 And when he had prayed these words, the Spirit of the Lord filled him and he said: Helam, I baptize you, having authority from Almighty God, as a demonstration that you've made a covenant to serve Him for the remainder of your mortal life. And may the Spirit of the Lord be poured out upon you, and may He grant you eternal life through Christ's redemption, which He prepared from the beginning of creation. 14 After Alma said these words, both Alma and Helam submerged in the water. And they resurfaced rejoicing, filled with the Spirit. 15 Then Alma took another and went into the water again and baptized him in the same way as the first, only he didn't submerge himself again. 16 He baptized every one in this way — about 204 people — who gathered at the place of Mormon. And they were baptized in the waters of Mormon and were filled with God's grace. 17 They were called the congregation of God, or the congregation of Christ, from that time forward. And whoever was baptized by God's power and authority was added to His congregation.

IX   18 And Alma, having authority from God, ordained priests, one priest for every 50. He ordained them to preach and teach concerning God's kingdom. 19 And he commanded them to only teach the things he and the holy prophets had taught. 20 To be clear, he commanded them to preach nothing but repentance and faith in the Lord, who had redeemed His people. 21 And he commanded them not to have any heated arguments with each other, but to look forward with one eye, having one faith and one baptism, having their hearts bound together in unity and love toward each other. 22 This is how he commanded them to preach. And so they became God's children.

X   23 He also commanded them to keep the Sabbath holy, and to give thanks to the Lord God every day. 24 He also commanded them that the priests he ordained were to work with their own hands for their support. 25 And there was one day in every week set apart for them to gather, to teach the people and to worship the Lord their God. They met as often as they could. 26 And the priests didn't depend on the people to pay them, but they were to receive God's grace as payment, so they could grow in faith, receiving inspiration from God, enabling them to teach with power and authority from God.

XI   27 Alma also commanded the congregation members to give freely of their material possessions, each one based upon what they had. If they had a lot, they were to give a lot. But only a little would be expected of those who only had a little. And those who had nothing were to receive. 28 So they were to give their donations voluntarily, out of their love for God, including to priests in need, and also to every needy, helpless soul. 29 He told them this was a commandment from God. And they obeyed God, giving to each other both temporally and spiritually according to their needs and circumstances.

XII   30 Now this was accomplished in the place called Mormon, by the waters of Mormon, in the forest that was near the waters of Mormon. The place of Mormon, the waters of Mormon, the forest of Mormon — how sacred a place for those who came to know their Redeemer there! How blessed they are! They'll sing praises to Him forever!

XIII   31 These things were done in the outskirts of the land to escape the notice of the king. 32 But the king, noticing the conduct of the people, sent his servants to follow them. So on the day they assembled to hear the Lord's word, they were betrayed and revealed to the king. 33 Now the king accused Alma of inciting the people to rebellion against him. So he sent his army to kill them. 34 But Alma and the Lord's people learned the king's army was coming. Therefore they took their tents and families and fled into the wilderness, 35 about 450 people in number.

XIV   19 And the king's army was unable to locate them and therefore returned. 2 Now the king's soldiers were reduced to only a few. A disagreement arose involving the rest of the people. 3 The minority started making threats against the king and a great struggle began. 4 Then a man named Gideon — a strong man who was an enemy of the king — drew his sword and swore in anger he would kill the king. 5 And he fought with the king. When the king saw Gideon was going to overpower him, he fled, running up the tower near the temple. 6 But Gideon chased him and was getting ready to climb the tower to kill the king when the king noticed a Lamanite army was invading from the land of Shemlon. 7 Now the king pleaded pitifully: Gideon, spare me! The Lamanites are about to attack us and they'll kill my people. 8 Now the king wasn't really concerned about his people but valued his own life. Nevertheless, Gideon spared his life.

XV   9 And the king ordered the people to flee from the Lamanites, and he ran in front of them. They fled into the wilderness with their women and children. 10 But the Lamanites pursued and caught up with them, and began killing them. 11 So the king ordered the men to abandon their wives and children and run from the Lamanites. 12 However, there were many who refused to leave them, preferring to stay and die with them. But the rest abandoned their wives and children and ran away.

XVI   13 Those who stayed with their wives and children had their beautiful daughters go out and beg the Lamanites not to kill them. 14 And because they were attracted by the beauty of their women, the Lamanites took pity on them. 15 So the Lamanites spared their lives, taking them prisoner. They took them back to the land of Nephi, allowing them to live there under the condition that they would hand over king Noah to the Lamanites and pay them half of everything they owned — half their gold, silver, and valuables. They would have to pay this tribute to the king of the Lamanites yearly. 16 One of king Noah's sons, named Limhi, was among the prisoners. 17 Although Limhi didn't want his father to be killed, he was aware of his father's iniquities. Limhi was a righteous man.

XVII   18 Gideon secretly sent men into the wilderness to search for the king and those with him. They located the missing people, all except for the king and his priests. 19 Now these people had vowed they would return to the land of Nephi; and if their wives, children, and those who remained with them had been killed, then they would take revenge and die with them. 20 But the king ordered them not to return, and they became so angry with the king they executed him by burning him to death. 21 They were about to execute the priests too, but they escaped.

XVIII   22 They were returning to the land of Nephi when they met Gideon's soldiers, who told them everything that had happened to their wives and children. They learned the Lamanites allowed them to live on the land as long as they paid them a tax of half of all they owned. 23 They informed Gideon's soldiers that they had killed the king and that his priests ran into the wilderness. 24 After they finished the discussion, they returned to the land of Nephi, rejoicing because their wives and children hadn't been killed; and they told Gideon they executed the king.

XIX   25 Following this the king of the Lamanites committed to them that his people wouldn't kill them. 26 And Limhi, the king's son, by a vote of the people, had the kingdom conferred on him. He also agreed with the king of the Lamanites that his people would pay taxes to him of half of everything they had.

XX   27 So Limhi began to administer the kingdom and there was peace among his people. 28 The king of the Lamanites put guards surrounding the land to confine Limhi's people, so they couldn't escape into the wilderness. He supported his guards from the taxes paid by the Nephites. 29 Now king Limhi had two years of peace in his kingdom, and the Lamanites didn't harass them or try to kill them during that time.

XXI   **20** There was a place in Shemlon where the Lamanite young women went to sing, dance, and entertain themselves. 2 One day a small number of them gathered to sing and dance. 3 Because king Noah's priests were ashamed to return to the city of Nephi, and fearing the people would kill them, they didn't dare return to their wives and children. 4 They hid in the wilderness and discovered the Lamanite young women, watching them and waiting in ambush. 5 When there were only a few of them gathered to dance, they emerged from their hiding place, took 24 of them, and forced them into the wilderness.

XXII   6 When the Lamanites found out their daughters were missing, they blamed Limhi's people, concluding that they were the ones who had kidnapped them. 7 So they sent their armies out — led by the king himself — and they went up to the land of Nephi to attack and kill Limhi's people. 8 Now Limhi saw them from the tower preparing to attack. So he gathered his people and waited in ambush for them in the fields and forests. 9 Then, when the Lamanites arrived, Limhi's people began to ambush and kill them.

XXIII   10 The battle became very severe, because they fought like lions for their prey. 11 And despite not being half as many as the Lamanites, Limhi's people began to prevail over the Lamanites, since they were fighting for their lives, wives, and children. Therefore they drove themselves onward, fighting like wild predators.

XXIV   12 After the battle was over, they found the king of the Lamanites alive among the bodies of the fallen Lamanites. His people abandoned the fight so quickly that he had been forgotten, wounded on the ground. 13 So they took him, bandaged his wounds, and brought him to Limhi, saying: Here is the king of the Lamanites. He was wounded and fell among their dead, and they left him. We've brought him here to you. Let's kill him! 14 But Limhi told them: Don't kill him, bring him here to see me. So they brought him, and Limhi asked: Why have you come up to fight my people? My people haven't broken the agreement

I had with you. So why have you broken the agreement you swore to my people? 15 The king replied: I've broken the agreement because your people kidnapped some of my people's daughters. I was furious because of that, and so I had my people attack your people. 16 Now Limhi had heard nothing about this. So he said: I'll search for them among my people, and whoever has done this will die. Therefore he searched for them among his people.

XXV   17 Now when Gideon, the king's captain, heard about this, he came and said to the king: Please don't bother investigating our people; don't accuse them of this. 18 Don't you remember your father's priests we tried to kill? Aren't they hiding in the wilderness? Isn't it apparent they've kidnapped the Lamanite young women? 19 Think about it and go tell the king about them, so that he can explain it to his people and they can be reassured about us. They're already getting ready to attack again and we have only a few able to fight. 20 Their large army outnumbers us and we will be killed unless their king explains we are innocent. 21 It's clear that Abinadi's prophesy against us is happening — all because we refused to listen to the Lord's word and turn from our iniquities. 22 So let's satisfy the king and fulfill the agreement we have made with him. Slavery is better than death. Therefore let's put a stop to all this killing. 23 Then Limhi told the king all about his father and the priests who had fled into the wilderness, attributing their daughters' kidnapping to them.

XXVI   24 So the king of the Lamanites was satisfied with Limhi's people, and he said to them: Let's go out unarmed to meet my people; and I give you my solemn oath that my people won't kill your people. 25 They followed the king, going out unarmed to meet the Lamanites. When they met the Lamanites, the king of the Lamanites bowed before them and pled on behalf of Limhi's people. 26 When the Lamanites saw Limhi's people were unarmed, they felt sympathy for them and were satisfied, and returned peacefully with their king to their own land.

XXVII   **21** Then Limhi and his people returned to the city of Nephi, living again in peace. 2 As time passed, however, the Lamanites once more became angry with the Nephites, and they began to cross the borders of the surrounding land. 3 Now they didn't dare kill them because of their king's commitment to Limhi, but they would hit them in the face, exercise authority over them, lay heavy loads on their backs, and drive them like pack mules. 4 This was all done to fulfill the Lord's word. 5 The Nephites were tormented. But there was no way for them to free themselves, since the Lamanites surrounded them on all sides.

XXVIII

6 The people began to complain to the king because of their afflictions, wishing to retaliate. They greatly troubled the king with their complaints, so that he let them do as they wanted. 7 They gathered again, put on their armor, and went out against the Lamanites to push them off their land. 8 But the Lamanites beat them, drove them back, and killed many of them. 9 That resulted in great mourning and lamentation among Limhi's people, the widow mourning her husband, the son and daughter mourning their father, and brothers mourning brothers.

XXIX

10 Now there were many widows in the land, and they complained continually every day, because a great fear of the Lamanites terrorized them. 11 Their continual complaining stirred up the rest of Limhi's people to be angry at the Lamanites, so they went once more to battle. But they were defeated again, and many were killed. 12 But they tried again a third time and suffered similarly, and those who survived returned to the city of Nephi. 13 Then they humbled themselves to the dust, submitting themselves to the burdens of slavery, letting themselves be beaten, herded here and there, and treated like pack mules, according to their enemies' whims. 14 They humbled themselves in the depths of humility, praying humbly to God — indeed, they prayed to God all day long, asking Him to end their suffering.

XXX

15 Now the Lord was slow to answer their prayers because of their iniquities. Nevertheless, the Lord answered their prayers and began to soften the Lamanites' hearts, and they began to ease their burdens. But the Lord didn't see fit to free them from slavery.

XXXI

16 Gradually they began to make progress in the land raising grain, flocks, and herds more successfully, so they didn't suffer hunger. 17 Now there were many more women than men. Therefore king Limhi ordered the men to help support the widows and their children, to prevent starvation. This was because so many had been killed. 18 Now Limhi's people stayed close together when possible to protect their grain and flocks. 19 And the king himself didn't feel safe outside the city walls unless he had his guards with him. He feared being captured by the Lamanites. 20 He had his people watch the surrounding land, hoping to capture those priests who had fled into the wilderness and kidnapped the Lamanite young women, causing them such great destruction. 21 They wanted to capture them to punish them. They came into the land of Nephi at night and stole their grain and valuable property. Therefore they set an ambush for them.

XXXII

22 There had been no more unrest between the Lamanites and Limhi's people, up to the time that Ammon and his men came into the land. 23 And the king, while outside the city gates with his guard,

encountered Ammon and his men. Thinking them to be Noah's priests, he had them arrested, tied up, and thrown in prison. Had they been Noah's priests, he would have had them executed. 24 But when he found they were not, and they were fellow Nephites who had come from Zarahemla, he was delighted.

XXXIII 25 Now king Limhi, before Ammon's coming, had sent a small number of men to search for the land of Zarahemla, but they couldn't find it. They got lost in the wilderness. 26 Despite that, they found a place that had been inhabited and was now covered with dry bones. It obviously had been occupied by people who were destroyed. They assumed it was Zarahemla, so they returned to the land of Nephi, arriving at the outskirts of the land only a few days before Ammon's arrival. 27 And they carried with them a record engraved on metal plates of the people whose bones they had found. 28 Now Limhi was again very pleased upon learning from Ammon that king Benjamin had a gift from God that let him interpret such engravings. Ammon was also pleased. 29 But Ammon and his men grieved because so many of Limhi's people had been killed 30 and that king Noah and his priests had led the people to commit so many sins and iniquities against God. They also mourned Abinadi's death and the departure of Alma and the people who went with him, who had formed a congregation of God through God's strength and power and through faith in the words spoken by Abinadi. 31 Indeed, they missed them because they didn't know where they could be found. If they knew how to locate them, they would have gladly joined them, since they too had made a covenant with God to serve Him and keep His commandments. 32 Since Ammon's arrival, king Limhi and many of his people had also made a covenant with God to serve Him and keep His commandments.

XXXIV 33 And king Limhi and many of his people wanted to be baptized, but there was no one available who had authority from God. Ammon declined to do it because he considered himself an unworthy servant. 34 Therefore they didn't form themselves into a congregation at that time, waiting on the Spirit of the Lord. Now they wanted to become just like Alma and his people who had fled into the wilderness. 35 They wanted to be baptized as a witness and testimony they were willing to serve God with all their hearts. Nevertheless, they waited, and an account of their baptism will be included later. 36 Now the entire focus and planning of Ammon, king Limhi, and his people was to escape from the Lamanites and get free from slavery.

Chapter 10

22 Ammon and king Limhi discussed with the people how to get free from slavery. They even brought everyone together to take a vote of the people about it. 2 But since there were so many Lamanites, it was impossible for Limhi's people to fight their way free from slavery by force, so they couldn't come up with a way to liberate themselves other than taking their women, children, flocks, herds, and tents and retreating into the wilderness.

II

3 Then Gideon came forward and addressed the king, saying: Your majesty, you've taken my advice many times before while we fought our Lamanite brothers. 4 And now, your majesty, if I haven't given you bad advice, or if you've listened to me before and found I gave you good counsel, I ask you to consider my counsel now; because I have a way to free this people from slavery. 5 The king wanted to hear him, and Gideon said: 6 Consider the back passageway through the back wall behind the city. The Lamanite guards get drunk at night. So let's announce to the people to gather their flocks and herds, so they can herd them into the wilderness at night. 7 And I'll go with your permission and pay the latest tribute of wine to the Lamanites, and they'll get drunk. Then we'll pass through the secluded pass on the left of their camp while they're passed-out drunk. 8 This is how we can leave with our women, children, flocks, and herds into the wilderness; and we'll avoid the land of Shilom. 9 The king adopted Gideon's plan 10 and had his people gather their flocks. And he sent the Lamanites the wine tribute, sending more wine as a gift to them. They drank the wine king Limhi sent them without restraint.

III

11 And so king Limhi's people ran away during the night into the wilderness with their flocks and herds. They avoided the land of Shilom while leaving and set their course toward the land of Zarahemla, letting Ammon and his men show the way. 12 They had taken all the gold, silver, valuable things, and supplies they could carry with them as they left, and they went on with their journey. 13 After traveling many days in the wilderness, they arrived in Zarahemla and joined Mosiah's people and became his subjects. 14 Mosiah gladly received them, and he also accepted their records and the records found by Limhi's people. 15 When the Lamanites discovered they had left the land at night, they sent an army into the wilderness to chase them. 16 After they had pursued them for two days, they lost their tracks and became completely disoriented in the wilderness.

Chapter 11

An account of Alma and the Lord's people, who were driven into the wilderness by king Noah's people.

23 The Lord warned Alma that king Noah's armies were coming to attack them, and Alma told his people. So they gathered their flocks, took their grain, and went into the wilderness ahead of king Noah's armies. 2 The Lord gave them strength, so they stayed ahead of king Noah's people coming to kill them. 3 They fled into the wilderness for eight days, 4 arriving at a very beautiful and pleasant land with fresh water. 5 They pitched their tents there and began to farm the ground and construct buildings, etc. — you see, they were productive and hard working.

II

6 And the people wanted Alma to be their king, since they loved and trusted him. 7 But he told them: It isn't advisable for us to have a king. This is what the Lord has said: You must not value one person over another, and no one should consider themselves better than another. Therefore I advise you against having a king. 8 However, if it were possible to always have ethical men as your kings, it would be worthwhile to have a king — 9 but remember the iniquity of king Noah and his priests. I was trapped in it and did many wicked things offensive to the Lord, that I now bitterly regret. 10 But after a lot of suffering, the Lord heard and answered my prayers and has turned me into an instrument in His hands to teach many of you knowledge about His truth. 11 Nevertheless, I don't expect praise for this, since I'm unworthy of taking any pride in myself. 12 Now I tell you: King Noah oppressed you, and he and his priests enslaved you and led you into iniquity, so you were captured with the chains of sin. 13 Now as God's power has freed you from these chains, from the control of king Noah and his people, and from the chains of sin, I want you to maintain your liberty, and never trust any man to be a king ruling you. 14 Don't trust anyone to be your teacher or minister unless he's called by God, walking in His ways, and following His commandments. 15 This is what Alma taught his people, that everyone should love their neighbor as themselves, and they shouldn't have any serious conflicts.

III

16 Now Alma, their congregation's founder, was their high priest. 17 And no one received authority to preach or teach unless it was from God and through Alma. He alone ordained all their priests and teachers, and no one was ordained unless they were ethical men. 18 So they cared for their people and taught them things required for righteousness. 19 And they began to thrive in the land, which they called Helam. 20 They increased in numbers and produced more than

they needed in the land of Helam. They built a city that they called the city of Helam. 21 However, the Lord disciplines His people; He requires them to be patient and faithful. 22 Nevertheless, whoever trusts Him will be rewarded on the last day; and this is how it was with Alma's people. 23 I'll show you that they were subjected to slavery, and no one could have freed them other than the Lord who is God: the God of Abraham, God of Isaac, and God of Jacob. 24 He freed them and demonstrated His mighty power to them, making them rejoice.

IV   25 What happened was that while they were in the land of Helam, in the city of Helam, while farming the surrounding land, a Lamanite army came into the outskirts of the land. 26 And Alma's people ran from their fields and gathered in the city of Helam, being very frightened at the Lamanites' arrival. 27 But Alma went out and joined with them and urged them to not be frightened, but to remember the Lord their God, that He would protect them. 28 So they subdued their fears and began to pray to the Lord to soften the Lamanites' hearts so they would spare them and their wives and children. 29 And the Lord softened the Lamanites' hearts. Alma and his people went out and surrendered to them, and the Lamanites took control of Helam.

V   30 Now the Lamanite armies, who had gone in pursuit of king Limhi's people, had been lost in the wilderness for many days. 31 But they had found those priests of king Noah in a place they called Amulon, where they had settled and farmed. 32 Now the name of the leader of those priests was Amulon. 33 And Amulon pled with the Lamanites and sent out their wives, who were the Lamanites' daughters, to plead with their relatives not to kill their husbands. 34 And the Lamanites had sympathy for Amulon and his men and didn't kill them because of their wives. 35 So Amulon and his men joined the Lamanites, and they were traveling in the wilderness in search of the land of Nephi when they discovered the land of Helam, where Alma and his people had settled.

VI   36 The Lamanites promised Alma and his people that if they would show them the way to the land of Nephi they would spare their lives and respect their liberty. 37 But after Alma had shown them the way leading to the land of Nephi, the Lamanites refused to keep their promise, and instead set guards over Alma and his people surrounding the land of Helam. 38 And the rest of them went to the land of Nephi; and some of those returned to Helam, bringing with them the wives and children of the guards who had been left behind. 39 The king of the Lamanites appointed Amulon to be a king and ruler over his people in Helam. However, he was only given power to obey the will of the king of the Lamanites.

VII   **24** And Amulon earned the trust of the king of the Lamanites, so the king allowed him and his men to be appointed teachers of his people in the lands of Shemlon, Shilom, and Amulon. 2 The Lamanites had control of all these lands; so the king of the Lamanites had appointed rulers over each of them. 3 Now the name of the king of the Lamanites was Laman, and he was named after his father, and was called king Laman. He ruled over many people. 4 He appointed teachers from Amulon's men in every land occupied by his people. So the Nephite language began to be taught to all the Lamanites. 5 And they were people that were friendly with each other. Nevertheless, they didn't know about God, and Amulon's men didn't teach them anything about the Lord God, the Law of Moses, or Abinadi's words. 6 But they taught them to write a record, enabling them to write to each other as well. 7 So the Lamanites became wealthier and began to trade with each other and grow strong and become shrewd and sly, like worldly men are — indeed, very sly, enjoying all kinds of wickedness and plunder, but they didn't cheat their own people.

VIII   8 Now Amulon began to abuse Alma and his people and persecute him and have his children mistreat and harass their children. 9 This was because Amulon recognized Alma had been one of the king's priests and was the one who believed Abinadi's words and was thrown out by the king. So he was very angry with him. Although he had to obey king Laman, Amulon still abused Alma's people, demanding work from them and putting taskmasters over them. 10 Their afflictions were so intense that they began to pray constantly to God. 11 Amulon ordered them to stop praying and put guards over them to watch them, to execute whoever was found calling upon God. 12 So Alma and his people didn't pray out loud to the Lord their God but instead poured out their hearts to Him, and He understood the thoughts of their hearts.

IX   13 And the Lord's voice came to them as they suffered, saying: Lift up your heads and be of good cheer. I'm aware of the covenant you made with Me. And I promise this people of Mine that I'll free you from slavery. 14 I'll also ease the burdens put upon your shoulders, so that you can't feel them on your backs, for as long as you remain in slavery. I'll do this so you can stand as witnesses for Me after this, and know for certain that I the Lord God am with My people as they suffer. 15 Now the burdens placed on Alma and his people were made light — the Lord gave them the strength to carry them with ease — and they submitted cheerfully and patiently to the Lord's will.

X   16 Their faith and patience were so great that the Lord's voice spoke again, saying: Be of good cheer, because I'll free you from slavery tomorrow. 17 He told Alma: You will lead this people, and I'll go with you and free them from slavery.

XI   18 Now Alma and his people gathered their flocks and grain at night — indeed, they spent the whole night herding their flocks. 19 And in the morning, the Lord caused a deep sleep to overcome the Lamanites, and all their taskmasters were sound asleep. 20 Then Alma and his people made their way into the wilderness. And when they had traveled all day, they pitched their tents in a valley, calling it Alma, because he led their way in the wilderness. 21 They poured out their thanks to God in the valley of Alma because He had been merciful to them and eased their burdens and freed them from slavery — and no one could have set them free from their enslavement except for the Lord who is God. 22 And they gave thanks to God — indeed, all the men, women, and children who could speak raised their voices, giving praise to God.

XII   23 Now the Lord told Alma: Act quickly and get yourself and these people out of this land. The Lamanites have reawakened and are pursuing you. So get out of this land, and I'll stop the Lamanites in this valley, so they don't come any further in pursuit of this people. 24 And they left the valley and traveled into the wilderness. 25 After they had been in the wilderness for twelve days, they arrived in Zarahemla, and king Mosiah also received them joyfully.

XIII   **25** Now king Mosiah called all the people together. 2 This included the people of Zarahemla who were descendants of Muloch and those who came with him into the wilderness, who outnumbered the children of Nephi or the descendants of Nephi. 3 But the Lamanites outnumbered the Nephites and Zarahemla's people by more than two to one. 4 Now all the Nephites and Zarahemla's people gathered, and they were divided into two groups.

XIV   5 Then Mosiah reviewed Zeniff's records and had them read to his people. Those records covered Zeniff's people from the time they left Zarahemla until they returned. 6 He also read the account of Alma and his people and all their difficulties, from the time they left Zarahemla until they returned. 7 When Mosiah had finished reading the records, the people who had remained in the land were shocked and amazed — 8 they didn't know what to think. When they saw those who had been freed from slavery, they were filled with overwhelming joy. 9 But when they thought of their relatives who had been killed by the Lamanites, they mourned and shed many tears. 10 When they thought of God's immediate goodness and His power in freeing Alma and his people from the Lamanites and from slavery, they sang and gave thanks to God. 11 But when they thought of the Lamanites, their relatives, of their sinful, polluted state, they were filled with pain and sorrow for their souls' well-being.

XV   12 And the children of Amulon and his men, who had married the Lamanite young women, were embarrassed at their fathers' conduct and didn't want to be associated with their fathers' name. So they changed their name to Nephi, so they could be called Nephi's children and be included with those who were called Nephites. 13 All of Zarahemla's people were included as Nephites, because Nephi's descendants governed the kingdom.

XVI   14 When Mosiah finished reading these records to the people, he wanted Alma to also speak to them. 15 So Alma spoke to them as they were gathered in large groups, going from one group to another, preaching repentance and faith in the Lord to the people. 16 And he urged Limhi's people and everyone who had been freed from slavery to remember it was the Lord who had rescued them. 17 After Alma finished teaching the people many things and concluded his preaching, king Limhi wanted to be baptized and so did all his people. 18 Therefore Alma went into the water and baptized them in the very same way he baptized his people in the waters of Mormon. And all those he baptized belonged to God's congregation — because of their belief in Alma's words.

XVII   19 Then king Mosiah authorized Alma to organize congregations throughout the land of Zarahemla, letting him ordain priests and teachers over each one. 20 Now they did this because there were too many people for only one teacher to guide them, or to be able to hear God's word in one group. 21 So they gathered in different groups called congregations, every congregation having priests and teachers, and every priest's messages repeating Alma's instruction. 22 And so, even though there were many congregations, they were all one congregation: God's congregation; because nothing was preached in any of the congregations except for repentance and faith in God. 23 Now there were seven congregations in the land of Zarahemla. And whoever wanted to take upon himself the name of Christ, or of God, joined the congregations of God; 24 and they were called God's people. The Lord poured out His Spirit upon them, and they were blessed and prospered in the land.

XVIII   **26** But many of the younger generation couldn't understand king Benjamin's words since they were little children when he addressed his people. They didn't believe their ancestors' traditions. 2 They didn't believe what had been said about the resurrection of the dead nor did they believe in Christ's coming. 3 Now because of their unbelief, they didn't accept God's word. And their hearts were hardened, 4 and they refused to be baptized or join the congregation. They were a separate people concerning their faith and remained separated from then on, staying in their carnal and sinful state because they wouldn't call on the Lord their God. 5 Now during Mosiah's rule they weren't half as numerous as God's people, but because of divisions in the congregation, they grew in numbers. 6 They misled many in the congregation with their persuasive words and led them to commit many sins. As a result, the congregation needed to admonish their members who committed sins.

XIX   7 So the teachers took the offenders to the priests; and the priests took them to Alma, the high priest. 8 King Mosiah gave Alma control over the congregation, 9 and Alma was aware of these offenders because there were many witnesses against them — indeed, many people came forward and testified of their iniquity. 10 Now nothing like this had happened before in the congregation, so Alma was deeply troubled and he took them to the king. 11 He said to the king: We've brought to you those who have been accused by their associates. They've been found committing various iniquities and won't repent of their iniquities. So we bring them to you, so you can judge them based on their crimes. 12 But king Mosiah told Alma: I'm not going to judge them. Therefore I give them back to you to be judged. 13 Now Alma was deeply troubled again. So he went and asked the Lord what to do about the problem, since he was afraid to do wrong in God's sight.

XX   14 After he had poured out his whole soul to God, the Lord's voice spoke to him, saying: 15 You are blessed, Alma. And those who were baptized in the waters of Mormon are blessed also. You are blessed because of your great faith based upon My servant Abinadi's words. 16 And they're blessed because of their great faith based upon the words you've taught them. 17 And you are blessed because you've established a congregation among this people. They will be strengthened and be My people. 18 And this people is blessed, those who are willing to bear My name; they'll be called in My name, and they're Mine. 19 Because you've asked Me about those who have done wrong, you are blessed. 20 You are My servant, and I covenant with you that you will have eternal life.

XXI   You will serve Me, go out in My name, and gather My sheep. 21 And any who hear My voice will be My sheep; and you will receive them into the congregation, and I'll also receive them. 22 This is My congregation. Whoever is baptized will be baptized as a sign of repentance; and whoever you receive must believe in My name, and I'll freely forgive them. 23 I Am the one who takes upon Myself the sins of the world, since I Am the one who created them. I Am the one who, in the end, will give to those who believe a place at My right hand. 24 They're called in My name; and if they know Me, they'll come forward and have a place eternally at My right hand. 25 And when the second trumpet sounds, those who never knew Me will arise and stand in front of Me. 26 And then they'll know that I Am the Lord their God, that I am their Redeemer, but they won't be redeemed. 27 Then I'll declare to them that I never knew them, and they'll go away into everlasting fire prepared for the accuser and his angels. 28 Therefore I tell you that you must not receive into My congregation any who refuse to hear My voice, because I won't welcome them on the last day.

XXII

29 Therefore I tell you: Go; you must judge whoever sins against Me according to the sins they've committed. And if a person confesses their sins before you and Me and repents in the sincerity of their heart, you must forgive them; and I'll forgive them also. 30 And as often as My people repent I'll forgive them of their offenses against Me. 31 And you must also forgive each other's offenses. I tell you truthfully: The person who doesn't forgive their neighbor's offenses when they say they repent, that person brings themselves under condemnation. 32 Now I tell you: Go; and whoever won't repent of their sins, the same won't be included among My people. And this shall be observed from now on.

XXIII

33 When Alma had heard these words, he wrote them down so he could preserve them and so he could judge the people of the congregation according to God's commandments. 34 And Alma went and judged those who had been caught in iniquity, according to the Lord's word. 35 Whoever repented of their sins and confessed them he counted among the congregation members. 36 But those who wouldn't confess their sins and repent of their iniquity, the same weren't included among the congregation members and their names were erased. 37 So Alma regulated the congregation's business. And they again began to have peace and abundance in the congregation, walking mindfully before God, receiving and baptizing many. 38 Now Alma and his fellow laborers who led the congregation did all these things, being very diligent, carefully teaching God's word, yet encountering many challenges, and being persecuted by those who didn't belong to God's congregation. 39 They admonished their brothers and sisters and each one was also admonished by God's word if they had erred or had sinned, being commanded by God to pray always and to give thanks in all things. 27 Now the unbelievers mistreated and harassed those of the congregation so much that they began to grumble and complain to their leaders about it, and they complained to Alma. And Alma brought the case before their king, Mosiah, who consulted with his counselors.

XXIV   2 King Mosiah sent a proclamation throughout the land that no unbeliever should mistreat or hurt anyone who belonged to God's congregation. 3 And a strict command went among all the congregations that there must not be any persecution among them, but there should be equality among all of them, 4 that they shouldn't let any pride or arrogance disrupt the peace, everyone should value their neighbor as themselves and work with their own hands to support themselves, 5 and their priests and teachers should work with their own hands for their support in every case except for sickness or extreme poverty. As they did these things, they abounded in God's grace. 6 And great peace began to prevail once more in the land. The people grew very numerous and began to spread out over the land — to the north, south, east, and west — building large cities and villages in every quarter of the land. 7 And the Lord blessed them and caused them to prosper, and they increased in number and became wealthy.

XXV   8 Now Mosiah's sons were included among the unbelievers, and so was one of Alma's sons, who was named Alma after his father. Nevertheless, he had become a very wicked man who worshiped idols, and he was eloquent and charmed the people with his persuasive language. Therefore he led many of them to follow him into sinning against God. 9 And he interfered with the prosperity of God's congregation, stealing away people's hearts, causing many strong disagreements among them, and giving God's enemy the opportunity to influence them.

XXVI   10 While he was out trying to destroy God's congregation (doing it secretly with Mosiah's sons), trying to destroy the congregation and lead the Lord's people astray, violating not only God's commandments but also the king's — 11 and as I told you, as they were going about rebelling against God, the angel of the Lord appeared to them, descending in what seemed like a cloud. He spoke with a voice like thunder, making the ground shake where they were standing. 12 Their astonishment was so great that they fell to the ground and didn't understand the words he spoke. 13 But he called out again, saying: Alma, get up and step forward. Why do you persecute God's congregation? Because the Lord has said: This is My congregation and I'll establish it, and nothing will destroy it except for My people's transgressions. 14 The angel also said: The Lord has heard His people's prayers and the prayers of His servant Alma, your father. He's prayed with great faith about you, so you could be brought to the knowledge of the truth. Therefore I've come to convince you of God's power and authority, so His servants' prayers will be answered according to their faith. 15 Can you challenge God's power? Does my voice not shake the earth? Can you not see me in front of you? I am sent from God. 16 Now I tell you: Go; and remember the slavery of your people in the lands of Helam and Nephi, and remember how He has done great things for them. They were enslaved and He set them free. Now I tell you, Alma: Go your way, and so that their prayers will be answered, end your efforts to destroy the congregation, unless you want to be destroyed! 17 Now these were the last words the angel said to Alma, as he left.

XXVII   18 Now Alma and those who were with him fell down on the ground again, since they were so astonished, having seen an angel of the Lord with their own eyes, and his voice was like thunder that shook the ground. They knew there was nothing except for God's power that could shake the ground and make it tremble as if it would split apart. 19 Alma was so dumbfounded that he couldn't talk or open his mouth. And he was weak and couldn't even move his hands. So those who were with him took him and carried him in a helpless condition, putting him down in front of his father. 20 They told his father all that had happened to them. And he was glad, because he knew that it was God's power. 21 And he had many people gather so they could witness what the Lord had done for his son and for those who were with him. 22 And he had the priests assemble and they began to fast and pray to the Lord their God that He would open Alma's mouth so he could speak, so his limbs could receive their strength, and so the people's eyes could be opened, to see and know about God's goodness and glory.

XXVIII   23 After they had fasted and prayed for two days and nights, Alma's arms and legs had their strength return. And he stood up and began to speak to them, telling them to be of good cheer. 24 He said: I've repented of my sins and have been redeemed by the Lord. I'm born of the Spirit. 25 And the Lord said to me: Don't be surprised that all mankind, men and women — people of every nation, tribe, and language — must be born again, born of God, changed from their carnal and fallen state to a state of righteousness, being redeemed by God, becoming His sons and daughters. 26 Therefore they become new creatures. And unless they do this, there's no way for them to inherit God's kingdom. 27 I tell you: If they don't follow God, they'll be rejected. I know this because I was on the verge of being rejected. 28 Nevertheless, after wading through great distress, repenting close to death, the Lord, in His mercy, has seen fit to rescue me suddenly from an everlasting burning; and I'm born of God. 29 My soul has been redeemed from a state of suffering in bondage of sin. I was in the darkest abyss, but now I see God's marvelous light. My soul was tortured with eternal torment, but I was quickly rescued, and my soul isn't pained anymore. 30 I rejected my Redeemer and denied what our fathers had said. But now I know that they correctly predicted He will come, and that He remembers every creature of His creation, and He will reveal Himself to everyone. 31 Every knee will bow and every tongue will acknowledge Him in His presence. They'll acknowledge He is God on the last day, when all mankind stands to be judged by Him. Then those who live on earth without God will acknowledge that the judgment they receive of everlasting punishment is right and fair. They'll shake, tremble, and recoil at a glance from His all-searching eye.

XXIX   32 Now Alma and those who were with him when the angel appeared to them began to teach the people from then on, traveling throughout the land, declaring to the people what they had heard and seen, preaching God's word in very trying circumstances: receiving very harsh treatment by unbelievers and getting beaten by many of them. 33 But despite all this, they imparted great comfort to the congregation, confirming their faith and urging them with long-suffering and consistent effort to keep God's commandments. 34 Four of them were Mosiah's sons: Ammon, Aaron, Omner, and Himni; these were the names of Mosiah's sons. 35 They traveled throughout the land of Zarahemla and among all the people who were under king Mosiah's rule, earnestly trying to repair all the harm they had done to the congregation, confessing their sins, explaining everything they had seen, and teaching the prophecies and scriptures to all who wanted to hear them. 36 So they were instruments in God's hands in bringing many to know the truth and their Redeemer. 37 And how blessed are they! Because they proclaimed peace and good news of good things, declaring to the people that the Lord reigns.

Chapter 12

28 After Mosiah's sons had done all this, they took a small number with them and went to their father the king and asked him to allow them to go up to the land of Nephi with those they had chosen, in order to preach what they had heard and share God's word with their Lamanite brothers and sisters, 2 so they could perhaps bring them to know the Lord who is God and convince them of their forefathers' iniquity. Perhaps to cure them of their hatred of the Nephites, and so they could also be brought to rejoice in the Lord who is God and be friendly to each other, and so there wouldn't be any more wars in the whole land that the Lord their God had given them. 3 Now they wanted salvation to be explained to every creature, because they couldn't stand for any human soul to perish. Indeed, the very thought that any soul might endure endless torment made them shake and tremble. 4 This is how the Spirit of the Lord acted upon them. They were once the vilest of sinners, but the Lord saw fit in His infinite mercy to spare them. Nevertheless, they suffered great anguish of soul because of their iniquities, experiencing terrible dread that they could be rejected forever.

II   5 They pled with their father for many days to be able to go up to the land of Nephi. 6 And king Mosiah went and asked the Lord if he should let his sons go among the Lamanites to preach the word. 7 The Lord said to Mosiah: Let them go there, because many will believe in their words; and they will have eternal life. And I'll protect your sons from the power of the Lamanites.

III   8 Mosiah gave them permission to go and do as they requested. 9 And so they went into the wilderness to preach the word among the Lamanites. I'll give an account of their labors later. 10 Now king Mosiah had no one to confer the kingdom on, since none of his sons would accept the kingdom. 11 So he took the records engraved on the brass plates, the plates of Nephi, and all the things that he had kept and preserved according to God's commandments. And he translated the records on the gold plates found by Limhi's people and then given to him by Limhi. He had the translation written down. 12 He did this because his people were eagerly wanting to know about the people who had been destroyed. 13 Now he translated the plates using those two stones fastened into the two rims of a frame for spectacles. 14 These things had been prepared from the beginning and handed down for generations for the purpose of translating languages. 15 And the hand of the Lord had preserved them to expose the iniquities and abominations of His people to any people who would inhabit the land. 16 And whoever has this instrument has always been called a seer.

IV   17 After Mosiah had finished translating these records, they learned it was an account of the people who were destroyed, from the time they were destroyed back to the time when the great tower was built, when the Lord confused the people's language and they were scattered across the whole earth, and went all the way back to Adam's creation. 18 Now this account distressed Mosiah's people — indeed, they were heartbroken. Nevertheless, it informed them a great deal, and they rejoiced because of that. 19 And this account will be written later; because it will benefit everyone to know what's written in that account.

Chapter 13

²⁰ Now, as I was saying, after king Mosiah had done these things, he took the brass plates and everything he had kept — all the records and the Interpreters as well — and conferred them on Alma's son Alma, and commanded him to maintain and protect them, adding to the record of the people. He was to hand them down from one generation to another, just as they had been handed down since Lehi left Jerusalem.

II   **29** When Mosiah had done this, he sent a message across the land, asking the people who they wanted as the next king. ² And the people voted and said: We want your son Aaron to govern as our king. ³ But he had left for the land of Nephi; so the kingdom couldn't be conferred on him. Besides, Aaron declined the kingdom anyway, and none of Mosiah's other sons were willing to take upon themselves the kingdom, either. ⁴ Therefore king Mosiah again sent a written message, asking: ⁵ My people or my brothers and sisters — because I consider you to be that — I want you to think carefully about what you decide. You want to have a king. ⁶ But I tell you that the one to whom the kingdom rightly belongs has declined and won't assume control of the kingdom. ⁷ Now if someone else is appointed in his place, I'm afraid that conflicts would arise among you. And who knows if my son, to whom the kingdom does belong, might become angry and draw away part of the people to follow him — causing wars and conflicts among you, which would lead to loss of life and turning away from the Lord's way, destroying many souls. ⁸ So let's be wise and think carefully about these things. Because we don't have any right to destroy my son or anyone else who might be appointed in his place. ⁹ If my son were to go back to being prideful and to his prior foolishness, he would change what he decided and claim his right to the kingdom, which would lead in turn to many sins. ¹⁰ So let's be wise, look to the future, and do what will bring peace to this people. ¹¹ Now I'll be your king for the rest of my days.

III   Nevertheless, let's appoint judges to judge this people according to our law, and we'll reorganize society. We'll appoint wise men to be judges who will judge the people according to God's commandments. ¹² Now it's better for a man to be judged by God than by man — because God's judgments are always just, but mankind's judgments aren't always appropriate and fair. ¹³ Therefore if it were possible for you to always have righteous men as your kings, who would establish God's laws and judge this people according to His commandments, if you could always have men for your kings who would act just like my father Benjamin did for us — I tell you that if this could always be the case, then it would fine for kings to rule us. 14 I myself have labored with all my strength to teach you God's commandments and establish peace throughout the land, so there wouldn't be any wars, conflicts, theft, plunder, murder, or any kind of iniquity. 15 And I've punished whoever has committed iniquity according to the crime they've committed and according to the law our forefathers gave us.

IV   16 Now I'm telling you that because not all men are just, it isn't good for you to have kings rule over you. 17 Because one wicked king causes so much iniquity to be committed and so much destruction! 18 Remember king Noah, his wickedness and abominations, and the resulting wickedness and abominations of his people. What great destruction fell upon them! Because of their iniquities they were also brought into slavery. 19 If it hadn't been for the intervention of their all-wise Creator — because of their sincere repentance — they would have inevitably remained in slavery until now. 20 But He rescued them because they humbled themselves before Him; because they prayed humbly to Him, He rescued them from slavery. And this is how the Lord's power is manifest in all cases among mankind, extending the arm of mercy toward those who put their trust in Him.

V   21 Now I tell you: You can't remove an iniquitous king from power without terrible conflict, bloodshed, and killing. 22 Because he has his friends in iniquity, and he keeps his guards around him, and he violates the laws of those who have ruled in righteousness before him, and he ignores God's commandments. 23 He enacts laws and forces them on his people — laws made according to his own wickedness. And he executes whoever doesn't obey his laws. He sends armies against anyone who disobeys him; and if he can, he'll kill them. And so an unrighteous king corrupts and perverts the ways of all righteousness. 24 Now I tell you: Such abominations are avoidable.

VI   25 Therefore choose for yourselves judges by your vote, so that you can be judged according to the laws that have been established by our forefathers, which are good and were given to them by the Lord. 26 Now it's not common for the majority of the people to want anything contrary to what's right, but it's common for the minority to want what isn't right. So you must observe this principle and make it your law, to do your business by the majority vote of the people.

VII   27 And if the time comes that the majority of the people choose iniquity, then that is when God's judgments will fall upon you and He'll cause great destruction, just like He's done upon this land up until now. 28 Now if you have judges and they don't judge you according to the law that's been given, you can make them be judged by a higher judge. 29 And if your higher judges don't make righteous judgments, you must cause a small number of your lower judges to convene, and they should then judge your higher judges based upon the vote of the people. 30 I've commanded you to do these things to respect the Lord; I've commanded you to do these things and to not have a king, and if these people commit sins and iniquities, they will be responsible for them. 31 I tell you: The sins of many people have resulted from their kings' iniquities; therefore their iniquities are their king's responsibility.

VIII   32 I don't want there to be any more inequality in this land, especially among my people. But I want this land to be a land of liberty and for everyone to enjoy their rights and privileges equally, so long as the Lord sees fit to allow us to live and to possess the land as an inheritance, and for as long as any of our descendants are on the land. 33 King Mosiah wrote many more things to them, explaining all the trials and troubles of a righteous king: the worrying for his people and the people's complaints to their king; he explained it all to them. 34 He told them these things shouldn't be like this, but the responsibility should rest on everyone and everyone should do their part. 35 He also explained the disadvantages they labored under by having an unrighteous king rule over them: 36 the risks of iniquities and abominations, and the wars, conflicts, slaughter, theft, plunder, whoredoms, and all kinds of sin which can't all be named, telling them these things should be avoided by them, that they were directly contrary to God's commandments.

IX   37 After king Mosiah sent this message to the people, they were convinced it was true. 38 So they gave up their desire to have a king and became very eager for equality for all. And everyone said they were willing to be responsible for their own sins. 39 So they assembled in groups throughout the land to vote for judges who would judge them based upon the given law. And they celebrated the liberty bestowed upon them. 40 Their love for Mosiah grew — indeed, they regarded him more highly than any other man. They didn't see him as a tyrant who was seeking power and money that corrupts the soul. He hadn't demanded and taken their wealth from them or casually killed others, but he had established peace in the land and allowed his people to be freed from all forms of slavery. So they cherished him as a leader. 41 And they appointed judges to rule over them, or to judge them according to the law, by voting throughout the land.

X   42 Alma, the high priest, was appointed to be the chief judge, his father having conferred the office upon him and given him responsibility over all the congregation's dealings. 43 Now Alma walked in the Lord's ways, kept His commandments, and passed righteous judgments. And there was continual peace throughout the land. ⁴⁴ And so began the judges' rule over the land of Zarahemla among all the people who were called Nephites; and Alma was the first and chief judge.

⁴⁵ Now his father died at age 82, having lived to fulfill God's commandments. ⁴⁶ And Mosiah died too, at age 63, in the 33rd year of his rule. In total, it had been 509 years since Lehi left Jerusalem. ⁴⁷ And that ended the rule of kings over the Nephites; and Alma's days also ended, who was the founder of their congregation.

The Book of Alma

THE SON OF ALMA

The account of Alma, who was the son of Alma, the first and chief judge over the Nephites, and high priest over the congregation. An account of the judges' rule and the wars and conflicts among the people. And an account of a war between the Nephites and Lamanites according to Alma's record, who was the first and chief judge.

Chapter 1

King Mosiah died and returned to the dust of the earth after fighting a good fight and living righteously before God. But no one was left to rule in his place. Nevertheless, the people accepted the laws he established. In the first year of the rule of the judges over the Nephites, the people followed the laws king Mosiah established. ² In the first year Alma occupied the judgment seat, a large man recognized for his strength was brought before him to be judged. ³ He had been preaching to the people what he called God's word, repeatedly attacking the congregation, declaring every priest and teacher should be chosen by the people and shouldn't have to work to support themselves, but should be paid by the people. ⁴ He also preached that all mankind would be saved on the last day, they didn't need to be afraid or worry, but they could relax and be happy. He claimed that because the Lord had created and redeemed everyone, in the end, everyone would have eternal life. ⁵ He successfully taught these things, and many believed what he said. People began to support him and give him money. ⁶ He became prideful and began to wear very expensive clothing. He even began to build up a church based on what he preached.

II   7 As he was on his way to preach to his followers, he met a man who belonged to the congregation of God and was one of their teachers. He started an intense argument with that teacher, hoping to mislead the congregation members. But the teacher opposed him, admonishing him with God's words. 8 This man's name was Gideon, the same one who had been an instrument in God's hands in freeing Limhi's people from slavery. 9 Now because Gideon opposed him with God's words, he was very angry with Gideon and drew his sword and attacked him. Because Gideon was quite old, he wasn't able to defend against the attack, and was killed. 10 The man who killed him was taken by the congregation members and brought to Alma to be judged for his crime. 11 He stood before Alma and boldly defended himself. 12 But Alma said to him: This is the first time that priestcraft has been introduced among this people. And you're not only guilty of priestcraft, but you've also tried to violently enforce it. If priestcraft were to be forced on the people, it would ensure their complete destruction. 13 You've killed a righteous man, one who's done a lot of good for the people. If we spare you, his murder would become our responsibility and God's vengeance would be directed at us. 14 Therefore you're condemned to die according to the law given by Mosiah, our last king. These laws have been approved by the people, so we must abide by them.

III   15 Then they took him — and his name was Nehor — and they brought him to the top of the hill Manti, where he confessed, or admitted between the heavens and earth, that what he had taught the people violated God's word. Then he was publicly executed.

IV   16 Despite this, it didn't put an end to the spread of priestcraft across the land, since there were many who loved worldly things. They went around preaching false doctrines, doing it for money and popularity. 17 However, they didn't dare lie — at least in public — for fear of the law, because liars were punished. So they pretended to preach according to their beliefs. Now the law punished no one for their beliefs. 18 They didn't dare steal for fear of the law, because thieves were punished. And they didn't dare rob or murder, because anyone who murdered was executed.

V   19 But those who didn't belong to God's congregation began to persecute those who belonged to it and had taken upon themselves the name of Christ. 20 They abused, harassed, and insulted them, knowing their humility. Members of the congregation were neither proud nor viewed themselves as superior. They shared God's word with each other freely, without money or cost. 21 There was a strict law among congregation members prohibiting persecution of those who didn't

belong to the congregation, as well as persecuting one another.
22 Nevertheless, there were many who were proud and who got into
heated arguments over disagreements, even sometimes getting into
fistfights. 23 This was during the second year of Alma's rule, and it
caused a considerable amount of trouble and difficulty for the
congregation. 24 The hearts of many were hardened, and their names
were removed, and they were no longer included as part of God's
people. Many also resigned from the congregation. 25 This was a
difficult test for those who were faithful. Despite this, they were firm
and immovable in keeping God's commandments, and they patiently
endured the persecution piled on them. 26 When their priests left their
work to share God's word with the people, the people also left their
work to hear God's word. When the priest had shared God's word with
them, they all returned diligently to their work, the priest not
regarding himself as better than his audience, since the preacher
wasn't any better than the hearer and the teacher wasn't any better
than the learner. They were all equal; and they all worked, each person
based on their ability. 27 They shared what they had based on their
ability to do so, with the poor, the needy, the sick, and the distressed.
And they didn't wear expensive clothing, yet they were well-dressed
and clean. 28 This is how they arranged things in the congregation and
they began to have peace again, despite all the persecution.

VI   29 Now because of the stability of the congregation, they became
wealthy, having plenty of everything they needed: flocks, herds, and
young, fattened animals; grain, gold, silver, valuables, furs, fine woven
linen, and all kinds of simple, comfortable cloth. 30 And in their
prosperous circumstances they didn't send away any who were naked,
hungry, thirsty, sick, or malnourished. And they didn't set their hearts
on wealth. They gave freely to all, old and young, slaves and free men,
male and female, whether in or out of the congregation, treating
everyone in need the same. 31 So they prospered and became far
wealthier than those who didn't belong to their congregation. 32 Those
who didn't belong to their congregation indulged in sorcery, idol
worship, laziness, gossip and foolish empty talk, jealousy, arguments,
wearing expensive clothes, proudly viewing themselves as superior,
persecution, lying, theft, robbery, committing whoredoms, murder,
and all kinds of evil. Nevertheless, those who broke the law were
prosecuted so far as it was possible.

VII   33 By making them accountable to the law (everyone received
punishment based on what they did), they became more peaceful, and
didn't dare commit violations that anyone would know about. So the

Nephites enjoyed considerable peace until the fifth year of the judges' rule.

VIII **2** At the start of the fifth year of their rule, a serious disagreement started among the people. A clever, worldly-wise man named Amlici had the same beliefs as the man who killed Gideon with his sword and was executed according to the law. 2 Now this Amlici had cleverly drawn away a large number of people to follow him. He had so many followers that they became very powerful and wanted to establish Amlici as their king. 3 Now this alarmed the congregation and everyone not persuaded by Amlici's arguments, because they realized that according to their law, such things were established by the voice of the people. 4 Consequently, if Amlici, an evil man, received enough support, he could deprive them of their right to worship as a congregation, because he intended to destroy God's congregation.

IX 5 The people gathered throughout the land in separate groups, according to whether they favored or opposed Amlici, everyone arguing at length and having heated disagreements with each other. 6 Then they voted about it, the votes being placed before the judges. 7 And the vote went against Amlici, so he wasn't made king over the people. 8 This made those who opposed him very happy, but Amlici persuaded those who supported him to be angry with those who didn't support him.

X 9 His supporters then anointed Amlici to be their king anyway. 10 After Amlici was made their king, he ordered them to go to war against their fellow Nephites, hoping to force them under his control. 11 Now Amlici's people called themselves the people of Amlici, or Amlicites, and the rest were called either Nephites or God's people. 12 The Nephites learned about the Amlicites' ambition and they armed themselves with swords, cimeters, bows, arrows, stones, slings, and every kind of weapon. 13 And they were ready to fight the Amlicites when they attacked. And captains, higher captains, and chief captains were appointed, depending on the number of soldiers.

XI 14 Amlici also armed his men with every kind of weapon, and appointed commanders and leaders over his people to lead them into battle against the Nephites. 15 The Amlicites attacked on the hill Amnihu, east of the Sidon River, which ran by the land of Zarahemla; there they began to fight the Nephites. 16 Since Alma was the chief judge and governor of the Nephites, he commanded his armed forces, with his soldiers, captains, and chief captains, in the battle against the Amlicites. 17 And they began to kill the Amlicites on the hill east of the Sidon River; the Amlicites fighting the Nephites very aggressively, so much so that many of the Nephites were killed by the Amlicites. 18 But the Lord helped the Nephites; with His strength, they massacred the Amlicites, and they began to retreat. 19 The Nephites chased them that whole day, killing a great number of them. In total, 12,532 Amlicites were killed and 6,562 Nephites were killed.

XII   20 When night came and Alma's pursuit of the Amlicites ended for the day, he had his people camp in the valley of Gideon. The valley was named after the Gideon Nehor had killed with his sword. The Nephites camped in this valley for the night. 21 Alma sent spies to follow the surviving Amlicites, so he could find out what their plans and schemes were to guard against them. His plan was to preserve his people from being destroyed. 22 Now the names of those he sent out to watch the Amlicite camp were Zeram, Amnor, Manti, and Limher; they, along with their spies, went to watch the Amlicites' camp.

XIII   23 On the following day, these men rushed back to the Nephites' camp. They were extremely surprised and frightened, reporting: 24 We followed the Amlicites' camp, and to our great surprise, in the land of Minon — above the land of Zarahemla and toward the land of Nephi — we saw a large Lamanite army, and the Amlicites have joined them! 25 They're attacking our people there, and our people are fleeing from them toward our city, with their flocks, wives, and children. Unless we hurry, they'll take our city, and kill our fathers, wives, and children.

XIV   26 The Nephites took their tents and left the valley of Gideon to return to their city of Zarahemla. 27 As they were crossing the Sidon River, the Lamanites and Amlicites, who seemed as countless as the sands of the sea, attacked them, intent on killing them. 28 However, trusting in the Lord, the Nephites prayed to Him with all their energy, asking Him to save them from their enemies. The Lord heard their prayers and strengthened them, and the Lamanites and Amlicites began to be slaughtered. 29 Alma and Amlici fought face to face with swords to the death.

XV   30 Being a man of God and relying on his faith, Alma prayed aloud: O Lord, have mercy and spare my life so I can be an instrument in Your hands to save and protect this people! 31 After Alma said this, he renewed his fight with Amlici; and he was able to overpower and kill Amlici with his sword. 32 He then fought the king of the Lamanites, but the king of the Lamanites retreated from Alma and sent his guards to fight him. 33 Alma's guards battled the king of the Lamanites' guards who were killed or ran away. 34 Then Alma cleared the ground on the west bank of the Sidon River, throwing the dead bodies of the Lamanites into the Sidon, to make room to cross and fight the Lamanites and Amlicites on the west side of the Sidon River.

XVI   35 When all the Nephites had crossed the Sidon River, the Lamanites and Amlicites ran from them, despite far outnumbering them. 36 They fled from the Nephites toward the wilderness to the west and north, beyond the land's frontier. The Nephites chased them with God's strength and killed them — 37 in fact, they killed on every battle front and scattered them to the west and north, until they reached a wilderness area called Hermounts. That area was infested by wild, dangerous predators. 38 Many died in the wilderness as a result of their wounds and then were eaten by those predators or by vultures. Their bones have been found and piled up on the ground.

XVII   3 Then the Nephite survivors of the battle buried their dead fellow soldiers. The total number of dead was far too many to be counted. After they finished burying their dead, they returned to their lands, houses, wives, and children. 2 Unfortunately, many women and children had been killed in the war, and many flocks and herds also died. Many fields of grain were also destroyed, being trampled by the armies. 3 And all the Lamanites and Amlicites that were killed on the bank of the Sidon River were thrown into the river. As a result, their bones — and there are many of them — went to the depths of the sea.

XVIII   4 The Amlicites were distinguished from the Nephites, since they had marked themselves with red on their foreheads to look like the Lamanites — yet they hadn't shaved their heads like the Lamanites did. 5 The Lamanites' heads were shaved; and they were naked except for animal skin, which was fastened around their waists. They did wear some armor also, which was securely fastened, and carried their bows, arrows, stones, slings, etc. 6 The Lamanites' dark countenance marked them since their forefathers. There was a curse on them because of their transgression and their rebellion against their brothers — Nephi, Jacob, Joseph, and Sam — who were righteous and holy men. 7 Their brothers tried to kill them, so they were cursed, and the Lord God set a mark upon them — upon Laman, Lemuel, Ishmael's sons, and the Ishmaelite women. 8 This was done so their descendants could be distinguished from their brothers' descendants. In this way the Lord God could keep His people separated, so they wouldn't mix and believe in incorrect traditions, resulting in their destruction.

XIX   9 Whoever intermarried with the Lamanites brought the same curse upon their descendants. 10 Therefore those who let themselves be led away by the Lamanites were called by that name and inherited that mark. 11 Those who rejected the Lamanites' tradition, believing instead in the records brought from Jerusalem, and in their forefathers' correct tradition, who believed in God's commandments and kept them, were called Nephites, or the people of Nephi, from then on.

¹² They're the ones who have kept the accurate records about them and the Lamanites.

XX   ¹³ We return now to the Amlicites, who also had a mark set on them. They marked themselves with red on their foreheads. ¹⁴ By this, God's word was fulfilled when He said to Nephi: I've cursed the Lamanites and I'll set a mark upon them, so they and their descendants will be separated from you and your descendants from this time forward and forever, unless they repent of their evil and turn to Me. Then I would have mercy on them. ¹⁵ I'll also set a mark on anyone who intermarries with your brothers' descendants, so they will be cursed as well. ¹⁶ In addition, I'll set a mark on those who fight against you and your descendants. ¹⁷ And those who separate themselves from you won't be included as your descendants anymore; and I'll bless you and your descendants, and whoever joins with your descendants, from this time forward and forever. These were promises made by the Lord to Nephi and his descendants. ¹⁸ Now the Amlicites didn't know they were fulfilling God's words when they began to mark themselves on their foreheads. However, as they had openly rebelled against God, it was fitting for the curse to fall on them. ¹⁹ I want you to understand they volunteered to be cursed. In similar fashion, so does everyone who's cursed — each person brings upon themselves their own condemnation.

XXI   ²⁰ Not many days after the battle fought in the land of Zarahemla against the Lamanites and Amlicites, another Lamanite army attacked the Nephites at the same place where the first army met the Amlicites. ²¹ The Nephites sent an army to drive them out. ²² Alma was suffering from a wound and didn't go out to battle against the Lamanites on this occasion, ²³ but he sent a large army against them. They went and killed many Lamanites and drove the rest of them from the borders of their land. ²⁴ Then they returned and began to establish peace in the land, without being troubled by their enemies for a time. ²⁵ Now all this happened — all these wars and conflicts started and ended — in the fifth year of the judges' rule. ²⁶ In one year, thousands and tens of thousands of souls were sent to the eternal world, to reap their reward according to their actions, whether they were good or bad. They would reap eternal happiness or eternal misery according to the spirit they chose to follow, whether it was a good spirit or a bad one. ²⁷ Because every person receives wages from the one they choose to follow — this is what the spirit of prophecy tells us, so it's the truth. That's how the fifth year of the judges' rule ended.

Chapter 2

4 In the sixth year of the judges' rule over the Nephites, there were no conflicts or wars in Zarahemla. 2 But the people mourned terribly over the loss of their relatives and fellow Nephites, over their flocks and herds being killed, and over damage to their farms from being trampled and destroyed by the Lamanites. 3 The disruption was so widespread that every one of them was directly impacted, and they believed God had sent His judgments against them because of their wickedness and abominations. So they were reminded to remember their duty 4 and renewed their commitment to the congregation. Then many were baptized in the Sidon River and joined God's congregation. Alma, who had been ordained by his father Alma as the high priest over the congregation, baptized them.

II   5 And in the seventh year of the judges' rule, about 3,500 souls joined God's congregation and were baptized. And the seventh year of the judges' rule over the Nephites ended, and there was continuous peace that year.

III   6 In the eighth year of the judges' rule, members of the congregation began to get proud because of their prosperity: wealth, fine clothing, woven linen, increasing flocks and herds, gold, silver, and all kinds of valuable property, which they gained through hard work. They thought of themselves as superior to others because of these things, and they showed off their wealth to be noticed, hoping to be envied. 7 Now this disappointed Alma immensely, as well as others Alma had ordained to be teachers, priests, and elders over the congregation. Many of them shared the disappointment and concern over the wickedness they could see growing among their people. 8 They regretted seeing congregation members devoted to getting rich and acting prideful — people who valued property over their fellow man, and gave more attention to what they owned than helping others in need. And as entertainment they randomly began to abuse those who didn't share their views. 9 So in this eighth year of the judges' rule, significant tensions developed among the congregation members; there was jealousy, arguments, malicious and abusive conduct, and pride, even worse than the pride of those who didn't belong to God's congregation. 10 So ended the eighth year of the judges' rule. The congregation's awful example was a big obstacle for those who didn't belong to the congregation; so the congregation began to decline.

IV   11 At the start of the ninth year, Alma could see the congregation's bad behavior. Their terrible example led unbelievers to go from one bad act to the next. That would ultimately result in destroying the people. 12 He also saw great inequality among the people: some proudly exalting themselves, despising others, turning their backs on the needy, the naked, and the hungry, thirsty, sick, and distressed. 13 This discouraged others. But he saw others were humbling themselves, assisting those needing help, sharing their possessions with the poor and the needy, feeding the hungry, and suffering all kinds of troubles and difficulties to obey Christ. They relied on the spirit of prophecy, trusted He would come, 14 and looked forward to the time of His arrival. As a result, their sins remained forgiven. They rejoiced over the resurrection of the dead, accomplished through the will, power, and deliverance from the chains of death by Jesus Christ.

v   15 Now Alma was very discouraged seeing the pains and troubles of God's humble followers, the abuse piled on them by others, and the growing inequality. Despite his discouragement, the Spirit of the Lord inspired him. 16 He appointed a wise man from the congregation's elders and the people voted to authorize him to adopt new laws, consistent with their existing law, to limit sinful, criminal behavior. 17 The man's name was Nephihah, and he was elected chief judge; he accepted the judgment seat to judge and govern the people. 18 Alma didn't authorize him to be the high priest over the congregation — he kept that office himself. Only the judgment seat was handed over to Nephihah. 19 He did this to free himself to go preach God's word to the Nephites, and urge them to remember their duty. He wanted to use God's word to confront all the pride, clever lies, and resulting conflicts among his people. He could see no way he could bring them back to the right way except by directly confronting them with pure testimony of the truth. 20 So at the start of the ninth year of the judges' rule over the Nephites, Alma handed over the judgment seat to Nephihah and devoted himself completely to the High Priesthood of the Holy Order of God, to teaching God's word according to the spirit of revelation and prophecy.

Chapter 3

The teaching Alma, the high priest belonging to the Holy Order of God, delivered to the people in their cities and villages throughout the land.

5 Alma started teaching God's word to the people, first in Zarahemla, and afterward throughout the land. 2 This is what he taught the congregation in the city of Zarahemla, according to his own record: 3 I Alma was ordained by my father Alma to be a high priest over God's congregation, since he had power and authority from God to do so. He started to establish a congregation in the land that

bordered the land of Nephi, a place called Mormon. He baptized his followers in the waters of Mormon. 4 I testify they were liberated from king Noah's control by God's mercy and power. 5 Subsequently they were enslaved by the Lamanites. But the Lord delivered them again from slavery by the power of His word. We were then led to this land and began to establish God's congregation here and throughout this land.

II   6 Now I ask all you who belong to this congregation: Have you remembered your fathers' captivity? Have you also remembered God's mercy and long-suffering toward them? Have you also carefully considered how He rescued their souls from hell? 7 He changed their hearts; He woke them from a deep sleep and they woke up to God. They were surrounded by darkness; but their souls emerged into the light of God's everlasting word. They were bound by the chains of death and hell, and faced everlasting destruction. 8 So I ask: Were they destroyed? I answer: No, they were not. 9 I also ask: Were the chains of death broken? Were the chains of hell surrounding them removed? I say: Yes, they were removed. And their souls grew in understanding and they sang of redeeming love. I testify they're saved. 10 Now I ask: What are the conditions for their salvation? On what basis did they hope for salvation? How were they freed from the chains of death and hell? 11 I'll tell you the answer: Didn't my father Alma believe in the words taught by Abinadi? And wasn't he a holy prophet? Didn't he speak God's words and my father Alma believed them? 12 Because of his faith, a powerful change happened in his heart. I testify this is all true. 13 He preached the word to your parents, and changed their hearts as well, and they humbled themselves and trusted the true and living God. Then they were faithful until the end; so they were saved.

III   14 Now I ask you, my brothers and sisters of the congregation: Have you spiritually been born of God? Have you received His image in your own countenances? Have you experienced this powerful change to your hearts? 15 Do you rely on faith in the redemption of the Lord who created you? Do you faithfully anticipate rising from the grave to immortality, freed from degeneration, illness, and corruption, to stand before God and be judged based on what you've done in the mortal body? 16 I ask: Can you expect to hear the Lord's voice then saying to you: Come to Me, blessed one; your works have been righteous on the earth? 17 Or do you imagine being able to lie to the Lord and claim: Lord, our works on earth have been righteous (even when they were not), and He'll save you? 18 Or can you instead foresee standing before God's judgment seat filled with guilt and remorse, remembering clearly all your guilt and wickedness, knowing you've defied God's commandments? 19 I ask: Can you look up to God on that day with a pure heart and clean hands? I ask: Can you look up, having the image of God engraved on your countenances? 20 I ask: Can you think of being saved when you've allowed yourselves to obey the accuser? 21 I say: You will then know you can't be saved; because no one can be saved unless their clothes are clean, purified, and every trace of sin and iniquity removed through the blood of Him our fathers testified was appointed to come to redeem His people from their sins.

IV   22 Now I ask you, my brothers and sisters: How will any of you feel when standing before God's judgment bar, with your clothes stained with blood and all kinds of filthiness? What will these things prove about you? 23 Won't they prove you are murderers, guilty of all kinds of wickedness? 24 My people, do you think anyone can have a place in God's kingdom with Abraham, Isaac, Jacob, and all the holy prophets, wearing clothes that aren't cleansed and spotless, pure, and white? 25 I'm telling you: That's impossible unless our Creator is a liar from the start, or you would have to believe He's a liar from the start. You can't think such a person will be welcome in the kingdom of heaven; they'll be thrown out since they belong in the accuser's kingdom.

V   26 Now, my people, consider this: If you've experienced a change of heart and felt moved to sing the song of redeeming love, I would ask, Do you still feel that way? 27 Have you been keeping yourselves innocent before God? If you were to die now, could you honestly say you've been humble enough, that your clothes have been cleansed and made white through the blood of Christ — who is coming to redeem His people from their sins? 28 Are you stripped of pride? I tell you that if you're not, then you aren't prepared to come face to face with God. You must prepare now; because the kingdom of heaven is coming soon, and you won't have eternal life. 29 Again I ask you: Is there any one of you not stripped of jealousy? I tell you anyone who's not, is not prepared and won't be found innocent. And I urge you to prepare quickly, since the time is near; and we don't know when the time arrives.

VI   30 I ask you again: Is there any one of you who mocks their brother or sister or who mistreats them? 31 Woe to anyone like this, because they aren't prepared; the time is short for them to repent or they can't be saved. 32 Indeed, woe to everyone who commits iniquity. Repent! Repent, because the Lord God requires it. 33 He invites all mankind — the arms of mercy are extended toward them. He pleads: Repent, and I will receive you. 34 He says: Come to Me and you'll partake of the fruit of the tree of life; you'll eat and drink freely of the bread and waters of life. 35 Come to Me and do righteous works and you won't be cut down and cast into the fire. 36 The time is near when anyone who's failed to produce good fruit or didn't do righteous works will have good reason to weep and mourn.

VII   37 All of you that commit iniquity, take pride in empty, worldly things and have claimed to understand righteousness: you've wandered off like sheep without a shepherd, while a shepherd has called and is still calling you back, but you ignore His voice. 38 I declare the Good Shepherd is calling to you. He is calling for you in His own name, which is the name of Christ. But if you won't respond to the Good Shepherd's voice, to the name you're called by, then you aren't His sheep. 39 Now if you aren't the sheep of the Good Shepherd, then to whose fold do you belong? I tell you the accuser is your shepherd, and you're part of his fold. Who can deny this? I'm telling you whoever denies this is a liar and a child of the accuser.

VIII   40 I testify whatever is good comes from God and whatever is evil comes from the accuser. 41 So if a person does good works, then they respond to the Good Shepherd's voice and follow Him. But whoever does evil works becomes a child of the accuser, since they follow his voice and obey him. 42 Whoever does this will get their payment from him. He'll compensate them with death as to righteousness, letting all good works in you die. 43 Now, my people, I want you to listen, because I sincerely plead from the core of my soul. I've spoken plainly to you so you won't miss the point, based upon God's commandments. 44 I'm called to speak in this way from the duty held by the Holy Order after the Order of the Son of God, Jesus Christ. It's my obligation to stand and testify to this people about what our fathers have prophesied about what will happen. 45 And this isn't all. Do you think I don't know personally about these things? I testify that everything I've spoken about is true. How do you think I know of their certainty? 46 I'll tell you: They were revealed to me by God's Holy Spirit. I've fasted and prayed many days to obtain personal knowledge of these things. And I know personally they're true, since the Lord God has revealed them to me by His Holy Spirit; which is the Spirit of revelation that's in me. 47 Just like it was revealed to me that the words of our fathers are true, the spirit of prophecy and revelation from the Spirit of God to me confirms 48 and therefore I personally know, what I told you about the future is true. I tell you that I know Jesus Christ, the Only Begotten of the Father, who's full of grace, mercy, and truth, will come. He is coming to take away the sins of the world, the sins of every person firmly believing in His name.

IX   49 I testify this is the Holy Order I've been ordained into to preach
to my dear people — and to everyone who lives in the land — to
preach to all: the old and the young, the enslaved and the free, the
middle-aged and the rising generation — to invite them all to repent
and be born again. 50 Indeed, the Spirit says: Repent, everyone
throughout the earth, because the kingdom of heaven is coming soon.
The Son of God will come in His glory, strength, majesty, power, and
dominion. My dear people, I tell you the Spirit says: The glory of the
King of the whole earth and of the King of heaven will very soon be
seen here with us. 51 And the Spirit directed me to go, use all my
energy, and warn the people bluntly, saying: Repent! Because, unless
you repent it's impossible to inherit the kingdom of heaven. 52 I also
testify the Spirit says: The ax is placed at the root of the tree, ready to
cut down and throw into the everlasting, unquenchable fire every tree
that doesn't produce good fruit. Listen and remember! The Holy One
has spoken it!

X   53 Now, my dear people, I ask you: Can you deny these words? Can
you set them aside and trample the Holy One under your feet? Can
you be filled with pride to your very core? Will you continue displaying
your extravagant clothes, setting your hearts on empty, worldly things
— on your material possessions? 54 Will you persist in thinking you're
better than others? Will you continue to mistreat your brothers and
sisters, who humble themselves and live according to the Holy Order
of God, which brought them into this congregation, having been
sanctified by the Holy Spirit? For they show by their works that they've
truly repented. 55 Again, will you continue turning your backs on the
poor and needy when you could easily help them? 56 Finally, all of you
who insist on continuing to do evil, I tell you unless you quickly repent,
this is what will get you cut down and thrown into the fire.

XI   57 Now all of you that wish to follow the voice of the Good
Shepherd: Come and separate yourselves from the wicked and don't
touch their unclean things. Their names will be erased, dividing the
names of the wicked from the names of the righteous, so that God's
word will be fulfilled, which says: The names of the wicked won't be
mixed in with the names of My people; 58 because the names of the
righteous will be included in the Book of Life, and I'll bestow upon
them an inheritance at My right hand. Now, my people, how can you
criticize this? I tell you: If you speak opposing it, it doesn't matter,
because God's word will certainly be fulfilled. 59 Indeed, does any
shepherd with a flock fail to watch over them to prevent wolves from
attacking and eating his flock? If a wolf enters his flock, doesn't he
drive it out? And ultimately, if he can, he'll kill it. 60 Now I tell you the

Good Shepherd is calling out to you. And if you're willing to respond to His voice, He'll bring you into His fold and you'll be His sheep. He commands you not to let any ravenous wolf enter among you, to prevent you from being destroyed.

XII   61 And I give you the same command He gave to me: You must take care to do what I've told you. 62 This is a commandment to the congregation. For those who don't belong to the congregation, I invite and ask you to come and be baptized as a sign of repentance, so you can also eat the fruit of the tree of life.

Chapter 4

6 After Alma had finished speaking to the congregation established in Zarahemla, he ordained priests and elders by placing his hands on them and ordaining them, according to God's Order, to protect and watch over the congregation. 2 Those who didn't belong to the congregation and repented of their sins were baptized as a sign of repentance and received into the congregation. 3 And those who belonged to the congregation and didn't repent of their sins and humble themselves before God (meaning those who were filled with pride to their core) were rejected and their names were erased, so they weren't included among those of the righteous. 4 This is how they began to establish order in the congregation in Zarahemla. 5 Now I want you to understand that God's word was freely available to everyone, so no one was deprived of the privilege of assembling to hear God's word. 6 Nevertheless, God's children were commanded to gather often and to join in fasting and humble prayer on behalf of the well-being of those souls who didn't know God.

II   7 When Alma had delivered these instructions, he left them — that is, the congregation in the city of Zarahemla — and went over to the east of the Sidon River into the valley of Gideon, where a city had been built called Gideon. It was located in the valley called Gideon, named after the man who had been killed with a sword by Nehor. 8 So Alma went to declare God's word to the congregation established in the valley of Gideon. He went to teach the revealed truth spoken by his fathers. And to follow the spirit of prophecy that was in him. Testifying of Jesus Christ, the Son of God, who would redeem His people from their sins. This followed the Holy Order in which he had been called to serve. That is according to the written record. Amen.

Chapter 5

Alma's teaching, which he delivered to the people in Gideon, according to his own record.

7 My dear people, since I've been permitted to come to see you, I'll attempt to teach in my own words, from my own mouth. This is the first time I've spoken to you in person, since I've been completely tied up handling the judgment seat solving many disputes, and therefore was unable to visit you. 2 I couldn't come now if the judgment seat wasn't handed over to my replacement. But the Lord in His mercy has allowed me to come see you. 3 I've come hoping and praying I would find that you had humbled yourselves before God and remained prayerful for His grace. I've prayed you were innocent before Him and weren't in the same awful predicament as our people at Zarahemla. 4 But may God's name be blessed, because He revealed the joyful news to me that they've returned to His righteous ways. 5 The Spirit of God lets me trust that you will also bring me joyful news.

II   I hope it won't require as much pain and sorrow here as did our brothers and sisters at Zarahemla. Indeed, my joy for them came after a lot of pain and sorrow. 6 But I trust you're not in the same state of unbelief as your brothers and sisters were. I trust you aren't prideful, and haven't set your hearts on wealth and worthless, worldly things. Further, I trust you don't worship idols, but you worship the true and living God, who is to come, looking forward to the remission of your sins with everlasting faith.

III   7 There are many things prophesied to happen. One of them is more important than all the others. For soon the Redeemer will come and live among His people. 8 I'm not saying He'll live with us while He's mortal, as the Spirit hasn't told me this will be the case. So I don't know about that. But I do know this much: that the Lord God has power to do all things according to His word, 9 and the Spirit has instructed me: Cry out to this people, saying: Repent! Repent, and prepare the way for the Lord and walk in His straight paths; because the kingdom of heaven is near, and the Son of God will soon come to earth. 10 He'll be born at Jerusalem, our ancestors' land, to Mary, a virgin, the exclusive, elect woman. She'll be overshadowed and conceive by the power of the Holy Ghost and will give birth to a Son — indeed, the Son of God. 11 He'll live among mankind, suffering pains, afflictions, and temptations of every kind. That fulfills the prophecy: He will take upon Himself His people's pains and sicknesses. 12 He will take death upon Himself, so He can break the chains of death that keep His people bound. He will take on their infirmities, so He can be compassionate to them by understanding the flesh, and know from experience in the flesh how to assist His people to accept and overcome their infirmities. 13 Now the Spirit knows everything. In any event, the Son of God will endure physical agony, so He can take upon Himself His people's sins and remove their transgressions through the power of His redemption. This is my testimony.

IV　　　　14 I warn you to repent and be born again, because the Spirit says: If you aren't born again, you can't inherit the kingdom of heaven. So come and be baptized as a sign of repentance, to be cleansed of your sins, to show your faith in the Lamb of God, who will take away the world's sins, who is powerful to save and cleanse from all unrighteousness. 15 Indeed, I say to you: Come and don't be afraid, and put away every sin that so easily entangles you, that ties you down to destruction. Come and take action and show God you're willing to repent of your sins and enter into a covenant with Him to keep His commandments, and show Him this today by entering the waters of baptism. 16 Whoever does this and keeps God's commandments from then on, should remember I assure them they will have eternal life. The Holy Spirit testifies this to you through me.

V　　　　17 Now, my dear people, do you believe this? I say: Yes, I know you believe this. The way I know you believe is because the Spirit reveals it to me. Now I'm full of joy because your faith is strong in what I've spoken. 18 As I said to you when I began, I hoped you weren't doubtful like your brothers and sisters. Thankfully I've found my hopes have been met. 19 I see you're on the path of righteousness. I see you're on the path leading to God's kingdom. I see you're on His straight path. 20 I can sense your confidence in the revealed testimony of His word that He can't lead into crooked paths. Nor does He deviate from what He's said, that He doesn't turn by so much as a shadow from the right to the left, or from what's right to what's wrong. His path is therefore one eternal round. 21 He doesn't dwell in unholy temples, and nothing filthy or even unclean can enter God's kingdom. Therefore I tell you: The time will come at that last day, when a person who's filthy will remain in their filth.

VI　　　　22 Now, my dear people, I've taught you this to help you understand your duty to God, to help you be blameless before Him, so you will let the Holy Order of God lead you, which is why God received you. 23 Now I want you to be humble, submissive, gentle, easy to persuade, full of patience and long-suffering, being self-controlled in all things, faithfully keeping God's commandments, asking for whatever you might need, both spiritual and temporal, always giving thanks to God for whatever you receive. 24 Make sure you have faith, hope, and charity, and then you will always be eager to do many good works. 25 May the Lord bless you and keep your clothes spotless, so you can, in the end, arrive with spotless clothes in the kingdom of heaven with Abraham, Isaac, Jacob, and all the holy prophets who have ever lived since the world began, to never leave.

VII   26 Now, dear people, I've taught you what the Spirit has led me to testify. My soul is overjoyed because of the great diligence and attention you've given to my teaching. 27 May God's peace rest upon you and your houses, farms, flocks and herds, and all you own, and on your women and children, according to your faith and good works, from now and forever. That is my message. Amen.

Chapter 6

8 Then Alma returned from the land of Gideon after teaching Gideon's people far too much to be written, having organized the congregation like he did before in Zarahemla. He went back to his own house at Zarahemla to rest. 2 So the ninth year of the judges' rule over the Nephites ended.

II   3 At the start of the 10th year, Alma went to Melek, west of the Sidon River, on the western border of the wilderness. 4 He began teaching there conforming to his calling in the Holy Order of God, teaching the people throughout the land of Melek.

III   5 The people came to him to be baptized from the entire area, including the outskirts of the land near the wilderness. 6 When he finished his work at Melek, he left there and traveled three days to the north of the land of Melek, arriving at a city called Ammonihah. 7 Now it was the Nephites' custom to call their lands, cities, and villages, even their small villages, after the person who first settled there. This was true of the land of Ammonihah.

IV   8 Once Alma arrived at Ammonihah, he began to preach God's word to them. 9 Now Satan had a firm hold on the hearts of the people of the city of Ammonihah; therefore they refused to listen to Alma. 10 Despite this, Alma looked to heaven for help, pleading with God to intervene, humbly asking for Him to help influence the people to open their hearts and see their need for repentance and baptism. 11 But they hardened their hearts and told him: We know you're Alma, and we know you're the high priest over the congregation, which you've established in many parts of the land based on your tradition. But we aren't part of your congregation, and we don't believe in such foolish traditions. 12 Because we don't belong to your congregation, we know you don't have any power over us. You've handed over the judgment seat to Nephihah, therefore you're no longer the chief judge over us. 13 When the people said this and rejected everything he said and ridiculed him, spit on him, and had him thrown out of their city, he left there and traveled toward a city named Aaron.

V   14 While he was on his way there, mourning and agonizing about the wickedness of the people in Ammonihah, while lamenting his failure, an angel of the Lord appeared to him, saying: 15 Alma, you are blessed. So look up and rejoice, because you have every reason to rejoice, since you've faithfully kept God's commandments from His first message to you. I'm the one who delivered it to you. 16 I now am sent to command you to return to Ammonihah and preach to them again, warning them that unless they repent, the Lord God will destroy them. 17 The Lord wants you to know that right now they're conspiring about how to destroy the freedom of your people. They violate the statutes, judgments, and commandments God has given His people.

VI   18 After Alma heard this from the angel of the Lord, he returned quickly to Ammonihah. He entered Ammonihah by a different way, on the south side of the city. 19 Because he was hungry when he entered, he asked a man: Will you give a humble servant of God something to eat? 20 The man replied: I'm a Nephite and I know you're a holy prophet of God. You're the man an angel told me in a vision I would meet and help. Come with me to my house, and I'll feed you. I know you'll bring a blessing for my household and me. 21 The man named Amulek took him into his house. He gave Alma bread and meat to eat.

VII   22 Then Alma ate bread until he was full; and he blessed Amulek and his household, and thanked God. 23 After eating his fill, he told Amulek: I'm Alma; I'm the high priest over the congregations of God throughout the land. 24 I was called by the spirit of revelation and prophesy to preach God's word to all these people. I was here before but they were unwilling to listen to me, and they threw me out. I was about to turn my back on this land forever. 25 But I've been commanded to return and prophesy to the people and testify against their iniquities. 26 Now Amulek, because you've fed me and taken me in, you are blessed. I was hungry because I had fasted for many days. 27 Alma stayed with Amulek for many days before he began to preach to the people.

VIII   28 Meanwhile the people grew more shameless in their iniquities. 29 Then the Lord told Alma: Go. Also, tell my servant Amulek: Go out and prophesy to the people, saying: Repent, because this warning is from the Lord: Unless you repent, I'll punish you people in My anger; and I won't abandon My fierce anger. ³⁰ Then Alma and Amulek went to tell the people God's warning to them. And they were filled with the Holy Ghost. ³¹ They had God's power and they couldn't be confined in dungeons or killed. Nevertheless, they didn't use their power until after they were tied up and thrown in prison, and only then to show the Lord's power was with them.

IX   ³² They went to preach and prophesy to the people obeying the Spirit and using the power the Lord gave them.

Chapter 7

The words of both Alma and Amulek that were proclaimed to the people living in Ammonihah. In addition, they're imprisoned and rescued by the miraculous power of God protecting them, according to Alma's record.

9 I Alma was commanded by God to take Amulek and again preach to the people in Ammonihah. As I started to preach to them, they argued with me. They asked, ² Who are you? Do you think we're going to believe one man's testimony, even if he preached to us the earth would pass away? ³ Now they didn't understand what they said, because they didn't understand the earth will pass away. ⁴ They also said: We won't believe your words, even if you were to prophesy this great city is going to be destroyed in a single day. ⁵ They didn't believe God could do such miraculous things, because they were a hard-hearted and stubborn people. ⁶ And they asked: If it were actually true, why wouldn't God send more authority than a single man to warn us about these important threats? ⁷ Then they started to arrest me, but hesitated.

II   I boldly stood my ground, fearlessly warning them: ⁸ You wicked and corrupt generation! How have you abandoned the tradition of your forefathers? Yes, how have you so quickly discarded God's commandments! ⁹ Don't you remember God rescued our father Lehi from Jerusalem? Don't you remember God led Lehi's people through the wilderness? ¹⁰ Have you so soon forgotten the many times He rescued our forefathers from enemies and saved their lives, including at the hands of their own brothers? ¹¹ If it hadn't been for His unequaled power, mercy, and long-suffering toward us, we would certainly have vanished from the earth long before now. We may have been condemned to a state of endless misery, pain, and sorrow. ¹² Now I tell you He commands you to repent. And unless you repent, there's no way for you to inherit God's kingdom. But this isn't all. He's commanded you to repent, or He'll completely destroy you from off the earth. He'll punish you in anger! He won't end His fierce anger at you.

III   13 Don't you remember what He told Lehi: that to the degree you keep My commandments, you'll prosper in the land. Also to the degree you don't keep My commandments, you'll be cut off from the Lord's presence. 14 Now I want you to remember that the Lamanites haven't kept God's commandments, and they've been cut off from the Lord's presence. Therefore the Lord's word on this has been vindicated, and the Lamanites were cut off from His presence from the start of their rebellion. 15 Nevertheless, I warn you that they'll be better off than you at judgment time if you remain in your sins. They're even better off in this life than you, unless you repent. 16 Indeed, many promises have been given to the Lamanites, because they remain ignorant due to their ancestors' traditions. Therefore the Lord will be merciful to them and patient with them living on the land. 17 At some time in the future, they'll be taught to believe in His word and understand their ancestors' traditions were wrong. Many of them will be saved because the Lord will forgive all those who call on His name.

IV   18 But I warn you if you persist in doing evil, your time on the land will end, because the Lamanites will attack you. If you don't repent, they'll come when you don't expect it, and you'll be punished and destroyed. It will be the result of the Lord's fierce anger. 19 He won't allow you to live in your iniquities, polluting His people. I tell you: No, He would choose to let the Lamanites destroy the entire Nephite nation if they were to fall into sin and transgression by rejecting so much light and knowledge given to them by the Lord their God. 20 You've been a greatly blessed people by the Lord, more blessed than people of other nations, tribes, and languages. You've had things revealed to you about the past, present, and future. You've had your desires, faith, and prayers answered. 21 You've been visited by the Spirit of God and heard the Lord's voice speak to you. You've talked with angels and received the spirit of prophecy and revelation. You've been given many gifts: the gift of speaking in tongues, the gift of preaching, the gift of the Holy Ghost, and the gift of translation; 22 you were rescued by God from the land of Jerusalem by His hand and then saved from famine, illness, and all kinds of diseases. The Nephites have been strengthened in battle so they couldn't be killed and have been repeatedly freed from slavery and watched over and preserved until now. You've prospered until you're now rich in many things.

V   23 I warn you that if this people, who have received so many blessings from the Lord, were to sin against the light and knowledge they have, if you fall into transgression, then it will be far more bearable for the Lamanites than for you. 24 Indeed, the Lord's promises are extended to the Lamanites, but if you sin they aren't extended to you. Hasn't the Lord expressly promised and firmly decreed that if you rebel against Him, you will be completely destroyed and removed from the earth?

VI   25 And now, to prevent you from being destroyed, the Lord has sent His angel to visit many of His people, instructing them to come and solemnly warn you: Repent! Repent, because the kingdom of heaven is coming soon. 26 Not many days from now the Son of God will come in His glory. His glory will be the glory of the Father's Only Begotten: full of grace, fairness, truth, patience, mercy, and long-suffering, and quick to hear His people's cries and answer their prayers. 27 He is coming to redeem those who are baptized as a sign of repentance, through faith in His name. 28 Therefore get ready for the coming Lord, because the time is near when everyone will reap a reward for their works based upon what they've been: If they've been righteous, they'll receive salvation through the power and redemption of Jesus Christ. But if they've been evil, they'll receive damnation through the power and captivity of the accuser. 29 This is the angel's message to you. 30 Now, my cherished people (because you are my people and you should be cherished), you must produce evidence of your repentance, because your hearts remain hardened against God's word, and you're now a lost and fallen people.

VII   31 When I said this, the people were furious with me because I told them they were hard-hearted and stubborn. 32 And because I also told them they were a lost and fallen people, they were angry and tried to take me by force and throw me into prison. 33 But at that time the Lord didn't let them throw me into prison.

VIII   34 Then Amulek spoke up and also began to preach to them. Not everything Amulek said has been written, but some of his words are included below.

Chapter 8

10 This is what Amulek preached to the people in Ammonihah: 2 I'm Amulek, the son of Gidanah, the son of Ishmael, a descendant of Aminadi — the same Aminadi who interpreted the writing on the temple wall, written by God's finger. 3 And Aminadi was a descendant of Nephi, the son of Lehi, who came from the land of Jerusalem and was a descendant of Manasseh, the son of Joseph, who was sold into Egypt by his brothers. 4 I'm also influential with those who know me. I have many relatives and friends. I've become wealthy through hard work. 5 Despite all this, I've never known much about the Lord's ways, mysteries, and awe-inspiring power. I said I didn't know much about these things, but that isn't completely accurate. I've watched His mysterious, miraculous power protecting the lives of this people. 6 But I hardened my heart. I had many opportunities to hear Him but refused to listen. Therefore, although I knew God did these things, I refused to acknowledge it. I kept rebelling against God in the wickedness of my heart, up until the fourth day of this seventh month, in the 10th year of the judges' rule.

II
7 As I went to see a close relative, an angel of the Lord appeared and said: Amulek, return to your own house. There you will feed a prophet of the Lord, a holy man who's a chosen man of God. He's fasted many days because of the sins of this people, and he's weakened by hunger. You're to welcome him into your house and feed him. He'll bless you and your family, and the Lord's blessing will then be on you and your family.

III
8 So I obeyed the angel's voice and returned to my house. I was on my way and met the man the angel told me to welcome to my house. He is this same man who's been telling you about the things of God. 9 The angel told me: He is a holy man. I know he's a holy man because God's angel said it. 10 I also know the things he's testified about are true. I tell you as the Lord lives, He absolutely sent His angel to reveal this to me, and He's blessed my house while this man named Alma has been there. 11 Indeed, God has blessed my household: me, the women of my family, my children, my father, and my relatives. God has even blessed all my relatives because we believed what Alma has taught us.

IV
12 Now when Amulek said this, the people were shocked, because there was now more than one witness who condemned them, confirming what was going to happen, based upon the spirit of prophecy in them. 13 Nevertheless, some of them were determined to challenge them, trying to trap them in a contradiction. They asked trick questions to find evidence against them. They hoped to hand them over to the judges, intending for them to be judged under the law and be executed or imprisoned for any crime they could accuse them of committing. Or for any crime they could make it appear they had committed.

V
14 Now their accusers trying to destroy them were lawyers who were hired or appointed to serve the law during their trials — civil and criminal — held before their judges. 15 These lawyers would argue artfully and debate deceptively, proving their proficiency in their

profession. 16 So they began to question Amulek to get him confused, hoping to hear a contradiction. 17 Now they didn't realize Amulek anticipated their evil plans. But when they began to question him, he understood their thoughts and told them: You wicked and corrupt generation, you lawyers and hypocrites! You're laying the accuser's foundations by planning traps and snares to entrap God's holy ones. 18 You're planning to corruptly misrepresent a righteous man. That will provoke God's wrath upon you, resulting in this people's complete destruction. 19 Mosiah, who was our last king, when he was about to give up the kingdom, had no one to confer it on. That resulted in this people being governed by our own choices. He was right when he said if the time comes when the people choose iniquity, or the people choose transgression, then they would be overdue for destruction. 20 I'm telling you the Lord is right to condemn you for your iniquities; He should warn the people with the message from His angels: Repent! Repent, because the kingdom of heaven approaches. 21 Indeed, He should warn you by the message of His angels: I'm coming to be with My people to implement fairness and justice. 22 I tell you if it weren't for the prayers of the righteous among you, you would be punished right now with complete destruction. It wouldn't come by a flood, as the people in Noah's time were killed, but it would be by famine, calamity, disease, and the sword. 23 You're only spared because of the prayers of the righteous. Therefore if you drive out the righteous from your community, the Lord won't hold back His hand, and He'll confront you in His fierce anger; and you'll be afflicted with famine, calamity, disease, and the sword. That is coming soon unless you repent.

VI   24 Then the people were even angrier with Amulek, shouting: This man is mocking our laws, that are fair; and our wise lawyers we've chosen! 25 But Amulek stretched out his hand and thundered back at them, saying: You wicked and corrupt generation, why has Satan got such firm control on your hearts? Why do you choose to submit to him? By trusting him, he is able to rule you, to blind your eyes, so you don't understand the truth when it's told to you. 26 I ask: Have I testified against your law? You're confused. You say I have spoken against your law, but I haven't; I've defended it, to your condemnation. 27 Now I tell you the reason this people will be destroyed is because of the unrighteous leadership of your lawyers and judges.

VII   28 When Amulek said this, the people condemned him: Now we know this man is a child of the accuser, because he's lied to us and broken our law. But he says he hasn't broken it. 29 He's denounced our lawyers and judges and others. 30 Now it was the lawyers who urged everyone to remember these accusations against him. 31 One of them, named Zeezrom, was the most eager one accusing Amulek and Alma. He was one of their best lawyers, in high demand in the community. 32 Now the aim of these lawyers was to make money, and they made money by staying busy.

VIII   **11** Mosiah's law paid appointed judges of the law based on the time required of them to decide a matter.

IX   2 If a man owed someone money, but refused to pay his debt, a complaint would be made to the judge. Then the judge would order him to be brought before him, and would send out officers to enforce the order. Then he would judge the man based on the law and evidence against him. So the debtor would be compelled to pay or be whipped, or even expelled from the community as a thief and robber. 3 The judge would be paid for the time he worked: being paid a senine of gold for a day, or a senum of silver, which was equal to a senine of gold. This was established by the law.

X   4 Now these were the names used by the Nephites for the different pieces of their gold and silver, and their values. They didn't use the same values as the Jews who lived at Jerusalem, nor the same measurements as the Jews either. Instead, they used changing calculations and measurements as people's choices and circumstances changed every generation till the rule of judges. Then king Mosiah standardized the system of calculations and measurements.

XI   5 Now the calculation was this: a senine, a seon, a shum, and a limnah of gold; 6 a senum, an amnor, an ezrum, and an onti of silver. 7 A senum of silver was equal to a senine of gold, and each was equal to a measure of barley or any kind of grain. 8 Now a seon of gold was twice the value of a senine. 9 A shum of gold was twice the value of a seon. 10 And a limnah of gold was worth all of them combined. 11 An amnor of silver was as valuable as two senums. 12 An ezrum of silver was the same value as four senums. 13 And an onti was worth all of them combined. 14 Now these are the lesser values in their calculation: 15 A shiblon was half a senum; so a shiblon equaled half a measure of barley. 16 A shilum was half a shiblon. 17 And a leah was half a shilum. 19 Now an antion of gold was equal to three shiblons. 18 These were the quantities used in their calculations.

XII   20 Now the lawyers' sole objective was to make money, because they received payment according to how much time they spent. They incited people to fight with one another, encouraging disturbances, with resulting wickedness, all so they could have more work, and make money from the resulting lawsuits. This was why they incited people to be angry with Alma and Amulek. 21 So Zeezrom started questioning Amulek: If I ask you a few questions, will you answer them for me? Now Zeezrom was a skilled accuser, serving Satan and opposing righteousness. That was why he asked Amulek: Will you answer the questions I ask you? 22 Amulek replied: Yes, I'll answer as the Spirit of the Lord inspires me to answer, because I'll say nothing opposing the Spirit of the Lord. Zeezrom offered to him: Here are six onties of silver; I'll give all these to you if you deny a Supreme Being exists.

XIII   23 Amulek responded: You child of hell, why are you trying to trick me? Don't you understand the righteous aren't tempted by bribes? 24 Do you really believe there's no God? I say: No, you know there's a God; but you corruptly love money more than Him. 25 You've lied before God. You made me the offer: I'll give you these six onties — which are very valuable — when you actually intended to keep them. You just wanted me to deny the true and living God, so you could have a reason to execute me. Now because of your great evil, you'll have your reward.

XIV   26 Then Zeezrom asked him: So you say there's a true and living God? 27 Amulek replied: Yes, there's a true and living God. 28 Next Zeezrom asked: Is there more than one God? 29 He answered: No. 30 Zeezrom asked him: How do you know these things? 31 He said: An angel has revealed them to me. 32 Zeezrom then asked: Who's the one who is to come? Is it the Son of God? 33 He answered: Yes. 34 And Zeezrom asked again: Will He save His people in their sins? And Amulek answered: I tell you that He will not, because it's impossible for Him to deny His word.

XV   35 Then Zeezrom told the people: See that you remember these things, because he says on the one hand there's only one God, but he says on the other hand the Son of God will come but He won't save His people, as if he had authority to command God. 36 Then Amulek rebuked him: You have lied! You say I speak as if I had authority to command God, because I said He won't save His people in their sins. 37 I repeat that He can't save them in their sins, because I can't deny His word. He has said no unclean thing can inherit the kingdom of heaven. So, how can you be saved unless you inherit the kingdom of heaven? Therefore you can't be saved in your sins. 38 Then Zeezrom asked him: Is the Son of God the very Eternal Father? 39 Amulek said to him: Yes, He's called the very Eternal Father of heaven, earth, and everything that's in them. He's the beginning and the end, the first and the last. 40 He'll come into the world to redeem His people. He'll take upon Himself the transgressions of those who believe in His name; these are the ones who will have eternal life, and salvation isn't available to anyone else. 41 So the wicked remain as if no redemption had been made, except for the chains of death being removed. Indeed, the day will come when all will rise from the dead and stand before God and be judged according to their works.

XVI
42 Now there is a mortal death, and Christ's death will release the chains of this mortal death, so everyone will be raised from this temporal death. 43 The spirit and body will be completely restored. Both limb and joint will be restored to their proper form, just like we are now formed; and we'll be brought to stand before God. We'll clearly understand right from wrong and truth from error, like we can now. We'll clearly remember all our guilt. 44 Now this restoration will come to all: old and young, enslaved and free, male and female, wicked and righteous. And not so much as a hair of their heads will be missing; but all things will be restored to their perfect form, the same as now, or in the restored body. Then everyone will stand before the judgment seat of Christ the Son, and God the Father, and the Holy Spirit, which collectively are one Eternal God. Then to be judged based on their works, whether they're good or whether they're evil.

XVII
45 Now I've told you about mortal death and the resurrection of the mortal body. This mortal body will be raised as an immortal body, from that first death back to life. Following that we'll no longer die, our spirits will unite with our bodies and not be separated again. Through this process, the restoration is spiritual and immortal, and we won't decay or die again.

XVIII
46 When Amulek finished saying this, the people were again surprised. Zeezrom began to tremble. That concludes everything I write from Amulek's talk.

Chapter 9

12 Alma saw that Amulek's words silenced Zeezrom. Zeezrom realized Amulek caught him lying and misleading, attempting to destroy him. Because Zeezrom was trembling in fear from his guilt, Alma spoke directly to him, confirming Amulek's words and elaborating and explaining the scriptures beyond what Amulek had covered. 2 What Alma told Zeezrom was overheard by everyone who gathered around them. He said this: 3 Now Zeezrom, your lies and misrepresentations have been exposed. But you haven't just lied to these people, you've also lied to God. He knows all your thoughts and God has revealed your thoughts to us by His Spirit. 4 You see we understand your plan. It was cunning, but follows Satan's pattern, hoping to use a lie to deceive these people, so you could turn them against us. You expected them to scorn us and throw us out. 5 Now this was your adversary's plan, and you've surrendered, letting him control you. Remember that what I tell you, I tell to everyone. 6 I warn all of you that this was a trap of the adversary he has used to control you. He hopes you follow him and get caught in his chains. He wants your everlasting destruction, which results from letting him control you.

II   7 When Alma had said this; Zeezrom began to tremble even more intensely, since he was convinced more and more of God's power. He also realized Alma and Amulek had exposed him. And he was convinced they knew the thoughts and secret intentions of his heart. They knew this because of the spirit of prophecy. 8 And Zeezrom began to ask them sincere questions, so he could learn more about God's kingdom. He asked Alma: What do Amulek's words about the resurrection of the dead mean? How will all rise from the dead, both the just and unjust, and be brought to stand before God to be judged according to their works?

III   9 Alma began to elaborate, saying: Many people are given knowledge of God's mysteries; however, they're placed under a strict command to only discuss that part of His word He allows to be given to mankind, corresponding to their obedience and diligence given to Him. 10 Those who harden their hearts receive less of His word. Those who don't harden their hearts are given a greater part of His word, until they understand God's mysteries. They can be given God's mysteries until everything is fully known. 11 However those who harden their hearts are given less of His word, until they know nothing about His mysteries. Then the accuser captures them and leads them by his will down to destruction. This is what the chains of hell mean.

IV   12 Amulek has spoken plainly about death and being changed from a state of mortality to a state of immortality and brought before God's seat to be judged for our works. 13 Then if we've hardened our hearts and rejected His word so that it isn't part of us, our judgment will be awful. At that point, we'll be condemned. 14 Our words will condemn us, our works will condemn us, our thoughts will condemn us, and we can't be found spotless. In that awful condition, we won't dare to look up to God. Under such circumstances, we would want to be able to command stones and mountains to fall on us and hide us from His presence. 15 But this can't be. We must appear and stand before Him in His glory, power, strength, majesty, and dominion, and acknowledge to our everlasting shame that all His judgments are righteous, that He is righteous in all He's done. He was merciful to mankind, and He has the power to save everyone who believes in His name and shows by their conduct they've actually repented.

V

16 Now there will also be a second death or a spiritual death for anyone whose mortal death happened while in their sins. They will also die spiritually. They die as to everything righteous. 17 That's when their torment will be like a fiery lake of lava, whose flames ascend from eternity to eternity. That's when they'll be chained down to everlasting destruction according to Satan's power and captivity, who will have subjugated them. That's his plan. 18 I tell you at that point they will be as if no redemption had been made, since they can't be redeemed according to God's justice; and they can't die, since there's no more decay.

VI

19 When Alma had finished speaking these words, the people became even more surprised. 20 But Antionah, who was a chief ruler, stepped forward and asked: What is this that you've said, that man would rise from the dead and be changed from this mortal state to an immortal state, so the soul can never die? 21 What does the scripture mean that says God placed cherubim and a sword of fire east of the Garden of Eden so our first parents couldn't enter and eat the fruit of the tree of life and live forever? Obviously it was impossible for them to live forever. 22 Alma replied: This is what I was about to explain. We see that Adam fell by eating the forbidden fruit, according to God's word. We see because of his fall all mankind became lost and fallen. 23 Now if it had been possible for Adam to have then eaten the fruit of the tree of life, there would be no death and God's word would have been empty, making God a liar, since He said: If you eat, you will certainly die. 24 And death has come upon mankind, the death mentioned by Amulek, which is the temporal death. Nevertheless, mankind is given time to repent. Therefore this life has become a probationary state, a time to prepare to come face to face with God. It's a time to prepare for the endless state we talked about, which is after the resurrection of the dead. 25 Now if it weren't for the plan of redemption established at the foundation of creation, there wouldn't be any resurrection of the dead. But there is a plan of redemption that provides the resurrection of the dead we mentioned.

VII

26 If it was possible for our first parents to have returned to eat from the tree of life, they would be miserable forever without any chance to prepare. The plan of redemption would be frustrated, and God would have broken His word. Redemption would have no effect. 27 But it wasn't so. Instead, mankind would die, and after death they face judgment. We told you about that judgment that happens at the end. 28 After God decreed these things would happen to mankind, He

wanted them to know about His plan to redeem them. 29 So He sent angels to explain it to them, who let mankind see His glory. 30 Once they understood, they began to call on His name. So God communicated with mankind to reveal the plan of redemption prepared from the foundation of creation. He revealed it to them based on their faith, repentance, and holy works.

VIII   31 He then gave commandments after they previously broke His first commandments involving temporal things. They had become like the Gods, knowing good from evil, putting themselves in a condition to act on their own choices, whether choosing evil or good. 32 Therefore after they understood the plan of redemption, God commanded them not to be evil, the penalty for it being a second death, an everlasting death as to righteousness. Because the plan of redemption couldn't help such a person, since according to God's decree justice can't be ignored. 33 And so God called on mankind in the name of His Son, as the ordained plan of redemption required. God announced: If you repent and don't harden your hearts, I'll have mercy on you through My Only Begotten Son. 34 Therefore any who repent and don't harden their hearts will qualify for mercy and remission of their sins through My Only Begotten Son and you will enter My rest. 35 But any who harden their hearts and commit iniquity, I swear in My wrath they won't enter My rest. 36 I tell you people that if you harden your hearts, you won't enter the Lord's rest. Indeed, your iniquity will provoke His wrath on you as when He was first provoked. He explained what would happen at both the first and at the last if mankind provoked His judgments. Now your souls face everlasting destruction according to His word, if you provoke the last death like the first death was provoked.

IX   37 Now, my people, since we know these things and since they're true, let's repent and not harden our hearts. We don't want to provoke the Lord our God to bring down His wrath on us by disobeying His second commandments to us. Let's enter God's rest, which according to His word is available for us.

X   13 In addition, my people, I would remind you of the moment the Lord God gave His children these commandments. Remember the Lord God ordained priests according to His Holy Order, which was according to the Order of His Son, to teach the people these things. 2 Such priests were ordained to the Order of His Son in such a way, so that by it the people would recognize how to look forward to His Son for redemption. 3 And this is how they were ordained: they were called and prepared from the foundation of creation according to God's foreknowledge, because of their great faith and good works. In the first place, since they were permitted to choose good or evil, they chose to do good and exercised great faith. As a result, they're called with a holy calling that had been prepared with and according to the planned redemption for those who qualified. 4 Therefore they were and are called to this holy calling because of their faith, while others chose to reject the Spirit of God because of their hard hearts and blind minds, and if it hadn't been for this, they could have had the same status as their brothers. 5 Or to be brief: in the first place they had the same opportunity as the others and this holy calling was available from the beginning of creation for any who chose not to harden their hearts. It was made available by the Only Begotten Son who was prepared to provide the atonement. 6 So they're called by this holy calling and ordained to the High Priesthood of the Holy Order of God to teach His commandments to mankind, so they also could enter His rest. 7 This High Priesthood is according to the Order of His Son, which Order existed from the foundation of creation. In other words, it is without beginning of days or end of years, having been prepared from eternity to all eternity according to His foreknowledge of all things. 8 Now this is how they were ordained: having qualified to receive a holy calling, they were ordained with a holy ordinance which confers upon them the High Priesthood of the Holy Order — which calling, ordinance, and High Priesthood has no beginning or end. 9 So they become high priests forever conforming to the Order of the Son, the Father's Only Begotten, who has no beginning of days or end of years, and who's full of grace, fairness, and truth. And so it is. Amen.

Chapter 10

10 As I said about the Holy Order, or this High Priesthood: many were ordained and became high priests of God. It was because of their great faith, repentance, and righteousness before God, choosing to repent and bring about righteousness rather than perish. 11 Therefore they were called according to this Holy Order and were sanctified, and their clothes were washed white through the Lamb's blood. 12 Now they — after being sanctified by the Holy Ghost, having their clothes made white, being pure and spotless before God — could only look upon sin with abhorrence. And there were many, a very great many, who were enabled to become pure and entered the rest of the Lord their God. 13 Now, my friends, I advise you to humble yourselves before God and show by your conduct that you've really repented, so you can also enter that rest. 14 Humble yourselves like the people in the time of Melchizedek, who was a high priest of this same Order I discussed, who also took upon himself the High Priesthood

eternally. 15 And it was this Melchizedek to whom Abraham paid tithes — yes, even our father Abraham paid one-tenth of all he owned. 16 Now these ordinances were given as a pattern to show the people how to anticipate and recognize the Son of God, since it demonstrated His Order, and in fact was His Order. These ordinances pointed forward to His coming and provided a remission of their sins, so they could enter the Lord's rest.

II   17 Now Melchizedek was ruler and teacher over the land of Salem. And his people had relapsed into iniquity and abominations; indeed, they had all gone astray and were involved in all kinds of wickedness. 18 But Melchizedek was a faithful, godly man ordained to the office of the High Priesthood according to the Holy Order of God, who preached repentance to his people. And they repented. And Melchizedek established peace in the land during his time; so he was called the Prince of Peace, because he was the King of Salem; and he ruled and taught under his father. 19 Now there were many before him and there were many after him, but no one was greater. Therefore he was identified specifically with this Order, more so than others. 20 Now I don't intend to explain this at length; what I've said is enough. The scriptures are readily available to you; if you deliberately misinterpret or distort them, it will be to your own destruction.

III   21 Now when Alma had said these words to them, he stretched out his hand to them and loudly proclaimed: Now is the time to repent, because the day of salvation is approaching. 22 And the Lord's voice, sent through angels, is declaring it to all nations, so they can hear this good news of great joy. Indeed, He's making this announcement of good news to all His people, including those scattered widely around the earth, and therefore we get this news too. 23 It's announced to us in plain terms so we can understand it and so we can't go wrong. We're included even though we're wanderers in a foreign land. We are very blessed since we're included in this good news coming to us here. 24 Right now angels are declaring it to many in our land, and this is to prepare hearts to welcome His message when He comes in His glory. 25 Now we await the joyful news of His arrival, announced to us by angels. Indeed, the time is coming, but we don't know how soon. I wish it would be in my lifetime; but whether it comes sooner or later, I'll rejoice in the news. 26 Angels will reveal the news to righteous and holy men when He arrives. Then the prophecies our fathers recorded about Him will be fulfilled.

IV   27 Now, my people, I plead with all my heart, with painful anxiety, that you listen to my words and abandon your sins and not delay the day you repent. 28 Please humble yourselves before the Lord, call upon

His holy name, and watch and pray continually, so you aren't tempted more than you can resist. Then you can be led by the Holy Spirit, becoming humble, meek, submissive, patient, full of love and all long-suffering. 29 I ask you to have faith in the Lord, and hope to receive eternal life, and have God's love always in your hearts, so you can be lifted up on the last day and enter His rest. 30 And may the Lord acknowledge your repentance, so you don't experience His wrath upon you, and you avoid the chains of hell, so you don't suffer the second death. 31 Alma said many more things to them, words that aren't written in this book.

V   **14** After Alma finished speaking to the people, many of them believed what he said and began to repent and study the scriptures. 2 But most of them wanted to kill Alma and Amulek, since they were angry with Alma because he had spoken bluntly to Zeezrom. They also accused Amulek of lying to them and mocking their law as well as their lawyers and judges. 3 They were also angry with both Alma and Amulek because they testified so openly and directly condemning their wickedness, and they attempted to kill them secretly. 4 But they didn't, and instead they arrested them, tied them up with ropes, and took them in front of the chief judge of their land. 5 People came to testify against them, declaring they had mocked the law, their lawyers and judges, and insulted the people who lived in the land, and claimed they testified there was only one God, who would send His Son among the people, but He wouldn't save them. The people made many other accusations against Alma and Amulek before the chief judge of the land. 6 But Zeezrom was very surprised by what was said. He also realized his lying words had blinded the people's minds. So his soul began to be tormented by the guilt he felt, like the pains of hell.

VI   7 Finally, he shouted to the people: I'm the guilty one, and these men are spotless before God. He began to defend them from that time forward. But the crowd yelled insults at him, saying: Are you also possessed by the devil? Then they spit on him and threw him out of their city, as well as anyone who believed in the words taught by Alma and Amulek. They expelled them and sent men to throw stones at them. 8 Then they gathered the wives and children of those they threw out, and anyone who remained in the city who believed in God's word, and threw them all into a bonfire. They also gathered their records containing the holy scriptures, and threw them into the fire to burn them up.

VII   9 Then they forced Alma and Amulek to go where they were killing the martyrs, to make them watch the people being killed in the fire. 10 When Amulek saw the pains of the women and children dying in the fire, he was shocked and pained. He said to Alma: How can we watch this awful scene? Let's stretch out our hands and use God's power given to us to save them from the flames. 11 But Alma replied: The Spirit restrains me from stretching out my hand. Understand that the Lord receives them up to Himself in glory. He allows them to do this thing — that is, He permits the people to do this to them because of the hardness of their hearts, so that His judgments punishing them in His wrath will be justified and righteous. The blood of the innocent will stand as a witness and testify powerfully against them at the last day. 12 Now Amulek said to Alma: Maybe they'll burn us too. 13 And Alma replied: If that's according to the Lord's will so be it. However, our work isn't finished; so they won't burn us.

VIII   14 When the bodies thrown in the fire were burned up, and also the records thrown in with them, the chief judge of the land came and stood in front of Alma and Amulek while they were tied up, hitting them with his hand on their cheeks and taunting them: After what you've seen, will you preach again to this people that they'll be thrown into a fiery lake that burns like lava? 15 You see you didn't have power to save these people who were thrown into the bonfire, and neither has God saved them, despite them being of your faith. And the judge struck them again on their cheeks and asked: What do you say for yourselves? 16 Now this judge belonged to the order and faith of Nehor, who killed Gideon. 17 And Alma and Amulek didn't answer him. So he struck them again and handed them over to the officers to be thrown in prison. 18 When they had been in prison three days, many lawyers, judges, priests, and teachers — all who were of Nehor's beliefs — entered the prison to confront them. They asked many questions, but they received no answers. 19 And the judge stood in front of them and asked: Why don't you answer their questions? Don't you realize I have the power to send you to be burned alive? And he ordered them to speak, but they said nothing.

IX   20 Then they left and went their way but returned the next day. And the judge hit them again on their cheeks; and many others came forward and hit them as well, asking: Will you stand before the people again and judge them and condemn our law? If you have such great power, why don't you free yourselves? 21 They said many similar things to them in uncontrolled rage, spitting on them and asking: What will it look like when we're damned? 22 They continued saying similar things mocking them like this for many days. They withheld food from them to starve them, and water so they would be thirsty. They also took their clothes from them, so they were naked, and they were tied up with strong ropes and confined in prison.

X   ²³ After they had suffered like this for many days, on the 12th day of the 10th month in the 10th year of the judges' rule over the Nephites, the chief judge over Ammonihah, as well as many of their teachers and lawyers, entered the prison where Alma and Amulek were tied up with ropes. ²⁴ The chief judge stood in front of them and struck them again, saying: If you have God's power, free yourselves from your restraints, then we'll believe what you said about the Lord destroying this people. ²⁵ After all of them came forward and struck them, saying the same thing, from the first to the last, when the last one had insulted them, God's power came upon Alma and Amulek, and they arose and stood on their feet. ²⁶ Then Alma declared: O Lord, how long must we suffer these great afflictions? O Lord, give us strength — according to our faith in Christ — to free ourselves. Then they broke apart the ropes that tied them. When the people saw this, they began to run away, because now they were afraid of being destroyed.

XI   ²⁷ They were so afraid they stumbled and fell to the ground and didn't reach the prison's outer door. The earth shook and quaked violently, and the prison walls began to fall apart to the ground; and the chief judge and the lawyers and priests and teachers who struck Alma and Amulek were killed in the collapse. ²⁸ But Alma and Amulek emerged from the prison unscathed, since the Lord had given them power according to their faith in Christ. They came immediately out of the prison, with no ropes tying them or walls confining them. But the prison had collapsed, and everyone within its walls was killed except for Alma and Amulek, who then walked directly into the city. ²⁹ Now the people heard a loud noise and came running together in large numbers to find out the cause. When they saw Alma and Amulek coming from the prison and the walls had fallen to the ground, they were very frightened and ran away from them, like a goat with her kids fleeing from two lions. And so they bolted from Alma and Amulek.

XII   **15** Then Alma and Amulek were commanded to leave that city. So they left and entered the land of Sidom. There they found the other people who had left Ammonihah, who had been thrown out and stoned because they believed in Alma's words. ² Alma and Amulek told them everything that had happened to their wives and children, and what happened to them, including how they were miraculously set free. ³ Now Zeezrom lay sick at Sidom with a burning fever caused by his great mental distress over his iniquity. He thought Alma and Amulek were dead and had been killed because of his evil. This great sin, and his many other sins, tormented his mind until he suffered in agony, finding no relief. Therefore he developed a scorching fever.

4 When he heard Alma and Amulek were in Sidom, his heart took courage. He immediately sent them a message, asking them to come and see him.

XIII   5 They responded and went immediately to see Zeezrom where he lay. They found him sick on his bed — very weak and depressed with a burning fever. His mind was also deeply troubled by his iniquities. When he saw them, he reached out his hand and begged them to heal him.

XIV   6 Then Alma took his hand and asked him: Do you believe in Christ's power to save? 7 He answered: Yes, I believe all the words you've taught. 8 And Alma said: If you believe in Christ's redemption, you can be healed. 9 And he said: Yes, I believe what you've taught. 10 Then Alma asked the Lord: O Lord our God, have mercy on this man and heal him according to his faith in Christ. 11 When Alma said these words, Zeezrom sprang to his feet and began to walk. This astonished all the people, and the news spread throughout the land of Sidom. 12 Then Alma baptized Zeezrom in the name of the Lord, and from then on he began to preach to the people. 13 Alma established a congregation in Sidom and ordained priests and teachers there, to baptize any who wished to be baptized in the name of the Lord.

XV   14 And there were many people who gathered from the region around Sidom and were baptized. 15 But as for the people in Ammonihah, they continued to be hard-hearted and stubborn. They didn't repent of their sins since they believed what Nehor taught, therefore they rejected any idea of repenting from sins, and they attributed Alma and Amulek's power to the devil.

XVI   16 Amulek left behind all his gold, silver, and valuables in Ammonihah for God's word, and was rejected by those who were once his friends, as well as by his father and family. 17 Then Alma established a congregation at Sidom. He saw the people stopped being proud. They began to humble themselves before God and assemble at their sanctuaries to worship God at the altar. They watched and prayed continually, so they could be saved from Satan, death, and destruction. 18 Once Alma saw all these things, he took Amulek and came over to the land of Zarahemla and took him to his own house and supported him in his needy circumstances, and strengthened him in the Lord. 19 And so ended the 10th year of the judges' rule over the Nephites.

Chapter 11

16 In the 11th year of the judges' rule over the Nephites, up until the fifth day of the second month there had been no wars or conflicts for a number of years and widespread peace had prevailed in the land of Zarahemla. But on the fifth day of the second month a cry of war was heard throughout the land. 2 Lamanite armies entered the outskirts of the land from the wilderness side, coming right into the city of Ammonihah, where they began to kill the people and destroy the city.

II   3 Before the Nephites could raise an adequate army to drive them from the land, they had killed the people in the city of Ammonihah, as well as some in the outskirts of Noah, taking others as prisoners and left into the wilderness.

III   4 The Nephites wanted to recover those who had been taken as prisoners and were now in the wilderness. 5 So the man named Zoram (whose two sons were named Lehi and Aha), was appointed chief captain over the Nephite armies. All three understood Alma was high priest over the congregation and heard he had the spirit of prophecy. Therefore Zoram went to him and asked him to find out where the Lord would direct them to go into the wilderness in search of their people who were Lamanite prisoners. 6 Alma asked the Lord.

IV   Alma then returned and informed them: The Lamanites will cross the Sidon River in the southern wilderness, beyond the outskirts of the land of Manti. You'll find them there, on the east side of the Sidon River. There the Lord will deliver to you all the Lamanite prisoners.

V   7 So Zoram and his sons crossed over to the east side of the Sidon River with their armies and marched beyond the outskirts of Manti into the southern wilderness. 8 They attacked the Lamanite armies, scattering them and driving them into the wilderness. Every one of the Lamanite prisoners was rescued, without a single prisoner killed. They were returned to their own lands. 9 That ended the 11th year of the judges, with the Lamanites removed from the land. Ammonihah's people were destroyed, every single one, and their great city which they claimed was too strong for God to destroy was gone. 10 In one day it was left deserted and ruined, and dogs and wild animals from the wilderness ate their corpses. 11 However, after many days their dead remains were piled up on the ground and covered with a thin layer of earth. The stench from it was so bad people didn't go in to reoccupy Ammonihah for many years. It was called Desolation of Nehors, because those who had been killed practiced Nehor's beliefs; and their lands remained uninhabited. 12 The Lamanites didn't attack the Nephites again until the 14th year of the judges' rule over the Nephites. So the Nephites enjoyed continuous peace throughout the land for three years.

VI   13 Alma and Amulek went about preaching repentance to the people in their temples and sanctuaries, and in their synagogues, which were built based on Jewish custom. 14 They continually shared God's word with any and all who would listen. 15 So Alma and Amulek continued preaching accompanied by many more chosen for the work. They taught in temples and synagogues throughout the land. And congregations were established widely throughout the land and in the surrounding areas where there were Nephites.

VII   16 The Spirit of the Lord was then equally and abundantly influencing everyone, preparing their minds and hearts to receive His message when He came. 17 They hoped to help the people avoid destruction by preaching against hard hearts and disbelief, to prepare them to joyfully accept the Lord's message, enter His rest, and be grafted as a branch into the true vine.

VIII   18 Now the priests denounced all lying, deceiving, jealousy, arguing, malicious and abusive behavior, theft, robbery, pillage, murder, committing adultery, and all kinds of lustfulness and indecent behavior, warning these things must not go on among them. 19 They explained the Son of God was coming soon. They described His suffering, death, and resulting resurrection of the dead. 20 Many asked about where the Son of God would come. They were taught He would appear to them after His resurrection, and this made the people joyful. 21 When the 14th year of the judges' rule over the Nephites ended, the congregation had been established throughout the land, the accuser defeated, God's word was being preached in its purest form, and the Lord was pouring out His blessings on the people.

Chapter 12

An account of Mosiah's sons, who rejected their rights to the kingdom for God's word and went up to the land of Nephi to preach to the Lamanites. Their times of suffering and their liberation, according to Alma's record. [Comprising chapters 12 to 14 RE.]

17 As Alma was traveling from Gideon southward to Manti, to his surprise he came upon Mosiah's sons on their way to Zarahemla. 2 Now these sons of Mosiah were with Alma when the angel first appeared to him. So Alma was overjoyed at seeing his friends again. They were still his faithful brothers in the Lord and that added to his joy. Their understanding of the truth had expanded greatly. They had grown from their experiences and from serious study of the scriptures. 3 But this isn't all; they also faithfully prayed and fasted, and as a result, they had the spirit of prophecy and revelation. When they taught, they taught with the power and authority of God. 4 They had been teaching God's word for 14 years among the Lamanites with a lot of success in bringing many of them to accept the truth. Indeed, by the power of their words many knelt in prayer before God, asking in His name for their sins to be forgiven. 5 They had encountered many afflictions during their missionary work. They suffered a great deal, both in body and mind, including hunger, thirst, fatigue, and many spiritual challenges. 6 This is the account of their journey: In the first year of the judges' rule, after refusing to be kings as their father and the people wanted, and saying goodbye to their father Mosiah, 7 they left Zarahemla. They brought their swords, spears, bows, arrows, and slings, to provide food while in the wilderness. 8 They went into the wilderness with a few chosen companions, to go to the land of Nephi and preach to the Lamanites.

II   9 They traveled for many days in the wilderness. To have a portion of the Spirit of the Lord accompany them, they fasted and prayed often, asking the Lord to let them be instruments in God's hands to persuade their Lamanite brothers and sisters to accept the truth, if at all possible. They hoped they would understand their ancestors' traditions were false and corrupt.

III   10 The Spirit of the Lord visited and told them: Take comfort. (And that comforted them to hear it.) 11 The Lord also said: Go to the Lamanites, your brothers and sisters, and convey My word. You must be patient, long-suffering, and endure afflictions, to set a good example for them. I'll make you messengers in My hands to save many souls. 12 Then Mosiah's sons and those with them resolved in their hearts to go to the Lamanites to teach them God's word.

IV   13 When they arrived at the outskirts of the Lamanites' land, each of them went their separate way, trusting in the Lord they would meet again when their harvest ended. They believed the work ahead of them was important, 14 and it was certainly tremendous, because they committed to preach God's word to a wild, hardened, savage people who took pleasure in murdering, robbing, and plundering the Nephites. Lamanite hearts were set on gold, silver, precious stones, and material possessions which they attempted to acquire through murder and plunder rather than working with their own hands for them. 15 They were a very lazy people, and many of them worshiped idols. God's curse had fallen upon them because of their ancestors' traditions, but despite that, if they would repent, the promises of the Lord were still offered to them. 16 This was the reason Mosiah's sons decided they needed to do the work to try to get them to repent. They hoped to let them understand the plan of redemption. 17 Then they separated and went their separate ways, each going individually, as they were led by the word and power of God directing them.

V   18 Their leader, Ammon, blessed them each for their missionary effort, as inspired by God, before departing. Then they went their separate ways. 19 Ammon went to the land of Ishmael, the land named for Ishmael's sons, who also became Lamanites. 20 As Ammon entered the land of Ishmael, the Lamanites took him and tied him up, since it was their practice to tie up all the Nephites who fell into their hands and bring them to the king. It was left up to the king whether to kill them, enslave them, imprison them, or expel them from his land, as he decided. 21 And so Ammon was brought to the king who was over the land of Ishmael — named Lamoni, a descendant of Ishmael. 22 The king asked Ammon if he wanted to live among his people, the Lamanites. 23 Ammon answered him: Yes, I want to live among your people for a while, maybe for the rest of my life.

VI   24 And king Lamoni was impressed with Ammon and had his restraints removed. He offered Ammon one of his daughters as a wife. 25 But Ammon said to him: No, but I only want to be your servant. So Ammon became one of king Lamoni's servants. He was sent to a group of servants assigned to watch Lamoni's flocks. 26 After he had served for three days, he went with the Lamanite servants taking the flocks to the waters of Sebus, a watering place. The Lamanites regularly took their flocks there to get water. 27 As Ammon and the king's servants were driving their flocks to that watering place, another group of Lamanites there watering flocks, blocked and scattered the flocks brought by Ammon and the king's servants. They scattered them in every direction.

VII   28 Then the king's servants began to complain, saying: Now the king will kill us just as he's killed our companions, because their flocks were scattered due to the wickedness of these men. They began to lament, saying: Our flocks are already scattered! 29 They were afraid of being killed, and wept. When Ammon saw this, he was encouraged and saw an opportunity. He said to himself: I'll make a show to my fellow servants of the power of God within me, by restoring these flocks for the king. That will impress my companions that I'm trustworthy, so they will believe me. 30 This is what occurred to Ammon as he saw the distress of those he regarded as his brothers.

VIII   31 He encouraged them, saying: My brothers, be of good cheer. Let's go and search for the flocks; we'll gather them and bring them back to the watering place. We'll save the flocks for the king and he won't kill us.

IX
32 So they went searching for the flocks; they followed Ammon and quickly located, surrounded, and herded the king's flocks back to the watering place, as Ammon had directed. 33 But those men returned to scatter the flocks again. Ammon said to his companions: Protect the flocks so they don't scatter, and I'll go and confront these men who are running them off. 34 So they did as Ammon had directed them. And he went out to fight them at the waters of Sebus, and there were many of them. 35 Therefore they weren't afraid of Ammon, since they thought that one of their men could easily kill him. They didn't know that the Lord had promised Mosiah that He would protect his sons from them; but they didn't know anything about the Lord, either. These men thought it fun to destroy even their fellow Lamanites — this is why they went out and scattered the king's flocks.

X
36 But Ammon stood his ground and began to throw stones at them with deadly accuracy using his sling. In this way, he killed a few of them — so many, in fact, that they were surprised at his ability. This made them angry because their companions were killed, and they wanted revenge and to kill him. But they were unable to hit him with their stones, and so they attacked him with clubs to kill him. 37 But Ammon, with his sword, cut off the arm of every man who lifted his club to strike him. He countered their blows by striking their arms with the edge of his sword; eventually, even though they outnumbered him, they became terrified and ran away. Despite their number, his skill and strength sent them running away in fear. 38 Now six of them were killed by his sling, but their leader was the only one killed by his sword. However, he had severed every arm raised against him, and there were many of them. 39 When he had chased them far away, he returned. After watering their flocks, they returned them to the king's pasture and then went to see the king, carrying the arms of those who had tried to kill Ammon, which he had cut off with his sword. They were carried in to the king as evidence of what was done.

XI
18 Then king Lamoni had his servants explain everything they had seen happen. 2 When they had all testified of what they had seen, and when the king had been informed of Ammon's faithfulness in preserving his flocks and of his great power in fighting those who tried to kill him, the king was astonished and said: This must be more than a man. He has to be the Great Spirit who punishes this people because of their murders. 3 And they replied to the king: Whether he's the Great Spirit or a man, we don't know. But we do know at least this much, that he can't be killed by the king's enemies, and they can't scatter the king's flocks either, when he's with us, because of his skill and great strength. So we know he's a friend of the king. Now, your

majesty, we don't believe that a man has such great power, since we know he can't be killed. 4 When the king heard these words, he said to them: Now I'm certain he's the Great Spirit. He's come down at this time to preserve your lives, so I wouldn't kill you like I did your fellow servants. This is the Great Spirit whom our fathers have spoken about. 5 Now this was the tradition Lamoni was taught by his father, that there was a Great Spirit; yet despite believing in a Great Spirit, they thought that whatever they did was right. However, Lamoni began to be overwhelmed with fear that he might have done wrong by killing his servants. 6 He had killed many of them because their fellow Lamanites had scattered their flocks at the watering place and he had them executed for failing to protect the flocks. 7 Now it was typical of these Lamanites to plunder flocks by waiting at the waters of Sebus to attack, scatter the flocks, raid, and remove them to their own land.

XII   8 King Lamoni asked his servants: Where is this man that has such great power? 9 And they replied: He's right now feeding your horses. Now the king had commanded his servants — before they watered their flocks — to prepare his horses and carriages and transport him to the land of Nephi. He planned to attend a great feast organized in the land of Nephi by Lamoni's father, the king over all the lands. 10 When king Lamoni heard that Ammon was preparing his horses and carriages, he was more surprised at Ammon's faithfulness. He said: Certainly no servant of mine has been as faithful as this man — he remembers all my commands and carries them out. 11 Now I know for certain this is the Great Spirit. I would ask him to come and see me, but I don't dare.

XIII   12 When Ammon had prepared the horses and carriages for the king and his servants, he went to see the king. He saw the king's countenance had changed; so he was about to turn around and depart. 13 But one of the king's servants said to him: Rabbanah, meaning powerful or great king — considering their kings to be powerful — and so he said to him: Rabbanah, the king would like you to stay. 14 So Ammon turned to face the king and asked him: What would you like me to do for you, your majesty? And the king didn't answer him for an hour, according to their time, because he didn't know what to say to him. 15 And Ammon asked him again: What do you wish me to do? But the king didn't answer him.

XIV   16 Because Ammon was filled with the Spirit of God, he discerned the king's thoughts and said to him: Is it because you've heard I defended your servants and flocks and killed seven of their fellow Lamanites with the sling and sword and cut off the arms of others in order to defend your flocks and servants? Is this what's causing your surprise? ¹⁷ I ask you: Why are you so surprised? I'm a man and your servant. So I'll do whatever you wish, if it's right. ¹⁸ Now when the king heard this, he was again surprised, seeing Ammon could discern his thoughts. Despite this, king Lamoni spoke up and asked him: Who are you? Are you that Great Spirit who knows all things? ¹⁹ Ammon answered: I'm not. ²⁰ Then the king said: How can you read my thoughts? Please speak freely and tell me about these things. Also, tell me how you were able to kill and cut off the arms of the people who raided my flocks. ²¹ If you explain these things, I'll give you whatever you ask. If it were needed, I would guard you with my armies. But I know you're more powerful than all of them. Still, whatever you ask of me, I'll grant it to you. ²² Since Ammon was wise yet harmless, he said to Lamoni: Will you listen to what I have to say if I explain the power enabling me to do these things? This is all I ask of you. ²³ And the king answered: Yes, I'll believe everything you say. And so Ammon cleverly caught the king's attention.

XV   ²⁴ And Ammon began to speak to him boldly and asked: Do you believe there's a God? ²⁵ And he answered: I don't know what that means. ²⁶ Then Ammon asked: Do you believe there's a Great Spirit? ²⁷ And he answered: Yes. ²⁸ And Ammon said: That's God. And Ammon asked him again: Do you believe this Great Spirit, who is God, created everything that's in heaven and on the earth? ²⁹ And he replied: Yes, I believe He created everything on the earth. But I know nothing about the heavens. ³⁰ Then Ammon said to him: The heavens are the place where God and His holy angels live. ³¹ And king Lamoni asked: Is it above the earth? ³² And Ammon replied: Yes, and He looks and sees all mankind; and He knows the thoughts and intents of their hearts, because they were all created by His hand from the beginning. ³³ And king Lamoni said: I believe everything you've said. Have you been sent from God? ³⁴ Ammon replied: I'm a man — and mankind, in the beginning, was created according to the image of God — and I've been called by His Holy Spirit to teach these things to this people, so they can learn about what's right and true. ³⁵ And a portion of that Spirit dwells within me, giving me knowledge and power based upon my hope and faith in God.

XVI   ³⁶ Now after Ammon said this, he started with the creation of the world and Adam, telling him all about the Fall of mankind. He described and explained the history and recited from the holy scriptures, quoting the prophets through the time when their father Lehi left Jerusalem. ³⁷ He also gave them an account — speaking to the king and his servants — of all the traveling their ancestors did in the wilderness, and of all the times they suffered from hunger and thirst, and of their hardships, etc. ³⁸ And he included the times that Laman, Lemuel, and Ishmael's sons rebelled; indeed, he told them about all their acts of rebellion. And he added information from the records and scriptures written from the time Lehi left Jerusalem down to the present time. ³⁹ Furthermore, he set out the plan of redemption that was prepared from the foundation of creation. He also told them about Christ's coming and about all the Lord's works.

XVII   ⁴⁰ After he had told all these things to the king, the king believed everything he said. ⁴¹ And he began to pray to the Lord, saying: O Lord, have mercy! According to the abundant mercy you've shown the Nephites, show it to me and my people! ⁴² When he had said this, he collapsed as if he were dead. ⁴³ Then his servants took him and carried him to his wife and placed him on a bed. He lay there, unconscious, for two days and nights. His wife, sons, and daughters mourned over him thinking he was dead, following the customs of the Lamanites, deeply grieving his loss.

XVIII   **19** After two days and nights, they were about to take his body and place it in a tomb made for burying their dead. ² Now the queen had heard of Ammon's reputation, so she sent him a message and asked him to visit her. ³ And Ammon did as he was commanded and went to see the queen and asked what she wanted. ⁴ She said: My husband's servants have told me that you're a prophet of a holy God and you have power to do many miracles in His name. ⁵ If this is so, I want you to go and see my husband — he's been on his bed for two days and nights. Some say he isn't dead, but others say that he is, and you can smell his decay and he should be placed in a tomb. But I personally don't think he smells of decay.

XIX   ⁶ Now this was what Ammon wanted, since he knew king Lamoni was under God's power. Ammon knew, because the dark veil of unbelief had been driven from the king's mind, that the light that lit up his mind — the light of God's glory and a marvelous light of His goodness — that this light had poured such joy into his soul, with the cloud of darkness dispersed, that the light of everlasting life was lit up in his soul. He knew this had overcome his physical body and he was carried away in God. ⁷ Because of this, what the queen asked of him was exactly what he had hoped. Therefore he went to see the king as the queen asked. And he saw the king and he knew he wasn't dead. ⁸ Then he said to the queen: He isn't dead, he is sleeping in God. Tomorrow he'll rise again, so don't bury him. ⁹ Then Ammon asked her: Do you believe this? She replied: I haven't received any information beyond what you've told me and what our servants have told me. Nevertheless, I believe it will happen as you've said. ¹⁰ And

Ammon said to her: Blessed are you because of your great faith. Indeed, I tell you such great faith isn't present among all the Nephites.

XX 11 And she watched over her husband's bed from then until the next day, until the time Ammon said he would arise. 12 And he did get up, just as Ammon had promised! As he stood up, he stretched out his hand to the queen and said: Blessed is the name of God! And blessed are you! 13 Just as sure as you're alive, I've seen my Redeemer. He'll come and be born of a woman, and He'll redeem everyone who believes in His name. When he had said these words, he was completely overcome and he dropped back down again with joy. And the queen dropped down as well, since she was also overpowered by the Spirit. 14 Then Ammon, seeing the Spirit of the Lord poured out according to his prayers on the Lamanites, now his fellow brothers and sisters — who before caused so much sorrow among the Nephites, or among all God's people, because of their iniquities and traditions — he fell to his knees and began to pour out his soul in prayer and thanksgiving to God for what He had done for his friends. Then he was overpowered with joy as well. And so all three of them had dropped to the ground. 15 When the king's servants saw they had fallen, they also began to pray to God, as the fear of the Lord had come over them as well. They were the ones who had stood before the king, testifying to him about Ammon's great power.

XXI 16 And they called on the Lord's name earnestly, until they had all collapsed onto the ground, except for one Lamanite woman named Abish. Even though she had been previously converted to the Lord for many years, because of a remarkable vision of her father (which had brought about her conversion), 17 she never told anyone. So when she saw Lamoni's servants had all fallen to the ground, and her mistress the queen and the king as well, and that Ammon was lying flat on the ground, she knew it was God's power. And thinking this opportunity — by telling the people what had happened to them — that their seeing this scene would cause them to believe in God's power, she ran from house to house telling the people. 18 And they began to gather at the king's house, so many that a crowd formed.

XXII And they were astonished to see the king and the queen and their servants lying on the ground; they all lay there as though they were dead. And they also saw Ammon — a Nephite. 19 Now the people began to complain, some saying a great evil had come upon them — or upon the king and his house — because he had allowed this Nephite to remain in the land. 20 But others reprimanded them, saying: The king has brought this evil upon his house because he killed his servants whose flocks had been scattered at the waters of Sebus.

21 They were also rebuked by those men who had been at the waters of Sebus and who had scattered the king's flocks, since they were angry with Ammon because of how many of their companions he had killed there while defending the king's flocks. 22 Now one of them, whose brother had been killed by Ammon's sword, was very angry with Ammon. So he drew his sword and came forward intending to kill Ammon. But as he lifted his sword to strike him, he was struck dead. 23 That showed that Ammon couldn't be killed, for the Lord had promised Mosiah his father: I'll spare him, and it will be so according to your faith. Therefore Mosiah entrusted him to the Lord.

XXIII   24 When the crowd saw the man who had lifted his sword to kill Ammon was struck dead, they were all frightened. They didn't dare touch him with their hands or touch any of the others lying there. And they were again astonished and asked each other what could have caused this great power or what all these things could mean.

XXIV   25 And there were many among them who said that Ammon was the Great Spirit. Others said he was sent by the Great Spirit. 26 But others reprimanded all of them, saying he was a monster who had been sent from the Nephites to torment them. 27 And there were some who said Ammon was sent by the Great Spirit to afflict them because of their iniquities and it was the Great Spirit who had always looked after the Nephites, who had always rescued them. And they said it was this Great Spirit who had killed so many of their people the Lamanites. 28 And their arguments grew very intense. While they were arguing with each other like this, the female servant, who had caused the crowd to gather, arrived. When she saw the crowd arguing, she was very sad and troubled, so much so that she started crying.

XXV   29 She went and took the queen by the hand, hoping to lift her up from the ground. As soon as she touched her hand, the queen got up and stood on her feet and shouted: O blessed Jesus, who's saved me from an awful hell! O blessed God, have mercy on this people! 30 When she had said this, she clapped her hands, since she was filled with joy, and said things the people didn't understand. When she finished, she took king Lamoni by the hand, and he got up and stood on his feet. 31 Seeing his people arguing, he immediately intervened and began to reprimand them and teach them the things he learned from Ammon. And everyone who paid attention to what he said believed and was converted to the Lord. 32 But a lot of them refused to listen; therefore they went on their way.

XXVI   33 When Ammon got up, he also ministered to them, and all of Lamoni's servants did as well. They all declared the very same thing to the people, that their hearts had been changed and they had no more desire to do evil. 34 And many of them declared to everyone that they had seen angels and had talked with them. And so they had told them about things of God and His righteousness. 35 And there were many who believed what they said. And all those who believed were baptized, and they became a righteous people; and they established a congregation among them. 36 And so the Lord's work began among the Lamanites; this was how the Lord began to pour out His Spirit upon them. And we see that He welcomes everyone who will repent and believe in His name.

XXVII   **20** When they had established a congregation in that land, king Lamoni wanted Ammon to go with him to the land of Nephi, so he could introduce him to his father. 2 The Lord's voice came to Ammon, saying: You must not go up to the land of Nephi, because the king there will try to take away your life; but you must go to Middoni, because your brother Aaron, and Muloki and Ammah are in prison there.

XXVIII   3 Now when Ammon had heard this, he said to Lamoni: My brother and his companions are in prison at Middoni; I will go there to free them. 4 Now Lamoni said to Ammon: I know you can do all things with the Lord's strength. But I'll go with you to Middoni, because the king of the land of Middoni, whose name is Antiomno, is a friend of mine. Therefore I will go there to persuade the king and he'll release your brother and his companions from prison. Then Lamoni asked him: Who told you your brother and his companions were in prison? 5 And Ammon replied: No one has told me except for God; He said to me: Go and free your brother and his companions; they're in prison in the land of Middoni. 6 When Lamoni had heard this, he had his servants prepare his horses and carriages. 7 Then he said to Ammon: Come, I'll go with you down to Middoni, and there I'll plead with the king to release your brother and his companions from prison.

XXIX   8 As Ammon and Lamoni were traveling there, they met Lamoni's father, who was king over the whole land. 9 Lamoni's father asked him: Why didn't you come to the feast on that great day when I made a feast for my sons and for my people? 10 He also asked: Where are you going with this Nephite, who's one of the descendants of a liar? 11 Lamoni answered him, explaining where he was going, not wanting to offend him. 12 He also told him exactly why he had stayed in his own kingdom, why he hadn't gone to see his father at the feast he had prepared. 13 When Lamoni had explained things to him, to his surprise his father got angry with him and said: Lamoni, you're traveling to free these Nephites, who are the descendants of a liar who robbed our ancestors. Now his children have also come among us so they can deceive us, by their cleverness and lies, so they can rob us once more of our property. 14 Then Lamoni's father commanded him to kill Ammon with the sword. He further commanded him not to go to Middoni, but to return with him to the land of Ishmael. 15 But Lamoni responded: I won't kill Ammon, and I won't return to the land of Ishmael either; on the contrary, I'm going to Middoni so I can release Ammon's brother and his companions, because I know they're righteous men and holy prophets of the true God.

XXX   16 When his father heard these words, he got angry and drew his sword so he could strike him to the ground. 17 But Ammon came forward and said to him: Do not kill your son. Still, it would be better for him to die than you, because he has repented of his sins; but if you were to die at this time in your anger, your soul couldn't be saved. 18 Besides, it would be right for you to show him mercy. Because if you were to kill your son, his blood would cry from the ground to the Lord who is God for vengeance to come upon you, since he's an innocent man, and perhaps you would lose your soul. 19 Now when Ammon said this to him, he replied: I know if I were to kill my son I would shed innocent blood, since you're the one who's tried to destroy him. 20 And he reached out his hand to kill Ammon, but Ammon deflected his blows and stabbed his arm so that he couldn't use it. 21 Now when the king saw Ammon could kill him, he began begging Ammon to spare his life. 22 But Ammon raised his sword and said to him: I'll strike you down unless you grant my request that my companions be released from prison. 23 Then, because the king was afraid he would lose his life, he said: If you're willing to spare me, I'll grant you whatever you ask, even up to half the kingdom.

XXXI   24 When Ammon saw that he had influenced the old king according to his desire, he said to him: If you're willing to agree to my companions being released from prison, and for Lamoni to keep his kingdom, and to stop being angry with him but let him act freely on his beliefs, then I'll spare you; otherwise, I'll strike you to the ground. 25 When Ammon had said these words, the king began to rejoice because his life was spared. 26 When he saw Ammon had no desire to kill him, and when he saw the great love he had for his son Lamoni, he was very surprised and said: Because this is all that you ask — for me to free your companions and to allow my son Lamoni to keep his kingdom — I'll grant your wish for my son to retain his kingdom from this time and forever, and I won't rule over him anymore. 27 I'll also grant your wish for your companions to be released from prison. And you and your companions are permitted to visit me in my kingdom,

because I'll be eager to see you. The king said this because he was
amazed by what he and his son Lamoni had said, therefore he wanted
to learn more about those things.

XXXII   28 Then Ammon and Lamoni continued traveling toward the land
of Middoni. And Lamoni gained the approval of the king of the land;
therefore Ammon's companions were freed from prison. 29 When
Ammon saw them in person, he was heartbroken — they were naked
and their skin was rubbed raw because they had been tied up with
strong ropes. They had also been starved, left thirsty, and been abused.
Yet they were patient in all their suffering. 30 As it happened, it was
their lot to have fallen into the hands of a more hardened and
stubborn people. Therefore they refused to listen to them, and they
had them thrown out, beaten, and driven from house to house and
from place to place, up until they had arrived at Middoni. There they
were arrested and thrown in prison and tied up with strong ropes and
imprisoned for many days, until they were rescued by Lamoni and
Ammon.

Chapter 13

An account of the preaching of Aaron, Muloki, and their companions to the
Lamanites. [Comprising chapters 13 and 14 RE.]

21 When Ammon and his companions split up in the border
region of the land of the Lamanites, Aaron traveled toward the place
called by the Lamanites Jerusalem, named after the place of their
ancestors' birth. It was adjoining the land of Mormon. 2 It was the
Lamanites, Amlicites, and the people of Amulon who built the city
called Jerusalem. 3 As for the Lamanites, they were quite hard-hearted
and set in their ways, but the Amlicites and the Amulonites were worse
and they led the Lamanites to harden their hearts, become
increasingly wicked, and practice abominations.

II   4 When Aaron arrived at the city of Jerusalem, he first began to
preach to the Amlicites. He started preaching in the synagogues they
had built for use by the followers of Nehor. Many of the Amlicites and
the Amulonites followed the teaching of Nehor and practiced it as a
religion. 5 Therefore when Aaron entered one of their synagogues to
preach to the people, and as he was speaking to them, an Amlicite
came forward confronting him by asking: What's this that you've
testified about? Have you seen an angel? Why don't angels appear to
us? Aren't we as good as your people? 6 You also say: Unless we repent,
we'll be doomed. How do you know the thoughts and intents of our
hearts? How do you know there are reasons why we should repent?

How do you know we aren't a righteous people? We've built sanctuaries, and we gather to worship God. We believe that God will save everyone.

III   7 Then Aaron asked him: Do you believe that the Son of God will come to redeem mankind from their sins? 8 And the man responded to him: We don't believe you know any such thing. We don't believe in these foolish traditions. We don't believe you know of future events, and we don't believe your ancestors or our ancestors knew about the things they spoke of either, about things to happen in the future.

IV   9 Now Aaron began to explain and interpret the scriptures for them regarding the Messiah's coming and about the resurrection of the dead and that there couldn't be any redemption for mankind unless it came about through the death and suffering of the Messiah and the atonement of His blood. 10 As he began to explain these things to them, they got angry with him and started to ridicule him; and they ignored the words he taught. 11 Therefore when he realized they ignored him, he left the synagogue and came over to a village called Ani-Anti. There he encountered Muloki actively preaching the word to them, and Ammah and his companions as well; and they debated the message of the gospel with as many of them as listened. 12 They realized the people intended to reject the message; so they left and came over into the land of Middoni. There they preached to many, but only a few of them believed what they taught. 13 Nonetheless, Aaron and some of his companions were arrested and thrown in prison; and the rest escaped from Middoni and fled to nearby areas. 14 Those who were thrown in prison endured many hardships; and they were freed by Lamoni and Ammon, who fed and clothed them. 15 Then they went out again to preach the word. This was how they were freed from prison the first time, and what they had suffered. 16 And they went as they were led by the Spirit of the Lord, preaching God's word in every synagogue of the Amlicites, or in every assembly of the Lamanites they were allowed to enter.

V   17 And the Lord began to bless them so much that they persuaded many to accept the truth. Many of them were convinced of their sins and that the traditions they believed were false.

VI   18 Then Ammon and Lamoni left the land of Middoni and returned to the land of Ishmael, which was their homeland. 19 And king Lamoni wouldn't permit Ammon to serve or be his servant. 20 But he had synagogues built in the land of Ishmael. And he had his people — or the people he ruled — meet together. 21 He told them how happy he was with them, and he taught them many things. He also declared to them that while he ruled, they would be free people, independent of the king, his father, because his father had given him the independent right to rule the people in the land of Ishmael and the surrounding area. 22 He announced to them that they were free to worship the Lord who is God as they wished, in any part of the land under the control of king Lamoni. 23 Ammon also preached to king Lamoni's people. He taught them the requirements for righteousness. And he diligently encouraged them daily; and they paid close attention to his message, and were eagerly devoted to keeping God's commandments. **22** While Ammon was busy teaching Lamoni's people, we turn to the account of Aaron and his other companions. After leaving Middoni, he was led by the Spirit to the land of Nephi, right to the house of the king who was over the whole land other than the land of Ishmael; and he was Lamoni's father.

VII   2 Aaron and his companions went to see him at the king's palace, bowed before the king, and said to him: Your majesty, we are Ammon's companions whom you've freed from prison. 3 And now, O king, if you will spare our lives, we will be your servants. And the king said to them: Stand up, for you are safe here. And I won't allow you to be my servants, but I'll insist that you minister to me. Indeed, I've been bothered because of the generosity and impressive words of your brother Ammon. I want to know why he hasn't come up from Middoni with you. 4 Aaron answered the king: The Spirit of the Lord has led him another way; he's gone to the land of Ishmael to teach Lamoni's people. 5 Then the king said: How do you explain the Spirit of the Lord? This is what troubles me. 6 And also, explain what Ammon said — if you repent, you will be saved; and if you don't repent, you will be rejected on the last day. 7 Then Aaron replied: Do you believe there's a God? And the king said: I know that the Amlicites say there's a God. And I've allowed them to build sanctuaries, so they could gather to worship Him. And if you say there's a God, I'll believe.

VIII   8 Now when Aaron heard this, his heart began to rejoice and he said: As surely as you live, your majesty, there is a God. 9 And the king said: Is God that Great Spirit who brought our ancestors out of the land of Jerusalem? 10 And Aaron replied: Yes, He is that Great Spirit. And He created all things, both in heaven and on earth. Do you believe this? 11 And he said: Yes, I believe that the Great Spirit created all things. And I want you to clarify for me all these things, and I'll trust your words.

IX   12 When Aaron saw the king was willing to believe his words, he began at the creation of Adam, reading the scriptures to the king, how God created mankind in His own image and likeness, and that God gave them commandments, and because of transgression, mankind had fallen. 13 Aaron explained the scriptures to him, from the creation of Adam, bringing to his attention the Fall of mankind and their mortal state, and also the plan of redemption that was prepared from the foundation of creation through the Messiah, for anyone who would believe in His name. 14 And since mankind had fallen, they weren't entitled to a reward based on anything they might do; but Christ's suffering and death atone for their sins through faith, repentance, etc., and He breaks the chains of death, so the grave will have no victory and so the bitterness of death will be replaced by the hope of glory. Aaron covered all these things in teaching the king. 15 After Aaron had explained these things to him, the king asked: What must I do so I can have this eternal life that you've spoken about? Indeed, what must I do so I can be born of God, so I can have this wicked spirit rooted out of my heart and receive His Spirit, so I can be filled with joy, so I won't be rejected on the last day? He said: I would give up all that I own; indeed, I'll renounce my kingdom if I can receive this great joy. 16 But Aaron said to him: If this is what you want, if you're willing to bow down to God — if you repent of all your sins and are willing to bow down to God and call on His name in faith, believing He'll respond to you, then you'll receive the hope that you long for.

X   17 When Aaron had said this, the king bowed down to the Lord on his knees, even lying face down on the ground, and prayed earnestly, saying: 18 O God, Aaron has told me that there is a God. And if there is a God and if you are God, will you make yourself known to me? I'll give up all my sins so I can know you and be raised from the dead and be saved on the last day. Now when the king had said these words, he passed out, and he looked like he was dead.

XI   19 His servants ran and told the queen everything that had happened to the king, and she went to see him. When she saw him lying there looking like he was dead, and Aaron and his companions on their feet, looking like they had killed him, she got angry and commanded her servants — or the king's servants — to take them and execute them. 20 But the servants had seen what caused the king to pass out. Therefore they didn't dare lay their hands on Aaron and his companions; and they begged the queen, saying: Why do you command us to kill these men when one of them is more powerful than all of us? Therefore we will die, not them. 21 When the queen saw the servants were afraid, she too became very afraid that something terrible might happen to her. So she commanded her servants to go call the people, and they could kill Aaron and his companions.

XII   22 When Aaron witnessed what the queen had decided, and knowing the hardness of the hearts of the people, he was afraid a crowd would gather and there would be a serious confrontation with them. So he put out his hand and helped the king up from the ground saying to him: Stand up! And he stood on his feet, regaining his strength. 23 Now this was done in the presence of the queen and many of his servants. When they saw it, they were amazed and became afraid. And the king stood up and began to testify to them, and he taught them so that his whole household was converted to the Lord. 24 Now a crowd gathered because of the queen's command, and many whispered complaints circulated between them because of Aaron and his companions. 25 But the king interrupted them and testified to them. He reconciled his people with Aaron and those with him.

XIII   26 When the king saw the people were reconciled, he had Aaron and his companions come and preach to them from the middle of the crowd. 27 Then the king sent a proclamation throughout the land, among everyone and all the surrounding areas, which extended from sea borders, east to the west, and divided from the land of Zarahemla by a narrow corridor of wilderness located there. It included everywhere by the seashore and the wilderness areas which were to the north by the land of Zarahemla to the area by the borders of Manti, by the headwaters of the Sidon River, running from the east toward the west; which was how the Lamanites and the Nephites were divided. 28 Now the less civilized part of the Lamanites lived in the wilderness, in tents. They occupied the western wilderness of the land of Nephi, and the western part of the land of Zarahemla by the border of the seashore, and to the west in the land of Nephi in the place their ancestors first landed and lived, bordering the seashore. 29 There were also many Lamanites to the east by the seashore where the Nephites had driven them. And so the Nephites were nearly surrounded by the Lamanites. Nevertheless, the Nephites had taken all the northern parts of the land bordering on the wilderness at the headwaters of the Sidon River, from the east to the west, around on the northern wilderness side, until they came to the land they called Bountiful. 30 And it was next to the land they called Desolation, since it was so far northward it came into the land that had been filled with people who were destroyed. We mentioned their bones were discovered by Zarahemla's people, at the place they first landed. 31 They spread from there up to the southern wilderness. The land to the north was called Desolation; and the land to the south was called Bountiful, since it was a wild region filled with all kinds of wild animals of every variety, some of which roamed from the north looking for food. ³² Now it was only the distance of a day and a half's travel for a Nephite on the line between the land of Bountiful and the land of Desolation, from the east to the western sea; accordingly, the land of Nephi and the land of Zarahemla were nearly surrounded by water, with a small neck of land running between the land to the north and the land to the south.

XIV   ³³ And the Nephites had inhabited the land of Bountiful, all the way from the east to the western sea. The Nephites, in their wisdom, had their armies guard the border that kept the Lamanites to the south, to prevent them from acquiring any more territory to the north, to prevent the northern lands from being overrun. ³⁴ Therefore the Lamanites couldn't conquer any more territory, except in the land of Nephi and the surrounding wilderness. The Nephites were wise to do this, since the Lamanites were their enemy; it prevented them from having to defend from every direction — and also so they had a way to retreat if they needed to escape. ³⁵ Now, after having said this, I return to the account of Ammon, and Aaron, Omner, and Himni, and their companions.

Chapter 14

23 Now the king of the Lamanites sent a proclamation to all his people that they were to leave Ammon, Aaron, Omner, and Himni alone, as well any of their companions who were preaching God's word, in any place they went, in any part of their land. ² He sent a decree prohibiting their arrest, or tying them up, or throwing them in prison, forbidding them from spitting on them, or beating them, or expelling them from their synagogues, or whipping them, or throwing rocks at them. Instead, they were to be given free access to their houses and to their temples and sanctuaries. ³ As a result they were permitted to go out and preach the word as they wished, because the king and his whole household had been converted to the Lord. He sent this proclamation across the land to control his people so God's word could go forth unimpeded, specifically so it would be spread throughout the land, so his people would be convinced to abandon their ancestors' wicked traditions, and be persuaded that they were all brothers and sisters and under an obligation not to murder, rob, steal, commit adultery, or commit any evil acts.

II   ⁴ Now after the king's proclamation, Aaron and his companions went from city to city and from one house of worship to another, establishing congregations and consecrating priests and teachers everywhere in the land among the Lamanites to preach and teach

God's word to them. They began to have great success. 5 In time thousands were brought to know the Lord; thousands accepted the Nephite traditions. They were taught the recorded prophecies that had been kept until the present time. 6 And as sure as the Lord lives, certainly all those who believed, or all those brought to accept the truth through the preaching, revelations, prophecy, and miracles of Ammon and his companions — indeed, I declare as the Lord lives, all the Lamanites who had been converted by their preaching to believe in the Lord never fell away. 7 They became a righteous people; they laid down weapons used in rebellion, and they didn't fight against God, or against any of their fellow Lamanites, or against the Nephites.

III   8 Now this is a list of the people who were converted to the Lord: 9 the Lamanites in Ishmael, 10 in Middoni, 11 in Nephi, 12 in Shilom and in Shemlon, and those in Lemuel, and people in Shimnilom. 13 These are the names of the Lamanite cities who were converted to the Lord. And all these people laid down the weapons used in rebellion — including every weapon of war — and they were all Lamanites. 14 However, the Amlicites weren't converted, except for one, and none of the Amulonites either. They hardened their hearts and persuaded the Lamanites living with them in their villages and cities to reject the message. 15 We've listed all the cities of the Lamanites where they repented and came to the knowledge of the truth and were converted.

IV   16 Now the king and those people who were converted wanted to be named, to be distinguished from their fellow Lamanites. So the king consulted with Aaron and a group of their priests about a new name to take upon themselves, so they could be recognized as distinct. 17 So they named themselves Anti-Nephi-Lehies, and were recognized by this name, and no longer called Lamanites. 18 And they began to be very productive people and were friendly to the Nephites. Therefore they opened communication with them, and the curse from God went away.

V   **24** Then the Amlicites, Amulonites, and Lamanites in Amulon, Helam, and Jerusalem — in short, in the entire surrounding area — who weren't converted and who rejected the name of Anti-Nephi-Lehi, were incited to anger against them by the Amlicites and Amulonites. 2 Their hatred for them became extreme, so much so they began to rebel against their king, rejecting him as their king. Consequently, they armed themselves to attack the people of Anti-Nephi-Lehi.

VI   3 Now the king conferred the kingdom on his son, and he named him Anti-Nephi-Lehi. 4 And the king died the very same year the Lamanites prepared for war against the people of God. 5 When

Ammon and his brothers and companions saw the Lamanites were preparing to kill their own people, they went to Midian. Ammon met all his companions there, and from there they went to the land of Ishmael so they could hold a council with Lamoni, and with his brother Anti-Nephi-Lehi too, about what they should do to defend themselves from the Lamanites. 6 Now none of the people who had been converted to the Lord would arm themselves to fight their own people. They refused to even prepare for war, and their king also commanded them not to do so.

VII   7 Now this is what he said to the people about the matter: I thank God, my dear people, that our great God has, in His goodness, sent these dear Nephites to us, to preach to us and convince us about the traditions of our wicked ancestors. 8 And I thank my great God that He's given us a portion of His Spirit to soften our hearts, so that we've listened to these fellow Nephites. 9 And I also thank God that by listening we've been convinced of our sins and the many murders that we've committed. 10 I also thank God, my great God, that He's permitted us to repent of these things, and He's forgiven us of our many sins and murders and taken away the guilt from our hearts through the merits of His Son. 11 Now, my people, since we were the most lost people and it has been all that we could do to repent of our sins and the many murders we committed and to get God to take them away from our hearts — for it took everything we could do to repent and receive God's forgiveness — 12 now, my most dearly beloved people, since God has removed our bloodstains and our swords have become clean, may we not stain our swords anymore with the blood of our brethren.

VIII   13 I tell you: No, let's not use our swords, so as to prevent any further stains from the blood of our brethren. I worry that perhaps if we stain our swords again, they can no longer be washed bright through the blood of the Son of our great God, which He will shed for the atonement of our sins. 14 And the great God has had mercy on us and revealed these things to us so we wouldn't perish. He has made these things known to us beforehand because He loves us, and He loves our children as well. Therefore in His mercy He visits us by His angels, teaching the plan of salvation to us as well as to future generations. 15 Oh how merciful is God! And now, since it has been as much as we could do to get our stains removed from us, and since our swords are now bright, let's hide them away so they can remain bright, as a testimony to God on the last day — or when we're brought to stand before Him to be judged — proving we haven't stained our swords with the blood of our brethren since He taught His word to us and through it He has made us clean. 16 Now, my people, if our brethren come to kill us, we won't use our swords; we'll even bury them deep in the ground, so they can be kept bright as a testimony at the day of judgment that we've never used them. And if our brethren kill us, we'll go to our God and be saved.

IX   17 When the king had finished saying these things, and all the people were assembled, they took their swords and weapons used to kill people and they buried them deep in the ground. 18 They did this precisely because it was in their view a testimony to God and to mankind that they would never use weapons again to kill people. They did this, pledging and covenanting with God that rather than killing their brethren, they would lose their own lives; and rather than take away, they would give to their fellow human beings; and rather than being idle, they would work hard with their hands. 19 As you can see, when these Lamanites were brought to accept and know the truth, they were determined and would even suffer death rather than commit sin. And we saw they buried their weapons of peace — or rather, they buried their weapons of war for peace.

X   20 Their brethren prepared for war and entered the land of Nephi to overthrow the king and put another in his place, and to destroy the people of Anti-Nephi-Lehi there. 21 Now when the people saw them coming against them, they went out to meet them and lay down on the ground in front of them and began to pray to the Lord. They were in this position when the Lamanites began to attack and kill them with the sword. 22 Without meeting any resistance, they killed 1,005 of them. And we know that they're blessed, for they've gone to live with God. 23 When the Lamanites saw their brethren wouldn't run away from the sword, and they also wouldn't move to the right or left, but were willing to lie down and die while they praised God, even while being killed by the sword — 24 when the Lamanites saw this, they stopped killing them. And there were many whose hearts were broken for their brethren who were killed by the sword, and they deeply regretted doing it.

XI   25 They threw down their weapons and refused to continue, since they were upset by the murders they had just committed. And they dropped to the ground, just like their brethren, relying on the mercy of those who were continuing the attack.

XII   26 The result was that God's people increased that day by more than the number who were killed. All those who had been killed were righteous; therefore we have no reason to doubt they were saved. 27 There wasn't a wicked person killed among them, but there were more than 1,000 brought to accept the truth. And so we see the Lord uses many ways to save His people. 28 Now most of the Lamanites who had done the killing of their brethren were Amlicites and Amulonites, and the majority of them followed the teachings of Nehor. 29 But of those who joined the Lord's people, none were Amlicites or Amulonites, or followed the teaching of Nehor, but they were actual descendants of Laman and Lemuel. 30 And so it becomes apparent that after people have been once enlightened by God's Spirit and possess great knowledge about the requirements of righteousness and then fall into sin and transgression, they become very hardened; and the result is worse than if they never had known the truth.

XIII   **25** Now these Lamanites became still more angry because they had killed some of their own people. Therefore they swore vengeance on the Nephites. And they didn't continue killing the people of Anti-Nephi-Lehi at that time, 2 but their armies went over into the area near the border of the land of Zarahemla and attacked the people living in Ammonihah and destroyed them. 3 Following that, they had many battles with the Nephites, in which they were driven and killed. 4 And of the Lamanites who were killed, almost all of them were descendants of Amulon and his companions, who had been the priests of Noah; and they were killed by the Nephites. 5 The survivors escaped to the eastern wilderness and seized power and authority over the Lamanites. They executed many of the Lamanites by burning because of their beliefs. 6 Now after having experienced so much loss and so many hardships, many of them began to remember the words Aaron and his companions had preached to them. Therefore they began to reject their ancestors' traditions and to believe in the Lord and conclude that He protected the Nephites; and as a result, many of them were converted while in the wilderness.

XIV   7 Then those rulers, who were the surviving descendants of Amulon, executed anyone who believed in these things. 8 This martyrdom made many of their fellow Lamanites angry. So fighting began in the wilderness, and the Lamanites began to hunt the descendants of Amulon and their supporters and kill them, but some escaped to the eastern wilderness. 9 And they're hunted to this day by the Lamanites. Clearly Abinadi's prophecy regarding the priests' descendants was fulfilled, words he said before he suffered death by fire. 10 Because he said to them: What you do with me after this will be the same fate you will suffer. 11 Now Abinadi was the first executed by fire because of his belief in God. And this is what he meant, that many would suffer death by fire just like him. 12 He told Noah's priests that their descendants would cause many to be put to death in the same way he was, and they would be scattered widely and killed, as a sheep without a shepherd that's driven and killed by wild animals. Now these words were confirmed, since they were driven, hunted, and struck down by the Lamanites.

XV ¹³ When the Lamanites saw that they couldn't overpower the Nephites, they returned to their own land; and many of them came over to live in the land of Ishmael and the land of Nephi and joined themselves to God's people, who were the people of Anti-Nephi-Lehi. ¹⁴ They also buried their weapons of war, just as their brothers had done. And they became a righteous people, and they walked in the ways of the Lord and paid attention to keeping His commandments and statutes. ¹⁵ Indeed, they kept the Law of Moses, as it was suitable and proper for them to still keep it, since it wasn't yet fulfilled. But despite the Law of Moses, they looked forward to the Messiah's coming, because the Law of Moses symbolized His coming and they believed they were obligated to perform those outward ordinances until He came to them. ¹⁶ Now they didn't believe salvation came by the Law of Moses, but the Law of Moses supported their faith in the Messiah. So they maintained a hope through faith of eternal salvation, relying on the spirit of prophecy, which foretold things to come. ¹⁷ Now Ammon, Aaron, Omner, Himni, and their companions were overjoyed at the success they saw among the Lamanites, since the Lord had answered their prayers and vindicated His word in every detail.

XVI **26** This is what Ammon said to his companions: My brothers and friends: What great reason we have to rejoice! Could we have thought, when we started out from Zarahemla, that God would have given us such great blessings? ² Now I ask: What are all the blessings He has bestowed on us? Can you even list them? ³ I'll answer for you: Our Lamanite brothers and sisters were in darkness, indeed, in the darkest abyss. Yet how many of them have been brought to see God's marvelous light! This is the blessing God has bestowed upon us: we've been made instruments in God's hands to bring about this great work. ⁴ Indeed, thousands of them are rejoicing and have been brought into God's fold. ⁵ The field was ripe. And you are blessed, because you took your sickles and reaped with your strength; indeed, you worked the whole day — and see how many bundles you have! They'll be gathered into the storehouses, so they aren't lost. ⁶ They won't be beaten down by the storm on the last day, or torn up by the tornadoes. But when the storm comes, they'll be brought together safely, so the storm can't reach them. And they won't be driven by angry winds to wherever the enemy might decide to scatter them. ⁷ Rather, they're in the hands of the Lord of the harvest. They are His, and He'll raise them up on the last day. ⁸ Blessed is the name of God! Let us sing to

His praise; let us give thanks to His holy name, because He brings about righteousness forever. 9 Consider that if we hadn't come up from Zarahemla, these dearly beloved brothers and sisters of ours, who have loved us in return, still would have been filled with hatred for us. And they would have been strangers to God as well.

XVII   10 When Ammon had said these words, his brother Aaron reprimanded him, saying: Ammon, I'm afraid your joy is making you brag. 11 But Ammon said to him: I'm not bragging about my own strength or wisdom; but my joy is full. My heart overflows with joy, and I'll rejoice in God. 12 I know that I'm nothing; as to my strength, I'm weak. So I won't brag about myself, but I'll brag about God; because I can do all things using His strength. Indeed, we've performed many powerful miracles in this land, for which we'll praise His name forever. 13 Consider how many thousands of our brothers and sisters He has delivered from the pains of hell! They're brought to sing redeeming love — and this is because of the power of His word given to us. Therefore don't we have great reason to rejoice? 14 Yes, we have reason to praise Him forever, because He is the Most High God and has released these fellow brothers and sisters of ours from the chains of hell. 15 They were surrounded by everlasting darkness and destruction; but He has brought them into His everlasting light, indeed, into everlasting salvation. And they're surrounded by the unmatched goodness and gift of His love. Indeed, we've been His instruments in bringing about this great and awe-inspiring work. 16 Therefore we should rejoice! We'll rejoice in the Lord; we'll truly rejoice, since our joy is full; we'll praise God forever.

XVIII   Who can rejoice too much in the Lord? Who can say too much of His great power and mercy and long-suffering toward mankind? I tell you: I can't say the smallest part of what I feel. 17 Who would have thought God was so merciful that He would rescue us from our awful, sinful, and polluted state? 18 We attempted to destroy His congregation, angrily making threats. 19 Then why didn't He condemn us to an awful destruction? Indeed, why didn't He let the sword of His justice fall upon us and doom us to eternal despair? 20 My soul almost runs away, as it were, at that thought. He didn't impose His justice on us, but instead showed His great mercy, taking us safely over the everlasting abyss of death and misery, all the way to the salvation of our souls. 21 And now, my friends, what person in their natural state knows these things? I tell you: No one knows these things except for the repentant. 22 Those who repent, exercise faith, do good works, and pray continually, these are the ones who are able to know God's mysteries. These are the ones who will be able to reveal things that have never been revealed. And these are the ones who will be granted the ability to bring thousands of souls to repentance, just as it has been granted to us to bring these brothers and sisters of ours to repentance.

XIX 23 Now, let's remember, my friends, we told our fellow Nephites in Zarahemla: We will go up to the land of Nephi to preach to our Lamanite brothers and sisters. And they laughed and ridiculed us. 24 They said to us: Do you believe you can convert the Lamanites to accept the truth? Do you think you can convince the Lamanites that their ancestors' traditions are incorrect, as stubborn a people as they are, who enjoy shedding blood, whose days have been spent in the worst iniquity, who have followed the pathway of transgression from the start? Now, my friends, remember this is what they told us. 25 And they also said: Let's arm ourselves to fight them, to destroy them and their iniquity from the land, so they don't overrun and destroy us. 26 But, my dear friends, we came into the wilderness, not with the intent to destroy our brothers and sisters, but to possibly save a few of their souls.

XX 27 When our hearts were depressed and we were about to turn back, the Lord comforted us and said: Go among your brothers and sisters and endure your troubles patiently; and I'll give you success. 28 Now we've gone out among them, and we've been patient in our sufferings. We've suffered every deprivation; we've traveled from house to house, relying on the mercy of the world — not just on the mercy of the world, but on God's mercy. 29 And we've gone to their houses and taught them; and we taught them in their streets; and we've taught them on their hills; and we entered their temples and synagogues and taught them. And we've been thrown out, mocked, spit upon, and hit in our faces. We've been stoned, taken by force, tied up with ropes, and thrown in prison; and through God's power and wisdom we've been set free again. 30 We've endured every kind of difficulty, and we've done all this to try to save some soul. And we thought our joy would be enough if perhaps we could be the means of saving some few.

XXI 31 Now we can look out and see the fruits of our labors. Are there only a few? I declare: No, there are many of them. And we can guarantee their sincerity because of their love for their brethren and for us. 32 Indeed, they're willing to sacrifice their own lives rather than take the life of an enemy. And they buried their weapons deep in the ground because of their love for their brethren. 33 Now I ask you: Has there been such great love in the whole land? I tell you: No, there hasn't been, not even among the Nephites. 34 Because Nephites arm themselves to fight against their brothers; they won't let themselves be killed. But how many of our converts have laid down their lives! And we know they've gone to their God because of their love and because of their hatred for sin. 35 Now, don't we have a reason to rejoice? Yes, I tell you, there's never been anyone since the world began with as great a reason to rejoice as us. I'm carried away in my joy, even to bragging about God. He has all power, all wisdom, and all understanding; He comprehends all things, and He's a merciful Being, bringing salvation to those who will repent and believe in His name. 36 Now if this is bragging, then I'll brag. Because this is my life and my light, my joy and my salvation and my redemption from everlasting pain and sorrow. Blessed is the name of God, who has watched over this people, a branch of Israel's tree, who were cut from its trunk and taken to an unfamiliar place. I say: Blessed is the name of God, who's been mindful of us, wanderers in this unfamiliar land. 37 Now, my friends, we see that God watches over every people, wherever they may live; indeed, He counts His people. And His tender mercy is offered to all the earth. Now this is my joy and my great thanksgiving. And I'll give thanks to God forever. Amen.

Chapter 15

27 When the Lamanites who went to war against the Nephites found — after many persistent attempts to destroy them — that it was useless to try to destroy them, they returned to the land of Nephi. 2 And because of losing, the Amlicites were very angry. When they saw they couldn't get revenge on the Nephites, they started to provoke the people to be angry with the former Lamanites, the people of Anti-Nephi-Lehi. So they again started to kill them. 3 Now they again refused to defend themselves, and they let themselves be killed by their enemy. 4 These were people Ammon and his companions dearly loved. They, in turn, treated Ammon and his companions as if they were angels sent from God to save them from everlasting destruction.

II   So when Ammon and his companions saw this brutal slaughter, they were overwhelmed with compassion, and they suggested to the king: 5 Let's gather this people of the Lord, and let's go down to the land of Zarahemla to the Nephites and escape from our enemies, so we won't be destroyed. 6 But the king responded: The Nephites will kill us because of the many murders and sins we've committed against them. 7 Then Ammon said: I'll ask the Lord. And if He says to us, Go down to the Nephites, will you go? 8 And the king replied: Yes, if the Lord says to go, we'll go down to the Nephites. We'll be their slaves until we make up to them the many murders and sins we've committed against them. 9 But Ammon said: It violates the law of the Nephites my father established for there to be any slavery. So let's go and rely on the mercy of the Nephites. 10 And so the king said: Then go ahead and ask the Lord, and if He tells us, Go, we'll go. Otherwise, we'll die here.

III   11 And Ammon went and asked the Lord, and the Lord said to him: 12 Remove the people from this land and save their lives, because Satan has a firm grip on the Amlicites' hearts, who incite the Lamanites to such anger against their brethren they will kill them; therefore leave this land. These people in this generation are blessed, therefore I'll preserve them.

IV   13 Now Ammon repeated to the king everything the Lord told him. 14 And they gathered all their people (the Lord's people), and together with their flocks and herds, departed into the wilderness separating the land of Nephi from the land of Zarahemla and approached the border of that land.

V   15 Then Ammon said to them: My companions and I will enter the land of Zarahemla, and you wait here until we return. We'll learn the Nephites' attitude to find out whether they're willing to let you enter their land.

VI   16 Just when Ammon entered the land, he and his brothers met Alma as was previously recorded in this account; and this was a joyful meeting. 17 Now Ammon was so joyful he was overcome. He was so emotional his strength failed him and he fell to the ground again. 18 Wouldn't you agree this is overwhelming joy? This kind of joy is only experienced by the truly repentant and humble candidate for hope in Christ. 19 Now Alma's joy in meeting his friends was truly great, and so was the joy of Aaron, Omner, and Himni; but their joy did not overcome their strength.

VII   20 Alma brought his brothers to his house in Zarahemla. Next, they went and recounted to the chief judge everything that had happened to them in the land of Nephi among their Lamanite brothers and sisters.

VIII   21 As a result, the chief judge sent an announcement throughout the land, asking for the vote of the people on whether to welcome these Lamanites, the people of Anti-Nephi-Lehi, to their land. 22 And the people voted, agreeing to let them settle in the land of Jershon. That land is east next to the sea, bordering Bountiful on the south. This land of Jershon was approved for their Lamanite brothers and sisters as their inheritance. 23 And they agreed to set their armies between the land of Jershon and the land of Nephi, to protect their Lamanite brothers and sisters in the land of Jershon. They voted to do this for them because the people of Anti-Nephi-Lehi were afraid of sinning if were to arm themselves to fight their brethren. Their fear over this came from the difficulty they experienced repenting of the many murders they committed and their prior awful wickedness. ²⁴ They agreed to do this for their Lamanite brothers and sisters so they could have the land of Jershon as their own. And they agreed to protect them from their enemies with Nephite armies, on the condition that they help support the armies by providing the required resources.

IX   ²⁵ After Ammon learned this, he returned with Alma to the people of Anti-Nephi-Lehi camping and waiting in the wilderness, and explained all this to them. And Alma also told them the story about his, Ammon's, Aaron's, and their brothers' conversion. ²⁶ Hearing the account made them rejoice. Then they settled into the land of Jershon. And the Nephites called them Ammon's people; so they were identified by that name from then on. ²⁷ They were recognized as Nephites and included among the people who belonged to God's congregation. They were also known for their devotion to God and respect for their fellow man, because they were entirely honest and upright in all things. They were firm in the faith of Christ, until the end. ²⁸ And they abhorred the idea of shedding the blood of their fellow human beings. They could never be persuaded to arm themselves to fight their fellowmen again. They weren't terrified of dying because of their hope and trust in Christ and the resurrection. For them, death was swallowed up by Christ's victory over it. ²⁹ That being so, they endured being killed in the most cruel and painful ways inflicted by their brethren and still wouldn't defend themselves with the sword or cimeter. ³⁰ They were a dedicated and dearly loved people, who were remarkably blessed by the Lord.

X   **28** After Ammon's people settled in Jershon — and a congregation also established for them — and after the Nephite armies began guarding the land of Jershon — and the border surrounding the land of Zarahemla also — it turned out that Lamanite armies had followed the Anti-Nephi-Lehies in the wilderness. ² It resulted in a tremendous battle, the worst warfare experienced by the entire population since Lehi departed Jerusalem. Tens of thousands of the Lamanites were killed, their bodies scattered on the ground. ³ There was also a terrible slaughter of the Nephites. Overall, the Lamanites lost and were chased away, and the Nephites returned home. ⁴ This was a terrible moment, a time of great mourning, lamenting, and weeping all over the land by all the Nephites. ⁵ There were widows mourning for their husbands, and fathers mourning for their sons, and daughters for brothers, and brothers for fathers. Every one of them wept and mourned their relatives who had been killed. ⁶ Up to this moment, this was the worst time in their history, a solemn moment when there was a great deal of fasting and prayer. 7 That's how the 15th year of the judges' rule over the Nephites came to an end.

XI   8 This covers the account of Ammon and his companions, their journey in the land of Nephi, their suffering there, their sorrows and hardships, and their overwhelming joy, the rescue to safety of the Anti-Nephi-Lehies into the land of Jershon. May the Lord, the Redeemer of all mankind, bless their souls forever. 9 This covers the account of the conflicts among the Nephites, and the wars between the Nephites and Lamanites, through the end of the 15th year of the judges' rule. 10 From the first to the 15th year, there were many thousands of people killed; lives squandered and terrible slaughter. 11 Thousands of their bodies were buried and thousands of other bodies are decaying in piles on the ground. And thousands are mourning lost relatives, fearing, according to the Lord's promises, that they were condemned to a state of endless misery, 12 but thousands of others mourn their lost relatives, but rejoice in the great hope, knowing the Lord's promises, that their lost ones will rise to dwell at God's right hand experiencing never-ending happiness. 13 From this record we witness the great disparity of mankind because of sin, transgression, and the power of the accuser, which happens because of the crafty and deceitful plans he uses to mislead people's souls. 14 It shows the continuing need for people to preach truth constantly in the Lord's vineyards. It shows the great reasons leading to sorrow and rejoicing: sorrow due to death and destruction among people, and joy from following the light of Christ to everlasting life.

XII   **29** I wish I were an angel and the wish of my heart could be granted: Then I would go out preaching with the trumpet of God, with a voice that would shake the earth, and shout: Repent! — to everyone! 2 I would proclaim repentance and the plan of salvation to every soul, with a voice like thunder, warning them to repent and draw near to God! Then there wouldn't be any more sorrow on the earth. 3 But I'm just a man and my wish is a sin, since I should be content with what the Lord has given me. 4 I shouldn't want to overthrow the plan of God thinking I know better, because I know He gives mankind what they desire, whether they choose death or choose life. I know He lets people choose between clearly ordained outcomes that they decide by their own choices: whether they choose salvation or choose destruction. 5 I know everyone chooses between good and evil; however, those who can't tell good from evil are innocent, but everyone who understands the difference between good and evil will get to experience, based on their choice, either good or evil, life or death, joy or regret.

XIII ⁶ Now, since I know this, why should I want anything more than to perform the work I've been asked to do? ⁷ Why should I want to be an angel, so I could preach to everyone, everywhere on earth? ⁸ The Lord gives to every nation, from their own people, using their own language, teachers delivering His message that He decides is relevant for them. Therefore we should trust that the Lord is wise enough to guide everyone to the truth appropriate for them. ⁹ I know the Lord's commandments to me, and I've found joy obeying. I'm not rejoicing in anything I've done, but I rejoice in doing as the Lord commanded me. To me it was glorious to serve as an instrument in God's hands to help others repent; this brought me joy. ¹⁰ When I see many others truly repent and drawing near to the Lord who is God, my soul is filled with joy; then I reflect on what the Lord did for me, that He answered my prayer. I reflect on His rescuing arm extended to me. ¹¹ I also reflect on the slavery of my ancestors; I'm grateful to know the Lord freed them from slavery and established His congregation among them. Indeed, the Lord God — the God of Abraham and the God of Isaac and the God of Jacob — freed them from slavery! ¹² I always reflect on the slavery of my ancestors. And the same God who liberated them from the Egyptians again freed my ancestors from slavery. ¹³ And the same God established His congregation among them. The same God called me by a holy calling to preach His message to this people. He gave me such tremendous success that my joy couldn't be greater. ¹⁴ I'm not only pleased at my own success, but I'm even more pleased at the success of my friends who taught in the land of Nephi. ¹⁵ They accomplished an amazing labor and have saved a great harvest for God. They will receive a great reward! ¹⁶ When I think of the success of these friends of mine, it's as if my spirit is swept away and carried up to God from my body, from this great joy.

XIV ¹⁷ I pray God grants these friends of mine an inheritance in God's kingdom, together with all those harvested through their labors, to everlastingly remain, so they can praise Him forever. May God grant my prayer, just as I've asked Him. Amen.

Chapter 16

30 Ammon's people had been settled in the land of Jershon, and the Lamanites had been driven out of the land and their dead had been buried by the residents. ² Because there were so many dead Lamanites they weren't counted. Neither were the Nephite dead counted. But following burying the dead and after time spent fasting, mourning, and praying, a time of peace arrived. This was in the 16th year of the judges' rule over the Nephites. Everywhere in the land there was peace. 3 And the people paid careful attention to keep the Lord's commandments; and they strictly followed God's ordinances in the Law of Moses, since they were taught to keep the Law of Moses until it was fulfilled. 4 There were no disturbances in the entire 16th year of the judges' rule over the Nephites.

II
5 At the beginning of the 17th year of the judges' rule, peace continued. 6 But toward the end of the 17th year, a man came to Zarahemla and he was an anti-Christ, because he denounced the prophecies of the prophets about Christ's coming. 7 Now there was no law prohibiting a person's belief. It was absolutely contrary to God's commandments to control or force beliefs. Everyone could choose equally for themselves. 8 The scripture states: Choose for yourselves today whom you will serve. 9 So if someone wanted to serve God, it was their right to do so. If they believed in God, they were free to serve Him. But if they didn't believe in Him, there was no law to punish them. 10 However if they murdered, they were executed; and if they robbed, they were punished; and likewise they were punished for stealing, adultery, and any other wickedness. 11 The law provided that people were only punished for their crimes, but not for their beliefs. Everyone was equally punished and equally free to believe as they wished.

III
12 And this anti-Christ, whose name was Korihor, couldn't be punished under the law. So he was free to preach to the people that there would be no Christ. He preached: 13 Why do you tie yourselves down with a foolish and useless hope? Why do you let such foolishness oppress you? Why do you look for a Messiah? It's impossible to know the future. 14 These ideas you call prophecies, that you say are handed down by holy prophets, are nothing more than your ancestors' foolish traditions. 15 How can you know they're true? You can't know about things you don't see, and so you can't know there will be a Messiah. 16 You anticipate you'll be forgiven of your sins, but this is a delusion of your troubled mind. You inherited this mental disorder from your ancestors' false traditions that convince you to believe in lies. 17 He said many more similar things, telling them there couldn't be any atonement made for mankind's sins, but that everyone experienced success or failure in this life based on the talent of each person. Therefore everyone's success or failure was based on their individual abilities, and they should enjoy life without feeling any guilt. 18 He preached these ideas to them, persuading many of them to go astray. It caused them to be proud of their wickedness. Many men and women engaged in whoredoms. He taught that death ended all existence and there was no afterlife.

IV   19 He took his message to Jershon to preach these things to Ammon's people, formerly Lamanites. 20 But they were wiser than many of the Nephites, and they arrested him, tied him up, and took him to Ammon, who was the high priest over that people.

V   21 He had him forcibly exiled. Next, he went to Gideon and began to preach to them as well. But here he didn't have much success, and he was arrested, tied up, and taken before both the high priest and the chief judge over the land.

VI   22 The high priest asked him: Why are you preaching these perversions that violate the Lord's commandments? Why do you teach there will be no Christ? Do you intend to make them hopeless? Why do you contradict the prophecies of the holy prophets? 23 Now the high priest's name was Giddonah, and Korihor responded: Because I don't teach your ancestors' foolish traditions. Because I don't teach this people to chain themselves with ridiculous ordinances and performances begun by ancient priests as a plan to seize power and authority, planning to keep them in ignorance, so they remain subservient and are controlled by your lies. 24 You claim these people are free. But I say these people are enslaved. You claim those ancient prophecies are true. But I say it's impossible for anyone to know they're true. 25 You claim these people are guilty and fallen because of a parent's transgression. I say no child is guilty because of their parents. 26 And you claim the Messiah will come. But it's impossible to know there will be a Messiah. And you also claim He'll be killed for the sins of the world. 27 You use that to indoctrinate the people to follow your ancestors' foolish traditions and obey your own wishes. You oppress them like they're your slaves so you can take for yourselves everything their work produces. They don't even dare to boldly confront you to reclaim their rights and privileges. 28 They don't dare to protect their property out of fear they might offend their priests, who control them to get what they want. The priests use traditions, dreams, whims, visions, and pretended mysteries to impose their beliefs. They threaten the people that if they don't do what they say, they'll offend some unknown being, who they say is God. Merely a false being who's never been seen or known, who never existed and will never exist. 29 When the high priest and the chief judge witnessed the hardness of his heart, and saw he would even denounce God, they refused to reply to anything he said, but they had him tied up; and they had the officers take him to Zarahemla, and brought before Alma and the chief judge who was governor over the whole land.

VII   30 When he was brought before Alma and the chief judge, he went on in the same way he had in Gideon, including blaspheming. 31 And he boldly advocated his arrogant ideas to Alma, insulting the priests and teachers, accusing them of brainwashing the people, to get them to follow their ancestors' silly traditions, in order to take everything that the people produced for themselves. 32 Now Alma said to him: You know we aren't paid by the people. Indeed, I've supported myself from the beginning of the judges' rule until now, supporting myself with my own labor, despite traveling around the land to teach God's word to my people. 33 And despite all my work performed in the congregation, I've never received so much as even one senine for my work, and none of my associates have either. The only exception is for the work of judges, and then any payment received is based on an established rate for our time. 34 So if we don't receive anything for our work in the congregation, how does it benefit us to work in the congregation except to declare the truth? We only do it to spread joy to our fellow beings. 35 Then how can you claim we preach to this people to become rich when you know we receive no financial benefit? Now, do you believe we deceive people and that lies cause such joy in their hearts? 36 And Korihor answered: Yes.

VIII   37 Then Alma asked him: Do you believe there's a God? 38 And he answered: No. 39 Then Alma asked him: Will you deny again there's a God and also deny Christ? Because I tell you: I know there's a God, and that Christ will come. 40 Now, what evidence do you have that there's no God or that Christ won't come? I tell you that you have nothing except for your word only. 41 But I have all things as a testimony that these things are true. And you also have all things as a testimony to you that they're true. And will you deny them? Do you believe these things are true? 42 I know you believe. But a lying spirit has power over you, and you've rejected God's Spirit so it can't have any place in you; but the accuser has power over you, and he leads you here and there, carrying out his evil plans to destroy God's children. 43 Now Korihor said to Alma: If you show me a sign to prove there's a God, and show me He has power, only then will I be convinced what you say is true.

IX   44 But Alma said to him: You've had plenty of signs. Will you put God to the test? Will you say, show me a sign, when you already have the testimony of your fellow Nephites and all the holy prophets? The scriptures are in front of you. And all things demonstrate there's a God: This earth and everything on it, and its motion, and all the planets moving in their appointed places — these all prove there's a Supreme Creator. 45 But you go around leading the hearts of this people astray, testifying to them that there's no God. While you ignore all the evidence. Then he said: Yes, I'll deny it unless you show me a sign.

X 46 Now Alma said to him: I mourn the hardness of your heart, that you're still determined to reject the spirit of the truth, resulting in your soul being destroyed. 47 But it's better for your soul to be lost than for you to bring many souls with you down to destruction. Your lying influence needs to end. Therefore if you deny again, God will strike you so you won't be able to speak, or teach, or preach your deceit to the people again. 48 Now Korihor responded: I don't deny the existence of a God, but I don't believe there's a God. And I also claim you don't know there's a God; and unless you show me a sign, I refuse to believe.

XI 49 Then Alma said to him: Here is the sign I'll give to you: God will vindicate my words and you will be unable to speak. I say, in the name of God, you will be struck mute, and will no longer speak. 50 When Alma said this, Korihor was struck mute, and he was unable to speak, vindicating Alma's words. 51 When the chief judge saw this, he wrote a note to Korihor asking: Are you convinced of God's power? How did you expect a sign to be given? Did you think God would target someone else to show you a sign? Now He has shown you a sign. Do you still disbelieve?

XII 52 Then Korihor wrote: I know that I'm mute, since I can't speak. And I know nothing except for God's power could bring this upon me. I always knew there was a God. 53 But the accuser deceived me, appearing to me in the form of an angel and saying to me: Go and reclaim this people, because they've all gone astray after an unknown God. He told me: There is no God. And he taught me what to say, and I've taught his words. I taught them because they were pleasing to the worldly mind. And I taught them until I had considerable success, then I honestly believed they were true. And for this reason I fought the truth, to the point I've now brought upon myself this great curse. 54 When he had said this, he begged Alma to pray to God so the curse would be removed from him. 55 But Alma said to him: If this curse were to be taken from you, you would return to leading the hearts of this people astray. Therefore what happens to you is up to the Lord.

XIII 56 And the curse wasn't taken from Korihor, but he was exiled and went around from house to house begging for food. 57 Now the knowledge of what happened to Korihor was spread throughout the land; a proclamation was sent out by the chief judge to everyone in the land, declaring to those who accepted Korihor's lies that they must quickly repent so the same judgments wouldn't come upon them.

XIV   ⁵⁸ That convinced them all of Korihor's wickedness. Therefore they were all converted again to the Lord. This put an end to Korihor's heresy. Meanwhile Korihor went from house to house begging for assistance.

XV   ⁵⁹ He wandered into a group of people that had separated themselves from the Nephites, and called themselves Zoramites, led by a man named Zoram. As he was walking in their community he was run over and trampled to death. ⁶⁰ This shows the fate of those who corrupt and pervert the ways of the Lord. We see the accuser won't support his children at the end but abandons them, and quickly drags them down to hell.

XVI   **31** Now after Korihor's death, Alma received the news that the Zoramites were perverting the ways of the Lord. Zoram, their leader, was leading the hearts of the people to worship idols that don't speak, etc. The news made Alma sick at heart because of the people's iniquity. ² Alma hated to hear about any iniquity among his people; so he mourned over the separation of the Zoramites from the Nephites. ³ Now the Zoramites were occupying a land they called Antionum, east of Zarahemla, nearly bordering the seashore south of the land Jershon, which also bordered the southern wilderness, a wilderness area with many Lamanites. ⁴ Now the Nephites were worried the Zoramites might begin to associate with the Lamanites, and that could result in more great losses suffered by the Nephites. ⁵ Now preaching the truth was more effective to lead the people to do what's right — indeed, it had greater effect on the minds of the people than the sword or anything else available — therefore Alma thought teaching God's word was their best alternative. ⁶ So he took Ammon, Aaron, and Omner — and he left Himni in the congregation in Zarahemla, but he took the first three with him — and Amulek and Zeezrom came too, who had been at Melek; and he also brought two of his sons. ⁷ Now he didn't bring his oldest son Helaman with him, but he did bring his sons Shiblon and Corianton. These are all the names of those who went with him to preach to the Zoramites.

XVII   ⁸ Now the Zoramites were previously part of the Nephites; so God's word had been preached to them. ⁹ But they had fallen into great errors, since they failed to carefully keep God's commandments and statutes according to the Law of Moses. ¹⁰ They also failed to follow the congregation's practice of regular prayer and worship of God daily to avoid temptation. ¹¹ In short, they perverted the ways of the Lord in many ways. To remedy this, Alma and his companions traveled to their land to preach the word to them.

12 When they had entered the land, to their astonishment they found the Zoramites had built synagogues and they came together on one day of the week, which they called the Lord's day, and they worshiped in a way Alma and his companions had never seen. 13 They had a high stand in the middle of their synagogue, high above the head; and the narrow top would only fit one person at a time. 14 Therefore anyone who wanted to worship had to go stand on top and raise their arms to heaven and say in a loud voice: 15 Holy, holy god, we believe that you are god. And we believe that you are holy, and that you were a spirit, and that you are a spirit and that you will be a spirit forever. 16 Holy god, we believe that you've separated us from our fellow Nephites. And we don't believe in the tradition of our fellow Nephites, handed down to them by the childishness of their ancestors, but we believe that you've chosen us to be your holy children, and that you've revealed to us that there will be no Messiah. 17 But you are the same yesterday, today, and forever. And you've chosen us to be saved, while everyone around us has been chosen to be sent down to hell by your wrath; and we thank you, O god, for this holiness. And we also thank you for choosing us, so we aren't led astray to follow the foolish traditions of our fellow Nephites, which tie them down to a belief in the Messiah, which leads their hearts to wander far from you, our god. 18 And again we thank you, O god, that we're a chosen and holy people. Amen.

XIX   19 Now after Alma, his companions, and his sons heard this prayer, they were shocked; 20 because everyone went there and offered up this same prayer. 21 Now they called the pulpit Rameumptom, which means the holy stand. 22 And from this stand they offered up, every single one of them, the very same prayer to god, thanking god they were chosen by him and he hadn't led them astray to follow the tradition of their fellow Nephites, and that their hearts weren't deceived to believe in things to come, which they didn't know anything about.

XX   23 Now when the people all had offered up their customary prayer, they returned to their homes, never speaking of their god again until they had gathered again at the holy stand to offer up thanks in their corrupt way. 24 Now when Alma saw this, his soul was troubled — since he realized they were a wicked and perverse people. He could see their hearts were set on gold, silver, and expensive things. 25 And it was clear their pride led them to arrogantly brag in their vanity. 26 And he cried out loudly to heaven, saying: How long, O Lord, will Your servants be left here to live and see such repulsive wickedness among mankind? 27 O God, they pray out loud to You, but their hearts are consumed by their pride. O God, they pray with their mouths while their hearts are filled with pride, because they value the worthless things of the world. 28 O God, their expensive clothing and their rings, bracelets, and ornaments of gold, and all the expensive things they're adorned with — their hearts are set upon them, while they pray to You saying: We thank you, O god, because we're a chosen people to you, while others will perish. 29 And they say You've told them there will be no Messiah. 30 O Lord God, how long will You allow such wickedness and unbelief to continue among this people? O Lord, will You give me the strength to endure my weaknesses! Because I'm weak, and such wickedness among this people pains my soul. 31 O Lord, my heart is very sorrowful. Will You comfort my soul in Christ! O Lord, will You give me the strength to patiently endure the coming afflictions because of this people's iniquity! 32 O Lord, will You comfort my soul and give me success! And also my fellow laborers Ammon, Aaron, and Omner, and Amulek and Zeezrom, and my two sons — O Lord, will You comfort all of them! Will You comfort their souls in Christ! 33 Will You give them the strength to endure the afflictions they'll encounter because of this people's iniquities! 34 O Lord, please grant us success in bringing them back to You in Christ! 35 O Lord, their souls are precious; and we're closely related to many of them. Therefore give us, O Lord, power and wisdom so we can bring these brothers and sisters back to You.

XXI 36 When Alma had said these words, he put his hands on everyone with him and blessed them to be filled with the Holy Spirit. 37 Afterward, they divided up without planning what they would eat, drink, or wear. 38 The Lord provided for them so they wouldn't be hungry or thirsty. And He provided the strength to cope with afflictions through the joy given by Christ. Now Alma prayed for this and it happened because he prayed in faith.

XXII **32** Then they went out and began to preach God's word to the people, entering their synagogues and houses; and they even preached the word in their streets. 2 After a great deal of work, they started to see some success among the poorer class of citizens, since they were expelled from the synagogues because they looked poor due to how they were dressed. 3 As a result, they weren't allowed to enter their synagogues to worship God, because they were regarded as unworthy. Because they were poor, the others living in Antionum treated them like trash. So they were both poor in material possessions and poor in spirit.

XXIII 4 While Alma was teaching and speaking to the people on the hill Onidah, a large crowd approached him. They were those just described, who were poor in spirit because of their poverty in material possessions; 5 and they came up to Alma. The one who was the most prominent among them asked him: What should these companions of mine do? They're despised by everyone, especially the priests, because of our poverty. They've thrown us out of our synagogues, which we worked hard to build with our own hands. They threw us out because of our poverty, now we don't have any place to worship God. What should we do?

XXIV   6 When Alma heard this, he turned around, facing him. Looking at them brought him hope and joy, because he could tell their difficulties had humbled them and prepared them to accept the word. 7 Therefore he abandoned his talk to the other crowd, and reached out his hand and declared to the penitent people before him: 8 I can tell you are humble in heart, and therefore you are blessed. 9 Your spokesman asked: What should you do? They threw you out because of your poverty, now you don't have any place to worship God. 10 I say: Do you think you can only worship God in your synagogues? 11 Furthermore, I ask: Do you think you can only worship God once a week? 12 I tell you: It benefits you to have been kicked out of your synagogues, to humble you so you can learn wisdom; because wisdom must be learned. It's because you're rejected and despised by others in your community, due to your great poverty, that you're humble of heart. You've been forced to be humble. 13 Now because you're forced to be humble you are blessed; because sometimes a person forced to be humble seeks repentance. Now certainly anyone who repents will find mercy. And everyone who finds mercy and endures to the end will be saved.

XXV   14 Now as I said, because you were forced to be humble you were blessed, but don't you think those who voluntarily humble themselves because of the word are more blessed? 15 Indeed, those who voluntarily humble themselves and repent of their sins, and persevere to the end will be far more blessed than those who are forced to be humble by their great poverty. 16 Therefore blessed are those who humble themselves without being forced to be humble. Or put differently, blessed are those who believe in God's word and are baptized while believing in their heart, without being humbled by their circumstances before they will believe. 17 There are those who say: If you show us a sign from heaven, then we'll know for sure; then we'll believe. 18 But I ask: Is this faith? I tell you: No. Because if someone knows a thing, they don't have any reason to believe, since they know it. 19 And now, how much more cursed is someone who knows God's will and doesn't do it than someone who only believes, or only has reason to believe, and falls into transgression? 20 You must decide this matter for yourself. I tell you it's on the one hand just like it's on the other, and everyone will inherit the consequences of their choices in this life.

XXVI   21 And now as I explained about faith: faith doesn't mean having a perfect knowledge of things; therefore if you have faith, you hope for things beforehand, which you haven't yet received. 22 Now I tell you and want you to remember that God is merciful to everyone who believes in His name. Therefore, in the first place, He wants you to believe based on His message. 23 Now He delivers His message using angels who teach men. Not only men but women as well, and even little children learn things that astonish the wise and the well-educated.

XXVII   24 Now, my new friends, as you've asked me what to do because you are downtrodden and religious outcasts — in describing you I'm not judging you, I only intend to accurately tell you the true circumstances you face — 25 I also don't mean all of you have been forced to be humble. I truly believe there are some of you who would humble themselves, whatever circumstances they might be in. 26 Now as I said, faith isn't perfect knowledge, and it's the same with my words. You can't know for certain when you first hear them, any more than faith is perfect knowledge. 27 But if you pay close attention and perform an experiment with my words, and start with the smallest particle of faith — even if you can't do anything more than want to believe — hold on to this desire, until you start to believe enough to trust my words a little.

XXVIII   28 Now we'll compare the word to a seed. If you let the seed be planted in your heart, if it's a true seed or a good seed, and you don't throw it out by your unbelief and resist the Spirit of the Lord — if you let it, a good seed will begin to grow within you. And when you feel growth begin, you'll start to realize, this has to be a good seed, or the word must be good, because it has started to enlarge my soul. It has started to increase my understanding. It has begun to be valuable to me. 29 Now, wouldn't this increase your faith? I tell you: Yes. Still, it hasn't grown to become perfect knowledge. 30 But as the seed swells, sprouts, and begins to grow, then you should recognize the seed is good, because it swells, sprouts, and begins to grow. Now won't this strengthen your faith? Of course it will strengthen your faith. You'll recognize this is a good seed because it lives and begins to increase. 31 Can you be sure this is a good seed? I answer: Yes! Because every living seed gives life. 32 Therefore if a seed grows, it's living. But if it doesn't grow, it's dead; therefore you throw it out. 33 And once you've tried my experiment and planted the seed and it swells, sprouts, and begins to grow, you must conclude that the seed is good.

XXIX   34 Does that give you perfect knowledge? Yes, your knowledge is perfect about that thing and your faith is dormant — and this is so because you know. You know the word has produced growth in your soul. You know this because it has sprouted up, your understanding begins to be enlightened, and your mind begins to expand. 35 Then isn't this real? I tell you: Yes, because it's light. And whatever is light is good, because it's recognizable; therefore you can be certain it's good.

XXX   Now after you've experienced this light, is your knowledge perfect? 36 I tell you: No. You have to continue on using your faith, since you've only exercised your faith to plant the seed as an experiment to understand whether the seed was good. 37 As a tree starts to grow, you'll want to nourish it carefully so it can take root, so it can grow up and produce fruit for us. Now if you cultivate it carefully, it will take root and grow up and produce fruit. 38 But if you neglect the tree and don't take care of it, it won't take root. Then the heat from the sun will scorch it, and it will wither away because it doesn't have any root. Then you'll pull it up and throw it out. 39 Now this isn't because the seed wasn't good, nor is it because its fruit wouldn't be good. But it's because your ground is barren and you're unwilling to care for the tree; therefore you won't harvest its fruit. 40 And so it is: if you don't give heed to the word, looking forward in faith for its fruit, you'll never gather fruit from the tree of life. 41 But if you cultivate the word — indeed, care for the tree as it starts to grow by faithfully, diligently, and patiently awaiting its fruit — it will take root. And it will be a tree springing up to everlasting life. 42 Because of your diligence, faith, and patience caring for (or obeying) the word so it can take root in you, in time you'll harvest its fruit. That harvest is most valuable: sweet over all that's sweet, white over all that's white, and pure over all that's pure; and you'll eat this fruit until you're filled, no longer hungry or thirsty, or without understanding the truth. 43 Then, my friends, you'll harvest the fruit of your faith, diligence, patience, and long-suffering, as you waited for the tree to produce fruit for you.

XXXI   33 Now after Alma taught this, they sent him a message, asking to know whether they were to believe in one God in order to obtain the fruit he spoke about; how they might plant the seed, or the word he had spoken about, which he said must be planted in their hearts; and in what way they should start to exercise their faith. 2 And Alma explained: You said you couldn't worship God because you were thrown out of your synagogues. But I tell you: If you think that prevents you from worshiping God, you're making a grave mistake.

You should carefully study the scriptures; because if you think they teach this, you're mistaken. 3 Do you remember reading what Zenos the prophet long ago said about prayer or worship? 4 He said: You are merciful, O God, because You've heard my prayer, even when I was in the wilderness. Indeed, You were merciful when I prayed about those who were my enemies, and You changed their hearts toward me. 5 Indeed, O God, You were merciful to me when I cried out to You in my field, when I cried out to You in my prayer, and You heard me. 6 And also, O God, when I returned to my house, You heard me in my prayer. 7 And when I returned to my room, O Lord, and prayed to You, You heard me. 8 Indeed, You are merciful to Your children when they cry out to You — to be heard by You and not by others — and You will hear them. 9 O God, You've been merciful to me and heard my cries in the middle of Your congregations. 10 And You've also heard me when I was driven out and hated by my enemies. You heard my cries and were angry with my enemies, and You visited them in Your anger with swift destruction. 11 And You heard me because of my effort and my sincerity. And it's because of Your Son that You've been merciful to me in this way. Therefore I'll cry out to You in all my troubles, because my joy is in You; You've turned Your judgments away from me because of Your Son.

XXXII   12 And now Alma said to them: Do you believe the scriptures written long ago? 13 If you do, you must believe what Zenos said: You've turned away Your judgments because of Your Son. 14 Now, my friends, haven't you read these scriptures? If you've read them, then how can you not believe in the Son of God? 15 The scriptures show Zenos wasn't the only one who spoke about these things — indeed, Zenoch also confirmed these things; 16 he was the one who said: You are angry, O Lord, with this people, because they refuse to understand the mercy You've freely given them because of Your Son. 17 And now, my friends, you see a second prophet long ago testified of the Son of God. And because the people refused to understand what he said, they stoned him to death. 18 But this isn't everything. These aren't the only ones who have spoken about the Son of God. 19 He was spoken of by Moses. And a symbol was raised up in the wilderness, so that anyone who was willing to look at it could live; and many looked and lived. 20 But few understood the meaning of those things, and this was because of their hard hearts. There were many who were so hardened they refused to look; therefore they died. Now the reason they refused to look is because they didn't believe it would heal them. 21 My friends, if you could merely turn your head to look at it and be healed, wouldn't you quickly look? Or would you prefer to harden your hearts in unbelief and be lazy, refusing to look around, risking your death? 22 If so, woe will come upon you. But if not, then look and begin to believe in the Son of God, that He will come to redeem His people and He will suffer and die to atone for their sins, and that He will rise again from the dead. That will bring to pass the resurrection, so everyone will stand before Him to be judged on the last day, the day of judgment, based on their works. 23 Now, my friends, I want you to plant this word in your hearts. And as it begins to grow, at that moment nourish it by your faith. And it will become a tree springing up in you to everlasting life. Then may God lighten your burdens through the joy of His Son. And you can accomplish this if you're willing. Amen.

XXXIII   34 Now after Alma finished this, he sat down on the ground. And Amulek stood up and began teaching, saying: 2 My friends, I think it's impossible for you not to have heard the prophecies about the coming of Christ, who we teach is the Son of God. I know this was taught to you many times before you separated yourselves from us. 3 And as you've asked my dear brother what you should do because of your difficulties, he's introduced you to truths that can prepare your minds, and he's urged you to want faith and patience — 4 asking you to have enough faith to plant the word in your heart, so you can test its goodness as an experiment. 5 And we've seen the great question you ponder is whether the word is in the Son of God or instead whether there will be no Christ. 6 And you heard my brother show you many examples of the word being in Christ for salvation. 7 My brother used the words of Zenos, that redemption comes through the Son of God, and also the words of Zenoch. And he's also used Moses to prove this is true.

XXXIV   8 Now let me testify and confirm to you I know this is true. I assure you I know Christ will come among mankind to take upon Himself the transgressions of His people, and He will atone for the sins of the world, because the Lord God has promised it. 9 An atonement must be made because the great plans of the Eternal God require it; otherwise all mankind would be unavoidably lost. Everyone has gone astray; all are fallen and lost and would certainly perish without the atonement — therefore it's necessary for it to happen. 10 Indeed, it's fitting for there to be a great and last sacrifice — not a sacrifice of a man or woman, nor of animals, nor of any kind of bird — because it can't be a mortal sacrifice, but it requires an infinite and eternal sacrifice. 11 Now there isn't anyone who can sacrifice their own blood and atone for the sins of someone else. If a person murders, will our law, which is equitable, execute a family member? I tell you: No. 12 But the law demands the execution of the one who has murdered. Therefore nothing short of an infinite atonement would be adequate for the sins of the world. 13 Therefore it's essential for there to be a great and last sacrifice. And then there will be an altogether appropriate end to the shedding of blood; because the Law of Moses will be fulfilled. Indeed, it will all be fulfilled, every single requirement, and none of it will remain incomplete. 14 The whole purpose of the law, every part of it, was designed to point to that great and last sacrifice; and that great and last sacrifice will be of the Son of God, infinite and eternal. 15 And so He'll bring salvation to all those who believe in His name, since this is what the last sacrifice accomplishes. Through it God can provide mercy, because every requirement of justice is satisfied and nothing more can be demanded by justice, and it makes a way for mankind to have faith that leads to repentance. 16 And so mercy can satisfy the demands of justice and embrace the penitent with arms of safety, while those who don't exercise any faith followed by repentance are exposed to all the punishment justice requires under the law. So the great and eternal plan of redemption only works for those who have faith followed by repentance.

XXXV   17 Therefore may God grant you, my friends, that you begin to exercise faith followed by repentance, so you begin to call on His holy name so He can give mercy to you. 18 Pray to Him for mercy, because He is powerful to save. 19 Humble yourselves and continue praying to Him. 20 Pray out loud to Him when you're in your fields, over all your flocks. 21 Pray out loud to Him in your houses, over all your household — morning, midday, and evening. 22 Pray aloud to Him against the power of your enemies. 23 Pray aloud to Him against Satan, who's an enemy of all righteousness. 24 Pray aloud to Him over the crops of your fields, that they thrive for you. 25 Pray aloud over the flocks of your fields, so they can increase. 26 But this isn't everything. You must pour out your souls in your private rooms and secret places and in your secluded retreats. 27 And when you don't pray aloud to the Lord, let your hearts be full, drawn out in silent prayer to Him continually for your well-being as well as the well-being of those who are around you.

XXXVI   28 Now, my friends, I say: Don't think that this is everything. Because after you've done all these things, if you turn away the needy and naked and don't visit the sick and afflicted and give a portion of what you can spare — if you have anything you can spare — to the needy, I'm telling you, if you don't do these other things too, then your prayer is useless and doesn't benefit you at all, and you're essentially hypocrites who deny the faith. 29 If you don't remember to be charitable, you're like the waste thrown away by refiners because it has no value, to be trampled underfoot.

XXXVII ³⁰ Now, my friends, you've received many witnesses, because the holy scriptures testify of these things, and therefore I want you to respond and produce evidence of your repentance. ³¹ I would like you to respond and not harden your hearts any longer. Because now is the time and the day of your salvation. And therefore if you repent and don't harden your hearts, the great plan of redemption will immediately take effect for you. ³² This life is the time for people to prepare to come face to face with God. Indeed, now is the time for people to perform their labors. ³³ And so, as I told you before, you have so many witnesses that I warn you not to delay your repentance until the end of your life. Because we've been provided our lifetime to let us prepare for eternity. If we squander that time, we pass into the dark night where no further work can be done. ³⁴ You can't say when that awful moment of crisis arrives that: I'll repent, I'll return to God. No, you can't say this. Because that same spirit that you listen to and obey while living in the flesh will, after your death, have the same power to influence you to listen to that spirit in the next life. ³⁵ Indeed, if you've delayed the day of your repentance until death, you've fallen under the power of the accuser's spirit, and he secures you as his own. Therefore the Spirit of the Lord has withdrawn from you and has no place in you, and the accuser has all power over you. This is the final state of the wicked. ³⁶ And I know this because the Lord said He doesn't dwell in unholy temples, but He dwells in the hearts of the righteous. He has also said that the righteous will arrive in His kingdom and never leave His presence again, but their clothes will be made white through the Lamb's blood.

XXXVIII ³⁷ Now, my dear friends, please remember this and work out your salvation in awe of God, and never deny Christ's coming. ³⁸ Stop resisting the Holy Ghost; on the contrary, welcome it and take upon yourselves the name of Christ. Humble yourselves, bow to the ground to worship God wherever you go, in spirit and truth, and live thanking Him every day for His mercy and blessings to you. ³⁹ I urge you, my friends, to remain watchful and prayerful so you aren't overtaken by the accuser's temptations. Don't let him overpower you, so you don't end up under his control on the last day. He won't reward you with anything good in return. ⁴⁰ Now, my dear friends, I would urge you to have patience and to endure every difficulty you face, and don't speak ill of those who reject you because of your great poverty and become sinners like them. ⁴¹ To the contrary, you must have patience and endure difficulties with a firm hope that you'll rest one day from all your difficulties.

XXXIX **35** Now after Amulek had finished teaching these things, they left the group that had gathered to listen and returned to Jershon. 2 And the rest of their companions, after they finished preaching the word to the Zoramites, also returned to Jershon.

XL 3 After the leaders of the Zoramites got together and deliberated about the words preached to them, they were angry because of the message, since it destroyed their dishonest profession; therefore they refused to accept what had been taught. 4 And they sent messages to have people meet so they could get their reaction to the things that had been taught. 5 Now their rulers, priests, and teachers didn't let the people know what they wanted to do, and so they secretly found out what the people were thinking.

XLI 6 Then, after they had found out what everyone was thinking, the many people who were in favor of the things taught by Alma and his companions were removed from the land and evacuated to Jershon. 7 Alma and his companions welcomed them.

XLII 8 Immediately the Zoramites were angry with Ammon's people in Jershon. The Zoramites' chief ruler, who was a very wicked man, sent a message to Ammon's people, demanding they banish all the Zoramites who arrived in Jershon. 9 He made violent threats against them. However, Ammon's people weren't afraid of the threats, and they didn't banish them, but they welcomed the impoverished Zoramites who arrived. They cared for them and clothed them and gave them lands to occupy. And they ministered to them given their circumstances. 10 This aroused the anger of the Zoramites against Ammon's people. And they befriended the Lamanites and provoked them to join their bitter resentment. 11 And so the Zoramites and the Lamanites prepared to go to war against both Ammon's people and the Nephites. 12 That was how the 17th year of the judges' rule over the Nephites ended.

XLIII 13 Ammon's people relocated from Jershon and went to Melek, letting Jershon be occupied by the Nephite armies in anticipation of the battle with the Lamanite and Zoramite armies. At the start of the 18th year of the judges' rule a war began between the Lamanites and the Nephites. An account of their wars will be given later.

XLIV 14 Anyway, Alma, Ammon, and their companions, and Alma's two sons, had returned to Zarahemla, after God used them as His method of bringing many Zoramites to repentance. The repentant converts were exiled from their land, but they were provided with their own lands in Jershon. And then they armed themselves to defend their wives, children, and lands.

XLV   15 Alma was very disturbed by his people's iniquity, because of the coming wars, slaughter, and conflicts facing them. He had been sent by God to preach the word in every city, but now as the people were preparing for war they began to harden their hearts and reject strict obedience to the word, which gravely disappointed him. 16 As a response, he brought his sons together so he could give each one of them his guidance for them to maintain individual righteousness. And next is an account of the instructions he gave them, taken from his own record.

Chapter 17

Alma's commandments to his son Helaman.

36 My son, listen carefully. I promise you that to the extent you keep God's commandments, you'll prosper in the land. 2 I want you to follow my example and always remember our ancestors' captivity. Because when they were slaves no one could save them except for the God of Abraham and the God of Isaac and the God of Jacob — He certainly rescued them from their misery. 3 Now Helaman my son, you are young, and I urge you to listen and learn what I tell you, because I've seen that anyone who puts their trust in God will have His assistance during their trials, troubles, and difficulties and will be saved on the last day. 4 Don't think I understand this just from what I've seen, because it isn't the result of earthly experience alone but has been confirmed by the Spirit: not from the carnal mind but from God.

II   5 Now I tell you: If I hadn't been born of God, I wouldn't have understood these things. Remember God revealed them to me by His holy angel, and not because I had done anything to be worthy of it. 6 Indeed, I went with Mosiah's sons trying to destroy God's congregation. But God sent His holy angel to stop us while we were making trouble. 7 He spoke to us as if with a voice of thunder — the whole earth shook beneath our feet. And we all fell to the ground because we all feared the Lord. 8 But the voice said to me: Get up. And I stood up on my feet and saw the angel. 9 And he said to me: End your efforts to destroy the congregation, unless you want to be destroyed!

III   10 Then I fell to the ground, and I couldn't open my mouth or use my limbs for three days and nights. 11 And the angel said more things to me, which were heard by my companions, but I didn't hear them. Because when I heard the words: End your efforts to destroy the congregation, unless you want to be destroyed! I was struck with such great fear and amazement thinking I might be destroyed, that I collapsed and didn't hear anything else. 12 But I was tortured with eternal torment — my soul suffered to the greatest extent and was tortured by guilt over all my sins. 13 I remembered every sin and all my iniquities, and they tormented me with the pains of hell. Indeed, I could see my rebellion against God and that I hadn't kept His holy commandments. 14 And I had effectively murdered many of His children by leading them away to destruction — to be clear, my iniquities had been so overwhelming that the very thought of coming into the presence of God tortured my soul with inexpressible horror. 15 I thought to myself: I wish I could vanish and cease all existence, both spirit and body, so I could avoid being brought to stand in the presence of God to be judged for my actions. 16 And now I was tortured with the pains of a damned soul for three days and nights.

IV 17 And as I was tortured like this, while I was pained by the memory of my many sins, I also remembered hearing my father prophesy to the people about the coming of one Jesus Christ, a Son of God, to atone for the world's sins. 18 Now as my mind took ahold of this thought, I cried out within my heart: O Jesus, Son of God, have mercy on me — I bitterly regret my life and I feel doomed to everlasting death. 19 Now when I prayed this, I was released from my pains; indeed, I was no longer tormented by the memory of my sins. 20 But then, I felt such joy, and I saw such light! My soul was filled with joy as great as had been my pains. 21 Indeed, I tell you, my son, nothing is as intense and bitter as were my pains.

V But my son, on the other hand, from my experience there's nothing as intense and sweet as was my joy. 22 And then I thought I saw — just like our forefather Lehi saw — God sitting on His throne, surrounded by numberless rings of angels engaged in singing and praising Him. And my soul longed to be there. 23 Then I recovered and my limbs got their strength back, and I stood on my feet and declared to the people that I had been born of God. 24 And from then on I've worked nonstop to bring souls to repentance, to bring them to taste the great joy I tasted, so they can also be born of God and be filled with the Holy Ghost.

VI 25 And now, my son, the Lord has given me satisfying joy from the results of my labors. 26 Because of the word He's freely given me, many have been born of God and have experienced what I have, and have seen with their own eyes as I have. Therefore they understand the things I've taught, just as I know they're true; and the knowledge I have comes from God. 27 I've been strengthened in the face of every one of my trials and troubles, and in all my suffering. Indeed, God has rescued me from prisons, chains, and death — yes, I put my trust in Him and know He'll always rescue me. 28 I know He'll raise me up on the last day to live with Him in glory, and I'll praise Him forever. He brought our ancestors out of Egypt, and He drowned the Egyptians in the Red Sea, and He led them by His power into the promised land. He has freed them from slavery and captivity from time to time. 29 He also led our ancestors out of the land of Jerusalem, and He has, by His everlasting power, freed them from slavery and captivity from time to time, all the way down to the present time. And I've always kept in mind their enslavement; and you also ought to remember their enslavement, as I have. 30 But, my son, this isn't everything. I promise you that to the extent you keep God's commandments, you'll prosper in the land; and I promise you that to the extent you don't keep God's commandments, you'll be cut off from His presence. Now this is based upon His word.

VII 　　**37** And now, my son Helaman, I command you to take the records that have been entrusted to me. 2 And I also command you to maintain a record of this people on the plates of Nephi, in the same way I have, and keep these things sacred which I've protected, just as I've kept them sacred. They've been maintained and kept safe for a wise purpose. 3 Also protect these brass plates containing these engravings, which have the records of the holy scriptures on them and our ancestors' genealogy, from the very beginning. 4 It has been prophesied by our forefathers that they're to be maintained and kept safe and handed down from one generation to another, to be protected and preserved by the Lord until they're published to all people of every nation, tribe, and language, to let them know of the mysteries they contain. 5 Now if they're protected and maintained, they'll absolutely retain their brilliance. And they will do so! So will all the plates containing sacred writings.

VIII 　　6 Now you may think that I'm being foolish. But I tell you great things are accomplished by ordinary, simple things. And simple methods, in many instances, prove the wise are wrong. 7 The Lord God can use anything to accomplish His great and eternal purposes. And by very simple methods the Lord proves the wise wrong and accomplishes the salvation of many souls. 8 Now it has been wisdom in God for these things to be kept safe until now. Because they've increased our people's memory and convinced many of the error of their ways and brought them to the knowledge of God, for the salvation of their souls. 9 Indeed, I tell you: If it weren't for the things contained in the records on these plates, Ammon and his companions wouldn't have convinced so many thousands of the Lamanites of their ancestors' false traditions. It was these records and their content that brought them to repentance; that is, they let them know of the Lord who is God and to rejoice in Jesus Christ their Redeemer. 10 And who knows whether they might turn out to be instruments in bringing many thousands more of them — and even many thousands of our stubborn fellow Nephites also, who are now hardening their hearts in sin and iniquities — to know of their Redeemer. 11 Now I don't fully know about that future, so I'll stop there. 12 It may be enough to simply say these records are kept safe for a wise purpose, a purpose that's known to God. Because He wisely guides all His works, and His direction is straight and He moves continually in one eternal round.

IX   13 Remember, remember, my son Helaman, how strict God's commandments are! He has said: To the extent you keep God's commandments, you'll prosper in the land; and to the extent you don't keep God's commandments, you'll be cut off from His presence. 14 And now remember, my son, that God trusts you with these sacred things, which He made sacred and which He'll watch over and keep safe for His own wise purpose, to preserve His influence with future generations.

X   15 Now I tell you by the spirit of prophecy that if you go against God's commandments, you'll lose these sacred things by God's power and you'll be handed over to Satan, and he'll abuse you. 16 But if you keep God's commandments and guard these sacred things as the Lord commands you (and you should always ask the Lord about how to accomplish your responsibilities), then no power of earth or hell can take them from you, since God has the power to vindicate all His words. 17 He's sure to fulfill any promise He may make to you, since He's kept the promise He made to our forefathers. 18 He promised them He would protect these things to preserve His influence with future generations.

XI   19 And now He has fulfilled one purpose: that is, to restore thousands of Lamanites to the knowledge of the truth. He's increased His influence with them. And He'll likewise yet exert His influence through them to future generations. Consequently, they will be preserved. 20 So I command you, my son Helaman, to be diligent in following all my words and diligent in keeping God's commandments as they're written.

XII   21 Now I'll tell you about those 24 plates: You must keep them safe, so that the mysteries and their dark, secret schemes, the conspiracies of those people who were destroyed, can be revealed to this nation. They will need to hear about all their murders, robberies, plundering, wickedness, and abominations. And you must preserve these Directors. 22 When the Lord saw His people began to fall into dark acts and to commit secret murders and abominations, the Lord warned that if they didn't repent, they would be altogether annihilated from the earth. 23 The Lord said: I'll prepare a stone for My servant Gazelem that will bring their dark acts into the light, so I can expose for the people who serve Me the errors, depravity, and abominations of the earlier believers who fell into secret wickedness and dark works. 24 And now, my son, these Directors were prepared to accomplish the prophecies of God, which He committed to have happen, saying: 25 I'll expose to public view, out of darkness into light, all their secret offenses and their abominations. And unless they repent, I'll destroy them and annihilate them from the earth. And I'll bring to light all their secrets and abominations to every nation who will inhabit the land after this. 26 And now, my son, we see they didn't repent; therefore they've been removed. And so far God's word has been fulfilled; indeed, their secret abominations have been brought out of darkness and revealed to us.

XIII   27 And now, my son, I command you to not publish all their oaths, covenants, and agreements used in their secret abominations; indeed, you must continue protecting this people from all their signs and conspiracies, so they don't learn them, so they can't risk falling into darkness as well, and also be destroyed. 28 Remember, there's a curse on all this land that any people who choose darkness until they're fully ripe in iniquity, will be destroyed by God's power. That being the case, I don't want this people to be destroyed. 29 So you must protect this people from these secret plans of their oaths and covenants. And only reveal to them the wickedness, murders, and abominations. You must teach them to reject and regard such wickedness, abominations, and murders with disgust. You must also teach them the reason those people were destroyed was due to their wickedness, abominations, and murders. 30 Indeed, they murdered all the Lord's prophets who came among them to condemn their iniquities. And the blood of those they murdered cried out to the Lord their God for vengeance upon their murderers. As a result, God's judgments were imposed upon those who practiced that darkness and were part of the secret conspiracies. 31 And may the land be cursed forever against those who work in darkness, to their utter destruction, unless they repent before they're fully ripe.

XIV   32 Now, my son, remember the words that I've spoken to you. Don't entrust those secret plans to this people, but teach them an everlasting hatred for sin and iniquity. 33 Preach to them repentance and faith in the Lord Jesus Christ. Teach them to humble themselves and to be meek and humble in heart. Teach them to resist every temptation of the accuser with their faith in the Lord Jesus Christ. 34 Teach them never to grow tired of doing good, but to be meek and humble in heart

— because then they'll find rest for their souls. 35 Remember, my son, and learn wisdom while you're young; indeed, learn to keep God's commandments while you're young. 36 Cry to God in prayer — in all that you do — for help, strength, and comfort; and do everything you do for the Lord. And no matter where you go, go with the Lord. Direct all your thoughts to the Lord and always place your heart's desires on the Lord. 37 Consult the Lord in everything you do, and He'll direct you for good. When you lie down at night, lie down directing your thoughts and feelings to the Lord, asking Him to watch over you in your sleep. When you get up in the morning, let your heart be full of thanks to God. And if you always do these things, you'll be lifted up on the last day.

XV   38 Now, my son, I want to discuss the thing our forefathers called a ball or Director — or rather, they called it Liahona, which translates to a compass — that the Lord provided. 39 And no one can accomplish such intricate workmanship. It was provided to point the way for our ancestors to travel in the wilderness. 40 And it worked for them based on their faith in God. As a result, if they had faith to believe God would make the pins point the way to go, then it happened. Therefore they saw this miracle, and many other miracles, performed by God's power day after day. 41 However, even though those miracles let them accomplish miraculous things, they happened by ordinary methods and they got lazy, took it for granted, and neglected to exercise their faith and diligence. So then the miracles stopped, and they didn't make progress in their journey. 42 Then they wandered in the wilderness, no longer traveling a direct path, and suffered hunger and thirst due to their faithlessness.

XVI   43 Now, my son, I want you to understand these things foreshadow coming events. As our ancestors were disinclined to pay attention to this physical compass, they didn't advance; so it is with spiritual things. 44 Because it's the same thing to pay attention to Christ's word, which will point out to you a straight path to eternal bliss, as it was for our ancestors to pay attention to this compass, which would point out to them a straight path to the promised land. 45 I ask you: Isn't the one symbolic of the other? Because just as surely as this Director brought our ancestors, by following the way it pointed, to the promised land, so will Christ's word, if we follow the way it points, take us beyond this valley of tears into a much better promised land.

XVII   46 My son, let's not get lazy because the way is simple, because our ancestors were like that. They had the way opened for them; if they would just look, they could live. And it's the same for us: the way is still open; and if we choose to look, we can live forever. 47 And now, my son, please care for these sacred things. Indeed, see that you look to God and live. Go minister to this people and declare the word, and be serious in mind and purpose. Farewell my son.

Chapter 18
Alma's commandments to his son Shiblon.

38 My son, listen to me carefully. I say to you, just as I said to Helaman, that to the extent you keep God's commandments, you'll prosper in the land; and to the extent you don't keep God's commandments, you'll be cut off from His presence. 2 Now, my son, I expect to have great joy because of you, as a result of your steadiness and your faithfulness to God. Since you began to look to the Lord who is God while you were young, I expect you'll continue to keep His commandments, and all who persevere to the end are blessed. 3 I tell you, my son, I have great joy in you already because of your faithfulness, diligence, patience, and long-suffering among the Zoramites. 4 I knew you were in chains; and I also knew you were stoned because of the word. And you endured all these things patiently because the Lord was with you. Now you realize the Lord rescued you.

II   5 Now, my son Shiblon, I want you to remember that to the extent you put your trust in God, to the same extent you'll be rescued from your trials, troubles, and difficulties, and you'll be lifted up on the last day. 6 My son, I don't want you to think I learned these things on my own — no, it was God's Spirit, within me, that revealed these things to me. If I hadn't been born of God, I wouldn't have understood these things. 7 The Lord, in His great mercy, sent His angel to declare to me that I must stop the work of destruction among His people. Indeed, I saw an angel face to face, and he spoke with me. His voice was like thunder, and it shook the whole earth.

III   8 At that time I experienced the most bitter pain and anguish of soul for three days and three nights. And I didn't receive a remission of my sins until I cried out to the Lord Jesus Christ for mercy. And once I cried out to Him, I found peace for my soul. 9 Now, my son, I've told you this so you can learn wisdom, so you can learn from me, that the only way and means by which mankind can be saved is in and through Christ. He is the life and light of the world. He is the word of truth and righteousness.

IV   10 Now, just like you began to teach the word, I want you to continue to teach in the very same way. And I want you to be diligent and even-tempered in all things. 11 Make sure not to be prideful; make sure you don't brag about your wisdom or great strength. 12 Be bold, but not overbearing. And make sure you keep your zeal in check, and let love fill your heart. Make sure you refrain from foolish behavior. 13 Don't pray like the Zoramites — you've seen they only pray to be heard by people and to be praised for their wisdom. 14 Don't say: O God, I thank You that we're better than our brothers and sisters. Instead, say: O Lord, forgive my unworthiness and remember my brothers and sisters in mercy. Always acknowledge your unworthiness before God. 15 And may the Lord bless your soul and permit you, on the last day, to enter His kingdom and arrive there in peace. Now go, my son, and teach the word to this people; be serious in mind and purpose. My son, farewell.

Chapter 19

Alma's commandments to his son Corianton.

39 Now, my son, I need to say a little more to you than I said to your brother. Haven't you observed your brother's steadiness, his faithfulness and diligence in keeping God's commandments? Hasn't he set a good example for you? 2 However, you didn't follow my instructions while with the Zoramites like your brother did. Now this is my complaint against you: You proceeded to brag of your strength and wisdom. 3 But this isn't everything, my son. You made me ashamed when you abandoned the ministry and traveled to Siron near the border of the Lamanites to chase the harlot Isabel. 4 Indeed, she broke a lot of hearts, but that doesn't excuse you, my son. You should have stayed with the ministry you were entrusted to perform. 5 Don't you know, my son, this conduct is an abomination to the Lord? Indeed, it's the most detestable of all sins other than shedding innocent blood or denying the Holy Ghost. 6 Because if you deny the Holy Ghost once it has had place in you — and you know that you deny it — this sin is unpardonable. And whoever murders against the light and knowledge of God, it isn't easy for them to obtain forgiveness. Oh no, I tell you, my son, it isn't easy for them to obtain forgiveness.

II   7 Now, my son, I wish you hadn't been guilty of such a great sin. I wouldn't dwell on your sins to distress your soul if it weren't for your good. 8 But you can't hide your sins from God. And unless you repent, they'll stand as a testimony against you at the day of judgment. 9 Now, my son, I want you to repent and abandon your sins and not follow the desires of your eyes, but control yourself. Because unless you do this, there isn't any way for you to inherit God's kingdom. Indeed, remember and take responsibility to control these things within yourself. 10 And I command you to take the initiative to consult your older brothers about your challenges in life, and to pay careful attention to their counsel, because you are young and need advice from your brothers. 11 Don't let yourself be led away into doing worthless or foolish things. Don't let the accuser lead you to ever chase after wicked harlots again. Look at how much wickedness your example caused among the Zoramites, my son! Because when they saw your conduct, they wouldn't believe anything I said. 12 Now the Spirit of the Lord tells me: Command your children to do good, so they don't lead away the hearts of many people to destruction. So I command you, my son, to respect and obey God, and stop your iniquities, 13 to turn to the Lord with all your mind, power, and strength, so you don't lead away the hearts of anyone else to do wickedly. Instead, go back to them and admit your mistakes and repair the wrong that you've done. 14 Don't try to acquire wealth or the worthless things of this world; because you can't take them with you.

III   15 Now, my son, I want to say a little more to you about Christ's coming. I tell you He is the one we know will come to take away the sins of the world. He'll come to declare good news of salvation to His people. 16 Now, my son, this was the ministry assigned to you: to declare this good news to this people, to prepare their minds — or rather, to save them, so they would in turn prepare their children's minds to hear the word when He comes. 17 Now I'll answer your concerns about this subject. You wonder why these things should be known so long beforehand. I tell you: Isn't a soul at this time as precious to God as a soul will be at the time of His coming? 18 Isn't it as necessary for the plan of redemption to be revealed to people now as well as later to their children? 19 Isn't it as easy, at this time, for the Lord to send His angel to declare this good news to us as it will be to our children, or even declare it after His coming?

IV   **40** Now, my son, there's a little more I would like to tell you, because I recognize you're worried about the resurrection of the dead. 2 I tell you there's no resurrection until after Christ's coming. To be clear, this mortal body doesn't put on immortality, this decaying flesh doesn't become free from decay, until after Christ's coming. 3 He brings to pass the resurrection of the dead. But, my son, the resurrection hasn't happened yet. Now I'll unfold to you a mystery. Understand, there are still many remaining mysteries that no one knows except God Himself. But I'll explain one thing to you that I've diligently inquired of God to know, which is about the resurrection. 4 There's a time appointed when all will rise from the dead. When this time might happen, no one knows; but God knows the time it's appointed to take place. 5 Now, whether there will be one time or a second time or a third time for people to rise from the dead, it doesn't matter, since God knows all about that. It's enough for me to know that there's a time appointed when everyone will rise from the dead.

V   6 Now there's necessarily a period of time between the time of death and the time of the resurrection. 7 Now I wanted to know about what becomes of the spirits of mankind from this time of death to the time appointed for the resurrection. 8 Now whether there's more than one time appointed for people to rise, it doesn't matter, because everyone doesn't die at once, and that doesn't matter. Everything is as one day with God, and time is only measured to mankind. 9 Therefore there's a time appointed to people when they will rise from the dead; and there's a period of time between the time of death and the resurrection.

VI   Now I prayed diligently to the Lord about this period of time following death and what becomes of the spirits of mankind; and this is what I've learned: 10 When the time comes when everyone rises, then they will know God planned all the times selected for mankind. 11 And so about the state of the spirit between death and the resurrection, it has been revealed to me by an angel that the spirits of all mankind, as soon as they've left this mortal body, the spirits of all people — whether they're good or evil — are taken home to that God who gave them life. 12 And then the spirits of those who are righteous will be received into a state of happiness, which is called paradise, a state of rest, a state of peace, where they'll rest from all their troubles and from all care and sorrow, etc. 13 Then the spirits of the wicked, who are evil — because they have no part or portion of the Spirit of the Lord, since they chose to do evil rather than good; therefore the accuser's spirit entered them and took possession of their bodies — these spirits will be thrown out into outer darkness. There will be weeping, wailing, regret, and anguish — and it will be like this because of their own iniquity, being led away captive by the accuser's will. 14 Now this is the state of the spirits of the wicked: in darkness and in a state of awful, fearful anticipation of the fiery indignation of God's wrath upon them. And so they remain in this state, as well as the righteous in paradise, while awaiting their resurrection.

VII   15 Now there are some who have understood that this state of happiness or misery of the spirit before the resurrection was a first resurrection. Yes, I suppose it may be called a resurrection, the raising of the spirit or soul and being assigned to a state of happiness or misery, according to what's been said. 16 But clearly we know there's a first resurrection — a resurrection of all those who have lived or who are living or who will live, down to Christ's resurrection from the dead.

17 I don't think we can assume the first resurrection described in this way can be when departing souls are divided and assigned to a state of happiness or misery. I wouldn't assume this is what it means. 18 I say to you: No. But it means the reuniting of the spirit with the body of those who lived from the days of Adam down to Christ's resurrection. 19 Now whether the spirits and bodies of those previously mentioned are to all be reunited at once, the wicked as well as the righteous, I don't say. Let it be enough for me to say that all who die before Christ will be resurrected before those who die after Christ's resurrection. 20 Now, my son, I don't promise their resurrection comes at the moment of Christ's resurrection. But I expect the spirits and bodies of the righteous to be reunited at Christ's resurrection and ascension into heaven. 21 But whether it happens at His resurrection or after, I can't say.

VIII   However, I'll say this, there's a time between death and the resurrection of the body where the spirit is in happiness or in misery, until the time appointed by God, when the dead rise and are reunited, both spirit and body, and are brought to stand before God and be judged according to their works. 22 This brings about the restoration of those things the prophets have spoken about. 23 The spirit will be restored to the body and the body to the spirit. And every limb and joint will be restored to every body — not even a hair of their heads will be lost, but all things will be restored to their proper and complete frame. 24 Now, my son, this is the restoration the prophets have spoken about. 25 And then the righteous will gloriously shine in God's kingdom. 26 But an awful death befalls the wicked, since they're separated from any connection to righteousness; they're unclean, and no unclean thing can inherit God's kingdom. They're thrown out and condemned to receive a portion of the fruits of their labors — or their evil works — and they drink to the bottom of a bitter cup.

IX   **41** Now, my son, I have a little more to say about the previously mentioned restoration. Some have twisted the scriptures and have gone far astray about this topic. And I can tell your mind has also been worried about this. So let me explain it to you. 2 I tell you, my son, God's justice requires the plan of restoration, because it's necessary for all things to be restored to their proper order. It's necessary and right, according to the power and resurrection of Christ, for a person's spirit to be restored to its body and for every part of the body to be restored to itself. 3 And it's also required by God's justice for people to be judged based upon their works in this life. If their works were good in this life and if the things they wanted were good, it's also necessary for them to be restored on the last day to that which is good. 4 And if their works were evil, they'll be restored to them for evil. Therefore everything will be restored to its proper order, everything to its natural state — mortality raised to immortality, what's perishable becoming imperishable — raised to endless happiness to inherit God's kingdom, or to endless misery to inherit the accuser's kingdom, one on the one hand and the other on the other hand, 5 one restored to happiness according to their desires of happiness — or to good according to their desires of good — and the other restored to evil according to their desires of evil. Because just as they've wanted to do evil all day long, in the very same way they'll have their reward of evil when the night comes. 6 And so it is on the other hand: if they've repented of their sins and desired righteousness until the end of their life, in the same way, they'll be rewarded for righteousness. 7 These are the ones who are redeemed by the Lord. These are the chosen ones who are rescued from that endless night of darkness, and so they will stand or fall. Because they decide for themselves, whether to do good or evil. 8 Now God's decrees are unalterable. Therefore the way is prepared so that whoever is willing can walk in the path and be saved.

X   9 Now, my son, don't risk one more offense against God by violating His doctrine as you've risked committing sin up to this time. 10 Don't assume that because a restoration has been spoken about that you'll be restored from sin to happiness. Indeed, I say to you: Wickedness never was happiness. 11 Now, my son, everyone who's in a state of nature — or I would say, in a carnal state — is suffering in bondage from sin. They're without God in the world, and they've gone contrary to God's nature. Therefore they're in a state contrary to the nature of happiness.

XI   12 And now, is the meaning of the word restoration to take a thing in a natural state and place it in an unnatural state, or to place it in a state opposite to its nature? 13 No, my son, this isn't the case. The meaning of the word restoration is to bring back evil for evil, or carnal for carnal, or devilish for devilish, good for that which is good, righteous for that which is righteous, just for that which is just, merciful for that which is merciful. 14 Therefore my son, see that you're merciful to your fellow human beings. Act justly, judge righteously, and do good continually. If you do all these things, then you'll receive your reward. You'll have mercy restored to you; you'll have justice restored to you; you'll have a righteous judgment restored to you; and you'll have good rewarded to you. 15 Because what you send out will return to you and be restored. Therefore the word restoration more fully condemns those who sin and doesn't justify them at all.

XII   **42** Now, my son, I perceive there's a little more that worries you, which you can't understand, which is about the justice of God in punishing those who sin. You assume it's unfair for those who sin to be condemned to a state of misery. 2 To answer you, my son, I'll explain it. You know that after the Lord God removed our first parents from the Garden of Eden to till the dust from which their bodies were organized, after He drove them out, He placed cherubim and a flaming sword at the east end of the Garden of Eden to prevent access to the tree of life. 3 Now we learned that they had, like God, become able to distinguish good from evil, and to prevent them from taking fruit from the tree of life, and eat, and live forever, the Lord God placed cherubim and the flaming sword to stop them. 4 And so this resulted in a time for mankind to repent, a probationary period, a time to repent and serve God. 5 Because if Adam and Eve had immediately reached out and eaten from the tree of life, they would have lived forever, according to God's word, having no time for repentance. And also God's word would be invalid, and the great plan of salvation would have been useless and powerless. 6 But mankind was appointed to die. Therefore just as they were cut off from the tree of life, they were destined to die and be cut off from life on the earth. So mankind became lost forever; they became fallen human beings.

XIII   7 Now we see by this that our first parents were cut off, both temporally and spiritually, from the Lord's presence. We see they were left on their own to follow after their own will. 8 Now it wasn't suitable and proper for mankind to be relieved from this temporal death, since that would destroy the great plan of happiness. 9 Therefore since souls could never die and the Fall had brought upon all mankind a spiritual death as well as a temporal one — that is, they were cut off from the Lord's presence — mankind needed to be rescued from this spiritual death. 10 So, once they had become worldly, carnal, and devilish by nature, this probationary state became a state for them to prepare; it became a preparatory state.

XIV   11 Now remember, my son, if it weren't for the plan of redemption — setting it aside — as soon as they were dead, their spirits would be miserable, being cut off from the Lord's presence. 12 Now there was no means to reclaim people from this fallen state, which they had brought upon themselves because of their own disobedience. 13 Therefore according to justice, the plan of redemption could only be brought about on the condition of mankind's repentance in this probationary state — that is, this preparatory state. This is the only condition that could allow mercy to take effect without destroying the requirements of justice. Now the requirements of justice couldn't be ignored. If so,

God would stop being God. 14 And so we see that all mankind had
fallen, and they were in the grasp of justice — indeed, God's justice —
which forever relegated them to be cut off from His presence. 15 Now
the plan of mercy couldn't be brought about unless an atonement
were made. Therefore God Himself will atone for the sins of the
world, to bring about the plan of mercy, to meet the demands of
justice, so that God can be a perfectly just God, and a merciful God as
well.

XV   16 Now repentance couldn't come to people unless punishment as
eternal as the life of man's soul, was imposed opposite to the plan of
happiness, also as eternal as the life of man's soul, in balance. 17 Now
how could a person repent unless they committed sin? How could they
commit sin if there wasn't any law? How could there be a law unless
there was a punishment? 18 Now a punishment was affixed and a just
law was established, which brought remorse of conscience to
mankind. 19 Now if there wasn't any law established stating that if a
person committed murder they must die, would they be afraid they
would die if they committed murder? 20 Furthermore, if there wasn't
any law established against sin, people wouldn't be afraid to sin. 21 And
if there wasn't any law established against people sinning, what could
justice do, or mercy either? Neither would have any claim on the
person. 22 But there's a law established and a punishment affixed, and
repentance granted — repentance that mercy claims. Otherwise,
justice claims the person and executes the law, and the law inflicts the
punishment. If it weren't so, justice itself would be undone; and God
would stop being God. 23 But God will not stop being God; and mercy
claims the repentant, and mercy comes because of the atonement, and
the atonement brings to pass the resurrection of the dead, and the
resurrection of the dead brings mankind back into God's presence. In
this way, they're restored into His presence, to be judged according to
their works, according to the law and justice. 24 Indeed, justice exercises
all his demands; and mercy also claims all those who are her own.
Therefore only the truly repentant are saved.

XVI   25 What? Do you imagine mercy can rob justice? I tell you: No, not
at all. If so, God would stop being God. 26 Accordingly, God brings
about His great and eternal purposes, which were in place from the
foundation of the creation. In this way, the salvation and redemption
of mankind are brought about, as well as their destruction and misery.
27 Therefore, my son, whoever wants to come is allowed to come and
freely receive the waters of life. And whoever doesn't want to come
isn't compelled to come. But on the last day, it will be restored to them
according to what they've done. 28 If they wanted to do evil and haven't

repented during their life, evil will come to them according to the restoration of God.

XVII   29 Now, my son, I don't want you to let these things trouble you anymore. Just let your sins trouble you with the fear that will humble you to repent. 30 My son, I don't want you to deny God's justice anymore. Don't try to excuse yourself in the least degree because of your sins by denying God's justice. On the contrary, let God's justice and mercy and long-suffering have full sway in your heart, and let them bring you down to the dust in humility. 31 Now, my son, you're called by God to preach the word to this people. My son, go on your way; declare the word with truth and seriousness of mind and purpose, so you can bring souls to repentance, so the great plan of mercy can benefit them. And may God guide you according to my words. Amen.

Chapter 20

43 Now Alma's sons went out to preach the word to the people. And Alma himself couldn't rest either, and he also went out. 2 Now we won't say anything else about their preaching except they preached the word and truth according to the spirit of prophecy and revelation, and they preached according to the Holy Order of God by which they were called.

II   3 And now I'll pick back up the account of the wars between the Nephites and Lamanites in the 18th year of the judges' rule mentioned earlier. 4 The Zoramites became Lamanites. Therefore at the start of the 18th year, the Nephites saw the Lamanites were coming to attack them. So they made preparations for war, and they gathered their armies in the land of Jershon. 5 And the Lamanites came with their thousands. They entered the land of Antionum, which was the land of the Zoramites; and a man by the name of Zerahemnah led them. 6 Because the Amlicites, in and of themselves had a more wicked and murderous disposition than the Lamanites, all the chief captains Zerahemnah appointed over the Lamanites were from the ranks of the Amlicites and Zoramites. 7 He did this so he could inspire their hatred of the Nephites, to bring them under his control in order to accomplish his plan, 8 which was to incite the Lamanites to be angry with the Nephites. He did this so he could seize great power over them, wanting power over the Nephites to enslave them, etc.

III   9 Now the Nephites' aim was to protect their lands and houses and their wives and children, to keep them out of the hands of their enemies, and to preserve their rights and privileges, and their liberty as well, so they could worship God according to their wishes. 10 They knew if they fell into the hands of the Lamanites, they would kill anyone who worshiped God in spirit and in truth, the true and living God. 11 They also knew of the Lamanites' extreme hatred of their former Lamanites who were the people of Anti-Nephi-Lehi, who were called Ammon's people. Those people refused to arm themselves; indeed, they had made a covenant and they wouldn't break it. Therefore if they fell into the hands of the Lamanites, they would be killed. 12 And the Nephites wouldn't allow them to be killed; so they gave them land to live on. 13 Ammon's people in return gave the Nephites a large part of their supplies to support their armies. And so the Nephites had to stand alone against the Lamanites, who were a mixture of Laman, Lemuel, Ishmael's sons, and all those who had defected from the Nephites, who were Amlicites, Zoramites, and the descendants of Noah's priests. 14 Now those who had defected were almost as numerous as the Nephites were. And so the Nephites had to engage them in conflict, knowing many would die.

IV   15 And when the Lamanite armies had gathered in the land of Antionum, the Nephite armies were prepared to meet them in the land of Jershon. 16 The leader of the Nephites, or the man who had been appointed to be the chief captain over them who would command all the Nephite armies, was named Moroni. 17 And Moroni took on the entire command and management of their wars; and he was only 25 years old when he was appointed chief commander over the Nephite armies.

V   18 He met the Lamanites at the border of Jershon. His people were armed with swords, cimeters, and a variety of other weapons. 19 When the Lamanite armies advanced, they saw Moroni had prepared the Nephites with breastplates and armshields and helmets to defend their heads, and they wore thick clothing. 20 Zerahemnah's army wasn't prepared with any such things; they only had swords and cimeters, bows and arrows, and stones and slings; and they were naked except for an animal skin that was secured around their waists; indeed, everyone was naked except for the Zoramites and Amlicites. 21 Yet even they didn't have breastplates or shields, and therefore they were very afraid of the Nephite armies because of their armor, despite far outnumbering them.

VI   22 Now they didn't dare come against the Nephites at the border of Jershon. So they left the land of Antionum and traveled through the wilderness, winding through a route taking them to the head of the Sidon River, so they could come into the land of Manti and take control of the land, since they didn't think Moroni's armies would know where they had gone. 23 But as soon as they had entered the wilderness, Moroni sent spies into the wilderness to watch their camp. And because Moroni also knew of Alma's prophecies, he sent some men to him, requesting him to ask the Lord where the Nephite armies should go to defend themselves against the Lamanites. 24 And the Lord's word came to Alma. Alma informed Moroni's messengers that the Lamanite armies were on the march, taking a route through the wilderness so they could come over into the land of Manti, planning to begin an attack on the weaker part of the people. And those messengers delivered the message to Moroni.

VII   25 Now Moroni left part of his army in the land of Jershon — fearing some of the Lamanites might somehow enter that land and take the city — and took the remaining part of his army and marched over into the land of Manti. 26 He had all the people in that region of the land come together to fight the Lamanites, to defend their lands and country, their rights and liberties. Therefore they were prepared for when the Lamanites would arrive. 27 Moroni had his army conceal themselves in the valley near the bank of the Sidon River, which was to the west of the Sidon River in the wilderness. 28 Moroni placed spies on all sides so he would know when the Lamanite army arrived.

VIII   29 Now, since Moroni knew the Lamanites' ultimate purpose was to kill the Nephites or to subjugate them and bring them into slavery, in order to establish a kingdom for themselves over the whole land, 30 and since he also knew the Nephites' only desire was to preserve their lands, liberty, and congregation, therefore he saw nothing wrong with using a military strategy against them. So he used his spies to find the route the Lamanites were going to take. 31 He divided his army and brought a part of it over into the valley and concealed them to the east and to the south of the hill Riplah. 32 And the rest he concealed in the valley toward the west, to the west of the Sidon River, and through the area bordering the land of Manti. 33 Then having placed his army according to his plan, he was prepared to meet them.

IX   34 The Lamanites approached on the north side of the hill, where part of Moroni's army was hiding. 35 When the Lamanites had passed the hill Riplah and entered the valley and began to cross the Sidon River, the army that was hiding on the south side of the hill, led by a man named Lehi, came out and surrounded the Lamanites on the east from behind.

X   36 Then the Lamanites, when they saw the Nephites coming toward them from behind, turned around and began to fight Lehi's army. 37 And the killing began on both sides, but it was more dreadful on the part of the Lamanites, since their naked bodies were exposed to the heavy blows of the Nephites with their swords and cimeters, which killed with almost every stroke. ³⁸ On the other hand, men occasionally fell among the Nephites from wounds and blood loss, since they were shielded on the more vital parts of the body from the strokes of the Lamanites by their breastplates, arm shields, and helmets. And so the Nephites continued killing the Lamanites. ³⁹ The Lamanites became frightened because of their great slaughter, which reached a point that they began to flee toward the Sidon River. ⁴⁰ And they were pursued by Lehi and his men. They were driven by Lehi into the Sidon River, and they crossed it. But Lehi stopped his armies at the bank of the Sidon River, and they didn't cross it.

XI   ⁴¹ Then Moroni and his army met the Lamanite army in the valley, on the other side of the Sidon River. Moroni and his army began to attack and kill them. ⁴² Then the Lamanites fled again before them toward the land of Manti, and they were met again by Moroni's armies. ⁴³ Now in this instance, the Lamanites fought fiercely. Indeed, the Lamanites had never been known to fight with such great strength and courage, not even from the beginning. ⁴⁴ They were inspired by the Zoramites and Amlicites, who were their chief captains and leaders, and by Zerahemnah, who was their chief captain, or their chief leader and commander. Indeed, they fought ferociously, like true warriors. And many of the Nephites were killed, since they broke many of their helmets in two and pierced many of their breastplates, and cut off many of their arms. So the Lamanites fought in their fury. ⁴⁵ Nevertheless, the Nephites were inspired by a better cause. They weren't fighting for monarchy or power, but they were fighting for their homes and liberty, their wives and children, and their way of life — indeed, for their rights of worship and their congregation. ⁴⁶ They were doing what they believed to be the duty owed to God; because the Lord had said to them and their forefathers that insofar as you aren't guilty of the first offense or the second, you must not allow yourselves to be killed by your enemies. ⁴⁷ Furthermore, the Lord said that you must defend your families even to the point of shedding blood. Therefore, for this reason, the Nephites were fighting the Lamanites, to defend themselves and their families and lands, their country and rights and religion.

XII   ⁴⁸ When Moroni's men saw the Lamanites' fury and anger, they were about to retreat and flee from them. But Moroni, recognizing their fear, reminded and inspired them with this rally cry: Remember your lands, your liberty, and your freedom from slavery. ⁴⁹ And they turned toward the Lamanites and they cried out in unison to the Lord their God, for their liberty and their freedom from slavery. 50 And they held their position against the Lamanites with renewed determination. In the very same hour they cried out to the Lord for their freedom, the Lamanites began to flee before them; and they went back all the way to the Sidon River. 51 Now the Lamanites outnumbered the Nephites by more than double their number. Yet despite that, they were forced back into one compact group in the valley, on the bank by the Sidon River. 52 So Moroni's armies surrounded them, on both sides of the river, with Lehi's men to the east. 53 Therefore when Zerahemnah saw Lehi's men to the east of the Sidon River and Moroni's armies to the west of the river — that they were surrounded by the Nephites — they were terrified. 54 Now Moroni, when he saw their terror, ordered his men to stop killing them.

XIII   **44** So they stopped and withdrew a pace from them; and then Moroni said to Zerahemnah: You can see, Zerahemnah, we don't want to be killers. You know that you are in our hands, yet we don't want to kill you. 2 We haven't come out to battle against you to shed your blood to get power. And we don't want to impose slavery on anyone, either. Yet this is the very reason you've come against us, and you're angry with us because of our religion. 3 But now you see with your eyes that the Lord is with us. And you see He's delivered you into our hands. Now I want you to understand this is accomplished by us because of our religion and our faith in Christ. Now you see you can't destroy this faith of ours. 4 You should realize this is the true faith of God. Indeed, you see God will support, watch over, and preserve us so long as we're faithful to Him and to our faith and religion. The Lord will never allow us to be destroyed unless we fall into transgression and deny our faith. 5 Now, Zerahemnah, I command you in the name of that all-powerful God who has strengthened our arms to give us power over you by our faith, by our religion and rights of worship and congregation, and by the sacred support we owe our wives and children, and by the liberty that binds us to our lands and country, and also by the upholding of God's sacred word, to which we owe all our happiness, and by all that is most dear to us, 6 furthermore, I command you by all your desire to live to give up your weapons to us and we'll stop the fight, and we'll spare your lives if you go your way and don't come against us to war again. 7 Now if you don't do this, you are in our hands. And I'll order my men to attack you and continue killing all of you with mortal wounds. And then we'll see who will have power over us. We'll see who will be sent into slavery.

XIV   8 When Zerahemnah had heard these words, he came forward and gave up his sword, cimeter, and bow to Moroni and said to him: Here are our weapons; we'll hand them over to you. But we won't agree to make an oath to you that we know we'll break, and our children as well. However, take our weapons and allow us to go away into the wilderness. Otherwise, we'll keep our swords, and we'll die or conquer. 9 We're not of your faith. We don't believe it's God who's delivered us into your hands. But we believe it's your clever precautions that have kept you safe from our swords; it's your breastplates and shields that have kept you alive.

XV   10 When Zerahemnah had finished saying this, Moroni gave the sword and weapons he had received back to Zerahemnah, saying: We'll continue the conflict until the end. 11 Now I won't renew the offer I've made. Therefore as the Lord lives, you shall not leave this place unless you leave with an oath that you won't come back against us to war. Now as you're in our hands, we'll spill your blood on the ground, or you'll submit to the conditions I've proposed. 12 When Moroni had said these words, Zerahemnah held onto his sword. And being angry with Moroni, he rushed forward to kill him. But as he raised his sword, one of Moroni's soldiers struck it right to the ground, and it broke at the hilt. He also struck Zerahemnah, so that he severed his scalp and it fell to the ground. And Zerahemnah retreated into the middle of his soldiers.

XVI   13 And the soldier who stood by, who cut off Zerahemnah's scalp, raised the scalp from the ground by the hair and placed it on the point of his sword and held it out to them, declaring to them in a loud voice: 14 Just as this scalp has fallen to the ground, which is your leader's scalp, so also will you fall to the ground unless you hand over your weapons and leave with a covenant of peace.

XVII   15 Now there were many — when they heard these words and saw the scalp on the sword — who suddenly became afraid. So, many came forward and threw down their weapons at Moroni's feet and made a covenant of peace. And they allowed all those who made a covenant to go away into the wilderness.

XVIII   16 Now Zerahemnah was furious. And he incited anger in the rest of his soldiers, to fight the Nephites more fiercely. 17 Moroni was angry because of the Lamanites' stubbornness. Therefore he ordered his people to attack them and kill them. So they began to kill them. And the Lamanites fought with their swords and with their strength. 18 But their naked skin and bare heads were exposed to the Nephites' sharp swords. Indeed, they were stabbed and slashed, and they fell very quickly before the Nephites' swords. They began to be swept down, just as Moroni's soldier had prophesied. 19 Now Zerahemnah, when he saw that they were all about to die, cried out loudly to Moroni, promising if they spared the lives of the rest of them that he and his people would covenant with them never to return to war against them. 20 And so Moroni again stopped the killing. And he took the Lamanites' weapons from them. After they had made a covenant of peace with him, they were allowed to go away into the wilderness.

XIX   21 Now their dead weren't counted because of how many there were. Unfortunately, the number of their dead was terribly high, on the part of both the Nephites and the Lamanites. 22 They threw their dead into the Sidon River, and they've gone downstream and are buried in the depths of the sea. 23 The armies of the Nephites led by Moroni went back to their houses and lands. 24 And so ended the 18th year of the judges' rule over the Nephites. That ends Alma's record, which was written on the plates of Nephi.

Chapter 21

The account of the Nephites and their wars and conflicts during Helaman's time, according to Helaman's record, which he kept during his life.

45 Now the Nephites were overjoyed because the Lord had again saved them from the power of their enemies. So they gave thanks to the Lord their God. And they fasted and prayed a great deal, and joyfully worshiped God.

II   2 In the 19th year of the judges' rule over the Nephites, Alma came to his son Helaman and asked him: Do you believe the words I said to you about those records that have been kept? 3 And Helaman answered him: Yes, I believe. 4 And Alma also asked: Do you believe in Jesus Christ, who is to come? 5 And he replied: Yes, I believe all the things you taught me. 6 Alma then asked him: Will you keep my commandments? 7 And he replied: Yes, I'll keep your commandments with all my heart. 8 Then Alma told him: You are blessed, and the Lord will make you prosperous in this land. 9 But I have something to prophesy to you. However, what I prophesy to you, you must not reveal; indeed, what I prophesy to you must not be revealed until the prophecy is fulfilled. Therefore write the words I tell you. 10 And this is what he prophesied: According to the spirit of revelation in me, this very people, the Nephites, 400 years following Jesus Christ's visit with them in person, will fall away in unbelief. 11 At that point they'll experience wars, plagues, disease, famine, and slaughter until the Nephites become completely extinct. 12 And it will happen like this because they'll fall away in unbelief and fall into works of darkness, lustful behaviors, and all kinds of iniquities. I know because they will sin against so great light and knowledge — indeed, I declare some of the fourth generation from Christ's appearance will still be living when this great iniquity comes. 13 And when that great day comes, then very soon after that those who are the descendants of people now included as Nephites won't be identified as Nephites anymore. 14 Anyone who remains and isn't killed on that great and terrible day will be called a Lamanite and will become like them, except for a few who will be called the Lord's disciples or followers. And the Lamanites will pursue them, until all of them are dead. Now because of iniquity, this prophecy will be fulfilled.

III   15 Then, after Alma had said these things to Helaman, he blessed him, and his other sons as well. He also blessed the earth for the benefit of the righteous. 16 He said: This is what the Lord God has said: The land will be cursed to destroy any people on this land who do evil, whether they belong to any nation, tribe, or language, when they're fully ripe. And just as I've said, so will it happen. Indeed, this is God's cursing and blessing on the land, because the Lord can't tolerate sin to any degree. 17 Now when Alma had said these words, he blessed the congregation, indeed, all those who would stand firmly in the faith from that time forward. 18 When Alma had done this, he left Zarahemla as if to go to Melek. And he was never heard of again. As to his death or burial, we don't have any knowledge. 19 But this we do know, that he was a righteous man. And the saying went abroad in the congregation that he was taken up by the Spirit or buried by the Lord, just like Moses was. But the scripture says the Lord took Moses to Himself. And we believe He has also received Alma in the spirit to Himself. Therefore, for this reason, we don't know anything about his death and burial.

IV   20 Now in the beginning of the 19th year of the judges' rule over the Nephites, Helaman went out among the people to declare the word to them. 21 And because of their wars with the Lamanites and the many little disagreements and disturbances that had occurred among the people, it became advisable for God's word to be declared among them, and for order to be established throughout the congregation. 22 So Helaman and his brothers went out to establish the congregation again in all parts of the land, in every city throughout the land of the Nephites. And they appointed priests and teachers over all the congregations.

V   23 Now after Helaman and his brothers had appointed priests and teachers over the congregations, disagreements arose among them, and they refused to pay any attention to the words of Helaman and his brothers; 24 and they grew proud: their hearts became lifted up because of their great wealth. So they grew wealthy in their own eyes and refused to pay any attention to the teachings to live righteously before God.

VI   **46** All those who refused to listen to Helaman and his brothers' instruction joined together against their fellow Nephites. 2 Now they were so angry with Helaman and his brothers that they were determined to kill them. 3 The leader of those who were very angry with their fellow Nephites was a large, strong man named Amalickiah. 4 Amalickiah wanted to be a king; and those people who were angry also wanted him to be their king. Most of them were the lower judges of the land who were looking for more power. 5 They had been persuaded by Amalickiah's promises that if they would support him and establish him to be their king, then he would make them rulers over the people. 6 In this way, Amalickiah persuaded them to begin fighting, despite Helaman and his brothers' preaching, and despite their great care over the congregation, since they were high priests over the congregation. 7 There were many in the congregation who believed the promises of Amalickiah; therefore they even split off from the congregation. And so the affairs of the Nephites were very precarious and dangerous, despite the great victory they had gained over the Lamanites, and the great feelings of joy they had experienced because the Lord had saved them. 8 So we see how quickly mankind forgets the Lord who is God, how quick they are to commit iniquity and to be led astray by the Evil One. 9 And we also see the great evil that one very wicked man can cause among mankind. 10 We see that Amalickiah, because he was a scheming, corrupt, and articulate man, led astray the hearts of many people to act wickedly, and to attempt to destroy God's congregation and also the foundation of liberty God had provided to them, or God's blessing sent upon the land because of the righteous.

VII   11 Now when Moroni, who was the chief commander of the Nephite armies, had heard of these conflicts, he was angry with Amalickiah. 12 He tore his outer garment and took a piece of it and wrote on it: In memory of our God, our religion and freedom and peace, our wives and children. He fastened it on the end of a pole. 13 And he put on his helmet, breastplate, and shields and secured his armor around his waist. Then he took the pole with his torn outer garment on the end of it, and he called it the Declaration of Liberty. And he bowed down to the ground and prayed to God with great energy for the blessings of liberty to rest on his fellow Nephites, as long as a group of Christians remained to inhabit the land 14 (because this was what all the true believers of Christ who belonged to God's congregation were called by those who didn't belong to the congregation). 15 And those who belonged to the congregation were faithful. All those who were true believers in Christ gladly took upon themselves the name of Christ, or the name of Christians, as they were called, because of their belief in Christ, who was to come. 16 Therefore at this time Moroni prayed for the Christian cause and for the freedom of the land to be upheld.

VIII   17 When he had poured out his soul to God in prayer, he identified all the land south of the land of Desolation — and in short, all the land, both to the north and to the south — as a chosen land and the land of liberty. 18 He said: Surely God won't allow us — who are despised because we take upon ourselves the name of Christ — to be trampled and killed, until we bring it upon ourselves by our own transgressions. 19 After Moroni said this, he rallied the people, waving the torn part of his garment in the air, so everyone could read what he had written on it, and shouting in a loud voice: 20 Anyone who wants to support this Declaration upon the land, may they come forward with the Lord's strength and make a covenant that they will defend their rights and religion, so that the Lord God will bless them.

IX   21 When Moroni had proclaimed these words, the people came running together with their armor secured around their waists, tearing their clothes as a sign, or as a covenant, that they wouldn't abandon the Lord their God. Or in other words, if they broke God's commandments — or fell into transgression — and were ashamed to take upon themselves the name of Christ, the Lord would tear them, just like they had torn their clothes. 22 Now this was the covenant they made; and they threw their clothes at Moroni's feet, saying: We covenant with God that we will have to be destroyed, just like our fellow inhabitants in the land northward were, if we fall into transgression. He can throw us at our enemies' feet, just like we've thrown our clothes at your feet, to be trampled underfoot if we fall into transgression. 23 Moroni said to them: We are a remnant of Jacob's descendants. And we are a remnant of Joseph's descendants, whose garment was torn into many pieces by his brothers. Now let's remember to keep God's commandments, or our clothes will be torn by our brothers and we'll be thrown in prison or sold or killed. 24 Let's preserve our liberty as a remnant of Joseph. Let's remember Jacob's words before his death. He saw a part of the remnant of Joseph's garment was preserved and hadn't decayed. He said: Just like this part of my son's garment has been preserved, so a part of my son's descendants will be preserved by God's power and will be taken to Him, while the rest of Joseph's descendants will perish, patterned after the remnant of his garment. 25 Now, this makes me sorrowful. Still, I have joy in my son, because of that part of his descendants who will be taken to God. 26 This was Jacob's language. 27 And now, it's possible the remnant of Joseph's descendants who will be lost like his garment are those who have defected from us; and it could be us as well, if we don't stand firmly in the faith of Christ.

X
28 When Moroni had said these words, he went about, and also sent out messages, to every part of the land where there were defections, and gathered all the people who wanted to maintain their liberty, to stand against Amalickiah and those who had defected, who were called Amalickiahites.

XI
29 When Amalickiah realized Moroni's people were greater than the Amalickiahites, and when he saw his people doubted the justice of the cause they had undertaken — and fearing he wouldn't achieve his objective — he took those of his people who were willing and made his way to the land of Nephi.

XII
30 Now Moroni thought it would be bad for the Lamanites to have any more strength. Therefore he planned to cut off Amalickiah's people, or to capture them and bring them back and put Amalickiah to death. Because he could see they would stir up the Lamanites to be angry with them and to come down to battle against them. And he knew Amalickiah would do this to accomplish his objectives. 31 Therefore Moroni thought it was advisable to utilize his armies, which had gathered and armed themselves and made a covenant to keep the peace. He led his army and marched into the wilderness with his tents to cut off Amalickiah's path in the wilderness.

XIII
32 He followed his plan and marched into the wilderness and got ahead of Amalickiah's armies. 33 Then Amalickiah fled with a small number of his men, and the rest surrendered to Moroni's control and were returned to Zarahemla. 34 Now because Moroni was a man who was appointed by the chief judges and the vote of the people, he had power to command and give orders to the Nephite armies as he thought best.

XIV
35 He had any Amalickiahites put to death who refused to make a covenant to support the cause of freedom, so they could maintain a free government. And there were only a few who refused the covenant of freedom.

XV
36 He also had the Declaration of Liberty hoisted on every tower throughout the land occupied by the Nephites. And so Moroni planted the flag of liberty among the Nephites. 37 And peace returned to the land. They maintained peace in the land until nearly the end of the 19th year of the judges' rule. 38 Helaman and the high priests also

established order in the congregation; indeed, for four years they enjoyed peace and rejoicing in the congregation.

XVI   39 There were many who died firmly believing their souls were redeemed by the Lord Jesus Christ, so they left the world rejoicing. 40 And there were some who died with fevers, which during some times of the year were very common in the land — but they could control the fevers because of the excellent qualities of the many plants and roots God provided to remove the cause of diseases which affected people due to the climate — 41 still there were many who died of old age. And those who died in the faith of Christ are happy in Him, as we understand.

XVII   47 Now we'll return in our record to Amalickiah and those who fled with him into the wilderness. He had taken those who were with him and gone up into the land of Nephi among the Lamanites, and there he stirred up the Lamanites to be angry with the Nephites; this resulted in the Lamanite king sending a proclamation throughout his land among all his people that they were to gather again to go to battle against the Nephites.

XVIII   2 When the proclamation went out to them, they were very afraid. They were afraid to displease the king; and they also were afraid to go to battle against the Nephites, fearing they might lose their lives. And so they refused — or most of them refused — to obey the king's command.

XIX   3 Now the king was furious because of their disobedience. So he gave Amalickiah the command over that part of his army who were obedient to his commands, and commanded him to compel them to obey and prepare for battle. 4 Now this was what Amalickiah wanted; and because he was evil and cunning, he planned in his heart to dethrone the Lamanite king. 5 Now he had obtained command over the king's loyal Lamanites, and he planned to get the trust of the disloyal. Therefore he went to the place called Oneidah, since all the Lamanites had fled there after they caught sight of the army coming; and thinking they were coming to kill them, they fled to Oneidah, where weapons were stored. 6 They had appointed a man as king and leader over them, because they were determined they wouldn't be forced to fight the Nephites.

XX   7 They gathered on the top of the hill called Antipas to prepare for battle. 8 Now it wasn't Amalickiah's objective to fight a battle as the king had commanded. But it was his plan to gain the favor of the Lamanite armies, so he could place himself at their head and dethrone the king and take the kingdom. 9 So he had his army pitch their tents in the valley near the hill Antipas. 10 When it was night, he sent a message in secret up to the leader of those on the hill Antipas, whose name was Lehonti. The message asked him to come down to the foot of the hill to speak with him.

XXI   11 When Lehonti received the message, he didn't dare go down to the foot of the hill. So Amalickiah sent a message a second time, asking him to come down. And Lehonti refused again. He sent a message a third time. 12 When Amalickiah realized he couldn't persuade Lehonti to come down off the hill, he went up the hill, nearly into Lehonti's camp. Then he sent his message a fourth time to Lehonti, asking him to meet and bring his guards with him.

XXII   13 When Lehonti went down to Amalickiah with his guards, Amalickiah asked him to come down with his army at night and surround those men, in their camps, which the king had given him to command. He promised to hand them over to Lehonti to command if he would appoint him, Amalickiah, the second in command of the whole army.

XXIII   14 Lehonti then led his men and surrounded Amalickiah's men, so that before they awoke at dawn, they were surrounded by Lehonti's armies. 15 When they saw they were surrounded, they pled with Amalickiah to let them join their fellow Lamanites, to avoid being slaughtered. Now this was exactly what Amalickiah wanted.

XXIV   16 He surrendered his men, against the king's commands. Now this was what Amalickiah wanted, so that he could accomplish his scheme to dethrone the king. 17 Now it was the custom among the Lamanites, if their first leader was killed, to appoint the second leader to be their chief leader.

XXV   18 Amalickiah had one of his servants administer poison little by little to Lehonti, so that he died. 19 When Lehonti was dead, the Lamanites appointed Amalickiah to be their leader and their chief commander. 20 And Amalickiah marched with his armies — since he had accomplished his plan — to the land of Nephi, to the city of Nephi, which was the main city. 21 And the king came out to meet him with his guards, because he thought Amalickiah had carried out his orders and Amalickiah had gathered the entire army to go battle the Nephites. 22 But as the king came out to meet him, Amalickiah had his servants go forward to meet the king. They went forward and bowed before the king, as if to show him respect for his prominence. 23 And the king put out his hand to raise them, as was the custom with the Lamanites and a sign of peace, imitating the Nephite custom. 24 When he had raised the first one from the ground, he stabbed the king in the heart and he fell to the ground. 25 Then the king's servants fled. And Amalickiah's servants cried out in a loud voice, saying: 26 The king's servants have stabbed him in the heart, and he's fallen and they've fled. Come and see!

XXVI 27 Amalickiah ordered his armies to march forward and see what had happened to the king. When they arrived at the spot and found the king lying in his blood, Amalickiah pretended to be very angry and said: Anyone who loved the king, let him go pursue his servants so they can be killed.

XXVII 28 And all those who loved the king, when they heard these words, came forward and went after the king's servants. 29 When the king's servants saw an army pursuing them, they were frightened again and fled into the wilderness and came over into the land of Zarahemla and joined Ammon's people. 30 The army that chased them returned, having lost their trail. And so Amalickiah by his fraud won the hearts of the people.

XXVIII 31 On the next day, he entered the city of Nephi with his armies and took the city. 32 Now the queen, when she had heard that the king was killed — for Amalickiah had sent a message to the queen informing her that the king had been killed by his servants, and that he had pursued them with his army, but it was in vain and they had escaped — 33 therefore when the queen had received this message, she sent a message to Amalickiah, asking him to spare the people of the city. And she also asked him to come see her. She also asked him to bring witnesses with him to testify about the king's death.

XXIX 34 Amalickiah took the same servant who killed the king, and also those who were with him, and went to see the queen at her throne. They all testified to her that the king was killed by his own servants. And they added: They've fled. Doesn't this testify against them? And so they satisfied the queen regarding the king's death.

XXX 35 Then Amalickiah worked to gain the queen's confidence and she agreed to marry him. And so by his fraud and with the assistance of his clever and deceitful servants, he obtained the kingdom. He was acknowledged king throughout the land among all the Lamanites, who were composed of Lamanites, Lemuelites, and Ishmaelites, and all the Nephite defectors from the time of Nephi's rule down to the present time. 36 Now these defectors had learned the same truths and prophecies from the Nephites and were taught the same knowledge of the Lord. Yet despite this, it's odd but true that, not long after defecting, they became more hardened, unrepentant, uncivilized, wicked, and savagely cruel than the Lamanites, eagerly adopting Lamanite traditions, giving in to laziness and all kinds of lustful behavior, indeed, entirely forgetting the Lord who is God.

XXXI   **48** As soon as Amalickiah obtained the kingdom, he began to manipulate the Lamanites against the Nephites. Indeed, he appointed men to speak to the Lamanites from their towers, accusing the Nephites. 2 In this way, he influenced them against the Nephites, so that in the latter end of the 19th year of the judges' rule, having carried out his scheme to that point, having been made king over the Lamanites, he also made it his aim to rule over the entire land, and all the people who lived there, the Nephites as well as the Lamanites. 3 So he had advanced his plan, since he had hardened the Lamanites' hearts and blinded their minds and stirred them up to anger, so much so that he collected a large army willing to attack the Nephites. 4 Indeed, he was determined, by virtue of the sheer size of his army, to overpower the Nephites and enslave them. 5 He appointed chief captains from the Zoramites, since they were the most acquainted with the Nephites' strength, safely reinforced places, and the weakest parts of their cities; therefore he made them chief captains over his armies. 6 And they set out with their army and advanced to the land of Zarahemla through the wilderness.

XXXII   7 Now while Amalickiah had, in this way, been obtaining power by fraud and deceit, on the other hand, Moroni had been engaged in preparing the minds of the people to be faithful to the Lord who is God. 8 He had been strengthening the Nephite armies and erecting small forts or reinforced places, throwing up banks of earth around them to protect his armies, and also building stone walls to surround them, around their cities and the borders of their lands, all throughout the land. 9 In their weakest fortifications he placed the greater number of men. He fortified and strengthened the land held by the Nephites. 10 By these preparations he intended to defend their liberty, their lands, their wives and children, and their peace, to live for the Lord their God, and maintain what was called by their enemies the cause of Christians.

XXXIII   11 Moroni was a strong and powerful man. He was a man of sound understanding; a man who didn't delight in slaughter, whose soul rejoiced in the liberty and freedom of his country and of his fellow Nephites from servitude and slavery, 12 whose heart swelled with thanksgiving to God for the many privileges and blessings He freely gave His people, who worked hard for his people's well-being and safety. 13 And he was a man who was firm in the faith of Christ. He had sworn an oath to defend his people, his rights, his country, and his religion, even to the point of losing his own life.

XXXIV   14 Now the Nephites were taught to defend themselves against their enemies, even if it required killing. But they were also taught never to go on the offensive, and never to fight with the sword except against an enemy, and only then if it was to preserve their lives. 15 And this was their faith, that by doing so God would give them prosperity in the land; or in other words, if they were faithful in keeping God's commandments, He would protect them by warning them to flee or to prepare for war, according to the danger they faced. 16 Also they believed God would reveal to them where they should go to defend themselves from their enemies, and by doing so the Lord would protect them. And this was Moroni's faith. His heart rejoiced in it — not in killing, but in doing good, in preserving his people, in keeping God's commandments, and resisting iniquity. 17 In truth I tell you: If all men had been, were, and would always be like Moroni, the very powers of hell would have been shaken forever. Indeed, the accuser would never have any power over people's hearts. 18 He was like Ammon the son of Mosiah, and like the other sons of Mosiah, and like Alma and his sons, since they were all men of God. 19 Now Helaman and his brothers weren't any less prepared to serve or any less engaged in serving the people than Moroni was: they preached God's word and baptized all those who were willing to listen to them as a sign of repentance. 20 So they went out; and the people humbled themselves because of their words, so much so that the Lord blessed them. And they were free from internal wars and conflicts for about four years.

XXXV   21 But as I've said, toward the end of the 19th year, despite the peace among themselves, they were reluctantly compelled to fight their Lamanite brothers. 22 Once it started, hostilities with the Lamanites never stopped for many years, despite Nephite reluctance. 23 They regretted having to fight the Lamanites, because they didn't like killing. That wasn't all, they also regretted being the ones who sent so many of their Lamanite brothers from this world into an eternal world, unprepared to come face to face with God. 24 Nevertheless, they couldn't simply give up their lives, or allow their wives and children to be slaughtered by the barbarous cruelty of those who were once their fellow Nephites, and who had split from their congregation and left them, and who had gone away in order to destroy them by joining the Lamanites. 25 Indeed, they couldn't bear for their Nephite or Lamanite brothers to rejoice over spilling Nephite blood, as long as any of them kept God's commandments — the Lord having promised that if they kept His commandments, they would prosper in the land.

XXXVI   **49** Now in the 11th month of the 19th year, on the 10th day of the month, the Lamanite armies were seen approaching Ammonihah. 2 The city had been rebuilt, and Moroni had stationed an army by the city's borders. They also had thrown up dirt around it to shield them from the Lamanites' arrows and stones, because they fought using stones and arrows. 3 Now the city of Ammonihah had been rebuilt, but only partially rebuilt. Because the Lamanites had destroyed it once, due to the people's iniquity, they expected it would again be an easy target for them. 4 But their hopes were dashed. The Nephites had dug up a ridge of earth around them so high the Lamanites couldn't throw their stones and shoot their arrows at them with any success, and they couldn't attack them either, unless they did it through the controlled entrance.

XXXVII   5 At this time the Lamanite chief captains were very surprised at the Nephites' thoughtful repairs to their defenses. 6 The Lamanite leaders had thought that because of their large numbers, it would again be a successful attack, as before. In preparing for the attack, they prepared themselves with shields and breastplates, and also with clothing made of leather, very thick clothing to cover their naked bodies. 7 Having prepared in this way, they thought they could easily overpower their Nephite relatives to enslave, or kill and slaughter them at will. 8 But to their complete surprise, they were prepared for them in a way unprecedented among all of Lehi's descendants; they were prepared for the Lamanites, to engage them in battle according to Moroni's instructions.

XXXVIII   9 The Lamanites, or the Amalickiahites, were shocked at how prepared they were for war. 10 Now if king Amalickiah had come down out of the land of Nephi at the head of his army, perhaps he would have had the Lamanites attack the Nephites at the city of Ammonihah, since he didn't care about his people's lives. 11 But Amalickiah himself didn't come down to battle. And his chief captains didn't dare attack the Nephites at the city of Ammonihah, since Moroni had adopted such a new defensive strategy for the Nephites that the Lamanites lost hope of defeating the fortifications, and they abandoned the attack. 12 Therefore they retreated into the wilderness and mobilized their armed forces and marched toward Noah, expecting it to be the next best place for them to attack the Nephites. 13 They didn't know Moroni had fortified — or had built forts of security for every city throughout the surrounding region. So they marched onward to Noah with firm determination. Indeed, their chief captains came forward and swore an oath they would destroy the people of that city. 14 But to their astonishment, the city of Noah, which had until then been a weak place, had become strong through Moroni's intervention, even surpassing the strength of the city of Ammonihah. 15 Now this was wise of Moroni. Because he anticipated they would be intimidated at the city of Ammonihah; and since the city of Noah had until then been the weakest part of the land, he expected they would march there to battle. And it happened as he had foreseen. 16 Moroni had appointed Lehi as chief captain over the men of that city; who was that same Lehi who fought with the Lamanites in the valley on the east side of the Sidon River.

XXXIX   17 Now when the Lamanites learned Lehi commanded the city, their hopes were again shattered, since they were very afraid of Lehi. Nevertheless, their chief captains had sworn an oath to attack the city, so they brought up their armies. 18 Now the Lamanites couldn't enter their secure forts by any other way except through the entrance, since the ridge of earth was raised quite high and the ditch excavated around the outside of it was quite deep, except near the entrance. 19 With this design the Nephites were prepared to kill all those who might attempt to climb up to enter the fort elsewhere, by throwing stones and shooting arrows down at them. 20 So they were prepared. Additionally, a group of their strongest men were ready with their swords and slings, to kill anyone who dared attempt to enter their fort through the entrance. Therefore they were prepared to defend themselves against the Lamanites.

XL   21 So the Lamanite captains attacked the front of the entrance and began to fight the Nephites, in order to invade the fortress. But they were driven back every time, with resulting deaths in an immense slaughter. 22 Now when they found they couldn't defeat the Nephites through the entry, they began to dig down their ridges of earth to create an opening for their armies, hoping for an equal chance to fight. But in these attempts they were swept down by the stones thrown and the arrows shot at them. Instead of filling up their ditches by pulling down the ridges of earth, they were filled up to a certain extent with their dead and wounded bodies. 23 So the Nephites completely overpowered their enemies. The Lamanites continued to attempt to kill the Nephites until their chief captains were all killed. Now more than 1,000 Lamanites were killed, while on the other side not a single Nephite was killed. 24 There were about 50 who were wounded, who had been exposed to the Lamanites' arrows at the entry. But they were protected by their shields, breastplates, and helmets, so their wounds were on their legs, many of which were very severe.

XLI   25 When the Lamanites saw all their chief captains were killed, they retreated into the wilderness. They returned to the land of Nephi to inform their king, Amalickiah, who was a Nephite by birth, about their great loss. 26 He was furious with his people because he hadn't achieved his objectives over the Nephites; he hadn't brought them under the burden of slavery. 27 Indeed, he was furious, and he cursed

God, and Moroni as well, swearing with an oath he would drink his blood. His reaction was because Moroni had kept God's commandments and had prepared for his people's protection. 28 In contrast, the Nephites thanked the Lord their God because of His miraculous power in freeing them from their enemies.

XLII   29 And so ended the 19th year of the judges' rule over the Nephites. 30 There was continual peace among them and great prosperity in the congregation because of the attention and diligence they gave God's word, which was preached to them by Helaman, Shiblon, Corianton, Ammon, his brothers, and so forth, and by all those who had been ordained by the Holy Order of God. They were baptized as a sign of repentance before they were sent out to preach among the people, and so on.

Chapter 22

50 Now Moroni didn't stop preparing for war or to defend his people against the Lamanites. Indeed, at the start of the 20th year of the judges' rule, he had his armies begin to dig up piles of earth around the outside of all the cities throughout the Nephites' lands. 2 On top of those ridges of earth around the outside of the cities, he had walls of timbers erected to the height of a man. 3 He had a frame of pointed stakes built upon those walls of timbers, around the outside of them; and they were strong and high. 4 And he built towers overlooking those pickets; and he had reinforced shelters on top of the towers, so the Lamanites' stones and arrows couldn't hurt them. 5 They were prepared to throw stones from the top of them at selected targets, using their arm strength to kill anyone who might attempt to approach the city walls. 6 In this way, Moroni prepared strongholds around the outside of every city in the whole land, in anticipation of their enemies' arrival.

II   7 Then Moroni had his armies enter the eastern wilderness. And they went out and drove all the Lamanites who were in the eastern wilderness into their own lands, which were south of the land of Zarahemla. 8 The land of Nephi ran in a straight line from the eastern sea to the west. 9 When Moroni had driven all the Lamanites from the eastern wilderness, which was north of their own lands, he made the inhabitants who were in the land of Zarahemla and in the surrounding regions go into the eastern wilderness, all the way to the shoreline, and occupy the land. 10 And he also placed armies to the south in the borders of their own lands and had them erect fortifications so they could guard their armies and their people from their enemies. 11 In this way he cut off all the Lamanite strongholds in the eastern wilderness, and also to the west, fortifying the line between the Nephites and Lamanites, between the land of Zarahemla and the land of Nephi, from the western sea running by the head of the Sidon River, the Nephites occupying all the land to the north, indeed, all the land to the north of the land of Bountiful, as they saw fit. 12 So Moroni with his armies, which increased daily because of the confidence in the protection his planning gave them, attempted to take away the Lamanites' ability to invade their lands. This was to prevent the Lamanites from gaining any power over their lands.

III   13 The Nephites began to build a city, and they called the city Moroni. It was by the eastern sea; and it was south, bordering the Lamanite frontier. 14 And they also began building a city between the cities of Moroni and Aaron, along the same border as Aaron and Moroni, and they called the name of that city and surrounding area Nephihah. 15 During that same year, they also began building many other cities in the north, one in a particular design they called Lehi, which was to the north near the seashore. 16 And so ended the 20th year. 17 And at the beginning of the 21st year of the judges' rule over the Nephites, the Nephites found themselves prospering. 18 In fact, they were very prosperous, and they became very rich. They increased in population and became strong in the land.

IV   19 Now we can see how merciful, fair, and true all the Lord's dealings are, fulfilling all His words for the benefit of mankind. We can see, even at this time, the words He spoke to Lehi are verified, saying: 20 Blessed are you, and your children as well. And they will be blessed! To the extent you keep God's commandments, you'll prosper in the land; and to the extent you don't keep God's commandments, you'll be cut off from His presence. 21 So we see these promises were kept for the Nephites; because it has been their quarrels and conflicts, their murders and thievery, their idol worship and whoredoms, and the abominations of the people that brought upon them armed conflict and destruction. 22 Those who were faithful in keeping the Lord's commandments were protected and saved every time, while thousands of their wicked fellow Nephites have been condemned to slavery or to die by the sword or to fall away in unbelief and mix with the Lamanites. 23 But there never was a happier time among the Nephites since Nephi's days than during Moroni's days, indeed, during the 21st year of the judges' rule. 24 And the 22nd year of the judges' rule also ended in peace, and the 23rd year as well.

V   25 At the start of the 24th year of the judges' rule, there also would have been peace among the Nephites if it hadn't been for a conflict that arose regarding the land of Lehi and the land of Morionton, which adjoined the borders of Lehi, both of which bordered the seashore. 26 The dispute came about because the people who lived in the land of Morionton claimed part of the land of Lehi. So a heated conflict arose between them, to the point that the people of Morionton armed themselves to fight their fellow Nephites, being determined to kill them with the sword. 27 But the people who lived in the land of Lehi fled to Moroni's camp and appealed to him for assistance. They did this because they weren't in the wrong.

VI   28 When the people of Morionton, who were led by a man named Morionton, discovered the people of Lehi had fled to Moroni's camp, they were very afraid that Moroni's army would attack and kill them. 29 So Morionton gave them the idea to flee northward, to the land covered with large bodies of water, and take the land to the north as their own. 30 They would have put this plan into effect, which would have been a matter of deep concern; but Morionton was a man of uncontrollable anger, and he got angry with one of his female servants and assaulted and severely beat her. 31 She fled and went to Moroni's camp and told Moroni everything about the events and about their intention to flee to the north. 32 Now the people of Bountiful, or rather Moroni was afraid the people of Bountiful, would listen to Morionton and unite with his people. That would result in him gaining control of those parts of the land, which would lead to serious consequences among the Nephites, consequences that would lead to the loss of their liberty. 33 Therefore Moroni sent an armed force to get ahead of Morionton's people, to stop their departure into the land to the north. 34 But they didn't get ahead of them until they had arrived at the border of the land of Desolation. They confronted them by the narrow pass beside the sea into the land to the north, between the sea on the west and on the east.

VII   35 And the army sent by Moroni, which was led by a man named Teancum, met Morionton's people. And Morionton's people, being influenced by his wickedness and persuasion, were so stubborn that a battle began, in which Teancum killed Morionton and defeated his army and took them prisoner and returned to Moroni's camp. And so ended the 24th year of the judges' rule over the Nephites. 36 This was how the people of Morionton were brought back. Once they covenanted to keep the peace, the land of Morionton was given back to them. And a general agreement was reached between them and the people of Lehi, and their lands were also given back to them.

VIII   37 In the same year that peace was restored among the Nephites, Nephihah the second chief judge died, having occupied the judgment seat with perfect uprightness before God. 38 Nevertheless, he had declined Alma's offer to take responsibility for those records and those things that Alma and his fathers considered most sacred. Therefore Alma had conferred them upon his son Helaman.

IX   39 Nephihah's son was appointed to fill the judgment seat in his father's place. He was appointed chief judge and governor over the people, with an oath and sacred ordinance to judge righteously, and to keep the peace and freedom of the people, and to grant them their sacred privileges to worship the Lord who is God, to support and maintain the cause of God while he ruled, and to bring the wicked to justice according to their crimes. 40 Now his name was Parhoron. Parhoron occupied his father's seat and began his rule over the Nephites at the end of the 24th year.

Chapter 23

51 Now at the start of the 25th year of the judges' rule over the Nephites, they had resolved the conflict between the peoples of Lehi and Morionton over their lands, and began the 25th year peacefully. 2 However, they didn't maintain complete peace in the land for long. Indeed, a dispute arose among the people over the chief judge Parhoron; some of the people wanted a few specific points of the law to be changed. 3 But Parhoron wouldn't allow the law to be changed. Therefore he didn't listen to or sympathize with those who petitioned to change the law. 4 As a result, those who wanted the law to be changed got angry with him and didn't want him to be chief judge over the land any longer. As a result, a heated dispute arose about the matter, but not to the point of violence.

II   5 And those who wanted Parhoron to be dethroned from the judgment seat were called kingmen, since they wanted the law to be changed to abandon the free government and establish a king over the land. 6 Those who wanted Parhoron to remain as chief judge over the land adopted the name of freemen. This divided the people into two factions, with the freemen having sworn or covenanted to maintain their rights and the privileges of their religion by a free government.

III   7 The dispute was settled by a vote of the people. The people's vote came out in the freemen's favor; and Parhoron retained the judgment seat, which caused celebrations among Parhoron's brothers and among the people of liberty as well, which silenced the kingmen, who didn't dare oppose the cause of freedom but were obligated to maintain it. 8 Now those who were in favor of kings were of high birth, and they made it their aim to be kings. They were supported by others who wanted power to control the people. 9 This was a critical time for any conflicts like this to be happening among the Nephites. Because

Amalickiah had again stirred up the hearts of the Lamanites against the Nephites; and he was gathering soldiers from all over his land and arming them and preparing for war, since he had sworn to drink Moroni's blood. 10 But we'll see that his promise was ill-advised. Nevertheless, he prepared himself and his armies to go against the Nephites in battle. 11 Now his armies had been reduced in number by the many thousands who had been killed by the Nephites. But despite their great loss, Amalickiah had assembled a surprisingly large army, therefore he wasn't afraid to come down to Zarahemla. 12 Indeed, Amalickiah himself led the Lamanites. And it was in the 25th year of the judges' rule; and it was while they were resolving their disputes over the chief judge, Parhoron.

IV   13 When the men who were called kingmen learned the Lamanites were coming down to battle against them, they were pleased. So they refused to go to battle, because they were so angry with the chief judge and with the people of liberty that they were determined not to participate in defending their country. 14 When Moroni saw this, and also saw the Lamanites were arriving at the outskirts of the land, he was extremely angry at the refusal of the people he fought so hard to protect. Indeed, he was furious with them. 15 And he sent a petition to the governor of the land expressing the people's will, asking him to give it his attention and to give him, Moroni, power to compel the separatists to either help defend their country or be executed. 16 Now he did this because his first concern was to put an end to conflicts and violent disagreements between the people. Indeed, up to that point, internal fighting had caused all their setbacks and had been their downfall. And the people approved his plan.

V   17 So Moroni commanded his army to confront the kingmen, to either put down their pride and nobility by cutting them down or compelling them to take up arms and support the cause of liberty. 18 The armies marched out against them, to put down their pride and nobility, and when they lifted their weapons to fight Moroni's men, they were cut down in a slaughter. 19 A total of 4,000 of those separatists were cut down by the sword. Any of their leaders who weren't killed in battle were taken and thrown in prison, since there was no time then for their trials. 20 The rest of those separatists, rather than be cut down by the sword, yielded to the flag of liberty and were compelled to raise the Declaration of Liberty on their towers and in their cities and to go to war in defense of their country. 21 And so Moroni put an end to those kingmen, so there weren't any known survivors of the kingmen. Through this he put an end to the stubborn pride of those people who claimed to have noble blood; they were brought down to humble themselves like their fellow Nephites and to fight valiantly for freedom from slavery.

VI
    22 While Moroni was in this way putting an end to the wars and conflicts between his own people and imposing peace and preserving their civilization and organizing a defense for the war against the Lamanites, the Lamanites invaded the land of Moroni, by the seashore.

VII
    23 Because the Nephites weren't strong enough in the city of Moroni, Amalickiah drove them out, killing many. And Amalickiah took the city and control over all their fortifications. 24 Those who fled the city of Moroni came to the city of Nephihah. The people of the city of Lehi also came together and made preparations and were ready to meet the Lamanites in battle.

VIII
    25 But Amalickiah wouldn't allow the Lamanites to go against the city of Nephihah to battle; instead, he kept them down by the seashore, putting his men in every city to maintain and defend it. 26 He went on taking many cities, including the cities of Moroni, Lehi, Morionton, Omner, Gid, and Mulek, all of which were near the eastern seashore. 27 And so with Amalickiah's leadership and superior numbers, the Lamanites had overtaken many cities, all of which were strongly reinforced using Moroni's fortifications, which then provided strongholds for the Lamanites.

IX
    28 Then they marched to the border of the land of Bountiful, driving the Nephites ahead of them and killing many of them. 29 But there they met Teancum, who had killed Morionton and stopped his people during Morionton's attempted departure. 30 So he confronted Amalickiah while he was marching with his large army to take the land of Bountiful and the land to the north. 31 But those hopes were thwarted when Teancum and his men, who were great warriors, drove them back. Indeed, every one of Teancum's men was superior to the Lamanites both in strength and ability to fight, so they defeated the Lamanites.

X
    32 They attacked the Lamanites repeatedly as they retreated, killing them until it was dark. Then Teancum and his men camped at the border of the land of Bountiful; and Amalickiah camped on the beach near the seashore, where they had been forced to retreat.

XI
    33 When it was night, Teancum and his assistant crept quietly in the dark into Amalickiah's camp. The fatigue from fighting and the daytime heat had put them into a sound sleep.

XII
    34 Teancum quietly entered the king's tent and impaled his heart with a javelin. The king died immediately without waking his servants. 35 Afterward, Teancum returned quietly to his own camp while his

men were sleeping. He woke them up and explained all he had done.
36 He then assembled his armies to stand ready in case the Lamanites
were up and preparing to attack them. 37 And so ended both the 25th
year of the judges' rule over the Nephites and Amalickiah's life.

Chapter 24

52 Now in the 26th year of the judges' rule over the Nephites,
when the Lamanites awoke on the first morning of the first month,
they found Amalickiah dead in his own tent. They also saw Teancum
was ready to give them battle on that day. 2 When the Lamanites saw
this, they were frightened; and they abandoned their plan to march
into the land to the north and retreated with their whole army into the
city of Mulek and the safety of their fortifications. 3 Amalickiah's
brother was appointed king, whose name was Ammoron. He assumed
control.

II   4 He ordered his people to maintain the cities that had cost lives to
occupy, and they lost a lot of lives taking every one of the cities. 5 Now
Teancum saw the Lamanites were determined to maintain the cities
and the parts of the land they had taken. He could see their forces far
outnumbered his, therefore Teancum thought it made no sense for
him to attempt to attack them in their forts. 6 But he kept his men
surrounding them, as if preparing to attack. And in fact, he was
preparing his defense against them by erecting walls on all sides and
preparing fortifications.

III   7 He kept preparing for battle in this way until Moroni sent a large
number of men to strengthen his army. 8 Moroni also sent an order for
him to retain all the prisoners that surrendered and were in his
custody. Now the Lamanites had taken many prisoners, and the order
to retain all the Lamanite prisoners was to use them in an exchange for
those the Lamanites held prisoner. 9 Moroni also sent orders for him to
fortify the land of Bountiful and to secure the narrow pass leading to
the land to the north, so the Lamanites didn't obtain that strategic
point and have power to repeatedly attack them on every side.
10 Moroni also sent him a message, asking him to be faithful in
maintaining that region and to look for every opportunity to afflict the
Lamanites as much as was in his power, so he could perhaps take back,
by military stratagem or some other way, those cities taken from them,
and to continue to fortify and strengthen the cities in the surrounding
area that hadn't fallen under the control of the Lamanites. 11 He also
said to him: I would come to you, but the Lamanites are gathering

against us by the western sea. I'll soon fight against them; therefore I can't come to you.

IV   12 Now the new king, Ammoron, left the land of Zarahemla after informing the queen about his brother's death. He brought a large number of men and marched against the Nephites in the area near the western sea. 13 He was making an effort to exhaust the Nephites with repeated attacks and draw away part of their forces to that region. At the same time, he also commanded those left to occupy the cities that had been taken to tire out the Nephites with repeated attacks near the eastern sea and to take additional land, as much as they might be able to do, as their armies' strength allowed. 14 And so the Nephites found themselves in these dangerous circumstances at the end of the 26th year of the judges' rule.

V   15 But in the 27th year of the judges' rule, Teancum followed the orders of Moroni. Moroni put armies in place to protect the southern and western limits of the land. He then began to march toward Bountiful, so he could assist Teancum. He planned to retake the cities they had lost. 16 Teancum was ordered to attack the city of Mulek and retake it, if possible.

VI   17 Teancum prepared to attack the city of Mulek and went with his army to attack the Lamanites. But he saw it was impossible to overpower them while they were behind their fortifications. Therefore he abandoned his plans and returned to the city of Bountiful to wait for Moroni's arrival, so he would have a larger force for the fight.

VII   18 Moroni arrived with his army in Bountiful near the end of the 27th year of the judges' rule. 19 At the start of the 28th year, Moroni and Teancum and many of the chief captains held a council of war, to decide what they could do to get the Lamanites to battle them in the open, or to coax them out of their strongholds, so they would have an advantage over them and take back the city of Mulek.

VIII   20 They sent messengers to the Lamanite army protecting the city of Mulek, to their leader, whose name was Jacob, asking him to come out with his armies to meet them on the open ground between the two cities. But Jacob, who was a Zoramite, refused to come out with his army to fight in the open.

IX   21 Then, because Moroni had no hope of meeting them on an even battlefield, he decided on a plan to lure the Lamanites out of their strongholds. 22 He had Teancum take a small number of men and march down near the seashore; and Moroni and his army marched at night into the wilderness to the west of the city of Mulek. And so the next day, when the Lamanite guards caught sight of Teancum, they ran and told Jacob, their leader.

X
²³ The Lamanite armies marched out against Teancum, expecting because of their superiority in numbers to overpower Teancum because of his small force. When Teancum saw the Lamanite armies coming out against him, he began to retreat down by the seashore, toward the north.

XI
²⁴ When the Lamanites saw he began to run away, they were encouraged and vigorously pursued them. While Teancum was luring away the Lamanites who were chasing them in vain, Moroni commanded a portion of his army who were with him to march into the city and take it over. ²⁵ They did so and killed all those who had been left to protect the city, indeed, that is, any who wouldn't give up their weapons. ²⁶ And so Moroni had taken the city of Mulek with part of his army while he marched with the rest to confront the Lamanites when they returned from chasing Teancum.

XII
²⁷ The Lamanites pursued Teancum until they got near the city of Bountiful, and there they encountered Lehi and a small army left to protect the city of Bountiful. ²⁸ When the Lamanite chief captains saw Lehi with his army coming against them, they fled in great confusion, for fear they might not reach the city of Mulek before Lehi overtook them, since they were exhausted from their march, and Lehi's men were fresh. ²⁹ Now the Lamanites didn't know Moroni had been behind them with his army — all they were afraid of was Lehi and his men. ³⁰ Now Lehi didn't want to overtake them until they met up with Moroni and his army. ³¹ Before the Lamanites had retreated very far, they were surrounded by the Nephites, by Moroni's men on the one hand and by Lehi's men on the other, all of whom were rested and full of strength, while the Lamanites were exhausted from their long march. ³² Moroni commanded his men to attack them until they had surrendered their weapons.

XIII
³³ Now Jacob, who was their leader — a Zoramite with an unconquerable spirit — led the Lamanites out to battle against Moroni with great fury. ³⁴ Because Moroni blocked their line of march, Jacob was determined to kill them and cut his way through to the city of Mulek. But Moroni and his men were more powerful; therefore they held the battle line against the Lamanites.

XIV
³⁵ They fought furiously on both sides, and many were killed on both sides; and Moroni was wounded and Jacob was killed. ³⁶ And Lehi attacked the back of their army with his strong men so fiercely that the Lamanites in the rear surrendered their weapons. And the rest of them, who were in a state of great confusion, didn't know where to go

or where to deliver a blow. 37 Moroni, seeing their confusion, said to them: If you bring your weapons forward and surrender them, we'll stop killing you. 38 When the Lamanites had heard these words, their chief captains — all those who weren't killed — came forward and threw down their weapons at Moroni's feet and commanded their men to do likewise. 39 But there were many who refused. Those who refused to give up their swords were taken and their hands tied; their weapons were removed from them, and they were marched under guard with their fellow Lamanites to Bountiful. 40 Now the number of prisoners who were taken exceeded the number of those who had been killed, indeed, more than those who had been killed on both sides.

XV   **53** As they guarded the Lamanite prisoners, they compelled them to gather and bury their dead, and the Nephite dead. And Moroni's men kept watch over them as they performed their work. 2 And Moroni went to the city of Mulek with Lehi and took command of the city and gave it to Lehi. Now Lehi was a man who had been with Moroni in the majority of his battles, and he was a man like Moroni. They rejoiced at seeing each other safe again; indeed, they loved one another dearly and they were dearly loved by all the Nephites.

XVI   3 After the Lamanites had finished burying their dead and the Nephite dead, they were marched back into Bountiful. And by Moroni's orders, Teancum made them begin working, digging a ditch around the land, or the city of Bountiful. 4 He made them build a barricade of timbers on the inner bank of the ditch; they piled up dirt from the ditch against the barricade of timbers. And so they made the Lamanites work until they had encircled the city of Bountiful with a strong wall of timbers and earth to a great height. 5 This city became a great stronghold from that time forward. They guarded the Lamanite prisoners in this city, inside a wall they had made them build with their own hands. Now Moroni was compelled to put the Lamanites to work because it was easy to guard them while they were working; and he needed all his forces to keep ready for an attack on the Lamanites.

XVII   6 In this way, Moroni had gained a victory over one of the largest Lamanite armies and had taken the city of Mulek, which was one of the strongest fortified places of the Lamanites in the land of Nephi. Additionally, he had built a stronghold to continue holding his prisoners. 7 He didn't attempt to engage the Lamanites in battle again that year, but he readied his men for war, built fortifications to defend against the Lamanites, kept their women and children fed and protected, and distributed food to their armies.

XVIII   8 In Moroni's absence there was a secret plot among the Nephites causing strong division that resulted in internal conflicts. Because of this, the Lamanite armies by the western sea to the south gained some ground over the Nephites and they took several of their cities there. 9 As a result of iniquity among themselves, because of their own violent disagreements and scheming, they ended up putting themselves into dangerous circumstances.

XIX   10 Now I have a little to say about Ammon's people, who in the beginning were Lamanites; but because of Ammon and his companions (more correctly because of the power and word of God), they had been converted to the Lord. They had been brought down into the land of Zarahemla and had been protected by the Nephites from then on. 11 Because of the oath they had made, they had been kept from going to battle against their Lamanite relatives, since they had taken an oath that they would never kill again. According to their oath, they would have died; they would have allowed themselves to fall into the hands of their Lamanite relatives if it hadn't been for Ammon and his companions' pity and great love for them. 12 For this reason they were brought down into the land of Zarahemla, and they had always been protected by the Nephites.

XX   13 But when they saw the danger and the many troubles and hardships the Nephites endured for them, they felt compassion for them and wanted to go to battle and join in defending their country. 14 But as they were preparing to use their weapons, they were convinced by Helaman and his brothers not to do it. Because it would require them to break the oath they had made, 15 Helaman was afraid that by doing so they might lose their souls. Therefore all those who had made this covenant were left to only watch their fellow Nephites face their difficulties in this dangerous time. 16 But they had many sons who hadn't made a covenant not to use weapons to defend themselves against their enemies. Therefore those who were able to fight got together and proclaimed themselves Nephites. 17 And they made a covenant to fight for the Nephites' liberty, to protect the land, at the peril of sacrificing their lives; indeed, they covenanted they would never give up their liberty, but they would fight in all circumstances to protect the Nephites and themselves from slavery.

XXI   18 Now there were 2,000 young men who made this covenant and took up weapons to defend their country. 19 And, although they had never been a disadvantage to the Nephites up to that point, they now became a great support. They took their weapons, and they asked Helaman to lead them. 20 They were all young men, very courageous, strong, and active as well. But this wasn't the best thing about them, because they were trustworthy in anything asked of them, 21 and they were truthful and serious-minded and focused, since they had been taught to keep God's commandments and live righteously.

XXII 22 Now Helaman led his 2,000 young soldiers to defend the people in the area to the south by the western sea. 23 So ended the 28th year of the judges' rule, etc.

Chapter 25

54 At the start of the 29th year of the judges, Ammoron sent a message to Moroni, asking him to exchange prisoners. 2 Moroni was overjoyed at this request, since he wanted the supplies used to maintain the Lamanite prisoners for his own people; and he also wanted his own people returned in order to strengthen his army. 3 Now the Lamanites had captured many women and children; but there wasn't a woman or child among all Moroni's prisoners, or the prisoners Moroni had captured. So Moroni resolved on a plan to obtain as many Nephite prisoners from the Lamanites as possible. 4 Therefore he wrote a letter and sent it with Ammoron's servant, who had brought his proposal to Moroni.

II Now this is what he wrote to Ammoron: 5 Ammoron, I write to you a few words about this war you've waged against my people, which was started by your brother and you're still determined to continue after his death. 6 I want to tell you something about God's justice and the sword of His almighty wrath, which hangs over you unless you repent and withdraw your armies back to your own lands, or the lands you inhabit, which is the land of Nephi. 7 Of course, I would explain it to you if you were capable of accepting it. I would explain to you about that awful hell prepared to receive such murderers as you and your brother have been, unless you repent and withdraw your murderous aims and return with your armies to your own lands. 8 But since you've previously rejected these things and have fought against the Lord's people, I expect you'll do that again.

III 9 Now we are fully prepared to defend against you; and unless you withdraw your aims, you will bring down on yourselves the wrath of that God whom you've rejected, resulting in your complete destruction. 10 And as the Lord lives, our armies will come against you unless you withdraw, and you will soon be killed. Indeed, we'll take back our cities and lands, and we'll maintain our religion and the cause of God. 11 But I suspect I'm wasting my time telling you about these things, because I suspect you're a child of hell. Therefore I'll end my letter by telling you I won't exchange prisoners unless it's on the condition that you turn over a man and his wife and children in exchange for one of our prisoners. If you're actually willing to do this, I will exchange. 12 But if you don't do this, I'll come against you with my armies, and I'll even arm my women and children; I'll come against you, and I'll follow you all the way into your own land, which is the land we first inherited. And it will be blood for blood, indeed, life for life. And I'll engage you in battle until you're annihilated. 13 I'm full of anger and so are my people. You've tried to murder us, and we've only tried to defend our lives. But if you attempt to kill us again, we'll attempt to kill you. And we'll try to recover our lands, the lands we first inherited. 14 Now I close my letter. I am Moroni; I am a leader of the Nephites.

IV   15 Now, when Ammoron had received this letter, he was angry, and he wrote another letter to Moroni. And these are the words he wrote: 16 I am Ammoron the king of the Lamanites. I'm the brother of Amalickiah, whom you've murdered. I'll avenge his blood upon you. And I'll come against you with my armies, because I'm not afraid of your threats. 17 Your forefathers treated their brothers unfairly, so much so that they robbed them of their right to govern when it rightfully belonged to them. 18 Now if you lay down your weapons and place yourselves under our control, to be governed by those to whom the government rightly belongs, then I'll have my people lay down their weapons and not carry on war any longer. 19 You've made a lot of fierce threats against me and my people. But we aren't afraid of your threats. 20 Nevertheless, I'll gladly agree to exchange prisoners according to your request, so I can preserve my food for my men of war. And we'll carry on a war that will be eternal, either to bring the Nephites under our control and authority or to bring about their eternal extinction. 21 As for that God whom you say we've rejected, we don't know such a being and neither do you. But if it's true that there's such a being, then it seems likely to us that He's made us as well as you. 22 And if it's true there's a devil and a hell, then won't He send you there to live with my brother, whom you've murdered, whom you suggest has been sent there? But these things don't matter. 23 I'm Ammoron and a descendant of Zoram, whom your forefathers seized and brought out of Jerusalem and forced into servitude. 24 I'm now a bold Lamanite. And this war has been waged to avenge their wrongs and to maintain and obtain their rights to the government. And so I end this letter to Moroni.

V   55 When Moroni had received this letter, he became even angrier, because he knew Ammoron knew what he wrote was a fraud. Indeed, he knew Ammoron understood what led him to this war against the

Nephites wasn't a just cause. 2 And he said: I won't exchange prisoners with Ammoron unless he abandons his intention, as I stated in my letter, because I won't give him any more power than he already has. 3 I know the place where the Lamanites guard my people, those they've taken prisoner. Since Ammoron refused to agree to the terms of my letter, I'll attack them according to my words; I'll pursue them with lethal force until they beg for peace. 4 When Moroni had said these words, he had a search made among his men to locate someone who was a descendant of Laman.

VI   5 They found one, named Laman, who had been one of the servants of the murdered king killed by Amalickiah. 6 Now Moroni had Laman and a small number of his men approach the guards who were over the Nephites. 7 They were guarded in the city of Gid; therefore Moroni had Laman, and a selected small number of men, accompany him.

VII   8 When it was evening, Laman went up to the guards who were over the Nephites. They saw him coming and called out, challenging him, but he said to them: Don't be afraid! I'm a Lamanite. We've escaped from the Nephites and they're asleep. And look, we've taken some of their wine and brought it with us. 9 When the Lamanites heard this, they gladly welcomed him. And they said to him: Give us some of your wine so we can drink. We're glad you've brought wine with you because we're tired. 10 But Laman said to them: Let's save our wine until we go to battle against the Nephites. But saying this just made them want to drink the wine even more. 11 They said: We're tired; so let's drink the wine. Soon we'll receive wine as part of our provisions, which we'll drink before going against the Nephites. 12 And Laman said to them: Do as you wish. 13 They drank the wine without restraint, and the taste was to their liking; so they drank even more of it. And it was strong, having been prepared in its strength.

VIII   14 They drank and enjoyed themselves, and before long all of them were drunk. 15 Laman and his men waited until they were all drunk and in a deep sleep, then they returned to Moroni and told him what had happened. 16 Now this was what Moroni had planned. Moroni had equipped his men with weapons, and he went to the city of Gid while the Lamanites were in a deep drunken sleep, and dropped the weapons inside to the prisoners, arming all of them, 17 even arming the women and all of their children, including anyone who could wield a weapon. When Moroni had silently armed all those prisoners, 18 even if they had awakened the drunk Lamanites, the Nephites could have killed them. 19 But this wasn't what Moroni wanted. He didn't enjoy murder or killing, but he took satisfaction in saving his people from ruin and death. In order to avoid any injustice himself, he wouldn't attack the Lamanites and kill them while they were drunk. 20 However he had achieved his objective, since he had armed the Nephite prisoners inside the city walls and provided them with the power to control the city inside — 21 then he had the men accompanying him move back a pace from them and surround the Lamanite armies. 22 Now this was done at night, and when the Lamanites woke up in the morning, they realized they were surrounded by the Nephites on the outside, and that their prisoners were armed on the inside. 23 So they saw the Nephites had power over them. And in these circumstances they could see it wasn't advisable for them to fight the Nephites. Therefore their chief captains asked for their weapons; and they brought them out and dropped them at the Nephites' feet, begging for mercy. 24 Now this was what Moroni wanted. He captured them as prisoners of war and took over the city and freed all the Nephite prisoners. They joined Moroni's army and added great strength to his army.

IX   25 He had the Lamanites he took prisoner begin to work on strengthening the fortifications around the outside of the city of Gid. 26 When he was satisfied with the fortifications for Gid, he had his prisoners taken to Bountiful. He also had that city guarded by a very strong force. 27 Despite all the Lamanites' schemes, the Nephites kept and protected all the prisoners they had captured and defended all the ground they had retaken and advantages they had gained. 28 So the Nephites again began to be victorious and reclaim their rights and privileges. 29 The Lamanites attempted to surround them at night many times, but in these attempts they lost many prisoners. 30 And they attempted to provide wine to the Nephites many times, to kill them with poison or by intoxication. 31 But the Nephites weren't slow to remember the Lord their God in these times of trouble. They couldn't be taken in by their traps. They refused to drink their wine; indeed, they wouldn't drink wine unless they had first given it to some of the Lamanite prisoners. 32 In this way they were careful that no poison was given to them. Because if their wine would poison a Lamanite, it would also poison a Nephite. So they tested all their drinks. 33 Now it was apparent to Moroni that they needed to retake the city of Morionton. Because the Lamanites had, through their work, fortified Morionton until it had become a very strong place of defense. 34 And they were continually bringing new forces into that city, and new supplies as well. 35 And so ended the 29th year of the judges' rule.

Chapter 26

56 Now at the start of the 30th year of the judges' rule, on the second day of the first month, Moroni received a letter from Helaman describing the affairs of the people in that region of the land. 2 This is what he wrote: My dearly loved brother Moroni, both in the Lord and in sharing the difficulties of our warfare: My dear brother, I will tell you an account of our warfare in this part of the land. 3 Two thousand of the sons of those people whom Ammon brought down out of the land of Nephi, descendants of Laman, who was the oldest son of our forefather Lehi, 4 — now I needn't tell you about their traditions or unbelief, since you know all about these things. 5 Instead, I want to tell you that 2,000 of these young men have taken their weapons and have asked me to lead them; and together we've defended our country.

II   6 Now you also know about the covenant their fathers made to not arm themselves in order to kill their Lamanite relatives. 7 But in the 26th year, when they saw the troubles and difficulties we were having on their behalf, they were on the verge of breaking the covenant and using weapons in our defense. 8 But I wouldn't let them break their covenant, believing God would strengthen us, so that we wouldn't suffer as a result of them keeping the oath they had taken. 9 But here's one thing to give you great joy: In the 26th year, I Helaman marched at the head of these 2,000 young men to the city of Judea to assist Antipus, whom you had appointed as a leader over the people of that part of the land. 10 And I added my 2,000 sons (and they're worthy to be called sons), to Antipus' army, and Antipus thanked us for this added strength. Indeed, his army had suffered many losses from the Lamanites because their overwhelming numbers had killed a great number of our men; and we have reason to mourn over this. 11 Still, we may console ourselves knowing they've died in the cause of their country and their God, and are happy. 12 Now the Lamanites held many prisoners, all of whom are chief captains, since they killed everyone else, and we think they're now in the land of Nephi; that is if they haven't already been killed.

III   13 Now these are the cities that the Lamanites have taken that cost the lives of so many of our valiant men: 14 the city of Manti, and the cities of Zeezrom, Cumeni, and Antiparah. 15 These were the cities they held when I arrived at the city of Judea. And I found Antipus and his men fortifying the city to the best of their ability. 16 They were discouraged physically and spiritually, since they had fought valiantly by day and worked strenuously at night to maintain their cities. And so they had suffered great hardships of every kind. 17 Now they were determined to conquer at this place or die. Therefore you can well imagine the little force I brought with me — those sons of mine — gave them a lot of hope and joy.

IV   18 Now when the Lamanites saw that Antipus had received added strength for his army, they were ordered by Ammoron not to come against the city of Judea or against us to battle. 19 So we were blessed by the Lord. Because if they had attacked us in this weak condition of ours, they might've destroyed our little army; but we were spared. 20 They were ordered by Ammoron to maintain those cities they had taken. And so ended the 26th year. At the start of the 27th year, we had prepared our city and ourselves for defense. 21 Now we wanted the Lamanites to attack us, since we didn't want to try to attack them in their strongholds. 22 We kept spies out on all sides to watch the Lamanites' movements, so they couldn't pass us at night or by day to make an attack on our other cities, which were to the north. 23 Because we knew that in those cities they weren't strong enough to defend against them. Therefore we wanted, if they passed us by, to attack them from behind; and so attacking from behind at the same time they were met in front, we thought we could defeat them. But our hopes were dashed. 24 They didn't dare pass us by with their entire army, nor to pass us by with a part of it either, since they were afraid they wouldn't be strong enough and would suffer a defeat. 25 They also didn't dare to march down against the city of Zarahemla, or dare to cross the head of the Sidon over to the city of Nephihah. 26 And so with their forces they were determined to defend the cities they had taken.

V   27 Now in the second month of this year, many supplies were brought to us from the parents of those 2,000 sons of mine. 28 And 2,000 men also joined us from Zarahemla. So we were prepared with 10,000 men and supplies for them, and for their wives and children as well. 29 Seeing our forces increase daily and supplies arrive for our support like this, the Lamanites began to be afraid and make periodic attacks, in order to interfere with us receiving supplies and strength. 30 When we saw how the Lamanites began to grow uneasy, we were eager to develop a strategy against them. So Antipus ordered me to march out with my little sons to a neighboring city as if we were taking supplies there. 31 The plan was for us to march near the city of Antiparah as if we were resupplying the city beyond it on the seashore. 32 We marched out as if with resupplies to go to that city. 33 Then Antipus marched out with a part of his army, leaving behind the rest to maintain the city. But he didn't march out until I with my little army came near the city of Antiparah. 34 Now the strongest Lamanite army was stationed in the city of Antiparah, indeed, the largest. 35 When they were told by their spies, they came out with their army and marched against us.

VI 36 We retreated ahead of them to the north. And so we led away the most powerful Lamanite army 37 for a considerable distance, so far away that when they saw Antipus' army behind them, they moved as fast as they could without turning right or left but marched straight after us. We concluded their aim was to kill us before Antipus caught up to them to avoid being surrounded by our forces. 38 And seeing our danger, Antipus increased the speed of his army's march. But at nightfall they hadn't overtaken us, and Antipus hadn't overtaken them either. So we camped for the night.

VII 39 Before daybreak, the Lamanites were already pursuing us. Now we weren't strong enough to fight them; indeed, I wouldn't allow my little sons to fall into their hands. So we kept marching, and we directed our march into the wilderness. 40 Now they didn't dare turn to the right or left, for fear of being surrounded; and I wouldn't turn to the right or left either, so we wouldn't be overtaken. We couldn't fight them without being killed, and then they would escape. And so we fled all that day into the wilderness, up until it was dark.

VIII 41 At daybreak, we saw the Lamanites were once again threatening us; and we fled just ahead of them. 42 But they didn't pursue us very far before they halted in the morning of the third day of the seventh month. 43 Now whether they were overtaken by Antipus, we didn't know. But I said to my men: They might have halted in order to get us to attack them, to catch us in a trap. 44 So what do you say, my sons? Will you go against them to battle? 45 Now I tell you, my dear brother Moroni, I had never seen such great courage, no, not among all the Nephites. 46 And because I had always called them my sons, since all of them were very young, they likewise said to me: Father, God is with us; He won't let us die; so let's go forward. We wouldn't kill our brothers if they would leave us alone. Therefore let's go so they don't overpower the army of Antipus. 47 Now they had never fought, yet they weren't afraid of death. And they thought more about the liberty of their families than they did about their own lives. They had been taught by their mothers that if they didn't doubt, God would protect them. 48 They told me their mothers' words, saying: We don't doubt that our mothers knew.

IX 49 So I returned with my 2,000 against the Lamanites who had pursued us. Now Antipus' armies had overtaken them, and a terrible battle had begun. 50 And being tired because of their long march in such a short time, Antipus' army was on the verge of defeat by the

Lamanites. Had I not returned with my 2,000, they would have achieved that end. 51 Because Antipus had died by the sword, and many of his leaders, on account of the fatigue brought on by the speed of their march. Therefore being confused because of the death of their leaders, Antipus' men began to retreat before the Lamanites.

X   52 The Lamanites were encouraged and began to overcome them. So the Lamanites were vigorously pursuing and attacking them when Helaman arrived from behind with his 2,000 and began to effectively kill them in great numbers, so the whole Lamanite army halted and turned to attack Helaman. 53 When Antipus' people realized the Lamanites had turned around, they regrouped and attacked the Lamanites from behind.

XI   54 Now we Nephites, including Antipus' force and I with my 2,000, surrounded the Lamanites and slaughtered them, so that they were compelled to hand over their weapons and surrender as prisoners of war.

XII   55 When they had surrendered to us, I counted those young men who had fought with me, fearing many of them had been killed. 56 But to my great joy, not one soul had died. They had fought as if with the strength of God; indeed, men were never known to have fought with such miraculous strength. And they attacked the Lamanites with such fury that they intimidated them; and because of this the Lamanites surrendered as prisoners of war. 57 But we had no place for our prisoners, where we could guard them to keep them from the Lamanite armies, so we sent them to Zarahemla, along with some of Antipus' men who survived. And I took the rest and added them to my young Ammonites and directed our march back to the city of Judea.

XIII   **57** Then I received a letter from king Ammoron offering that if I would hand over the prisoners of war we had taken, then he would give the city of Antiparah back to us. 2 But I sent a letter to the king telling him we were sure our forces were adequate to take the city of Antiparah by force, and therefore handing over prisoners for that city would be unwise of us, and we would only hand over our prisoners in an exchange. 3 And because Ammoron refused my letter since he wouldn't exchange prisoners, we began to prepare to go against the city of Antiparah. 4 But the people of Antiparah left the city and fled to the other controlled cities, to fortify them. So the city of Antiparah fell into our hands. 5 And so ended the 28th year of the judges' rule.

XIV   6 At the start of the 29th year, we received a set of supplies and an addition to our army from Zarahemla and the surrounding area adding 6,000 men, and another 60 of the sons of the Ammonites who had come to join their fellow Ammonites, my little band of 2,000.

Now we were reinforced, and we also had plenty of supplies brought to us.

XV   7 At that point we planned to take the battle against the army stationed to protect the city of Cumeni. 8 I have to tell you we soon achieved that objective. Indeed, with a part of our strong force we surrounded the city of Cumeni at night, a little while before they were going to receive a delivery of supplies. 9 We camped on all sides of the city for many nights, sleeping on our swords and keeping guards so the Lamanites couldn't attack us at night by surprise, which they attempted to do many times. But every time they attempted this, they were killed. 10 In the end, their supplies arrived for delivery to the city at night. But instead of being Lamanites, we were Nephites who captured the delivery and took it for ourselves. 11 Yet despite being cut off from their support like this, the Lamanites were still determined to maintain the city. So we thought it best for us to send these supplies to Judea and send our prisoners to Zarahemla.

XVI   12 Not many days had gone by before the Lamanites started to lose all hope of aid; therefore they surrendered the city to us. And so we had achieved our goal of obtaining the city of Cumeni. 13 But we had so many prisoners that despite our own huge numbers, we had to employ all our force guarding them or put them to death. 14 Indeed, they would break out in great numbers and would fight with stones and clubs, or with whatever they could get their hands on, so we had to kill more than 2,000 of them after they had surrendered as prisoners of war. 15 Therefore we had to either put an end to their lives or guard them sword in hand down to Zarahemla. Moreover, our supplies were only enough for our own people, despite what we had taken from the Lamanites. 16 Now in these crucial circumstances it became a very serious matter to make a decision regarding those prisoners of war. Nevertheless, we decided to send them down to Zarahemla. So we chose some of our men and gave them responsibility over our prisoners to take them to Zarahemla.

XVII   17 But they came back the very next day. Now we didn't ask them about the prisoners, since the Lamanites were closing in on us, and they returned just in time to save us from being overtaken. For Ammoron had sent fresh supplies and large reinforcements for their support.

XVIII   18 The men we sent with the prisoners arrived just at the right time to stop them as they were beginning to overpower us. 19 But my little band of 2,060 fought most desperately. Indeed, they were resolute before the Lamanites and delivered death to any who fought them. 20 As the rest of our army was about to give way before the Lamanites, these 2,060 were firm and undaunted. 21 And they obeyed and took care to strictly perform every word of command. Everything happened to them according to their faith. I remembered the words they told me their mothers had taught them. 22 Now it was these sons of mine together with the men chosen to transport the prisoners to whom we owe this great victory, because they were the ones who defeated the Lamanites. Therefore they were driven back to the city of Manti. 23 And we held onto our city of Cumeni and weren't all killed by the sword; however, we had suffered great loss.

XIX 24 After the Lamanites fled, I immediately gave orders for my wounded men to be separated and recovered from the dead lying on the ground, and to have their wounds treated. 25 There were 200 out of my 2,060 who had fainted from blood loss. Nevertheless, according to God's goodness and to our great astonishment and the joy of our whole army, not one of them died. But there wasn't a single one of them who hadn't received many wounds. 26 Now their preservation was astonishing to our entire army. They were all spared while a thousand of our fellow soldiers were killed. And we rightly ascribe it to God's miraculous power because of their great faith in what they had been taught to believe, that there was a just God, and that whoever didn't doubt would be kept safe by His miraculous power. 27 Now this was the faith of these men I'm telling you about. They are young and their minds are firm, and they put their trust in God continually.

XX 28 Now after we had taken care of our wounded men and buried our dead and the many dead Lamanites, we asked Gid about the prisoners they had set out with for Zarahemla. 29 Now Gid was the chief captain over the company appointed to guard them down to that land. 30 Gid told me: We set out to go down to Zarahemla with our prisoners. And we met the spies of our armies, who had been watching the Lamanite camp. 31 They called out to us, saying: the Lamanite armies are right now marching toward the city of Cumeni. And they're going to attack them and kill our people.

XXI 32 Our prisoners heard their shouts, which encouraged them, and they rose up in rebellion against us. 33 Because of their rebellion, we attacked them with our swords. They all ran together, as one, upon our swords, and as a result most of them were killed. The rest broke through and fled. 34 When they were gone and we were unable to catch up to them, we started quickly to the city of Cumeni. We arrived in time to assist our fellow Nephites in holding onto the city. 35 And we have once again been freed from the power of our enemies. And blessed is the name of God; He's the one who's rescued us, who's done this great thing for us.

XXII   ³⁶ Now when I Helaman had heard Gid's words, I was filled with great joy because of God's goodness in keeping us safe, so we didn't all die. I trust that the spirits of those who have been killed have entered God's rest.

XXIII   **58** Now our next objective was to take control of the city of Manti. Yet there wasn't any way for us to lure them out of the city with our small force. They remembered how we had defeated them before. That being the case, we couldn't lure them away from their strongholds. ² They were so much more numerous than our army that we didn't dare go attack their strongholds. ³ Also it was essential for us to keep our men protecting the parts of our land we had recovered. Therefore we needed to wait, so we could receive more strength from Zarahemla and also a fresh set of supplies.

XXIV   ⁴ And so I reported by messenger to the chief governor of our land to acquaint him with the state of affairs of our people. We waited to receive supplies and strength from Zarahemla. ⁵ But this only helped a little, and was offset by the Lamanites also receiving reinforcements from day to day and many supplies as well. These were our circumstances at this time. ⁶ The Lamanites were making surprise attacks against us from time to time, trying to kill us with this new approach. However, we couldn't really engage them in a battle because of their protected strongholds.

XXV   ⁷ We were left in these difficult circumstances for many months, until we were about to starve for lack of food. ⁸ Eventually we received food brought to us under guard by an army of 2,000 men who came to join us. This limited assistance was all we received to defend ourselves and our country against an almost innumerable enemy. ⁹ Now we didn't understand what caused these difficulties we faced, or the reason why they didn't send us more strength. Therefore it troubled us and we were afraid God's judgments might fall upon our land and let us be overthrown and completely destroyed. ¹⁰ Therefore we poured out our souls in prayer to God that He would strengthen us and rescue us from our enemies, and give us strength, so we could maintain our cities, lands, and property to save our people. ¹¹ The Lord our God gave us assurances He would liberate us, speaking peace to our souls, giving us renewed faith, and letting us look forward to Him liberating us. ¹² We were satisfied with the small force we received and were firmly resolved to defeat our enemies and to maintain our lands and possessions and our wives and children and our liberty. ¹³ And so we went with all our strength to battle the Lamanites in the city of Manti. We pitched our tents beside the wilderness near the city. ¹⁴ On the following day, when the Lamanites saw we camped beside the wilderness near the city, they sent spies to count the number and estimate the strength of our army.

XXVI   15 When they saw we were few in number, and fearing we would intercept their supplies unless they came out to fight and kill us, and believing they could easily kill us with their much larger armies, therefore they prepared to attack. 16,17 When we saw they were preparing to attack, I had Gid, with a few chosen men, hide on the right flank in the wilderness. I also had Teomner, with a few chosen men, hide on the left flank. When they were in place, I remained with the rest of my army in the same place where we originally camped, waiting for the Lamanites to attack.

XXVII   18 The Lamanites came out in their strength against us. When they arrived and were about to attack us with their swords, I had those men who were with me retreat into the wilderness.

XXVIII   19 The Lamanites quickly chased us, since they needed to catch up to us so they could kill us. Therefore they followed us into the wilderness. And we passed between Gid and Teomner's men, who went unnoticed by the Lamanites.

XXIX   20 When the Lamanites passed, meaning the army had passed by, Gid and Teomner emerged from their hiding places and killed their lookouts, to prevent any Lamanite messengers from sending word, thereby preventing a retreat to the city. 21 After cutting them off, they ran to the city and attacked the guards left to guard the city, killing them and taking the city. 22 Now this was accomplished because the Lamanites sent their whole army, except for only a few guards, after our decoy into the wilderness.

XXX   23 And by means of this, Gid and Teomner had taken their stronghold. Then, after having traveled a great deal in the wilderness, we changed our course toward Zarahemla. 24 When the Lamanites saw they were marching toward Zarahemla, they were very afraid our plan was to lure them to their destruction. So they began to retreat into the wilderness, returning the way they had come. 25 Then at night they camped. Now the chief captains of the Lamanites thought the Nephites would be tired from their march; and because they thought they chased our whole army away, they didn't worry about the city of Manti.

XXXI   26 Once it was dark, I had my men, instead of sleeping, march by a different route back to Manti. 27 And because we moved during the night, the next day we were well ahead of the Lamanites, arriving before them at the city of Manti. 28 And so using this strategy we took the city of Manti without losing any men.

XXXII

²⁹ When the Lamanite armies approached the city and saw we were there prepared to battle, they were shocked, extremely frightened, and so taken off guard that they fled into the wilderness. ³⁰ Other Lamanite armies followed and abandoned this entire region of the land. But they took away many women and children with them. ³¹ And now all the cities taken by the Lamanites have returned to our hands. And our parents, wives, and children are returning to their homes, everyone except those who have been captured and removed by the Lamanites. ³² But our armies are too small to protect so many cities and lands. ³³ We believe it's God who's given us victory over these lands, letting us again control our cities and lands that were originally ours.

XXXIII

³⁴ Now we don't understand the reason the government doesn't provide more support for us; and the men who came up to join us don't know why we haven't received more support, either. ³⁵ We don't know whether your struggles have taken priority and received more support for your region. If so, we don't want to complain. ³⁶ But if that's not the case, we're afraid there might be some faction in the government interfering with them sending more men to help us. Because we know they have more men than the ones they've sent. ³⁷ But it doesn't matter. We trust God will save us, despite our armies' weakness, and rescue us from our enemies. ³⁸ This is toward the end of the 29th year, and we now control our lands and the Lamanites have retreated to the land of Nephi.

XXXIV

³⁹ And those sons of Ammon's people I've spoken so highly about, are with me in the city of Manti. The Lord has protected them, and kept them from dying by the sword, and not even one soul has been killed. ⁴⁰ But they've suffered many wounds. Despite that, they remain committed to the liberty God has given them. They're continually faithful to the Lord who is God. They make sure to always keep His statutes, judgments, and commandments. And they have absolute faith in the prophecies about what's to come. ⁴¹ Now, my dear brother Moroni, may the Lord our God, who's redeemed us and made us free, keep you continually in His presence, and may He favor this people, giving you success in retaking control of everything God gave us, and which the Lamanites took from us. Now I end my letter. I am Helaman, Alma's son.

Chapter 27

59 Now in the 30th year of the judges' rule over the Nephites, after Moroni received and read Helaman's letter, he rejoiced over

Helaman's success in regaining the lands that had been lost. 2 He let all his people know throughout the surrounding area so they could also celebrate.

II   3 Then he immediately sent a letter to Parhoron, asking him to send men to reinforce Helaman, or Helaman's armies, so he could better protect that part of the land he had so miraculously regained. 4 After Moroni sent this letter to Zarahemla, he started to plan how to regain control of the rest of the lands and cities the Lamanites had taken.

III   5 While Moroni was preparing his plan to battle the Lamanites, the people of Nephihah, who had gathered from the cities of Moroni, Lehi, and Morionton, were attacked by the Lamanites. 6 Everyone who had fled from Manti and the surrounding area had joined with the Lamanites. 7 There were many of them, and were reinforced daily by Ammoron's command, so they attacked the people of Nephihah; and they began to kill them with a massive slaughter. 8 Their armies had so many fighters that the rest of the people of Nephihah had to flee from them, and they came over and joined Moroni's army. 9 Now since Moroni expected to send men to the city of Nephihah to keep that city, because it was easier to keep the city from falling into the hands of the Lamanites than to retake it, he thought they would easily keep that city. 10 But now he kept all his forces to protect the places he had recovered.

IV   11 When Moroni learned the city of Nephihah was lost, he mourned and began to doubt, because of the people's wickedness, if they could defeat the Lamanites. 12 Now all his chief captains also doubted. They were unsure and extremely surprised by the people's wickedness, assuming this was why the Lamanites succeeded in taking Nephihah. 13 And Moroni was angry with the government because of their indifference to the freedom of their country.

V   **60** He wrote another letter to governor Parhoron. This is what he wrote: I address my letter to Parhoron in the city of Zarahemla, who is the chief judge and the governor over the land, and to all those who have been chosen by this people to govern and support the requirements of this war. 2 I have some complaints about you. You know you have the obligation to assemble men and furnish them with swords, cimeters, and other weapons to defend against the Lamanites, wherever they trespass on our land. 3 Now I tell you my men and I, and Helaman and his men also, have suffered tremendously from hunger, thirst, fatigue, and all the difficulties of defending the people. 4 But if this were all we suffered, we wouldn't criticize or complain. 5 However, the thousands of our slaughtered people who died by the sword might've been spared if you had given our armies adequate strength and aid. Your great neglect of us is unexplained.

VI   6 Now we want to know the reason for your severe neglect. We want to know why you are so thoughtless. 7 Can you possibly sit thoughtlessly on your thrones while your enemies are spreading death all around you, while they're murdering thousands of your fellow Nephites? 8 The very people who have expected your protection, who have put you in a position of trust to help them? Indeed, you could have sent reinforcements to them to help them and could have saved thousands of them from dying by the sword. 9 But this isn't all. You've withheld provisions from them, while many have fought and bled to death hoping to protect this people. And they did this when they were about to die from hunger because of your absolute neglect of them. 10 Now, my dearly loved people (because you ought to be loved by us), you should've acted more diligently to care for and protect the freedom of this people. But you've neglected them, so much so that the blood of thousands will come upon your heads for vengeance. Indeed, all their cries and suffering were seen by God. 11 Could you possibly think you could sit on your thrones and because of God's great kindness you could do nothing and He would save you? If you have believed this, then you believed in vain. 12 Do you think that because so many of your fellow Nephites have been killed, it's because of their wickedness? I tell you: If you have believed this, then your belief is wrong. I tell you: There are many who have died by the sword, and it condemns you. 13 Because the Lord tolerates the righteous being killed so His justice and judgment can come upon the wicked. Therefore there's no need to think the righteous are lost because they're killed; on the contrary, they enter the rest of the Lord their God.

VII   14 Now I tell you: I'm very fearful God's judgments will overtake this people because of their indifference and neglect, including the indifference and neglect of our government and their abandonment of their fellow Nephites who have now been killed. 15 If it weren't for the wickedness that began at the top of our government, we could have defeated our enemies, and they wouldn't have gained any power over us. 16 We've been punished because of our own warring between ourselves caused by the kingmen, which resulted in so much slaughter of ourselves. We were fighting among ourselves instead of uniting our strength as we had before. We were divided by the ambitions of the kingmen for power and authority to control us. Instead of being true to the cause of our freedom and joining with us to fight against our enemies, they took up their swords to fight against us. This was what caused so much slaughter among ourselves. If we had instead gone together to defend ourselves with the Lord's strength, we would have defeated our enemies, since God had promised us that is what would happen, and His word would certainly have been fulfilled. 17 But now the Lamanites attack us and are murdering our people with the sword, including our women and children, and removing them as prisoners, afflicting sorrow, distress, and pain, and taking our lands; and this is a result of the great wickedness of the kingmen who are attempting to seize power and authority.

VIII   18 But why should I say very much about this? Because it appears likely to us you are the ones attempting to seize authority. It appears likely you are also traitors to your country. 19 Or have you neglected us because you're in the heart of our country and surrounded by security, and that's the reason you don't have food sent to us, as well as men to strengthen our armies? 20 Have you forgotten the commandments of the Lord your God? Have you forgotten our ancestors were slaves? Have you forgotten the many times we've been rescued from our enemies? 21 Or do you imagine the Lord will repeatedly save us as we idly sit on our thrones and fail to use the resources given to us by the Lord? 22 Will you sit complacently surrounded by thousands of people, even tens of thousands who join your complacency, while there are thousands around the borders of the land who are dying by the sword, wounded and bleeding? 23 Do you imagine God will consider you guiltless while you do nothing but watch these things? I tell you: No.

IX   Now I want you to remember God said to first cleanse the inner vessel, and then the outer vessel afterward. 24 Now unless you repent, and start actively sending food and men to us and also to Helaman, so he can maintain the parts of our country that he has regained, and so we can also recover the rest of our lands in these parts, we should stop fighting the Lamanites until we've first cleansed our inner vessel, including the top of our government. 25 Unless you start doing what I ask and begin to show me the true spirit of freedom and make the effort to help and support our armies and give them the necessary food for their survival, I'll leave some of my freemen to maintain this part of our land. I'll leave the strength and blessings of God upon them, so no other power can work against them 26 — and I'll do this because of their great faith and their patience in their tribulations — 27 and I'll take the fight to you. And if there are any among you who have a desire for freedom, if there's even a spark of freedom remaining, I'll incite insurrections against you, up until all those wanting power and authority are dead. 28 I'm not afraid of your power or authority, but it's God whom I fear. It's to obey His commandments that I take up my sword to defend the cause of my country. And it's because of your iniquity we've suffered these losses.

x   29 It is time, this very moment, that unless you start defending your country and your little ones, the sword of justice won't just threaten you, but it will strike you down in punishment, and you'll be destroyed. 30 I'm waiting for assistance from you. Unless you resupply us, I'll come against you, right to Zarahemla, and I'll strike you with the sword, and end all your power to interfere with this people's defense of our freedom. 31 Indeed, the Lord won't let you live while your increasing iniquities are causing the destruction of His righteous people. 32 Can you possibly believe the Lord will spare you and punish the Lamanites, when their ancestors' traditions have caused their hatred? And that hatred has grown because of those who have split from us. But your iniquity is because of your love of glory and worldly things of no lasting value. 33 You know you're breaking God's laws, and you know you're trampling them underfoot. The Lord has told me: If those whom you've appointed as your governors don't repent of their sins and iniquities, you must go up to battle against them.

XI   34 Now I'm obligated, based on the covenant I made, to keep the commandments of God. Therefore I ask you to obey God's word and immediately send some provisions and men to me, and to Helaman as well. 35 If you refuse, I'll immediately come against you, because God won't let us die from hunger. Therefore He'll feed us with your food, even if the sword must be used. Now see that you obey God's word. 36 I am Moroni your chief captain. I don't seek power, but to pull it down. I don't seek the world's honor but the glory of God and the freedom and prosperity of my country. And so I close my letter.

Chapter 28

61 Soon after Moroni had sent his letter to the chief governor, he received a letter from Parhoron the chief governor. This is what it said: 2 I Parhoron, the chief governor of this land, send this to Moroni, the chief captain over the army. I tell you, Moroni, I have no pleasure in your great difficulties; they distress me. 3 But there are some who are pleased by your troubles. There is a rebellion underway against me and against all the freemen. Our opponents are very numerous. 4 They have attempted to remove me from the judgment seat, and have caused all of the resulting difficulties by their iniquity. Their rhetoric and deceit have confused and misled many people to sympathize with them, resulting in our many difficulties. They have interfered with resupplying you, and have intimidated our freemen so that they haven't joined you. 5 I've been exiled and have fled to Gideon with as many men as I could. 6 From here I've sent a proclamation throughout this part of the land. People are flocking to us daily, with their weapons, in defense of their country and their freedom and to pay back our wrongs. 7 Indeed, so many have joined us that those insurrectionists now face stiff resistance; they're now afraid of us and don't dare start the battle against us. 8 But they control the city of Zarahemla, and they have appointed a king to now rule. He has written to the Lamanite king and made an alliance with him. As part of their alliance, he has agreed to hold and defend the city of Zarahemla, expecting that will enable the Lamanites to conquer the rest of the land. He anticipates he will be appointed king over this people after they're conquered by the Lamanites.

II   9 Now in your letter you have criticized and judged me, but it doesn't matter. I'm not angry, but am pleased by your patriotic heart. I don't seek power, only to retain my judgment seat to protect my people's rights and liberty. I stand firmly in the liberty that God has given us.

III   10 Now we will oppose wickedness, even to the death. We wouldn't kill the Lamanites if they would stay in their own land. 11 We wouldn't kill our fellow Nephites if they didn't rise up in rebellion and lift their sword against us. 12 We would submit to the burden of slavery if God's justice demanded it, or if He commanded us to do so. 13 But He doesn't command us to put ourselves under the control of our enemies, but to put our trust in Him and He'll rescue us. 14 Therefore my dear brother Moroni, let us resist evil. And any evil we can't resist with our words, including rebellions and defections, let us resist with our swords, to preserve our freedom, so we can have joy worshiping in our congregation and obeying our Redeemer and our God. 15 Therefore come quickly to join me with a few of your men, and leave the rest in Lehi and Teancum's charge. Give them orders to follow God's Spirit in conducting the war in that part of the land, for that's the very spirit of freedom within them. 16 I've sent a few provisions to them, to feed them while you come to aid me. 17 Recruit any force you can while on your march here; and we'll immediately go against those defectors in God's strength, directed by the faith we share. 18 We'll take Zarahemla, get control of provisions, and then relieve Lehi and Teancum. We'll strike them with the Lord's strength, and put an end to this sinful rebellion.

IV   19 Your letter made me rejoice, Moroni. Because I was a little worried about what to do, whether it was right for us to attack fellow Nephites. 20 However, as you said: Unless they repent, the Lord has commanded you to go against them. 21 See that you bless Lehi and Teancum in the Lord. Tell them not to be afraid, since God will protect them, and all those who stand firmly in the liberty God has given us. Now I end my letter to my dear brother Moroni.

Chapter 29

62 Now when Moroni received this letter, he was encouraged and filled with joy because of Parhoron's faithfulness, learning he wasn't a traitor to the freedom and cause of his country. 2 On the other hand, he was also very sad for the iniquity of those who had driven Parhoron from the judgment seat who clearly had rebelled against their country and God.

II

3 Moroni took a small number of men, as Parhoron requested, and put Lehi and Teancum in command of the rest of his army and then marched to Gideon. 4 He raised the Declaration of Liberty every place he went and recruited all the force he could during his march to Gideon.

III

5 Thousands flocked to his banner and took up their swords in defense of their freedom, refusing to be slaves. 6 After Moroni recruited all the men he could during his march, he arrived at Gideon. After combining his forces with Parhoron's, they were very strong, clearly stronger than the men of Pachus, the defectors' king. He was the one who chased away the freemen from Zarahemla and now ruled there.

IV

7 So Moroni and Parhoron led their armies to Zarahemla and took the battle to the city and confronted Pachus' followers. 8 Then Pachus was killed and his men taken prisoners; and Parhoron was restored to his judgment seat. 9 Pachus' followers and any captured and imprisoned kingmen were tried under the law. Then they were executed according to the law. Not only Pachus' men and the kingmen were put to death, but also anyone who refused to take up arms to defend their country and instead decided to fight against it. 10 It was absolutely necessary for this law to be enforced for the safety of their country. Anyone who was found denying the people's freedom was quickly executed under the law. 11 That ended the 30th year of the judges' rule over the Nephites, with Moroni and Parhoron having restored peace to Zarahemla among their own people, having imposed the death penalty on everyone unfaithful to the cause of freedom.

V

12 At the start of the 31st year of the judges' rule, Moroni immediately had supplies and an army of 6,000 men sent to Helaman

to assist him in preserving that part of the land. 13 He also had an army of 6,000 men with enough food sent to the armies of Lehi and Teancum. This was done to fortify the land against the Lamanites.

VI   14 Then Moroni and Parhoron left a large army in Zarahemla and marched with a large army to Nephihah. They were resolved to remove the Lamanites from that city.

VII   15 As they marched to the land, they captured a large group of Lamanites after killing many of them and took their supplies and weapons. 16 After they had captured them, they had them covenant that they would never again take up weapons against the Nephites. 17 When they had made this covenant, they sent them to live with Ammon's people. Those who hadn't been killed numbered about 4,000.

VIII   18 After sending them away, they resumed the march to Nephihah. When they arrived at Nephihah, they camped in the plains of Nephihah near the city. 19 Now Moroni wanted the Lamanites to fight the battle on the plains. But the Lamanites knew how committed and fearless they were, and could see the size of their armed forces, so they didn't dare come out against them; therefore the battle didn't start that day. 20 When night came, Moroni went under the cover of darkness and climbed up the wall to observe the area where the Lamanites camped with their army.

IX   21 They were all asleep by the east entrance. Then Moroni returned to his army and made them quickly assemble ropes and ladders to get over the wall and inside the city.

X   22 Moroni led his men over the wall into the west side of the city opposite to where the Lamanites' army camped.

XI   23 So they infiltrated the city at night using ropes and ladders to scale the wall. When morning came, they were all inside the city walls. 24 When the Lamanites woke up and saw Moroni's armies inside the walls, they were extremely frightened, and they ran out through the gate. 25 When Moroni saw them running away, he had his men chase them, and they killed many and surrounded many others and took them prisoner. The rest escaped to the land of Moroni, by the seashore. 26 In this way, Moroni and Parhoron had taken the city of Nephihah without the loss of one life; but many of the Lamanites were killed.

XII   27 Now many of the Lamanite prisoners wanted to join Ammon's people and become free, 28 and everyone who wanted to join them was allowed to do so, if they wished. 29 Therefore Lamanite prisoners joined Ammon's people and started working extremely hard, tilling the ground and raising all kinds of grain, as well as flocks and herds of every kind. And so the Nephites were relieved of a great burden, and didn't need to deal with the Lamanite prisoners.

XIII   30 Now Moroni had taken the city of Nephihah, and captured many prisoners. That substantially reduced the Lamanite armies. He also recovered many of the Nephite prisoners, which substantially strengthened Moroni's army. Afterward, he left Nephihah to go to the land of Lehi.

XIV   31 When the Lamanites saw Moroni was heading directly toward them, they were again frightened and ran away from Moroni's army. 32 Moroni and his army chased them from city to city until they encountered Lehi and Teancum. And the Lamanites retreated from Lehi and Teancum, going all the way to the seashore and the land of Moroni. 33 There the Lamanite armies consolidated into one single, large body in the land of Moroni. Now Ammoron the Lamanite king was also there.

XV   34 Moroni, Lehi, and Teancum camped with their armies surrounding the Lamanites at the land of Moroni, by the south and east borders of the wilderness. 35 And so they camped for the night, since both the Nephites and the Lamanites were tired from the long march. No conflict began that night, except for Teancum. He was bitterly angry with Ammoron, because he considered Ammoron and his brother Amalickiah to be responsible for this great unending war with the Lamanites, which resulted in so much fighting, slaughter, and hunger.

XVI   36 In his bitter anger, Teancum crept into the Lamanite camp and over the city walls. He climbed from place to place, until he found the king; and he threw a javelin at him, which pierced him near the heart. But the king woke up his servant before he died, and he chased Teancum and killed him.

XVII   37 When Lehi and Moroni learned Teancum was killed, they were heartbroken. He was a man who fought valiantly for his country — a true friend of liberty — and he had endured terrible hardships. But now he was dead, his life departing from this earth.

XVIII   38 On the following day, Moroni attacked the Lamanites with such fury that there was a great slaughter, and they retreated out of the land. They fled and didn't return again to fight the Nephites. 39 And so ended the 31st year of the judges' rule over the Nephites. They had endured wars, carnage, hunger, and hardships for many years. 40 There had been murders, conflicts, defections, and all kinds of iniquity among the Nephites. Nevertheless, because of the prayers of the righteous they were spared. ⁴¹ But because of the years of war between the Nephites and Lamanites, many had become coldhearted; and others were softened by their hardships and were deeply humbled before God.

XIX   ⁴² After Moroni fortified the areas most exposed to the Lamanites with an adequate defense, he returned to the city of Zarahemla. Helaman also returned to his place. And peace returned to the Nephites. ⁴³ Moroni turned over command of his armies to his son, named Moronihah. He retired to his house, to spend the rest of his days in peace. ⁴⁴ Parhoron returned to his judgment seat. Helaman returned to preaching God's word to the people. Indeed, because there had been so many wars and conflicts, the congregation needed to receive attention. ⁴⁵ Therefore Helaman and his brothers traveled and taught God's word with authority, convincing many people of their wickedness, which led them to repent of their sins and be baptized in the name of the Lord who is God.

XX   ⁴⁶ And so they once more established God's congregation throughout the land. ⁴⁷ The administration of their laws received attention, with new judges and chief judges being chosen. ⁴⁸ And the Nephites began to flourish and increase in numbers and grow strong in the land once more, and they began to grow very rich. ⁴⁹ But despite their wealth, strength, or prosperity, they weren't prideful, and no one thought themselves better than another. They weren't slow to remember the Lord their God, either, but they sincerely humbled themselves before Him. ⁵⁰ They remembered how the Lord had done great things for them, He rescued them from death, chains, prisons, and from so many difficulties; He had rescued them from their enemies. ⁵¹ And they prayed to the Lord their God continually, and the Lord blessed them as He promised, and they grew strong and flourished in the land. ⁵² All this was accomplished before Helaman died, in the 35th year of the judges' rule.

Chapter 30

63 At the start of the 36th year of the judges' rule over the Nephites, Shiblon took possession of the sacred artifacts given to Helaman by Alma. ² He was a good man who lived righteously before God and took care to be good and keep the commandments of the Lord his God, like his brother had done.

II   ³ Then Moroni also died. And so ended the 36th year of the judges' rule. ⁴ In the 37th year of the judges' rule, there was a large group of men — up to 5,400 of them, along with their wives and children — who left Zarahemla and traveled to the land to the north.

III   5 There was an ingenious man named Hagoth who built a very large ship on the shore beside Bountiful, bordering the land of Desolation, and launched it into the western sea at the narrow neck of land leading to the north. 6 Many Nephites went with him, sailing out to sea with supplies, including many women and children; and they sailed north. And so ended the 37th year. 7 In the 38th year, this man built more ships. And the first ship returned as well; and many more people sailed off with many supplies for the land to the north.

IV   8 They never were heard of again. We think they drowned in the deep sea. And another ship sailed out to sea as well, and we have no idea where she went. 9 During this year, many people migrated north. And so ended the 38th year.

V   10 In the 39th year of the judges' rule, Shiblon died as well. And Corianton had sailed to the north, to take supplies for the people who went there. 11 Therefore it was necessary for Shiblon, prior to his death, to confer those sacred things on Helaman's son, who was named Helaman after his father. 12 Now all the engravings in Helaman's possession were transcribed and sent to the people throughout the land, except for the parts Alma commanded not to be made public. 13 (Those parts were kept sacred and handed down from one generation to another.) Therefore in this year they were delivered to Helaman before Shiblon's death.

VI   14 Also in this year, some defectors had gone and joined the Lamanites; and they were once again stirred up to be angry at the Nephites. 15 In this same year, they once more came down, with a large army, to fight Moronihah's people, or Moronihah's army, and in this battle they were defeated and driven back to their own lands, losing a lot of lives. 16 And so ended the 39th year of the judges' rule over the Nephites. 17 And so ended Alma's account, as well as the account of his two sons, Helaman and Shiblon.

The Book of Helaman

Chapter 1

An account of the Nephites, their wars, conflicts, and disagreements, as well as the prophecies of many holy prophets before Christ's coming, according to the record of Helaman the son of Helaman, and according to the records of his sons, up to Christ's coming.

In addition, many of the Lamanites are converted — an account of their conversion, describing the righteousness of the Lamanites and the wickedness and abominations of the Nephites, etc.

At the start of the 40th year of the judges' rule over the Nephites, a serious problem arose among the Nephites. 2 Parhoron died and departed this earth. A serious fight began between the brothers (Parhoron's sons) about who would occupy the judgment seat. 3 Now the names of those fighting for the judgment seat were Parhoron, Paanchi, and Pacumeni. This resulted in the people fighting. 4 Now the fighting didn't involve all Parhoron's sons, since he had many, but these were the ones competing for the judgment seat. This caused three divisions of the people. 5 Nevertheless, Parhoron was chosen by the people's vote to be the chief judge and governor over the Nephites.

II

6 And Pacumeni, when he saw he would lose the judgment seat, joined with the vote of the people. 7 But Paanchi and his supporters who wanted him to be governor were disappointed and angry. Therefore he actively planned to lead people in a rebellion against their fellow Nephites.

III

8 As he was planning this, he was captured, tried under the approved law, and was sentenced to death, because he planned a rebellion and attempted to destroy the people's liberty. 9 When his supporters for the governorship learned he was sentenced to death, they were so angry that they assigned a person named Kishcumen to go to Parhoron's judgment seat to murder him. 10 He was chased by Parhoron's servants, but Kishcumen's escape was so quick no one caught him. 11 And he returned to those who sent him, and they all made a covenant swearing by their everlasting Maker they wouldn't tell anyone Kishcumen had murdered Parhoron. 12 Therefore Kishcumen remained unknown to the Nephites, since he had been disguised when he murdered Parhoron. Kishcumen and his gang, who covenanted with him, blended in with the people so well that not all of them were identified, but all those who were identified were sentenced to death. 13 Now Pacumeni was elected by the people's vote to be the chief judge and governor over the people, replacing his brother

Parhoron, following the right of succession. And all this occurred in the 40th year of the judges' rule, and the year ended.

IV
14 In the 41st year of the judges' rule, the Lamanites gathered an innumerable army of men equipped with swords, cimeters, bows, arrows, helmets, breastplates, and a variety of shields. 15 They attacked the Nephites. Their leader was named Coriantumr, a descendant of Zarahemla. He was a Nephite defector, and was a large, powerful man. 16 Therefore the Lamanite king, named Tubaloth, the son of Ammoron, trusted that Coriantumr, being so powerful, could take on the Nephites. He believed that by sending so strong and wise a leader he could defeat the Nephites. 17 Therefore he aroused the anger of his people, assembled an army, appointed Coriantumr as their leader, and sent them marching to war against the Nephites in Zarahemla.

V
18 Because the Nephites had been distracted by internal conflict and fighting for control of the government, they neglected to keep enough guards for Zarahemla, thinking the Lamanites wouldn't dare attack the great city of Zarahemla in the heart of their lands. 19 But Coriantumr led his large army and attacked the city, and their attack was so sudden there wasn't any time for the Nephites to assemble their armed forces. 20 Therefore Coriantumr cut down the guards by the city entrance and led his whole army right into the city. They killed everyone who opposed them, taking control of the entire city. 21 Pacumeni, who was the chief judge, ran from Coriantumr to the city wall. Coriantumr killed him against the wall, ending Pacumeni's life.

VI
22 When Coriantumr realized he not only held the city of Zarahemla, but that the Nephites had run away, were killed, captured, and thrown into prison, and he had overtaken the strongest fortification in the whole land, he was so confident that he prepared to conquer the whole land. 23 So he didn't pause in Zarahemla, but quickly marched a large army directly to the city of Bountiful. He was determined to act quickly and cut his way through with the sword, planning to take the entire north part of the land. 24 Because he mistakenly believed their greatest strength was in the center of the land, he immediately attacked, not giving them any time to gather their defense except in small companies. By quickly attacking them in small companies he cut them down.

VII
25 But Coriantumr's campaign through the center of the land gave Moronihah a great advantage, despite the many Nephites who were killed. 26 Moronihah thought the Lamanites would never dare to attack the center of the land, but that they would invade cities along the border, as they had always done before. Therefore Moronihah positioned their strongest armed forces to protect the border, away

from the center. 27 But the Lamanites weren't afraid to attack the center, as he had hoped; instead, they surprisingly invaded the center of the land and captured the capital, the city of Zarahemla, and were attacking throughout the center of the land, slaughtering the people — men, women, and children — and overtaking many cities and fortresses. 28 But when Moronihah realized this, he immediately dispatched Lehi with an army on a route to intercept them before they reached Bountiful. 29 He intercepted them before they reached Bountiful, and successfully attacked, forcing their retreat. 30 Moronihah intercepted them in their retreat and fought them in a very bloody battle costing many lives. Coriantumr was one of those who were killed. 31 Then the Lamanites couldn't retreat in any direction — not to the north, south, east, or west — since they were surrounded on every side by the Nephites. 32 Coriantumr had put the Lamanites into the middle of the Nephites, clearly vulnerable to the Nephites; and he had been killed. So the Lamanites surrendered to the Nephites.

VIII   33 Moronihah retook Zarahemla and the Lamanite prisoners left peacefully. 34 And the 41st year of the judges' rule ended.

IX   **2** In the 42nd year of the judges' rule, after Moronihah reestablished peace between the Nephites and Lamanites, no one occupied the judgment seat. So the people debated who would fill the position. 2 Helaman, who was the son of Helaman, was elected by the people's vote. 3 But Kishcumen, who had murdered Parhoron, set a trap to kill Helaman as well. He was supported by his gang, who had made a covenant to keep their murderous conspiracy secret. 4 A man named Gaddianton led Kishcumen's gang, and he was persuasive, careful in planning killings and robbery, and very cunning in protecting the gang. 5 He promised them if they would place him in the judgment seat, Kishcumen and other gang members would be appointed to positions of power and authority. Therefore Kishcumen planned to kill Helaman.

X   6 An official loyal to Helaman spied on the gang the night the murder was planned, knew of the plan, and met Kishcumen on his way to kill Helaman on the judgment seat. 7 He gave Kishcumen a sign he was a gang member, and so Kishcumen explained his purpose, and asked him to take him to the judgment seat so he could murder Helaman. 8 After Helaman's loyal official heard all of Kishcumen's secret plans, about the planned murder, and how gang members intended to murder, rob, and rise to power as the objective of their conspiracy, then Helaman's loyalist said to Kishcumen: I'll take you to the judgment seat. 9 Now that really pleased Kishcumen, because he thought he would accomplish his plan. But Helaman's servant, as they were going to the judgment seat, stabbed Kishcumen in the heart, and he fell dead without a groan. And he ran and told Helaman everything he had seen, heard, and done.

XI   10 Helaman sent out forces to arrest this gang of robbers and secret assassins, so they could be executed according to the law. 11 But when Gaddianton saw Kishcumen didn't return, he was afraid he might be killed. So he led his gang and they quickly fled the land in secret, entering the wilderness. As a result, when Helaman sent out forces to arrest them, they were nowhere to be found. 12 You'll learn more about this Gaddianton later. And so the 42nd year of the judges' rule ended. 13 At the end of this book, you'll learn Gaddianton ultimately caused the overthrow, and almost caused the entire annihilation of the Nephites. 14 Now I don't mean the end of the Book of Helaman, but I mean the end of the record of Nephi, from which I've taken the entire account written here.

Chapter 2

3 In the 43rd year of the judges' rule, there was no fighting among the Nephites except for some minor disagreements among the people caused by a little pride in the congregation, which were settled by the end of the 43rd year. 2 There wasn't any conflict among the people in the 44th year, and only a little in the 45th year. 3 In the 46th year, however, there were many conflicts and divisions, and consequently, a very large number of people left Zarahemla and went to the north to settle land of their own. 4 They traveled a considerable distance, arriving at large bodies of water and many rivers. 5 They spread out over the whole land, wherever it hadn't been laid waste and stripped of timber by the many earlier inhabitants of the land. 6 Now other than the lack of timber, etc. nothing about the land was actually desolate. But because of the complete destruction of the earlier occupants, it was called desolate. 7 Due to the lack of timber on the land, the people who went there developed skill in making cement; and they built cement houses to live in.

II   8 Their population increased and spread out across the land from the south to the north and started to cover the whole region, from the southern sea to the northern sea, and from the western sea to the eastern sea. 9 They lived in tents and cement houses and they protected any tree that sprouted there, planning for the future to have timber to build their houses, cities, temples, synagogues, sanctuaries, and other buildings.

III   10 Because timber was very scarce in the land to the north, they imported a great deal of it. 11 This let the people in the north build many cities, using both wood and cement. 12 Many of Ammon's people, who were born Lamanites, relocated there also.

IV   13 Many people have kept detailed records of this nation's activities. 14 But not even one percent of events are included in this book, such as an account of the Lamanites and Nephites wars, conflicts, divisions, preaching, prophecies, shipping, shipbuilding, building of temples, synagogues, and sanctuaries, and their righteousness and wickedness, and their acts of murder, robbery, and plunder, and all kinds of abominations and whoredoms and idol worship. 15 There are many different books and records, for the most part kept by the Nephites. 16 They were being handed down from one generation to another by the Nephites, until the Nephites fell into transgression and were murdered, plundered, hunted, and driven out and killed and scattered upon the earth, and then mixed with the Lamanites, until they're no longer called Nephites, becoming wicked, wild, and ferocious, finally becoming actual Lamanites.

V   17 Now I return to my account: After what I recorded last took place, and following other great conflicts, disturbances, wars, and divisions among the Nephites, 18 the 46th year of the judges' rule ended. 19 There were still great conflicts in the land, in the 47th year, and in the 48th year as well. 20 Nevertheless, Helaman served in the judgment seat with justice and fairness. He paid careful attention to obey God's statutes, judgments, and commandments, and he did what was right in God's eyes continually, living like his father had lived; so he prospered in the land.

VI   21 He had two sons. He named the oldest Nephi and the youngest Lehi. They grew up obeying the Lord. 22 The wars and conflicts lessened among the Nephites in the last part of the 48th year of the judges' rule over the Nephites. 23 In the 49th year of the judges' rule, peace prevailed in the land, except for the secret societies Gaddianton the bandit had organized in the more populated areas, which were concealed from those in charge of the government; therefore they weren't captured and executed.

VII   24 In this same year there was tremendous growth in the congregation, resulting in thousands joining with the congregation after being baptized as a sign of repentance. 25 The congregation's prosperity was so great and so many blessings were poured out upon the people that even the high priests and teachers were very surprised. 26 The Lord's work prospered, resulting in many souls, tens of thousands in fact, being baptized and joining God's congregation.

27 So we see the Lord is merciful to all those who call on His holy name in the sincerity of their hearts; 28 we see heaven's gate is open to all, that is to say, to those who believe in the name of Jesus Christ, who is the Son of God, 29 open to anyone who accepts God's salvation, which gives life and has power. It will cut through all the accuser's deceitfulness, traps, and tricks, and then it will lead Christ's followers along a straight and narrow path to safely cross over that endless abyss of misery prepared to engulf the wicked, 30 taking their immortal souls to stand at God's right hand in the kingdom of heaven, to join Abraham, Isaac, Jacob, and all our holy fathers, and never to leave. 31 In this year, there was continual rejoicing in Zarahemla and in the surrounding areas, even in the entire land inhabited by the Nephites. 32 There was peace and immense joy during the rest of the 49th year. Indeed, there was also continuous peace and great joy in the 50th year of the judges' rule.

VIII   33 In the 51st year of the judges' rule, there was also peace, except for pride that started entering the congregation — not God's congregation, but into the hearts of those claiming to belong to God's congregation. 34 They were lifted up in pride, to such an extent they persecuted many of their fellow members. Now as a result of this great evil, the more humble part of the people were persecuted and abused. 35 But in response they fasted and prayed often, growing increasingly stronger in their humility and increasingly firmer in the faith of Christ. Their souls rejoiced and they were consoled by the purification and sanctification of their hearts; the kind of sanctification that results from letting God into your heart. 36 The 52nd year also ended in peace, except for the great pride within the wealthy, prosperous people's hearts that over time increasingly influenced them.

IX   37 In the 53rd year of the judges' rule, Helaman died, and was replaced by his oldest son Nephi. He served in the judgment seat with justice and fairness. Indeed, he kept God's commandments and followed his father's example. 4 In the 54th year, there were many strong arguments in the congregation. There was also fighting among the people, resulting in a substantial amount of killing. 2 And a violent rebellion was defeated, lives were lost, and the surviving rebels exiled. These rebels went to see the Lamanite king.

X   3 They attempted to incite the Lamanites to attack the Nephites; but the Lamanites were intimidated and refused to listen to what the defectors said. 4 But in the 56th year of the judges' rule, another body of defectors left the Nephites to join the Lamanites; and they, along with the earlier rebels, together succeeded in inciting them to be angry with the Nephites; and that whole year they prepared and armed themselves to go to war. 5 In the 57th year, they attacked the Nephites, spreading death; so much that in the 58th year of the judges' rule they succeeded in taking Zarahemla, as well as the lands near Bountiful. 6 The Nephites and Moronihah's armies were driven back, all the way to Bountiful. 7 There they fortified their positions to defend against the Lamanites, from the west to the east seas, which was a day's journey for a Nephite on the fortified borderline defending their northern country. 8 So the Nephite defectors with the large Lamanite army captured all the Nephite lands to the south. All this took place in the 58th and 59th years of the judges' rule.

XI   9 In the 60th year of the judges' rule, Moronihah, with his armies, succeeded in regaining many parts of the land. They took back many cities from Lamanite control.

XII   10 In the 61st year of the judges' rule, they succeeded in taking back half of their territory. 11 Now the Nephites' losses and their many deaths wouldn't have happened if not for the wickedness and abomination that continued among them, including those who claimed to belong to God's congregation. 12 It was because of the pride of their hearts, because of their great wealth; indeed, it was because they oppressed the poor, withholding their food from the hungry, withholding their clothing from the naked, and hitting their lowly fellow Nephites in the face, mocking what was sacred, rejecting the spirit of prophecy and revelation, murdering, plundering, lying, stealing, committing adultery, engaging in intense disputes, and defecting to the land of Nephi to join the Lamanites. 13 Because of their great wickedness, and boasting in their own strength, they were left with only their own strength. Therefore they didn't prosper, but were afflicted, struck down, and driven by the Lamanites until they lost control of almost all their lands. 14 But Moronihah preached continually to the people, denouncing their iniquities. And Nephi and Lehi, who were Helaman's sons, also preached continually to the people, and prophesied many things to them about their iniquities and what would happen to them if they didn't repent of their sins. 15 Some repented; and to the degree they repented, they began to prosper. 16 When Moronihah saw they repented, he was inspired to lead them onward from place to place and from city to city, until they had regained half their property and half their lands. 17 And so ended the 61st year of the judges' rule.

XIII   18 In the 62nd year of the judges' rule, Moronihah was unable to regain any more of their lands from the Lamanites. 19 Therefore they abandoned their plan to get the rest of their lands, since the Lamanites were so numerous it was impossible for the Nephites to defeat them.

Therefore Moronihah used all his armed forces to defend those places he had retaken.

XIV 20 Because of the extremely large number of Lamanites, the Nephites feared they would be overpowered, trampled, killed, and destroyed. 21 They began to remember Alma's prophecies and Mosiah's words as well. They saw they had been a stubborn and unyielding people and had treated God's commandments as meaningless 22 and they had changed and ignored Mosiah's laws, the very laws the Lord commanded him to give the people. So they realized their laws had become corrupted and they had become a wicked people, no different than the Lamanites. 23 Due to their iniquity, the congregation was falling apart. They began to disbelieve in the spirit of prophecy and in the spirit of revelation. God's judgments stared them in the face. 24 They saw they were now weak like their Lamanite brothers and sisters and the Spirit of the Lord no longer protected them. It had withdrawn from them because the Spirit of the Lord doesn't reside in unholy temples. 25 Therefore the Lord stopped protecting them with His miraculous and unmatched power, since they fell into unbelief and awful wickedness. They could see the Lamanites were far more numerous than they were; and unless they held firmly to the Lord their God, they faced unavoidable destruction. 26 They saw the Lamanites' strength matched theirs comparing man to man. They were in a weakened condition because of their transgressions; indeed, it only took a few years for them to be weakened by their transgressions.

XV 5 That same year, Nephi turned the judgment seat over to a man named Cezoram. 2 Because their laws and how they were administered was controlled by the will of the people, and there were more who chose evil than those who chose good, their entire society was ripening for destruction, since the laws had become corrupted. 3 But this wasn't the only thing. They were so stubborn and defiant that if you enforced the law or imposed justice, they deserved to be destroyed.

XVI 4 Nephi was sick at heart because of this; so he turned over the judgment seat and assumed the responsibility to preach God's word for the rest of his life, and his brother Lehi joined him, for the rest of his life also. 5 They remembered what their father Helaman told them. He said: 6 My sons, I want you to remember to keep God's commandments. And I want you to explain to the people that I named you after our first parents who came from the land of Jerusalem. I've done this so your names will remind you of them. When you remember them, you'll remember their works. When you remember their works, you know it's said, and also written, that they were good.

7 Therefore, my sons, I want you to be good, so the same thing will be said and written about you, as it has been said and written of them. 8 Now, my sons, I ask of you one more thing, which is that you don't set a good example so you can brag about it. Only do what's right to store up for yourselves a treasure in heaven, which is eternal and won't fade away, so you can have the precious gift of eternal life. We have every reason to believe our fathers received that gift.

XVII   9 Remember, remember, my sons, the words king Benjamin taught his people. Remember there isn't any other way or means by which mankind can be saved, except through the atoning blood of Jesus Christ, who's sure to come. Remember He is coming to redeem the world. 10 Remember also what Amulek said to Zeezrom in the city of Ammonihah. He told him the Lord would certainly come to redeem His people, but He wouldn't come to redeem them in their sins, but He would come to redeem them from their sins. 11 He has power given to Him from the Father to redeem them from their sins if they repent. Therefore He has sent His angels to declare the requirement for repentance, which permits the power of the Redeemer to save their souls. 12 Now, my sons, remember, remember it's on the rock of our Redeemer, who is Christ, the Son of God, you must build your foundation, so that when the accuser attacks with powerful winds, lightning, a tornado, hail, and his turbulent storm to defeat you, none of it will have the power to drag you down to the abyss of misery and endless suffering, because the rock you're built on is a stable foundation that will never fail.

XVIII   13 This was what Helaman taught to his sons, but he also went on with things not written down, and taught other things from this record and from written scriptures; 14,15,16 and they remembered his words. Then they departed to teach God's word throughout the Nephite communities, beginning at Bountiful, then the city of Gid, and from there to Mulek, all in keeping with God's commandments. They taught from one city to another until they had traveled to all the Nephites in the land to the south, and then went from there into the land of Zarahemla among the Lamanites.

XIX   17 They preached powerfully, convincing many of the defectors who had departed from the Nephites that they had been wrong. As a result, they publicly confessed their sins and were baptized as a sign of repentance and immediately returned to the Nephites to attempt to repair the wrongs they had committed. 18 Additionally Nephi and Lehi preached powerfully with a voice of authority to the Lamanites, since God's power and authority was His gift to them. Their words were inspired through that gift. 19 Therefore their messages were astonishing and so convincing to the Lamanites that 8,000 of them in Zarahemla and the surrounding area were baptized as a sign of repentance because they had been convinced of the wickedness of their fathers' traditions.

XX   20 Then Nephi and Lehi went on from there to the land of Nephi. 21 And there they were captured by a Lamanite army and thrown into prison, the same prison where Ammon and his brothers were put by Limhi's servants. 22 After they had been confined in prison many days without food, the captors went into the prison to take and kill them. 23 But Nephi and Lehi were surrounded as if by fire, and so they didn't dare touch them for fear of being burned. However, Nephi and Lehi weren't burned although they were standing unharmed in the middle of fire. 24 When they saw they were surrounded by a pillar of fire and it didn't burn them, their hearts took courage; 25 they saw the Lamanites didn't dare touch them, or even dare to approach them; instead, they stood dumbstruck in amazement.

XXI   26 Nephi and Lehi got up and spoke to them, saying: Don't be afraid! It's God who's shown you this miraculous thing, showing you that you can't take and kill us. 27 These words were followed by a strong earthquake. The prison walls shook as if they were about to fall to the ground, but they didn't fall. The crowd who entered the prison were Lamanites and Nephite defectors. 28 Thick darkness surrounded them, and they were filled with ominous fear. 29 They heard a voice speaking as if from above the thick cloud of darkness, saying: Repent, repent! Stop trying to kill My servants, whom I've sent to you to declare the gospel.

XXII   30 What they heard wasn't a voice like thunder, nor a deafening, loud voice, but it was a quiet voice of perfect mildness, almost a whisper; and it pierced right to the very core — 31 and yet despite the mildness of the voice, the earth shook terribly. The prison walls quaked again as if they were about to fall to the ground. The thick darkness overshadowing them remained. 32 And the voice spoke again, saying: Repent, repent, because the kingdom of heaven is near. Stop trying to kill My servants. And again the earth and walls shook and quaked. 33 The voice spoke a third time and said astonishing words to them that we are unable to record. The walls quaked again, and the earth shook as if it were about to split in two.

XXIII   34 The Lamanites couldn't see to flee because of the thick darkness surrounding them, and they were also paralyzed by fear. 35 Now one of them, a Nephite by birth, had once belonged to God's congregation but had split from them. 36 He turned around, and could see through the darkness the faces of Nephi and Lehi. They were brightly shining like the faces of angels. He saw them looking up to heaven and they seemed to be talking or addressing someone they could see.

XXIV ³⁷ This man yelled out to the crowd to turn around and look. And they turned around and looked and they also saw the faces of Nephi and Lehi. ³⁸ They asked the man: What does all this mean? Who are these men talking to? ³⁹ Now the man's name was Aminadab. And Aminadab answered: They're talking with God's angels. ⁴⁰ The Lamanites asked him: How can we get this thick darkness removed from surrounding us? ⁴¹ Aminadab answered: You must repent and pray to the voice until you have faith in Christ, which was taught to you by Alma, Amulek, and Zeezrom. When you do this, the thick darkness will be lifted from you.

XXV ⁴² They all began to pray to the voice of the One who had shaken the earth. Indeed, they prayed until the thick darkness dispersed. ⁴³ When they looked around and saw the thick darkness was removed from surrounding them, they realized they all were surrounded by a pillar of fire. ⁴⁴ Nephi and Lehi were in the center of the crowd. Yet even though they were surrounded and in the middle of a flaming fire it didn't hurt them, and it didn't harm the prison walls, either. They felt joy that's unspeakable and glorious. ⁴⁵ The Holy Spirit of God descended from heaven and entered their hearts. They were filled as if with fire, enabling them to speak of breathtaking, glorious things.

XXVI ⁴⁶ The voice spoke to them again, cheerfully and softly, saying: ⁴⁷ Peace, peace be with you because of your faith in My Well Beloved, who existed from the foundation of creation. ⁴⁸ When they heard this, they looked up trying to see who was speaking. The heavens opened as angels descended from heaven and ministered to them. ⁴⁹ There were about 300 souls who witnessed these things. They were told to not question or doubt their experience. ⁵⁰ They went out and testified to the people, declaring throughout the surrounding area everything they had heard and seen, and the majority of the Lamanites were convinced by their testimony. ⁵¹ All those who were convinced gave up their weapons, their hatred, and ancestors' traditions as well. ⁵² And they returned the lands they had taken back to the Nephites.

XXVII **6** All these things had happened by the time the 62nd year of the judges' rule had ended; and the majority of the Lamanites had become righteous, so much so that their righteousness exceeded the Nephites', because they were firm and steady in their faith. ² In contrast, there were many Nephites who had become hardened, unrepentant, and excessively wicked, rejecting God's word and all the preaching and prophesying provided to them. ³ Nevertheless, the congregation members felt tremendous joy about the conversion of the Lamanites, and for God's congregation now established among them. They fellowshipped with each other, rejoiced with each other, and shared the joy. 4 Many of the Lamanites went to Zarahemla and testified to the Nephites about their conversion and urged them to be faithful and repent. 5 Many preached effectively and persuasively, which humbled many of them and converted them to again follow God and the Lamb.

XXVIII   6 Many of the Lamanites went north along with Nephi and Lehi to preach to the people there. And so ended the 63rd year. 7 There was peace throughout all the land, allowing the Nephites to travel anywhere they wished, whether it was among the Nephites or the Lamanites. 8 The Lamanites could do likewise, also among the Lamanites or the Nephites. All had free communication and trade with one another, letting them buy, sell, and profit, as they wanted.

XXIX   9 They became very rich, both the Lamanites and the Nephites; they accumulated gold, silver, and precious metals, both in the south and in the north. 10 Now the land to the south was called Lehi; and to the north was called Muloch, after Zedekiah's son. Because the Lord originally led Muloch to settle the land to the north and Lehi settled the south. 11 There was a variety of gold, silver, and precious ores in both areas. The skilled workmen refined a variety of metals resulting in their wealth. 12 Others raised grain in abundance, both in the north and in the south. They prospered both in the north and in the south. The population grew and society was strong in the land. They raised many flocks and herds, providing many fattened calves. 13 Their women worked hard and made thread, all kinds of cloth, woven linen, and a variety of material to clothe themselves. And so the 64th year ended in peace. 14 In the 65th year, they also had great joy and peace and continual preaching and many prophecies about the future. And so ended the 65th year.

XXX   15 In the 66th year of the judges' rule, Cezoram was murdered by an unidentified person while the judgment seat was his. That same year his son, who had been appointed by the people to replace his father, was also murdered. And so ended the 66th year. 16 At the start of the 67th year, the people began to grow very wicked again. 17 The Lord had blessed them with material possessions for so long that they were never angry, started a war, or caused any bloodshed. Therefore they began to make their material possessions their only priority. Indeed, they began acquiring wealth and status so they could think of themselves as better than the next person. Then secret murders started, and people started robbing and stealing to make money. 18 Now the murderers and thieves were from that gang started by

Kishcumen and Gaddianton. There were many, even among the
Nephites, who joined Gaddianton's gang. But there were far more
among the more wicked part of the Lamanites. They were called
Gaddianton's robbers and murderers. 19 They were the ones who
murdered the chief judge Cezoram and his son while responsible for
the judgment seat. But they went unidentified.

XXXI   20 When the Lamanites discovered there were robbers among
them, they were dismayed. They used every means within their ability
to find and execute them. 21 But Satan inspired most of the Nephites
to join with those gangs of robbers and commit themselves through
covenants and oaths, promising to protect and defend one another no
matter the circumstances they were caught in, so they could escape
punishment for their murders, robberies, and thefts.

XXXII   22 They used their secret signs and words to identify any fellow
gang member who had made the covenant. It didn't matter what
crime his fellow gang member committed, he would be protected by
the other gang members. 23 They were able to murder, rob, steal, and
commit whoredoms and all kinds of evil, violating the laws of the land
and laws of God also. 24 Anyone who belonged to their gang and
revealed their wickedness and corruption to the world was to be tried,
not according to their country's laws, but according to the rules of
their gang society, which had been established by Gaddianton and
Kishcumen. 25 Now these were the secret oaths and covenants Alma
commanded his son not to make public, to prevent the resulting
destruction.

XXXIII   26 But Gaddianton didn't get his secret oaths and covenants from
the records delivered to Helaman; he got them from that same being
who tempted our first parents to eat the forbidden fruit — 27 the same
one who plotted with Cain to murder his brother Abel, promising
others wouldn't find out about it. He plotted with Cain and his
followers from then on. 28 It's also the same one who inspired people's
hearts to build a tower high enough to get to heaven. It was the same
being who deceived the people who came from that tower to this land,
and then spread works of darkness and abominations over the whole
land till the people destroyed themselves and fell into an everlasting
hell. 29 It was him, the same one, who put it in Gaddianton's heart to
do the same evil and continue with secret murders. And he's promoted
it since the beginning of mankind, all the way up to now. 30 He's the
original advocate for every sin. He renews his dark works and secret
murders by passing down the plots, oaths, covenants, and their wicked,
destructive plans to generation after generation, whenever he can take
hold of mankind's hearts. 31 Now he got a great hold on the hearts of

the Nephites, so much so that they became very wicked. Indeed, the majority of them turned from the way of righteousness and stomped on God's commandments, gratified their ambitions, and made gold and silver idols for themselves.

XXXIV ³² All these iniquities erupted in just a few years, with most of it beginning in the 67th year of the judges' rule over the Nephites. ³³ They increased their iniquities in the 68th year, while the righteous mourned and agonized over it. ³⁴ And so the Nephites began to fall away in unbelief and grow increasingly in wickedness and abominations, while the Lamanites grew increasingly in their knowledge of God; they obeyed His ordinances and commandments and walked uprightly in truth before Him. ³⁵ But the Spirit of the Lord began withdrawing from the Nephites because of the wickedness and hardness of their hearts. ³⁶ On the other hand the Lord began to pour out His Spirit on the Lamanites because they were willing and readily believed in His word.

XXXV ³⁷ The Lamanites hunted the secret society of Gaddianton's robbers. And they preached God's word among the most wicked of them, so this gang of robbers was completely destroyed among the Lamanites. ³⁸ On the other hand, the Nephites built them up and supported them, beginning with the most wicked of them, until they spread over the entire Nephite territory and had persuaded most of the righteous, until they started adopting their scheme and sharing in their spoils and participated in their secret murders and conspiracies. ³⁹ This resulted in the complete control of the government with resulting oppression and exploitation of the poor, the meek, and the humble followers of God. ⁴⁰ They were in an awful state and ripening for everlasting destruction. ⁴¹ And so ended the 68th year of the judges' rule over the Nephites.

Chapter 3

THE PROPHECY OF NEPHI, THE SON OF HELAMAN

God warns the Nephites that He will punish them in His anger to their complete destruction unless they repent of their wickedness. God punishes the Nephites; they repent and turn to Him. Samuel, a Lamanite, prophesies to the Nephites.

7 In the 69th year of the judges' rule over the Nephites, Nephi, the son of Helaman, returned from the north to Zarahemla. ² He taught God's word and prophesied many things to the people there. ³ But they rejected everything he said, so he left them and returned to his native land. ⁴ He found the people had become awful and corrupt. There were Gaddianton robbers filling the judgment seats. They had seized control of the land. They disregarded God's commandments. They defied Him and acted abusively to people. 5 They condemned the righteous because of their righteousness. They let the guilty and wicked go unpunished because of their money. They were given control over the government to do anything they wanted, and they wanted money and adoration from the public, which allowed them to commit adultery, steal, kill, and indulge themselves. 6 It had only taken a few years for this widespread iniquity to be welcomed by the Nephites. When Nephi saw it, it broke his heart. He lamented: 7 I wish I could have lived during the time when my forefather Nephi first came from the land of Jerusalem; I wish I could have felt joy with him in the promised land. At that time, his people were easy to persuade, firm in keeping God's commandments, and slow to want to commit iniquity. And they were quick to listen and obey the Lord's words. 8 Indeed, if my days could have been in those days, my soul would have rejoiced in the righteousness of my fellow Nephites. 9 But I was born at this time and live at a time that fills me with sorrow because of the wickedness of my fellow Nephites.

II   10 Now Nephi was on a tower in his garden, next to the highway leading to the main marketplace of the city of Zarahemla. As Nephi prayed on the garden tower next to his garden gate by the highway, 11 some men were passing by and saw him lamenting to God. They ran and told the people what they had seen. And a big group of people went to learn the reason for him lamenting over the people's wickedness.

III   12 When Nephi got up, he saw a crowd had gathered. 13 He asked them: Why have you come here? You want me to tell you about your iniquities? 14 Is it because I've gotten on my tower in order to lament to God as I mourn over your terrible iniquities? 15 Is it because of my mourning and lamentation you've come here and act surprised? Indeed, you should be surprised! You should be surprised by how you've surrendered to the accuser and given him complete control over your hearts. 16 Why have you surrendered to the lies of someone who wants to drag your souls down to everlasting misery and endless suffering?

IV   17 O repent, repent! Why are you determined to die? Turn back, turn back to the Lord who is God! Do you know why He's abandoned you? 18 It's because you've hardened your hearts. Indeed, you ignore the Good Shepherd's voice. You've made Him angry at you. 19 Therefore instead of gathering you, He'll exterminate you and feed dogs and scavengers with your carcasses, unless you repent. 20 How could you turn your back on God in the very moment He saved you?

21 It's because you want wealth, to be envied for your gold and silver. You only value wealth and worldly things of no real value, and to get it you're willing to murder, rob, steal, and tell lies about your neighbor and do every kind of evil. 22 Because of this, you're headed for misery and calamity unless you repent. If you don't repent, this great city and all the other great cities throughout our land will be lost, leaving you no place to live. Because the Lord won't protect you against your enemies, as He's done until now. 23 This is what the Lord says: I won't support the wicked with My protection for any one more than another, but I protect only those who repent of their sins and obey Me.

V   So now my friends you'll find it will be better for the Lamanites than for you unless you repent. 24 They're more righteous than you, since they haven't sinned against the great knowledge given to you. Therefore the Lord will be merciful to them. He'll lengthen out their days and increase their offspring, while you'll be completely destroyed unless you repent. 25 Woe to you because you welcome the great abomination founded by Gaddianton which you've embraced by joining that gang. 26 You're doomed to misery and calamity because you're full of pride, which has corrupted you as a result of your great wealth. 27 Woe to you because you are wicked and abominable, 28 and unless you repent, you will perish; and you'll lose all your lands, and you'll be annihilated. 29 Now I'm giving this warning not from myself, but from God. God sent me to warn you, otherwise I wouldn't know this is your doom.

VI   **8** When Nephi finished these words, there were judges who belonged to the secret society of Gaddianton who were angry and shouted to the people: Why don't you arrest this man and bring him to trial, so he can be condemned for the crime he's committed? 2 Why are you looking at and listening to this man, when he's denouncing you people and our laws? 3 They said this because Nephi had spoken to them about how corrupt their laws were. Indeed, Nephi said many things that can't be written here. But he didn't say anything contrary to God's commandments. 4 And those judges were angry with him because he was blunt about their secret works of darkness. Nevertheless, they didn't dare arrest him, since they were afraid the people might not support them. 5 Therefore they appealed to the people: Why are you letting this man ridicule us? He's threatening this whole nation with destruction, and he claims we'll lose our great cities, and we won't have any place left to live. 6 Now we know this is impossible. Because we are powerful and our cities are great; therefore our enemies can't prevail against us.

VII   7 So they inflamed the people until they argued over Nephi, some denounced him and some objected saying: Leave this man alone, because he's a good man; and the things he said are certain to happen unless we repent. 8 All the judgments of God he said are coming are going to come to us, since we can see he's right about our many iniquities. He also knows everything that will happen to us because he identified our iniquities. 9 Indeed, if he wasn't a prophet, he wouldn't have testified about these things.

VIII   10 The people who wanted to kill Nephi were intimidated, so they didn't arrest him. Therefore he began to prophesy again, seeing he had some support, so that the rest of them were intimidated. 11 Therefore he was inspired to say to them: My friends, haven't you read God gave power to the man Moses to divide the water of the Red Sea? And the water parted to one side and the other, so our ancestor Israelites walked through on dry ground. Then the water fell upon the Egyptian armies, swallowing them up.

IX   12 Now if God guided this man, then why do you argue among yourselves and refuse to accept He guided me so I know about His coming judgments upon you unless you repent? 13 You not only reject my words, but you also reject all the words of our forefathers, and also the words of Moses, who clearly had great power given to him; and he testified about Christ's coming. 14 Indeed, didn't he testify the Son of God was to come? He lifted up the brass serpent in the wilderness, as a sign that He who was to come would be lifted up. 15 Just as all those who looked on that serpent would live, similarly, all those who look to the Son of God with faith, having a repentant spirit, will live, and even receive life which is eternal. 16 Now Moses wasn't the only one who testified of these things, but all the holy prophets from his day back to the days of Abraham did as well. 17 And Abraham saw His coming and was filled with gladness and rejoiced. 18 I tell you Abraham wasn't the only one who knew of these things, there were many before Abraham's time who were called by the Order of God, according to the Holy Order of His Son, and this was to show to the people thousands of years before His coming that redemption was available to them. 19 Now I want you to know that ever since Abraham's time there have been many prophets who have testified about this. The prophet Zenos testified boldly — and for that he was killed — 20 and Zenoch, Ezaias, Isaiah, and Jeremiah as well. Jeremiah was the same prophet who testified about Jerusalem's destruction. We've learned Jerusalem was destroyed according to Jeremiah's words. So why won't the Son of God come according to his prophecy? 21 Will you argue Jerusalem wasn't destroyed? Will you say Zedekiah's sons weren't killed, all except for Muloch? Indeed, can't you see Zedekiah's descendants are here and they were led from the land of Jerusalem? But this isn't everything. 22 Our father Lehi was forced out of Jerusalem because he testified of these things. Nephi and nearly all our forefathers down to today have all testified about it as well. They've testified of Christ's coming and have looked forward rejoicing at His coming day. 23 And He is God; and He is with them, and He revealed Himself to them, and He redeemed them. They worshiped Him because of what's to happen.

X   24 Now seeing as you know this and will lie if you deny it, which is your sin because you've rejected all these things, despite the clear evidence given to you. Indeed, you've been given evidence both in heaven and on earth as a witness that they're true. 25 But you've rejected the truth and rebelled against your holy God. Right now, instead of storing up for yourselves treasures in heaven — where nothing can destroy and where nothing unclean can enter — you've earned condemnation for yourselves on judgment day. 26 Indeed, right now you're ripening — because of your murders, sexual immorality, and wickedness — for everlasting destruction. Unless you repent, it's coming soon. 27 It's at your doorstep. Go to the judgment seat and investigate what's happened there; your judge has been murdered, and he's lying in his blood. His brother, whose goal is to sit in the judgment seat, has murdered him. 28 They both belong to your secret society, founded by Gaddianton and the Evil One, whose goal is to destroy people's souls.

XI   **9** Now when Nephi said this, five men who were there ran to the judgment seat. They said to each other as they were going: 2 Now we'll know for certain whether this man is a prophet and whether God has commanded him to prophesy such astonishing things to us. We don't believe that He has; and we don't believe he's a prophet. However, if what he's said about the chief judge is true, that he's dead, then we'll believe the other things he's said are true. 3 And they ran quickly to the judgment seat where the chief judge was on the ground lying in his blood. 4 When they saw this, they were shocked, so much so they fainted, since they hadn't believed the things Nephi had said about the chief judge. 5 But when they saw this, they believed; and they feared all the judgments Nephi predicted. So they trembled with fear and fainted.

XII   6 Now the judge was stabbed by his brother, who then escaped using a disguise. As soon as the judge was murdered, the servants ran and told the people, yelling a murder had happened. 7 And the people gathered at the judgment seat. To their astonishment, they saw the five men who had fainted. 8 Now the people didn't know anything about the crowd gathered at Nephi's garden. Therefore they said to each other: These men are the ones who have murdered the judge; and God has struck them down to prevent their escape.

XIII   9 So they took them, tied them up, and threw them into prison. And it was announced the judge was killed and the murderers were captured and were being held in prison. 10 The next day, the people assembled to mourn and fast at the burial of the murdered highest and chief judge. 11 The judges who were at Nephi's garden and overheard him also attended the burial.

XIV   12 And they asked the others: Where are the five who were sent to ask about the chief judge, to find out whether he was dead? And they answered: We don't know about the five you sent, but we have five murderers now in our prison. 13 Then the judges asked to see them, and they were brought out. Then they recognized the five who had been sent. The judges questioned them about the matter. And they explained: 14 We ran to the judgment seat. When we saw everything just like Nephi described, we were shocked and we fainted. When we had recovered from our shock, they threw us in prison. 15 Now as to this man's murder, we don't know who did it. We only know this much: we ran and came just as you asked, and he was dead just as Nephi had said.

XV   16 Now the judges described the matter in detail to the people and accused Nephi, saying: We know Nephi must have conspired with someone to kill the judge; then he would be able to tell it to us, so he could convert us to his faith, so he could raise himself to be a great man, chosen by God and a prophet. 17 Now we'll expose this man, and get his confession and reveal the judge's true murderer. 18 The five were set free on the day of the burial. However, they rebuked the judges for speaking against Nephi, confronting them one after another, countering their arguments and proving them wrong.

XVI   19 Nevertheless, they had Nephi arrested, tied up, and brought before the crowd who had gathered. And they began to question him in various ways trying to get him to contradict himself, so they could condemn him to death, 20 asking him: You're part of a conspiracy, an accomplice! Who's your associate that committed this murder? Tell us and admit your guilt! And they also offered: Here's some money! We'll let you live if you tell us and admit you've made an agreement with someone. 21 But Nephi responded: You fools, you unconverted in heart, you blind and stubborn people, do you have any idea how long the Lord your God will let you continue in your sinful ways? 22 You ought to begin weeping and wailing over the destruction now coming for you, unless you repent. 23 You say I conspired with a man to murder Seezoram, our chief judge. But I told you because I wanted you to know it had happened. You need to realize I know of all your wickedness and abominations. 24 Because I've exposed your wickedness, you accuse me of conspiring with a man to commit this murder. Because I showed you this sign, you're angry and want to have me killed.

XVII   25 Now I'll show you another sign, and we'll see if you want to kill me for this one as well. 26 I tell you: Go to the house of Seantum, who is Seezoram's brother, and ask him: 27 Has Nephi, the so-called prophet, who prophesies so much evil about us, conspired with you, and as part of this conspiracy have you murdered your brother Seezoram? 28 And he'll tell you: No. 29 Then ask him: Did you murder your brother? 30 And he'll stand there afraid, not knowing what to say. And he'll deny he did it; and he'll pretend to be surprised. Nevertheless, he'll tell you he's innocent. 31 But when you examine him, you'll find blood on the bottom part of his cloak. 32 When you see this, you should ask: Where does this blood come from? Isn't this your brother's blood? 33 And then he'll shake with fear and his face will lose its color and look as pale as death. 34 Then you should say: Because of how afraid and pale you look, we know you're guilty. 35 Then he'll be even more afraid; and he'll confess and no longer deny he committed this murder. 36 And then he'll tell you that I, Nephi couldn't know anything about it unless it was revealed to me by God's power. Then you'll know I'm honest and I'm sent to you from God.

XVIII   37 And they went and did just as Nephi had said to them. The things he predicted were true; because just as he described, Seantum denied, and then like he predicted, he confessed. 38 He was exposed as the actual murderer, so the five were vindicated, and Nephi proven innocent. 39 Some of the Nephites believed in Nephi's words. Others believed because of the testimony of the five, who had been converted while they were in prison. 40 Some of the people said Nephi was a prophet. 41 And others said: He's a god; because if he wasn't a god, he couldn't know about everything. Indeed, he's told us the thoughts of our hearts, and he's foretold things to us as well, and he's even identified the murderer of our chief judge.

XIX   **10** This resulted in an argument among the people, so they split up, going away and leaving Nephi standing alone. 2 Nephi went to return to his own house, pondering about what the Lord had shown him. 3 As he was pondering this, regretting the Nephites' wickedness, their secret works of darkness, murders, robberies, and all their iniquities; reviewing these in his heart, a voice spoke to him, saying:

4 You are blessed, Nephi, because of the things you've done. I've seen how you've tirelessly declared the word I gave you to this people. You haven't been afraid of them and haven't tried to save your own life, but have tried to learn My will and to keep My commandments. 5 Now because you've done this so tirelessly, I'll bless you forever. And I'll make you powerful in word and deed, in faith and works, so that all things will happen to you as you ask, since you won't ask anything contrary to My will. 6 You are Nephi and I Am God. I declare this to you in front of My angels as witnesses: You are given power over this people and will strike the earth with famine, disease, and destruction in response to this people's wickedness. 7 Indeed, I give you power that whatever you seal on earth will be sealed in heaven, and whatever you set loose on earth will be set loose in heaven, and so you will hold this power over this people. 8 And so if you say to this temple: Split in two! — it will happen. 9 And if you say to this mountain: Fall down and be leveled! — it will happen. 10 And if you say for God to afflict this people, it will happen. 11 Now I command you to go and warn these people that the Lord God, the All-Powerful One, decrees: Unless you repent, you will be afflicted and destroyed.

xx   12 Now when the Lord said this to Nephi, he stopped, turned around, and didn't go to his house, but warned the many people spread across the land about the Lord's words promising to destroy them if they didn't repent. 13 Now despite the great miracle of Nephi telling them about the murder of the chief judge, they hardened their hearts and refused to pay any attention to the Lord's words. 14 But Nephi declared to them the Lord's word, saying: Unless you repent, the Lord says you will be afflicted and destroyed. 15 When Nephi delivered this message, they still hardened their hearts and ignored what he said. The people mocked him and attempted to seize him so they could throw him in prison. 16 But God's power was with him, and they were unable to grab him and put him in prison because he was taken by the Spirit and carried away from them.

xxi   17 And so he went forth in the Spirit from gathering to gathering declaring God's word, until all of them heard it directly or indirectly. 18 But they refused to respond to his warning. But there began to be heated arguments, so much so that they fought among themselves and began to kill each other with the sword. 19 And so ended the 71st year of the judges' rule over the Nephites.

Chapter 4

11 Now in the 72nd year of the judges' rule, the arguments increased and resulted in armed conflicts throughout the whole

Nephite territory. 2 And it was this secret gang of robbers that led the violence and wickedness. This conflict lasted that whole year, and in the 73rd year it continued.

II   3 In this year, Nephi approached the Lord in prayer, saying: 4 O Lord, don't let this people die by the sword. But, O Lord, let there instead be a famine in the land to prompt them to remember the Lord their God; and perhaps they will repent and turn to You. 5 Then it happened according to Nephi's words, and there was a great famine in the land among all the Nephites. And in the 74th year the famine continued; and the violence stopped because famine was now killing people. 6 This ruin continued in the 75th year also, because a drought destroyed their crops and grain. The entire land suffered, both the Lamanites as well as the Nephites, resulting in both being struck down, dying by the thousands in the more wicked areas.

III   7 Then the people realized they were about to die by famine. They began to remember the Lord who is God and began to remember Nephi's words. 8 The people began to beg their chief judges and leaders to ask Nephi: We know you're a man of God. Therefore call upon the Lord who is God and ask Him to end this famine for us, so what you said about our destruction won't happen. 9 The judges made that request of Nephi. When Nephi saw the people changed and sincerely humbled themselves and repented, he again prayed to the Lord, saying: 10 O Lord, the people have repented. And they've eliminated Gaddianton's gang from them, so they no longer exist; and they've buried their secret plans. 11 Now, O Lord, because of their humility, will You turn away Your anger and let Your anger end with the destruction of those wicked men who've already died? 12 O Lord, please turn away Your great anger —and put an end to the drought and famine. 13 O Lord, let my request persuade You to send rain upon the earth, so she can produce her fruit and her grain for the harvest. 14 O Lord, You listened to me when I said: Let there be a famine to stop the killing by the sword. And I know You'll listen to me now since You promised if the people repent, You will spare them. 15 O Lord, they've repented because of the famine, disease, and destruction imposed on them. 16 Now, O Lord, will You turn away Your anger and see once more whether they'll serve You? And if so, O Lord, You can bless them as You've promised.

IV   17 In the 76th year, the Lord turned away His anger and caused rain to fall on the earth, and it produced her fruit in the season of her fruit. It produced her grain in the season of her grain. 18 And the people rejoiced and glorified God, and the whole land was covered with rejoicing. They no longer attempted to kill Nephi; instead, they considered him to be a great prophet and a man of God, having great power and authority given to him from God. 19 Now Lehi his brother was no less righteous than him. 20 So the Nephites again began to prosper in the land and began to rebuild their desolate places and began to increase in numbers and spread out, until they covered the whole land, both to the north and the south, from the western to the eastern sea. 21 The 76th year ended in peace; and the 77th year began in peace. And the congregation spread throughout the whole land. Most of the people, both the Nephites and the Lamanites, belonged to the congregation. They had great peace in the land. And so ended the 77th year. 22 They had peace in the 78th year as well, except for a few conflicts about the points of doctrine taught by the prophets. 23 In the 79th year, there was a great deal more conflict. But Nephi and Lehi and many of their associates, who knew about the true points of doctrine, since they had many revelations daily, preached to the people, putting an end to their disputes in that same year.

V   24 In the 80th year of the judges' rule over the Nephites, a small number of Nephite defectors, who had some years earlier gone over to the Lamanites and taken upon themselves the name of Lamanites, along with a small number who were actual descendants of the Lamanites — being stirred up to anger by those defectors — therefore they began a war with the Nephites. 25 They committed murder and robbery; and then they would retreat into the mountains and wilderness, and to secret places, hiding out so they wouldn't be caught, receiving additional defectors daily who came to join them. 26 And so in a very few years they became a very large gang of robbers. They searched in order to learn all of Gaddianton's secret plans, becoming robbers of Gaddianton.

VI   27 Now these robbers made great havoc, causing great destruction among both the Nephites and the Lamanites. 28 It was necessary to end their work of destruction. Therefore they sent an army of strong men into the wilderness and mountains to find this gang of robbers and kill them. 29 But in that same year they were driven back, all the way into their own lands. So ended the 80th year of the judges' rule over the Nephites.

VII   30 As the 81st year began, they again attacked this gang of robbers and killed many of them. But they also experienced widespread losses; 31 and so they again had to retreat from the wilderness and mountains back to their own lands, because of the many robbers there. 32 And so ended that year.

VIII   The robbers continued to increase and gain strength, reaching a point where they defied the entire Nephite army, and the entire

Lamanite army as well. Everyone throughout the land was afraid of them. 33 They raided many parts of the land and inflicted great ruin upon them; indeed, they killed many and carried away others captive into the wilderness, particularly their women and children. 34 Now this great evil, which resulted from the people's iniquity, again reminded them to remember the Lord their God. 35 And so ended the 81st year of the judges' rule. 36 But in the 82nd year they again began neglecting the Lord their God. In the 83rd year, they grew worse in their iniquity. In the 84th year, they didn't change their ways. 37 In the 85th year, they got increasingly prideful and wicked. They were again ripening for destruction. 38 Thus ended the 85th year.

IX   **12** This is an example of how false and unsteady mankind's hearts are and shows that the Lord in His great infinite goodness blesses and prospers those who trust in Him. 2 It shows how, at the very time He blesses His people with expanding crops, flocks, herds, gold, silver, and every kind of valuable, sparing their lives and rescuing them from the power of their enemies, softening the hearts of their enemies, so they don't start wars against them, and in short, doing everything for His people's well-being and happiness, that's when they harden their hearts, forget the Lord their God, and turn their backs on the Holy One. They do this because their lives are easy, comfortable, and prosperous. 3 It shows us that unless the Lord disciplines His people using hardships, including the threats of death, terror, famine, and diseases, they forget Him. 4 How foolish, vain, evil, and devilish are mankind; how quick to commit iniquity and slow to do good; how quick to follow the words of the Evil One and to set their hearts on the worthless things of the world; 5 how quick to be prideful; how quick to brag and become evil; and how slow they are to remember the Lord who is God and to follow His counsel; indeed, how slow they are to let Wisdom guide them. 6 They don't allow the Lord who is God, who created them, to rule and reign over them. Despite His great goodness and His mercy toward them, they treat His advice as worthless and they refuse to let Him guide them.

X   7 How insignificant are mankind; indeed, they're even less than the dust of the earth. 8 The dust of the earth obeys the everlasting God, responding to His command when told to move or divide. 9 At His command, the hills and mountains tremble and quake. 10 At His voice the peaks are broken up and leveled and made into a valley. 11 And by the power of His voice, the whole earth shakes; 12 indeed, by the power of His voice the foundations rock, right to the very core. 13 If He says to the earth: Move! — then it moves. 14 If He says to the earth: You must go back, to lengthen a day for many hours — then it happens.

15 And so the earth goes backward, obeying His word, and it looks to people as if the sun is standing still. This is because the earth moves and not the sun. 16 In addition, if He says to the waters of the sea: Be dried up! — then it is done. 17 If He says to this mountain: Rise up and move over and bury that city! — then it happens. 18 If a person hides a treasure in the ground and the Lord says: Let it be cursed because of the iniquity of the person who hid it! — then it will be cursed. 19 If the Lord says: It is cursed to prevent anyone from recovering it from this time forward and forever! — then it will be lost from this time forward and forever. 20 And if the Lord tells someone: Because of your iniquities you will be cursed forever — then it will happen. 21 If the Lord says: Because of your iniquities you will be cut off from My presence — then He'll make it so. 22 And woe to anyone who hears Him say that; because it will happen to those who are committed to iniquity, and they can't be saved. To save people from this doom, repentance has been provided.

XI   23 Therefore blessed are those who repent and listen to the voice of the Lord who is God, because these are the ones who will be saved. 24 And may God in His infinite wisdom do whatever is required for mankind to be led to repent and do good works, so they can be restored to grace for grace based on their works. 25 I want all mankind to be saved. But we realize that on that great and last day some will be rejected and driven out of the Lord's presence, 26 and condemned to endless misery, vindicating the prophecy: Those who have done good will have everlasting life, and those who have done evil will have everlasting damnation. And so it is. Amen.

Chapter 5

Samuel the Lamanite's prophecy to the Nephites.

13 In the 86th year, the Nephites remained unrepentant, indeed, persistently wicked, while the Lamanites were careful to strictly keep God's commandments according to the Law of Moses. 2 In this year a man named Samuel, a Lamanite, came to Zarahemla and began to preach to the people. He preached repentance to the people for many days, but they threw him out, and as he was returning to his own land, 3 the Lord's voice spoke to him, telling him to return and prophesy to the people everything that would enter his heart.

II   4 But they wouldn't let him reenter the city. Therefore he climbed atop the city wall and reached out his arm and shouted in a loud voice, prophesying to the people everything the Lord put into his heart. 5 He declared to them: I'm Samuel, a Lamanite, and I'm telling you the words the Lord puts into my heart. He has this message for this people: The sword of justice hangs over you. And before 400 years have passed, the sword of justice will fall upon you. 6 Indeed, terrible destruction awaits you. It will certainly come for you, and nothing can save you except repentance and faith in the Lord Jesus Christ. He is assuredly coming into the world to suffer many things and be killed on behalf of His people. 7 An angel of the Lord testified of this to me; he's brought me this good news. I was sent to testify of it to you as well, so you also hear this good news. But you refused to listen to me.

III   8 Therefore the Lord now says: Because of the hardness of the hearts of the Nephites, unless they repent, I'll take away My salvation from them and I'll withdraw My Spirit from them. I won't put up with them any longer, and I'll let the hearts of their Lamanite brothers and sisters turn against them. 9 And before 400 years have passed, I'll bring afflictions, punishing them with the sword, famine, and with disease; 10 indeed, they'll bring down My fury. And there will be those of the fourth generation of your enemies, who will live to see your complete destruction. The Lord warns: This is certain to happen unless you repent to avoid the fourth generation seeing your destruction. 11 But the Lord says: If you repent and return to the Lord your God, I'll turn My anger away. Indeed, the Lord says: Blessed are those who repent and turn to Me, but woe upon those who don't repent. 12 Woe to this great city of Zarahemla! It's only because of the righteous that it's saved. Woe to this great city! The Lord says: I see that many, indeed, the majority of the inhabitants of this great city, have chosen to harden their hearts against Me. 13 But blessed are those who repent, since I'll spare them. If it weren't for the few righteous in this great city, I would send fire down from heaven and destroy it. 14 But it's spared because of the righteous. The Lord says: The time will come, once you drive away the righteous, you will be ripe for destruction.

IV   Woe to this great city because of the wickedness and abominations that are in her. 15 Woe to the city of Gideon because of the wickedness and abominations in her. 16 Woe to all the cities, in every direction, inhabited by the Nephites, because of the wickedness and abominations in them. 17 A curse will fall on the land, says the Lord of Hosts, because of the wickedness and abominations of the people living there.

V   18 And it will happen, says the Lord of Hosts (our great and true God), that any who protect their wealth by hiding it in the ground will never recover it because the land will be cursed. Only the righteous will be able to protect what's stored for the Lord's sake. 19 The Lord says: I want them to protect their valuable possessions for My purposes. But everyone who doesn't safeguard their wealth for My sake is cursed, because only the righteous protect their valuable things for My sake. Any others who hoard their wealth are cursed, both them and their wealth, for it will be lost because of the curse upon the land. 20 The day is coming when they'll hoard wealth because they've set their hearts on their property. Because they've set their hearts on their property and will hide it away when they flee from their enemies, they and their property will be cursed, and everything and everyone will be lost on that day, says the Lord.

VI   21 People of this great city, listen to me. Listen to the words of the Lord. He says your wealth has become a curse to you; you and your wealth are both cursed because that's all you value, and you won't listen to the words of the One who gave it to you. 22 You've forgotten the Lord who is God because of what He's blessed you with. However, you always remember your property, never thanking the Lord your God for it. Your hearts never focus on the Lord; instead, you're full of great pride leading to bragging and awful arrogance, to jealousy, conflicts, malice, persecutions, murders, and all kinds of iniquities. 23 For this reason, the Lord God has cursed the land and your property also — and this is because of your iniquities. 24 Woe to this people because you now drive out the prophets, ridicule them, throw stones at them, kill them, and abuse them, just like they've done before.

VII   25 When you mention it, you claim: If we had lived during the time of our ancestors long ago, we wouldn't have killed the prophets; we wouldn't have stoned them and driven them out. 26 But you're worse than them. Because as the Lord lives, if a prophet comes to you and declares the Lord's word, telling of your sins and iniquities, you're enraged at him and throw him out and look for a way to kill him. Indeed, you'll claim he's a false prophet, a sinner, and follows the accuser because he testifies about your evils. 27 But if a man tells you: Do this; it isn't iniquity! Do that; you won't suffer for it! Indeed, if he says: Live your life proudly; never be ashamed of what others see you doing, and do as you please. When someone is teaching this, you want to hear it. You'll say he's a prophet; 28 you'll support him. You'll give him some of your wealth and pay him with your gold and silver; you'll clothe him with expensive clothing. And because he assures you and says everything is fine, you won't find any fault with him.

VIII   29 You wicked and perverse generation, you hardened and stubborn people, how long do you think the Lord will put up with you? How long will you allow yourselves to be led by foolish and blind guides? How long will you choose darkness rather than light? 30 The Lord's anger is already aroused against you. He's cursed the land because of your iniquity. 31 The time is coming when He'll curse your wealth; it will slip away and you won't be able to hold onto it; and when poverty overtakes you, your wealth won't come back. 32 In the days of your poverty you'll appeal to the Lord, but that won't help; because desolation will have arrived, and your destruction is certain. You'll weep and howl on that day, says the Lord of Hosts. Then you'll lament and say: 33 I wish I had repented and hadn't killed, stoned, and driven out the prophets. Then you'll ask: Why didn't we remember the Lord our God at the time He blessed us with abundance? Then our wealth wouldn't have slipped away and been lost, and now we suffer poverty. 34 We put a tool here, and the next day it disappears. We can't find our swords in the day of battle as we search for them. 35 We've stored our valuable things, and they've slipped away from us because of the curse on the land. 36 Why didn't we repent when the Lord's word came to us? The land is cursed; everything is unstable, and we can't hold onto anything. 37 We're surrounded by demons, surrounded by the angels of him who attempts to destroy our souls. Indeed, we've sinned terribly. O Lord, we beg You to turn Your anger away from us! This will be your plea in those days.

IX   38 But the days of your probation have ended. You've procrastinated the day of your salvation until it's everlastingly too late and your destruction is now certain. You've tried your whole lives to get what's impossible: You've tried to find happiness in committing iniquity, which violates the nature of the righteousness of our great and eternal Head. 39 People of this land, I wish you would listen to me! I pray the Lord's anger can still be turned away from you, and ask you to repent and be saved.

X   **14** Now Samuel the Lamanite prophesied many more things that can't be written. 2 But he did tell them: I'll give you a sign. Five years from now, the Son of God will come to redeem all those who believe in His name. 3 I'll give you this as a sign of when He comes. There will be great lights in heaven, and in the night before He comes there will be no darkness, so it will seem to people as if it's still daytime. 4 Therefore there will be a day, a night, and a day, as a single daytime without any night. This is a signal to you, since you'll observe the rising and setting of the sun. Therefore it will be obvious there were two days and a night; nevertheless, the night won't be dark. That will be on the night before He's born. 5 A new star will arise, unlike anything you've seen; and this will be another signal to you. 6 But this isn't all, because there will be many signals and astonishing things in heaven. 7 All of you will be amazed and astonished, so much so that you'll fall to the ground. 8 Those who believe in the Son of God will have everlasting life.

XI   9 The Lord has commanded me by His angel to come and tell you this. He's commanded me to prophesy these things to you; He directed me: Proclaim to this people: Repent and prepare to follow the Lord. 10 Now, because I'm a Lamanite and told you the words the Lord commanded me to speak which condemn you, you're angry with me, are trying to kill me, and have driven me away. 11 Despite this, you're going to hear my words, which is why I've climbed atop the walls of this city: so you would hear and know of God's judgments awaiting you because of your iniquities; so you could know the offenses requiring your repentance; 12 and so you know about the coming of Jesus Christ, the Son of God the Father of heaven and of earth, the Creator of all things from the beginning; and so you are aware of the signs of His coming, so you can believe in His name. 13 If you believe in His name, you'll repent of all your sins, to receive a remission of your sins through Him.

XII   14 In addition, I'll tell you of another sign coming at His death. 15 Because He certainly must die to bring salvation. It's necessary and proper for Him to die in order to bring about the resurrection of the dead, so that mankind can return to the Lord's presence. 16 His death precedes His resurrection and will redeem everyone from the first death, that spiritual death. Because all mankind was cut off from the Lord's presence when Adam fell, they're effectively dead both physically and spiritually. 17 But Christ's resurrection redeems all mankind and returns them to the Lord's presence. 18 And it establishes the conditions for repentance, so whoever repents isn't cut down and thrown into the fire. But whoever doesn't repent is cut down and thrown into the fire. Then a second, spiritual death happens to them, because they're cut off again from all righteousness. 19 Therefore repent, repent, or else by knowing these things and failing to do them, you'll come under condemnation and bring this second death down upon you.

XIII   20 But as I told you about another sign, a sign of His death: On the day of His death, the sun will become dark and refuse to give his light to you, and the moon and stars as well. There won't be any light on this land for three days, from the time when He suffers death to the time when He rises from the dead. 21 When He dies, when He breathes His last, there will be thunder and lightning for many hours. The earth will shake and tremble, and the rock of the earth, both above the ground and beneath it, which you see is now solid, or most of it is one solid mass, will be fractured apart; 22 it will be broken apart into grooves, cracks, and broken fragments from then on, across the whole earth, both above the ground and beneath it. 23 And there will be great storms. Many mountains will be laid low like a valley. Many places now called valleys will become very high mountains. 24 Many highways will be broken up, and many cities will be decimated. 25 And many graves will be opened and will give up many of their dead; with many holy ones seen by many witnesses. 26 The angel has told me the following: He said there would be thunder and lightning for many hours. 27 He told me that while the thunder and lightning and storm lasted, as this takes place darkness will cover the entire land for three days. 28 The angel also told me many would see greater things than these, in order for them to believe — that these signs and these wonders would happen throughout this land, so there wouldn't be any reason for unbelief by mankind — 29 and so that whoever chose to believe could be saved and whoever didn't believe could have a righteous judgment imposed on them; and so if they're condemned, they chose their own condemnation.

XIV   30 Now remember, remember, my friends, that whoever perishes, perishes by their own choice and whoever does evil does it to themselves. Because you're free; you're permitted to act for yourselves. God has given you a choice, and He lets you freely make it. 31 He's made you capable of distinguishing good from evil. He lets you choose life or death. You can do good and be restored to what's good or have what's good restored to you; or you can do evil and have what's evil restored to you. **15** Now, my dear people, I declare to you that unless you repent, your houses will be left completely abandoned. 2 Unless you repent, your women will have good reason to mourn when they nurse their young. You'll attempt to escape and there won't be any safe place to go. Woe to those who are pregnant, since pregnancy will slow them down and they won't be able to escape; they will struggle, fall down, and be left to die. 3 Woe to you people called Nephites, unless you repent when you see all the signs and astonishing things that will be shown to you. Because you've been a chosen people of the Lord. He's loved the Nephites. And He's corrected you as well when you strayed because He loves you.

XV   4 But, my friends, He's detested the Lamanites because they've continually done evil — but only because of their ancestors' wicked traditions. But salvation has come to them through the Nephites' preaching; and because of this, the Lord will assure their descendants' survival. 5 I tell you the majority of them are following their duty faithfully, living carefully before God, taking care to keep His commandments, statutes, and judgments according to the Law of

Moses. 6 I tell you the majority of them do this. They continue tirelessly to work on converting the rest of their fellow Lamanites to the truth. Therefore many others join them daily. 7 You've seen and know that all who are converted to the truth, abandon the wicked and perverse traditions of their ancestors, and are persuaded to believe the holy scriptures (the prophecies of the holy prophets written there), which led them to faith in the Lord and to repentance, which faith and repentance bring them a change of heart; 8 therefore you know all of them are firm and resolute in the liberty God has given them. 9 You also know they've buried their weapons, and they're afraid to use them because they might sin in some way. You can see they're afraid to commit sin. They'll allow themselves to be cut down and killed by their enemies and won't resist them. They refuse because of their faith in Christ.

XVI   10 Now because once converted to the truth they're steadfast in their beliefs, and because they're firm once they accept the truth, the Lord will bless them and preserve their descendants, despite their iniquity. 11 Indeed, even if they fall away into unbelief, the Lord will watch over their posterity until the time arrives prophesied by our forefathers, and by the prophet Zenos, and many other prophets as well, about the restoration of the Lamanites to the knowledge of the truth. 12 I tell you that in the last days the Lord's promises cover the Lamanites, our friends and relatives. Despite coming hardships for them, and despite being driven here and there on the earth, hunted, afflicted, and scattered about, having no place for refuge, still, the Lord is going to be merciful to them. 13 This will fulfill the prophecy that they will return to the true knowledge, meaning the knowledge of their Redeemer, their great and true Shepherd, and be included as His sheep. 14 Therefore I tell you: It's going to be better for them than for you unless you repent. 15 Because if the powerful miracles had been shown to them that have been shown to you, you can see for yourselves they wouldn't have fallen away in unbelief ever again. No, they only fell away into unbelief because of their ancestors' traditions. 16 Therefore the Lord says: I won't completely destroy them, but in the day of My wisdom I'll lead them back to Me, says the Lord. 17 Now the Lord says to the Nephites: If you don't repent and take care to do My will, I'll completely destroy you, says the Lord, because of your unbelief, despite the many powerful miracles I performed among you. And as surely as the Lord lives, these things will happen, says the Lord.

XVII   16 Now there were many who heard what Samuel the Lamanite said from the city walls. All those who believed what he said went looking for Nephi. When they found him, they confessed their sins to him and didn't deny them, asking to be baptized in the name of the Lord. 2 But all those who didn't believe Samuel's message were angry at him. They threw stones, and many also shot arrows at him as he stood on the wall. But the Spirit of the Lord was with him, so they missed him with their stones or arrows.

XVIII   3 When they saw they couldn't hit him, many more believed what he said, so they also went to Nephi to be baptized. 4 Nephi was baptizing, prophesying, preaching, crying repentance to the people, showing them signs and awe-inspiring things, and performing miracles among the people, so they would know Christ was sure to come soon. 5 He taught them about other things that would happen soon, so that when they happened they would remember they had been revealed to them beforehand, and would believe. Therefore all who believed in Samuel's words went to Nephi to be baptized, because they came repenting and confessing their sins.

XIX   6 But the majority didn't believe what Samuel said. Therefore when they saw they couldn't hit him with stones and arrows, they yelled to their captains: Arrest this man and tie him up. He's possessed by a devil; and because of the power of the accuser protecting him, we can't hit him with our stones and arrows! So arrest him and tie him up and take him away! 7 As they went to lay their hands on him, he jumped down from the wall and escaped from their lands, returning to his own country, where he continued to preach and prophesy among his own people. 8 He was never heard from again by the Nephites. And this tells you the condition of the people. 9 So ended the 86th year of the judges' rule over the Nephites. 10 And so ended also the 87th year of the judges' rule — most of the people remaining prideful and wicked and a minority living carefully before God. 11 It was the same in the 88th year of the judges' rule. 12 In the 89th year of the judges' rule, there was little change in the people's affairs, except that the people began to be more entrenched in iniquity and increasingly disobedient to God's commandments.

XX   13 But in the 90th year of the judges' rule, great signs were given to the people, and other awe-inspiring things as the prophet's words began to be fulfilled. 14 Angels appeared to wise men declaring to them good news of great joy. In this year, the scriptures began to be fulfilled. 15 Nevertheless, the people still hardened their hearts, except for the most believing of them, among both the Nephites and the Lamanites. They began to rely on their own reasoning and foolishness, saying: 16 They may have guessed right about a few things among so many. But certainly, all the great and miraculous things predicted will never happen. 17 They began to reason and argue among themselves,

¹⁸ saying it wasn't at all reasonable for any Messiah to come, but if he does come, and he really is the son of God the Father of heaven and of earth, as claimed, then why won't he show himself to us as well as to those at Jerusalem? ¹⁹ Why won't he come to this land as well as to the land of Jerusalem? ²⁰ But clearly this is a wicked tradition handed down to us by our ancestors, to make us believe in some great and miraculous thing to happen, but not among us, but in a land that's far away, a land we know nothing about. Therefore they can keep us in ignorance, since we can't witness with our own eyes when it happens. ²¹ And using this clever and unseen trick from the Evil One, they'll make claims we'll never be able to disprove, which will be used to control us as servants to them and their false tradition, since we depend on them as our teachers. So they'll keep us in ignorance our whole lives, if we let them.

XXI

²² The people imagined many other foolish, vain lies to believe. And they were very agitated, since Satan constantly stirred them up to sin. He went around spreading rumors and starting conflicts everywhere, in order to harden the people's hearts toward the truth and to reject the prophesies. ²³ Despite the signs and marvelous things that happened among the Lord's people and the many miracles they experienced, Satan controlled the people's hearts throughout the land. ²⁴ And so ended the 90th year of the judges' rule. ²⁵ And so ended the Book of Helaman, based on the record of Helaman and his sons.

THE THIRD BOOK OF NEPHI

THE SON OF NEPHI, WHO WAS THE SON

OF HELAMAN

Helaman was the son of Helaman, who was the son of Alma, who was the son of Alma, a descendant of Nephi, who was the son of Lehi, who came from Jerusalem in the first year of the rule of Zedekiah, king of Judah.

Chapter 1

Now the 91st year ended and it had been 600 years since Lehi left Jerusalem. That year Lachoneus was chief judge and governor over the land. ² And Nephi the son of Helaman left Zarahemla, giving his eldest son Nephi possession of the brass plates and all other records, along with every item regarded as sacred since Lehi's departure from Jerusalem. ³ Then he left the land. No one knows where he went. His son Nephi maintained the record of this people after him.

II   4 At the start of the 92nd year, the events prophesied by the prophets were taking place more frequently with greater signs and miracles happening among the people. 5 But there were some who said the time was past for the fulfillment of what Samuel the Lamanite said would happen. 6 They began to celebrate the defeat of their fellow Nephites, saying: The time is past, and Samuel's words haven't been fulfilled. Therefore your joy and anticipation of it happening have been foolish. 7 They stirred up turmoil throughout the land. And the people who believed were very disheartened, fearing that perhaps the prophesied things might not happen. 8 But they watched, still hoping for the day and night and day that would be like one day, with no nighttime, so they would know their faith hadn't been misplaced.

III   9 Now there was a day set by the unbelievers on which everyone who still believed in those traditions was to be executed, unless the sign given by Samuel the prophet happened. 10 When Nephi the son of Nephi saw this wickedness of his people, he was distressed. 11 So he went to pray, knelt on the ground, and prayed mightily to God on behalf of his people who were about to be killed because of their faith in their fathers' traditions. 12 He prayed powerfully to the Lord all that day, and the Lord's voice spoke to him, saying: 13 Lift up your head and be of good cheer, because the time has arrived, and the sign will be given tonight. I'll come into the world tomorrow, to show to the world that I'll fulfill everything I had My holy prophets declare. 14 I'm coming to My own to fulfill everything I've revealed to mankind from the foundation of creation, and to obey the will of both the Father and of the Son — of the Father because of Me, and of the Son because of My flesh. The time has arrived, and the sign will be given tonight.

IV   15 The words told to Nephi were fulfilled, just as they had been spoken. There was no darkness at sunset. And the people were astonished because there was no darkness when the night came. 16 Many who hadn't believed the prophet's words collapsed and appeared to be lifeless, since they realized their big plan to kill those who believed the prophet's words had been crushed — the promised sign had already arrived. 17 They began to realize the Son of God would soon appear. And in short, everyone throughout the land — from the west to the east, both in the north and south — was so astonished that they fell to the ground. 18 They knew the prophets had testified of these things for many years and the promised sign had just occurred. They began to be afraid because of their iniquity and unbelief.

V   19 There was no darkness during the entire night, but it was as light as if it was midday. Then the sun rose in the morning again, in regular order. They knew it was the day the Lord would be born, because the promised sign happened. 20 And it followed in every detail exactly as the prophets had foretold. 21 A new star appeared as well, as was foretold. 22 Immediately lies from Satan began to circulate, to harden their hearts, so they wouldn't believe in the signs they saw and their awe-inspiring meaning. But despite these lies and deceptions, most of the people believed and were converted to the Lord.

VI   23 Nephi went out to teach the people, and so did many others, baptizing as a sign of repentance, and there were many sins forgiven. So the people again experienced peace in the land. 24 There were no disputes except for one involving a few who started to preach, claiming to prove from the scriptures that the Law of Moses no longer applied. But they were wrong about this and didn't understand the scriptures. 25 But they soon were converted and convinced of their error because the Law wasn't yet fulfilled, and must be fulfilled completely. It was revealed to them that not even the smallest detail or part would end until it was all fulfilled. Therefore in this same year they realized their error and admitted their mistakes. 26 So the 92nd year came to an end, bringing good news to the people because of the signs that happened vindicating the words of the prophecy of all the holy prophets.

VII   27 The 93rd year ended in peace as well, except there were still Gaddianton robbers, who lived in the mountains and defiled the land. Their fortifications and secret places were too well defended for the people to defeat them; therefore they got away with murder and slaughtered many people. 28 In the 94th year, their numbers increased somewhat because there were many Nephite defectors who joined them, which very much disappointed the Nephites who remained. 29 The Lamanites were also very disappointed by their children who grew into adulthood and were persuaded by the convincing lies of the Zoramites to also join the Gaddianton robbers. 30 So the Lamanites were afflicted also, and began to lose faith and commitment because of the growing wickedness of the rising generation.

VIII   **2** The 95th year ended. The people started to forget the signs and marvelous things they had been taught. They became increasingly less impressed by signs or miracles from heaven. Their hearts grew hard, their minds blinded, and they started to disbelieve everything they had heard and seen, 2 foolishly imagining it was just something people, using the accuser's power, did to mislead and deceive everyone's hearts and minds. So Satan once again influenced the people's hearts, blinding their eyes and persuading them to believe Christ's doctrine was foolish and worthless.

IX   3 The people increasingly drifted into wickedness and abominations. They refused to believe there would be more signs or miracles. Satan succeeded in leading away the people's hearts, tempting them to do great evil in the land. 4 This developed over the 96th year, as well as the 97th year, the 98th year, and the 99th year. 5 It had been 100 years since the time king Mosiah led the Nephites. 6 And 609 years had elapsed since Lehi left Jerusalem. 7 It was nine years since the sign foretold by the prophets marked the birth of Christ into the world. 8 Now the Nephites began to measure time from when the sign was given, or from Christ's birth; therefore nine years ended. 9 This was when Nephi, who had responsibility for the records, the father of Nephi, didn't return to Zarahemla and couldn't be found anywhere in the whole land.

X   10 The people remained wicked despite the preaching and prophesying constantly provided to them. The 10th year ended; and the 11th year also ended with continuing iniquity. 11 In the 13th year, wars and conflicts started everywhere, because the Gaddianton robbers were so numerous, killed so many people, ruined so many cities, and spread so much death and carnage throughout the land that it was necessary for all the people, both the Nephites and the Lamanites, to fight against them. 12 So all the Lamanite converts to the Lord united with the Nephites, and for the mutual protection of themselves and their women and children, they took up arms against the Gaddianton gang of robbers. They fought to maintain their rights, the privilege of their congregation to worship, and their freedom and liberty.

XI   13 Before this 13th year ended, the Nephites faced the threat of complete destruction because of the terrible, widespread war. 14 Now the Lamanites who had joined with the Nephites were included as part of the Nephites. 15 Their curse was removed, and their countenance became pure and radiant like the Nephites. 16 Their young men and women became very beautiful and were included as and called Nephites. And so ended the 13th year.

XII   17 At the start of the 14th year, the war between the robbers and the Nephites continued and worsened. Nevertheless, the Nephites gained some advantage over the robbers, driving them back out of their lands into the mountains and hiding places. 18 And so ended the 14th year. And in the 15th year, they again attacked the Nephites. Because of the Nephites' wickedness and their many conflicts and defections, the Gaddianton robbers had many advantages over them. 19 And so ended the 15th year. The people found themselves facing many hardships; and the sword of destruction hung over them, and they were about to be struck down; and this was the result of their iniquity.

Chapter 2

3 In the 16th year from Christ's coming, Lachoneus the governor of the land received a letter from the leader of the gang of robbers. This is what he wrote: 2 Lachoneus, most noble and chief governor of the land, I write this letter to praise you and your people because of the firmness shown in maintaining what you believe are your rights and liberty. Indeed, you remain resolute as though supported by a god's hand in defending what you call your liberty, property, and country. 3 It seems a pity to me, most noble Lachoneus, that you're so foolish and unwise as to think you can stand against so many brave men who are at my command, who are right now ready for action and await anxiously for the command: Attack the Nephites and destroy them! 4 I know of their invincible spirit, having tested them on the battlefield, and of their eternal hatred for you because of the many wrongs you've done to them. So if they were to attack you, they would completely destroy you. 5 Therefore I've written this letter, signing it myself, out of concern for your well-being because of your firmness in what you believe to be right, and your noble spirit on the battlefield.

II   6 Therefore I'm writing to you, asking you to surrender your cities, lands, and property to my people, rather than having them take vengeance upon you with the sword and destroy you. 7 In other words, surrender to us and unite with us and become acquainted with our secret doings and become our associates, so that you can be like us, not our slaves, but our kin and partners in all our wealth. 8 I swear to you: If you do this with an oath, then you won't be destroyed. But if you don't do this, I swear to you with an oath that next month I'll order my armies to come down and attack you, and they won't hold back and spare you, but they'll kill you and cause the sword to fall upon you, until you're all dead. 9 I'm Giddianhi, the governor of this secret society of Gaddianton. And I know this society and what it does are good. We follow an ancient practice and tradition, which has been handed down to us. 10 I'm writing this letter to you Lachoneus; and I hope you surrender your lands and property without bloodshed, so that my people, who have split from you because of your wickedness in keeping their rights of government from them, can regain their rights and government. Unless you do this, I'll avenge their wrongs. I am Giddianhi.

III   11 When Lachoneus received this letter, he was shocked at Giddianhi's boldness in demanding control over the Nephites' land, in threatening the people, and in claiming to avenge imagined wrongs. Their only harm was brought upon themselves by joining the wicked, despicable robbers. 12 Now the governor Lachoneus was a righteous man and couldn't be frightened by a robber's demands and threats. Therefore he gave no attention to the letter from Giddianhi, the robbers' governor, but he had his people call upon the Lord for strength in preparation for when the robbers attacked them. 13 Indeed, he sent a proclamation among all the people to gather their women, children, flocks, herds, and all their belongings, leaving their lands behind, and gather into one place. 14 He had fortifications built all around them, and he reinforced that place. He also had Nephite and Lamanite armed forces (meaning all of them also included as Nephites), look out in every direction to watch and guard against the robbers, day and night. 15 He declared to them: As the Lord lives, unless you repent of all your iniquities and cry out to the Lord, there's no way you'll be saved from these Gaddianton robbers. 16 Lachoneus' words and prophecies were so alarming that they made everyone afraid. Therefore they made every effort to do what Lachoneus said.

IV

17 Lachoneus appointed chief captains to command all the Nephite armed forces in preparation for when the robbers came down out of the wilderness to attack. 18 Now the overall commander was appointed to be the supreme commander of all the Nephite armed forces, and his name was Gidgiddoni. 19 It was a Nephite custom, except during times of wickedness, to appoint as their chief captains those who had the spirit of revelation and the spirit of prophecy. Accordingly, Gidgiddoni, a great prophet, was appointed, and so too was the chief judge.

V

20 Now the people said to Gidgiddoni: Pray to the Lord and then let's go up into the mountains and the wilderness and attack the robbers and kill them in their own lands. 21 But Gidgiddoni said to them: Heaven forbid! If we attacked them, the Lord would hand us over to them. Therefore we'll prepare ourselves in the center of our lands and we'll consolidate our armies. But we won't attack them; we'll wait until they attack us. As the Lord lives, if we do this, He will put them in our power.

VI

22 In the 17th year, toward the end of the year, Lachoneus' proclamation had gone out throughout the whole land. They had taken their horses, wagons, cattle, flocks, herds, grain, and all their belongings and marched out by thousands and tens of thousands until they reached the gathering place to defend themselves against their enemies. 23 And the designated place was the land of Zarahemla and the region between the land of Zarahemla and the land of Bountiful,

to the line between the land of Bountiful and the land of Desolation. 24 Tens of thousands of Nephites gathered together there. Now Lachoneus had them gather in the land to the south because of the great curse on the land to the north. 25 They fortified themselves against their enemies and lived in one area, as a single large group. And they obeyed the words of Lachoneus, repenting of all their sins. They offered prayers to the Lord their God, asking Him to protect them when their enemies came down to attack them. 26 They mourned because of their enemy. And Gidgiddoni had them make a variety of weapons, so they would be protected with armor, shields, and bucklers, according to his instructions.

VII **4** Toward the end of the 18th year, the robbers' armed forces had prepared for battle and started to make sudden attacks from the hills, mountains, and wilderness areas, and from their strongholds and secret places, and began to get control of the land, both in the south and in the north. They occupied all the lands deserted by the Nephites, as well as the abandoned cities. 2 But there were no wild animals or wild game in the areas deserted by the Nephites; and there was no wild game for the robbers except in the wilderness. 3 The robbers couldn't survive except in the wilderness due to a lack of food. This was because the Nephites left their lands bare, taking all their flocks, herds, and belongings, and consolidated into a single large group. 4 Therefore it was impossible for the robbers to steal food, other than by engaging the Nephites in open battle. The Nephites were gathered into a single large group, and they had stored up enough supplies, horses, cattle, and flocks of every kind to survive for seven years, and during this time they hoped to drive the robbers out of the land — and so the 18th year ended.

VIII 5 In the 19th year, Giddianhi concluded it was necessary to go up to battle against the Nephites, since there was no way for them to survive except to steal, rob, and murder. 6 They didn't dare spread out on the land in order to raise grain, fearing the Nephites would attack and kill them. So in this year Giddianhi ordered his armed forces to attack the Nephites.

IX 7 They came up to battle in the sixth month, and the day they came up to battle was great and terrible. They were outfitted like robbers: they had lambskins around their waists, which were dyed in blood, and their heads were shaved, and they had helmets on. The look of Giddianhi's army, because of their armor and being dyed in blood, was threatening. 8 Then the Nephite armed forces — when they saw Giddianhi's army come into view — fell to their knees and cried out loudly to the Lord their God that He would spare them and save them from their enemies. 9 When Giddianhi's army saw this, they began to shout loudly for joy. They thought the Nephites had fallen to the ground with fear because of the terror produced by their warriors. 10 But these hopes were unwarranted, since the Nephites weren't afraid of them, but they respected God and humbly and earnestly asked Him for protection. Therefore when Giddianhi's armies rushed upon them, they were ready to resist them; and they fought them with the Lord's strength.

X   11 The battle began in this sixth month, and it was great and terrible; indeed, the resulting slaughter was immense, so much that there had never been so much killing among all of Lehi's people since he left Jerusalem. 12 Despite the threats and oaths Giddianhi made, the Nephites defeated them, and they retreated.

XI   13 Then Gidgiddoni ordered his armies to pursue them to the wilderness boundary and not to spare any that fell into their hands along the way. So they chased them and killed them to the edge of the wilderness, obeying Gidgiddoni's order. 14 And Giddianhi, who had fought boldly, was chased as he ran away. Because he was exhausted from the fighting, he was caught and killed. That was how Giddianhi the robber died. 15 And the Nephite armies returned to their secure location.

XII   The 19th year came to an end and the robbers didn't come again to battle, then or in the 20th year either. 16 In the 21st year, they didn't start a battle, but they surrounded and besieged the Nephites. They thought that if they cut off the Nephites from their lands and surrounded them, and cut them off from the outside, they could make them surrender according to their wishes. 17 Now they had appointed a replacement leader over them named Zemnarihah. Therefore it was Zemnarihah who ordered the siege to take place. 18 But this was an advantage for the Nephites. Because it was impossible for the robbers to lay siege long enough to have any effect on the Nephites, because of their abundant supplies they had stored 19 in contrast to the robbers' insufficient supplies. Indeed, they had nothing for their survival except meat, which they hunted in the wilderness. 20 Wild game grew increasingly scarce, so much that the robbers were starving. 21 The Nephites were repeatedly attacking their armed forces — both during the day and at night — killing them by the thousands and tens of thousands.

XIII   22 So Zemnarihah's people now wanted to abandon their plan because of the great losses they experienced both at night and during the day. 23 Zemnarihah ordered his people to abandon the siege and go to the most remote parts of the land to the north. 24 Now Gidgiddoni learned of their plan and knew they were weakened from hunger and from the casualties inflicted upon them, so he sent out his armies at night to block their retreat and placed his armed forces in the direct path of their retreat. 25 They did this at night and got ahead of the robbers, so on the next day, when the robbers began their journey, they encountered Nephite armed forces in both their front and their rear. 26 The robbers to the south were also cut off from their retreat. All this was done at Gidgiddoni's command.

XIV 27 Many thousands surrendered as prisoners to the Nephites, and the rest of them were killed. 28 Their leader Zemnarihah was captured and hanged from the top of a tree until he was dead. When they had hanged him to death, they cut the tree down and shouted: 29 May the Lord preserve His people in righteousness and holiness of heart, so they can cut down all who attempt to kill them to gain power and join secret conspiracies, just as this man has been cut down to the ground. 30 They rejoiced and shouted again together, saying: May the God of Abraham and the God of Isaac and the God of Jacob protect this people in righteousness, so long as they call on God's name for protection. 31 And they burst out as one, singing and praising God for the great thing He had done for them in preserving them from falling into their enemies' hands. 32 Indeed, they cried out: Hallelujah to the Most High God! They cried out: May the Lord God Almighty's name be blessed, the Most High God! 33 Their hearts were joyful to the point they were brought to tears because of God's great goodness in freeing them from their enemies. They knew it was because of their repentance and humility that they were saved from everlasting destruction. 5 Now there wasn't a living soul among the Nephites who had any doubt about the words spoken by the holy prophets. They knew they must necessarily be fulfilled. 2 They knew Christ must necessarily have come, because of the many signs given, fulfilling the prophets' words. Because of the things that had already happened, they knew all the rest of the things would happen just as it had been foretold. 3 So they abandoned all their sins, abominations, and whoredoms and served God diligently day and night.

XV 4 When they had captured all the robbers, so that not one of them escaped alive, they imprisoned them and preached God's word to them. Those who repented of their sins and made a covenant not to murder again were freed. 5 But those who didn't make a covenant and who continued to have thoughts of murdering in secret — indeed, all those who were found threatening their fellow Nephites — were condemned and punished according to the law. 6 So they put an end to those evil, secret, and despicable conspiracies resulting in so much evil and so many murders. 7 The 22nd year had come to an end, and the 23rd year as well, and the 24th, and the 25th. And so 25 years had come and gone.

XVI   8 Many things, which some would consider to be great and awe-inspiring, had taken place. However, they can't all be written in this book. Indeed, this book can't contain even one percent of what occurred among so many people in 25 years. 9 But there are records containing accounts of everything this people did. And Nephi gave a shorter but true account. 10 Therefore I've made my record of these things using Nephi's record, which was engraved on the plates called the plates of Nephi.

XVII   11 I'm making this record on plates I made myself, with my own hands. 12 My name is Mormon; I was named after the land of Mormon, where Alma established the congregation among this people, the first congregation established among them after their transgression. 13 I'm a follower of Jesus Christ, the Son of God. I've been called by Him to declare His word among His people, so they can have everlasting life. 14 It has become important for me, according to God's will, to answer the prayers of those who went before, to make this record. This answers the prayers of those holy ones, 15 comprising a small record of what's happened since Lehi left Jerusalem, until now. 16 Therefore I base my record from the earlier accounts of those who went before, up to the beginning of my time. 17 And then I'll add a record of what I've seen with my own eyes. 18 I know the record I'm making is a fair, correct, and true record. Nevertheless, our language limits us from writing many things.

XVIII   19 Now I'll bring my remarks about myself to an end and continue to give my account of what's happened before my time. 20 I'm Mormon and a pure descendant of Lehi. I have reason to praise God and my Savior Jesus Christ, for bringing our ancestors out of the land of Jerusalem — and no one knew it except Him and those He brought out of that land — and for giving me and my people so much knowledge for the salvation of our souls. 21 He's certainly blessed Jacob's family and been merciful to Joseph's descendants. 22 And to the degree Lehi's children have kept His commandments, He's blessed them and prospered them as He promised. 23 He will certainly return a remnant of Joseph's descendants to know the Lord their God again. 24 As surely as the Lord lives, He will gather in from the four quarters of the earth all the remnant of Jacob's descendants who are scattered throughout the whole earth. 25 He has covenanted with all of Jacob's family, and that covenant will likewise be fulfilled when He decides it's the right time, restoring all of Jacob's family to know of the covenant

He's made with them. 26 Then they will know their Redeemer — Jesus Christ, the Son of God — and be gathered in from the four quarters of the earth to their own lands, from where they've been scattered. Indeed, as the Lord lives, it will happen. Amen.

Chapter 3

6 Now the Nephites all returned to their own lands in the 26th year, every one with their family, flocks and herds, horses and cattle, and everything they owned. 2 They hadn't consumed all their provisions, so they took with them all the grain they hadn't eaten, of every kind, as well as their gold, silver, and valuables. And they returned to their own lands and property, toward the north and south, and in the land to the north and south. 3 They allowed those robbers who had made a covenant to keep peace in the land (they wanted to remain Lamanites), to have land based on their numbers, so they could have something to survive on. In this way, they established peace throughout the land; 4 and they again started to flourish and grow strong. And the 26th and 27th years came to an end. Social order returned to the land, and their laws, based upon fairness and justice, were again enforced. 5 At this time nothing in the whole land would prevent their continuing prosperity, other than if they again fell into transgression. 6 Now it was Gidgiddoni and Lachoneus, the chief judge, and those who had been appointed to be their leaders, who led in establishing this great peace in the land.

II   7 Many cities were rebuilt and many old cities were repaired. 8 Many highways were constructed and new roads connected city to city, land to land, and area to area. 9 The 28th year ended in abiding peace. 10 But in the 29th year, some controversies arose between people, and some were now proud and boastful because of their great wealth, so much so that they actively persecuted others. 11 Now there were many merchants, many lawyers, and officials also. 12 The people began to be divided into classes based on wealth and their opportunities for education. Unfortunately, some were uneducated due to their poverty; and others were highly educated because of their wealth. 13 Some were very prideful and others very humble. Some met verbal abuse by returning verbal abuse, while others tolerated abuse, persecution, and other mistreatment without retaliating; but to the contrary, they were humble and repentant before God. 14 Therefore inequality increased throughout the land, with even the congregation becoming divided, so much so that in the 30th year the congregation broke apart throughout the land with the exception of a few Lamanites who remained committed to the true faith. They refused to abandon it, since they were firm, resolute, and immovable, willing to diligently keep the Lord's commandments.

III   15 Now the cause of the people's iniquity was that Satan had such influence that people began to commit all kinds of iniquity; to become prideful, and tempting them to seek power, authority, wealth, and property with no eternal value. 16 Satan led the hearts of the people into all kinds of iniquity. Therefore they had only enjoyed peace for a few short years. 17 At the start of the 30th year, the people were in an awful state of wickedness. They submitted to the accuser's temptations, doing as he led them, participating in exactly the sins he urged upon them. 18 Now they didn't sin ignorantly; they knew God's will for them, since it had been taught to them. Therefore they willfully rebelled against God.

IV   19 Now Lachoneus the son of Lachoneus replaced his father in the governor's seat, and was serving at the time. 20 Then men began to be inspired by heaven and sent out, warning the people all over the land, preaching and exposing the people's sins and iniquities, and telling them about the redemption the Lord would provide for His people through Christ's resurrection. They taught clearly about His death and suffering. 21 Now many people got very angry because of the men who testified of these things. Those who were angry included the chief judges and those who had been high priests and lawyers. All the lawyers were angry with those who testified of these things. 22 Now, no lawyer, judge, or high priest had the authority to condemn anyone to death until the death order was signed by the governor. 23 But many of those who taught about Christ, testifying boldly, were taken and put to death secretly by the judges, so the governor didn't learn of their deaths until after they had been killed. 24 Now it violated the laws of the land for anyone to be put to death without the governor's approval.

25 Therefore a complaint was sent to Zarahemla, to the governor, accusing the judges who had condemned the Lord's prophets to death of violating the law.

V   26 They were arrested and brought before the judge to be judged for the crime they had committed, according to the law adopted by the people. 27 Now these judges had many friends and relatives. Those others, including almost all the lawyers and high priests, joined with the relatives of the judges facing a trial for violating the law. 28 They entered into a covenant with each other, the same as the one made long ago, which was given and administered by the accuser, to conspire against all righteousness. 29 Therefore they conspired against the Lord's people and made a covenant to kill them and to free the guilty murderers from the justice to be imposed under the law. 30 They defied the law and the rights of their country. And they covenanted with one another to kill the governor and set up a king over the land, to destroy liberty and establish control by kings.

VI **7** Now you should know they didn't establish a king, but in that 30th year they murdered the chief judge while on the judgment seat. 2 Then the people divided against each other. They separated into tribes, everyone gathering with family, relatives, and friends. And the government was destroyed. 3 Each tribe had a ruler or leader over them, resulting in tribes forming around tribal leaders. 4 Now every man had many family members and many relatives and friends; therefore the resulting tribes were quite large. 5 Now when this happened, at first there were no wars among them. All these terrible consequences happened because the people submitted to Satan's power. 6 The secret conspiracy of the friends and relatives of those who murdered the prophets destroyed all governmental order. 7 They caused a great conflict in the land, but there was still a small righteous part of the people, despite the overwhelming majority becoming wicked; yet there were a few righteous among them. 8 In less than six years most of the people had abandoned their righteousness like the dog to his vomit, or like a sow to her wallowing in the mire.

VII 9 Now the secret society of conspirators who had led them into iniquity united together to put a man in charge named Jacob. 10 They called him their king. Therefore he was king over this evil society. He was one of the most vocal opponents of the prophets who testified of Jesus. 11 Yet his group wasn't as large as the combined tribes of the people. Each tribe was led separately, with its own laws, but they united to oppose the evil society as their common enemy. Despite not being righteous, the people were united in their hatred of those who had made the covenant to destroy the government. 12 Therefore when Jacob realized their enemies were more numerous than they were, using his position as king of the group, he ordered his people to flee into the northernmost part of the land to establish a kingdom for themselves where they would await defectors. He persuaded them there would be many defectors. With additional defectors he said they would become strong enough to defeat the other tribes. His group then followed his plan. 13 Their departure was so quick it couldn't be intercepted before they were beyond the people's reach. That's how the 30th year ended in this state of affairs among the Nephites.

VIII 14 In the 31st year, they remained divided into tribes, every one according to their family, relatives, and friends. Nevertheless, they agreed they wouldn't go to war with each other. But they weren't united in their laws or in their ways of governing, because their rulers and leaders decided those matters. But they adopted very strict laws against one tribe doing wrong to another, so to some degree they had peace in the land. Nevertheless, their hearts were against the Lord their God; and they stoned the prophets and drove them away.

IX   15 Nephi, who had been visited by angels and heard the Lord's voice, had seen angels, and was an eyewitness, then had power given to him to let them know about Christ's ministry. He was also an eyewitness of the swift fall from righteousness to wickedness and abominations. 16 Because he was troubled at the hardness of their hearts and the blindness of their minds, he went out to preach to them that same year. He boldly testified of the need for repentance and remission of sins through faith in the Lord Jesus Christ. 17 He warned them of many things. Because they can't all be written, and a part wouldn't be sufficient, they aren't written in this book. Nephi taught with power and great authority.

X   18 They were angry with him, because he truly had greater power than they did. So it was impossible for them to refute the truth of his words. His faith in the Lord Jesus Christ was so deep that angels ministered to him daily. 19 He drove out devils and unclean spirits in Jesus' name and even raised his brother from the dead after he had been stoned and killed by the people. 20 They saw it with their own eyes and were angry with him because of his power. He also performed many more miracles in the people's sight, in Jesus' name.

XI   21 And the 31st year came to an end. Only a few were converted to the Lord. But all those who were converted, truthfully declared to the people they had been visited by the power and Spirit of God that was in Jesus Christ, in whom they believed. 22 All those who had devils driven out of them and who were healed of sickness and disease truthfully declared to the people it was the Spirit of God given to them that let them be healed. Signs followed them as well, and people saw them also perform some miracles.

XII   23 So the 32nd year came to an end as well. Nephi cried out to the people at the start of the 33rd year, preaching repentance and remission of sins to them. 24 Now I would like you to remember there wasn't anyone who repented who wasn't baptized with water. 25 Therefore Nephi ordained other men to this ministry, to let everyone be baptized with water who came forward. This was done as a witness and testimony before God and the people that they had repented and received a remission of their sins. 26 Many repented and were baptized at the start of this year. And so most of the year went by.

Chapter 4

8 According to our record, which we know is true because it was kept by a righteous man — he really performed many miracles in Jesus' name, and no one could perform a miracle in His name unless they were completely cleansed of their iniquity — 2 now if this man didn't make a mistake in calculating our time, the 33rd year came to an end. 3 The people began to anxiously watch for the sign given by the prophet Samuel the Lamanite, meaning the time when darkness would cover the land for three days. 4 There was a lot of uncertainty and arguments among the people, despite the fact so many signs had already been given.

II

5 In the 34th year, on the 14th day of the first month, a great storm arose, the kind of storm that had never been experienced before in that land. 6 There were great and terrible winds; and terrible thunder, so much so that it shook the whole earth as if it were about to split apart. 7 There was very sharp lightning, the kind of lightning never before experienced in that land. 8 The city of Zarahemla caught fire. 9 The city of Moroni sank into the depths of the sea and its inhabitants drowned. 10 And earth overwhelmed the city of Moronihah, so that a great mountain rose up in its place. 11 There was great and terrible destruction in the land to the south. 12 But the destruction was greater and more terrible in the land to the north since the whole surface of the land was changed because of the storms, tornadoes, thunder, lightning, and very strong earthquakes. 13 Highways were broken up, level roads were damaged, and many flat areas became uneven. 14 Many prominent cities were sunk, many were burned, and many were shaken until their buildings had fallen to the ground and their inhabitants were killed and they were left empty. 15 Some cities remained, but they were heavily damaged, and many of the occupants were killed. 16 Some were taken away by tornadoes; and no one knows where they went, except they know they were removed. 17 So the surface of the whole land was deformed because of the storms, thunder, lightning, and earthquakes. 18 The solid ground was split apart — indeed, the land was broken up all over, being left in broken fragments, grooves, and cracks everywhere.

III

19 When the thunder, lightning, storms, violent wind, and earthquakes stopped after approximately three hours, although some said it lasted much longer, nevertheless all these great and terrible things happened over the course of about three hours and then darkness covered the land.

IV
20 Thick darkness covered the whole land, so that those who survived could feel the vapor of darkness. 21 That dark vapor prevented any light, even from candles or torches. And fires couldn't be lit either, not even with their best and very dry wood, so there wasn't any light at all. 22 So no light was seen, not a fire or a spark, nor the sun, moon, or stars, as thick mists of darkness covered the land.

V
23 No light was seen for three days. There was continuous, intense mourning, howling, and weeping by the people; indeed, their deep cries of anguish echoed loudly, because of the darkness and devastation that had befallen them. 24 In one place they were heard crying out: Why didn't we repent before this great and terrible day! If we had repented, then our people would have been spared and they wouldn't have been burned in that great city of Zarahemla! 25 In another place they were heard crying out and mourning: Why didn't we repent before this great and terrible day! Why did we kill and stone the prophets and drive them away! If we hadn't done this, then our mothers and beautiful daughters and children would have been spared and wouldn't have been buried in that great city of Moronihah. And so they lamented loudly.

VI
9 Then a voice was heard among all the inhabitants of the land, crying out: 2 Woe, woe, woe to this people! Woe to the inhabitants of the whole earth unless they repent. The accuser is laughing and his angels are rejoicing because of the beautiful sons and daughters of My people who have been killed. It's because of their iniquity and their abominations that they've fallen. 3 I've burned that great city of Zarahemla, along with its inhabitants. 4 I've caused that great city of Moroni to be sunk in the depths of the sea and its inhabitants to be drowned. 5 I've covered that great city of Moronihah with earth, along with its inhabitants, to hide their iniquities and abominations from My sight, so the blood of the prophets and holy ones won't protest to Me against them anymore. 6 I've caused the city of Gilgal to be sunk and its inhabitants to be buried deep in the earth — 7 and the city of Onihah and its inhabitants, and the city of Mocum and its inhabitants, and the city of Jerusalem and its inhabitants; and I've caused water to come up in their place, to hide their wickedness and abominations from My sight, so the blood of the prophets and holy ones won't protest to Me against them anymore. 8 And the city of Gadiandi, the city of Gadiomnah, the city of Jacob, and the city of Gimgimno — I've caused all these cities to be sunk and have made hills and valleys where they used to be. And I've buried their inhabitants deep in the earth, to hide their wickedness and abominations from My sight, so the blood of the prophets and holy

ones won't protest to Me against them anymore. 9 That great city Jacob-Ugath, which was inhabited by king Jacob's people, I've caused to be burned with fire because of their sins and wickedness, which was above all the wickedness of the whole earth because of their secret murders and conspiracies: they were the ones who destroyed the peace of My people and the government of the land. Therefore I caused them to be burned, to remove them from My sight, so the blood of the prophets and holy ones wouldn't protest to Me against them anymore. 10 I've caused the city of Laman, the city of Josh, the city of Gad, and the city of Kishcumen to be burned with fire, along with their inhabitants, because of their wickedness in driving out the prophets and stoning those whom I sent to declare to them regarding their wickedness and abominations. 11 Because they drove them all out, so there weren't any righteous people remaining, I sent down fire and destroyed them, so their wickedness and abominations would be hidden from My sight, so the blood of the prophets and holy ones I sent among them wouldn't cry to Me from the ground against them. 12 All this devastation of this land and its people has been necessary because of their wickedness and abominations.

VII   13 All you that have been spared because you were more righteous than they were, will you return to Me now and repent of your sins and be converted, so I can heal you? 14 I promise you: If you come to Me, you will have eternal life. My arm of mercy is reaching for you. Anyone who comes to Me, I'll receive them; those who come to Me will be blessed. 15 I Am Jesus Christ, the Son of God. I created the heavens, the earth, and everything that's in them. I was with the Father since the beginning. I Am in the Father and the Father in Me; and the Father has glorified His name in Me. 16 I came to My own, and My own rejected Me; and the scriptures promising My coming are fulfilled. 17 I've given power to all those who have received Me, to become sons and daughters of God. Likewise, I'll give power to all those who believe in My name. Because redemption comes through Me, and the Law of Moses has been concluded by Me. 18 I Am the light and the life of the world. I Am first and last, the beginning and the end. 19 You must no longer shed blood as an offering to Me; indeed, your sacrifices and burnt offerings must end now, because I'll no longer accept any of your sacrifices or burnt offerings. 20 You must offer Me a broken heart and a contrite spirit as a sacrifice. Whoever comes to Me with a broken heart and a contrite spirit, I'll baptize them with fire and the Holy Ghost, just like the Lamanites were baptized with fire and the Holy Ghost because of their faith in Me at the time of their conversion, and yet they didn't understand what it was. 21 I've come into the world to bring redemption to the world, to save the world from sin. 22 Therefore whoever repents and comes to Me as a little child, I will receive them, because God's kingdom is made up of people like this. I've given My life for such people, and I've taken it up again. Therefore repent and come to Me, everyone throughout the world, and be saved.

VIII

10 Now all the people of the land heard these words and were witnesses of them. After these things were said, there was silence in the land for many hours. 2 The silence was because the people's astonishment was so great they stopped mourning and howling about losing their relatives. So there was silence throughout the land for many hours.

IX

3 Then a voice spoke again to the people, and everyone heard it and testified of it. The voice said: 4 You people of these great cities that have fallen, who are descendants of Jacob, who belong to the house of Israel; you people of the house of Israel, how often I've gathered you as a hen gathers her chicks under her wings and how often I've guided you! 5 Again, how often I've tried to gather you as a hen gathers her chicks under her wings! You people of the house of Israel who have fallen, O house of Israel who live at Jerusalem as well as you that have fallen: how often I would have gathered you as a hen gathers her chicks, but you refused! 6 You people of the house of Israel whom I've spared, how often I will gather you as a hen gathers her chicks under her wings, if you repent and return to Me with all your heart! 7 But if not, O house of Israel, your dwelling places will become desolate until the time when the covenant to your fathers is kept.

X

8 After the people heard this, they again began to weep and howl because of lost relatives and friends, 9 and for three days this continued. Then in the morning, the darkness dispersed from the land and the ground stabilized, stopped splitting, the terrible groaning stopped, and all the tumult of noises ended. 10 The ground held firmly together once more and stood still. The mourning, weeping, and wailing of the survivors stopped. Their mourning changed into joy and their lamentations changed into praise and thanksgiving to the Lord Jesus Christ their Redeemer. 11 At that point the scriptures spoken by the prophets were fulfilled. 12 It was the more righteous who were saved; they were the ones who received the prophets and didn't stone them. Those who were spared were the ones who hadn't killed the holy ones. 13 They were spared and weren't sunk and buried deep in the ground, they weren't drowned in the depths of the sea, they weren't burned by fire, they weren't fallen upon and crushed to death, they

weren't carried away in the tornadoes, and they weren't overcome by the vapor of smoke and darkness.

XI   14 Now whoever reads this, please understand; if you have the scriptures, please carefully study them and notice if all these deaths and this destruction by fire, smoke, storms, tornadoes, and the opening of the earth to bury them, whether all of it fulfills the prophecies of so many of the holy prophets. 15 I tell you: Many testified about these things at Christ's coming and were killed because of their testimony about these things. 16 This includes the prophet Zenos, and Zenoch who both spoke about these things, and they testified specifically about us, who are a remnant of their descendants. 17 Our father Jacob also testified about a remnant of Joseph's descendants. And aren't we a remnant of Joseph's descendants? These things that testify of us, aren't they written on the brass plates our father Lehi brought from Jerusalem? 18 At the end of the 34th year, I'll show you that the Nephites who were spared, as well as those who had been called Lamanites, were favored and greatly blessed, to such an extent that soon after Christ's ascension into heaven He actually visited them, 19 showing His body to them and ministering to them. An account of His ministry will follow after this. Therefore I'm finishing my remarks for now.

Chapter 5

Jesus Christ showed Himself to the Nephites when a large number of people had gathered in Bountiful; and He ministered to them. He appeared to them as described in the following account.

11 Now a large number of Nephites gathered around the temple in Bountiful. They were astonished, talking to each other in amazement, pointing out to each other the remarkable changes that had taken place. 2 They were also talking with each other about Jesus Christ, of whom the sign had been given about His death.

II   3 While they were conversing about this, they heard a voice as if it came out of heaven. And they looked around, since they didn't understand the voice they heard. It wasn't a harsh voice or a loud voice. But despite being a quiet voice, it pierced those who heard it to the core, so much that they trembled. It cut them to the core and melted their hearts. 4 They heard the voice again but didn't understand it. 5 And they heard the voice a third time and understood and listened attentively to it. They looked toward the sound, looking steadily toward heaven, where it originated. 6 At the third time, they understood the voice, and it said to them: 7 Here is My Beloved Son, in whom I'm well pleased, in whom I've glorified My name. Listen to Him!

III   8 When they understood, they looked up again to heaven. They saw a man descending from heaven, and He was dressed in a white robe. He came down and stood among them, and the whole crowd was looking at Him. They didn't dare speak, not even to each other, and they didn't know what it meant, since they thought it was an angel appearing to them.

IV   9 He stretched out His hand and spoke to them, saying: 10 I Am Jesus Christ, whom the prophets testified would come into the world. 11 I Am the light and the life of the world. And I've drunk out of the bitter cup the Father has given Me and have glorified the Father by taking upon Myself the sins of the world, in which I've submitted to the Father's will in all things from the beginning. 12 When Jesus said this, the whole crowd fell to the ground, since they remembered it had been prophesied to them that Christ would show Himself to them after His ascension into heaven.

V   13 And the Lord spoke to them, saying: 14 Stand up and come up to Me, so you can put your hands in My side and you can feel the nail marks in My hands and feet, so you will know I Am the God of Israel and the God of the whole earth who was killed for the sins of the world.

VI   15 And the people went up and put their hands in His side and felt the nail marks in His hands and feet. They did this — going up one by one until they had all gone up — and saw with their eyes and felt with their hands and knew for certain and testified it was He the prophets wrote about, who was to come. 16 When they had all gone up and witnessed for themselves, they cried out as one: 17 Hallelujah! Blessed is the name of the Most High God! And they fell down at Jesus' feet to worship Him.

VII   18 Then He spoke to Nephi who was in the crowd, and commanded him to approach. 19 So Nephi stood up and went to Him and bowed before the Lord, and he kissed His feet. 20 Then the Lord commanded him to stand up, and he got up and stood in front of Him. 21 And the Lord said to him: I give you power to baptize this people when I've ascended into heaven again.

VIII   22 Then the Lord called up others and said the same thing, giving them power to baptize. He instructed them: You must baptize in the following manner, and there must not be any controversies about this. 23 I instruct you that anyone who repents of their sins because of your words and wishes to be baptized in My name, you must baptize them in the following way: You must go down and stand in the water and baptize them in My name. ²⁴ Now these are the words that you must say, calling them by name, saying: ²⁵ Having authority given to me by Jesus Christ, I baptize you in the name of the Father, and of the Son, and of the Holy Ghost. Amen. ²⁶ And then you must immerse them under the water and bring them back out of the water. ²⁷ This is the way you must baptize in My name. Truly I tell you that the Father and the Son and the Holy Ghost are united as one; I am in the Father and the Father in Me, and the Father and I are united as one. ²⁸ And exactly as I've commanded you, so you must baptize. You must not argue about this as you've done before, and you must not argue about the points of My doctrine either, as you've done before. ²⁹ In truth I tell you: Anyone who welcomes the spirit of conflict doesn't follow Me, but is following the accuser, who's the father of conflict. He incites people to angrily fight with each other. ³⁰ This isn't My doctrine, to incite angry fighting by people. But this is My doctrine, everything like that should end.

IX   ³¹ Listen carefully to what I tell you: I will declare to you My doctrine. ³² This is My doctrine, and it is the doctrine that the Father has given to Me: I testify of the Father, and the Father testifies of Me, and the Holy Ghost testifies of the Father and Me. I also testify the Father commands all people everywhere to repent and believe in Me. ³³ And anyone who believes in Me and is baptized will be saved, and they are who will inherit God's kingdom. ³⁴ But anyone who doesn't believe in Me and isn't baptized will be damned. ³⁵ In truth I tell you this is My doctrine, and I testify of it from the Father. Anyone who believes in Me also believes in the Father, and the Father will testify to them of Me, since He will visit them with fire and with the Holy Ghost. ³⁶ In this way the Father will testify of Me, and the Holy Ghost will testify to them of the Father and Me, because the Father and I and the Holy Ghost are united as one. ³⁷ In addition, I say to you: You must repent and become as a little child and be baptized in My name, or under no circumstance can you receive these things. ³⁸ And again, I say to you: You must repent and be baptized in My name and become as a little child, or under no circumstances can you inherit God's kingdom. ³⁹ In truth I tell you this is My doctrine. Whoever builds on this builds on My rock, and the gates of hell will not prevail against them. ⁴⁰ And those who declare more or less than this and establish it as My doctrine advocate evil and are not built upon My rock, but are built on a sandy foundation, and the gates of hell stand open to receive them when the floods come and the wind pounds them. ⁴¹ Therefore go to this people and declare to the farthest reaches of the earth the words that I've spoken.

x   **12** When Jesus had spoken these words to Nephi and to the twelve who had been called and received power and authority to baptize, He reached out His hand to the crowd and cried out to them: Blessed are you if you pay close attention to the words of these twelve whom I've chosen from this people, to minister to you and to be your servants. I've given them power so they can baptize you with water. And after you're baptized with water, I'll baptize you with fire and the Holy Ghost. Therefore blessed are you if you believe in Me and are baptized, after seeing Me and knowing that I Am.

XI   2 In addition, more blessed are those who believe in your words because you testify that you've seen Me and you know that I Am. Indeed, blessed are those who believe in your words and come down into the depths of humility and are baptized, since they will be visited with fire and the Holy Ghost and will receive a remission of their sins.

XII   3 Yes, God is with the poor in spirit who come to Me, for the kingdom of heaven belongs to them.

XIII   4 And also, God is with all those who mourn, for they will be comforted.

XIV   5 And God remembers the meek, for they will inherit the earth.

XV   6 And God accompanies all those who hunger and thirst for righteousness, for they will be filled with the Holy Ghost.

XVI   7 And God loves the merciful, for they will obtain mercy.

XVII   8 And God blesses the pure in heart, for they will see God.

XVIII   9 And God is with all the peacemakers, for they will be called the children of God.

XIX   10 And God is beside all those who are persecuted for being called by My name, for the kingdom of heaven is theirs. 11 And God stands with all of you when people revile, persecute, and say all manner of evil against you falsely, because of following Me, 12 for you should all have great joy and be very glad, because a great reward awaits you in heaven; the prophets who lived before you were persecuted in the same way.

XX   13 In truth I tell you: I guide you to be the salt of the earth, but if the salt loses its useful flavor, what will the earth be salted with? The salt will from then on be good for nothing but to be thrown out and trampled by people's feet.

XXI   14 In truth I tell you: I guide you to be the light of this people. A city that's built on a hill can't be hidden. 15 Ask yourself: do people light a lamp and hide it under a basket? No, they put it on a lampstand, and it gives light to everyone in the house. 16 Therefore let your light shine in the same way before this people, so they can see your good works and glorify your Father who is in heaven.

XXII   17 Don't think I've come to destroy the Law or the prophets. I didn't come to destroy, but to fulfill. 18 Truly I tell you: Not even the smallest part or requirement of the Law has gone unfulfilled, but in Me it has all been accomplished.

XXIII   19 And know this, I've given you the law and the commandments of My Father, that everyone is to believe in Me, and all must repent of their sins, and come to Me with a broken heart and a contrite spirit. Everyone has the commandments before them and the law is accomplished. 20 Therefore come to Me and everyone can be saved. For in truth I tell you that unless you obey My commandments which I've commanded you at this time, you'll never enter into the kingdom of heaven.

XXIV   21 All have heard what was said since ancient time, and have also seen it written before you, that you shall not murder, and whoever murders will incur condemnation by God. 22 But I say to you whoever is angry with his brother will be in danger of His judgment. And whoever calls his brother, Worthless, will risk offending the Heavenly Council, and whoever will say, You fool! — risks the fires of hell.

XXV   23 Therefore if any of you will come to Me, or will start to come to Me, and remembers that your brother or sister holds anything against you, 24 go your way first to your brother or sister to be reconciled with them, and then come to Me with full commitment in your heart and I'll welcome you.

XXVI   25 Accept accountability for your misconduct the instant it's brought to your attention, to avoid leaving this life unrepentant and risking condemnation. 26 I warn you: You'll discover no way to escape before paying fully for every sin; and while in prison under condemnation, are you able to redeem yourself? I warn you that you cannot.

XXVII   27 Remember also, it was written since ancient time that you shall not commit adultery; 28 but I say to you that anyone who engages in deliberate planning to seduce a woman to sin sexually has already committed adultery in his heart. 29 Hear now: I command you to not let any of these things enter your heart, 30 for it's better to stop doing any of these things, and carry your own cross, rather than to be cast into hell.

XXVIII   31 It has been written that whoever leaves his wife, let him give her a written divorce. 32 But I say, unless it's because of unfaithfulness, whoever leaves his wife causes her to be unfaithful. Whoever marries her after such a divorce also betrays the marriage covenant.

XXIX   33 And the Law also decrees: You are never to renounce, but always strictly do anything you swear unto God. 34 But now I warn you: Don't swear at all, either by heaven, for it's God's throne, 35 or by the earth, for it's His footstool, 36 neither swear by your head, because you can't even make one hair black or white, 37 but only say: Yes, yes, no, no; for whatever results from more than that will prove to be evil.

XXX   38 And the scriptures state: An eye for an eye and a tooth for a tooth; 39 but I say instead: Accept life's injustices gracefully, and when someone hits your right cheek, turn to him the other also. 40 And if someone sues you under the law to get your coat, let them have your overcoat too. 41 And whoever orders you to go a mile, go two. 42 Give to any that ask of you, and if someone wants to borrow from you, never turn them down.

XXXI   43 The Law also says for you to love your neighbor, and lets you even hate your enemy. 44 But now I say to you: Love your enemies also, bless them that curse you, do good to them that hate you, and pray for them who despitefully use you and persecute you, 45 so you may become the children of your Father who is in heaven, for He makes His sun to rise on the evil and on the good. 46 Therefore everything ordained anciently under the Law of Moses has all been fulfilled through Me. 47 Those prior things are over and I implement these new things. 48 Therefore I want you to be perfect, just as I or your Father who is in heaven is perfect.

XXXII   **13** I categorically say that I want you, whenever you contribute to the poor, to be careful not to make that a public show for others to see; otherwise, you have no reward from your Father who is in heaven. 2 Therefore when you contribute help, don't blow a trumpet to announce it, as hypocrites do in the synagogues and in the streets to impress others. I'm warning you: They have their only reward. 3 But when you give charitably, don't even let your left hand know what your right hand does, 4 so your donations are kept in secret; and your Father who sees that secret will Himself openly reward you.

XXXIII   5 And when you pray, don't imitate the hypocrites, for they love to pray standing in the synagogues and on the street corners, hoping to be noticed by others. I'm warning you: They have their only reward. 6 But when you pray, go into your closet, and after shutting the door, pray to your Father in secret; and your Father who sees that secrecy will openly reward you. 7 When you pray, don't use arrogant chanting like the heathen, for they think they're noticed because of their conspicuous noise. 8 Absolutely do not be like them, for your Father knows everything you need before you even ask Him.

XXXIV   9 So follow this example when you offer prayer: Our Father in heaven, let Your name remain Holy. 10 May Your will be done on earth as it is in heaven. 11 And forgive us our debts as we forgive our debtors. 12 And don't let us fall into temptation, but rescue us from evil. 13 For Yours is the kingdom, and the power, and the glory, forever. Amen. 14 For if you forgive others' offenses, your Heavenly Father will also forgive yours, 15 but if you don't forgive others' offenses, your Father won't forgive yours either.

XXXV   16 Furthermore, when you fast, don't imitate the hypocrites, acting distressed, for they act as if they're suffering to be admired by others. I'm warning you: They have their only reward. 17 But when you are fasting, clean up, wash up, dress up, 18 avoid any appearance of fasting, let only your Father know in secret; and your Father who sees in secret will openly reward you.

XXXVI   19 Don't accumulate treasures on earth, where moths damage, rust corrodes, and thieves break in and steal, 20 but instead accumulate treasures in Heaven, where there are no damaging moths, corrosive rust, and thieves don't break in and steal; 21 because what you treasure reveals what's in your heart.

XXXVII   22 The light enters the body through your eyes; if, therefore, your eyes look to God, your whole body is full of His light. 23 But if your eye looks for evil, your whole body is then full of darkness. Therefore if the light within you looks for the darkness, how overwhelming that darkness becomes.

XXXVIII   24 No one can serve two masters, for they'll either hate the one and love the other, or at least they'll follow the one and ignore the other. You can't serve God and covet.

Chapter 6

25 And now after Jesus said these words, He looked at the twelve He had chosen and said unto them: Remember the words I've spoken. Realize you are the ones I've chosen as ministers to this people.

II   Therefore I tell you: Don't focus on yourself, worrying about what you'll eat or what you'll drink, nor for yourself and what you'll wear. Isn't life more than food? And the body more than clothes? 26 Notice the birds in the air. They don't plant, nor do they harvest and store in barns, but your Heavenly Father feeds them. Don't you matter more than them?

III   27 Which of you, by wanting it, can add one inch to his height? 28 And why do you think about clothing yourself? Look at the lilies of the field, how they grow. They make no effort to cover themselves;

29 and yet I tell you even Solomon at the height of his glory wasn't as splendid as one of these. 30 Accordingly, if God clothes the grass of the field like that, which grows today and tomorrow is burned in an oven, He will also clothe you if you aren't faithless. 31 Therefore don't worry and ask: What will we eat? Or, What will we drink? Or, What will we wear? 32 For your Heavenly Father knows you need all these things. 33 But you should first seek the kingdom of God and His righteousness, and all these other things will be provided for you.

IV
34 Therefore don't worry about tomorrow, for the next day will have its demands. Each day will have enough challenges to occupy you.

V
14 And now after Jesus had said this, He turned back to the crowd and addressed them again, saying: I warn you not to condemn others so that you aren't condemned; 2 for the reason you condemn anyone else will be the reason you're also condemned — your standards for others will be used against you.

VI
3 And why do you focus on the bit of sawdust in your brother's eye, but ignore the log in your own eye? 4 Or how can you say to your brother: Let me pull the sawdust out of your eye, while there's a log in your own eye? 5 You hypocrite, first get the log out of your own eye, and then you can see clearly enough to remove the bit of sawdust out of your brother's eye. 6 Don't give anything holy to dogs, nor place your pearls in front of pigs and watch them be trampled underfoot, because then the pigs turn and attack you.

VII
7 Ask and it will be given to you, seek and you will find, knock and it will be opened to you; 8 indeed, everyone that asks, receives, and anyone that seeks, finds, and to the one that knocks, it will be opened.

VIII
9 Or who of you, if your child asks for bread, will give them a stone? 10 Or if your child asks for a fish, will give them a snake? 11 If you then, with all your faults, still understand how to respond to your children's requests, how much more does your Father who is in heaven know how to respond kindly to things asked of Him? 12 Therefore everything you expect others to do for you, do that for them, for that will satisfy the law and the prophets.

IX
13 You should enter through the narrow gate, for the gate is wide and the road is vast that leads to destruction, and many enter through those; 14 because the gate is narrow and the pathway tight leading to life, and very few find it.

X
15 Beware of false prophets who come to you in sheep's clothing, but inside they're ravenous wolves. 16 You can identify them by their results. Can you gather grapes from thorns? Or figs from thistles?

17 Likewise you know that every good fruit tree produces good fruit, but diseased trees produce diseased fruit. 18 A good tree doesn't produce bad fruit, neither does a diseased tree produce good fruit. 19 Every tree that fails to produce good fruit is cut down and thrown into the fire. 20 Therefore by the fruit produced you can identify them.

XI

21 Not everyone that says to Me, Lord! Lord! will enter the kingdom of heaven, but only those who obey the will of My Father who is in heaven. 22 Many will say to Me on that day: Lord, Lord, have we not prophesied in Your name? And in Your name cast out devils? And in Your name accomplished many wonderful things? 23 And I'll respond to them: I never knew you. Get away from Me, you that embraced iniquity.

XII

24 Therefore anyone who hears these teachings from Me and obeys them, I'll compare to a wise man who built his house on bedrock; 25 and the rain fell, the floods came, and the tempests beat against that house, but it remained unharmed, because it was built on bedrock. 26 In contrast, everyone that hears these teachings from Me and disobeys them I'll compare to a foolish man who built his house on the sand; 27 and the rain fell, the floods came, and the tempests beat against that house, and it failed, and its collapse was terrible.

Chapter 7

15 When Jesus finished saying this, He looked around at the large crowd and said to them: You've now heard what I taught before I ascended to My Father. Therefore anyone who remembers these teachings of Mine and obeys them, I'll raise that person up on the last day.

II

2 When Jesus had said this, He could tell some of them were surprised and wondered what He intended for the Law of Moses, since they didn't understand what He meant that old things had come to an end and all things had become new. 3 And He explained to them: Don't be surprised I said that old things had come to an end and everything had become new. 4 I assure you the Law that was given to Moses is now completed. 5 I Am the one who gave the Law, and I Am the one who covenanted with My people Israel. Therefore the Law is now completed by My coming to conclude the Law. Therefore it now ends. 6 I haven't destroyed what the prophets foretold, since anything not yet accomplished by Me will all happen, I promise you. 7 When I said old things have ended, I don't mean that those prophecies yet to happen won't occur. 8 Because there are still covenants I've made with My people that aren't yet fulfilled, but the Law given to Moses ends

with Me. 9 I Am the Law and the light. Look to Me and endure to the end, and you will live; indeed, I'll give eternal life to all who endure to the end. 10 I've given you the commandments. Therefore keep My commandments; they're what the law and the teachings of the prophets intended, because they truthfully pointed to Me.

III   11 When Jesus said that, He said to the twelve He had chosen: 12 You are My disciples, and you are a light to this people, who are a remnant of Joseph's family. 13 This is your inherited land; the Father has given it to you. 14 And the Father has never commanded Me to tell that to your fellow Israelites at Jerusalem. 15 Nor has the Father ever commanded Me to tell them about the other tribes of the house of Israel the Father led away from the land. 16 But the Father did command Me to tell them this: 17 I have other sheep that aren't part of this fold. I will visit them and they will also hear My voice, and I will make all My sheep into one fold, following one Shepherd. 18 Now because of stubbornness and unbelief they didn't understand what I said. Therefore the Father commanded Me not to say anything else about this subject to them. 19 But truly I tell you the Father has commanded Me, and I'm telling it to you, that you were separated away from them because of their iniquity. Therefore it's because of their iniquity that they don't know about you. 20 Moreover, and I'm telling you this truth: the Father has separated other tribes away from them. And it's because of their iniquity that they don't know about them. 21 Now I tell you truthfully that you are the ones I spoke of when I said: I have other sheep that aren't part of this fold; I will visit them, and they will also hear My voice; then I will make all My sheep into one fold, following one Shepherd. 22 And they didn't understand Me, since they thought I was talking about the Gentiles. They didn't understand that the Gentiles were to be converted through their preaching. 23 And they didn't understand Me when I said that they would hear My voice. And they didn't understand Me that the Gentiles wouldn't hear My voice at this time, and that I wouldn't reveal Myself to them except by the Holy Ghost. 24 But you've both heard My voice and seen Me, and you are My sheep, and you are included with those the Father has given to Me. **16** And again I testify to you I have other sheep that don't live in this land, nor in the land of Jerusalem, nor in any of the areas where I went to minister. 2 The ones I'm speaking about are those who haven't heard My voice yet; and I haven't revealed Myself to them either. 3 But I've received a commandment from the Father to go to them: that they're to hear My voice and be included among My sheep, so there can be one fold following one Shepherd. Therefore I will go in order to reveal Myself to them.

IV   4 And I command you to write these words when I leave, so that if My people at Jerusalem — those who saw Me and were with Me during My ministry — if they don't ask the Father in My name to learn about you by the Holy Ghost, and about the other lost tribes also, then what you will write will be protected until they will be given to the Gentiles. Then through the fullness of the Gentiles a remnant of their descendants can be recovered from those scattered across the earth because of their unbelief. They will learn to know Me, their Redeemer. 5 Then I'll gather them in from the four quarters of the earth; and I'll keep the covenant the Father has made to all the people of the house of Israel. 6 The Gentiles will be blessed because of their belief in Me, through and as a result of the Holy Ghost, which testifies to them of Me and of the Father. 7 The Father says: Because of their belief in Me and because of your unbelief, O house of Israel, in the latter days the truth will come to the Gentiles, so that the fullness of these things will be revealed to them.

V   8 But woe, says the Father, to the unbelieving Gentiles, because despite having come to this land and scattering My people who are part of the house of Israel: And My people of the house of Israel will have been banished from their society and been trampled underfoot by them. 9 But because of the Father's mercy to the Gentiles and also the Father's judgments imposed on My people of the house of Israel, I promise you that after all this, including that I will cause My people of the house of Israel to be driven, afflicted, killed, and banished from their society, and to be hated, mocked, and ridiculed by them. 10 The Father commands Me to tell you: At the time when the Gentiles sin against My gospel and reject the fullness of My gospel and are filled with pride to their very center above all nations, more proud of themselves than anyone on earth, and are full of all kinds of lying, deceit, mischief, all kinds of hypocrisy, murder, priestcraft, whoredoms, and secret abominations — if they do all these things and reject the fullness of My gospel, says the Father, I'll take the fullness of My gospel away from them. 11 Then I'll return to the covenant I made with My people of the house of Israel, and I'll bring them My gospel. 12 And I'll show you, O house of Israel, that the Gentiles no longer have power over you, but I'll keep My covenant with you, O house of Israel, and you'll understand the fullness of My gospel. 13 But if the Gentiles repent and return to Me, says the Father, they'll be included with My people of the house of Israel. 14 And I won't let My people, who are part of the house of Israel, go among them and trample them down, says the Father. 15 But if they won't return to Me and obey My voice, I'll let My people, O house of Israel, go through them and trample them down. They'll be like salt that's become useless, which is then good for nothing but to be thrown out and trampled underfoot by My people, O house of Israel.

VI

16 In truth I tell you: The Father has commanded Me to give this people this land as their inheritance. 17 And then the prophet Isaiah's words will be fulfilled, which say: 18 Your watchmen will raise their voice, with a chorus together they'll sing, for they'll see eye to eye when the Lord brings back Zion. 19 Announce with joy, sing together you abandoned places of Jerusalem, for the Lord has comforted His people, He has redeemed Jerusalem. 20 The Lord has shown His power before the eyes of all the nations and everywhere to the end of the earth will see the salvation of God.

Chapter 8

17 When Jesus had said these words, He again looked around at the crowd of people and said to them: It's time for Me to leave. 2 I can tell you're weak, and that right now you can't understand everything the Father commanded Me to say to you. 3 So go to your homes and ponder what I've said and ask the Father in My name to help you understand, and prepare your minds for tomorrow, and I'll come back to you. 4 But right now I'm returning to the Father, and to also show Myself to the lost tribes of Israel, who were never lost to the Father, for He knows where He has led them.

II

5 When Jesus had said this, He again looked around at the people, who were in tears and looking steadily at Him, as if they wanted to ask Him to remain a little longer with them. 6 He said to them: My heart is full of compassion for you. 7 Are there any of you who are sick? Bring them here. Are there any of you who are lame, blind, crippled, injured, leprous, or infirm, deaf, or that suffer from anything? Bring them here and I'll heal them, because of the compassion I feel for you; My heart is full of mercy. 8 Yes, I can see you want Me to show you what I did for your fellow Israelites at Jerusalem, since I see you have faith enough to let Me heal you.

III

9 When He had said this, the whole crowd together, brought to Him everyone who was sick, suffering, crippled, blind, mute, or unwell in any way; and He healed every one of them as they were brought up to Him. 10 All of them, including both those who had been healed and those who were healthy, bowed down at His feet and worshiped Him.

And everyone who was able to come, despite the size of the crowd, kissed His feet, bathing His feet with their tears.

IV   11 Then He commanded for their little children to be brought. 12 So they brought their little children and sat them down on the ground around Him, and Jesus stood in the middle of them; and the crowd made room until they had all been brought to Him. 13 When they were all brought and Jesus stood in the middle of them, He commanded the crowd to kneel on the ground. 14 When they had knelt on the ground, Jesus groaned to Himself and said: Father, the wickedness of the people of the house of Israel troubles Me. 15 After He said this, He also knelt on the ground. And He prayed to the Father, and what He prayed can't be written. Those that heard Him testified about it; 16 and they testified to the following: The eye has never seen and the ear has never heard such great and awe-inspiring things we saw and heard Jesus speak to the Father. 17 And no tongue can speak, neither can anyone write, neither can people's hearts conceive such great and astonishing things as we both saw and heard Jesus speak. No one can conceive of the joy that filled our souls when we heard Him pray to the Father for us.

V   18 When Jesus finished praying to the Father, He got up. But the crowd's joy overwhelmed them. 19 Jesus told them to stand back up; 20 and they got up from the ground. Then He told them: Blessed are you because of your faith. Now My joy is complete. 21 When He had said these words, He wept; and the crowd testified of it. Then He took their little children, one by one, and blessed them and prayed to the Father for them. 22 When He had done this, He again wept. 23 He told the crowd: Notice your little ones. 24 As they looked at them, their eyes were drawn up to heaven; and they saw the heavens open, and they saw angels descending from heaven as if they descended in a pillar of fire. And they descended and surrounded the little ones, who then were also surrounded by fire, and the angels ministered to them. 25 And the crowd saw, heard, and testified. They know their record is true, because all of them saw and heard, everyone for themselves. In total, there were about 2,500 people, who consisted of men, women, and children.

VI   **18** Then Jesus commanded His disciples to bring Him some bread and wine. 2 And while they were gone for bread and wine, He commanded the crowd to sit down on the ground. 3 When the disciples returned with bread and wine, He took the bread and broke it and blessed it, and He gave it to the disciples and commanded them to eat. 4 When they had eaten and were filled, He commanded them to give it to the crowd. 5 When the crowd had eaten and were filled, He said to the disciples: one of you will be ordained, and I'll give him power to break bread and bless it and give it to the people of My congregation, to all who believe and are baptized in My name. 6 You must always make a practice of doing this, just as I've done, just as I've broken bread and blessed it and given it to you. 7 And you must do this in remembrance of My body, which I've shown you. It will be a testimony to the Father that you always remember Me. And if you always remember Me, you'll have My Spirit to be with you.

VII   8 After He said this, He commanded His disciples to take the cup of wine and drink from it, and also to give it to the crowd so they could drink. 9 And they did so and drank and were filled. Then they gave it to the crowd and they drank and were filled. 10 After the disciples completed this, Jesus said to them: Blessed are you for this thing that you've done, because this fulfills My commandments. This shows the Father that you're willing to do what I've commanded you. 11 You must always do this for those who repent and are baptized in My name. You must do it in remembrance of My blood, which I've shed for you, so you can show to the Father that you always remember Me. And if you always remember Me, My Spirit will be with you. 12 I command you to do these things. If you always do these things, you'll be blessed, since you're built on My bedrock. 13 But any of you who do more or less than these things aren't built on My bedrock; you've built on a sandy foundation. When the rain falls, the floods come, and the tempests beat against them, they will fall; and the gates of hell are already open to welcome them. 14 Therefore you are blessed if you keep My commandments, which the Father has commanded Me to give you. 15 I warn you: You must be watchful and always pray for strength against the accuser's temptations, so you aren't led away by him as his prisoner. 16 And just as I've prayed among you, so you must likewise pray in My congregation, with My people who repent and are baptized in My name. I Am the light; I've set an example for you.

VIII   17 When Jesus had said this to His disciples, He turned back to the crowd and said to them: 18 I truthfully warn you: You must be watchful and always pray so that you won't fall into temptation, because Satan longs to have you, so he can sift you like wheat. 19 Therefore you must always pray to the Father in My name. 20 And anything you ask the Father in My name that's right, believing you will receive, it will be given to you. 21 Pray in your families to the Father always in My name, so your wives and your children can be blessed. 22 You must meet together often. And you must not exclude anyone from joining you when you meet together, but let them join you and don't prohibit them from doing so; 23 but you must pray for them and not throw them out.

If they frequently join you, you must pray to the Father for them in My name. 24 Therefore hold up your light, so it can shine to the world. I Am the light that you must hold up, what you've seen Me do. You see that I've prayed to the Father, and all of you have witnessed it. 25 And you see I haven't commanded any of you to leave; instead, I've commanded you to come to Me, so you could feel and see; you must do the same for the world. Anyone that breaks this commandment allows themselves to be led into temptation.

IX   26 When Jesus had said these words, He again looked at the disciples He had chosen and said to them: 27 I now tell you: I'll give you another commandment; and then I must go to My Father, so I can fulfill other commandments He has given Me. 28 Now this is the commandment I give you: you must never allow anyone to knowingly partake of My flesh and blood unworthily when you administer it. 29 Because anyone that eats and drinks My flesh and blood unworthily eats and drinks damnation to their soul. Therefore if you know someone is unworthy to eat and drink My flesh and blood, you must prevent them from doing so. 30 Nevertheless, you must not banish them from your fellowship, but you must minister to them and pray to the Father for them in My name. And if they repent and are baptized in My name, then you must accept them and administer My flesh and blood to them. 31 But if they don't repent, they can't be included as part of My people, to prevent them from destroying My people. Because I know My sheep and they're counted. 32 Nevertheless, you must not drive them out of your meetings or places of worship, since you must continue to minister to them. Because you don't know whether they will return, repent, and come to Me with all their heart and I will heal them, and you'll be the means of bringing them to salvation. 33 Therefore obey what I've commanded you, so you don't come under condemnation. For woe to those whom the Father condemns! 34 I'm giving you these commandments because of the arguments that have occurred between you. Blessed are you if you don't have any disputes. 35 Now I'm going to the Father because it's necessary for Me to return to the Father for your benefit.

X   36 When Jesus had finished saying these things, He touched the disciples He had chosen with His hand, one by one, until He had touched them all; and He spoke to them while He touched them. 37 And the crowd didn't hear what He said; therefore they didn't testify about it. But the disciples testified that He gave them power to give the Holy Ghost. Later in this record I'll show you this testimony is true. 38 When Jesus had touched them all, a cloud came and overshadowed the crowd, so they couldn't see Jesus. 39 While they were overshadowed,

He left them and ascended into heaven. The disciples saw and testified that He ascended into heaven again.

Chapter 9

19 After Jesus ascended into heaven, the people dispersed; and every man took his wife and children and returned to his own home. ² And it was immediately and widely reported among the people, before it was dark, that they had seen Jesus and He had ministered to them and He would visit them the next day as well. ³ News about Jesus spread the whole night. The news spread abroad so much that there were many, a great many, who traveled all that night to be at the place on the next day where Jesus would visit the people.

⁴ The next day, when a large crowd of people had gathered, Nephi and his brother he had raised from the dead, whose name was Timothy, and also his son whose name was Jonas, and the brothers Mathoni and Mathonihah, and Kumen, Kumenonhi, Jeremiah, Shemnon, Jonas, Zedekiah, and Isaiah which are the names of the disciples whom Jesus had chosen, went forward to stand in the middle of the crowd. ⁵ But the crowd was so large that they had them separated into 12 groups. ⁶ And the twelve taught the crowd. They had the crowd kneel on the ground and pray to the Father in the name of Jesus. ⁷ The disciples also prayed to the Father in the name of Jesus. Then they got up and ministered to the people. ⁸ When they had reiterated the same words Jesus had spoken, not varying from what Jesus had said, they knelt down once more and prayed to the Father in the name of Jesus. ⁹ And they prayed for what they most desired: they asked for the Holy Ghost to be given to them. ¹⁰ After they had prayed for this, they went down to the water's edge; and the crowd followed them. ¹¹ Then Nephi went down into the water and was baptized. ¹² And he came up out of the water and began to baptize, and he baptized all those Jesus had chosen. ¹³ When they were all baptized and had come up out of the water, the Holy Ghost fell upon them; and they were filled with the Holy Ghost and with fire. ¹⁴ And they were surrounded by what seemed to be fire, which came down from heaven. The crowd witnessed it and testified of it. Angels came down from heaven and ministered to them. ¹⁵ While the angels were ministering to the disciples, Jesus came and stood in the middle of them and ministered to them. ¹⁶ He spoke to the crowd and commanded them to kneel again on the ground, and also for His disciples to kneel down on the ground. ¹⁷ When they all knelt down, He commanded His disciples to pray. ¹⁸ And they began to pray; and they prayed to Jesus, calling Him their Lord and God.

III   19 Jesus left them and went a little way off and bowed down on the
ground, saying: 20 Father, I thank You that You've given the Holy Ghost
to these whom I've chosen. And it's because of their belief in Me that
I've chosen them out of the world. 21 Father, I ask You to give the Holy
Ghost to all those who will believe in their words. 22 Father, You've
given them the Holy Ghost because they believe in Me. And You see
that they believe in Me because You hear them, and they pray to Me;
and they pray to Me because I'm with them. 23 Now Father, I pray to
You for them, and for all those who will believe in their words, so they
can believe in Me, so I can be in them as You Father are in Me, so we
can be united as one.

IV   24 When Jesus had prayed this to the Father, He came to His
disciples, and they continued to pray to Him without stopping. Yet
they didn't repeat any words, since the things they were to pray for
were inspired; and they were filled with hope. 25 Jesus blessed them as
they prayed to Him. And His countenance smiled upon them, and the
light of His countenance shined on them. They were as bright as Jesus'
countenance and clothes. And its brightness exceeded everything that
is white; indeed, nothing on earth could be as brilliantly white. 26 Then
Jesus said to them: Pray on. And they never did stop praying. 27 Then
He turned away from them again and went a little way off and bowed
down on the ground, praying again to the Father: 28 Father, I thank
You that You've purified these that I've chosen because of their faith.
I pray for them and also for those who will believe in their words, so
they can be purified in Me through faith in their words, like these are
purified in Me. 29 Father, I don't pray for the world but for those whom
You've given to Me out of the world because of their faith, so they can
be purified in Me, so I can be in them as You Father are in Me, so we
can be united as one, so I can be glorified in them. 30 When Jesus had
said these things, He went back to His disciples, and they prayed to
Him intently, without stopping. He smiled upon them again. And they
were shining, just like Jesus.

V   31 Then He went again a little way off and prayed to the Father.
32 And no tongue can speak the words He prayed, neither can anyone
write the words He prayed. 33 But the crowd heard and testified of it.
Their hearts were open, and they understood in their hearts the words
He prayed. 34 Nevertheless, the words He prayed were so great and
awe-inspiring that they can't be written, neither can they be spoken by
any person. 35 When Jesus had finished praying, He went back to the
disciples and said to them: I've never seen such great faith as yours
among the Jews. Therefore I couldn't show them such great miracles
because of their unbelief. 36 Truly I say to you: None of them saw such

great things as you've seen, neither have they heard such great things as you've heard.

VI   **20** Then He commanded the crowd of people to stop praying, and His disciples as well. But He commanded them to continue praying in their hearts. 2 And He commanded them to get up and stand on their feet. They arose and stood on their feet. 3 Then He broke bread again and blessed it and gave it to the disciples to eat. 4 When they had eaten, He commanded them to break bread and give it to the large crowd of people. 5 When they had given it to the people, He also gave them wine to drink and commanded them to give it to the people. 6 Now no bread or wine had been brought by the disciples, or by the people either. 7 But He truly gave them bread to eat and wine to drink. 8 He said to them: Anyone who eats this bread eats of My body to their soul. And anyone who drinks this wine drinks of My blood to their soul. And their soul will never be hungry or thirsty but will be filled. 9 When the people had all eaten and drunk, they were filled with the Spirit. And they cried out loudly as one, giving glory to Jesus, whom they both saw and heard.

VII   10 When they had all given glory to Jesus, He said to them: Now I'll fulfill the commandment of the Father to Me regarding this people, who are a remnant of the house of Israel. 11 You remember I spoke to you about when Isaiah's words will be fulfilled. You can see they're written down and you have them. Therefore study them carefully. 12 In truth I tell you: When they're fulfilled, then the covenant the Father has made for His people, O house of Israel, is also fulfilled. 13 Then the remnant scattered throughout the earth will be gathered in from the east, west, south, and north. They'll be brought to know the Lord their God who has redeemed them. 14 And the Father has commanded Me to give you this land as your inheritance. 15 I tell you that if the Gentiles don't repent after the blessing they will receive after having scattered My people, 16 then you, a remnant of the house of Jacob will rise up from them. You'll be mixed in with them, who will outnumber you. You'll be among them like a lion among his prey in the forest, and as a young lion among the flocks of sheep, who moves unopposed to take down and tear to pieces. 17 Your hand will be against your opponents and all your enemies will be cut down. 18 I'll then gather My people together like a farmer harvesting grain to the storehouse, 19 for I'll empower those of the Father's covenant with iron horns and brass hooves to beat down many people. I'll use their wealth to honor the Lord and take their property for the Lord of the whole earth. And I Am the one who does it. 20 The sword of My justice, says the Father, will then threaten them. And unless they repent, it will strike them, says the Father, including all the Gentile nations.

VIII   21 I'll establish My people, O house of Israel. 22 I'll establish you in this land to vindicate the covenant I made with your father Jacob; that includes a New Jerusalem. And the Powers of heaven will help you, and I'll also be helping you. 23 I Am the one Moses described, saying: The Lord God will raise up a prophet to you from your brethren, like me; listen to whatever He'll say to you. And it will follow that every soul who will not hear that prophet will be cut off from among the people. 24 Truthfully I say to you: All the prophets from Samuel and those following after, as many as have prophesied, have testified of Me. 25 And now you are the children of the prophets, and part of the house of Israel, and you have part in the covenant the Father made with your fathers, when He promised to Abraham: Through your posterity all the families of the earth will be blessed. 26 The Father has raised Me up before all men and sent Me to you covenant children first, to bless you and turn you from your sin. 27 Now this blessing to you is to keep the Father's covenant He made with Abraham, saying: Through your posterity all the families of the earth will be blessed. The Holy Ghost will be poured out on the Gentiles through Me, and this blessing given to the Gentiles will give them power to scatter My people, the house of Israel. 28 However after they receive the fullness of My gospel, then if they harden their hearts against Me, I'll cause them to experience the same fate of being scattered, says the Father. 29 I'll remember the covenant I made with My people. I've covenanted with them that I would bring them back together at the right time; I'll give them back the land of their ancestors as their inheritance, which is the land of Jerusalem, which is the promised land for them forever, says the Father.

IX   30 The time will come when the fullness of My gospel will be preached to them. 31 And they will believe in Me, that I Am Jesus Christ, the Son of God, and they will pray to the Father in My name. 32 Then their lookouts will sing the same message together as a chorus, agreeing eye to eye. 33 Then the Father will gather them together again and give Jerusalem to them as an inherited land. 34 Then they'll break out in joyful song, singing together with all the scattered remnants from Jerusalem, for the Father has brought comfort to His people, He has redeemed Jerusalem. 35 The Father has vindicated His covenant for all to witness, and everyone to the ends of the earth will see He has saved His people. And the Father and I are united as one. 36 Then this prophecy will be fulfilled: Wake up, wake up again and dress yourself with strength, O Zion. Put on your clean garments, O Jerusalem, the holy city. From now on none of the faithless or uncircumcised will try to enter. 37 Shake all the dust off yourself, stand up and then rest, O Jerusalem. Take the chains off your neck, O imprisoned daughter of Zion. 38 For the Lord declares: You've sold yourselves for nothing and you'll be set free without charge.

39 For I declare to you that My people will know My name, and on that day they'll recognize I Am the one who told you about this. 40 And then they'll say: How beautiful shall His presence be upon the mountains! For He brings good news, announces peace, proclaims deliverance, brings salvation, and declares to Zion: Your God reigns! 41 And then the shout will be heard: Depart, depart, get yourself out of there, and don't touch anything unclean, get away and be clean before you receive the sacred rites of the Lord. 42 But you can't act in haste, nor run faster than your ability, for the Lord will lead you and the God of Israel will move you along. 43 You'll see that My servant will proceed wisely, He'll be exalted and extolled, and be above others. 44 People are astonished at Your appearance, Your suffering was greater than any man can endure, for it would kill all other men — 45 so He'll cleanse many nations. The kings will be at a loss for words not knowing what to say because of Him, for they'll see what they were never told, and be forced to consider what they never expected. 46 Now I promise you: All these things will happen exactly as the Father has commanded Me to declare. This will conform to the Father's covenant with His people; and Jerusalem will again be inhabited by My people, as a land of their inheritance.

21 I tell you the truth. And I'll give you a sign to identify the time when these things are about to happen, when I will gather My people, the house of Israel, from their long-scattered state, and will again establish My Zion among them. 2 This is the sign for you: When the things that I'm declaring to you now and after this by the power of the Holy Ghost that are given to you by the Father are then revealed to the Gentiles, and taken as a message through them to you, that is when the Father's covenant is being fulfilled. You are descendants of Jacob and will be scattered by the Gentiles. 3 But the Father will reveal these things first to the Gentiles, then from them to you. 4 It's the Father's plan for the Gentiles to be established in this land as a free people through His power, to allow the history and prophecies to come from them to a remnant of your descendants. That vindicates the Father's covenant with His people, O house of Israel. 5 Therefore the record of these events, and the events that will take place among you after this, will come from the Gentiles to your descendants. But your descendants will first fall away in unbelief because of iniquity. 6 That's an essential part of the Father's plan. The covenant requires this record to come

from the Gentiles, so the Gentiles will understand His direct involvement. Then the Gentiles, provided they don't harden their hearts, will be able to repent and come to Me and be baptized in My name and know the true points of My doctrine, so they can be included with My people, the house of Israel. 7 When these things happen, and your descendants begin to know these things, it will be a sign to let them know the Father's work is underway, to fulfill the covenant He made to everyone who's part of the house of Israel. 8 When that time comes, kings will be at a loss for words not knowing what to say, for they'll see what they were never told about and be forced to consider what they never expected.

XII

9 At that time, to advance My cause, the Father will begin a work, which will be a great and awe-inspiring work among them. There will be many who won't believe it, although a man will tell it to them. 10 But the ministry of My servant will be led by My hand; therefore they won't be able to harm his work, although he'll be opposed and discredited by them. Yet I'll support him; I'll show them My wisdom is greater than the accuser's deceitful scheming. 11 Therefore those who won't believe in My words, and I Am Jesus Christ, which the Father will give and empower that servant to set before the Gentiles, it will result exactly as Moses said: They will be cut off from My people who are part of the covenant. 12 And then you, a remnant of the house of Jacob, will rise up from them. And you'll be mixed in with them who will outnumber you. You'll be among them like a lion among his prey in the forest, and as a young lion among the flocks of sheep, who moves unopposed to take down and tear to pieces. 13 Your hand will be against your opponents and all your enemies will be cut down. 14 Yes, woe to the Gentiles unless they repent: For when that day comes, says the Father, I'll take away your strength from you, and I'll destroy your security. 15 Your cities will fall and I'll break open your guarded borders. 16 Your sciences and learning will turn into foolishness, and your false beliefs will cause your failure. 17 I'll expose the fraud of those in authority, and your trusted institutions will lose everyone's loyalty. 18 False prophets and false ministers will be brought to shame and humiliation. 19 All lying, deceiving, envying, strife, priestcraft, and whoredoms will come to an end. 20 At that time, says the Father, I'll cut down anyone who won't repent and draw near to My Beloved Son to preserve My people, the house of Israel. 21 I'll take vengeance and unleash My fierce anger on all the unbelieving, beyond anything they expect.

Chapter 10

22 But if the Gentiles repent and hearken to My words and don't harden their hearts, I'll establish My congregation among them. And they will enter the covenant and be included with the remnant of Jacob, to whom I've given this land as their inheritance. 23 They will join with My people, the remnant of Jacob, and all those of the house of Israel who come, so they can build a city that will be called the New Jerusalem. 24 Then they will join with My people who are scattered throughout the land so they can be brought in together to the New Jerusalem. 25 Then the Powers of heaven will come down among them, and I will be with them as well. 26 Then the Father's work will be underway, when this gospel is preached among the remnant of this people. Truly I say to you: At that time, the Father's work will be taught among the scattered portion of My people, even the tribes that have been lost, whom the Father led away out of Jerusalem. 27 The Father will work with My scattered people, to enable them to come to Me, so they can call on the Father in My name. 28 Truly the work of the Father will be underway in all nations, clearing the way to let His people be gathered home to the land of their inheritance. 29 They will go out from all nations. And they won't go hastily or at a run, because I will go in front of them, says the Father, and I will guard them from behind.

II   **22** Then what's written will happen: Sing, O barren, you who never gave birth; break into song and cry aloud, you who never struggled in labor to give birth; for there will be more children of the barren than children of the married wife, says the Lord. 2 You'll need a bigger tent, let your communities spread out; keep growing, get longer tent cords and stronger poles, 3 for you'll gather from the south and the north, and your posterity will adopt the Gentiles and fill the desolated cities again. 4 Don't be afraid, for you'll never be embarrassed or confused, nor ashamed; for you'll forget your youthful shame and won't remember mourning as a widow anymore. 5 For your Creator, your Husband, His name is the Lord of Hosts; and your Redeemer will be called the Holy One of Israel, the God of the whole earth. 6 For the Lord has invited you as an abandoned and forlorn woman, and a wife who married young and now abandoned, explains the Lord. 7 It was only a momentary departure by Me, but now with kindness and forgiveness I embrace you again. 8 I was only upset and left you for a moment, but My affection and loyalty to you will never end, declares the Lord your Redeemer. 9 It's like when I promised the flood of Noah will never be repeated, I likewise promise I will never abandon you again. 10 Although the mountains will erode away, and the hills disappear, My protection and care for you will never end, nor will My covenant of peace be revoked, for I your Lord have mercy on you.

III 11 O you afflicted, storm-tossed, and suffering one, know that I will provide a foundation as sturdy as rock and beautiful as sapphire. 12 I'll make your towers more valuable than rubies, doors that are precious, surrounded by heavenly designs upon the walls. 13 All your children will be taught about the Lord, and your children will learn and understand. 14 I'll govern you righteously; you won't be oppressed, live in fear, or feel threatened, for none of that will return to you. 15 If anyone were to dare attack you it will offend Me, and they'll be defeated before your eyes. 16 I provided the blacksmith that fans the coals to forge the weapons, and I have control over invading armies. 17 No weapon turned against you will succeed, and every accusation against you will be disproven, for My servants will be vindicated. This is the heritage of My servants, and their defense comes from Me, says the Lord.

IV 23 Now I tell you that you ought to carefully study these things. In fact, I give you a commandment to study these things diligently, because Isaiah's prophecies are critical. 2 He clearly focused his prophecy on My people who are part of the house of Israel. Therefore he necessarily prophesied about the Gentiles. 3 And everything he prophesied has happened, or will happen, precisely as he foretold. 4 Therefore pay careful attention to My words. Write down the things I've told you. At the time decided by the Father, they will be provided to the Gentiles. 5 And anyone who obeys My words, repents, and is baptized, will be saved. Carefully study the teachings of the prophets, because many of them explain these things.

V 6 After Jesus said this, He explained the scriptures to them and told them: There are other scriptures I want you to write that you don't have. 7 He asked Nephi: Bring out the records you've kept. 8 Then Nephi brought out the records and put them in front of Him; He glanced at them and said: 9 The truth is that I commanded My servant, Samuel the Lamanite, to tell this people that at the time the Father glorified His name in Me, there would be many holy ones who would rise from the dead and appear to many and minister to them. He asked them: Wasn't this the case? 10 His disciples answered: Yes, Lord, Samuel prophesied as you've said, and everything happened accordingly. 11 Jesus asked them: Then why haven't you written it down — that many holy ones rose from the dead and appeared to many and ministered to them? 12 And Nephi remembered this wasn't written down. 13 And Jesus commanded it to be added and this was written as He commanded.

Chapter 11

14 After Jesus explained all the scriptures as one consistent whole to them, He commanded them to teach what He had explained to them. 24 Then He required them to write down the prophecy Malachi received from the Father. After it was written, He explained what it meant. This is what the Father said to Malachi: I'll send My messenger and He'll prepare the way before Me, and the Lord whom you seek will suddenly come to His temple, the messenger of the covenant whom you delight in, He will come, says the Lord of Hosts. 2 But who can endure the day of His coming? And who will be able to stand when He appears? For He's like a refiner's fire and like launderers' soap. 3 He'll sit as a refiner and purifier of silver, and He'll purify the sons of Levi and refine them as gold and silver, that they may offer to the Lord an offering in righteousness. 4 Then will the offering of Judah and Jerusalem be accepted by the Lord, as in the days of old and as in former years. 5 And I'll conduct a trial in which I'll testify against their false ministers, and against the adulterers, and against those who lie under oath, and against those that cheat the laborer by underpaying his wages, cheat widows, and orphans, and are cruel to foreigners, disobeying Me, says the Lord of Hosts. 6 I the Lord, do not change; that's why you children of Jacob aren't already destroyed.

II

7 Ever since the time of your ancestors you've disobeyed Me and changed the ordinances instead of respecting them. Come back to Me and I'll come back to you, says the Lord of Hosts. But you ask: What do You mean, return? 8 Can a person rob God? Yet you've robbed Me. But you ask: How have we robbed You? You've stolen tithes and offerings. 9 You're cursed with a curse, because you've robbed Me, including this whole nation. 10 Bring all your tithes into the storehouse, so there's food in My temple, and test Me, whether I, the Lord of Hosts, won't open the windows of heaven and pour out a blessing upon you so great you won't have enough room to store it. 11 And I'll drive away pests, protecting your crops, and your vineyards will produce in abundance, says the Lord of Hosts. 12 Then every nation will call you blessed, for you'll occupy a delightful land, says the Lord of Hosts.

III

13 Your words have been arrogant against Me, says the Lord. But you ask: What have we said against You? 14 You've said: It's useless to serve God. What benefit have we gotten from keeping His ordinances

and repenting before the Lord of Hosts? ¹⁵ We can see the arrogant are blessed, cheaters get rich, evildoers aren't punished, and those who dare God to punish them aren't punished.

IV ¹⁶ Then those who respected the Lord prayed about it, and the Lord listened and was persuaded. An account was written up and presented to Him on behalf of those who worshiped the Lord and respected His name. ¹⁷ I'll protect them in the day of judgment as My treasured fruit, says the Lord of Hosts. And I'll have compassion for them like a father has compassion for his own faithful son. ¹⁸ Then you'll see the distinction between the righteous and the wicked, between one who serves God and one who does not. **25** There's a day coming that will burn like an oven, and all the proud, and all that are wicked, will burn like straw; entirely burned up, roots, branches, and all.

V ² But for everyone who reveres My name, the Son of Righteousness will rise with healing in His wings. And you'll go out like calves leaping joyfully when let out of the stall; ³ and you'll trample over the wicked, as if they were ashes under the soles of your feet in the day I accomplish this, says the Lord of Hosts. ⁴ Remember the Law of my servant Moses, the statutes and ordinances I commanded him at Horeb for all Israel to follow. ⁵ Know this, I will send you Elijah the prophet before the coming of the great and dreadful day of the Lord, ⁶ and he'll turn the heart of the fathers to the children and the hearts of the children to their fathers, otherwise I will return and utterly curse the earth.

VI **26** When Jesus had said this, He explained it to the crowd. He explained everything to them, both great and small. ² He said: These scriptures, which you didn't have, the Father commanded Me to give to you. Because He wisely wants them to be given to future generations. ³ Then He explained everything, from the very beginning until the time when He would return in His glory — indeed, everything that would happen on earth — until the elements are melted with intense heat, the earth is rolled together like a scroll, and the heavens and earth end, ⁴ everything leading to the great and last day when all people of every nation, tribe, and language will stand in front of God to be judged for their works, whether they're good or evil. ⁵ If they're good, to the resurrection of everlasting life; and if they're evil, to the resurrection of damnation, balanced, the one on the one hand and the other on the other hand. This conforms to the mercy, justice, and holiness in Christ, who existed before the world began.

Chapter 12

6 And now not even one percent of what Jesus taught the people can be written in this book. 7 But the plates of Nephi contain most of what He taught the people. 8 I've written these few things He taught the people, intending for them to be brought back to this people from the Gentiles, as Jesus has explained. 9 After they get this first to test their faith, if they believe this record, then greater things will be added to them. 10 If they refuse to believe this record, then the greater things will be withheld from them to their condemnation. 11 I was about to write everything that was engraved on the plates of Nephi, but the Lord forbids it, saying: I'll test the faith of My people. 12 Therefore I'm writing only the things I've been commanded to write by the Lord. Now I will finish this by adding what I've been commanded to write. 13 Therefore I want you to know the Lord truly taught the people for three days. After that, He showed Himself to them frequently: breaking bread with them, blessing it, and giving it to them.

II   14 He taught their children and ministered to them as mentioned previously, and He inspired their tongues. They said great and astonishing things to their parents, including greater things than He had revealed to the people; and He inspired their tongues so they could speak. 15 He ascended into heaven to the Father a second time following His visit with them during which He healed their sick and crippled, opened the eyes of the blind, unstopped the ears of the deaf, and performed many cures for them, including raising a man from the dead, displaying His power to them before ascending again to the Father. 16 The next day many people assembled. And they both saw and heard the children, including very young children, who opened their mouths and said astonishing things. What they said was forbidden for anyone to write.

III   17 And Jesus' disciples began from then on to baptize and teach anyone who came to them. Those who were baptized in the name of Jesus were filled with the Holy Ghost. 18 Many of them saw and heard unspeakable things that aren't lawful to be written. 19 They taught and ministered to each other; and they had all things common among them, everyone dealing fairly with each other. 20 And they did everything just as Jesus had commanded them. 21 Those who were baptized in the name of Jesus were called the congregation of Christ.

IV   **27** As the disciples of Jesus were traveling and preaching the things they had both heard and seen and were baptizing in Jesus' name, the disciples had gathered and were united in powerful prayer and fasting. 2 Jesus showed Himself to them again, since they were praying to the Father in His name. Jesus came and stood among them, asking them: What would you like Me to give you? ³ They answered Him: Lord, we would like You to tell us the name we should give this congregation, because the people are arguing about this. ⁴ The Lord answered them: In truth I tell you: Why are the people complaining and arguing about this? ⁵ Haven't they read the scripture that says: You must take upon yourself the name of Christ, which is My name. For this is the name you'll be called by on the last day. ⁶ Whoever takes upon them My name and continues faithful to the end will be saved on the last day. ⁷ Therefore whatever you do, you must do in My name. Therefore you must give the congregation My name. You must call on the Father in My name, so He will bless the congregation because of Me. ⁸ How can it be My congregation unless it's given My name? If a congregation is given Moses' name, then it's Moses' congregation. Or if it's given the name of a man, then it's the congregation of a man. But if it's given My name, then it's My congregation, if they're actually built on My gospel. ⁹ Truly I tell you that you're built on My gospel; therefore you must do everything you do in My name. Therefore if you call on the Father on behalf of the congregation, the Father will hear you if you do it in My name. ¹⁰ If the congregation is built on My gospel, then the Father will display His own works in it. ¹¹ But if it's not built on My gospel and is built on the works that men do or on the works that the accuser does, truly I tell you, their works will bring them joy for a time; but soon the end will come, and they'll be cut down and thrown into the fire from where there's no return. ¹² Their works will follow them; since it's because of their works they'll be cut down. Therefore remember what I've told you.

V   ¹³ I've given you My gospel. This is the gospel I've given to you, that I came into the world to do the will of My Father, because My Father sent Me. ¹⁴ And My Father sent Me so I could be lifted up on the cross — and after I've been lifted up on the cross, I can bring all people to Me, so that as I've been lifted up by people, likewise people will be lifted up by the Father to stand before Me to be judged according to their works, whether they were good or whether they were evil. ¹⁵ This is why I've been lifted up. Therefore, according to the Father's power, I will draw everyone to Me so they can be judged according to their works. ¹⁶ Those who repent and are baptized in My name will be fully rewarded. If they continue faithful to the end, I'll hold them guiltless in the presence of My Father when I stand to judge the world. ¹⁷ Those who don't continue faithful to the end, they're the ones who will also be cut down and thrown into the fire from which they can't return again because of the Father's justice. ¹⁸ This is the message He's given to mankind. This is why He acts consistent with the message He's given; He doesn't lie but fulfills all His words. 19 No unclean thing can enter His kingdom. Therefore no one enters His rest except those who have washed their clothes in My blood because of their faith, and repentance of all their sins, and their faithfulness to the end. 20 Now this is the commandment: Repent, everyone, throughout the earth, and come to Me and be baptized in My name, so you can be sanctified by receiving the Holy Ghost, so you can stand spotless in My presence on the last day. 21 Therefore I tell you: This is My gospel. You know what you must do in My congregation. You must do the works that you've seen Me do; because what you've seen Me do is precisely what you must also do. 22 Therefore if you do these things, you are blessed, since you'll be lifted up on the last day.

Chapter 13

23 Write what you've seen and heard, but don't write those things that are forbidden. 24 Write the things the people do in the future, just as what's happened has been written. 25 Because this people will be judged from the books that have been written and will be written, everyone will learn about their works through them. 26 The Father keeps a record of everything. Therefore the world will be judged from the books that will be written. 27 And you should understand you'll be judges of this people, following the judgment I'll provide to you, which will be just and true. Therefore what type of men should you be? Truly I say to you: Precisely as I Am. 28 Now I will go to the Father. Truthfully I tell you: Anything you ask the Father in My name will be given to you. 29 Therefore ask and you will receive; knock and it will be opened to you. Because those who ask receive; and those who knock, it will be opened to them. 30 Now My joy is great, to the point of being completely filled with joy, because of you and this generation. Now even the Father rejoices, and the holy angels also, because of you and this generation, because none of them are lost. 31 I want to clarify that I mean those of this generation who are currently alive. None of them are lost, and I have a fullness of joy in them. 32 But I feel sadness for the fourth generation from you, because they will be led away captive by the accuser, just as the son of perdition was. They will sell Me for silver and gold and for things that moths destroy and thieves can break in and steal. And I'll punish them at that time and let the violent experience violence.

II   33 When Jesus had finished saying this, He advised His disciples: Enter through the narrow gate. Because the gate is narrow and the pathway tight leading to life, and very few find it. But the gate is wide and the way is easy leading to death, and a great number follow it until the night comes when no one can work.

III   **28** After Jesus said this, He spoke to His disciples one by one, asking them: What is it that you would ask from Me after I've gone to the Father? 2 They all answered, except for three, saying: We would ask that once the ministry you've called us to comes to an end, and we've lived to a suitable age, that we can speedily go to join You in Your kingdom. 3 He said to them: You're blessed for asking this of Me. Therefore after you're 72 years old, you'll join Me in My kingdom, to rest there with Me. 4 When He had spoken to them, He turned around to the three and asked them: What would you like Me to do for you when I've gone to the Father? 5 They were afraid and unwilling to ask Him what it was they wanted. 6 And He said to them: I know your thoughts. You want the same thing John My beloved — who was with Me in My ministry before I was lifted up by the Jews — asked from Me. 7 Therefore you're more blessed. You'll never experience death, but you'll live to observe everything the Father does for mankind, until all things are fulfilled according to the Father's will, and I return in My glory with the Powers of heaven. 8 You'll never experience the pains of death. But when I come in My glory, you'll be changed in the blink of an eye from mortality to immortality. Then you'll be blessed in My Father's kingdom. 9 In addition, you won't feel pain while you remain on earth as mortals, nor any sadness other than for the sins of the world. I'll do all this because of what you've asked of Me since you've asked to bring souls to Me while the world lasts. 10 You'll have a full measure of joy because of this, and you'll arrive in My Father's kingdom. Your joy will be full, just like the Father has given Me fullness of joy. And you'll be just like I am, and I am just like the Father, and the Father and I are united as one. 11 And the Holy Ghost testifies of the Father and Me. And the Father gives the Holy Ghost to mankind because of Me.

IV   12 When Jesus had spoken these words, He touched each of them with His finger, all except for the three who were to remain; and then He left. 13 The heavens opened, and the three were taken up to heaven and saw and heard unspeakable things. 14 They were forbidden to reveal it, neither were they given power to explain the things they saw and heard. 15 Whether they remained in their bodies or left their bodies, they couldn't tell. But it seemed to them that they had been transfigured, and were changed from this body of flesh into an immortal state, so they could behold the things of God. 16 Afterward, they ministered once more on the earth. Nevertheless, they didn't teach about the things they had heard and seen because of the commandment given to them in heaven. 17 Now whether they were mortal or immortal from the day of their transfiguration, I don't know. 18 But I do know this much based on the record that's been given: they traveled throughout the land and ministered to all the people, bringing into the congregation those who believed their preaching, baptizing them; and those who were baptized received the Holy Ghost. 19 Those who didn't belong to the congregation threw them in prison. But prisons couldn't hold them and were split apart. 20 They were thrown into pits, but they struck the earth with God's word, and by His power they were freed from these deep pits. No one was able to dig pits deep enough to hold them. 21 They were thrown into a furnace three times and weren't harmed. 22 They were thrown into a den of wild animals twice, and they played with the animals like a child with a nursing lamb and weren't harmed. 23 So they traveled among all the Nephites and preached Christ's gospel to everyone in the land, and the people were converted to the Lord and were united to Christ's congregation. Therefore the people of that generation were blessed as Jesus foretold.

V   24 Now I Mormon will conclude these things. 25 I was about to write the names of those who were never to experience death, but the Lord forbids it. Therefore I won't write them, because they're hidden from the world. 26 But I've seen them, and they've ministered to me. 27 In the future, they'll be among the Gentiles, and yet the Gentiles won't know who they are. 28 They'll also be among the Jews, and yet the Jews won't know who they are either. 29 When the Lord in His wisdom determines it's the right time, they'll minister to the scattered tribes of Israel and to people of every nation, tribe, and language, and they'll bring many souls to Jesus, as they requested, because of the persuading power of God that's in them. 30 They're just like God's angels. And if they pray to the Father in the name of Jesus, they can show themselves to anyone they think it advisable. 31 Therefore they will do great and awe-inspiring things before the great day arrives when all people will certainly stand before Christ's judgment seat. 32 They will even do a great and awe-inspiring work among the Gentiles before that judgment day. 33 And if you had all the scriptures that give an account of every one of Christ's awe-inspiring works, then you would realize every one of Christ's words have and will certainly take place. 34 Woe to anyone who refuses to listen to Jesus' words and the words of those He has chosen and sent to them. Anyone who doesn't receive Jesus' words and the words of those He sends, doesn't accept Him, and therefore He won't accept them on the last day. 35 It would be better for them if they hadn't been born. Do you think you can gain salvation after trampling God underfoot as you ignore the God you offend?

VI   36 Now as I spoke about those whom the Lord had chosen — the three who were caught up into the heavens — that I didn't know whether they were changed from mortality to immortality — 37 but since I wrote, I asked the Lord; and He's informed me there had to be a change made to their bodies, otherwise, they would have died. 38 Therefore to avoid their death, a change was made to their bodies so they wouldn't suffer pain or sorrow, except for the sins of the world. 39 Now this change wasn't equivalent to the one that will take place on the last day, but a change was still made to them, so Satan couldn't have any power over them, and he couldn't tempt them. They were sanctified in the flesh and made holy so that earthly decline no longer affected them. 40 They'll remain in this state until the judgment day of Christ. Then at that time they'll receive a greater change and be taken into the Father's kingdom, never to leave, but to live with God eternally in the heavens.

VII   **29** Now I tell you when the Lord in His wisdom decides it's the right time for this record to be given to the Gentiles according to His word, then know the covenant the Father made with the children of Israel regarding them being restored to their lands of inheritance is already happening. 2 You should realize the Lord's prophecies by the holy prophets will all be fulfilled. There won't be any reason for you to say the Lord is delaying His coming to the children of Israel; 3 there won't be any reason for you to imagine the prophecies are meaningless. Indeed, the Lord will remember the covenant He made for His people of the house of Israel. 4 When you read this record, you should no longer ignore everything the Lord has done. His sword of justice is already in His right hand. Then, if you betray and ignore Him, His justice will quickly overtake you.

VIII   5 Woe to those who treat the things the Lord does with contempt. Woe to those who deny Christ and His sacrifices for you. 6 Woe to those who deny the Lord's revelations and say: The Lord no longer inspires revelation, prophecy, gifts, tongues, healings, or the power of the Holy Ghost. 7 Woe to those who claim Jesus Christ can't perform miracles, seeking to get paid. Those claiming this will be like the son of perdition, for whom there's no mercy, according to Christ's words. 8 Moreover, there will no longer be any reason to mock, despise, or ridicule the Jews or any remnant of the house of Israel. The Lord remembers His covenant to them, and He'll vindicate what He has promised. 9 Therefore there's no reason for you to think you can turn the Lord's right hand to the left, or that He isn't able to execute judgment in order to fulfill the covenant He made to the house of Israel.

Chapter 14

30 Listen all you Gentiles; hear the words of Jesus Christ, the Son of the living God, which He commanded me to write about you. He commands me to write this: 2 Turn away, all you Gentiles, from your wicked ways and repent of your evil deeds, your lying and deceiving, your whoredoms, your secret abominations and idolatrous ways, your murders, priestcrafts, envying, and strife, and from all your wickedness and abominations, and come to Me and be baptized in My name, so you can receive a remission of your sins and receive the Holy Ghost, so you can be included with My people of the house of Israel.

THE FOURTH BOOK OF NEPHI

WHO WAS THE SON OF NEPHI, ONE OF CHRIST'S DISCIPLES

An account of the Nephites according to his record.

The 34th year came to an end and the 35th year as well, and Jesus' disciples had formed a congregation of Christ in every surrounding land. Those who came to them and truly repented of their sins were baptized in Jesus' name and received the Holy Ghost. 2 In the 36th year, the people were all converted to the Lord throughout the land, both Nephites and Lamanites. There were no conflicts or disputes among them. Everyone dealt fairly and honestly with each other. 3 They had all things in common, so there weren't any rich or poor people, enslaved or free people, but they were all given their freedom and allowed to share in the heavenly gift.

II   4 The 37th year came to an end as well, and peace still prevailed in the land. 5 Jesus' disciples performed great miracles, as they healed the sick, raised the dead, and caused the crippled to walk, the blind to see, and the deaf to hear. And they performed all kinds of miracles among the people, and they didn't do any miracles without doing them in Jesus' name. 6 So the 38th year ended, and the 39th as well, and the 41st and 42nd, up until 49 years had come to an end, and the 51st and 52nd, until 59 years also ended. 7 The Lord blessed them with great prosperity in the land, so they built cities again where they had been burned. 8 They rebuilt that great city of Zarahemla again. 9 But there were many cities that had been sunk and water came up in their place, therefore these cities couldn't be restored. 10 The Nephites grew strong and very quickly increased in numbers and became a very beautiful and delightful people. 11 They were married and given in marriage, and were blessed according to the many promises the Lord had made to them. 12 They didn't perform the rites and ordinances of the Law of Moses anymore, but they obeyed the commandments they received from their Lord and God, continuing in fasting and prayer and in meeting together often, both to pray and hear the Lord's word. 13 There were no conflicts among the people in the whole land, but there were mighty miracles happening among Jesus' disciples.

III   14 The 71st year came to an end, and the 72nd year as well, and in short, up to the 79th year passed by; indeed, 100 years came and went. And the disciples of Jesus, whom He had chosen, had all gone to God's paradise, except for the three who were to remain. Other disciples were ordained to replace them, and many of that generation also died. 15 There were no conflicts in the land because of God's love that filled the people's hearts. 16 There was no envying or disputes or disturbances or whoredoms or lying or murder or any kind of unrestrained, lustful conduct. There certainly couldn't have been a happier people among all the people created by God. 17 There were no robbers or murderers, neither were there Lamanites or any kind of ites, but they were united, Christ's children, and heirs to God's kingdom. 18 How they were blessed! The Lord blessed them in everything they did, and they were blessed and given prosperity until 110 years had ended. And the first generation after Christ had died, and there were no conflicts in the whole land.

IV   19 And Nephi — the one who kept this last record, and he kept it on the plates of Nephi — died, and his son Amos kept it in his place. He also kept it on the plates of Nephi; 20 and he kept it for 84 years. There was still peace in the land except for a small part of the people who had revolted from the congregation and taken upon themselves the name of Lamanites. So there were once again Lamanites in the land. 21 And Amos died as well. And it was 194 years from Christ's coming, and his son Amos kept the record in his place. He also kept it on the plates of Nephi; and it was also recorded in Nephi's book, meaning this book. 22 And 200 years ended, and the second generation had all died except for a few.

V   23 Now I Mormon want you to know the number of people increased to such an extent that they had spread throughout the land, and they had become very wealthy because Christ blessed them with prosperity. 24 In the 201st year, some began to be lifted up in pride, such as wearing expensive clothing and all kinds of fine pearls and wealthy possessions. 25 From then on, they no longer shared their goods and material possessions equally. 26 They began to be divided into classes. They began to build up churches to themselves to make money, and they began to deny Christ's true congregation.

VI   27 When 210 years had ended, there were many churches in the land. There were churches that claimed to know Christ, yet denied most of His gospel, so that they accepted all kinds of wickedness and administered sacred things to those to whom it had been forbidden, because of unworthiness. 28 This church grew tremendously in size because of iniquity and the power of Satan, who had seized control of their hearts. 29 There was another church that denied Christ. They persecuted those who belonged to Christ's true congregation because of their humility and belief in Christ. They despised them because of the many miracles that happened among them. 30 So they exerted power and control over Jesus' disciples who remained with them. They threw them in prison; but by the power of God's word that was in them, the prisons were split apart; and they went out performing mighty miracles. 31 Nevertheless — and despite all these miracles — the people hardened their hearts and tried to kill them, just as the Jews at Jerusalem decided to kill Jesus, according to His testimony. 32 They threw them in blazing furnaces, yet they emerged unharmed. 33 They also threw them in the dens of wild animals, but they played with the wild animals just like a child with a lamb; and they emerged unharmed. 34 The people, however, hardened their hearts, because many priests and false prophets led them to build up many churches and do all kinds of iniquity. They would hit the people of Jesus, but the people of Jesus wouldn't hit back. And so they dwindled away into unbelief and wickedness from year to year, until 230 years came to an end.

VII   35 Now in the 231st year there was a great separation among the people. 36 In this year some people began calling themselves Nephites, and they were true believers in Christ. Among them were others the Lamanites called Jacobites, Josephites, and Zoramites. 37 Therefore the true believers in Christ and the true worshipers of Christ, which included the three disciples of Jesus who were divinely appointed to remain on earth, were called Nephites, Jacobites, Josephites, and Zoramites. 38 Those who rejected the gospel were called Lamanites, Lemuelites, and Ishmaelites. They didn't slowly dwindle into unbelief, but they willfully rebelled against Christ's gospel. They taught their children not to believe, just as their ancestors fell away at the beginning. 39 It was because of their parents' wickedness and abominations, just like it was at the beginning. They were taught to hate God's children, just as the Lamanites were taught to hate Nephi's children from the beginning. 40 And 244 years had ended, and this was the state of affairs among the people. The more wicked part of the people grew in strength and outnumbered God's people. 41 They continued to build up churches for themselves and decorate them with a variety of precious things. So 250 years ended, and 260 years as well.

VIII   42 Then the wicked part of the people again began to build up Gaddianton's secret oaths and conspiracies. 43 And the Nephites began to be prideful as well, because of their great wealth, and they became vain like their fellow Lamanites. 44 Starting at this time, the disciples began to grieve for the world's sins. 45 When 300 years had ended, both the Nephites and Lamanites had become very wicked, the one like the other. 46 And Gaddianton's robbers spread throughout the land. No one was righteous, except for Jesus' disciples. The people accumulated gold and silver in abundance and traded all kinds of goods.

IX   47 After 305 years had ended — and the people persisted in doing evil — Amos died, and his brother Ammaron kept the record in his place. 48 When 320 years came to an end, Ammaron, compelled by the Holy Ghost, hid all the sacred records that had been handed down from generation to generation until the 320th year from Christ's coming. 49 He concealed them with the Lord's protection so that they could be returned to the remnant of Jacob's family, according to the Lord's prophecies and promises. This is the end of Ammaron's record.

THE BOOK OF MORMON

Chapter 1

Now I Mormon will make a record of what I've both seen and heard, calling it the Book of Mormon. 2 Around the time Ammaron concealed the records under the Lord's care, he came to talk to me. I was about 10 years old and had by then begun to be somewhat educated in the way my people were taught. Ammaron said to me: I can see you're a dependable and mindful child. 3 Therefore when you're about 24 years old, I want you to remember what you've seen about this people. When you reach that age, go to the land of Antum to a hill called Shim. There I've deposited with the Lord's protection all the sacred records regarding this people. 4 You must take possession of the plates of Nephi, leaving the rest where they are. Then you must add to the plates of Nephi everything you've observed about this people. 5 I'm a descendant of Nephi, and my father's name was Mormon, and I remembered what Ammaron commanded me.

II   6 When I was 11 years old, I was taken by my father to the south land, all the way to Zarahemla. 7 The whole land was covered with buildings; and the people seemed to be as numerous as the sand of the sea.

III   8,9 In this year, a war broke out between the Nephites and Lamanites — that is, between the Nephites, Jacobites, Josephites, and Zoramites on the one hand, and the Lamanites, Lemuelites, and Ishmaelites on the other. 10 The war began between them at the border of Zarahemla by the Sidon River. 11 The Nephites had gathered a large number of men, more than thirty thousand. In this same year there were several battles, in which the Nephites defeated the Lamanites and killed many of them.

IV   12 The Lamanites withdrew their plans, and peace was achieved in the land. The peace lasted for about four years, in which there was no killing. 13 But wickedness abounded throughout the land, so much so that the Lord removed His beloved disciples; and the work of miracles and healing stopped because of the people's iniquity. 14 And there were no gifts from the Lord. The Holy Ghost didn't come upon anyone because of their wickedness and unbelief. 15 When I was 15 years old, and because I was fairly serious-minded and mature, the Lord visited me, and I experienced and understood the goodness of Jesus. 16 I tried to preach to the people, but my mouth was shut. I was forbidden to preach to them because they had willfully rebelled against God. The beloved disciples departed from the land because of the people's iniquity. 17 I remained among them, but I was forbidden to preach to them because of the hardness of their hearts. Because of the hardness of their hearts, the land was cursed. 18 And the Gaddianton robbers, who were among the Lamanites, raided the land, so much so the inhabitants began to hide their valuables in the earth; and they slipped away because the Lord had cursed the land, so they couldn't hold onto them or recover them. 19 There was sorcery, witchcraft, and dark magic; and the power of the Evil One spread throughout the land, as prophesied by Abinadi and Samuel the Lamanite.

V   2 In that same year, a war began again between the Nephites and Lamanites. Despite being young, I was big and strong, so the Nephites appointed me to lead their armed forces. 2 Therefore in my 16th year, at the end of the 326th year, I led a Nephite army against the Lamanites. 3 In the 327th year, the Lamanites attacked us with enormous strength, to such a degree they intimidated my armed forces. As a result, they refused to fight and began to retreat to the northern regions. 4 We arrived at the city of Angolah and took control of it and prepared to defend ourselves against the Lamanites. We fortified the city to the utmost of our ability. But despite our fortifications, the Lamanites attacked, overwhelmed us, and drove us out of the city. 5 They also drove us out of the land of David. 6 And we marched until we arrived in the land of Joshua, which was to the west bordering the seashore. 7 We gathered our people as fast as possible, so we could get them in a single group. 8 But the land was filled with robbers and Lamanites. Despite the great destruction hanging over my people, they didn't repent of their evildoing. Therefore blood and carnage spread everywhere on that land, slaughtering both the Nephites and Lamanites. The entire government was completely overthrown throughout the land. 9 Now the Lamanites had a king, and his name was Aaron. He attacked us with an army of 44,000. I fought him with 42,000. I beat him with my army, causing him to hastily retreat. All this took place, and 330 years ended.

VI   10 Then the Nephites began to repent of their iniquity and cry out in anguish, just as Samuel the prophet had prophesied. No one could keep what belonged to them because of the thieves, robbers, murderers, magic art, and witchcraft in the land. 11 So everyone throughout the land — but particularly the Nephites — began to mourn and regret these circumstances. 12 When I saw their grief, mourning, and sorrow before the Lord, my heart began to rejoice. I personally knew of the Lord's mercy and long-suffering, and so I believed He would be merciful to them and they could again become a righteous people. 13 But my joy was futile; their sorrow wasn't toward repentance because of God's goodness, but they were experiencing instead the sorrow of the damned because the Lord wouldn't let them be happy in their sins. 14 They didn't come to Jesus with a broken heart and contrite spirit, but they cursed God and wished to die. Still, they were willing to fight with the sword for their lives. 15 So my sadness returned. I realized the day of grace had ended for them, both temporally and spiritually. I saw thousands of them cut down in open rebellion against God and piled up like manure on the land. And so 344 years concluded.

VII   16 In the 345th year, the Nephites began to retreat from the Lamanites, and were chased all the way to Jashon before it became possible to stop them in their retreat. 17 Now the city of Jashon was near the place Ammaron had deposited the records under the Lord's protection to prevent them from being destroyed. So I followed Ammaron's directions and went and retrieved the plates of Nephi and added to the record as he asked. 18 I made a full account of all the wickedness and abominations on the plates of Nephi; but on these plates I refrained from making a full account. I've been an eyewitness of continual wickedness and abominations ever since I was able to observe people's behavior. 19 I mourn because of their wickedness; my heart has been filled with sorrow my whole life because of their wickedness. Nevertheless, I know I'll be lifted up on the last day.

VIII   20 During this year, the Nephites were again hunted and driven. We were pushed back until we arrived northward to the land called Shem. 21 We fortified the city of Shem and gathered our people there as much as possible, so we could try to protect and save them. 22 In the 346th year, they attacked us again. 23 And I spoke to my people and tried hard to rally them to bravely confront the Lamanites and fight for their wives, children, houses, and homes. 24 My words to a degree stirred them to action so that they didn't flee from the Lamanites but stood bravely against them. 25 We fought against an army of 50,000 with an army of 30,000. We successfully withstood their attack and they retreated hastily. 26 When they ran away, we chased them with our armed forces and fought again and beat them. Still, the Lord's strength wasn't with us. We were left to ourselves, so the Spirit of the Lord didn't assist us. Therefore we were as weak as our Lamanite brothers. 27 I mourned over the terrible misfortune of my people caused by their wickedness and abominations. Yet we took the fight to the Lamanites and the Gaddianton robbers until we regained possession of our own lands. 28 And the 349th year ended. In the 350th year, we made a treaty with the Lamanites and the Gaddianton robbers, in which we divided up our lands. 29 The Lamanites gave us the land to the north, as far as the narrow passage leading to the land to the south. We gave the Lamanites all the land to the south.

IX   3 The Lamanites didn't come to battle again until ten more years had passed. During that time, I had the Nephites work on preparing their lands and weapons for the next battle. 2 The Lord said to me: Proclaim to this people: Repent and come to Me and be baptized, build up my congregation again, and you'll be spared. 3 I proclaimed this to my people, but it was useless. They didn't realize it was the Lord who had spared them and given them a chance for repentance. So they hardened their hearts against the Lord their God. 4 After this 10th year had ended, making a total of 360 years since Christ's coming, the Lamanite king sent me a letter informing me they were preparing to attack us again. 5 I had my people gather at the land of Desolation at a city near the border, at the narrow pass leading into the land to the south. 6 We placed our armies there so we could stop the Lamanite armies, to prevent losing any of our lands. Therefore we fortified against the attack to the best of our ability.

x   7 In the 361st year, the Lamanites attacked the city of Desolation.
We defeated them in that year, and they returned to their own lands.
8 In the 362nd year, they returned and attacked again. We defeated
them again and killed a large number of them, and their dead were
thrown into the sea. 9 Now because of this great accomplishment by
my people the Nephites, they started boasting about their strength and
they swore an oath before the heavens that they would avenge
themselves of the blood of their brothers who were killed by their
enemies. 10 They swore an oath by the heavens and by God's throne
that they would attack their enemies, destroy them, and remove them
from the land.

xi   11 I absolutely refused from that time on to be a commander and
leader of this people because of their wickedness and abominations.
12 I had led them into battle many times, despite their wickedness, and
I had loved them, with a godly love and all my heart. I had poured out
my soul in prayer to God all day long for them. However, I did this
without any hope because of the hardness of their hearts. 13 For I had
saved them from their enemies three times and they didn't repent of
their sins. 14 When they had sworn an oath by all that had been
forbidden them by our Lord and Savior Jesus Christ, that they would
go against their enemies in battle and avenge themselves of their
brothers' blood, the Lord said to me: 15 Vengeance is Mine; I will repay.
And because this people didn't repent after I had saved them, they will
be destroyed and removed from the earth.

xii   16 So I absolutely refused to lead the attack against my enemies. I
did just as the Lord had commanded me, standing and witnessing as a
bystander in order to document for the world what I saw and heard,
following the Spirit that told me what was coming. 17 Therefore I'm
writing to you Gentiles, and to the house of Israel as well, when the
work begins, you'll be at the beginning of preparing to return to the
land of your inheritance. 18 I'm writing for the twelve tribes of Israel
scattered everywhere on earth, who will be judged according to your
works by the Twelve whom Jesus chose to be His disciples in the land
of Jerusalem. 19 I'm also writing to the remnant of this people, who will
be judged by the twelve whom Jesus chose in this land, who in turn will
be judged by the other Twelve whom Jesus chose in the land of
Jerusalem. 20 And it's the Spirit teaching these things to me. Therefore
I'm writing to all of you; I'm writing to let you know that all of you will
stand before Christ's judgment seat, every soul belonging to the whole
human family of Adam: You'll stand to be judged for your works,
whether they were good or evil. 21 Also I want you to believe the gospel
of Jesus Christ, which will be available to you, and also so the Jews, the

Lord's covenant people, will have another witness, in addition to Him they saw and heard, that Jesus, whom they killed, was the true Messiah and the true God. ²² It's my wish to be able to persuade everyone, all over the earth, to repent and prepare to stand before Christ's judgment seat.

Chapter 2

4 In the 363rd year, the Nephites attacked the Lamanites with their armed forces from the land of Desolation. ² But the Nephite forces were pushed back to the land of Desolation. While they were exhausted, a fresh Lamanite army attacked them. They had a fierce battle, resulting in the Lamanites taking the city of Desolation and killing many Nephites, and taking many prisoners. ³ The survivors fled and joined the inhabitants of the city of Teancum. Now the city of Teancum was near the seashore, and close to the city of Desolation. ⁴ It was because the Nephite armies attacked the Lamanites that they began to be destroyed; otherwise, the Lamanites wouldn't have been able to defeat them. ⁵ But God's judgments will overtake the wicked. And it's by the wicked that the wicked are punished. Because it's the wicked who incite mankind to violence. ⁶ And the Lamanites prepared to attack the city of Teancum.

II ⁷ In the 364th year, the Lamanites attacked the city of Teancum, trying to take control of it. ⁸ But they were repulsed and driven back by the Nephites. When the Nephites saw they had driven the Lamanites back, they again boasted about their strength. They went out relying on their own strength and retook the city of Desolation. ⁹ Now thousands had been killed on both sides, on the part of both the Nephites and Lamanites while all this happened. ¹⁰ And the 366th year ended, and the Lamanites once again attacked the Nephites. Yet the Nephites didn't repent but persisted in their wickedness. ¹¹ It's impossible for the tongue to describe or for a person to write a complete description of the horrible scene of blood and carnage that occurred among both the Nephites and Lamanites. Every heart was hardened so that they enjoyed killing continually. ¹² There had never been such great wickedness among Lehi's descendants, not even among the whole house of Israel, according to the Lord's words, as took place among this people.

III ¹³ The Lamanites took the city of Desolation — and this was because they outnumbered the Nephites. ¹⁴ They also marched against the city of Teancum and drove out the inhabitants and took many women and children prisoners, and then offered them up as sacrifices to their idol gods. 15 In the 367th year, the Nephites were angry because the Lamanites had sacrificed their women and children. And they attacked the Lamanites with fury, and again beat the Lamanites and drove them out of their lands. 16 The Lamanites didn't return to attack the Nephites until the 375th year. 17 In that year, they came down and attacked them with all their power; there were so many they weren't counted. 18 From that time on, the Nephites never had any success against the Lamanites, but began to be swept away like dew exposed to the sun. 19 The Lamanites attacked the city of Desolation. A terrible battle was fought in the land of Desolation, in which they defeated the Nephites. 20 The Nephites ran away to the city of Boaz. There they stood bravely against the Lamanites, and the Lamanites didn't defeat them until a second attack. 21 When they attacked a second time, the Nephites were defeated and killed in a truly great slaughter, and their women and children were again sacrificed to idols. 22 The Nephites again fled, taking all the inhabitants with them, in both towns and villages. 23 When I could see the Lamanites were about to overthrow the land, I went to the hill Shim and recovered all the records Ammaron had hidden away under the Lord's protection.

IV

5 I then united with the Nephites and changed my mind about the oath I made not to help them anymore. They again gave me command of their armies because they looked on me as if I could rescue them from their terrible predicament. 2 But I didn't have any hope; I knew the Lord's judgments would come upon them because they didn't repent of their iniquities but fought for their lives without calling on that Being who had created them. 3 The Lamanites attacked us after we had fled to the city of Jordan. But they were driven back and they didn't take the city at that time. 4 They attacked us again, and we kept the city. There were also other cities defended by the Nephites, and these strongholds stopped their advance, preventing them from entering the countryside behind this line to slaughter the inhabitants of our land. 5 But any place we passed without bringing the inhabitants with us was destroyed by the Lamanites; all the towns, villages, and cities were burned down. And so 379 years came to an end. 6 In the 380th year, the Lamanites attacked us again. We confronted them boldly. But it was useless, because their numbers were so large that they trampled the Nephites underfoot. 7 And we fled again. Those who were faster than the Lamanites escaped; but those who weren't faster were overtaken and killed.

V

8 Now I don't intend to distress people's souls by describing such an awful scene of blood and carnage as I witnessed. But I know these things must be made known. Everything hidden must be revealed on

the housetops. 9 Information about these events must be given to the remnant of this people and to the Gentiles the Lord said would scatter this people like they were nothing. Therefore I write a short summary because I was commanded to do this, not daring to give a full account of the things I've seen because it would be too distressing to describe fully the wickedness of this people.

VI   10 This account is for their descendants and for the Gentiles who care about the house of Israel and realize where their blessings come from. 11 I know the Gentiles will mourn over the misfortunes of the house of Israel. Indeed, they'll grieve over this people's destruction. They'll mourn that this people didn't repent, to then be embraced in the arms of Jesus. 12 Now this record is for the remnant of Jacob's family. This account exists because God knows it was wicked to try and prevent it from being openly exposed. These things are to be hidden away with the Lord's protection, so they can come forth when He decides it's the right time. 13 This is the commandment I've received. They'll become available according to the Lord's commandment when in His wisdom He determines it's proper. 14 This record will go to the unbelieving Jews. They'll get it to persuade them that Jesus is the Messiah, the Son of the living God. This is so the Father through His Most Beloved can accomplish His great commitment to restore the Jews and the whole house of Israel to the lands of their inheritance, which the Lord their God has given them, to fulfill His covenant. 15 It's also for the descendants of this people to more fully believe in His gospel taught to them by the Gentiles. This people will be scattered and become a dark, filthy, and repulsive people, beyond the description of anything before among us or what happened among the Lamanites. This is the result of their unbelief and idol worship. 16 The Spirit of the Lord has already stopped influencing their fathers. They're without Christ and God in the world, and they're driven about by the wind like chaff. 17 They were once a delightful people. They had Christ for their shepherd; indeed, they were even led by God the Father. 18 But now they're led about by Satan, just like chaff is driven by the wind, or like a vessel tossed about on the waves without a sail, anchor, or anything to steer her with; just as she is, so are they. 19 The Lord has reserved the blessing they could have received in the land for the Gentiles who will occupy the land. 20 They'll be driven and scattered by the Gentiles. After they've been driven and scattered by the Gentiles, then the Lord will remember the covenant He made with Abraham for the whole house of Israel. 21 The Lord will also remember the prayers of the righteous offered to Him on their behalf.

VII   22 Then, all you Gentiles, how will you survive against God's power
unless you repent and turn away from doing evil? 23 Don't you realize
you're in God's hands? Don't you realize He has all power and at His
great command the earth will be rolled together as a scroll?
24 Therefore repent and humble yourselves before Him so His
judgment isn't imposed also on you, with the remnant of Jacob's
descendants coming among you as a young lion to tear you apart, with
no one to rescue you.

Chapter 3

6 Now I'll finish my record about the destruction of my people the
Nephites. We marched out to confront the Lamanites. 2 I wrote a letter
to the Lamanite king, asking him to permit us to gather our people to
the land of Cumorah by a hill called Cumorah, where we would
engage them in battle. 3 And the Lamanite king granted my request.
4 We marched to the land of Cumorah and pitched our tents around
the hill Cumorah. It was in a land of many lakes, rivers, and springs.
Here we hoped to gain some advantage over the Lamanites. 5 When
384 years had ended, we had finished gathering the rest of our people
to the land of Cumorah.

II   6 When we finished gathering everyone to the land of Cumorah, I
was old. And because I knew it would be my people's last struggle and
because I had been commanded by the Lord not to allow the sacred
records handed down by our forefathers to fall into Lamanite hands
who would destroy them, I made this record from the plates of Nephi
and hid away all the records entrusted to me by the Lord in the hill
Cumorah, except for these few plates I gave my son, Moroni.

III   7 Then my people, including their wives and children, saw the
Lamanite armies approaching. They waited for the attack with that
awful fear of death that fills the hearts of the wicked. 8 They attacked
us, and every one was terrified because of their overwhelming
numbers. 9 They attacked my people with the sword, bow, arrow, ax,
and all kinds of weapons. 10 My men were cut down, all 10,000 who
were with me, and I was wounded and fell in the middle of them. And
they passed me by and didn't kill me. 11 After they cut down all my
people except for 24 of us, including my son Moroni, on the next day
after the Lamanites had returned to their camps, the survivors of the
slaughter of our people surveyed from the top of the hill Cumorah the
10,000 of my people who were dead. It included all those I led into
battle. 12 We also surveyed the 10,000 led by my son Moroni. 13 And
Gidgiddonah's 10,000 were dead, with him in the middle of them.

¹⁴ And Lamah had died with his 10,000, and Gilgal had died with his 10,000, and Limhah had died with his 10,000, and Joneum had died with his 10,000; and Cumenihah, Moronihah, Antionum, Shiblom, Shem, and Josh had died with their 10,000 each. ¹⁵ There were ten more who died by the sword with their 10,000 each; indeed, everyone except for the 24 who were with me, and a few who had escaped to lands in the south, and another few who defected to the Lamanites. All others were dead. Their flesh, bones, and blood lay on the ground, left by those who killed them to decay on the land and to decompose and return to their mother earth.

IV ¹⁶ My soul was torn with anguish for those of my people who had been killed, and I cried out: ¹⁷ O you beautiful people, how could you have departed from the Lord's ways! O you beautiful people, how could you have rejected that Jesus who stood with open arms to receive you! ¹⁸ If you hadn't done this, you wouldn't have fallen. But you've fallen, and I mourn your loss. ¹⁹ O you beautiful sons and daughters, you fathers and mothers, you husbands and wives, you beautiful people — how is it that you could have fallen! ²⁰ But you're gone, and my sorrow can't bring you back. ²¹ The day will soon come when your mortal body will put on immortality. These decomposing bodies must soon become bodies free from decay. Then you must stand before Christ's judgment seat to be judged according to your works. If you were righteous, then you will be blessed with your forefathers who have gone before you. ²² If only you had repented before this great destruction overtook you! But you're gone. And the Father — indeed, the Eternal Father of heaven — knows your circumstances; He'll do with you according to His justice and mercy.

V **7** Now I would like to speak a little to the remnant of this people who are spared, if God gives them my words, so they can learn about their forefathers. Yes, I speak to you that remain of the house of Israel. This is my message for you: ² Know that you're part of the house of Israel. ³ Know you must repent or you can't be saved. ⁴ Know you must lay down your weapons and never pick them up again, unless God commands you, and you must never enjoy shedding blood. ⁵ Know you must learn about your forefathers and repent of all your sins and iniquities and believe in Jesus Christ, that He is the Son of God and He was killed by the Jews, and that by the power of the Father He has risen again, by which He's gained the victory over the grave. In Him the bitterness of death is swallowed up. ⁶ He brings about the resurrection of the dead, through which mankind will certainly be raised to stand before His judgment seat. ⁷ He has accomplished the world's redemption, so that any who are found guiltless before Him at the judgment day will live in God's presence in His kingdom, to sing unending praises with the choirs above, to the Father, the Son, and the Holy Ghost, which are united as one God, in a state of endless happiness. 8 Therefore repent, be baptized in Jesus' name, and hold firmly to Christ's gospel, which will be set before you, not only in this record but also in the record the Gentiles receive from the Jews, a record the Gentiles will provide to you. 9 Indeed, this record is written so you'll believe that record. If you believe that one, then you'll believe this one also. If you believe this, you'll know about your forefathers and the miraculous works that were done among them by God's power. 10 You'll also know you're a remnant of Jacob's descendants. Therefore you're included among the people of the first covenant. If you believe in Christ and are baptized — first with water, then with fire and the Holy Ghost, following our Savior's example, as He has commanded us — it will be well with you at the judgment day. Amen.

Chapter 4

8 Now I Moroni will finish my father Mormon's record. I only have a few things to write, things I was commanded to write by my father. 2 After the great and awful battle at Cumorah, any Nephites who escaped to the south were hunted by the Lamanites and all killed. 3 They killed my father also. As a result, I'm the only one who remains to write the sad tale of my people's destruction. They're gone, and I will follow my father's commandment. I don't know whether they'll kill me. 4 Therefore I'll write and conceal the records in the ground. It doesn't matter what happens to me. 5 My father has made this record, and he has described its purpose. I would also write about it if I had room on the plates, but I don't. I don't have any ore, as I'm alone. My father was killed in battle, along with all my relatives. I don't have any friends or anywhere to go. I don't know how long the Lord will let me live. 6 Four hundred years have come and gone since the coming of our Lord and Savior. 7 The Lamanites have hunted down my people the Nephites from city to city and place to place until they're all dead. Their fall was immense; indeed, the destruction of my people the Nephites is remarkable and astonishing. 8 It's the Lord's hand that's done it. The Lamanites are now at war with each other — the whole land is one continual round of murder and killing, and no one knows when the war will end.

II   9 Now I won't describe them further, since there isn't anyone living now except Lamanites and robbers. 10 There isn't anyone who knows the true God, except for Jesus' disciples who stayed in the land until the people's wickedness was so great the Lord wouldn't let them remain

with the people. No one knows where they are. 11 But my father and I
have seen them, and they've ministered to us. 12 Whoever receives this
record and doesn't condemn it because of its imperfections will learn
of greater things than these. I'm Moroni. If it were possible, I would
make all things known to you.

III   13 Now I'll finish writing about this people. I'm Mormon's son, and
my father was a descendant of Nephi. 14 I'm the same one who will
hide away this record under the Lord's care. The plates themselves
aren't valuable because of the commandment of the Lord, for He
truly said no one will have them for the purpose of getting rich. But
the record written on them is very valuable. And the Lord will bless
whoever brings it to light. 15 No one can have power to bring it to light
unless God gives it to him, because God ordains it can only be done
with an eye toward His glory or to benefit the Lord's ancient and long-
dispersed covenant people. 16 Blessed is the one who brings this thing
to light; it will be brought out of darkness to light, according to God's
word. Indeed, it will be brought out of the ground. It will shine out
from darkness and come to the knowledge of the people. It will be
done by God's power. 17 If there are any errors, they're human
mistakes; but we don't know of any error. Nevertheless, God knows all
things. Therefore any who condemn, let them be careful not to put
themselves in danger of hell fire. 18 Those who say: Show it to me or
I'll strike you down! Let them be careful not to demand what the Lord
forbids. 19 Because those who judge rashly will in turn be judged rashly;
they'll be paid according to their works. Therefore, those who strike
will in turn be struck by the Lord. 20 Take note of what the scripture
says: People must not inflict harm or judge. The Lord has said:
Judgment is Mine, and vengeance is Mine as well; I will repay. 21 Those
who, in great anger, fight against the Lord's work and against the
Lord's covenant people, who are the house of Israel, and say: We will
destroy the Lord's work, and the Lord won't remember the covenant
He's made to the house of Israel — they're in danger of being cut
down and thrown into the fire. 22 Because the Lord's eternal purposes
will roll on until all His promises are fulfilled.

IV   23 Though I can't write them, study Isaiah's prophecies. Indeed, I
tell you that those holy ones who have come before me and inhabited
this land will cry out to the Lord, even from the dust. As the Lord lives,
He will remember the covenant He made with them. 24 He knows their
prayers on behalf of their fellow brothers and sisters. He knows their
faith, because in His name they could remove mountains, and in His
name they could make the earth shake; and by the power of His word
they made prisons fall to the ground. Not even hot furnaces, wild

animals, or venomous snakes could harm them, because of the power of His word. 25 Their prayers were also on behalf of him whom the Lord will allow to bring this record to light. 26 No one should say that it won't come forth because it surely will, since the Lord has spoken it. It will come out of the earth by the Lord's power, and no one can prevent it. It will appear at a time when people will say miracles are over. It will come just as if one had spoken from the dead. 27 It will come at a time when the blood of holy ones will cry out to the Lord because of secret conspiracies and works of darkness; 28 indeed, at a time when God's power will be denied and churches will have become polluted and consumed with pride to their very center, when church leaders and teachers will be filled with pride to their very center, to the point of being envied by those who belong to their churches. 29 It will come at a time when people will hear of fires, storms, and vapors of smoke in foreign lands. 30 And people will hear of wars, reports of wars, and earthquakes in various places. 31 It will come at a time when there will be great pollutions on the earth: there will be murders, robbing, lying, deceiving, whoredoms, and all kinds of abominations; when there will be many who will say: Do this or do that, it doesn't matter; the Lord will defend you on the last day. But woe to such people: they're bitterly corrupted by sin. 32 It will come at a time when there will be churches built up that will say: Come to me, and for your money you'll be forgiven of your sins.

v   33 O you wicked, perverse, and stubborn people, why have you built up churches to yourselves to get money? Why have you altered God's holy word so as to bring condemnation on your souls? Look to God's revelations, because the time is coming when all these things will certainly be fulfilled. 34 The Lord has shown me great and awe-inspiring things about what's going to take place soon after these words appear among you. 35 Now, I speak to you as though you were present, yet you are not. But Jesus Christ has shown you to me, and I know the things you do. 36 I know you live pridefully. There are none, except for a few, who aren't lifted up in pride to their very center, to the point of wearing very fine clothing, and to the point of envying and strife, malice, persecution, and all kinds of iniquity. Your congregations and churches — every single one of them — have become polluted because of the pride of your hearts. 37 You love money and your material possessions and your fine clothing and decorating your houses of worship more than you love the poor and the needy, the sick and the afflicted. 38 You pollutions, hypocrites, and you teachers who sell yourselves for things that will corrode and decay, why have you polluted God's holy congregation? Why are you ashamed to take upon yourselves the name of Christ? Why don't you consider that the value of an endless happiness is greater than misery that never dies? Isn't it because of the world's praise? 39 Why do you adorn yourselves with things that have no life, and yet allow the hungry, the needy, the naked, the sick, and the afflicted to pass you by and not notice them? 40 Why do you build up your secret abominations for the purpose of getting rich and cause widows and orphans to mourn before the Lord, and make the blood of their fathers and husbands cry to the Lord from the ground for vengeance on your heads? 41 The sword of vengeance hangs over you; and the time is soon coming when He'll avenge the blood of the holy ones upon you, since He won't endure their cries any longer.

VI   **9** Now I'll also speak to those who don't believe in Christ. 2 Will you believe when He returns again? When the Lord comes — indeed, on that great day when the earth is rolled together as a scroll and the material elements melt with intense heat — on that great day when you're brought to stand before the Lamb of God, will you then claim there's no God? 3 Will you then continue to deny Christ, even when you behold the Lamb of God? Do you think you'll live with Him under a consciousness of your guilt? Do you think you could be happy living with that holy Being when your souls are tormented with a consciousness of your guilt, that you've continually abused His laws? 4 I tell you that you would be more miserable living with a holy and righteous God under a consciousness of your filthiness before Him than you would be living with the damned souls in hell. 5 Indeed, when you're brought to see your nakedness before God, as well as the glory of God and the holiness of Jesus Christ, it will light a flame of unquenchable fire in you. 6 O then, you who don't believe, turn to the Lord! Cry powerfully to the Father in Jesus' name, so perhaps you can be found spotless, pure, beautiful, and white on that great and last day, having been cleansed by the Lamb's blood.

VII   7 Again I speak to you that deny God's revelations and say they've ended, that there are no more revelations, prophecies, gifts, healing, speaking in tongues, or the interpretation of tongues. 8 I say to you: Those who deny these things don't know Christ's gospel. Indeed, they haven't read the scriptures; if they have, they don't understand them. 9 Don't we read that God is the same yesterday, today, and forever, and there's no variability or hint of changing in Him? 10 Now if you've pictured to yourselves a god who changes and there's even a trace of changing in him, then you've imagined a god who isn't a God of miracles. 11 But I'll show you a God of miracles — indeed, the God of Abraham, and the God of Isaac, and the God of Jacob. That same

God who created the heavens, the earth, and everything that's in them.
12 He created Adam, and by Adam came the Fall of mankind. And
because of the Fall of mankind came Jesus Christ, namely, the Father
and the Son. Because of Jesus Christ we receive mankind's
redemption. 13 Because of mankind's redemption, which came by Jesus
Christ, they're brought back into the Lord's presence. This is how all
people are redeemed, because Christ's death brings about the
resurrection, which brings about a redemption from an endless sleep,
a sleep from which all people will be awakened by God's power when
the trumpet sounds. They will appear, both small and great, and all
will stand at His place of judgment, being redeemed and freed from
the eternal chains of death, a temporal death. 14 Then the judgment of
the Holy One will be imposed upon them. The time will come when
those that are filthy will remain filthy, and those that are righteous will
remain righteous, and those that are happy will remain happy, and
those that are unhappy will remain unhappy.

VIII   15 Now, all of you that have pictured to yourselves a god who can't
perform any miracles, I want to ask you: Have all these things I've
spoken about ended? Has the end come yet? I tell you: No. God hasn't
stopped being a God of miracles. 16 Doesn't everything created by God
inspire awe? Who can comprehend God's miraculous works? 17 Who
will say it wasn't a miracle that by His word heaven and earth came
into existence, and by the power of His word mankind was created
from the dust of the earth, and by the power of His word miracles
have been performed? 18 Who will say Jesus Christ didn't do many
powerful miracles? And His disciples did many powerful miracles also.
19 If miracles were done, then how has God stopped being a God of
miracles, and yet is an unchangeable Being? I tell you: He doesn't
change; if so, He would stop being God. And He hasn't stopped being
God and is a God of miracles. 20 The reason He stops doing miracles
among mankind is because they fall away in unbelief and turn from
the right way, and don't know the God they should trust.

IX   21 I say to you whoever believes in Christ, without doubting,
anything they ask the Father in the name of Christ will be given to
them. This promise is for everyone, even the whole earth. 22 Now Jesus
Christ, the Son of God, instructed His disciples who were to remain,
and also to all His disciples, which was overheard by the crowd: You
are to go across the world and preach the gospel to everyone.
23 Anyone who believes and is baptized will be saved, but anyone who
doesn't believe will be damned. 24 And these signs will follow those who
believe: In My name they'll cast out devils, they'll speak with new
tongues, they'll handle snakes, and if they drink anything deadly, it

won't hurt them; they'll lay hands on the sick, and they'll recover. 25 And those who believe in My name, who don't doubt, to them I'll confirm all My words, to the farthest reaches of the earth. 26 Now who can stand against the Lord's works? Who can deny His words? Who will rise up against the Lord's almighty power? Who will treat the Lord's works with contempt? Who will treat Christ's children with contempt? Take note, all you that treat the Lord's works with contempt: you will die and be astonished.

X   27 Therefore don't disregard these things, treat them with contempt, or be astonished by them, but pay attention to the Lord's words and ask the Father in Jesus' name for whatever you might need. Don't doubt, but be believing. Begin as in former times and come to the Lord with your whole heart and work out your own salvation before Him with awe and reverence. 28 Be wise in the days of your probation. Rid yourselves of all uncleanliness. Don't ask in order to satisfy your lusts, but ask with unshaken firmness not to yield to any temptation, and to serve the true and living God. 29 Make sure you aren't baptized unworthily. Make sure you don't take the sacrament of Christ unworthily. But make sure you do all things in worthiness and do them in the name of Jesus Christ, the Son of the living God. If you do this and persevere to the end, you won't under any circumstances be thrown out. 30 I speak to you as though I spoke from the dead because I know you'll have my words.

XI   31 Don't condemn me because of my imperfection, or my father because of his imperfection, or those who have written before him, but rather give thanks to God that He has shown you our imperfections, so you can learn to be wiser than we've been. 32 We've written this record, according to our knowledge, in characters we call reformed Egyptian, handed down and adapted by us to fit our speech. 33 If our plates had been large enough, we would have written in Hebrew; but the Hebrew characters have been adapted by us as well. If we could have written in Hebrew, however, there wouldn't have been any miscommunications in our record. 34 But the Lord knows what we've written and that no other people understand our language. Because no other people understand our language, He has prepared instruments for its translation. 35 These things are written so we can rid our clothes of the blood of our fellow brothers and sisters, who have fallen away in unbelief. 36 What we want for them is their restoration to the knowledge of Christ, consistent with the prayers of all the holy ones who have lived in the land. 37 May the Lord Jesus Christ let their prayers be answered according to their faith. And may God the Father remember the covenant He's made with the house of Israel, and may

He bless them forever through faith in the name of Jesus Christ. Amen.

The Book of Ether

Chapter 1

Now I Moroni will next give an account of those ancient inhabitants who were destroyed by the Lord's hand in this northern land. 2 I'm taking my account from the 24 plates found by Limhi's people — and this is called the book of Ether. 3 Because I believe the first part of this record is also part of the record of the Jews (which has to do with the creation of the world and Adam, and contains an account from that time up until the great tower, and everything that happened among mankind up to that time), 4 I'm not including anything that happened from Adam's time until then. But they're included on the plates, and whoever finds them will be able to read the full account. 5 Therefore I'm not giving the full account, only a partial account, from the time of the tower until they were destroyed.

II

6 This is how I summarize their record: The one who wrote this record was Ether, and he was a descendant of Coriantor. 7 Coriantor was the son of Moron; 8 Moron was the son of Ethem; 9 Ethem was the son of Ahah; 10 Ahah was the son of Seth; 11 Seth was the son of Shiblon; 12 Shiblon was the son of Com; 13 Com was the son of Coriantum; 14 Coriantum was the son of Amnigaddah; 15 and Amnigaddah was the son of Aaron. 16 Aaron was a descendant of Heth, who was the son of Hearthom. 17 Hearthom was the son of Lib; 18 Lib was the son of Kish; 19 Kish was the son of Corom; 20 Corom was the son of Levi; 21 Levi was the son of Kim, 22 and Kim was the son of Morianton. 23 Morianton was a descendant of Riplakish; 24 Riplakish was the son of Shez; 25 Shez was the son of Heth; 26 Heth was the son of Com; 27 Com was the son of Coriantum; 28 Coriantum was the son of Emer; 29 Emer was the son of Omer; 30 Omer was the son of Shule; 31 Shule was the son of Kib; 32 Kib was the son of Orihah, who was the son of Jared, 33 and this Jared came out from the great tower with his brother and their families, along with some others and their families, when the Lord confused the people's language and made an oath, in His wrath, to scatter them throughout the world; and so the people were scattered.

III

34 Jared's brother was a large and powerful man, and because he was very blessed by the Lord, Jared said to him: Cry to the Lord in prayer and ask Him to not let us become confused and unable to keep

a clear understanding of our language. ³⁵ Jared's brother cried to the Lord in prayer, and the Lord had compassion on Jared. As a result, He didn't confuse Jared's language, and Jared and his brother weren't disconnected. ³⁶ Then Jared told his brother: Cry to the Lord again in prayer — perhaps He'll turn His anger away from those who are our friends and not confuse their language. ³⁷ Jared's brother cried to the Lord in prayer, and the Lord had compassion on their friends and families as well so that they weren't divided and disconnected. ³⁸ Jared again said to his brother: Go and ask the Lord whether He intends to lead us out of the land. If He does intend to lead us out of the land, ask Him: Where are we to go? And who knows, it's possible the Lord will lead us to a land that's specially chosen and better than all other places on earth. If so, let's be faithful to the Lord, so we can receive it from Him. ³⁹ And Jared's brother cried to the Lord in prayer, in accordance with what Jared asked. ⁴⁰ The Lord heard Jared's brother and had sympathy on him and told him: ⁴¹ Get to work and gather your flocks of every kind, both male and female; and seeds of every kind; and your family, and your brother Jared and his family, and your friends and their families, and Jared's friends and their families.

IV   ⁴² When you've done this, you must lead them down into the valley to the north. I'll meet you there and lead you to a land that's specially chosen and better than all other places on earth. ⁴³ I'll bless you and your descendants there and raise up a great nation to Me from your descendants, your brother's descendants, and from those who go with you. No other nation on earth will be greater than the one I'll raise up to Me from your descendants. I'll do this for you because of your persistent prayers.

V   **2** Then Jared and his brother and their families, as well as the friends of Jared and his brother and their families, went down into the valley to the north. The name of the valley was Nimrod, being named for the powerful hunter. They traveled with their flocks of every kind they had gathered, male and female. ² They also laid snares and caught birds. They also prepared a vessel, in which they carried fish. ³ They also took with them deseret — a word that means honey bee. So they took with them swarms of bees and a variety of seeds they gathered from the land.

VI   ⁴ When they had come down into the valley of Nimrod, the Lord came down and talked with Jared's brother. He was in a cloud and Jared's brother didn't see Him. ⁵ The Lord commanded them to travel into the wilderness, to a region where no one had ever been. The Lord led them, talking with them as He stood in a cloud, giving them directions on where to travel. ⁶ They traveled in the wilderness and built small ships, crossing many bodies of water in these ships while being continually guided by the Lord. 7 The Lord wouldn't allow them to remain in the wilderness beyond the sea, but His desire was for them to proceed all the way to the land of promise, which was specially chosen and better than all other places on earth, which the Lord God had saved for a righteous people. 8 He had sworn in His wrath to Jared's brother that whoever occupied this land of promise, from that time forward and forever, must serve Him, the true and only God, or they would be swept away when they provoked His full wrath upon them.

VII   9 Now we'll witness God's decrees concerning this land, and whoever occupies this land of promise must serve God, or they'll be swept away when they provoke His full wrath upon them. The full extent of God's wrath will be provoked when they've ripened in iniquity. 10 This is a land that's specially chosen and better than all other places on earth. That being the case, those who inhabit it must serve God or they'll be swept away because of God's everlasting decree. But they aren't swept away until there's a fullness of iniquity among the occupants of the land. 11 This is coming to you, Gentiles, so you can know God's decrees, so you can repent and not continue in your iniquities until the fullness has come, so you don't provoke the full extent of God's wrath upon you as the inhabitants of the land have all done before. 12 This is a choice land; and any nation that inhabits it will be free from enslavement and captivity and from all other nations under heaven if they will only serve the God of the land, who is Jesus Christ, who's been revealed to you through the things we've written.

VIII   13 Now I'll continue with my record. The Lord brought Jared and his companions all the way to the great sea separating land masses. When they arrived at the sea, they pitched their tents and named the place Moriancumer. They lived in tents at the seashore for four years. 14 Then at the end of the four years, the Lord again came to Jared's brother and stood in a cloud and talked with him. The Lord talked with Jared's brother for three hours and chastised him because he didn't remember to call on the Lord's name. 15 Jared's brother repented of that evil and called on the Lord's name on behalf of his companions who were with him. The Lord said to him: I'll forgive you and your companions of their sins, but you must not sin anymore. You must remember that My Spirit won't always influence mankind. Therefore if you persist in doing evil until you're fully ripe, you'll be cut off from the Lord's presence. These are My conditions for the land I'll give you as an inheritance, since it will be a specially chosen land better than all other places on earth.

IX
16 Then the Lord said: Go to work and build small ships like you've built before. And Jared's brother began to work along with his companions and built ships patterned after those built previously, following the Lord's instructions. They were small and light on the water, just like the buoyancy of waterfowl. 17 They were built watertight, so they would hold water like a bowl. The bottom part of each ship was watertight like a bowl, and the sides were also watertight like a bowl, and the ends were peaked, and the top was watertight like a bowl, and the length of each ship was the length of a tree, and the doors — when shut — were watertight, like a bowl. 18 Then Jared's brother cried out to the Lord, saying: O Lord, I've finished the work You've commanded me to do, and I've made the ships as You've directed me. 19 But, O Lord, there's no light in them. How will we steer? We'll suffocate, because we only have the limited air inside them to breathe; therefore we'll die. 20 The Lord said to Jared's brother: Make a hole in the front and back of each ship. Whenever you need more air, unplug the holes to let in air. If water rushes in on you, plug the hole so you don't sink from the water that comes pouring in.

X
21 Jared's brother did as the Lord commanded. 22 Then he cried out again to the Lord, saying: O Lord, I've done just as You've commanded and prepared the ships for my people. But there's no light in them. O Lord, are You going to let us cross the sea in darkness? 23 The Lord asked Jared's brother: What do you want Me to do to provide light in your ships? You can't have windows, since they would be dashed into pieces. You aren't to use fire, since you can't light a fire. 24 You'll be like a whale in the sea, with mountainous waves crashing over you. However, I'll protect you as you cross the deep sea; because the winds blow at My word, and I also control the rains and floods. 25 I'll prepare you; and unless I prepare you for the ocean waves, the blowing winds, and the floods that are coming, you won't be able to cross. Therefore what other preparation do you want from me in order to light the vessels to cross the depths of the sea?

XI
3 Now there were eight ships prepared. Jared's brother went to the mountain, which they called Mount Shelem because of its great height, and smelted from a rock 16 small stones; they were white and clear, like transparent glass. He carried them in his hands up to the top of the mountain and cried out again to the Lord, saying: 2 O Lord, You've said the sea will surround us. Now, O Lord, don't be angry with Your weak servant, because we recognize You are holy and live in the heavens and we are unworthy, and because of the Fall, our natures have become evil continually. Nevertheless, O Lord, You've given us a commandment to call on You, so we can receive from You what we

ask. 3 O Lord, because of our iniquity You've led us out through difficulties and afflictions, and for many years we've lived in the wilderness, but You've continually been merciful to us. O Lord, take pity on me and take away Your anger toward us, Your people. Don't let us cross the sea in darkness, but use these stones I've smelted from the rock. 4 I know, O Lord, that You have all power and can use anything You want as a blessing for mankind. Therefore touch these stones with Your finger, O Lord, and prepare them so they can shine in the dark; and they'll give light for us in the ships we've prepared, so we can have light as we cross the sea. 5 O Lord, You're able to do this. We know that You're able to display great power that looks ordinary to people's understanding.

XII

6 When Jared's brother had said these words, the Lord stretched out His hand and touched the stones one by one with His finger. And the veil was taken from the eyes of Jared's brother, and he saw the Lord's finger. It was like a man's finger, like flesh and blood; and Jared's brother fell down before the Lord because he was afraid. 7 The Lord saw the brother of Jared had fallen to the ground and He said to him: Get up. Why have you fallen down? 8 He answered the Lord: I saw the Lord's finger and I was afraid He would strike me, because I didn't know the Lord had flesh and blood. 9 The Lord said to him: Because of your faith you've seen that I'll take upon Myself flesh and blood. None of those now living have approached Me with such great faith as you have; otherwise, you couldn't have seen My finger. Did you see more than this? 10 He answered: No, Lord. Show Yourself to me. 11 And the Lord asked him: Do you believe the words I will speak? 12 He replied: Yes, Lord, I know that You speak the truth, since You're a God of truth and can't lie.

XIII

13 When he had said these words, the Lord showed Himself to him and said: Because you know these things, you are redeemed from the Fall. Therefore you're brought back into My presence, so I show Myself to you. 14 I Am the one who was prepared from the foundation of creation to redeem My people. I Am Jesus Christ, I Am the Father and the Son. In Me all mankind, who believe in My name, will have life, and they'll have it eternally; they'll become My sons and daughters. 15 I have never shown Myself to those I created who are now living, because none of them have believed in Me as you have. Do you see you're created according to My own image? Indeed, all mankind were created in the beginning in My own image. 16 This body you see right now is the body of My Spirit. I formed mankind in the image of My Spirit body. As I appear to you in the Spirit, so will I appear to My people in the flesh.

XIV   17 Now as I Moroni told you I couldn't make a full account of this
record, therefore it's enough for me to say Jesus showed Himself to this
man in the Spirit, in the same way and in the same bodily form as He
showed Himself to the Nephites. 18 He ministered to him just as He
ministered to the Nephites — and He did this to let this man
understand He was God because of the many great things the Lord
revealed to him. 19 Because of this man's knowledge, he couldn't be
kept from seeing inside the veil. And he saw Jesus' finger, and when he
saw it, fear came over him and he fell down, because he knew it was
the Lord's finger. His faith was replaced by knowledge, since he knew
without any doubt. 20 So because he had this perfect knowledge of
God, he couldn't be kept outside the veil. Therefore he saw Jesus, and
Jesus ministered to him.

XV   21 The Lord said to Jared's brother: You must not allow these
things that you've seen and heard to be revealed to the world until the
time comes when I glorify My name in the flesh. Therefore you must
carefully preserve what you've seen and heard, and show it to no one.
22 At the end of your life, you must write these things down and seal
them up, so no one can translate them; and you'll write them in a
language that can't be understood. 23 And I provide you with these two
stones to also seal up with the things you write. 24 I made the language
you write in impossible for others to understand. Therefore I'll use
these stones, at the right time, to let people understand what you write.
25 When the Lord said this, He showed Jared's brother everyone who
had lived and would live on earth. The Lord didn't keep them from his
sight, not even those living in the farthest parts of the earth. 26 The
Lord had previously told him that if he would believe in Him, if he
would believe He could show him all things, then they would be shown
to him. Therefore the Lord couldn't keep anything from him since he
knew the Lord could show him all things.

XVI   27 The Lord told him: Write these things down and seal them up
under My care; I'll reveal them at the right time to mankind. 28 And
the Lord commanded him to seal up the two stones he had received
and hide them until the Lord provides them to mankind. 4 Then the
Lord commanded Jared's brother to descend the mountain from the
Lord's presence and write everything he had seen. And they were
forbidden to come to mankind until after He had been lifted up on the
cross. This is the reason king Benjamin kept them secure, so they
wouldn't be known to the world until after Christ showed Himself to
His people. 2 After Christ had truly shown Himself to His people, He
commanded them to be revealed.

XVII   ³ Now after they've all dwindled in unbelief and only Lamanites remain, who have rejected Christ's gospel — I've been commanded to hide them away again in the ground. ⁴ I've written on these plates the very things Jared's brother saw. Greater things were never revealed than those things revealed to Jared's brother. ⁵ Therefore the Lord has commanded me to write them down and I've written them. He also commanded me to seal them up under His care. He has also commanded me to protect the ability to translate them, so I've sealed the Interpreters according to the Lord's commandment. ⁶ The Lord told me: They must not go to the Gentiles until they repent of their iniquity and become clean before the Lord. ⁷ The Lord said: When they exercise faith in Me, just as Jared's brother did, so that they become sanctified in Me, then I'll show them the things Jared's brother saw, even providing all My revelations to them. This is what Jesus Christ said, who's the Son of God the Father of the heavens and the earth, and everything in them.

XVIII   ⁸ Let any who fight against the Lord's word be cursed. And any who deny these things, let them be cursed, as Jesus Christ has said: I won't show any greater things to them for I Am the one who speaks. ⁹ At My command, the heavens open and shut, and at My word the earth will shake. At My command, those living on earth will die by fire. ¹⁰ Those who don't believe My words don't believe My disciples. If you think I don't speak, decide for yourself; but you'll know on the last day that I Am the one who speaks. ¹¹ And I'll visit those who believe the things I've spoken by the manifestations of My Spirit. They'll know and testify; because of My Spirit, they'll know these things are true, since they persuade mankind to do good. ¹² Anything that persuades people to do good comes from Me, because good comes from no one other than Me. I Am the same one who leads people to everything good.

XIX   Those who refuse to believe My words won't believe in Me, that I Am. And those who refuse to believe in Me won't believe in the Father, who sent Me. For I Am the Father. I Am the light, the life, and the truth of the world. ¹³ Come to Me, Gentiles, and I'll show you the greater things, knowledge that's hidden away because of unbelief. ¹⁴ Come to Me, O house of Israel, and it will be revealed to you how the Father has great things in store for you from the foundation of creation that you haven't received because of unbelief. ¹⁵ When you move aside the veil of unbelief that causes you to remain in your awful state of wickedness and hardness of heart and blindness of mind, then the great and miraculous things that have been hidden away from you from the foundation of creation will come to you. When you call on the Father in My name with a broken heart and a contrite spirit, then you'll know, O house of Israel, that the Father remembers the covenant He made to your fathers. 16 Then the revelations I had My servant John write will be understood by everyone. Remember, when you see these things, you'll know that the time is near when they will be revealed. 17 Therefore when you receive this record, you can know the Father's work has begun throughout the land. 18 So repent, everyone, throughout the world. Come to Me, believe in My gospel, and be baptized in My name. Because anyone who believes and is baptized will be saved, but anyone who doesn't believe will be condemned. Signs will follow those who believe in My name. 19 Those who are found faithful to My name on the last day will be blessed, for they'll be lifted up to live in the kingdom prepared for them from the foundation of creation. I Am the one who has spoken it. Amen.

Chapter 2

5 I Moroni have written the commandments given to me, based on my memory. And I've told you about the things I sealed up under the Lord's care. So don't translate them, since you're forbidden to do so unless God in His wisdom decides otherwise. 2 And then you'll have the opportunity and direction to show the plates to those who help bring this book to light. 3 The plates will be shown to three witnesses by God's power; as a result, they'll know for sure these things are true. 4 The word of three witnesses will confirm these things. The testimony of three, and this book — in which God's power will be displayed and His word revealed, which the Father, the Son, and the Holy Ghost testify of — all this will stand as a testimony against the world on the last day. 5 If they repent and come to the Father in Jesus' name, they will be received into God's kingdom. 6 Now if I don't have any authority to say these things, decide for yourself; you'll know I have authority when you see me and we stand before God on the last day. Amen.

Chapter 3

6 Now I'll continue to give the record of Jared and his brother. 2 After the Lord had prepared the stones that Jared's brother had taken up to the mountain, he came down from the mountain and placed the stones in the ships, one at each end of the ships. And they gave light to their ships. 3 So the Lord caused stones to give out light in the dark, to provide light for men, women, and children, so they wouldn't have to cross the sea in darkness.

II   4 They prepared all kinds of food, so they could survive on the sea
— as well as food for their flocks, herds, and any other livestock or
animal or bird they brought with them — when they had done all this,
they boarded their vessels or small ships and set out on the sea,
entrusting themselves to the Lord their God. 5 The Lord God sent a
furious wind blowing over the sea toward the promised land; and so
they were tossed on the waves by the wind. 6 They were buried in the
sea many times because of the mountainous waves that broke upon
them, and because of the powerful storms accompanying the violent
wind.

III   7 When they were buried in the deep sea, no water could hurt
them, since their ships were watertight like a bowl, and they were also
watertight like Noah's ark. When they were entirely under the water,
they cried out to the Lord, and He returned them to the surface.

IV   8 The wind never stopped blowing toward the promised land while
they were on the water, and they were always driven onward by the
wind. 9 And they sang praises to the Lord. Jared's brother sang praises
to the Lord, thanking and praising Him throughout the day. When
night came, they didn't stop praising the Lord. 10 And so they were
driven onward, and no sea creature could wreck them, and no whale
could stop them. They had light continually, whether above or under
the water. 11 And so they were driven onward upon the sea for 344
days. 12 Then they landed on the shore of the promised land. When
they set foot on the shore of the promised land, they bowed down to
the ground and humbled themselves before the Lord and shed tears of
joy before the Lord because of His many tender mercies over them.
13 Then they went out on the land and began to cultivate the earth.

V   14 Jared had four sons: their names were Jacom, Gilgah, Mahah,
and Orihah. 15 Jared's brother had sons and daughters as well.
16 Jared's friends and his brother's friends numbered about 22. They
also had sons and daughters before they came to the promised land.
And so they began to multiply. 17 They were taught to live with
humility and obey the Lord, and they were also taught from above.
18 They began to spread throughout the land, increasing in numbers
and cultivating the earth, and growing strong upon the land.

VI   19 Then Jared's brother became old and sensed he would soon die.
So he said to Jared: Let's gather our people in order to count them and
find out what they want from us before we die. 20 And in due course the
people were gathered. Now Jared's brother had 22 children and Jared
had 12, four of whom were sons. 21 They counted their people, and
after they had counted them, they asked them what they wanted them
to do before they died. 22 The people asked them to anoint one of their

sons to be a king over them. 23 This request deeply troubled them, and so Jared's brother told them: This will certainly lead to slavery. 24 But Jared told his brother: Let them have a king. So he said to them: Choose a king from our sons, whomever you wish.

VII   25 They chose the first born of Jared's brother, whose name was Pagag. But he refused, not wanting to be their king. And yet the people wanted his father to compel him, but his father refused to do so, ordering them not to force any man to be their king. 26 Then they chose each of Pagag's brothers, but they all declined. 27 Jared's sons declined as well, all except for one. So Orihah was anointed to be king over the people. 28 He began to rule and the people began to prosper, becoming very wealthy.

VIII   29 Then Jared died and so did his brother. 30 Orihah lived humbly and obeyed the Lord, remembering the Lord had done great things for his father, and teaching his people how the Lord had done great things for their fathers. **7** Orihah administered justice over the land in righteousness his whole life, which was very long. 2 He had sons and daughters; indeed, he had 31 children, 23 of whom were sons.

IX   3 He also had a son named Kib in his old age, who ruled as his successor, and Kib had a son named Corihor. 4 When Corihor was 32 years old, he rebelled against his father and went over and lived in the land of Nehor. He had sons and daughters who grew up to be very attractive, so Corihor drew away many people to join him. 5 When he had assembled an army, he came up to the land of Moron, where the king lived, and took him prisoner, fulfilling the words of Jared's brother, that they would be brought into slavery. 6 Now the land of Moron, where the king lived, was near the land later called Desolation by the Nephites. 7 Kib lived in captivity, and so did his people under the rule of his son Corihor, until he became very old. Nevertheless, Kib had a son named Shule in his old age, while he was still in captivity.

X   8 Shule was angry with his brother; he grew strong and powerful as a man; and he was also skilled in judgment. 9 So he went to the hill Ephraim and smelted ore from the hill, making steel swords for those he had drawn away with him. After he had armed them with swords, he returned to the city of Nehor and attacked his brother Corihor, in this way obtaining the kingdom and restoring it to his father Kib. 10 Now because of what Shule had done, his father conferred the kingdom upon him; so he began to rule as his father's successor. 11 He administered justice in righteousness and spread his kingdom throughout the land since the people were very numerous. 12 Shule also had many sons and daughters. 13 And Corihor felt regret for the many evil things he had done, so Shule trusted him with power in his kingdom. 14 Corihor had many sons and daughters. One of Corihor's sons was named Noah.

XI   15 Noah rebelled against king Shule and his father Corihor and drew away his brother Cohor, all his siblings, and many of the people. 16 He fought king Shule in battle, by which he gained the land they first inherited; and he became a king over that part of the land. 17 Noah attacked king Shule again, capturing him and taking him away as a prisoner into Moron. 18 When Noah was about to put him to death, Shule's sons crept into Noah's house at night and killed him, broke down the prison door, brought their father out, and placed him on his throne in his own kingdom. 19 Therefore Noah's son built up his father's kingdom as his successor. However, they lost control over king Shule. The people who were under the rule of king Shule benefited and grew strong. 20 The land was divided and there were two kingdoms: the kingdom of Shule and the kingdom of Cohor, Noah's son. 21 Cohor had his people attack Shule in which Shule defeated them and killed Cohor. 22 Now Cohor had a son named Nimrod. And Nimrod surrendered Cohor's kingdom to Shule, gaining Shule's confidence; so Shule granted privileges to him, and Nimrod did what he wanted in Shule's kingdom. 23 During Shule's reign, prophets came among the people; they were sent from the Lord and prophesied that the people's wickedness and idol worship were bringing a curse upon the land, and they would be destroyed if they didn't repent.

XII   24 But the people abused and mocked the prophets. And king Shule administered justice against all those who abused the prophets. 25 He made a law throughout the land that authorized the prophets to go wherever they wished. Because of this, the people were brought to repentance. 26 Because the people repented of their iniquities and idol worship, the Lord spared them, and they again began to flourish in the land.

XIII   Shule had sons and daughters in his old age. 27 And there were no more wars during Shule's time. He remembered the great things the Lord had done for his ancestors in bringing them across the sea to the promised land; therefore he administered justice in righteousness his whole life. **8** He had a son named Omer, who ruled as his successor. Omer had a son named Jared, and Jared had sons and daughters.

XIV   2 Jared rebelled against his father and went to live in the land of Heth. He deceived a great number of people because of his sly, deceitful words until he had gained half the kingdom. 3 Once he had gained half the kingdom, he attacked his father, took his father by force as a prisoner, and made him work as a slave. 4 Omer was held in captivity half the time that he ruled. He had sons and daughters, among whom were Esrom and Coriantumr. 5 They were very angry because of what their brother Jared had done, so much so that they raised an army and attacked Jared by night. 6 When they had destroyed Jared's army, they were about to kill him as well. But he begged them not to kill him, promising them that he would surrender the kingdom to his father. And they allowed him to live.

XV 7 Now Jared became despondent because he had lost the kingdom, since he had set his heart on the kingdom and the world's glory. 8 But Jared's daughter was very astute, and seeing her father's unhappiness, she devised a plan to recover the kingdom for her father. 9 Now Jared's daughter was very beautiful. She talked with her father and asked him: Why is my father so sad? Hasn't he read the record that our ancestors brought across the sea? Isn't there an account about people long ago who obtained kingdoms and great glory using secret plans? 10 Therefore send for Akish the son of Kimnor. I'm beautiful and I'll dance in front of him. And I'll impress him so that he'll want to marry me. Therefore if he asks you to give me to him to be his wife, you must say: I'll give her away if you agree to bring me the head of my father the king.

XVI 11 Now Omer was Akish's friend. So when Jared had sent for Akish, Jared's daughter danced in front of him, impressing him so much he wanted her to be his wife. He asked Jared: Give her to me to be my wife. 12 But Jared said to him: I'll give her away if you agree to bring me the head of my father the king. 13 So Akish gathered all his relatives to Jared's house and asked them: Will you swear allegiance to me in what I ask of you? 14 They all swore to him by the God of heaven, and by the heavens, the earth, and their heads, that anyone who deviated from what Akish wanted would lose their head, and anyone who divulged anything Akish revealed to them would lose their life.

XVII 15 In this way they made an agreement with Akish. And Akish administered to them the oaths like the people long ago, who also tried to obtain power, oaths that had been handed down from Cain, who was a murderer from the beginning. 16 They were maintained by the accuser's power in order to administer these oaths to the people, and to keep those who made these oaths concealed, and to help those who sought power to obtain it, resulting in murder, pillaging, lying, and committing all kinds of wickedness and whoredoms. 17 It was Jared's daughter who gave her father the idea to search out these ancient things. Jared gave Akish the idea. So Akish passed it on to his relatives and friends, persuading them by pleasing promises to do anything he wanted. 18 They formed a secret society, as they did long ago, a society God considers most corrupt and wicked of all. 19 Because the Lord doesn't operate by secret conspiracies, neither does He want people to kill; on the contrary, He has always forbidden it since mankind's beginning.

XVIII   20 I Moroni am not writing the details of their oaths and conspiracies, since it has been revealed to me that they exist among all people; and they exist among the Lamanites. 21 And they've brought about the people's destruction, whom I'm now writing about, as well as the Nephites' destruction. 22 Any nation that upholds such secret conspiracies, to get power and wealth, until they spread throughout the nation, will be destroyed. Because the Lord won't permit the blood of His holy ones, which will be shed by them, to always cry out to him from the ground for vengeance without avenging them. 23 Therefore, you Gentiles, it's God's wisdom for you to be shown these things, so you'll repent of your sins and not allow these murderous conspiracies, that are always set up for power and money, to control you, so that you won't provoke your own destruction. Indeed, the sword of the justice of the Eternal God will fall upon you, to your ruin and destruction, if you allow these things to continue. 24 Therefore the Lord commands you, when you see these things come among you, to wake up to a sense of your awful situation because of this secret society that's come into existence among you. Woe to this conspiracy on account of the blood of those who have been killed; they cry out from the dust for vengeance upon it, and upon those who make and support it.

XIX   25 Indeed, whoever builds it up hopes to overthrow the freedom of all lands, nations, and countries. These conspiracies bring about everyone's destruction since they're built up by the accuser, who's the father of all lies. He's the same liar who deceived our first parents, who caused people from the start to commit murder. He's hardened people's hearts so that they've murdered the prophets, stoned them, and banished them. 26 As a result, I've been commanded to write these things so evil can be ended. And so the time will come when Satan won't have any power over people's hearts, so they can be persuaded to always do good and come to the Source of all righteousness and be saved.

Chapter 4

9 Now I'll continue with my record. Because of Akish and his friends' secret alliance, they overthrew Omer's kingdom. 2 Still, the Lord was merciful to Omer, and to his children who didn't want to kill him. 3 The Lord warned Omer in a dream to leave the land. So Omer left the land with his family and traveled many days and came over and passed by the hill Shim and went over near the place where the Nephites were slaughtered, and from there eastward, arriving at a place called Ablom, by the seashore. He pitched his tent there, along with his children and his whole household except for Jared and his family.

II   4 Jared was anointed king over the people using wicked means and he gave his daughter to be Akish's wife. 5 Then Akish plotted to take his father-in-law's life, using those he had sworn to secrecy with an ancient oath. And they cut off his father-in-law's head while he sat on his throne listening to his people. 6 Indeed, this evil, secret society had spread so much it had corrupted the hearts and minds of everyone. As a result, Jared was murdered on his throne, and Akish ruled in his place.

III   7 Then Akish got jealous of his son. So he imprisoned him and provided him with little or no food until he died. 8 Now the one who had died had a brother named Nimrah, and he was angry with his father because of what he had done to his brother. 9 So Nimrah gathered a small number of men and escaped from the land and came over and lived with Omer. 10 Then Akish had other sons, who won the hearts of the people, despite having sworn to Akish to follow his orders to commit all kinds of iniquity. 11 Now Akish's people wanted to become rich, just as Akish wanted power. So Akish's sons offered them money, and in this way they drew away the majority of the people to follow them. 12 A war began between Akish and his sons, lasting many years, resulting in nearly everyone in the kingdom being killed. Only 30 people survived, besides those who had escaped with Omer's household. 13 So Omer was restored to his own land.

IV   14 Then Omer grew old. Nevertheless, in his old age he had a son named Emer, whom he anointed to be king, to rule as his successor. 15 After he had anointed Emer to be king, Omer had peace in the land for two years. Then he died, having lived through many unhappy years. Emer ruled in his place and followed his father's example. 16 The Lord again began to remove the curse from the land. Emer's household prospered greatly under his rule. In 62 years they had become very prosperous, so much so that they became very wealthy, 17 having all kinds of fruit and grain, textiles, fine linen, gold, silver, and valuables, 18 and all kinds of cattle, oxen, cows, sheep, swine, goats, and many other kinds of animals useful for man's food. 19 They also had horses and donkeys, as well as elephants, cureloms, and cumoms, all useful to man, but especially the elephants, cureloms, and cumoms.

²⁰ So the Lord poured out His blessings on this land, which was specially chosen above all other lands. He commanded all who might live on the land to live there in obedience to the Lord, or they would be swept away when they had ripened in iniquity. The Lord said: I'll pour out the full extent of My wrath upon them.

V
     ²¹ Emer administered justice in righteousness his whole life, and he had many sons and daughters. Among them he had a son named Coriantum, whom he anointed to rule as his successor. ²² After he had anointed Coriantum to rule in his place, he lived four years, experiencing peace in the land. He even saw the Son of Righteousness and was glad and rejoiced in his day, and he died in peace.

VI
     ²³ Coriantum followed his father's example, and he built many great cities and administered good things to his people his whole life. He didn't have any children until he was very old. ²⁴ His wife died when she was 102 years old. Then Coriantum married a young woman in his old age and had sons and daughters. He lived until he was 142 years old. ²⁵ He had a son named Com, who ruled as his successor. He ruled 49 years, and he had a son named Heth; and he also had other sons and daughters. ²⁶ The people had spread again over the whole land. And a very great wickedness returned to the land again. Heth began to embrace the secret, ancient plans once more, in order to kill his father. ²⁷ He dethroned his father, killing him with his own sword. And he ruled in his place.

VII
     ²⁸ Prophets came into the land again, crying out repentance to them, that they must prepare the way for the Lord, or a curse would descend upon the land; indeed, there would be a great famine and they would die if they didn't repent. ²⁹ But the people didn't believe the prophets' words, and they exiled them. They threw some of them into pits and left them to die. They did all these things following king Heth's command. ³⁰ Then a severe famine arose in the land. The people began to die very quickly from the famine, since it didn't rain. ³¹ Venomous snakes appeared on the land, poisoning many people. Their flocks started fleeing from the snakes toward the land to the south, which the Nephites later called Zarahemla. ³² And many flocks died while fleeing. But some of them escaped into the land southward. ³³ The Lord caused the snakes to stop pursuing them and instead, they blocked the way, so the people couldn't pass, and any who tried to get through died from the venomous snakes. ³⁴ The people followed the path of the animals and ate the carcasses of those that died as they were fleeing, until they had devoured them all.

VIII
     When the people saw they were going to die, they began to repent of their iniquities and cry out to the Lord. ³⁵ When they had humbled

themselves sufficiently before the Lord, the Lord sent rain on the earth. And the people began to recover, and fruit began to grow in the north country and the surrounding regions. The Lord reminded them of His power by saving them from famine.

IX   **10** Heth as well as his whole household had died from the famine except for his descendant Shez. Then Shez began to rebuild a broken people. 2 He remembered the destruction of his forefathers, and he established a righteous kingdom, remembering what the Lord had done in bringing Jared and his brother across the sea. He lived the way the Lord commanded, and he had sons and daughters. 3 But his oldest son, whose name was also Shez, rebelled against him. However, he was struck down and killed by a robber because of his great wealth, giving his father peace once more. 4 His father built many cities on the land. The people again began to spread over the land. Shez lived to be very old, and he had a son named Riplakish. Then Shez died, and Riplakish ruled as his successor.

X   5 But Riplakish didn't live righteously in the Lord's eyes, since he had many wives and concubines, and he oppressed the people with burdens difficult to bear. He imposed heavy taxes and built many spacious buildings with the tax revenue. 6 He erected a very beautiful throne for himself and built many prisons. He imprisoned any who refused to pay taxes. He threw any who were unable to pay taxes into prison, making them work continually for their support. He had any who refused to work put to death. 7 He obtained all his fine things, including pure gold that was refined in prison. He had a variety of fine pieces of craftsmanship made in prison.

XI   He afflicted the people with his whoredoms and abominations. 8 When he had ruled 42 years, the people rose up in rebellion against him. War broke out again in the land to such an extent that Riplakish was killed and his descendants were driven from the land. 9 After many years, Morianton, a descendant of Riplakish, gathered an army of exiles and attacked, gaining power over many cities. The war became severe and lasted many years, and he obtained power over the whole land and set himself up as king over the whole land. 10 After he had set himself up as king, he eased the people's burdens, in this way winning their approval; and they anointed him to be their king. 11 He did what was right for the people, but not for himself, on account of his many whoredoms; so he was cut off from the Lord's presence.

XII   12 Morianton established many cities. The people became very wealthy under his rule, in buildings, in gold and silver, in raising grain, in flocks and herds, and in those things that had been restored to them. 13 Morianton lived to a very old age, and then he had a son named

Kim. Kim ruled as his father's successor. He ruled eight years and his father died. But Kim didn't rule in righteousness, and so the Lord didn't bless him. 14 His brother rose up in rebellion against him, and as a result of the rebellion he captured him and enslaved him. He remained in captivity his whole life, having sons and daughters while living in captivity. In his old age, he had a son named Levi, just before he died.

XIII   15 Levi worked as a slave after his father's death for 42 years. Then he made war against the king of the land and as a result he obtained for himself the kingdom. 16 After he had obtained the kingdom for himself, he did what was right in the Lord's eyes. And the people prospered in the land. He lived a very long time and had sons and daughters. He also had a son named Corom, whom he anointed king in his place.

XIV   17 Corom did what was right in the Lord's eyes throughout his life, and he had many sons and daughters. After he had lived a long time, he died, like everyone else on earth, and Kish ruled as his successor. 18 Then Kish also died, and Lib ruled as his successor. 19 Lib also did what was right in the Lord's eyes. During Lib's time, the venomous snakes were eliminated. As a consequence, they went into the land to the south to hunt food for the people of the land, because the land was filled with forest animals. And Lib became a great hunter. 20 They built a large city by the narrow neck of land, where the sea divides the land. 21 They preserved the land to the south as a wilderness area where they could hunt wild game. And the whole land to the north was filled with inhabitants. 22 They were very industrious, and they bought, sold, and traded with each other in order to make money. 23 They processed all kinds of ore, and they refined gold, silver, iron, bronze, and all kinds of metals; and they dug these out of the ground. So they threw up great mounds of earth in order to recover ore of gold, silver, iron, and copper. They fashioned a variety of fine pieces of craftsmanship. 24 They had textiles and fine woven linen, and they made all kinds of cloth so they had clothes to wear and to dress themselves with. 25 They made all types of tools to cultivate the earth, to plow and sow, to reap and hoe, and to thresh. 26 They made all kinds of tools to use with their animals. 27 They made all types of weapons. They also made all kinds of elaborately worked objects. 28 No nation was ever more blessed than they were or given more prosperity by the Lord. And they were in a land specially chosen and better than all other places on earth, because the Lord had declared it.

XV   29 Lib lived many years and had sons and daughters, and he also had a son named Hearthom. 30 Hearthom ruled as his father's successor. When Hearthom had ruled for 24 years, he lost the kingdom. He worked as a slave for many years, all the way to the end of his life. 31 He had a son named Heth. Heth lived in captivity his whole life, and he had a son named Aaron. Aaron lived in captivity his whole life, and he had a son named Amnigaddah. Amnigaddah also lived in captivity his whole life, and he had a son named Coriantum. And Coriantum lived in captivity his whole life, and he had a son named Com.

XVI   32 Com drew away half the kingdom and ruled over half the kingdom for 42 years. He went to battle against king Amgid, and they fought for many years, during which time Com gained power over Amgid and got control of the rest of the kingdom. 33 In Com's days, robbers began to appear in the land, and they adopted the ancient plans, and administered oaths like those long ago did, again attempting to destroy the kingdom. 34 Now Com fought them a great deal, but he didn't succeed in defeating them.

XVII   **11** During Com's time, many prophets returned again, prophesying of that great nation's destruction unless they repented and turned to the Lord and gave up committing murder and doing evil. 2 But the people rejected the prophets. And they fled to Com for protection, because the people tried to kill them. 3 They prophesied many things to Com, and he was blessed for the rest of his life. 4 Com lived a very long time and had a son named Shiblon; and Shiblon ruled as his successor.

XVIII   But Shiblon's brother rebelled against him, and a massive war developed throughout the land. 5 Shiblon's brother had all the prophets who prophesied of the people's destruction put to death. 6 There were great difficulties and misery throughout the land since they had testified a great curse would come upon the land and upon the people and there would be terrible destruction among them, such as never had occurred on earth, and that their bones would be piled up on the land as mounds of earth unless they repented of their wickedness. 7 But they didn't listen to the Lord's voice because of their wicked conspiracies. As a result, wars and conflicts occurred throughout the land, and also famines, diseases, and calamities, so many it resulted in terrible destruction, unlike anything experienced before on earth. All this happened during Shiblon's days. 8 And the people began to repent of their iniquity. To the degree they did, the Lord had mercy on them.

XIX   9 Then Shiblon was killed, and Seth was captured, and he lived in captivity throughout his life. 10 His son Ahah obtained the kingdom, and he ruled over the people his whole life. He committed all kinds of iniquity during his life, resulting in the deaths of many people; and his life was short. 11 Ethem, a descendant of Ahah, obtained the kingdom; and he also acted wickedly during his life. 12 During Ethem's time, many prophets came again and prophesied to the people. They prophesied the Lord would completely destroy them and remove them from the earth unless they repented of their iniquities. 13 But the people hardened their hearts and refused to listen. And the prophets mourned and withdrew from the people.

xx   14 Ethem executed the laws in wickedness his whole life; and he had a son named Moron, who ruled as his successor. Moron lived wickedly in the Lord's eyes. 15 A rebellion arose among the people because of the secret conspiracy that was established in order to obtain power and wealth. A strong man arose among them, powerful in evil, who engaged Moron in battle, by which he conquered half the kingdom; and he held onto half the kingdom for many years. 16 At length Moron defeated him and regained the kingdom. 17 Another powerful man rose up in rebellion, and he was a descendant of Jared's brother. 18 He defeated Moron and obtained the kingdom. As a result, Moron lived in captivity the rest of his life, and he had a son named Coriantor.

xxi   19 And Coriantor lived in captivity his whole life. 20 During his time, many prophets also came, prophesying of great and miraculous things and begging the people to repent — that unless they repented, the Lord God would execute judgment against them to their complete destruction, 21 and the Lord God would send or bring forth another people to live there, by His power and in the same way He brought their ancestors. 22 But they rejected everything the prophets said because of their secret society and their wicked abominations. 23 Coriantor had a son named Ether; and he died, having lived in captivity his whole life.

Chapter 5

12 Ether lived during Coriantumr's rule, who was king over the whole land. 2 Ether was a prophet of the Lord; therefore he came forward during Coriantumr's time and began to prophesy to the people, since he couldn't be restrained because of the Spirit of the Lord in him. 3 He cried out from morning until the sun went down, urging the people to believe in God to bring them to repentance, so they wouldn't be destroyed, telling them that all things are accomplished by faith. 4 Therefore anyone who believes in God can, with confidence, hope for a better world, even a place at God's right hand. This hope comes from faith and becomes an anchor to people's souls, which would make them sure and resolute, always abounding in doing good, being led to glorify God. 5 Ether prophesied great and miraculous things to the people, things they didn't believe because they didn't see them.

II

6 Now I Moroni would like to speak a little about these things. I would like to show the world that faith is things that are hoped for and not seen. So don't resist or argue that you don't believe because you don't see, because you don't receive any witness until after your faith is tested. 7 Indeed, it was by faith that Christ visited our ancestors in person after He had risen from the dead. He didn't visit them until after they had faith in Him. That being the case, it was necessary for some to have faith in Him, since He didn't show Himself to the world unless the people had faith. 8 Because of people's faith He has shown Himself to the world and glorified the Father's name and prepared a way so that others could share in the heavenly gift, so they could hope for those things they haven't seen. 9 Therefore you may also have hope and share in the gift if only you have faith. 10 It was by faith that men long ago were called according to God's Holy Order. 11 Therefore the Law of Moses was given by faith. But God has prepared a better way in the gift of His Son, and it has been fulfilled by faith. 12 Because if there isn't any faith among mankind, God can't do any miracle among them; consequently, He didn't show Himself until after they had faith.

III

13 It was Alma and Amulek's faith that caused the prison to collapse to the ground. 14 It was Nephi and Lehi's faith that brought about the conversion of the Lamanites, so they were baptized with fire and the Holy Ghost. 15 It was the faith of Ammon and his brothers and their companions that brought about such a great miracle among the Lamanites. 16 All those who performed miracles did them by faith, both those who lived before Christ and those who lived after. 17 It was by faith the three disciples obtained a promise that they wouldn't experience death, and they didn't obtain the promise until after they had faith. 18 No one at any time has performed any miracles until after they had faith; therefore they first believed in the Son of God. 19 There were many whose faith was so strong, even before Christ came, who couldn't be kept outside the veil but truly saw with their eyes the things they had seen first with an eye of faith; and they were glad. 20 We've seen in this record one of these was Jared's brother: his faith in God was so great that when God put forward His finger, He couldn't hide it from Jared's brother because of the promise He made to him, which he had obtained by faith. 21 After Jared's brother had seen the Lord's finger, because of the promise Jared's brother had obtained by faith, the Lord couldn't hold anything back from his sight. So He showed

him all things since he could no longer be kept outside the veil. 22 It's by faith that my forefathers have obtained the promise that these things would come to their descendants through the Gentiles. Therefore the Lord, even Jesus Christ, has commanded me.

IV   23 And I said to Him: Lord, the Gentiles will ridicule these things because of our weakness in writing; You've made us powerful in speaking, by faith; however, You haven't made us powerful in writing. You've made this people able to speak great things because of the Holy Ghost, which You've given them. 24 Yet You've made us able to write only a little because of the difficulty of inscribing and You haven't made us gifted in composing like Jared's brother. You endowed the things he wrote with power, just as You are, to such a degree as to overpower the people who read them. 25 You've also inspired our sermons to be powerful and great, so that we can't even write them. Therefore when we write, we see only our weakness and hesitate because of the contrast in our writing. I'm afraid the Gentiles will mock our record.

V   26 When I had said this, the Lord told me: Fools mock, but they will mourn. And My grace is sufficient for the meek, so that they won't find an excuse in your weaknesses. 27 If people come to Me, I'll show them their weaknesses. I give people weaknesses so they can be humble. And My grace is sufficient for all people who humble themselves before Me. If they humble themselves before Me and have faith in Me, then I'll make weak things become strong for them. 28 I'll show the Gentiles their weaknesses. I'll show them that faith, hope, and charity lead to Me, the Source of all righteousness.

VI   29 Having heard these words, I was comforted and said: O Lord, may Your righteous will be done. I know You act according to people's faith for their benefit. 30 Indeed, Jared's brother said to the mountain Zerin: Move out of the way! — and it was moved out of the way. If he hadn't had faith, it wouldn't have moved. Therefore You act after people have faith. 31 In this way You revealed Yourself to Your disciples. After they had faith and spoke in Your name, You showed Yourself to them in great power. 32 I also remember You've said that You've prepared a place for mankind in Your Father's kingdom, confirming our hope. So mankind must hope or they can't inherit the place You've prepared. 33 I remember You've said You've loved the world, so much You laid down Your life for the world so that You could take it back, in order to prepare a place for mankind. 34 Now I know this love You have for mankind is charity. Therefore unless people have charity, they can't inherit the place You've prepared in Your Father's kingdom. 35 I know by what You've said that if the Gentiles don't have charity because of our weaknesses, it will test them and may cost them the gift, and even result in losing a blessing that will then be given to those grateful and willing to accept Your gifts.

VII   36 Then I prayed to the Lord that He would give the Gentiles grace, so they could have charity. 37 The Lord said to me: If they don't have charity, it's no loss for you. You've been faithful; therefore your clothes will be washed clean. Because you've seen your weaknesses, you'll be made strong; this will let you arrive in peace at the place I've prepared for you in My Father's kingdom.

VIII   38 Now I'll say farewell to the Gentiles, and to my people as well, whom I love, until we come face to face before Christ's judgment seat, where everyone will know my clothes aren't stained with your blood. 39 Then you'll know I've seen Jesus and He has talked with me face to face, and He told me about these things in plain humility in my own language, just as one person tells another. 40 I've written only a few of them because of my weakness in writing. 41 Now I would urge you to investigate this Jesus whom the prophets and His messengers have written about, so that the grace of God the Father and the Lord Jesus Christ and the Holy Ghost, which testifies of Them, can be and dwell in you forever. Amen.

Chapter 6

13 Now I'll conclude my record covering the destruction of the people I've been writing about. 2 They rejected all of Ether's words, since he truthfully told them everything from mankind's beginning, and when the floodwaters receded from this land, it became a choice land better than all other places on earth, a land chosen by the Lord. Therefore the Lord requires everyone who lives there to follow Him. 3 It was destined to be the place of the New Jerusalem, where the Lord's holy sanctuary would come down out of heaven.

II   4 Ether saw Christ's days, and he spoke about a New Jerusalem on this land. 5 He also spoke about the house of Israel and the Jerusalem where Lehi would come from — that after it was destroyed, it would be rebuilt as a holy city to the Lord; so it couldn't be a New Jerusalem since it had existed before. However, it would be rebuilt and become a holy city of the Lord; and it would be founded for the house of Israel. 6 And also a New Jerusalem would be founded on this land for the remnant of Joseph's descendants. And earlier events depicted this: 7 Think of how Joseph brought his father down into Egypt, where he later died; likewise, the Lord brought a remnant of Joseph's descendants out of the land of Jerusalem, to be merciful to Joseph's descendants, so they wouldn't be killed, just as He was merciful to Joseph's father, so he wouldn't perish.

III   8 Therefore the remnant of Joseph's family will be established on this land, and it will be their land by inheritance. They'll establish a holy city to the Lord like the old Jerusalem. And they won't be left in doubt anymore through the end, when the earth passes away. 9 There will be a new heaven and a new earth; and they will be like the old ones, except the old ones will have ended and all things will have become new. 10 Then the New Jerusalem will come; and those who live there are blessed since they're the ones whose clothes are spotless through the Lamb's blood; and they're included with the remnant of Joseph's descendants, who are part of the house of Israel. 11 Then the old Jerusalem will also return; and its inhabitants are blessed since they've been washed clean in the Lamb's blood; they're the ones who were scattered and gathered in from the four quarters of the earth and from the north countries and share in the fulfillment of the covenant God made with their father Abraham. 12 When these things happen, it will accomplish the scripture that says: There are those who were first who will be last, and there are those who were last who will be first.

IV   13 I was about to write more, but I'm forbidden to do so; however, Ether's prophecies were great and marvelous. But they regarded him as worthless and cast him out. So he hid himself in a cave by day, and at night he went out, viewing what was happening to the people. 14 While he lived in a cave, he made the rest of this record, watching at night the destruction that overtook the people.

V   15 In the same year the people banished him, a great war began among the people since many powerful men rose up in rebellion and tried to kill Coriantumr using their secret plans of wickedness, which have been mentioned before. 16 Now because Coriantumr had thoroughly studied the art of war and the learning of the world, he attacked those who tried to kill him in battle. 17 Yet he didn't repent, and neither did his beautiful sons and daughters, and neither did the beautiful sons and daughters of Cohor, and neither did the beautiful sons and daughters of Corihor. In short, none of the beautiful sons and daughters in all the land repented of their sins. 18 That being the case, during the first year Ether lived in the cave, many people were killed by the sword by those secret societies that fought against Coriantumr, trying to obtain the kingdom. 19 And Coriantumr's sons fought and bled a great deal. 20 In the second year, the Lord's word came to Ether that he was to go and prophesy to Coriantumr that if he and his whole household repented, the Lord would give him his kingdom and spare the people. 21 Otherwise, they would be destroyed, as well as his whole household, all except for him. Only he would survive long enough to see the fulfillment of the prophecies about another people inheriting the land as their own, and Coriantumr would be buried by them, and every soul would be killed except for Coriantumr. 22 But Coriantumr didn't repent, and neither did his household, and neither did the people; and the wars didn't stop. They tried to kill Ether, but he escaped from them and hid again in the cave.

VI   23 Shared rose up in rebellion and he also attacked Coriantumr and defeated him, so in the third year he captured and confined him. 24 In the fourth year, Coriantumr's sons defeated Shared and reclaimed the kingdom for their father. 25 Now a war began throughout the land, every man with an armed band of men fighting for what they wanted. 26 There were also robbers, and in short, all kinds of wickedness throughout the land. 27 Coriantumr was very angry with Shared, and so he went out to attack him in battle with his armed forces. They met in great anger, in the valley of Gilgal, and the battle became severe. 28 Shared fought him for three days. And Coriantumr beat him and pursued him until he came to the plains of Heshlon. 29 Shared attacked him again on the plains. And he defeated Coriantumr and drove him back to the valley of Gilgal. 30 Coriantumr engaged Shared in battle again in the valley of Gilgal, in which he beat Shared and killed him. 31 But Shared wounded Coriantumr in the thigh, and as a result, he didn't return to fight again for two years. During that time, everyone throughout the land was killing each other and no one could restrain them.

VII   **14** A great curse came upon the land because of the people's iniquity. The curse on the land was so great that if a man placed his tool or sword on a shelf, or wherever he might keep it, he couldn't find it the next day. 2 As a result, everyone clung with their hands to those things that were theirs and wouldn't borrow or lend. Every man kept the hilt of his sword in his right hand, in defense of his property and life, as well as the property and life of his wife and children. 3 Now after two years and following Shared's death, Shared's brother rose up in rebellion and attacked Coriantumr. In that battle Coriantumr beat him and pursued him to the wilderness of Akish. 4 Shared's brother attacked him in the wilderness of Akish, and the battle became very heated, and many thousands fell by the sword. 5 Then Coriantumr laid siege to the wilderness. But Shared's brother marched out from the wilderness at night and destroyed part of Coriantumr's army while they were drunk. 6 Then he went to the land of Moron and set himself up as king in Coriantumr's place. 7 Coriantumr lived with his army in the wilderness for two years, adding great strength to his army during that time.

VIII   8 Now Shared's brother, whose name was Gilead, also added great strength to his army because of secret conspiracies. 9,10 But Lib, his high priest, who was a member of a secret society, murdered him in a secret pass as he ruled over the kingdom, and Lib obtained the kingdom for himself. He was a man of great stature, more than any other man among all the people. 11 In Lib's first year, Coriantumr came up to Moron and engaged Lib in battle. 12 He fought with Lib, and in the battle Lib struck him and wounded his arm. Nevertheless, Coriantumr's army pressed hard against Lib, so he fled to the area by the seashore. 13 Coriantumr pursued him, and Lib engaged him in battle on the seashore. 14 Lib furiously attacked Coriantumr's army, so they fled again to the wilderness of Akish. 15 Lib then pursued him until he came to the plains of Agosh. Coriantumr brought all the people with him as he fled ahead of Lib from that part of the land where he escaped. 16 When he arrived on the plains of Agosh, he attacked Lib; and he struck him repeatedly until he died. Nevertheless, Lib's brother, acting in his place, came against Coriantumr; and the battle became very heated, during which Coriantumr fled again from the army of Lib's brother.

IX   17 Now the name of Lib's brother was Shiz. And Shiz pursued Coriantumr; he conquered many cities, killing men, women, and children, and burning their cities. 18 The fear of Shiz ran through the whole land; indeed, a cry of terror ran throughout the land: Who can stand before Shiz's army? He sweeps the earth before him!

X   19 The people then began to assemble into armed forces throughout the land. 20 They were divided: some fled to Shiz's army and others fled to Coriantumr's army. 21 The war had been so great and long lasting, and the slaughter and carnage had gone on so long, that the whole land was littered with dead bodies. 22 The war was so swift and speedy no one was left to bury the dead, but they marched out from slaughter to slaughter, leaving the bodies of men, women, and children scattered over the land, to feed the maggots. 23 The stench from it spread over the whole land. So the people were bothered, both during the day and at night, because of the smell of rotting flesh. 24 Nevertheless, Shiz didn't stop pursuing Coriantumr, having sworn to avenge himself on Coriantumr for the blood of his brother, who had been killed; however, the Lord's word came to Ether that Coriantumr wouldn't die by the sword. 25 We see from this the Lord let them experience the full extent of His wrath. Their wickedness and abominations had paved the way for their everlasting destruction.

XI

²⁶ Shiz pursued Coriantumr eastward, all the way to the area by the seashore. There he engaged Shiz in battle for three days. ²⁷ The destruction was so terrible among Shiz's armed forces that they became frightened and began to flee from Coriantumr's army. They fled to the land of Corihor and swept off the inhabitants in front of them, all those who refused to join them. ²⁸ They pitched their tents in the valley of Corihor, and Coriantumr pitched his tents in the valley of Shurr. Now the valley of Shurr was near the hill Comron, so Coriantumr gathered his armed forces on the hill Comron and sounded a trumpet to Shiz's army to summon them to battle. ²⁹ They came forward but were driven back. They came a second time, and they were driven back a second time. They came back a third time, and the battle grew very fierce. ³⁰ Shiz struck Coriantumr repeatedly, giving him many deep wounds. Coriantumr, having lost a lot of blood, fainted and was taken away, as if dead. ³¹ Now the loss of men, women, and children on both sides was so great that Shiz ordered his people not to pursue Coriantumr's army; so they returned to their camp.

XII

15 When Coriantumr had recovered from his wounds, he began to remember the words that Ether had spoken to him. ² He saw the sword had already killed nearly two million of his people. He began to feel great regret — indeed, two million strong men had been killed, and their wives and children as well. ³ He began to feel sorrow for the evil he had done. He began to remember the words the prophets had spoken; and he saw they had been completely fulfilled, up to that point. And his soul mourned and refused to be comforted.

XIII

⁴ He wrote Shiz a letter, asking him to spare the people, saying he was willing to give up the kingdom for the sake of the people's lives. ⁵ When Shiz received his letter, he wrote Coriantumr a letter, saying if he would give himself up so he could kill him with his own sword, he would spare the people's lives. ⁶ But the people didn't repent of their iniquity. And Coriantumr's people were stirred up to anger toward Shiz's people, and Shiz's people were stirred up to anger toward Coriantumr's people; so Shiz's people attacked Coriantumr's people.

XIV

⁷ When Coriantumr saw he was about to be defeated, he fled again from Shiz's people. ⁸ He came to a body of water known as Ripliancum, which means large or to exceed all. When they arrived at this body of water, they pitched their tents; and Shiz also pitched his tents near them. On the following day, they came together for battle. ⁹ They fought a very heated battle, during which Coriantumr was wounded again; and he fainted from blood loss. ¹⁰ Coriantumr's armed forces bore down heavily against Shiz's armed forces, defeating them

and causing them to flee. They fled southward and pitched their tents in a place called Ogath. 11 Coriantumr's army pitched their tents by the hill Ramah, that same hill where my father Mormon hid away the sacred records under the Lord's care. 12 And they gathered everyone throughout the land who hadn't been killed, all except for Ether.

XV   13 Ether saw everything the people did. He saw the people who were on Coriantumr's side joined Coriantumr's army and the people who were on Shiz's side joined Shiz's army. 14 They spent four years bringing the people together, getting everyone in the land, so they could receive all the strength it was possible to receive. 15 When they had all assembled, everyone to the army of their choice, with their wives and children — men, women, and children being armed with weapons: having shields, breastplates, and headplates, and being clothed and equipped for war — they marched out against each other to battle. They fought all that day and neither side emerged victorious.

XVI   16 When night came, they were tired and retired to their camps. After they had retired to their camps, they began to howl and mourn for those who had been killed. Their cries, howls, and lamentations were so great that they filled the air. 17 They went again to battle the next day. And awful and terrible was that day. Nevertheless, neither side was victorious. When night came, they again filled the air with their cries, wails, and mourning for those who had been killed.

XVII   18 Coriantumr again wrote Shiz a letter, asking him not to return to battle, but to take the kingdom and spare the people's lives. 19 But the Spirit of the Lord had stopped struggling with them. Satan had complete power over the people's hearts — they were abandoned to the hardness of their hearts and the blindness of their minds, so they could be destroyed. Therefore they returned to battle. 20 And they fought the whole day. When night came, they slept on their swords. 21 On the following day, they fought until night came. 22 When night came, they were drunk with anger, like someone who's drunk with wine. They slept again on their swords.

XVIII   23 On the next day, they fought again. When night came, they had all died by the sword, all except 52 of Coriantumr's people and 69 of Shiz's people. 24 And they slept on their swords that night. On the next day, they fought again; and they struggled powerfully with their swords and shields the whole day. 25 When night came, 32 of Shiz's people remained and 27 of Coriantumr's people remained. 26 And they ate and slept, and prepared for death the following day. They were large and powerful men as to men's strength. 27 They fought for three hours and fainted from blood loss. 28 When Coriantumr's men had recovered enough energy so they could walk, they were about to flee for their lives. But Shiz and his men got up, and Shiz swore in anger he would kill Coriantumr or he would die by the sword; ²⁹ so he pursued them.

XIX On the next day he overtook them, and they fought again with the sword. When they had all died by the sword, all except for Coriantumr and Shiz, it turned out that Shiz had fainted from blood loss. ³⁰ When Coriantumr had leaned on his sword and rested a little, he struck Shiz's head. ³¹ After he had cracked Shiz's head, Shiz rose up on his hands and fell. After struggling for breath, he died. ³² And Coriantumr fell to the ground as if lifeless.

XX ³³ The Lord spoke to Ether and told him: Go out and look. And he went out and saw the Lord's words had all been fulfilled. Then he ended his record, but I haven't written one percent of it, and he hid the plates where Limhi's people found them. ³⁴ Now the last words written by Ether are these: It doesn't matter whether the Lord intends for me to be translated or that I submit to the Lord's will in the flesh, as long as I'm saved in God's kingdom. Amen.

THE BOOK OF MORONI

Chapter 1

1 After I finished summarizing the account of Jared's people, I hadn't expected to write anything else, but I haven't died yet. And I'm not revealing my whereabouts to the Lamanites, so they don't kill me. ² Now their own battles among themselves are brutal. Because of their hatred, they put to death every Nephite who refuses to deny Christ. ³ And I won't deny Christ, so I move around carefully for the safety of my own life. ⁴ So I'll write a few more things, contrary to what I expected, since I hadn't anticipated adding anything else. But I'll write a few more things, which might one day be of some value for my Lamanite brothers and sisters, if it's the Lord's will.

Chapter 2

2 The words that Christ spoke to His disciples, the twelve He had chosen, as He laid His hands on them. ² He called them by name, saying: You must call on the Father in My name in mighty prayer. After you've done this, you'll have power to give the Holy Ghost to anyone you lay your hands on. And you must confer the Holy Ghost in My name since this is what My messengers do. ³ Now Christ told them this when He first appeared to them. But the crowd of people didn't hear it; however, the disciples did. And the Holy Ghost descended upon anyone they laid their hands on.

Chapter 3

3 The way in which the disciples, who were called the elders of the congregation, ordained priests and teachers. ² After they had prayed to the Father in the name of Christ, they laid their hands on them and said: ³ In the name of Jesus Christ, I ordain you to be a priest — or if he was a teacher, I ordain you to be a teacher — to preach repentance and remission of sins through Jesus Christ by enduring faith in His name to the end. Amen. ⁴ This is how they ordained priests and teachers, according to God's gifts and callings to men. And they ordained them by the power of the Holy Ghost which was in them.

Chapter 4

4 The way in which their elders and priests administered Christ's flesh and blood to the congregation. They administered it according to Christ's commandments, so we know that the way they did it is correct. The elder or priest administered it. ² They knelt down with the congregation and prayed to the Father in the name of Christ, saying: ³ O God the Eternal Father, we ask You in the name of Your Son Jesus Christ to bless and sanctify this bread for the souls of all those who partake of it, so they can eat in remembrance of Your Son's body and show to You, O God the Eternal Father, that they are willing to take upon themselves the name of Your Son, and always remember Him, and keep His commandments He has given them, so they can always have His Spirit to be with them. Amen

Chapter 5

5 The way in which the wine was administered. They took the cup and said: ² O God the Eternal Father, we ask You in the name of Your Son Jesus Christ to bless and sanctify this wine for the souls of all those who drink of it, so they can do it in remembrance of Your Son's blood, which was shed for them, so they can show to You, O God the Eternal Father, that they always remember Him, so they can have His Spirit to be with them. Amen.

Chapter 6

6 Now I'll speak about baptism. Elders, priests, and teachers were baptized; and they weren't baptized unless they produced suitable evidence that they were worthy of it. ² They didn't receive any for baptism unless they came forward with a broken heart and a contrite spirit and testified to the congregation that they had truly repented of all their sins. ³ No one was received for baptism unless they took upon themselves the name of Christ, having made up their minds to serve Him to the end. 4 After they had been received for baptism and were influenced and cleansed by the power of the Holy Ghost, they were included as being part of Christ's congregation and their names were taken down, so they could be remembered and fed by the good word of God, to keep them on the right way, and to always keep them vigilant, in a state of prayer, relying exclusively on the merits of Christ, who was the author and finisher of their faith.

II   5 The congregation met together often to fast, pray, and speak with each other about the well-being of their souls, 6 and they met together often to partake of bread and wine in remembrance of the Lord Jesus. 7 They were vigilant in making sure there was no iniquity among them. And whoever was found to commit iniquity — and three congregation witnesses gave testimony against them before the elders — and if they didn't repent or confess, their names were erased and they weren't included as belonging to Christ's people. 8 But as often as they repented and asked for forgiveness, with real intent, they were forgiven. 9 Their meetings were conducted by the congregation according to the operation of the Spirit and by the power of the Holy Ghost. They would do as the Holy Ghost inspired them, whether it was to preach, admonish, pray, humbly petition, or sing, that's what they would do.

Chapter 7

7 Now I'll write a few of the words that my father Mormon spoke about faith, hope, and charity. This is what he said to the people as he taught them in the synagogue they had built for a place of worship:

II   2 I Mormon will now speak to you, my dear people. And it's by the grace of God the Father and our Lord Jesus Christ and His holy will, because of the gift of His calling to me, that I'm permitted to speak to you at this time. 3 I would like to speak to you who belong to the congregation, who are the peaceable followers of Christ, and who have obtained a sufficient hope to enter the Lord's rest, from now until you rest with Him in heaven. 4 Now, my people, I judge these things of you because of your peaceable walk with mankind. 5 For I remember God's word that says: You'll know them by how they live. Because if their actions are good, then they're good. 6 God has said: A person who's evil can't do good. Because if they offer a gift or pray to God, unless they do it with real intent, it's of no benefit to them — 7 it isn't credited to them for righteousness. 8 If a person who's evil gives a gift, they do it grudgingly; so it's credited to them the same as if they had retained the gift. Therefore they're considered evil before God. 9 And it's similarly counted as evil if a person prays without real intent of heart. It's of no benefit to them since God doesn't accept such a person. 10 So a person who's evil can't do good, and they can't give a good gift either. 11 Indeed, a bitter spring can't produce good water and a good spring can't produce bitter water. Therefore a person who's the accuser's servant can't follow Christ; and if they follow Christ, they can't be a servant of the accuser. 12 So everything good comes from God and everything evil comes from the accuser. Because the accuser is an enemy of God and constantly fights against Him and constantly invites and entices to commit sin and to do what's evil. 13 But godly things constantly invite and persuade to do good.

III   So everything that invites and persuades to do good and to love God and to serve Him is inspired by God. 14 Therefore be careful, my dear people, not to judge what's evil to come from God, or what's good and from God to come from the accuser. 15 You are required to determine, so you can distinguish good from evil. The way to determine things is as plain as the daylight is from the dark night, so you can know it clearly. 16 Because the Spirit of Christ is given to everyone so they can tell good from evil. Therefore I'll show you how to decide. Everything that invites to do good and persuades to believe in Christ is sent out by the power and gift of Christ. Therefore you're able to know clearly it comes from God. 17 But anything that persuades people to do evil and not to believe in Christ and deny Him and not to serve God, then you're able to know clearly that it comes from the accuser. This is how the accuser works; he doesn't persuade anyone to do good — no, not one — and neither do his angels or those who subject themselves to him. 18 Now, since you understand the light by which you can decide things, and this light is the light of Christ, take care you don't make the wrong decision; because you'll be judged by the standard you judge with. 19 So I implore you to search diligently using the light of Christ in order to know good from evil. And if you embrace every good thing and don't condemn it, you'll certainly be a child of Christ.

IV   20 Now, how is it possible you can hold firmly to every good thing? 21 Now I come to that faith I said I would speak about. I'll tell you the way by which you can hold firmly onto every good thing. 22 God, since He knows all things and exists from everlasting to everlasting, sent angels to minister to mankind, to prophesy about Christ's coming, and to reveal that every good thing would come in Christ. 23 God also declared to prophets with His own words that Christ was to come. 24 There were various ways He revealed good things to mankind; and everything that's good comes from Christ. Otherwise, people would have remained fallen and nothing good could have come to them. 25 So people began to exercise faith in Christ through the ministering of angels and by means of every word that came from God. In this way they take hold of every good thing by faith, and this is how it was until Christ's coming. 26 After He came, people were also saved by faith in His name, and by faith they became the sons and daughters of God.

V   As surely as Christ lives, He said these words to our ancestors: Anything you ask the Father in My name that's good, in faith believing you will receive, it will be done to you. 27 Therefore, my dear people, have miracles stopped just because Christ has ascended into heaven and arrived at God's right hand, to claim from the Father His rights of mercy, which He has upon mankind? 28 He has answered the requirements of the law, and He claims all those who have faith in Him. And those who have faith in Him will hold firmly to every good thing. Therefore He acts as an advocate for the benefit of mankind, and He lives eternally in the heavens.

VI   29 And because He's done this, my dear people, have miracles stopped? I tell you: No. And neither have angels stopped ministering to mankind. 30 They are obedient to Him, to minister according to His commands, revealing themselves to those of strong faith and of a firm mind in every form of godliness. 31 The responsibility of their ministry is to call people to repentance, and to fulfill and do the work of the Father's covenants that He's made to mankind, to prepare the way among people by declaring Christ's word to the Lord's chosen vessels, so they can bear testimony of Him. 32 And by doing this, the Lord God prepares the way for the remainder of mankind to have faith in Christ, so the Holy Ghost can have a place in their hearts according to the power of the Holy Ghost. This is how the Father vindicates the covenants He's made to mankind. 33 Christ has said: If you have faith in Me, you'll have power to do whatever I consider needed and proper. 34 And He's said to everyone on earth: Repent and come to Me and be baptized in My name and have faith in Me, so you can be saved.

VII   35 Now, my dear people, if these things I've told you are indeed true — and God will show you on the last day, with power and great glory, that they're true — has the day of miracles ended? 36 Or have angels stopped appearing to mankind? Or has He withheld the power of the Holy Ghost from them? Or will He so long as time lasts or the earth stands or there's one person to be saved? 37 I tell you, No. Because it's by faith miracles are performed, and it's by faith angels appear and minister to mankind. So if these things have come to an end, woe to mankind, since it's because of unbelief; and everything is wasted, 38 because no one can be saved, according to Christ's words, unless they have faith in His name. So if these things have come to an end, then so has faith; and mankind's condition will be awful, since it will be as if no redemption had been made for them.

VIII   39 But I hold a higher opinion of you. I conclude you have faith in Christ because of your meekness. Because if you don't have faith in Him, then you aren't fit to be included among the people of His congregation. 40 Again, I want to speak to you about hope. How can you attain faith without having hope? 41 So what will you hope for? You must have hope through Christ's atonement and the power of His resurrection to be raised to life eternal, and you'll have this hope because of your faith in Him, according to the promise. 42 So if a person has faith, they must have hope, since without faith there can't be any hope. 43 Again, I tell you a person can't have faith and hope unless they're meek and humble of heart. 44 Otherwise, their faith and hope are useless, since no one is acceptable before God except the meek and humble of heart.

IX   If a person is meek and humble in heart and confesses by the power of the Holy Ghost that Jesus is the Christ, they must have charity. Because if they don't have charity, they're nothing; so they must have charity. 45 Charity is long-suffering and kind; it doesn't envy or brag; it doesn't insist on its own way; it isn't easily angered; it doesn't keep track of wrongs; it takes no pleasure in evil, but rejoices in the truth; it patiently bears all things, always believes, always hopes, and always endures. 46 So, my dear people, if you don't have charity, you're nothing, since charity never fails. Therefore hold firmly to charity, which is the greatest of all. Because everything will pass away; 47 but charity is Christ's pure love, and it endures forever. Those who are found to possess it on the last day, it will go well with them. 48 So, my dear people, pray earnestly to the Father so you can be filled with this love that He's freely given to all who are true followers of His Son Jesus Christ, so you can become the sons and daughters of God, so when He appears, we'll be like Him and we'll see and comprehend Him, so we can have this hope, so we can be purified, just as He is pure. Amen.

Chapter 8

8 A letter from my father Mormon, written to me, Moroni, soon after my calling to the ministry. He wrote this to me: 2 My dear son Moroni, I'm overjoyed that your Lord Jesus Christ has been mindful of you and called you to His ministry and to His holy work. 3 I'm mindful of you always in my prayers, continually praying to God the Father in the name of His Holy Child Jesus that He through His infinite goodness and grace will protect you through enduring faith in His name to the end.

II

⁴ Now, my son, I'll speak to you about something that distresses me greatly — indeed, it troubles me that you're seeing serious disagreements. ⁵ If what I've heard is the truth, there have been arguments among you about baptizing your little children. ⁶ Now, my son, I want you to work diligently to root out this blatant error from your people — this is why I've written this letter. ⁷ As soon as I had learned about this from you, I asked the Lord about the matter. The Lord's word came to me by the power of the Holy Ghost, saying: ⁸ Listen to the words of Christ your Redeemer, your Lord and your God. I didn't enter the world to call the righteous to repentance, but sinners. The healthy don't need a physician, only those who are sick. Little children aren't sick, since they're incapable of committing sin. Therefore Adam's curse is taken from them because of Me, and it doesn't have any power over them. And the Law of Moses has been ended by Me. ⁹ This is what the Holy Ghost revealed as God's word to me.

III

So, my dear son, I know it's solemn mockery before God for you to baptize little children. ¹⁰ I tell you to teach the following: repentance and baptism for those who are accountable and capable of committing sin. Indeed, teach parents they must repent and be baptized and humble themselves like their little children, and they will all be saved with their little children. ¹¹ Their little children don't need repentance or baptism. Baptism is a sign of repentance, in order to fulfill the commandments, for the remission of sins. ¹² But little children are alive in Christ, from the very foundation of creation. If it weren't so, God would be a biased God and a changeable God, and one who showed favoritism in His treatment of people. Indeed, how many little children have died without baptism! ¹³ So if little children couldn't be saved without baptism, they would have necessarily gone to an endless hell. ¹⁴ I tell you those who think little children need baptism are bitterly corrupted by sin, since they don't have faith, hope, or charity. If they were to die with these thoughts, they would certainly go down to hell. ¹⁵ Indeed, it's awful wickedness to think God will save one child because of baptism and another child will be punished because they haven't been baptized. ¹⁶ Woe to those who corrupt and pervert the Lord's ways in this fashion, since they will perish unless they repent.

IV

I'm speaking boldly since I have authority from God. I'm not afraid of what people can do, since perfect love drives out all fear. ¹⁷ And I'm filled with charity, which is everlasting love. Therefore to me, all children are equal. I love little children with a perfect love, and they're all equal before God and take part in salvation. 18 I know God isn't a biased God, nor a changeable being; on the contrary, He's unchangeable from all eternity to all eternity. 19 Little children can't repent. So it's awful wickedness to deny them God's pure mercies; they're all alive in Him because of His mercy. 20 Those who say little children need baptism deny Christ's mercy and forgiveness and regard His atonement and the power of His redemption as worthless. 21 Woe to such people — they're in danger of death, hell, and an endless torment. I'm speaking boldly; God has commanded me to do so. Listen and pay careful attention to these things, or they'll stand against you at Christ's judgment seat. 22 All little children are alive in Christ, as well as all those who haven't had any law, since the power of redemption comes upon all those who don't have any law. Those who aren't condemned or under any condemnation can't repent, and baptism doesn't help them. 23 But it's mockery in God's eyes, denying Christ's mercy and forgiveness and the power of His Holy Spirit, and it puts trust in dead works.

V 24 My son, this thing shouldn't be. Because repentance is for those who are under condemnation and the curse of a broken law. 25 The beginning step following repentance is baptism. And baptism comes through faith in order to fulfill the commandments; and fulfilling the commandments brings remission of sins; 26 and the remission of sins brings meekness and a humble heart. And because of meekness and a humble heart comes the presence and gift of the Holy Ghost, and this Comforter fills with hope and perfect love, and this love endures by being diligent in prayer until the end comes, when all the holy ones will live with God. 27 My son, I'll write to you again if I don't return soon to battle the Lamanites. The pride of this nation — that is, the Nephites — has made their destruction certain, unless they repent. 28 Pray for them, my son, so that repentance can come to them. But I'm afraid the Spirit has stopped struggling with them. And in this part of the land, they're also attempting to put an end to all power and authority that comes from God, and they're denying the Holy Ghost. 29 After rejecting such great knowledge, my son, they will soon be lost, fulfilling the prophecies spoken by the prophets as well as the words of our Savior Himself. 30 Goodbye, my son, until I write to you or meet you again. Amen.

Chapter 9
Mormon's second letter to his son Moroni.

9 My dear son, I'm writing to you again, so you know I'm still alive, but I'm writing about serious and upsetting matters. 2 I've had a severe battle with the Lamanites from which we didn't emerge victorious. Archeantus has died by the sword, as well as Luram and Emron; indeed, we've lost a large number of our best men. 3 And now, my son, I'm afraid the Lamanites will destroy this people since they don't repent. And Satan is continually stirring them up to be angry with each other. 4 So I'm working with them constantly. When I speak God's word with sharpness, they're offended and grow angry with me. When I don't use any sharpness, they harden their hearts against it. I'm afraid the Spirit of the Lord has stopped struggling with them. 5 Indeed, they become so incredibly angry that it seems to me they aren't even afraid of death. They've lost their love for each other and constantly thirst for blood and revenge. 6 Now, my dear son, despite their hardness, let's work diligently, because if we were to stop working, we would come under condemnation. We have a labor to perform while we inhabit our mortal bodies, so we can overcome the enemy of all righteousness and rest our souls in God's kingdom.

II   7 Now I'll write a little about this people's suffering. According to the intelligence I've received from Amoron, the Lamanites have many prisoners that they took from the tower of Sherrizah — and there were men, women, and children. 8 They've killed the husbands and fathers of those women and children. And they feed the women with their husbands' flesh, and the children with their fathers' flesh. And they only give them a little water. 9 Despite this great abomination of the Lamanites, it doesn't exceed that of our people in Moriantum. There they took many Lamanite young women prisoner. After depriving them of what was most dear and precious above all things — chastity and virtue — 10 they murdered them in a most cruel manner, torturing their bodies until they died. After they've done this, they devour their flesh like wild animals because of their hard hearts, and they do it as a sign of bravery. 11 My dear son, how can a people like this, who are uncivilized — 12 and only a few years ago they were a civil and delightful people — 13 how can a people like this, who take pleasure in so much abomination, 14 how can we expect God to hold back His hand in judgment against us? 15 My heart cries out: Woe to this people! O God, bring down Your judgment, and hide their sins, wickedness, and abominations from Your face!

III   16 Also, my son, there are many widows and their daughters who remain in Sherrizah. And that part of the supplies the Lamanites didn't take, Zenephi's army has taken, leaving them to wander wherever they can looking for food. Many old women faint as they go and die. 17 The army that's with me is weak. The Lamanite armies are between me and Sherrizah. All those who have fled to Aaron's army have fallen victim to their awful brutality. 18 Oh the depravity of my people! They don't follow the rule of law and they don't show any mercy. I'm only a man and I only have a man's strength. I can no longer enforce my commands. 19 They've become strong in their perversion. They're brutal as well, sparing no one, neither old nor young. And they take pleasure in everything except for what's good. The suffering of our women and children throughout this land surpasses all. Indeed, words can't describe it, and it can't be written either.

IV   20 Now, my son, I won't dwell any longer on this horrible scene. You know this people's wickedness, that they're without principle and no longer capable of feeling, and their wickedness exceeds that of the Lamanites. 21 I can't recommend them to God, for fear He might strike me down. 22 But, my son, I recommend you to God. And I trust in Christ that you'll be saved. I pray to God that He'll spare your life so you can see in person either the return of His people to Him or their complete destruction. Because I know they will die unless they repent and return to Him. 23 If they die, it will be like the Jaredites, because of their determination to pursue blood and revenge. 24 If they die, we know many of our people have defected and joined the Lamanites, and many more will defect and join the Lamanites as well. So, write a few things if you're spared, in case I happen to die and don't see you. But I trust I can see you soon since I have sacred records I wish to hand over to you.

V   25 My son, be faithful to Christ. Don't allow what I've written to upset you and weigh you down to death, but allow Christ to lift you up. May His suffering and death, and His appearance in person to our ancestors, and His mercy and long-suffering, and the hope of His glory and eternal life, rest in your mind forever. 26 And may the grace of God the Father — whose throne is high in the heavens — and of our Lord Jesus Christ — who sits on the right hand of His power until all things become subject to Him — may Their grace be with you and stay with you forever. Amen.

Chapter 10

10 Now I Moroni will write something that seems worthwhile to me. I'm writing to my Lamanite brothers and sisters. I want them to know that more than 420 years have come to an end since the sign of Christ's coming was given. 2 After I give a few words of counsel to you, I'll seal up these records.

II   3 I would urge you that when you read these things, if it's wisdom in God for you to read them, to remember how merciful the Lord has been to mankind, from the creation of Adam all the way down until you consider these things and ponder them in your hearts. 4 When you consider these things, I would urge you to ask God the Eternal Father in the name of Christ: Aren't these things true? And if you ask with a sincere heart, with real intent, having faith in Christ, He'll reveal the truth of it to you by the power of the Holy Ghost. 5 And by the power of the Holy Ghost, you can know the truth of all things. 6 Anything that's good is righteous and true. Therefore nothing good denies Christ; on the contrary, it acknowledges that He exists. 7 And you can know He exists by the power of the Holy Ghost. Therefore I would urge you not to deny God's power — indeed, He works by power according to mankind's faith, the same today, tomorrow, and forever.

III   8 Furthermore, my brothers and sisters, I urge you not to deny God's gifts — there are many of them and they come from the same God. There are different ways these gifts are administered, but it's the same God who brings about all things in all respects. And they're given to people by the manifestations of God's Spirit in order to benefit them. 9 To one a gift is given by God's Spirit so they can teach words of wisdom, 10 and to another so they can teach words of knowledge by the same Spirit, 11 and to another great faith, and to another the gifts of healing by the same Spirit; 12 in addition, to another a gift is given so they can perform powerful miracles, 13 and to another so they can prophesy about all things, 14 and to another the gift of seeing angels and ministering spirits, 15 and to another the gift of speaking in tongues, 16 and to another the interpretation of languages and a variety of tongues. 17 All these gifts come through Christ's Spirit, and they come to every person individually, according to their desires. 18 I would urge you, my dear people, to remember every good gift comes from Christ.

IV   19 I would urge you, my dear people, to remember He is the same yesterday, today, and forever, and all these gifts I've mentioned, which are spiritual, will never come to an end as long as the world lasts, except in accordance with mankind's unbelief. 20 So there must be faith; and if there must be faith, there must also be hope; and if there must be hope, there must also be charity. 21 And unless you have charity, there's no way for you to be saved in God's kingdom. Nor can you be saved in God's kingdom if you don't have faith. Nor can you, if you don't have hope. 22 And if you have no hope, you must necessarily be in despair; and despair comes because of iniquity. 23 Christ truthfully told our fathers: If you have faith, you can do everything that I consider suitable and proper.

V
24 Now I'm speaking to the farthest reaches of the earth, that if the time comes when God's power and gifts are put to an end among you, it will be because of unbelief. 25 Woe to mankind if this is so, since there won't be anyone who does good among you — no, not one — because if there's someone among you who does good, they'll do it by God's power and gifts. 26 Woe to those who dismiss these things and die, because they will die in their sins and can't be saved in God's kingdom. I say this according to Christ's words, and I don't lie. 27 I urge you to remember these things, because the time will quickly come when you'll know I don't lie, since you'll see me at God's place of judgment. And the Lord God will tell you: Didn't I declare My words to you, which were written by this man, like someone crying out from the dead, indeed, like someone speaking from the dust? 28 I declare these things to fulfill the prophecies. They will go out from the mouth of the everlasting God, and His word will call out sharply from generation to generation. 29 God will show you that what I've written is true.

VI
30 Again, I would urge you to come to Christ and hold firmly to every good gift, and avoid every evil or unclean thought. 31 Wake up and arise from the dust, O Jerusalem! Put on your beautiful clothes, daughter of Zion, and strengthen your tent stakes and extend your borders out forever, so you won't be lost anymore, so the covenants the Eternal Father has made with you, O house of Israel, can be fulfilled. 32 Come to Christ and be made complete in Him, and reject all ungodliness. And if you reject all ungodliness and love God with all your might, mind, and strength, then His grace is sufficient for you, so that by His grace you can be complete in Christ. If by God's grace you're complete in Christ, there's no way you can deny God's power. 33 Moreover, if you're complete in Christ by God's grace and don't deny His power, then you're sanctified in Christ by God's grace through the shedding of Christ's blood, which is part of the Father's covenant, to accomplish the remission of your sins, so that you become holy, without stain.

VII
34 Now I'll say goodbye to all. I soon go to rest in God's paradise, until my spirit and body reunite and I'm brought forth triumphant

through the air to come face to face with you at the judgment seat of
the great Jehovah, the Eternal Judge of both living and dead. Amen.

—————•—————

THE TESTIMONY OF THREE WITNESSES

Be it known unto all nations, kindreds, tongues, and people, unto whom this work shall come, that we, through the grace of God the Father and our Lord Jesus Christ, have seen the plates which contain this record, which is a record of the people of Nephi, and also of the Lamanites, their brethren, and also of the people of Jared, who came from the tower of which hath been spoken. And we also know that they have been translated by the gift and power of God, for his voice hath declared it unto us; wherefore, we know of a surety that the work is true. And we also testify that we have seen the engravings which are upon the plates, and they have been shown unto us by the power of God and not of man. And we declare with words of soberness that an angel of God came down from heaven, and he brought and laid before our eyes, that we beheld and saw the plates, and the engravings thereon; and we know that it is by the grace of God the Father and our Lord Jesus Christ that we beheld and bear record that these things are true; and it is marvelous in our eyes. Nevertheless, the voice of the Lord commanded us that we should bear record of it; wherefore, to be obedient unto the commandments of God, we bear testimony of these things. And we know that if we are faithful in Christ, we shall rid our garments of the blood of all men, and be found spotless before the judgment seat of Christ, and shall dwell with him eternally in the heavens. And the honor be to the Father, and to the Son, and to the Holy Ghost, which is one God. Amen.

Oliver Cowdery
David Whitmer
Martin Harris

And also the Testimony of Eight Witnesses

Be it known unto all nations, kindreds, tongues, and people, unto whom this work shall come, that Joseph Smith, Jr., the translator of this work, has shown unto us the plates of which hath been spoken, which have the appearance of gold; and as many of the leaves as the said Smith has translated, we did handle with our hands. And we also saw the engravings thereon, all of which has the appearance of ancient work and of curious workmanship. And this we bear record with words of soberness, that the said Smith has shown unto us, for we have seen, and hefted, and know of a surety that the said Smith has got the plates of which we have spoken. And we give our names unto the world to witness unto the world that which we have seen; and we lie not, God bearing witness of it.

Christian Whitmer
Jacob Whitmer
Peter Whitmer, Junior
John Whitmer
Hiram Page
Joseph Smith, Senior
Hyrum Smith
Samuel H. Smith

The Testimonies of the First Witnesses

Before any formal witnessing to the Book of Mormon took place in late June 1829, there were two initial witnesses that should be recognized:

EMMA SMITH

"The plates often lay on the table without any attempt at concealment, wrapped in a small linen tablecloth, which I had given him to fold them in. I once felt of the plates as they thus lay on the table, tracing their outline and shape. They seemed to be pliable like thick paper, and would rustle with a metallic sound when the edges were moved by the thumb, as one does sometimes thumb the edges of a book. . . I did not attempt to handle the plates, other than I have told you, nor uncover them to look at them. I was satisfied that it was the work of God, and therefore did not feel it to be necessary to do so."[1]

MARY WHITMER

Acknowledging that there are only secondhand accounts of her story, Mary Whitmer, wife of Peter Whitmer, Sr., was visited in June 1829 by the angel, whom her grandson said she always referred to as "Brother Nephi." Nephi stated to her, "You have been very faithful and diligent in your labors, but you are tired because of the increase of your toil. It is proper therefore that you should receive a witness, that your faith may be strengthened."[2] This angelic messenger then personally showed her the Book of Mormon record, turning "the leaves of the book of plates over, leaf after leaf, and also showed her the engravings upon them."[3]

---

[1] Emma Smith interview, *The Saints' Herald*, vol. 26, 289, 290 [1 Oct 1879] cited in Joseph Smith, Heman Conoman Smith, and F. Henry Edwards, *The History of the Reorganized Church of Jesus Christ of Latter Day Saints* (Independence, MO: Herald House, 1967), 3:353–358.

[2] David Whitmer's account, according to an interview with Orson Pratt and Joseph F. Smith in September 1878, published 16 November 1878 in the *Deseret News*.

[3] Interview of John C. Whitmer with Edward Stevenson and Andrew Jenson in Richmond, Missouri, 1888, in Andrew Jenson, *Latter-day Saints Biographical Encyclopedia*, vol. 1, 283; *Historical Record*, vol. 7, 621; *Juvenile Instructor*, vol. 24, 22; *The Children's Friend*, Deseret News, vol. II, 1903, 190–191. See also Interview with David Whitmer by Orson Pratt and Joseph F. Smith, September 1878. Source: "Report of Elders Orson Pratt and Joseph F. Smith," *Millennial Star*, 40 (9 Dec 1878), 771–74; *Deseret News*, 16 Nov 1878; Cook, *David Whitmer Interviews*, 42–43.

A Selected Glossary

This glossary provides only brief descriptions of selected words and does not include all possible definitions or meanings or explanations. A more expansive treatment of some of these words can be found in *A Glossary of Gospel Terms* at www.scriptures.info.

Abomination Something that is practiced that is wrong, done as a religious belief. Celebrating something false as a religious sacrament not sanctioned by God or approved by Him. Something becomes abominable when it is motivated by a false form of religious observance.

Accuser One of many titles for Satan or the Devil. The Latin word is from the Ecclesiastical Greek *diabolos*, which in Jewish and Christian use was "the Devil, Satan," and which in general use meant "accuser, slanderer." Satan is a title that means "accuser," "opponent," and "adversary"; hence, once he fell, Lucifer became — or in other words, was called — Satan because he accuses others and opposes the Father (*see* Revelation 4:4; 8:6 RE). *See* Satan.

Angel A messenger is one who brings a message from the Lord. It includes not only pre-mortal and post-mortal spirits and beings, but also living men. When anyone, man or angel, is entrusted with a message from God, the message is God's.

Anoint To place oil (typically, olive oil) that is consecrated and set apart for a special purpose upon the head or other important parts of the body or upon instruments of ceremonial worship. The term comes from the Hebrew word *mashiach* (Messiah) and the Greek word *christos* (Christ), both meaning "anointed one." Throughout history, anointing has been used for the blessing of the sick, the formal ordination of priests, and the investiture of kings to their position. *See also* Christ, Messiah.

Anti-Christ One who denies or opposes Christ. They teach false doctrine and deliberately seek followers and supporters.

Anti-Nephi-Lehi *Anti* appears to be a proper noun or proper name in the Nephite-Lamanite language. It means the people of Nephi and Lehi. It was originally a name given to the brother of the king Lamoni. *Anti* means a "combination or face-to-face meeting." The Latin *ante* means "standing in front of a person and facing him," so *Anti-Nephi-Lehi* means the people of Nephi brought face-to-face or joined together with the other descendants of Lehi. It's bringing together the peoples of Nephi and Lehi.

Ascension An ascension is an ancient text that narrates the journey of a patriarch, prophet, or other significant figure into heaven or through the cosmos, followed by their return to earth to share their visions and experiences. Notable examples of those who have ascended and left a written record are Abraham, Enoch, Moses, Ezekiel, Isaiah, John the Revelator, and Lehi and Nephi. There are two ascents. One is temporary and happens when men are "caught up" but then return to this world. It represents overcoming the world and returning the individual back to the presence of God. It is called *redemption from the Fall* (Ether 1:13 RE) because it brings the individual back into God's presence. This form of temporary ascent is designed to establish a covenant or promise related to the other, more gradual ascent through development of the individual. The temporary mortal ascent secures a promise for the individual that they will be permitted to make the eternal ascent to where God and Christ dwell in the afterlife and is possible for all mortals. The scriptures, in particular the *Covenant of Christ*, contain accounts of those who have ascended to God's presence and overcome the Fall of mankind. The second form is the actual ascent, involving redemption, and securing eternal life and cannot happen in mortality but is accomplished over time.

Atonement The great work performed by Jesus Christ that describes the redemption of all mankind from death, and the possibility that all mankind may be saved by obedience to the laws and ordinances of the Gospel of Jesus Christ. Without the atonement, the possibility of a return to the presence of God could not take place. The atonement was accomplished by His sinless life, the suffering in the garden of Gethsemane, and His death on the cross and resurrection from the grave.

Babylon The capital city of the ancient kingdom Babylonia which ruled much of the Near East in biblical times. Babylon is identified symbolically to represent "the world" and its evil. It includes and symbolizes all the false religious, philosophical, educational, and governmental systems of the world. Its counterpart in the scriptures is Zion.

Baptism The ordinance is performed by following the instructions taught by Christ in 3 Nephi 5:8 RE. One must be put under the water and then *come forth again out of the water*. The purpose of baptism is to follow Christ's example. It symbolizes the death of the old man of sin and the resurrection into a new life in Christ. It must involve immersion. One is placed below the surface of the water, in the same way the dead are buried below ground. The breath of life is cut off while under the water and restored anew when coming forth again out of the water. The officiator, having obtained power and authority from God is the one who immerses and then brings the recipient up out of the water. Christ prescribes the exact words to be used in the ordinance. Authorization comes from Jesus Christ, but the ordinance is performed in the name of the Father, and of the Son, and of the Holy Ghost.

Baptism of Fire and the Holy Ghost A sign of redemption, purification, and holiness that is included in the "gate" for entering into God's presence. The baptism of fire and the Holy Ghost, as taught by Christ in the Doctrine of Christ (*see* 2 Nephi 13:3 RE), is given without man's involvement, comes from heaven, and is promised by both the Father and the Son. The fire and the Holy Ghost are given as a sign to the recipient that they may know it is safe for them to enter into God's presence and not be consumed. The baptism of fire purges and removes sin. In effect, you receive holiness through the sanctifying power of the Holy Spirit.

Belief Understanding and accepting true doctrine (see 3 Nephi 7:4 RE). Belief leads to faith and faith to knowledge. But the process is initiated by one's belief and correct understanding of His teachings. Belief is only possible by receiving the truth. It is important to have the truth in order to acquire belief.

Book of Mormon A volume of scripture Joseph Smith attributed to his translation of a set of metal plates. The plates were originally written by aboriginal inhabitants of the Americas, then buried by the last contributing author approximately A.D. 421. Originally written by a prophetic family from the tribe of Joseph, who fled Jerusalem in 601 B.C., prior to the Babylonian destruction. The high point of the text is the post-resurrection visit of the Messiah — or Jesus Christ — to the Americas. Smith claimed the location of these buried plates was revealed to him by an angel, and the translation was accomplished by "the gift and power of God." The original account was abridged by a man or prophet named "Mormon" and the book takes its name from him.

Borders of the Red Sea A proper name, and therefore, capitalized, for the area of the range of mountains that has been called the *Jabal*, which means "the Borders." Nephi 1:7 RE; 1 Nephi 2:5 LE. *See also* 1 Nephi 1:8 RE, 1 Nephi 5:6 RE.

Broken Heart and Contrite Spirit Repentance is accompanied by a broken heart and contrite spirit. If you had to bear your sins into His presence it would make you burn with regret and fear. Your own heart must break. When you behold how little you have to offer Him, your spirit becomes contrite.

Charity The pure love of Christ. The Apostle Paul elevated charity (the pure love of Christ) to such high importance that salvation itself depends upon a person's charity (*see* 1 Corinthians 1:51 RE). It is through grace that one obtains charity. It is through charity that one can bless others. Charity is a determination to live a certain way and to not allow oneself to be overcome by the jealousies, envies, and all the negative things that make it so easy to excuse giving kindness to others. In a very real sense, charity is trying to see others in the same way that the Father sees them.

Christ A title meaning "anointed one." It is the anglicized form of the Greek word *Christos* (χριστός), which means "Messiah." Jesus Christ is a name with a title as is Jesus the Anointed (One) or Jesus the Messiah. *See also* Messiah.

Church In this book the term church is usually used as an institution organized by men and used in a negative sense, as opposed to the term congregation. *See* Congregation.

Church, The Wealthy, Corrupt, and Utterly Wicked Mankind is commanded to not unite with this church, which is described as wealthy, corrupt, and utterly wicked (1 Nephi 3:27 RE). This church is symbolically described as Babylon — or the world. Using a typological comparison, the prophet Nephi prophesied that the world in the last days will be separated into two divisions. One is this corrupt and utterly wicked church, and the other is the Congregation of the Lamb of God (Christ) (1 Nephi 3:27-28 RE). The other utterly wicked church, described originally in the 1830 translation as "great and abominable," is all-inclusive and comprised of all philosophies, all belief systems, all unbelief systems, all rationalizations, all theories, and all vanities that distract people from repenting and following Christ. These vary from very good things that are uplifting (and possess even great portions of truth) to the degrading and perverse. This all-inclusive church is a "whore" because she is completely indiscriminate and open for all to have her acceptance and affection. She welcomes all, the only requirement being that one have false beliefs.

Cimeter A weapon of war. When Cortés invaded Mexico, he faced fierce resistance from the native population, which he could only conquer due to the devastating impact of smallpox and other European diseases. Despite having the best European arms and armor, including armored war horses, his forces encountered native weapons like the *macuahuitl*. This weapon, a wooden club embedded with sharp obsidian blades capable of having an edge sharper than steel razor blades, could sever limbs and decapitate both men and horses. Skilled users wielded these with great effect. (This historical example doesn't support any Book of Mormon geographical interpretation or preference.) The Middle Eastern scimitar, with its curved shape ideal for slashing rather than stabbing, had a similar function in battle. Therefore, this book likely references a weapon used for slicing blows, not a specific curved metal blade. Nephite knowledge of metallurgy, derived from Nephi, often gave them an advantage, such as using armor while the Lamanites fought nearly naked. However, this knowledge was sometimes lost in cycles of war and apostasy, leading both sides to use various weapons, both metal and non-metal. The unique spelling cimeter preserves its distinction and avoids the misconception of referring to a specific type of curved metal blade, emphasizing function over form.

Commandment A direction from the Lord on how to live and behave. Commandments are given to teach men and women how they can continue to receive and renew a continuing conversion to Christ's way of life. Commandments are not a burden to bear, but a roadmap to follow.

Congregation In this book a *congregation* is defined as a group, community, or fellowship of believers. Denotes followers of Christ, obeying His commandments, in contrast to the term *church*.

Consecrate To set something or someone apart as sacred or holy; to pronounce clean; to purify or sanctify. The antonym is *desecrate*.

Covenant A *covenant*, simply put, is a promise. It involves committing to fulfill an expectation with the understanding that something will be received in return when certain conditions are met or completed. Mankind does not make covenants with God. God alone offers a covenant, and people either accept or reject God's offer. But until God makes the offer, mankind can do nothing to create a covenant with God.

Covenant People Descendants of the patriarch Jacob, later renamed Israel by God, who are not merely biological descendants but are Israel by covenant; and those today who belong to the house of Israel because of their covenant relationship with God.

Destroy In the vernacular of this book, to destroy does not always mean annihilation. It can mean mean to end the organized existence of a people or to terminate their government, deprive them of a land, and end their cultural dominance. People were destroyed when they lost control over their government and land.

Disciple A person who follows Jesus Christ. In this book it can refer to the twelve disciples who were called and chosen by Christ in the Americas.

Doctrine of Christ Christ explained His Doctrine immediately following His instruction on baptism: *This is My doctrine, and it is the doctrine that the Father has given to Me: I testify of the Father, and the Father testifies of Me, and the Holy Ghost testifies of the Father and Me. I also testify the Father commands all people everywhere to repent and believe in Me. And anyone who believes in Me and is baptized will be saved, and they are who will inherit God's kingdom. But anyone who doesn't believe in Me and isn't baptized will be damned. In truth I tell you this is My doctrine, and I testify of it from the Father. Anyone who believes in Me also believes in the Father, and the Father will testify to them of Me, since He will visit them with fire and with the Holy Ghost* (3 Nephi 5:9 RE). This doctrine of Christ will bring you in contact with God. You were meant to return to the Family you came from. It is the homecoming you have always felt was needed. You do not belong here. There is something higher, something more holy calling to you. It is not found in an institution, or program, or a ward, or office. It is only found in God, who is your home. The Doctrine of Christ is the doctrine of God's return to be with you and abide with you. *See* Gospel of Jesus Christ.

Eternal Life The definition of *Eternal life* was given by the Savior and recorded by John, who wrote: *Jesus spoke these words, and lifted up his eyes to Heaven and said, Father, the hour has come. Glorify your Son, that your Son also may glorify you, as you have given him power over all flesh, that he should give eternal life to as many as you have given him. And this is life eternal: that they might know you, the only true God, and Jesus Christ whom you have sent* (John 9:19 RE). To know God is Eternal life.

Faith More than belief; a principle of action that requires one to act on belief in order to produce faith. Faith is defined as a principle of power through action, in which one puts those beliefs into action and thereby acquires power. Before belief can turn into faith, action is required. Belief becomes faith, and faith becomes knowledge.

Fall (of Mankind) The state of God's withdrawal from Adam, causing mankind's spiritual death or separation from God. *Therefore all mankind was and always would be in a lost and fallen state unless they relied on this Redeemer* (1 Nephi 3:2 RE). *[Christ's] death precedes His resurrection and will redeem everyone from the first death, that spiritual death. Because all mankind was cut off from the Lord's presence when Adam fell, they're effectively dead both physically and spiritually* (Helaman 5:12 RE). Redemption from the Fall happens when one is brought back into the presence of God.

Filthy Mankind will be judged for what they have done while on earth during their mortal life. If they were to die in their wickedness, they would be outcast from spiritual things involving righteousness and brought to stand before God to be judged for what they did. If the things they did involve *filthy* thoughts and behavior, they'll certainly be *filthy*, and it would be impossible for them to live in God's kingdom, because God's kingdom would become polluted and *filthy* as well. But God's kingdom isn't *filthy*, and no unclean thing can enter God's kingdom (*See* 1 Nephi 4:6 RE).

Gentiles Historically identified as non-Jews or non-Israelites but defined within this book to include great numbers of descendants of Israel who have lost their identity or knowledge of their original birthright, as well as present-day *Gentiles* who become included within the house of Israel after conversion. The Messiah taught: *But if the Gentiles will repent and return unto me, saith the Father, behold they shall be numbered among my people, O house of Israel* (3 Nephi 16:13 RE). When they convert, they are restored through covenant to their status as Israel. The *Gentiles* make up the majority of readers of this book in the present era.

Gift of the Holy Ghost The Holy Ghost can come and visit with a person but not remain with them. If it comes and visits with them, then it is said the person has "received" the Holy Ghost. This kind of visit is conditional.

It is dependent upon the worthiness and desire of the recipient. For the Holy Ghost to become a constant companion which remains, it is said to be *the gift of the Holy Ghost*, because the one with this endowment has received a gift from God, and it is given to them by God to be theirs. Baptism and the Holy Ghost have always been linked together, but laying on hands has not always been included. Baptism and the Holy Ghost are linked whether or not there is someone who can lay on hands to give the gift. Baptism precedes the Holy Ghost, and the Holy Ghost always follows, if the baptism was proper. The only condition for receiving the Holy Ghost is sincere repentance before baptism. If a person is sincere, then the gift follows automatically.

Gospel of Jesus Christ Jesus Christ defines His gospel in the Book of Mormon: *This is the gospel I've given to you, that I came into the world to do the will of My Father, because My Father sent Me. And My Father sent Me so I could be lifted up on the cross — and after I've been lifted up on the cross, I can bring all people to Me, so that as I've been lifted up by people, likewise people will be lifted up by the Father to stand before Me to be judged according to their works, whether they were good or whether they were evil. This is why I've been lifted up. Therefore, according to the Father's power, I will draw everyone to Me so they can be judged according to their works. Those who repent and are baptized in My name will be fully rewarded. If they continue faithful to the end, I'll hold them guiltless in the presence of My Father when I stand to judge the world... No unclean thing can enter His kingdom. Therefore no one enters His rest except those who have washed their clothes in My blood because of their faith, and repentance of all their sins, and their faithfulness to the end. Now this is the commandment: Repent, everyone, throughout the earth, and come to Me and be baptized in My name, so you can be sanctified by receiving the Holy Ghost, so you can stand spotless in My presence on the last day. Therefore I tell you: This is My gospel* (3 Nephi 12:5 RE). *See* Doctrine of Christ.

High Priesthood of the Holy Order Priesthood or priestly authority is the association between mankind and those on the other side of the veil. It is a fellowship wherein mortals are connected with "the Powers of Heaven" — a title referring to a specific group in heaven. Priesthood, in its highest form, is an opportunity to serve and bless others. It is a call to save, redeem, and rescue others from destruction. Men do not make priests; God does. The purpose of priesthood is to accomplish two things: first, to have valid ordinances, such as baptism and blessing the sacrament; second, to obtain answers or direction from heaven. The High Priesthood is conferred upon those who exercise exceeding faith, repentance, and righteousness before God, choosing to repent and work righteousness. Ordination to the High Priesthood reckons from before the foundation of the earth. Power in that priesthood is derived from heaven. These powerful doctrines are not even imagined by other faiths or traditions. It is apparent that an ordination to even the High Priesthood cannot guarantee a recipient will have faith sufficient to gain power in the priesthood. For that, like every other blessing, it is always required for the man to obtain it directly from heaven. The priesthood is predicated on a relationship with "the Powers of Heaven." Priesthood authority cannot be abused. If the one ordained does not secure such a relationship with the Powers of Heaven, then the ordination will not produce the expected results.

Holy Ghost The Holy Ghost is most correctly understood as the individual spirit within each man or woman — it is the heavenly record from each one's prior experiences, although now veiled. The Holy Ghost is the light of truth. The Holy Ghost is also the received communication, inspiration, or light from above, and the source of that light can be any number of *holy beings* sent to shed that light upon mankind. The Holy Ghost is a personage. It is an individual. It is a spirit that will dwell inside a man, a woman, or a child. The Holy Ghost, which resides inside of each person, receives intelligence from Christ. The Holy Ghost is the *Record of Heaven* that man has lost contact with because of the veil. It is a personage of spirit who resides inside each man or woman, and one must "receive" it after baptism by finally listening to that inner *truth of all things* or *record of the Father and the Son* (Genesis 4:9–10). From Adam until Christ, the Holy Ghost was the primary voice by which revelation was delivered from God to mankind. It is active and has been active in delivering the words of prophecy to "holy men" throughout history. The scriptures have explained that the Holy Ghost which dwells in man — this personage of spirit — has the following other descriptions or attributes: *the Record of Heaven, the Comforter, the keys of the kingdom of Heaven, the truth of all things, that which quickens all things — which makes alive all things, that which knows all things, and has all power according to Wisdom, mercy, truth, justice and judgment* (Genesis 4:9). This is a description of the personage of spirit that dwells inside each person. This is the Holy Ghost. This is something that can be in contact with the Holy Spirit, or the *mind of the Father and Son.*

Holy Ones/Saints *Holy Ones* are the righteous ones, also known as the saints of the Holy One of Israel. (*See* 2 Nephi 6:7 RE.) Holy ones or saints are supposed to be identified as baptized followers of Christ — holy, sacred, consecrated, and pure — and in the scriptures they often are, but historically they have also fallen short of that description. Sanctification is the process of becoming a *holy one. See* Sanctification.

Holy Order The Holy Order is the channel through which all knowledge, doctrine, the plan of salvation, and every important matter is revealed from heaven. Among other things, the purpose of the Holy Order is to put in place a mechanism by which God can reveal from heaven what is necessary for the salvation of man on Earth. It may serve everyone but will never be held by everyone. It conveys blessings and information that are withheld from the world. *See* High Priesthood, Priesthood.

Holy Spirit   The power of God which fills the immensity of space. Sometimes the Holy Spirit is called the "Light of Christ" rather than the Holy Spirit.

House of Israel   The descendants of the patriarch Jacob of the Old Testament (whose name was changed to Israel) who have an active covenant with God, which excludes those descendants of Israel who have abandoned the faith, broken the covenant, and gone off to serve false gods. The Messiah has given His promise that He would gather and restore the house of Israel. It includes the descendants of Israel's twelve sons or the twelve tribes of Israel.

Holy One of Israel   The Lord God Almighty, the true Messiah and Redeemer who has a covenant relationship with those faithful to Him (*see* 2 Nephi 1:2 RE). And the gatekeeper is the Holy One of Israel, and He doesn't use any servant there (2 Nephi 6:11 RE).

Idol Worship   Idols can take the form of other men and women, ourselves, false educational ideas, or organizations. Idolatry is anything that separates mankind from God.

Iniquity   The Book of Mormon usage may be confined to the following: The willful act of disobedience or rebellion that represents the most extreme form of unrighteous behavior — premeditated, ongoing, and tending to escalate. Those who commit iniquity exert their power over the powerless. *See* Ripe in Iniquity.

Isaiah   An Old Testament prophet who ministered from around 740 B.C. to 701 B.C. Because of his important writings, he is quoted or paraphrased extensively by Nephite prophets, as well as Jesus Christ, who commands us to diligently study his writings, *because Isaiah's prophecies are critical* (3 Nephi 10:4 RE).

Islands of the Sea   Everything that is not part of the great Euro-Asian-African land mass. Although North America is currently regarded as a continent, in the Book of Mormon vernacular, it is an *island of the sea*. Further, most of Israel was relocated onto the *islands of the sea*. When the Lord affirms that He speaks to those on the *islands of the sea*, He is confirming that there are multiple locations, involving multiple parties, each one of which has received sacred communication from Him. We think of *islands* apart from continents. This book explains that the American continents are in reality one of the *islands of the sea*.

Israel, Gathering of   An event that is foretold to happen at the end of the times, when Christ returns. All the house of Israel, the descendants of Jacob (Israel), will be gathered from their scattered condition.

Jaredites A pre-Israelite, pre-Nephite civilization that migrated to America, named after the patriarch Jared, whose brother was a prophet and exhibited great faith as described in the book of Ether.

Jesus Christ The name *Jesus*, which derives from the Hebrew, *Yeshua* or *Joshua*, and means "the Lord is salvation" or "God saves." The word *Christ* is a title that originates from the Greek word meaning the "anointed one." *See* Christ, Messiah.

Jews The Jews, or those of the Jewish race or religion, who trace their lineage back to the house of Israel through Judah, the son of Jacob or Israel.

Lamanites In broad terms, those people who descended from Laman, the eldest son of Lehi and Sariah, and who were part of the Lamanite civilization that was in continual conflict with the Nephites. In our day, they are characterized as the descendants of Book of Mormon people who belong to the house of Israel and who are broadly defined to include native or indigenous covenant people of the Americas.

Law of Circumcision The *law of circumcision* was instituted with Abraham before the time of Moses as a token of the covenant between God and His chosen people and the practice was incorporated into the Mosaic law. It is important to note that the *law of circumcision* is a traditional short-hand way to refer to the Law of Moses.

Law of Moses When the children of Israel refused to live a higher law, they were given the Law of Moses. This law, in a general view, consisted of a collection of commandments, statutes, performances, rituals, sacrifices, and ceremonies. The focus of the Law of Moses was ritual purity, but Christ replaced that earlier ritual-based purity with internal purity. In Christ the Law of Moses was fulfilled and will not return.

Long-suffering An adjective meaning to be patient, tolerant, accommodating, forgiving, and charitable.

Meekness A difficult attribute to recognize, it is found in the relationship between man and God, not between man and man; to be meek is to follow the Lord's will, even when one doesn't want to do so, even when it brings one into conflict with friends, family, or community. Meekness is measured as between the servant and the Lord, not as between the servant and his critics. Meekness means a person voluntarily restrains himself and uses the absolute minimum control or authority over others. It is related to humility. *And God remembers the meek, for they will inherit the earth* (3 Nephi 5:14 RE).

Messiah A title meaning "anointed one," from the Hebrew *mashiach*. *See also* Christ.

Mulochites A people discovered by Mosiah, known as the people of Zarehemla, that were descendants of Muloch, or Mulek, who was a son of the last king of Judah, Zedekiah. Muloch and his party escaped the destruction of Jerusalem by the Babylonians and were led by the Lord to the promised land.

Nation A title for a people or ethnicity, like the Israelites. *Nations* does not refer to modern states, but to family divisions or subsets, like the ancient tribes of Israel. They were called nations. The terms *nations, kindreds, tongues, and people* have a family meaning; they specifically have the family of Israel — in its scattered condition — in mind. The gospel is intended primarily for one family of redeemed souls.

Nephites In broad terms, those people who descended from Nephi, the son of Lehi and Sariah, or followed his teachings, or were part of his civilization.

Ordinance It is through covenant-forming ordinances — including rituals — that the power of godliness has been manifested to mankind. The ordinances, such as baptism, the gift of the Holy Ghost, the sacrament, etc., are helps, symbols, and requirements. *Helps* in that they establish milestones that memorialize passage from one stage of development to the next. *Symbols* in that they point to a deeper meaning or spiritual reality almost always grounded in the atonement of Jesus Christ. *Requirements* in that they mark the defined route taken by Christ as a mortal to fulfill all righteousness. The ordinances as symbols point to the real thing. The real thing is Jesus Christ and His Gospel.

Persevere/Endure/Persist to the End Persevering, enduring, or persisting to the end, is the fixed purpose to always serve God so that you may always have His spirit to be with you and is essential to salvation. Nephi tells us that his words persuade people to *persist to the end, which is life eternal* (2 Nephi 15:1 RE).

Pollutions To pollute is to defile, violate the sanctity of, or render something ceremonially unclean. The use of pollute to contaminate the environment hadn't emerged until 1860. *And people will hear of wars, reports of wars, and earthquakes in various places. It will come at a time when there will be great pollutions on the earth: there will be murders, robbing, lying, deceiving, whoredoms, and all kinds of abominations* (Mormon 4:4 RE). *You pollutions, hypocrites, and you teachers who sell yourselves for things that will corrode and decay, why have you polluted God's holy congregation?* (Mormon 4:5 RE).

Priest One who has authority to perform ordinances, as described in the *Covenant of Christ*. See High Priesthood, Priesthood, Holy Order.

Priestcraft The exploitation of religious authority for personal gain and prestige (*see* 2 Nephi 11:17 RE). Any person who tries to put themselves between another person and heaven, claiming that they are the source of religious truth, is practicing priestcraft and will in the end lead both to damnation.

Priesthood   *Priesthood* or priestly authority is the association between mankind and those on the other side of the veil. It is a fellowship wherein mortals are connected with "the Powers of Heaven" — a title referring to a specific group in heaven. Priesthood, in its highest form, is an opportunity to serve and bless others. It is a call to save, redeem, and rescue others from destruction. Men do not make priests; God does. The purpose of priesthood is to accomplish two things: first, to have valid ordinances, such as baptism and blessing the sacrament; second, to obtain answers or direction from heaven. *See* High Priesthood, Holy Order.

Promised Land   Every time the full covenant is given, it includes a promised land. The Americas are the land God covenanted to give His people. The Gentiles must repent and accept His gospel, to be part of His covenant people. This was a covenant made by God to Lehi, as a dispensational head. The beneficiaries of the covenant included Lehi's family and those who came with them, as well as generations of Lehi's family who came thereafter. This land in particular, is a land of promise to those who serve the God of this land, who is Jesus Christ (*see* Ether 1:7 RE).

Prophet   A true messenger or teacher sent with authority by God to minister. All the prophets had authority and were ordained by God himself. The portion of the high priesthood authority which let men speak face to face with God was bestowed by God directly upon the prophets, independent of the mainstream of the people and their leadership. The Messiah takes ownership of the prophets by declaring, "I send unto you prophets!" (Matthew 10:35 RE). The prophet's role is always to cry repentance. Priests may preside and kings may rule, but the prophet's voice is always crying repentance.

Repentance   To repent is to turn to God. To turn to Him is to face Him, listen to Him, heed Him, and pay attention to what He is, says, and does. It is to seek to be in contact with Him. If one is in contact with Him, He will teach him all things he should do (*see* 2 Nephi 14:1 RE).

Ripe in Iniquity   That moment in time when people can no longer repent, when they have reached the limit when judgment will overtake them. Fruit is fully ripe at that moment when further ripening would not mean improvement but only deterioration. When the fruit is ripe there is no point in letting it remain longer on the tree. Ripeness is that state of things when nothing further remains to be done in the direction of ripening, and the process has reached the end. A society has reached such a point when it can no longer go in the direction it has been taking, when the only hope of motion lies in a change or a direct reversal of direction. *See* Iniquity.

Sacrament/Lord's Supper/Bread and Wine   Christ instituted the sacrament during the Passover meal. It was His "last supper" with His closest followers. All the accounts agree on the purpose: to remember the body and blood He would sacrifice on behalf of mankind. When the Lord appeared to the Nephites, He proclaimed He had fulfilled the Law (*see* 3 Nephi 7:2 RE). All the rites and sacrifices added through Moses pointed to His great sacrifice of His body and blood. The purpose of the sacrament is to remember Christ, His body that was broken to fulfill the required sacrifice, and His blood that was shed for man's redemption. When the bread is broken and blessed, those who qualify (by having repented and been baptized) receive it as a gift or token from Christ — it is His body. This is to be done *in remembrance of [His] body* (Moroni 4:1 RE). It is through His body that He, the living sacrifice, shows the way to all. "A loving God has died for us. His body is a testimony of life, obedience, sacrifice, cruelty, forgiveness, death, resurrection, immortality, power, and glory. When you remember His life, you should remember all that is associated with it. When the Lord visited the Nephites, *He commanded that they should eat* (3 Nephi 8:6 RE). This is more than an invitation; it is more than an offering. It is a commandment.

Sanctification To be sanctified is to be qualified to stand in the presence of God without sin, clean of all blood and sin. The baptism of fire and the Holy Ghost is for sanctification. It is done upon the body and the Spirit within each person. The work of this "baptism of fire" is always sanctification. It brings the recipient into greater contact with God. In effect, you receive holiness through the sanctifying power of the Holy Spirit. This in turn makes your own spirit holy. Man is unworthy to enter into God's presence and, therefore, requires a power higher than his own from which to borrow purity. This purifying agent is the Holy Ghost (*see* 3 Nephi 9:3–4 RE). Christ sanctifies mankind; they don't sanctify themselves. To be purified, to be sanctified by the Lamb — removing from you, and taking upon Himself the responsibility to answer for whatever failings you have — this is not ritual purity. This is purity in fact.

Satan One of many titles for the Devil or Lucifer. A title that means "accuser," "opponent," and "adversary"; hence, once he fell, Lucifer became — or in other words, was called — Satan because he accuses others and opposes the Father (*see* Revelation 4:4; 8:6 RE). *See* Accuser.

Seashore The term seashore can mean the land that lies adjacent to an ocean, lake, or body of water. The word sea originally meant a sheet of water, sea, lake, or pool, and often made no distinction between sea and lake, either large or small, by inland or open, salt or fresh.

Secret Conspiracy An evil *conspiracy* that works in darkness and whose overall objective is "power and gain," but especially "the control over the government," often using political office to rule and do according to their will, that they might get gain and glory of the world (*see* Helaman 3:1 RE). Even though these completely corrupt *conspiracies* may work in secret, their works are often displayed in the open or to public view without any regard to concealment. These conspiracies have existed since the time of Cain, are inspired by Satan, and often use covert signs and oaths as they convert blood to cash and cash to blood: using the treasures of the earth "to rule with blood and horror on the earth." This book characterizes the creating of a secret combination or conspiracy as the most abominable and wicked above all, in the sight of God (Ether 3:17 RE) because of the intent to commit murder, secret murder (*see* Alma 37:22 RE; 3 Nephi 4:6 RE; Helaman 2:30, 33, 35 RE), and secret works of darkness (see 2 Nephi 6:3, 7:3, 11:15 RE; Alma 17:12 RE; Helaman 2:33, 3:6, 19 RE; Mormon 4:4 RE).

Seer A seer is someone who has knowledge of things which cannot be seen with the natural eye. *He possesses the means that allow him to see and translate ancient records, and this ability is a gift from God. These things are known as Interpreters, and no man can look into them unless God commands him to do so, in order to prevent him from seeing something he shouldn't see and perishing. Whoever is commanded to look in them is called a seer* (Mosiah 5:8 RE). When anyone has possession of such an instrument as Interpreters or the Urim and Thummim, they are, by definition, a seer; the instrument itself allows the possessor to see the past, present, and future. However, it is not necessary to possess this instrument to be a seer.

Sin Missing the mark, failing, making a mistake, violating a commandment, disobeying, or doing one thing when one should be doing other and better things.

Transgression It should be noted that the terms sin and transgression are often used interchangeably, permitting mutual substitution. The use of the term in scripture may vary based on context, but it is often used to indicate a deliberate offense. At times, transgression can be interpreted to mean an offense committed in innocent ignorance, whereas the word sin is used primarily for an offense committed deliberately, with the knowledge that an eternal law is being violated. Transgression requires repentance, just as does sin.

Translate To operate under the power of the Spirit through revelation to restore that which has been lost and to clarify that which is in the mind of the Lord. In all of the revelations that deal with the Scriptures, the fullness of the Scriptures, and the revision of the Bible by inspiration through Joseph Smith under the direction of the Lord, which imparted the Scriptures, the word that gets used continually to describe that effort is translate, and it has a highly particularized meaning. It does not mean taking an ancient text and re-working it by moving it from one language into another.

Twelve Witnesses What this book refers to as the Twelve Apostles of Jesus in the New Testament. In this edition, when the word "Twelve" is capitalized, it refers to the Twelve Apostles of Jerusalem.

Unbelief As used in this book, it means one does not understand and has not accepted true doctrine. The word *unbelief* means to accept false doctrine or to have an incomplete and inaccurate understanding of correct doctrine.

Wickedness The state of being evil or immoral, not only in actions but also as a state of one's mindset; harboring an evil disposition, consistently causing deliberate harm; the ultimate condition of unrighteousness. Wickedness is also distinguished by those engaging in abominable practices.

Woe When one woe is pronounced upon a people, it is a warning of condemnation in this life. A three-fold condemnation (woe, woe, woe) is more serious and extends beyond this life in the hereafter.

Wrath There are two levels of wrath. One is temporal — here and now. The wicked are often punished here by letting them pursue their own evil course until it destroys them — unless they repent. The other is eternal — meaning coming after this life, and is a result of leaving this life with accountability for what happened here and the lack of preparation for the moment when judgment is rendered. What mortals perceive as God's "feelings" (such as anger or wrath) cannot be adequately defined in human terms. We think God is very loving and benign because of the sacrifice of Christ. But consider how God's wrath is manifested. He withdraws, He withdraws His spirit. When you want Him present and He withdraws, that disapproval can feel terrible.

Zion A prophesied last-days community of saints to which the City of Enoch will return, and where Christ will dwell. Zion consists of people living in harmony with God. It is defined in revelation as *the pure in heart* (T&C 96:5–7), but prophecy also confirms it will be an actual location and a place of gathering. Zion and a New Jerusalem will exist before the Lord's return in glory. Zion is something that has only been accomplished in the known history of the world by two communities. It is prophesied that there will be a third.

Background of the Covenant of Christ

Source Groups

The *Covenant of Christ* text primarily spans a period of approximately one thousand years, between 600 B.C. and A.D. 400. Numerous prophets wrote the record, and one of the final writers, Mormon, abridged or condensed the lengthy history into a single book, which was subsequently completed by his son, Moroni. Then in approximately A.D. 420 Moroni buried the abridged record in what is now the state of New York, in the United States of America.

Joseph Smith Jr. (1805-1844) was shown the site of the hidden record by an angel. Joseph was given the record and the means to translate it in 1827. Joseph completed the translation and published the book three years later, in 1830. The first published work was named The Book of Mormon after that prophet, Mormon, who had compiled and abridged it.

The source text consisted of records engraved on metal referred to as "plates." The plates detail the ancient migrations of three specific groups to the American continent:

• **The people of Lehi** left Jerusalem in 601 B.C. and later divided into two main groups known as the Nephites and the Lamanites, each named for one of Lehi's sons. This is the primary group that created and kept this record.

• **The people of Muloch** also left Jerusalem at the time of the Babylonian destruction. Muloch was one of the sons of King Zedekiah, the last king of Judah (*see* Jer. 39:1–2 RE). Internal evidence in the text suggests the group that came with Muloch (commonly called Mulochites) may have spoken Aramaic. The Mulochites joined with the Nephites and became one people (*see* Omni 1:8 RE).

• **The people of Jared** (commonly called the Jaredites) left the Tower of Babel at the time of the confounding of languages and traveled to the American continent. Their civilization ended around the time the Mulochites arrived.

Source Records

The *Covenant of Christ* mentions several sources that added to the final text, all of which are ancient records kept on metal plates. Though several of the sets of plates overlapped as to time period or the group keeping the record, each is unique in purpose and content. The text references the following plates, all of which contributed material to the *Covenant of Christ:*

• The *Plates of Brass* are a record containing *the five books of Moses…and a record of the Jews from the beginning…and the prophecies of the holy prophets* up to and including some of the prophecies of Jeremiah (see 1 Nephi 1:10, 22 RE). These plates were taken from Jerusalem by Nephi, son of Lehi, and brought to the American continent with Lehi's family.

• The *Small Plates of Nephi* are a record started by Nephi covering events leading up to and including his family's travels from Jerusalem to the American continent, as well as the ministry of Nephi and his brother Jacob. Subsequent prophets and writers continued this record until the plates were full. Their purpose was to record the ministry and the *things of God*, rather than a secular history (*see* 1 Nephi 2:1, 14 RE; 2 Nephi 3:6 RE; Words of Mormon 1:2–3 RE). This content was included, unabridged, and used to replace lost 116 pages of manuscript of the Book of Mormon and encompass the books of 1 Nephi, 2 Nephi, Jacob, Enos, Jarom, and Omni.

• The *Large Plates of Nephi* are a historical record kept by Nephi, son of Lehi, and subsequently added to by other writers. This record contains more political and secular information than the *Small Plates of Nephi*, including the history of the kings, the wars, and the conflicts of the Nephite people (*see* 1 Nephi 2:14 RE). These records were abridged by Mormon to create his record (*see Covenant of Christ* Dedication).

• The *Plates of Ether* are a record of an earlier civilization called the Jaredite people who left the Tower of Babel at the time of the confusion of tongues and traveled to the American continent. Their record was recorded by the prophet Ether on twenty-four gold plates (*see* Mosiah 5:12 RE; Ether 1:1 RE). Their civilization ended with the destruction of their people, during the lifetime of Nephi, son of Lehi.

• The *Plates of Mormon* is the abridgment, made by Mormon, of the *Large Plates of Nephi* and were subsequently added to by Mormon's son, Moroni, who also included the above *Small Plates of Nephi* and an abridgment of the *Plates of Ether*. Mormon's abridgment of the *Large Plates of Nephi* begins at The Words of Mormon and ends at Mormon 3:5 RE. Moroni's completion of the record includes Mormon 4, Ether, and Moroni. The *Plates of Mormon* were buried by Moroni ca. A.D. 421, following the destruction of the Nephite civilization. These plates were given to Joseph Smith in 1827 by the resurrected Nephi, son of Lehi. While in the possession of Joseph Smith, the *Plates of Mormon* were commonly called the "Gold Plates" or "Gold Bible." The unsealed portion of the plates was translated by the gift and power of God, and the sealed portion of the plates was left untranslated. When the work of translation was completed, Joseph reburied the plates (*see* 2 Nephi 11:20 RE).

Covenant of Christ is primarily the work of three authors: Nephi (son of Lehi), Mormon, and Moroni. Nephi's small plates are included without abridgment, while the rest of the record consists of Mormon and Moroni's abridgments of prior records written by other authors, as well as their own writings. Because the majority of the abridging work was done by Mormon, the original book bears his name. The translation of the plates was given to Joseph Smith by the gift and power of God. Though Joseph Smith was initially listed as author for copyright purposes, he claimed only to have received the translation and did not claim original authorship of any part of the book. Joseph stated the Book of Mormon (or now, *Covenant of Christ*) was the *most correct of any book on earth*, because it was received directly from God. All other volumes of scripture are vastly inferior due to the changes and emendations made to them by men. *Covenant of Christ* is the covenant that mankind has been condemned for neglecting, and it is a great loss when it is defined as just another volume of scripture or just another book. It contains the means for mankind to return to the presence of the Lord.